CRIME & JUSTICE IN AMERICA

Present Realities and Future Prospects

PAUL F. CROMWELL
Wichita State University

ROGER G. DUNHAM
University of Miami

Prentice Hall, Upper Saddle River, New Jersey 07458

Library of Congress Cataloging-in-Publication Data

Crime and justice in America: present realities and future prospects
/edited by Paul Cromwell and Roger Dunham.
    p. cm.
  ISBN 0-13-228636-X
  1. Crime-United States   2. Criminal justice, Administration of—
United States.   I. Cromwell, Paul F.   II. Dunham, Roger G.
HV6789.C6882   1997
364.964—dc20   96-9690
                                                           CIP

Editorial/production supervision
    and electronic page composition: *Janet M. McGillicuddy*
Template design: *Janet M. McGillicuddy*
Director of manufacturing and production: *Bruce Johnson*
Managing editor: *Mary Carnis*
Cover design: *Miguel Ortiz*
Charts and graphs: *Stephen Hartner*
Manufacturing buyer: *Ed O'Dougherty*
Acquisitions editor: *Neil Marquardt*
Marketing manager: *Frank Mortimer, Jr.*
Editorial assistant: *Rose Mary Florio*

HV6789
.C6882
1997

 © 1997 by Prentice-Hall, Inc.
A Simon & Schuster Company
Upper Saddle River, NJ 07458

Printed in the United States of America
10 9 8 7 6 5 4 3 2 1

ISBN 0-13-228636-X

Prentice-Hall International (UK) Limited, *London*
Prentice-Hall of Australia Pty. Limited, *Sydney*
Prentice-Hall Canada, Inc., *Toronto*
Prentice-Hall Hispanoamericana, S.A., *Mexico*
Prentice-Hall of India Private Limited, *New Delhi*
Prentice-Hall of Japan, Inc., *Tokyo*
Prentice-Hall Asia Pte. Ltd., *Singapore*
Editora Prentice-Hall do Brasil, Ltda., *Rio de Janeiro*

To my wife and best friend, Jimmie Cromwell, and to my newest grandchild, Victoria Anne Pettis.

—Paul F. Cromwell

To my wife Vicki, and our children, Jenny, Jason, Joshua, Ben, Seth and Zack.

—Roger G. Dunham

CONTENTS

SECTION 3   Adjudication and Sentencing   180

SECTION 4   Jails, Prisons, and Community-Based Corrections   261

ACKNOWLEDGMENTS

Many people helped make this volume a reality. First, we would like to offer our thanks to the authors and publishers of the articles selected for inclusion here. Their scholarship is the core of this anthology and we greatly appreciate their allowing us to include their work in our book.

We were aided by those who reviewed the work and offered their critical analyses and suggestions for improvement. Foremost among these was Frank Schmalleger, the Justice Research Association, Hilton Head, South Carolina. He graciously gave of his time and expertise and many of his suggestions found their way into the anthology. Specifically, he suggested the inclusion of materials on criminal justice ethics, careers, and the section on the future of criminal justice. Other reviewers whose suggestions and criticisms immeasurably improved the book include John Chuvala, Western Illinois University; Leon Cantin, Huron University; Thomas Winfree, New Mexico State University; Frederick VanDusen, Palm Beach Community College; Larry Andrews, Missouri Western State College; Steve Brodt, Ball State University; Mark J. Addesa, West Virginia State College; Wayne L. Wolf, South Suburban College; Beverly H. Strickland, Fayetteville Tech Community College; and Carl E. Russell, Scottsdale Community College. Others contributing their expertise to the project were Frederic Faust, Florida State University and George Wilson, University of Miami.

Finally, our editors at Prentice Hall, Robin Baliszewski, Neal Marquardt, Janet McGillicuddy, and editorial assistant Rose Mary Florio were a source of encouragement and inspiration. Without them this book would not have come to fruition.

Paul Cromwell
Wichita, Kansas

Roger M. Dunham
Coral Gables, Florida

PREFACE

The criminal fascinates us even as he repels us. Like Cain, he is not his brother's keeper. Like the serpent, he tempts us to guilty knowledge and disobedience. He is to men what Lucifer was to the angels, the eternal outcast and rebel, challenging all the assumptions of the moral order and risking heaven to do so. We are dismayed by his often dark and bloody deeds, and we run from him when the sun goes down, leaving the streets of our central cities dark and deserted. But even as we escape in terror, we seek him out in our imagination, as though he held locked within him some dirty secret of our own. He is, after all, a brother, acting out the primitive part in us that we struggle to keep dark. He is hated for being too much like us; he is envied for his freedom and the blessed gift of unrepentance.

Ysabel Rennie

The purpose of this volume is to provide a comprehensive range of perspectives on topics and issues critical to the study of criminal justice. We have selected readings from many sources, including recent criminal justice research monographs and articles from the professional and academic literature, case studies, sociological, psychological, and criminological analyses, the popular media and literature, as well as historical and philosophical approaches to understanding the complex issues confronting criminal justice today. This interdisciplinary approach provides a broad coverage of the various topics and issues, presented in an interesting and readable format. We believe that the selections will capture the students' and teachers' imagination and help make the fascinating study of criminal justice even more appealing.

The book is divided into five sections or topic areas: (1) Crime and Justice in America; (2) The Police in America; (3) Adjudication and Sentencing; (4) Jails, Prisons, and Community-Based Corrections; and (5) Looking Toward the 21st Century: The Future of Crime and Criminal Justice. Each section contains selected discussions and analyses of current issues and problems, ethical considerations, and materials related to criminal justice career opportunities, including employment standards and qualifications, and strategies for pursuing employment in the public or private sector of criminal justice. Each section is preceded by brief comments by the editors and is followed by questions to stimulate classroom discussion. *Crime and Justice in America: Present Realities and Future Prospects* also contains an index to assist the reader in locating topics of interest. This volume may readily be used as a stand-alone text for introductory criminal justice courses or as a supplement to most introductory texts. We have also sought to provide readings that create a balance between theory and practice; that promote critical thought about current criminal justice issues; and that encourage a vision for the future. As criminal justice teachers with a combined thirty years teaching and research and over two decades of experience in criminal justice practice and administration, we realize the need to present students with materials that challenge their minds yet keep their interest and make them want to read further. We believe we have accomplished that goal in this volume.

Section 1

Crime and Justice in America

Introduction

Every known society or group has rules for its members to follow, and, as a result of this and simple human nature, every known society or group has rule-breakers. Once some members break the rules, it is only natural for the remaining members to respond to the rule-breakage. If the sentiment is strong concerning the importance of the rules to the group, the response will be severe. This is the bottom-line of crime and justice. Crime is nothing more than the breaking of rules we consider important to our society, and justice is the official response to breaking those rules. The focus of Section I is on these more general aspects of crime and justice.

In the first selection, entitled "The Evolution of Criminal Law," criminologist C. Ray Jeffery traces the origins of the criminal law from the customs of primitive tribal society to modern concepts of law. He explains the change from law as private vengeance to crime as offenses against the state, and how its focus changed from restitution and compensation to punishment and justice. This is especially relevant today in light of the criticism that our justice system needs to focus more on the plight of victims.

The second selection, "Fallacies and Truths About Crime" by Rutgers University criminologist Marcus Felson, is a unique and provocative analysis of crime in America with particular reference to the misunderstandings and outright erroneous information that many Americans use as a foundation for their concepts of crime and punishment. Marcus Felson provides a general perspective or image of crime and criminals that he sums up as temptation and control. Society provides both temptations and controls, and it is the balance of the two that dictates the amount and nature of our crime problem.

"Highlights From 20 Years of Surveying Crime Victims" chronicles much information that is only available through the National Crime Victimization Survey. This report includes crime rates in the United States. Who are the victims of crime? What is the relationship of victim and offender? Where and when does crime occur? How much crime occurs in schools? Trends over the past two decades are also discussed and analyzed in this important overview that addresses victims, one of the most neglected subjects in the study of crime.

The fourth selection, "Racism in the Criminal Justice System: Two Sides of a Controversy" by William Wilbanks and Coramae Richey Mann, presents two sides of a

1

longstanding controversy. Mann argues that racism pervades the criminal justice system, while Wilbanks suggests that the system discriminates in favor of African-Americans. Each author makes his or her case and then points out "flaws" in the other argument. The debate introduces more questions than definitive answers, which provides a catalyst for all those interested in racial justice.

The final selection in this section is entitled "Drugs, Crime, and the Justice System." This report presents a detailed discussion of the relationship between drug use and crime. Currently, drugs are thought to stimulate crimes beyond the illegal use of drugs. It would be futile to try and understand the crime problem without understanding illegal drug use and its role in the criminal enterprise. The authors of this selection analyze the linkages between drug use and violent crime and between drug use and income-generating crime. Their presentation of extensive empirical evidence supports their conclusion that drug use has a strong influence on crime.

THE EVOLUTION
OF CRIMINAL LAW

C. Ray Jeffery

Tribal Law

The transition in social organization was from tribal to state, from simple to complex, and from hunting and fishing to agricultural to industrial and urban. Law as we know it emerged from this transition from a tribal society to a state society.

Primitive tribes are governed by custom, tradition, magic, and witchcraft. Anthropologists have taken two different approaches to the nature of primitive law. One view maintains that all custom is law, and therefore primitives have a legal system. Malinowski argued, for example, that primitive social systems are governed by custom, which is enforced by reciprocity or "a body of binding obligations...kept in force by specific mechanisms of reciprocity and publicity inherent in the structure of their society" (Malinowski, 1926:58).

The problem with the definition of law as custom is that it equates law with all social norms. All laws are social norms, not all social norms are laws. Custom is enforced by ridicule, tradition, social pressure, public opinion, and threats of ostracism from the group. Law is enforced by the use of force and coercion. Seagle (1941:7) wrote that "it is the fact that the sanction is applied exclusively by organized political government that distinguishes law from religion, morals, and custom." Hoebel (1954:28) stated that "a social norm is legal if its neglect or infraction is regularly met by the application of physical force by an individual or group possessing the socially recognized privilege of so acting." In commenting on the sociological and anthropological usages of the term "law," Roscoe Pound (1945:300) said: "This broader usage (law as custom) is common with sociologists. But certainly for jurists, and I suspect for sociologists, it is expedient to avoid adding to the burden of the term of too many meanings, and to use 'law' for social control through the systematic application of the force of politically organized society."

Primitive people had little or no law because they are controlled by custom, religion, magic, and witchcraft, and the basic unit of society is the kinship group, not the political state (Redfield, 1967; Bohannon, 1967b; Seagle, 1941; Radcliffe-Brown, 1935; Llewellyn

C. Ray Jeffery, *Criminology: An Interdisciplinary Approach*, Englewood Cliffs, NJ: Prentice-Hall, 1990, pp. 49–56. Used by permission of the publisher.

and Hoebel, 1941). The shift from *tribal law* to *state law* is one of the basic changes in institutional structure that occurred in the history of human social organization.

The Nature of Tribal Law

Primitive law is based on the principle of *self-help*. Primitive law is private law, and it is enforced by the tribal group. In most primitive societies the *feud* is carried on by groups related to one another by blood or by social obligation. An injury to a member of tribe *A* by a member of tribe *B* led to a retaliatory strike against a member of tribe *B* (Barton, 1949; Llewellyn and Hoebel, 1941; Popisil, 1967; 1971).

Early Egyptian and Greek law was organized along tribal principles, based on a doctrine of "lex talionis," or an eye for an eye, a tooth for a tooth. This principle is found in the Code of Hammurabi (2400 B.C.) (Koschaker, 1935), which placed a limitation on revenge since the offended party could take no more than an eye for an eye. Out of early tribal law we find the historical beginnings of a major justification for punishment: that revenge is justice and that punishment must fit the crime. We discuss retribution and revenge in later chapters.

The feud was very costly in terms of lives and injuries, so limitations were placed on the conditions under which the feud could be carried out. The feud was limited in many societies by the use of ridicule and the singing duel, in which the litigants insulted one another until satisfaction was obtained (Bohannan, 1967b).

A common way to limit the blood feud was through a system of compensation, or payment of damages to the injured party. The amount of the payment depended on the extent and nature of the injuries (Barton, 1949). Among the Comanche Indians restitution often took place in the form of horses. The military societies of the Cheyenne Indians performed police functions, especially during the communal buffalo hunts, and these military societies were an important step toward the development of the state system (Hoebel, 1954; Llewellyn and Hoebel, 1941).

The Teutonic tribes of northern Europe had a system of self-help and the blood feud. A system of compensation for injuries developed to assure peace between the conflicting parties (von Bar, 1916; Huebner, 1918). The Teutonic tribes who settled England (Angles, Saxons, Danes) brought with them the Germanic system of tribal law. The Anglo-Saxons developed a detailed system of compensation, called the *wergild*, money paid for the death of a tribal member. The payment schedule corresponds to our modern insurance contract, whereby a person is paid so much for the loss of an eye or an arm or a life (Thorpe, 1840; Attenborough, 1922; Rightmire, 1932; Kemble, 1879; Pollack and Maitland, 1899; Robertson, 1925; Seebohm, 1902).

From Tribal to State Law

As discussed above, the pattern of social evolution was from a hunting and fishing economy to an agricultural economy. Villages, population growth, and a more complex division of labor resulted in the decay of the tribal groups. Territorial groups replaced kinship groups. These territorial groups took the form of feudal kingdoms governed by lords, and eventually by a unification of kingdoms under a lord, which became the modern nation-state system (Stubbs, 1891; Traill, 1899; Rightmire, 1932; Kemble, 1879). *Land* replaced *blood* as the basis for social control. Individuals now owed allegiance not to the kinship group but to the land. The person who owned the land judged the person who had no land. Under a feudal system this was the lord-serf relationship, and anyone who lived on the land owed the lord services and allegiance. Under the state system the citizen owed the king services and allegiance.

In his *Ancient Law*, Sir Henry Maine (1906) referred to this shift from tribalism to state sovereignty as a shift from "status to contract." Under a status system rights are determined by one's membership in a family; under a contract system one's rights are determined by individual contractual relationships worked out within the framework of the political state. In his *Ancient Society*, Lewis Henry Morgan (1878) called this movement one of "savagery to civilization." "A tremendous change takes place when the tribal tie gives way to the territorial tie" (Kocourek and Wigmore, 1915). "Legal controls came to be associated with locality rather than with bloodstock or descent" [Goebel (1937a); see also Barton (1949) and Titiev (1954)]. Simpson and Stone (1948) summarize this movement as follows: "The cardinal characteristics of an emergent political society is that kinship is no longer the main bond of social cohesion. Stated affirmatively, this means that political organization has been superimposed upon kin organization." Mueller and Besharov (1986) have traced the growth of the criminal law from the family to the clan to the nation-state and finally to international bodies such as the United Nations.

THE EMERGENCE OF STATE LAW

The Unification of England

The political unification of the feudalistic settlements in England came about as a result of feudal warfare and conquests by one lord of another lord. The emergence of Christianity in England was also a unifying force. The conquest of England by the Normans under William the Conqueror (A.D. 1066) united the kingdoms of England under one king for the first time in history (Traill, 1899; Rightmire, 1932; Stubbs, 1891; Kemble, 1879).

The King's Peace

After the conquest William the Conqueror became the source of law and authority. The concept of the "king's peace" emerged; that is, any violations of the peace, such as fighting or thievery, were punished by the king as violations of the rights and authority of the king. The guilty party had to pay compensation to the king for these violations (Pollack and Maitland, 1932; Seagle, 1941).

By the time of Henry II (1154–1189) the Court of the King's Bench was open to citizens who had the proper legal writ, known as Pleas of the Crown. The Court of Common Pleas was established for pleas not involving the king directly (Maitland, 1931).

The king appointed local judges to represent him in local courts, and these judges made decisions that were recorded on the Pipe Rolls. In time these many judicial decisions came to be known as the common law of England. Common law is judge-made law with the authority of the king behind it; it is not customary law or tribal law.

Trial Procedures

The doctrine of self-help was based on the *appeal* of the injured party, where an accusation was made against the accused by the injured party. This was a private procedure that was replaced by a trial procedure by which the innocence or guilt of the accused party was determined. These trials originally involved trial by *ordeal*, a physical test involving the hot iron ordeal, the cold water ordeal, or the dry cereal ordeal. If the accused did not suffer injury from the ordeal, it was assumed that he was innocent. The ordeal depended on divine intervention, and clergy played an important part in the ordeal until the Fourth Latern Council of A.D. 1215 forbade clerical participation in the ordeal.

The Normans introduced the trial by *battle*, whereby the two litigants fought one another until one was killed or injured. The trial by battle also took the form of the *duel*, by which men of honor settled their differences (Radin, 1936; Attenborough, 1922).

The *indictment* came into existence at this time also, whereby local officials would take testimony from witnesses as to the type of crimes committed in the county. This led to the modern grand jury and became a means of public prosecution of criminal cases. The indictment led to a *trial by jury* in place of the ordeal, and such trials were held in the king's court (Holdsworth, 1923).

Compensation to the King

The old system of compensation to the victim or his/her family was replaced by compensation to the king. Crimes were no longer family or tribal affairs, but were offenses against the king. "The very core of the revolution in finance and law that took place in Henry II's reign was the transfer of the initiative in criminal matters from the kindred of the injured man to the king as public prosecutor" (Jeudwine, 1917:84; Pollock and Maitland, 1899). The payment made to the king as part of the king's peace was called an *amercement*.

Gradually, the law of wrongs was differentiated into the law of torts and the law of crimes. Tort law involves compensation for injuries done to another party for which private responsibility exists; criminal law involves punishment done for injuries done to the general public or to the state. A distinction was now made between those offenses for which compensation was made and those for which compensation was not made. For those guilty of a criminal offense who could not pay the compensation to the king, a different kind of punishment had to be used, such as mutilation, outlawry, transportation, and death. The inability of a defendant to pay for the crime was a basis for the development of criminal sanctions (Potter, 1943). Pollock and Maitland (1899) wrote: "Gradually more and more offenses became emendable; outlawry remained for those who could not or would not pay." They cite the case of a forger who was saved from the gallows by the payment of the amercement to the king. A murderer could buy back his life, although a thief without the means of restitution was hanged. There can be no tort law for a judgment-proof population [Pike (1873); see also von Bar (1916)]. The fact that the compensation went to the king and not the victim discouraged victims from pursuing criminal cases in the court system, and the initiative to prosecute criminal cases was left to the king and his agents.

Punishment

As was noted above, the death penalty developed for those who were unable to pay the compensation due to the king. Executions were carried out for a great variety of offenses and they were public affairs attended by huge crowds in a holiday spirit. Cruel and ingenious methods of torture and death were used at these executions. By the time of Henry VIII there were over 200 capital offenses, and children, women, and animals were executed as well as men (Holdsworth, 1923; Plucknett, 1948; Radzinowicz, 1948–1957; Stephens, 1883).

Although many capital offenses and many executions occurred, the number of executions to the number of eligible offenders was small. Criminous clerks (priests) were exempted from the criminal law of the king under the benefit of clergy doctrine. Sanctuary was granted to a fleeing criminal by the monasteries, and a criminal who reached the safety of the church could leave the country, usually at Dover, for a foreign land (Plucknett, 1948; Holdsworth, 1923).

In capital cases the judges would interpret the statutes narrowly, or fail to apply the death penalty. Juries would return verdicts which required less than the death penalty, or they would find the defendant not guilty. Prosecutors would reduce charges through plea bargaining. All of these practices are still to be found in the criminal justice system. Such legal practices made the use of capital punishment most capricious and uncertain (Hall, 1952).

Transportation as a punishment was introduced in the late seventeenth century. Inmates were shipped to colonies, such as Botany Bay in Australia. Alexander Maconschie, a British penal reformer, made his reputation at the penal colony in Australia (Mannheim, 1970). In the nineteenth century imprisonment and the growth of our present prison system replaced the use of capital punishment and transportation as a major means of dealing with the crime problem. The development of the modern prison system, probation and parole, and treatment techniques are the subject matter of corrections and the criminal justice system (see Chapters 8 and 9).

The Police System

The disintegration of the tribal system left the community without a means of enforcing law and order. A system of local control was developed called the *hundred*, 100 men designated as responsible for the good behavior of the people in the community. A body of armed citizens, called the *posse comitatus*, pursued the criminal, and local political units were responsible for police protection, which was in the hands of private citizens (Pike, 1873; Pollack and Maitland, 1899).

As the crown gained power it extended this power into each local county government. The king's reeve or shire reeve (a shire is a county) watched over the king's financial and legal affairs in each shire, and he presided over the county court. The shire reeve came to be known as the sheriff, who is still the police officer at the county level in most states (Stubbs, 1891; Jeudwine, 1917).

From 1300 to 1900 there was no strong public police force in England. Pike, Stephens, Radzinowicz, and other legal historians described this period as one of lawlessness and violence. Local merchants organized private police forces to combat crime. John and Henry Fielding and Patrick Colquhoun led a movement to establish a strong centralized police force in England. John Fielding established the Bow Street Runners as a police unit in London, and in 1829 Sir Robert Peel organized a centralized police force for England, which at this time was limited to the city of London. Scotland Yard was also established during this period (Radzinowicz, 1948–1957).

The police system, like the court system, shifted from private to public during this period. Today we still depend on public police agencies—but with an increase in the usage of private police forces since public resources are not adequate to deal with the crime problem.

Later Developments in the Criminal Law

The enclosure movement, by which land was taken by the lords from the peasants and enclosed for herding sheep rather than for growing crops, led to a shift in population from rural to urban areas. Peasants moved from farms to towns and villages, and a new class of vagrants was created, forming the basis for some major social problems. A growing population and industrialization also contributed to this rural-to-urban shift. The Statutes of Labourers of 1349 ordered men to remain on their jobs and in the township. The Elizabethan Poor Laws of 1598 and 1601 attempted to provide relief for a population of poor and destitute people. Workhouses and houses of correction were established, one to provide work for the able bodied, the other to provide punishment for those who would not work. However, in practice the two institutions were never clearly distinguished. The Settlement Act of 1662 made each parish responsible for the welfare of those residing in the parish, which meant residence by birth. Crowded slum areas were characterized by vagrancy, begging, gambling, drunkenness, prostitution, and theft (Pike, 1873; Stephens, 1883).

At this time a number of criminal laws were passed aimed at controlling vagrancy, theft, poverty, drinking, and gambling. Eighty percent of the executions of the day were for property offenses. "Sending paupers to Bridewell" was a common expression. The Waltham Black Act made it a capital offense for anyone to have a face blacked while doing injury to person or property. This act was aimed at the highwaymen and robbers of that time, and it extended the death penalty to many new areas of theft (Radzinowicz, 1948–1957). The Gin Act of 1736 was an attempt to control the public gin houses, and it caused so much popular resentment that rioting occurred as a result. Many rebellions and riots involving political and religious groups, such as the Lollards and Anabaptists, occurred at this time (Radzinowicz, 1948–1957; Pike, 1873). The criminal law was shaped to handle the many social problems created by urbanization and industrialization.

In *Theft, Law and Society*, Jerome Hall (1952) traces the changes that occurred in the law of theft due to the impact of urbanization and industrialization. His study begins with the *Carrier's Case* of 1473. In this case the defendant had been hired to carry goods to Southhampton. During the course of the journey he broke the bales and took the content. The concept of larceny as it developed in common law included the element of trespass. A person who is a bailee is in legal possession of goods; therefore, he cannot be held to be guilty of larceny. In the *Carrier's Case* the court found that the breaking of the bales constituted trespass, and the defendant was convicted of larceny by bailee. The common law was thus extended into a new area, a move made necessary by the development of trade and commerce and the use of bailments in modern industrial societies. Hall (1952:10) states that the "door was opened to admit into the law of larceny a whole series of acts which had up to that time been purely civil wrongs."

Receiving stolen property was a major criminal problem at this time. Jonathan Wild organized a trade in stolen property which extended overseas as well as in England. He had a well-organized and effective criminal syndicate for the purpose of trading in stolen goods. By 1827 a series of statutory changes and judicial interpretations of the law placed receiving stolen property in the category of a felony (Hall, 1952).

The development of banking, a money economy with its use of credit, and the violation of the trust placed in persons dealing with money made it necessary to extend the criminal law to cover new areas of business and commerce. In the eighteenth century criminal law came to be the means by which offenses involving the business system were controlled. Civil offenses were made criminal offenses when servants, bailees, bank tellers, and clerks came into possession of money and property legally, which they then converted to illegal use. Civil actions against such persons were not adequate since these people were for the most part judgment-proof.

TYPES OF LAW

Common Law

The first type of state law was common law, the law found in the decisions of judges. The doctrine of *stare decisis* developed, that is, following the precedent of earlier case law. Lawyers cite earlier decisions similar in fact and argue that the precedent in that case should govern in the present case. Since judges make contradictory decisions in similar cases, the new case may be resolved in several different ways, thus setting more precedent. Some decisions are overturned by appellate courts, and in many instances the minority opinion in one case will become a majority opinion in a later case.

Since judges are constantly making and changing the law, it is hard to argue that the law embodies eternal and absolute values. The best explanations of the power of judges to make law are to be found in the positive law doctrine, where law is the command of the sovereign, and the legal realist doctrine, where law is viewed as the behavior of the judges.

Statutory Law

The second type of law is statutory law, law made by state and federal legislatures. Most states have gone to a statutory form of law. This means that another source of state power makes the law, namely, the legislators. This raises the question of the power of politics and the fact that legislators vote to support certain private interest groups. Governors and legislators support the death penalty because of public support and votes.

In the final analysis judges decide on the legality of legislation according to the doctrine of judicial review and the separation of executive, legislative, and judicial functions. The courts also review the activities of the executive branch of government.

Constitutional Law

The third type of law is constitutional law, including the law used to create a new government. Basic to the U.S. Constitution is the Declaration of Independence (1776), which states: "We hold these Truths to be self-evident, that all Men are created equal, that they are endowed by their Creator with certain inalienable Rights, that among these are Life, Liberty, and the Pursuit of Happiness." In this statement is the idea of natural and inalienable rights, or rights to be found in natural law. These rights were originally expressed in the writings of John Locke. Constitutional law is thought of as "higher law," not positive or human-made law. Corwin (1929) argued that constitutional law contained the idea of a higher law. Constitutional law is higher law in another sense. The law applied in any given case can be appealed to the Supreme Court, which will determine whether it is constitutional. Thus the Constitution ranks higher than common law or statutory law.

Some political scientists and lawyers view the Constitution as natural law embodying higher moral principles, but we can also regard such law as positive law or human-made law. U.S. Supreme Court judges are appointed by the president through a political process. The president selects men and women who are politically conservative or liberal, depending on the president's own political views. When a new justice is appointed, there is speculation as to how the Court will vote on critical issues, such as the death penalty, or abortion, or school desegregation. This is especially true in those cases where the Court in the past has voted 5–4 or 6–3 on the issue. When a new president is elected, the future of the Supreme Court may be at stake.

Rather than being an apolitical body, the Supreme Court is as political a body as exists in our form of government. Behavioral scientists study the behavior of Supreme Court justices as they do the behavior of other political figures (Dye and Zeigler, 1978; Schubert, 1965; Glick, 1983).

The Evolution of Criminal Law: Summary

The evolution of criminal law was from tribal law to feudal law to state law. Law emerged from private vengeance and the blood feud to criminal law in which the king was the offended party. Crimes became offenses against the king; the king prosecuted the case, and the king gained compensation or revenge from the criminal. The victim no longer benefited from the conviction of the criminal.

If the criminal could not pay the compensation, he/she was usually executed. In later history transportation and imprisonment replaced the death penalty as the major means of controlling criminal behavior. The modern criminal justice system is a product of the growth of the state system, along with the agricultural-industrial-urban complex which now characterized western European nation-states. Criminal law moved from restitution and compensation to punishment and justice. This is a basic characteristic of modern criminal law.

REFERENCES

ATTENBOROUGH, F. L. (1922). *The Laws of the Earliest English Kings.* Cambridge: Cambridge University Press.

BARTON, R. F. (1949). *The Kalingas.* Chicago: University of Chicago Press.

BOHANNAN, P. (1967a). "The Differing Realms of the Law." In *Law and Warfare,* ed. Paul Bohannan. New York: Natural History Press.

BOHANNAN, P. (1967b). *Law and Warfare.* New York: Natural History Press.

CAMPBELL, B. G. (1979). *Humankind Emerging.* Boston: Little, Brown.

COHEN, R. and E. R. SERVICE (1978). *Origins of the States: The Anthropology of Political Evolution.* Philadelphia: Institute for the Study of Human Issues.

CORWIN, E. S. (1929). *The "Higher Law" Background of American Constitutional Law.* Ithaca, N.Y.: Great Seal Books.

DYE, T. R., and L. E. ZEIGLER (1978). *The Irony of Democracy,* 4th ed. North Scituate, Mass.: Duxbury Press.

FRIEDL, E. (1975). *Women and Men.* New York: Holt, Rinehart and Winston.

GERSTEIN, D. R., ET AL. (1988). *The Behavioral and Social Sciences.* Washington, D.C.: National Academy Press.

GLICK, H. (1983). *Courts, Politics, and Justice.* New York: McGraw-Hill.

GOEBEL, J., JR., ed. (1937a). *Cases and Materials on the Development of Legal Institutions.* New York: Columbia Law Review.

GOEBEL, J. (1937b). *Felony and Misdemeanor.* New York: Commonwealth Fund.

HAAS, J. (1982). *The Evolution of the Prehistoric State.* New York: Columbia University Press.

HALL, J. (1952). *Theft, Law and Society,* 3rd ed. Indianapolis, Ind.: Bobbs-Merrill.

HARRIS, M. (1977). *Cannibals and Kings: The Origins of Culture.* New York: Vintage.

HOEBEL, E. A. (1954). *The Law of Primitive Man.* Cambridge, Mass.: Harvard University Press.

HOLDSWORTH, W. S. (1923). *A History of English Law,* Vols. 1–7. Boston: Little, Brown.

HUEBNER, R. (1918). *A History of Germanic Private Law.* Boston: Little, Brown.

JEUDWINE, J. W. (1917). *Tort, Crime and the Police in Medieval Britain.* London: Williams & Norgate.

KEMBLE, J. M. (1879). *The Saxons in England.* London: Bernard Quartich.

KOCOUREK, A., and J. H. WIGMORE (1915). *Primitive and Ancient Legal Institutions.* Boston: Little, Brown.

KOSCHAKER, P. (1935). "Law: Cuneiform." In *Encyclopedia of the Social Sciences,* Vol. 9. New York: Macmillan.

LAWICK-GOODALL, J. (1971). *In the Shadow of Man.* Boston: Houghton Mifflin.

LENSKI, G., and J. LENSKI (1982). *Human Societies,* 4th ed. New York: McGraw-Hill.

LEWELLEN, T. (1983). *Political Anthropology.* South Hadley, Mass.: Bergin and Garvey.

Lewin, R. (1984). *Human Evolution.* San Francisco: W. H. Freeman.

Llewellyn, K. N., and E. A. Hoebel (1941). *The Cheyenne Way.* Norman: University of Oklahoma Press.

Maine, Henry (1906). *Ancient Law,* 10th ed. London: J. Murray.

Stephen, J. F. (1983). *A History of the Criminal Law of England.* Vols. 1–3. London: Macmillan.

Stubbs, W. (1891). *The Constitutional History of England,* Vol. 1. Oxford: Clarendon Press.

Thorpe, B., ed. (1840). *Ancient Laws and Institutes of England.* London: Royal Commission of Public Records.

Titiev, M. (1954). *The Science of Man.* New York: Holt.

Traill, H. D. (1899). *Social England.* Vols. 1–6. New York: Putnam.

von Bar, C. L. (1916). *A History of Continental Criminal Law.* Boston: Little, Brown.

Wright, H. T. (1977). "Recent Research on the Origin of the State." In *Annual Review of Anthropology,* Vol. 6. Palo Alto, Calif.: Annual Reviews.

QUESTIONS FOR THOUGHT AND DISCUSSION

1. How is tribal law different from our legal system today (state law)? Have we become overdependent on formal law?
2. Should the focus of the criminal justice system change from the current emphasis on punishment and justice to more emphasis on restitution and compensation?
3. What are the differences among common law, statutory law, and constitutional law?

FALLACIES AND TRUTHS ABOUT CRIME

Marcus Felson

Education consists mainly in what we have unlearned.

—*Mark Twain Notebook (1935)*

Many people begin studying crime with a mind full of distracting emotions and misconceptions.[1] The emotions might include extreme sympathy for or antipathy against offenders, victims, police officers, or the criminal justice system. Perhaps because of these emotions, many people make sweeping generalizations about crime, such as the following:

- "We ought to lock up all the criminals and throw away the key."
- "Most rape victims bring it on themselves."
- "Racism is the cause of most of our crime."
- "Americans are taught to be violent."

Perhaps such statements deserve discussion, but the strong emotions underlying them often interfere with that discussion and make it hard to sift out that grain. The purpose of this chapter is to try to take a more objective view.

Emotions are not the only problem in studying crime. Because crime is so widely discussed, incorrect information about crime is widely believed. The reader has to re-examine some "common knowledge." Fortunately, most people also have some correct information about crime. This chapter is devoted to not only helping overcome misinformation, but also reinforcing correct information about crime.

This volume builds a general perspective that helps to organize crime information: "the routine activity approach."[2] This perspective treats crime as a routine activity that draws on other routine activities. The chapter plan is first to present fallacies about crime and then to present truths, before summarizing what we have covered.

Our first step is to try to free ourselves from mass media images of crime.[3]

Marcus Felson, *Crime in Everyday Life*, Thousand Oaks, CA: Pine Forge Press, pp. 1–19. Copyright © 1995 by Pine Forge Press. Reprinted by permission of Pine Forge Press.

SOURCES SHOWING CRIME AS ORDINARY

Crimes are generally dramatic and serious in police adventure shows on television and when reported as news. Violent incidents predominate. This leads to the *dramatic fallacy* of crime analysis, because crime is portrayed as much more dramatic than it usually is. For example, watching television at night or reading the newspaper in the morning, one is likely to see a great deal of murder, especially romantic murders by jealous lovers, as well as felons and police officers shooting at one another.

To understand the dramatic fallacy, it is important to learn more about crime in its ordinary forms. The following three standard sources of crime data can help us.[4]

1. *Official police reports.* Each local police department collects crime data and reports it routinely to the Federal Bureau of Investigation in Washington, D.C. The FBI compiles these statistics for the United States as a whole and publishes them annually in its *Uniform Crime Reports* (all data refer to the year preceding the report date).
2. *Victim surveys.* Data on crime are collected through such efforts as the National Crime Survey, which interviews a general sample of citizens about their own and their households' victimization experiences. This survey is conducted by the U.S. Bureau of the Census and turns up at least twice as many crimes (in the categories asked) as official police data.
3. *Self-reports.* Based on interviews with youths or others about their own lawbreaking, these surveys report many more crimes than do official police data. They are especially effective in turning up reports of underage crimes (status offenses), minor drug abuse, and minor thefts.

All three types of crime data lead to the conclusion that most crime is very ordinary.

Official Data

To establish this point, we begin with data from the FBI's *Uniform Crime Reports* for 1990. These include a total of 14.5 million offenses reported for eight major crime categories alone: homicide,[5] forcible rape, aggravated assault, robbery, motor vehicle theft, larceny-theft, and arson.[6] Yet almost 9 out of 10 of these crimes are property crimes: burglaries, motor vehicle thefts, and larceny-thefts. Homicides are only two-tenths of 1% of the major crime total—and we have not yet begun to consider all the minor offenses.

Most of the 20,045 homicides in the United States in 1990 would not interest Sherlock Holmes: Only 312 were by strangulation, 36 by drowning, 14 by explosives, and 11 by poison. Only 65 of these homicides were killings of law enforcement officers: only one-third of 1% of all homicides in the United States that year. Only 2% of 1990 homicides involved romantic triangles, and only 6.5% involved narcotics felons. And not all of these offenses were very interesting. This is not to deny the significance of these deaths, but it does point out that interesting homicides are such a small share of total homicides and an even tinier share of major crimes.

Now if we turn to the 9 million arrests in 1990 for all reasons, four out of five were not even for the eight major crimes. For example, more than 1 million were for driving under the influence of alcohol, and another 1.5 million arrests were for drunkenness, disorderly conduct, and liquor law violations. In other words, for every homicide in the United States, there are some 500 arrests of all types and many more crimes that never lead to arrest.

Victim Reports

The National Crime Survey indicated approximately 34 million victimizations in the United States in 1990.[7] Some 81% of the victimizations reported were nonviolent. If we compare the 20,045 homicides officially reported to the 4.7 million assaults from the National Crime Survey, we see that for every homicide there are at least 230 nonlethal assaults mentioned by respondents.

Self-Reports

Again, survey responses are dominated by relatively minor crimes. For example, 88% of high school students reported illegal alcohol use; another 31% reported having used marijuana.[8] Yet less than 7% reported ever having used cocaine, for which current use is reported by 2% of respondents. Again, minor offenses greatly outnumber major ones.

Thus the vast majority of crimes are very ordinary, undramatic, and certainly nonviolent. Examples of common criminal acts are shoplifting, public drunkenness, disturbing the peace, breaking and entering, smoking small amounts of marijuana, stealing car accessories or contents, vandalizing park property, and stealing company property from the workplace. Even when there is violence, it usually is minor and leaves no lasting physical harm. Indeed, an incident in which two drunk fellows ineptly shove one another is much more typical than a gunfight.

These common offenses are not the stuff of television. So-called cop shows prefer dramatic plots, interesting offenses, stunning fights, and thrilling car chases—anything but ordinary criminal acts. Even homicide is treated not in its ordinary form: the tragic result of a stupid little quarrel.[9] The television medium is more likely to present a clever and dramatic murder with a plot that fills a half-hour or hour time slot and a level of drama and excitement that are absent from the ordinary real life murder or mugging.

Police officers will tell you that their work involves hours and hours of boredom that are interrupted by moments of sheer terror. Yet most police officers never fire their weapons on the job and only a tiny fraction have ever shot or much less killed anybody. For example, compared to almost 3,900 homicides in California in 1991, there were only 131 cases of police officers killing suspects in what were judged to be "justifiable" homicides.[10] That means there were 30 ordinary homicides for every police killing.

In recent years, several television networks have discovered that they can film and present live police activities.[11] These shows give a better portrayal of the daily life of police officers and offenders than had previous cop shows. However, even these shows have a natural bias toward action. One would never guess from them that police spend a lot of time driving around waiting for something to happen. The more ordinary encounters with citizens are not likely to be included. Thus the new cop shows compress what action there is into a kaleidoscope of excitement and quick diversity. Even these rather realistic shows miss one important point about real crime: The majority of crime is either never reported to the police or results in no police action when it is reported. Thus even the most realistic cop show is still a kind of fiction. If the producers tried to show the boredom of everyday police work, their programs would have no viewers.

Newspapers offer more space than does television for covering ordinary criminal events, but only college, community, or small-town newspapers take the trouble to write about an ordinary break-in or theft of a car stereo. Major newspapers in big cities will not cover these incidents. Even commonplace murders (such as those resulting from ordinary arguments) are usually given short shrift in big city newspapers or are left out entirely; it is the unusual gang slaying and the drive-by shooting that is featured.[12] Such coverage leads many people to believe that they know a lot more about crime than they really do.

THE BRILLIANT AND DARING CRIMINAL?

Closely related to the dramatic fallacy is the *ingenuity fallacy*. This is the tendency to exaggerate the offender's cleverness. In the adventures of Sherlock Holmes, Professor Moriarty is an example of an evil and brilliant daredevil, whom Sherlock Holmes can only catch after an epic struggle.[13]

Another example of the skilled criminal is the cat burglar, who can slip into a room while his victims sleep, quietly pocket their valuables, and then slip out.[14] Yet most residential burglaries are conducted mainly in daytime when homes are deserted, not at night when greater skill would be required. Those that do occur at night generally occur when people are out for the evening or away on vacation. Paul Cromwell and his associates (1991) carried out an elaborate and clever ethnographic study of known burglars. The researchers drove around with their subjects to stage imaginary burglaries, asking such questions as:

- Would you break into that house?
- Why would you not break into that other house?
- What attracts you to the house on the corner?
- Why would you not break in right now?

Almost all of the burglars said that they would never enter a residence that they knew to be occupied! This is why they probe to make sure nobody is home. The most common method for probing is to knock on the door or ring the doorbell. But first these burglars drive around awhile to pick their targets. They take a look, think quickly, home in on the target, and then act. Although many of their decisions are intuitive, they have an underlying rationale: They pick times and places that offer good targets but have little chance of getting caught.

On numerous occasions, crime victims have stated, "It must have been a professional who broke into our house." Yet after they recite the facts of the case, it becomes clear that almost anybody could have committed the crime. Almost anybody knows to look for jewels hidden in the bathroom or kitchen. Almost any teenage offender can get into the house in less than a minute and out in another minute or two with some loot. Almost anybody can succeed at burglary in a neighborhood largely abandoned during the daytime.

The "de-skilling" of crime in recent history is an important insight of Maurice Cusson of the University of Montreal.[15] During the era of the convergent city, household density was so high that only a skilled burglar could sneak in and out successfully. Before the self-service store existed, only a skilled thief could slip the merchandise out from under a shopkeeper's nose. The changes in household activity patterns and marketing patterns provided great new crime opportunities that required little or no skill. Even bank robberies today are mostly unplanned, with the offender typically robbing the bank after seeing it for the first time.[16]

The ingenuity fallacy also leads many people to overestimate the amount of centrally organized crime in society, the role of gangs, the role of organized crime, and the role of conspiracy. Even though many crimes are committed by groups, this does not mean that such groups are well organized, carefully coordinated, or widely linked.

Malcolm Klein, an expert on juvenile gangs, reports that such gangs are typically loose networks with unstable membership. Few are well organized or persistent, and those that do persist have subgangs that come and go. In addition, most of the crime committed in gang territories are not organized by gangs. This misconception has led much of the public to see gangs as the central crime problem rather than putting them into the larger perspective of a generally high crime rate.[17]

The same issue is relevant for organized crime. The news media and many movies depict "the Mafia" as a centrally organized group functioning much as a business board. Although this may be true in Sicily and southern Italy, the American version of organized crime is much less centralized and more a network of people who act illegally but do not work from the same location. Some but not all of these criminals know one another, sharing illegal acts but not acting as a board of directors. This point is made most effectively by Peter Reuter (1984). A senior economist at the Rand Corporation, Reuter has examined illegal markets and attempts by organized crime to control them. These markets include bookmaking, "numbers" rackets, and loan sharking. These markets are not controlled in a centralized fashion as they are with a television Mafia.[18]

How Old Are Criminals?

A third fallacy is the *age fallacy*, which leads people to think that both offenders and victims of crime are older than criminologists know them to be.[19] Television often presents offenders and victims of crime who are middle-aged or older. Yet victim surveys repeatedly show that ordinary crime victimization risk is highest among teenagers and those in their early 20s. This risk declines noticeably in the late 20s, and the decline continues into the later ages. Except for purse snatching, the relative victimization risk is very low for senior citizens, however much their suffering may interest the mass media.

Offending also shows a young pattern. When victims of violence in the National Crime Survey were asked to estimate the ages of their attackers, 61% of victims younger than 21 reported that the offenders were 21 or younger. For victims 21 to 29 years of age, only one in four report the offenders to be older than their own age group. In general, the tendency to participate in crime shoots up with the onset of adolescence, peaks in the mid to later teens, and declines from there on. After age 30, the decline in crime participation is especially marked.

The age pattern of crime can be offset by changes in the opportunity to carry out crime. For example, those too young to have a job do not get a chance to engage in employee theft, so these crimes will not begin until they enter the labor force. The lack of opportunity may also explain why 54% of those arrested for murder are older than 25, even though other assaults have a younger pattern. Think of murder as a special case of assault in which the victim usually dies because the offender uses a more lethal weapon. Survey data indicate that aging brings higher levels of gun ownership, hence a greater chance for an assault to become a murder.[20]

Criminal justice system data tend to overestimate the age of offenders, because so many are transferred quickly to the juvenile system and treated leniently. Even so, four-fifths of arrested burglars are younger than 30 and two-thirds are younger than 25.

To sum up, we have reviewed fallacies about both crime and criminals. Both are quite ordinary. Offenders tend to be adolescents or young adults. Although they may act in groups, seldom are they sophisticated in their organization. We now turn to the role of the criminal justice system.

ARE THE POLICE AND COURTS CENTRAL TO CRIME?

The *constabulary fallacy* is the unfortunate tendency to think that the police know about crimes that have been committed and are the key to crime prevention. To be sure, crime is very important for police, but how important are police for crime? The same general question can be asked about judges, prosecutors, and corrections personnel.

Reporting Crime

Respondents to the National Crime Survey report that 63% of their victimizations were never reported to police. For thefts and household larceny victimizations, this figure exceeded 70%. Self-report data turn up even greater numbers of illegal acts never gaining the attention of police, notably in the area of smoking marijuana and underage use of alcohol.[21] When so much crime never comes to the attention of police, we have to begin putting police power and the criminal justice system as a whole into a smaller perspective.

The Short Arm of the Law

Of those crimes that police know to exist, the vast majority result in no arrest; of those arrested, most do not lead to trial or a guilty plea; of those that get to trial, most do not result in incarceration. For example, some 5.1 million household burglaries were estimated nationally from the 1990 National Crime Survey. Table 1.1 shows what happens with every 1,000 of these burglaries: More than 600 are never reported to the police, 960 do not result in arrest, 987 do not lead to conviction for burglary, and some 990 are never sentenced to jail or prison. Of those who are sentenced, not all are actually locked up, because of jail and prison overcrowding.

The fallout from start to finish is even greater for some other crimes. For example, the National Crime Survey estimates 21 million larcenies nationally in 1990, but only 61,918 people were sentenced to incarceration for larceny (3 per 1,000). These data sug-

TABLE 1.1   DISPOSITIONS OF HOUSEHOLD BURGLARIES

Household Burglaries	1,000
Burglaries reported*	390
Burglary arrests	40
Burglary convictions (state courts)	13
Incarceration	10

*Uniform Crime Reports

Derived from 1991 *Sourcebook*, Tables 3.1, 3.2, 3.127, 4.1, 4.2, 5.46, 5.47, and 5.49. The table does not present true rates, because of time lags and differences in definition. These calculations should be treated as estimates only.

gest that the criminal justice system is actually quite marginal in its direct effect on everyday crime.

Delays in Punishment

Even when the criminal justice system delivers punishment, it does so after long delays. For example, the median time elapsing between arrest for larceny and conviction in state courts in 1988 was five months, with a mean of eight months! These delays occur despite the fact that 93% of larceny convictions involve a guilty plea and do not even require trial.[22] And most trials are bench trials (before a judge and without a jury).[23]

To put our system of punishment into perspective, consider what happens when you touch a hot stove: You receive quick, certain, but minor pain. After being burned once, you will not touch a hot stove again. Now think of an imaginary hot stove that burns you only once every 500 times you touch it, with the burn not hurting until five months later. Psychological research and common sense alike tell us this imaginary stove will not be as effective in punishing us as the real stove. Such a pattern of rewards and punishments is called a *reinforcement schedule*.[24] Psychologists have established the following:

- rewards work better than punishments,
- reinforcements work better when they quickly follow the event,
- reinforcements work better when they are frequent, and
- extreme reinforcements are not very effective.

We can see that the U.S. criminal justice system does everything wrong: It gives punishments rather than rewards and relies on rare and delayed—but extreme—penalties. Meanwhile, crime gives sure and quick rewards to offenders. It should come as no surprise that so many people continue to commit crimes.

Patrol and Protect?

Even without punishment, police theoretically can reduce crime by patrolling and thus, by their sheer presence on the streets, reduce crime. The Kansas City Patrol Experiment investigated this point by making major increases in police patrols and then testing the impact of such increases. The experiment discovered that intensified police patrols are scarcely noticed by offenders or citizens and have no impact on crime rates.[25]

The problem is not that police on patrol do something wrong, but rather that we are giving them a ridiculously impossible task and should not be surprised when they do not gain success. We are asking them to protect one quarter of 1 billion people and billions of pieces of property dispersed over vast amounts of space. The modern metropolis as we know it is so spread out that it defeats effective policing.

To illustrate how difficult it is to cover a police beat for all 168 hours in a week, let us do some calculations. Note that at least one third of sworn police officers have special assignments or full-time desk duties and cannot patrol at all. Consider also that each patrol officer works approximately 10 hours per week on roll call, paperwork, court appearances, instruction, consultation, and breaks, leaving 30 hours per week for actual patrol. Assume that each officer patrols alone.

Consider Los Angeles County as an example. Its 8.8 million people live in 4,070 square miles at a density of 2,178 persons per square mile or approximately 1,000 households per square mile. Los Angeles County has some 15,000 police officers who must cover (by the above arithmetic) approximately 1,670 beats of some 2.4 square miles each. That means that each officer on patrol has to "protect" approximately 2,400 households and several hundred businesses, schools, and other locations every day. Round it off to some 3,000 locations that must be protected by each officer on patrol. Each location can expect daily coverage of approximately 29 seconds.[26]

That is not only precious little direct protection, but also little time for an officer to learn who has a right to be walking out of your place and who does not. It is not surprising that less than 1% of offenses end with the offender "caught in the act" by police on patrol. Doubling the number of police in a U.S. metropolis is like doubling a drop in a bucket.

DOES BAD COME FROM BAD?

We now turn to misconceptions about how crime relates to other phenomena in society.

This section examines the *pestilence fallacy*, which states that bad things come from other bad things. Crime is bad. Therefore it must emerge from other ills, such as unemployment, poverty, cruelty, and the like. Moreover, prosperity ought to bring lower crime rates.

Why then do the most prosperous nations of the world, including the United States, have high property crime rates? Why do the poor nations of the world have generally low property crime rates? Why does the United States, despite its prosperity, have such high violent crime rates? Why does the Netherlands, despite its high level of social welfare spending and emphasis on social equality, also have high violent crime rates? Why was the major period of crime rate increase in the United States, 1963 to 1975, also a period of healthy economic growth and relatively low unemployment?[27]

Why did Sweden's crime rates increase greatly as its Social Democratic government brought more and more programs to enhance equality and protect the poor? For example, Sweden had some 8,000 violent crimes in 1950, which increased to nearly 40,000 in 1988.[28] During the same period, burglaries grew to 7 times their former number, and robberies increased to 20 times their former level! This is not to argue that

Sweden's welfare state contributed to its crime rate (nonwelfare states also had proliferating crime), but to show that crime seems to march to its own drummer, largely ignoring social justice, inequality, government social policy, welfare systems, poverty, unemployment, and the like. To the extent that crime rates respond at all to these phenomena, they may actually rise somewhat with prosperity. In any case, crime does not simply flow from other ills. This is not an argument against fighting poverty, discrimination, or unemployment. Rather, it is an attempt to detach criminology from a knee-jerk link to other social problems.

These points show that we still have a puzzle to piece together.

LIBERALS, CONSERVATIVES, OR NEITHER?

All too many observers tend to link crime to their larger political or religious agenda. This might be called the *agenda fallacy*. For example, a "liberal" agenda promises to reduce crime by enacting poverty programs and increasing social or economic justice. A "conservative" agenda offers to reduce crime by decreasing welfare support or by using capital punishment (even though it does not apply to most crimes).[29] Some religious groups claim that conversion to their faith or values will prevent crime. In each case, crime is treated not for its own sake but rather for how it can be added to a larger agenda.

If you are in favor of a minimum wage as part of your agenda, then why not argue that it will prevent crime? If you are in favor of more emphasis on sexual morality, tell people this will lead to crime prevention. If you are a feminist, proclaim that rape is produced by antifeminism. If you dislike pornography, link it to sexual or other crimes. If the entertainment media offend your sensibilities, blame them for crime and demand censorship as a crime prevention method. Right-wing, left-wing, or whatever your agenda, if there is something you oppose, blame that for crime; if there is something you favor, link that to crime prevention! These are political tactics, but they are not the tactics for gaining more knowledge. Indeed, they may eventually do harm to the agenda when promises are not fulfilled.

Those who really want to learn about crime should observe the following advice:

1. Learn everything you can about crime—for its own sake rather than to satisfy ulterior motives, such as gaining political power or religious converts.
2. Set your agenda aside while learning about crime. If your political and religious ideas are worthwhile, they should stand on their own merits.

MORALITY AMONG MORTALS

A special case of the pestilence fallacy is the *morality fallacy*. This is the belief that crime is produced by declining morality. The fallacy follows from this line of thinking:

Crime is immoral.

Crime is widespread.

Thus moral training is lacking.

The above reasoning forgets about hypocrisy. People are quite able to believe in and even to preach in favor of the very rules that they violate.

Moral *training* does not guarantee moral *behavior*, any more than the lack of moral behavior proves the absence of moral training. More specifically, the high murder rate in the United States does not prove that Americans believe in murder or that they are trained to commit murder. If that were the case, why do U.S. laws set such high levels of punishment for murder? Why would U.S. public opinion show such outrage at murderers and other serious criminals?

Consider a parallel question: Why do people become overweight? This set of statements is analogous to the earlier triplet of crime statements:

Being overweight is bad.

Being overweight is widespread.

Thus thinness training is lacking.

If this conclusion is true, then why do so many overweight people want to lose weight? They must already know that it is better to be thin but find it difficult to accomplish their goal. Temptations to eat are widespread. The problem for eating is the same as for drinking, drugs, and crime: to resist temptations.

The many fallacies reviewed so far fit a pattern. All of them point toward a general image of crime and criminals based on a moral struggle between evil offenders and the criminal justice system, which acts on behalf of society. Although we would like to think that the image is only present in the popular media, it is also found within criminology itself.[30]

CRIMINOLOGY IS VULNERABLE

As Table 1.2 indicates, theories of criminality found in standard criminology textbooks are sometimes influenced by the same fallacies, if not in their original theoretical formulations, then at least as the theories are actually used by the policy world.[31]

Deterrence theory emphasizes using the criminal justice system to punish offenders. Ignoring the low probability of punishment in the United States (the constabulary fallacy), the theory's interest in capital punishment commits the dramatic fallacy, because most ordinary crimes are not even subject to capital punishment and ordinary murders are not likely to lead to capital sentences. Deterrence theory has become part of a self-righteousness political agenda from the right wing (agenda and morality fallacies).

Incapacitation theory advocates locking up "career" criminals to reduce crime. It exaggerates the criminal efficiency of a few people (the ingenuity fallacy) and forgets that these people will be locked up relatively late in their "criminal careers," after most of their damage has already been done (age fallacy). It relies too much on a criminal justice system (constabulary fallacy), is part of a right-wing political agenda, and depends too heavily on condemnation of a few (agenda and morality fallacies).

Differential association theory is based on the notion that delinquency is passed through associations. Thus delinquents are thought to "breed" other delinquents (pesti-

TABLE 1.2   FALLACIES IN CRIMINALITY THEORIES

Theory	Policy Emphasis	Fallacies
Deterrence	Impact of punishment for deterring offenders; use capital punishment	A C D M
Incapacitation	Locking up "career" offenders	A C G I M
Differential association	"Bad company" creates delinquency; break up delinquency groups	A C P
Labeling	The criminal justice system labels people as deviant, thus reinforcing their criminal behavior	A C M P
Strain	Poverty and inequality produce crime	A M P

Fallacy types

A: agenda fallacy   I: ingenuity fallacy
C: constabulary fallacy   M: morality fallacy
D: dramatic fallacy   P: pestilence fallacy
G: age fallacy

lence fallacy). When the theory leads to a policy of having police try to break up delinquency groupings, the constabulary fallacy comes to play. When the theory is used to justify urban renewal of poor neighborhoods to "break the cycle of crime," the agenda fallacy is operating. Despite this critique of differential association theory, we shall draw a useful idea from it later in this chapter.

Labeling theory blames the criminal justice system for producing crime and delinquency as it "labels" individuals as deviant. Like deterrence and incapacitation theory, labeling theory greatly overestimates the power of the criminal justice system (constabulary fallacy). It treats crime as one ill arising from another, the evil of state power (hence the pestilence fallacy). The theory treats punishment in immoral terms and is part of a left-wing agenda.

Strain theory examines the strains in society as the cause of crime. Its central argument is that poor people seek the goals of society but cannot meet them by legitimate means; they then turn to illegitimate means. Crime prevention must therefore rely on reducing poverty. Strain theory commits the pestilence fallacy by linking crime to poverty. A moral tone underlies its approach, and it is part of a liberal agenda.

Control theory avoids most of the fallacies of the other theories. Rather than asking "Why does that bad boy commit crime?" control theory asks, "Why doesn't everyone commit crime?" The answer is that social controls influence people to follow society's rules. Thus control theory avoids reliance on the police, considers undramatic crimes, and minimizes moralistic analysis of crime and agenda fallacies. Control theory is taken up later in this chapter.

So far we have found some pieces of the crime puzzle: the ordinary nature of crime and criminals, the youthfulness of offenders and victims, the limited powers of police and the justice system, that crime can come from social goods as well as from ills, and that agendas and morality are not very helpful in approaching crime. Many other insights and facts about crime can help us to continue building our understanding of how crime occurs and how crime rates change. The next part of the chapter gathers some of these "truths."

COMMON INSIGHTS ABOUT CRIME

This section presents six related common insights about human beings. These insights will help us examine how human situations vary and how they contribute to our understanding of crime. Some of the most useful insights about the human race in general can be applied to understand criminal behavior in particular.

First, consider the insight of *basic human frailty*. This is nothing more than the biblical notion that human beings are morally weak and that each individual needs help from society in order to withstand immoral temptations and pressures. Thus people with moral beliefs have difficulty meeting their own standards in practice, being capable of good and evil. The practical problem is to help people overcome their weaknesses by structuring society to reduce temptation. To be sure, some people are more "frail" than others, but all people have some frailty and temptability. This is quite different from saying people do not have strong enough beliefs about right and wrong. Rather it states that people have difficulty putting their moral beliefs into action, that is, in resisting temptations.

Second, related to the frailty insight, individuals vary greatly in their behavior from one situation to another. This *situational insight* is that each individual varies, not only over a lifetime but also in different situations on any given day. Almost everyone has ups and downs, ins and outs, anger and calm, conformity and defiance, and legal and illegal behavior. This insight has been incorporated into a whole social science field known as *situational social psychology*. Although they do not deny that individuals have personalities, situational social psychologists believe that the stability of personality is often exaggerated, that specific situations also have powerful effects on individuals.

Are youths as likely to get drunk with their parents present or absent? Are they as likely to smoke marijuana with peers as with their grandparents? Are those who are well behaved at home equally well behaved at school? Is sexual intercourse no more likely to occur when a couple is alone than when they are encumbered by the presence of others? Is juvenile delinquency no more likely to occur among a group of juveniles than it is when one juvenile is alone? Do the same students who are quiet in a college class remain quiet at a college football game? Are employees as likely to follow company rules when the boss is absent as when he or she is present? Do people drink as much alone as in a group? Are males no more rowdy among other males than they are in the presence of females?

If you answer "no" to several of these questions, then you accept the basic notion that much of human behavior is situational. That means that such behavior depends in part on who is present, where, and when.

The situational insight also helps us to think about the human frailty insight. Some situations will tend to bring out human weaknesses, including a weakness for crime.

Third, a special case of the situational insight is the *temptation insight*. In some situations, individuals are exposed to tremendous temptations. For example, self-service stores often place valuable and popular consumer goods within easy reach. This temptation helps to produce criminal acts that almost surely would not otherwise occur. One saying, "Opportunity makes the thief," reflects this insight. Flashing money among strangers, putting valuables in highly visible places, leaving keys in the car—all are examples of how to tempt someone to commit a crime that might not otherwise occur. Under some circumstances, one can be drawn to violate one's own beliefs.

Fourth, another special case of the situational insight is the *provocation insight*, which recognizes that an otherwise calm person can be provoked into a nasty, even violent, response. Provocation is sometimes carried out by a third party who acts as a troublemaker by egging on two others until they have little choice but to fight or lose face. As we shall see, young males are more likely to create provocative situations, thus encouraging fights to happen.

Fifth, the *bad company insight* is the widespread recognition that going around with the "wrong crowd" is somehow associated with criminal behavior and delinquency. This insight was taken up in the previous section, which discussed differential association theory. This theory states that associating with other delinquents teaches an individual to become a delinquent and thus is a cause of delinquency. However, this theory has a problem: Like the chicken and the egg, it is difficult to measure which came first, bad company or one's own bad behavior. The expression "Birds of a feather fly together" may help explain why delinquents spend time together. In other words, an individual who seeks trouble may find a delinquent group to join him; but it is not clear that the others are any more or less at fault. Each parent may think "My child is a good child; it's those others who are a bad influence." This interpretation may make a parent feel better, but it does not tell us where delinquency starts.

Can each parent be correct? *Is it possible for all the boys to have a bad influence on one another?* Rather than being one-sided, bad influence is symmetrical; boys get into trouble together they would not get into separately. This "symmetrically bad influence" combines readily with the idea that human behavior is highly situational and that individuals are morally frail and subject to temptations and provocations. It is indeed possible for each boy to be a "good boy" at home but a "bad boy" when he runs with his peers. The issue is not so much bad company as adolescent company. *Each* boy is influenced by the group to do "bad" things. *Each* parent underestimates the situational variations and each child's potential for mischief.

Moreover, for technical reasons alone, groups can be better for carrying out some delinquent acts. It is easier to break into a house when there is a big boy to kick in the door, a fast boy as a lookout to run in with a warning, a dexterous boy to pick locks, and a large enough group to provide safety in numbers and mutual reinforcement of courage to break the law.

Sixth, consider the *idleness insight*. The expression "Idle hands are the devil's workshop" is central to control theory. Youths with nothing to do have a tendency to get into more trouble, while youths with a tight and busy schedule are more likely to stay out of trouble. Keeping busy might be accomplished by spending time at school, in family settings, in recreation, or at work. However, the idleness insight is not always so easy to apply in practice.

These six insights about human behavior are consistent with one another. They tell us that human beings are morally frail, temptable, provocative, responsive to situations and to one another, and influenced by idleness or activity. These six different points of departure all converge on the same image of human beings and the same image of the criminal as a human being.

Understanding our common humanity is important for studying how we as human beings can go wrong. But we also need to understand human variations.

THE INDIVIDUAL STILL EXISTS

Traditionally, criminology has focused on variations among individuals and neglected variations among situations. This book does not propose to turn the tables all the way. Some features of individuals remain important to criminology and need to be understood. Unfortunately, it is very difficult to explain why some individuals tend more to commit crime than others. Even though criminology has not yet "solved" this problem, more active offenders do have some traits that distinguish them from the rest of the population. In particular, we would find that the most active criminal offenders have a strong tendency to get into all kinds of trouble, criminal or not. Very active offenders are more likely, for example, to be crime victims, smokers, alcohol abusers, and bad drivers and to have trouble in school, work, and family relationships.[32]

In addition, frequent offenders have strong tendencies to commit a great variety of offenses rather than to specialize, say, in robbery or in burglary. Robbers usually have committed burglary or theft or have been caught speeding or charged with disorderly conduct. A look at criminal records of offenders displays this great variety of illegal experience, as does self-reported delinquency. Although some frequent offenders tend not to perform violent crimes, the violent offender's crime record usually includes more nonviolent crimes than violent crimes.

In general, we can say that some individuals have more trouble than others in resisting temptations of various kinds. The attraction of *self-control* is that it sums up the efforts of parents, teachers, and others to counteract human frailty. We are all born weak, but year after year we are taught self-control to help us resist the various temptations; to keep us studying or working, out of the kitchen, or away from the bottle; to help keep the mouth shut when the boss, customer, spouse, or teacher says something that tempts a nasty reply; to avoid fights, drugs, and thefts; and to keep doing one's homework or one's work.

The self-control insight recognizes that some people often have a general tendency to get into trouble, especially by going for the pleasure of the moment. Other people have a general tendency to stay out of trouble and to perform those tasks that require delayed gratification—that is, giving up some pleasure now in order to improve things later. However, all people are subject to some temptation some of the time.

IMPORTANCE OF THE FAMILY

The *family insight* is the widely held notion that strong families impair crime and that weak families contribute to more crime.[33] Robert Sampson argues that family life—rather than poverty itself—is the driving force of crime production. The correlation between poverty and family problems is important, but it can also mislead us into thinking that poverty itself is the cause of crime when family problems contribute most directly to crime. By making clear when poverty is and is not associated with weak families, one can resolve the poverty fallacy and fit some more pieces of the "puzzle" together.

The family insight fits well with the other common insights.[34] Favorable families tend to combat basic human frailty, keep youths away from unfavorable situations, lead them away from bad company, idleness, undesirable temptations, risks, and provocations, while developing self-control when it is needed. Moreover, control theory tells us that children are often afraid to embarrass their parents by getting into trouble. Family life also serves to reduce crime victimization risk.

SUMMARY THUS FAR

In sum, crime and delinquency are ordinary and undramatic, involve little ingenuity, draw offenders and victims who are much younger than is commonly believed, and are far less tied to the police and criminal justice system than is commonly stated. Crime derives from many of the good aspects of society, independent of popular agendas that wish to subsume it, is neither determined by poverty nor totally unrelated to it, and does not depend on morality as commonly portrayed.

Crime and delinquency feed on human frailty; depend on widespread situational variations in human behavior; are fed by temptations, provocations, exposure to bad company and idleness; and are countered by the development of self-control to resist temptation and strong family life. Even though these developments may contribute to a pattern of criminal behavior for certain individuals, that should not distract us from studying crime as a set of specific acts tempting a broad range of population.

IT IS NOT WHO YOU ARE, BUT WHAT YOU DID

A cornerstone of the U.S. legal system is that a person cannot be charged with a crime based on *who* he or she is, only for *what* he or she has done. Thus the state cannot charge a citizen with the crime of "being a drug abuser" or "a burglar." The state could charge him or her with "breaking into the residence at 341 Bryant Street on May 5, 1993." Specifics are required in search warrants and arrest warrants, as well as in the prosecution of the case. Only after someone is convicted of a specific crime and is ready for sentencing can the court make use of a previous criminal record.[35]

A lawyer's job is to take each case one at a time. A criminologist, in contrast, studies many cases to learn generalizations about crime. This often tempts criminologists to describe a world of criminals distinct from the world of general citizens.[36] We must resist that temptation. In the words of British scholar Susan Smith (1986, p. 98), "Empirical research is increasingly gnawing away at the concept of mutually exclusive offender and victim populations, showing it to be a figment of political imagination and a sop to social conscience." In an excellent collection of evidence on this point, Ezzat Fattah (1991) explains that both offenders and victims tend to be in the same groups: young, male, and unmarried. Offenders themselves have very high rates of crime victimization. In addition, the very high rates of self-reported delinquency among American youths and the arrest of adults without significant previous criminal records also tell us to abandon the notion that crime is the province of a small segment of the population.[37]

In the old cowboy movies, the roles were clearly divided into good guys (white hats and white horses) and bad guys (black hats and black horses). Criminology should not follow such a simpleminded script; what we know about crime does not justify that. Even though a few people commit a disproportionate share of crimes, millions of Americans commit a very few crimes each, which adds to millions of crimes in the aggregate.

This chapter has provided a general perspective, an image of crime and criminals. That image could be summed up in two words: *temptation* and *control*. Society provides temptations to commit crime as well as controls to prevent people from following these temptations. Some temptations are implicit in the human race and all human society, other temptations are generated by all modern societies, and still others are unique to our society. As any society generates more temptations but fewer controls, it invites a crime wave.

The task of the rest of this book is to study the structure of temptation and control. Society offers such a structure by organizing everyday life: work, school, shopping, streets, and transport. This daily organization influences crime by determining which of the two forces, temptation or control, has the upper hand in any given setting or in society as a whole.

ENDNOTES

1. See Walker (1989) for a discussion of the emotional and sensational treatment of crime.
2. See Cohen and Felson (1979) and Felson (1987a). See also the landmark work on life-styles and crime: Hindelang, Gottfredson, and Garafolo (1978). Important related work on similar theories is reviewed in the introduction to Clarke and Felson (1993).
3. On myth making of crime by media and others, see Kappeler, Blumberg, and Potter (1993).
4. The four main statistical sources of information on crime used for this text are (a) *official police data*, which are collected in the FBI's annual *Uniform Crime Reports* (all data refer to the year preceding the report date); (b) *victimization data*, which are from the National Crime Survey and are found in the U.S. Department of Justice's *Criminal Victimization in the United States*, various years (data from this large survey are used to estimate numbers for the entire nation); (c) *self-report data* from various sources, most notably Johnston, O'Malley, and Bachman (1992); and (d) *convenient compilations* of crime data found in the Department of Justice's annual *Sourcebook of Criminal Justice Statistics* (hereafter cited as *Sourcebook*).
5. Here the words *homicide* and *murder* are used interchangeably; technically speaking, however, homicide includes more than murder. We intend to follow the *Uniform Crime Reports*, which combines murder with nonnegligent homicides. This excludes negligent manslaughters, such as an automobile driver accidentally but negligently killing someone with his or her car. (For the technical uses and definitions of these and other words, see the 1991 *Sourcebook*, Appendix 3, or the *Uniform Crime Reports*.)
6. Each crime statistic is taken from the 1990 *Uniform Crime Reports*; for the number of major offenses and number of homicides, see Table 21; for methods and types of homicide (including romantic triangles and those involving narcotics felons) and total numbers and types of arrests, see Table 27.

7. The victim reports are compiled in the 1991 *Sourcebook*. See Table 3.1 and numerous tables following that.

8. Discussion of ordinary self-report data is based on statistics drawn from Johnston et al. (1992), which include high school students' use of alcohol, marijuana, and cocaine, including "ever used" and current use. The same statistics are covered in the 1991 *Sourcebook*, Tables 3.91 through 3.98. Student self-report of miscellaneous crimes is examined in Tables 3.77 through 3.90.

9. Quarrels leading to homicide are depicted on page 13 of the 1990 *Uniform Crime Reports*.

10. The number of justifiable homicides by police is presented in California Office of the Attorney General (1989). The 1991 updated data were obtained by telephone from Charlotte Rhe of the Bureau of Criminal Statistics and Special Services. There are also substantial data on police as victims of both homicides and assaults; see 1991 *Sourcebook*, Tables 3.159–3.164, 3.166–3.177. On the ordinariness of police work, see Moore (1992), especially pages 114–115. Also see Wycoff (1982).

11. For examples of current police shows on television, see the weekly television listings of your local newspaper or the weekly *TV Guide*.

12. For an example of large versus small newspaper coverage of crime, compare the daily "Security Roundup," in the *Daily Trojan*, the newspaper of the University of Southern California, to crime presented in the front and Metro sections of the daily *Los Angeles Times*.

13. Sherlock Holmes tales are anthologized in Doyle (1984). Examples of crime tales for television are in Hitchcock (1959).

14. For a description of the skilled thief of the past, see Sutherland (1956). Another important burglar study is by Bennett and Wright (1984).

15. See Cusson (1993). Be sure to compare with Sutherland (1956) and then compare both Cromwell and Cusson to Akerstrom (1993). See especially Chapter 4 on crime as work and Chapter 6 on social skills of offenders.

16. The ease of robbery is taken up in Bellot (1983); also see Gabor, Baril, Cusson, Elie, LeBlanc, and Normandeau (1987).

17. On the loose nature of most street gangs, see Klein (1971). For more misconceptions about gangs, see Klein, Maxson, and Cunningham (1991) and Maxson, Gordon, and Klein (1985).

18. Concerning exaggerations about organized crime, see Reuter (1984). On the basis for the organized crime myth making, consult Kappeler, Blumberg, and Potter (1993), pages 11–14.

19. On the age fallacy, see Chapter 6 of Gottfredson and Hirschi (1990). For age and victimization data, as well as victim reports of ages of assailants, see the 1991 *Sourcebook*, Table 3.33. Age arrest data are found in the 1990 *Uniform Crime Reports*, Table 27, and in the 1991 *Sourcebook*, Tables 4.3, 4.4, 4.5, 4.8, 4.9, 4.11, and 4.13.

20. For evidence that the age pattern for crime is offset by weapons ownership, see methods of murder on page 13 of the 1991 *Uniform Crime Reports*. Survey data on gun ownership by age are found in the 1991 *Sourcebook*, Tables 2.49 and 2.50.

21. Nonreporting of crime to the police is a central issue in reports of the National Crime Survey. See the 1991 *Sourcebook*, Tables 3.12 through 3.15. To verify police nondiscovery of most instances of illegal drug use, compare incidents of drug abuse from Johnston, O'Malley, and Bachman (1992) with arrests shown in Table 27 of the 1991 *Uniform Crime Reports*. Also see Gottfredson and Hirschi (1990) for how lack of opportunity to commit crime influences age data.

22. On delay in court, the days elapsing between arrest for larceny and conviction in state courts can be found in Table 5.52 of the 1991 *Sourcebook*. The statistics reported in the text include auto theft (not separated by the survey) and are based only on cases disposed of by

trial. More modest statistics result if guilty pleas (which are far more numerous) are included. The median then becomes four months and the mean becomes six months.

23. On types of trials, see Table 5.48 of the 1991 *Sourcebook*, which documents the predominance of guilty pleas and bench trials.

24. Reinforcement schedules are covered in any introductory psychology textbook, but the special linkage to crime is thoroughly discussed in Gibbs (1975).

25. On the Kansas City Preventive Patrol Experiment, see Kelling, Pate, Dieckman, and Brown (1974). For research designed to help plan better patrols, see Larson (1972). A review of the patrol issue is found in Sherman (1983).

26. The number of sworn police officers per square mile of territory is from Table 1.35 in the 1989 *Sourcebook*. Los Angeles County's population and density are from U.S. census as reported in the *World Almanac and Book of Facts, 1992* (New York: Pharos, 1991), page 110.

27. See Cohen and Felson (1979) for links between crime rates and prosperity. On the United States' highest homicide rate among developed countries, see U.S. Department of Justice (1988). When taken in a broader international perspective, including very high homicide rates in several less developed countries, the U.S. homicide rate does not look quite as bad; on this, see Brantingham and Brantingham (1984), Figure 10.1. About inconsistency and complexity of linkages between economics and crime, see Thornberry and Christiansen (1984) and Messner and Tardiff (1986). For doubts about links between inequality and crime rates, see Cohen and Felson (1979). Evidence that prosperous nations have high property crime rates is presented in Brantingham and Brantingham (1984), Figure 10-2, p. 254.

28. Sweden's crime wave is covered in Dolmen (1990). See also Wikstrom (1985).

29. On the liberal and conservative agendas, see Walker (1989). Also see Barlow (1990), pages 28–31 and 61–71. On crime for its own sake as the necessary focus, see Gottfredson and Hirschi (1990), especially Chapter 2.

30. On moralizing via social science, see Wrong (1961).

31. For a more extensive critique of the theories of crime in Table 1.2, see Chapter 1 of Hirschi (1969). Standard crime theories are found in the following sources. On *deterrence*, see Bentham (1948). On *incapacitation*, see Assembly of Behavioral and Social Sciences (1978). For a spirited and thoughtful attack on incapacitation policies, see Hirsch (1976). On *differential association*, see Cohen (1955) and Sutherland and Cressey (1974). For another approach, see Cloward and Ohlin (1960). On *labeling theory*, see Lemert (1972). On *strain theory*, see Merton (1957). On *control theory*, see Hirschi (1969). The insight of basic human frailty is a part of control theory. On *situational insight*, see Luckenbill (1970) plus references in Chapter 2. Check also Briar and Piliavin (1965). For entry into the social psychology literature on situations, see Bandura (1985). Also see Argyle, Furnham, and Graham (1981). The *temptation insight* is given more attention in Chapters 2 and 8; the latter provides references on reducing temptation to prevent crime. *Provocations* are discussed in Luckenbill (1970) and at greater length in Chapter 2. The *bad company insight* is an issue taken up in Chapter 1 of Hirschi (1969). Delinquency as a group activity is considered, for example, in Erickson and Jensen (1977), Reiss (1988), and Tremblay (forthcoming). The *idleness insight* is examined at great length in Hirschi (1969).

32. The tendency of some individuals to get in many types of trouble is a central issue in Gottfredson and Hirschi (1990). For an update with numerous additional references, see Grasmick, Tittle, Bursik, and Arneklev (1993), as well as Keane, Maxim, and Teevan (1993); the same issue of the *Journal of Research in Crime and Delinquency* has commentary from Gottfredson and Hirschi. On linkages among various "delinquencies," see Akers

(1984); Hirschi (1969); Kandel (1978); Johnston, O'Malley, and Bachman (1992); Hindelang, Hirschi, and Weis (1981); Schoff (1915); and Ferri (1897). On the nonspecialization of offenders, see Klein (1984).

33. On family problems and delinquency, see Sampson (1987). On social area analysis with family problems included, see Shaw and McKay (1931, 1942). For nuances about how families influence delinquency, see pages 97–105 in Gottfredson and Hirschi (1990).

34. Marriage "intactness" may miss the point in studying how strong families reduce crime. The problem is that "intact" families—those with a husband and wife still married—do not always provide a strong family life. Some "intact" families have a father or mother or both who are largely absent, while some single parents perform double duty, join with other single parents, or enlist other relatives to help deliver more adult time for children. Or, after separating, two parents may provide joint custody or regularly visit their children.

Given that "intactness" is too crude and inaccurate to define or measure family strength, what better indicator can we find? We suggest that actual time that parents or other adult family members spend with children is a far better approach to defining family strength. Not denying that families can have a bad time together, we suggest that from a population viewpoint, more time means less crime.

The issue of marriage intactness is considered in Hirschi (1983); that short chapter takes up several nuances about family life and crime. The time that families spend together is investigated by Medrich, Roizen, Rubin, and Buckley (1982).

35. The American legal system and its dealings with crime and criminals is very well reviewed in handbooks for lawyers and students produced for various states. A very good example is Katz (1987).

36. For arguments against criminals as a specific subset of the human race, see Fattah (1991), who includes review of details on the age and social composition of victims, which are in turn drawn from the United States' National Crime Survey and similar victim surveys in other nations.

37. That crime is not the province of a small segment of the population, see Gottfredson and Hirschi (1990).

QUESTIONS FOR THOUGHT AND DISCUSSION

1. What are the most serious misunderstandings we have about crime and criminals? How do these misunderstandings lead us to ineffective solutions to the crime problem?

2. Does the author's argument imply a complete change in the relationship between criminology and morality? Is this a proposal for a new criminology that is entirely amoral?

3. What does this reading imply about the role of police and the rest of the criminal justice system?

HIGHLIGHTS FROM 20 YEARS OF SURVEYING CRIME VICTIMS

The National Crime Victimization Survey, 1973–92y

Marianne W. Zawitz
Patsy A. Klaus
Ronet Bachman
Lisa D. Bastian
Marshall M. DeBerry, Jr.
Michael R. Rand
Bruce M. Taylor

THE NATION'S TWO CRIME MEASURES

The National Crime Victimization Survey (NCVS) and the FBI's Uniform Crime Reports (UCR) measure various aspects of crime at the national level. These complementary series each contribute to providing a complete picture about the extent and nature of crime in the United States. Together the NCVS and UCR provide a more comprehensive assessment of crime in the United States than could be obtained from either statistical series alone.

The National Crime Victimization Survey

Using stable data collection methods since 1973, the NCVS has the following strengths:

- It measures both reported and unreported crimes.
- It is not affected by changes in the extent to which people report crime to police or improvements in police record-keeping technology.

From Bureau of Justice Statistics, Highlights from 20 Years of Surveying Crime Victims, Washington, D.C.: United States Department of Justice, October, 1993.

Violent crimes measured by NCVS and UCR*

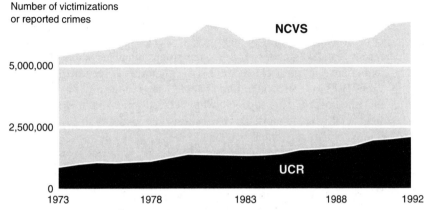

Number of victimizations
or reported crimes

*Includes NCVS violent crimes of rape, robbery, aggravated assault, and simple assault; and UCR violent crimes of murder and nonnegligent manslaughter, forcible rape, robbery, and aggravated assault.

NCVS provides information on both reported and unreported crime.

- It collects information that is not available when the initial police report is made including contacts the victim has with the criminal justice system after the crime, extent and costs of medical treatment, and recovery of property.
- It collects detailed information about victims and characteristics of the victimization including who the victims are, what their relationship is to the offender, whether the crime was part of a series of crimes occurring over a 6-month period, what self-protective measures were used and how the victims assess their effectiveness, and what the victim was doing when victimized.
- On occasion, it includes special supplements about particular topics such as school crime and the severity of crime.

The Uniform Crime Reports

The UCR program measures police workload and activity. Local police departments voluntarily report information to the Federal Bureau of Investigation (FBI) including the numbers of crimes reported to police, arrests made by police and other administrative information. The UCR program has the following strengths:

- It can provide local data about States, counties, cities, and towns.
- It measures crimes affecting children under age 12, a segment of the population that experts agree cannot be reliably interviewed in the NCVS.
- It includes crimes against commercial establishments.
- It collects information about the number of arrests and who was arrested.
- It counts the number of homicides (murders and nonnegligent manslaughters), crimes that cannot be counted in a survey that interviews victims. UCR also collects detailed information about the circumstances surrounding homicides and the characteristics of homicide victims.

HIGHLIGHTS FROM 20 YEARS OF SURVEYING CRIME VICTIMS

- Overall crime rates have been stable or declining in recent years; however, violent crime has increased for some groups. Violent crime rates for teenagers increased in recent years, while rates for other age groups remained stable or declined. The violent crime rate for blacks in 1992 is the highest ever recorded.
- From 1973 to 1991, 36.6 million people were injured as a result of violent crime including over 6 million people who received serious injuries.
- In general, you are more likely to become the victim of a violent crime than to be injured in a motor vehicle accident.
- One in four households in the United States is victimized by one or more crimes each year.
- About half of all violent crimes and more than a third of all crimes are reported to police.
- Teenagers and young adults consistently have the highest victimization rates.
- Handguns are used in about 10% of all violent crimes. Handgun crime rates are above the 1986 low but have not returned to the 1982 high.
- In 1991, an estimated $19.1 billion was lost directly from personal and household crime.
- The average dollar loss per crime increased from $142 in 1975 to $550 in 1991, a substantial increase even when adjusted for inflation.
- 9% of violent victimizations were series crimes where the victim experienced three or more similar victimizations within a 6-month period, but was unable to describe them separately.
- Males are much more likely to be victimized by strangers than by family members or other intimates. Females are as likely to be victims of violence by intimates as they are by strangers.
- About 30% of violent crimes and 25% of burglaries occur when the victim is engaged in a leisure activity away from home.

HOW MUCH CRIME IS THERE?

Almost 34 Million Victimizations Occurred in the United States in 1992

	Number of Victimizations	Rate per 1,000 Persons or Households
Personal crimes	18,831,980	91.2
Violent crime	6,621,140	32.1
Rape	140,930	.7
Robbery	1,225,510	5.9
Assault	5,254,690	25.5
Personal theft	12,210,830	59.2

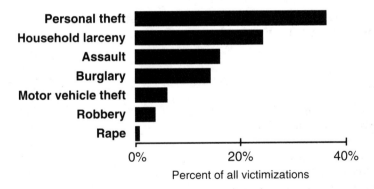

Most crime is property crime

	Number of Victimizations	Rate per 1,000 Persons or Households
Household crimes	14,817,360	152.2
Burglary	4,757,420	48.9
Larceny	8,101,150	83.2
Motor vehicle theft	1,958,780	20.1

About One in Four U.S. Households Was Victimized by a Crime in 1992

In 1992—

- 23% of U.S. households were victimized by a crime of violence or theft.
- 5% of all households had at least one member age 12 or older who was a violent crime victim.
- Black households, Hispanic households, and urban households were the most likely to experience crime.

Some Victims Are Repeatedly Victimized

Series victimizations are defined as three or more similar victimizations occurring within a 6-month period, which the victim is unable to describe separately. Victims reported series victimizations in—

- 9% of all violent crimes.
- 2% of personal thefts.
- 3% of household crimes.

How Do Crime Rates Compare with the Rates of Other Life Events?

Events	Rate per 1,000 Adults per Year
Accidental injury, all circumstances	220
Accidental injury at home	66
Personal theft	61
Accidental injury at work	47
Violent victimization	31
Assault (aggravated and simple)	25
Injury in motor vehicle accident	22
Death, all causes	11
Victimization with injury	11
Serious (aggravated) assault	8
Robbery	6
Heart disease death	5
Cancer death	3
Rape (women only)	1
Accidental death, all circumstances	.4
Pneumonia/influenza death	.4
Motor vehicle accident death	.2
Suicide	.2
HIV infection death	.1
Homicide/legal intervention	.1

Sources: See the Appendix for detailed sources, time periods, and calculations used for these data.

The Vast Majority of Violent Crimes Involve One Victim Rather Than Multiple Victims

Of all violent crimes, 92% had only one victim. The crimes of aggravated assault and robbery had more incidents with more than one victim than the other personal crimes.

A crime incident can have multiple victims. The National Crime Victimization Survey covers both incidents and victims. Some measures such as where the crime occurred are analyzed based on incidents; other measures such as the number of injured victims are based on the number of victimizations.

WHAT ARE THE TRENDS IN CRIME?

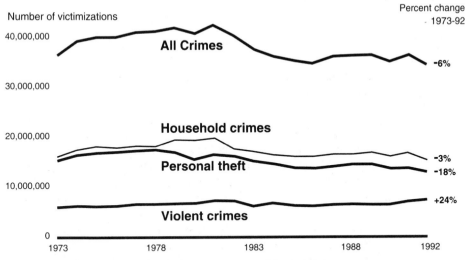

Note: Household crimes include burglary, larceny, and motor vehicle theft.
Violent crimes include rape, robbery, and assault.

The number of victimizations rose from 1973 until the early 1980s and has since declined

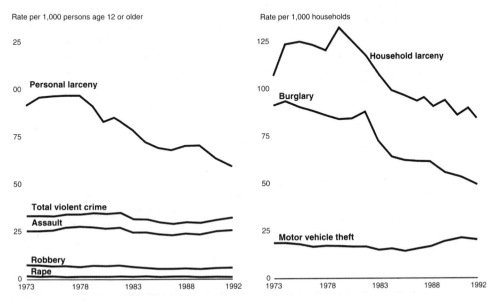

Victimization rates for most property crimes have also declined

WHAT ARE THE CHARACTERISTICS OF THE CRIMES MEASURED BY NCVS?

Rape

DEFINITION   Carnal knowledge through the use of force or the threat of force, including attempts. Both heterosexual and homosexual rape are included.

FACTS ABOUT RAPE

- In 1992, 141,000 rapes were reported to the NCVS. Rapes of males account for about 8% of all rapes measured by the survey. Crimes including rapes that occur in an institutionalized setting (such as a prison, hospital, or the military) are not measured in the survey.
- About half of all rapes of females were perpetrated by someone known to the victim.
- The offender was armed in about one-fifth of rapes of females. A higher proportion of stranger rapists were armed with some type of weapon (29%) compared to non-stranger rapists (17%). About the same proportion of handguns were used in stranger rapes as were knives or other sharp instruments. Nonstranger rapists were more likely to be armed with knives or sharp instruments.
- Of female rape victims who took some type of self-protective action such as fighting back and yelling and screaming, most reported that it helped the situation rather than made it worse.
- Slightly more than half of female rape victims report their victimizations to the police. They are more likely to report the crime if the perpetrator was armed, if they sustained additional injuries, and if they received medical care for these injuries. The relationship the victim had with the offender (intimate, acquaintance, stranger) does not affect whether the victimization is reported to the police.

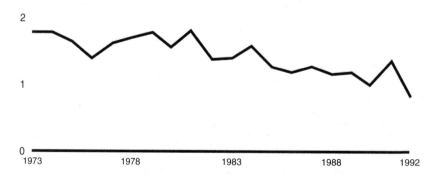

Number of rapes per 1,000 females age 12 or over

The rape rate fluctuated over the past 20 years

Number of robberies per 1,000 persons age 12 or over

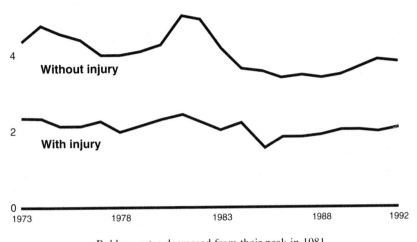

Robbery rates decreased from their peak in 1981

Robbery

DEFINITION Completed or attempted theft of property or cash directly from a person by force or threat of force, with or without a weapon.

FACTS ABOUT ROBBERY

- In 1992, 1.2 million robbery victimizations occurred in the United States. Property was lost in two-thirds of these robberies.
- For the period 1987–90, four of every five robberies measured by the NCVS were committed by persons who were strangers to the victim.
- The most common outcome in robberies committed by strangers (42%) was for the victim to lose property but to sustain no injury. The victim suffered a serious injury and lost property to the offender in 1 in 20 robberies. In 25% of all stranger robberies, the victim escaped from the incident without being injured or losing property.
- Offenders were armed with handguns in 21% of all stranger robberies. The offender's weapon was a knife in 19%, and an object used as a weapon (such as a stick, rock, etc.) in 10% of stranger robberies. The offender was unarmed in a third of all robberies committed by strangers.

Weapon Type	1987–90 Stranger Robberies	
	Number	Percent
Total robberies	3,514,600	100
Handgun	743,900	21
Other gun	53,900	2

Weapon Type	1987–90 Stranger Robberies Number	Percent
Knives, sharp objects	657,000	19
Other weapons	361,200	10
Unarmed	1,138,700	32
Weapon type not known or not known whether offender was armed	560,000	16

Assault

DEFINITION   The intentional inflicting, or attempted inflicting of injury upon another person. Aggravated assault involves serious injury and includes all assaults or threats of injury with a deadly or dangerous weapon. Simple assault involves less serious injury and by definition does not include any assaults involving weapons.

FACTS ABOUT ASSAULT

- In 1992, over 5 million assaults were committed; two-thirds of these assaults were simple assaults.
- Over 1.5 million assaults in 1991 resulted in some sort of injury.
- Over half of the injured assault victims who receive medical care receive their care in a clinic or hospital.
- Most assaults by armed offenders occur at night, usually before midnight. Most assaults by unarmed offenders occur during the day.
- About 7% of assaults occur inside a bar, restaurant, or nightclub. The most common places where both simple and aggravated assaults occur are on the street; in a parking lot or garage; at or in the victim's home; or at, in, or near a friend's, relative's, or neighbor's home.
- About a third of the aggravated assaults involve the use of a gun. However, those resulting in injury are more likely to involve a blunt object than any other weapon.
- The victim used some form of self-protection in almost three-fourths of all assaults. These findings are the same for both stranger and nonstranger assaults.
- When self-protection was used, 72% of victims felt that it helped the situation, 7% thought it hurt the situation, 7% thought it both helped and hurt, and 13% thought it neither helped nor hurt.
- More than half of victims who said that self-protection helped felt it avoided injury or greater injury. Of those who thought self-protection was harmful, 67% said it made the offender angrier or more aggressive.

Burglary

DEFINITION   Unlawful or forcible entry or attempted entry of a residence. This crime usually, but not always, involves theft. As long as the person has no legal right to be present in the structure a burglary has occurred.

Number of assaults per 1,000 persons age 12 or over

Percent change
1973-92*

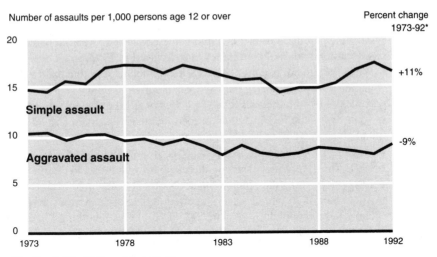

*Significant at the 90% confidence level

The rate for simple assault has increased over 1973 levels while the rate for aggravated assault has declined

Number of burglaries per 1,000 households

Percent change
1973-92

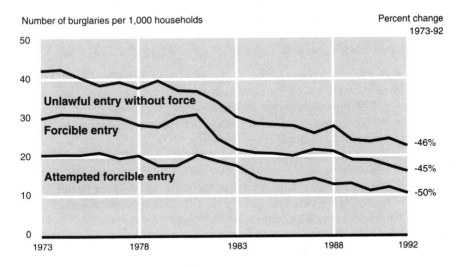

The rates for all types of household burglaries have been decreasing

The structure may be a house, garage, shed, or any other structure on the premises. If it occurs in a vacation residence or hotel occupied by the household, it is still classified as a burglary for the household.

FACTS ABOUT BURGLARY

- About 4% of all households in the United States experienced one or more of the 4.8 million household burglaries that occurred in 1992.
- When the time of occurrence was known, victims reported that over half of all burglaries took place during the day from 6 a.m. to 6 p.m.
- Almost 3 in 10 burglaries result in losses of $500 or more.
- Some economic loss including property damage occurs in 86% of all burglaries and about 95% of all forcible entry burglaries.
- The estimated economic loss to victims of household burglaries was $4.2 billion in 1991. This figure includes only direct costs to victims and does not measure such costs as operating the criminal justice system or increased insurance premiums.
- About half of all burglaries are reported to the police. Serious burglaries are more likely to be reported; more than 70% of burglaries involving forcible entry are reported to police but 42% of the burglaries when the offender enters without force are reported.

Larceny

DEFINITION   Theft or attempted theft of property or cash without involving force or illegal entry. If the property is taken from a residence by someone who has a legal right to be there, it is a household larceny. If it is taken from a person either with contact but no direct force or without contact it is a personal larceny. Personal larceny with contact includes purse snatching and pocket picking.

FACTS ABOUT LARCENY

- In 1992, a total of 12,210,830 personal larcenies and 8,101,150 household larcenies occurred. Of the personal larcenies, 152,300 involved purse snatching and 332,500 involved pocket picking.
- Personal larcenies without contact are the least likely crimes to be reported to the police.
- The estimated direct losses to victims of personal and household larceny were $5.4 billion in 1991.
- Personal larceny with contact (purse snatching or pocket picking) is the one crime measured by NCVS that affects the elderly to the same extent as it affects younger persons in the population.

Motor Vehicle Theft

DEFINITION   Stealing or unauthorized taking of a motor vehicle, including attempted thefts.

MOTOR VEHICLE THEFT FACTS

- A total of about 2 million motor vehicle thefts occurred in the United States in 1992. When based upon the number of vehicles owned the motor vehicle theft rate was about 13 motor vehicle thefts per 1,000 vehicles.

Number of personal larcenies per 1,000 persons age 12 or over   Percent change
                                                                                  1973-92

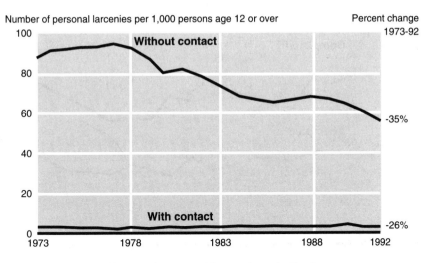

The rates for personal larceny have declined

Number of household larcenies per 1,000 households   Percent change
                                                                                  1973-92

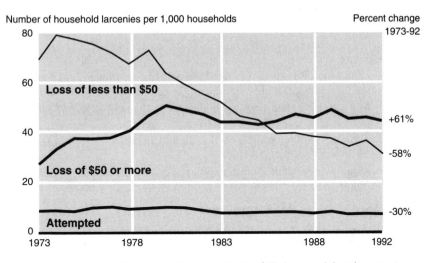

Rates for household larceny with a loss of under $50 decreased, but the rate
for larcenies with a loss of $50 or more increased

- Of all households in the United States, 2% were the victims of one or more motor
  vehicle thefts during 1992.
- Of all crimes measured by the NCVS, completed motor vehicle thefts are the most
  likely to be reported to the police (92%).
- The most common place for a motor vehicle theft to occur is in a parking lot or
  garage (36%).
- In 1991, motor vehicle theft resulted in an estimated $8.5 billion in direct losses to
  victims.

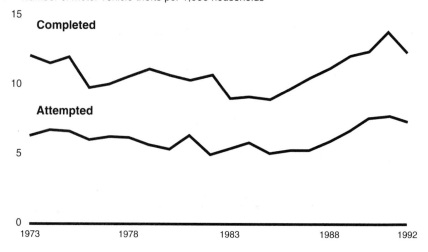

Number of motor vehicle thefts per 1,000 households

Completed

Attempted

The rates for motor vehicle theft declined through the 1970s and early 1980s, but began rising in the late 1980s

- Motor vehicle theft rates are higher for households headed by blacks (37 per 1,000) than for whites (19 per 1,000). When calculated based upon vehicles owned the rates are still higher for blacks (31 per 1,000) than for whites (11 per 1,000).
- Motor vehicle theft rates are higher for Hispanics (42 per 1,000 households) than for non-Hispanics (20 per 1,000).
- The rate of motor vehicle theft is higher for renters (29 per 1,000) than for home-owners (18 per 1,000).
- Motor vehicle theft rates are higher in central cities (37 per 1,000 households) than suburban areas (21 per 1,000) or rural areas (6 per 1,000).

WHO ARE THE VICTIMS OF CRIME?

WHO ARE THE VICTIMS OF PERSONAL CRIME?

Rate per 1,000 Persons
Age 12 or Over

	Violence	*Theft*
Sex		
Male	40	65
Female	23	58

Males have higher personal crime victimization rates than females, except for the crimes of rape and personal larceny involving contact.

Rate per 1,000 Persons
Age 12 or Over

	Violence	Theft	
Age			
12–15	63	101	The elderly (those age 65 or older) are
16–19	91	94	significantly less likely than younger
20–24	75	115	age groups to become the victims of most
25–34	35	71	types of crime.
35–49	20	56	
50–64	10	35	
65 and older	4	20	
Race			
White	30	61	Blacks have significantly higher violent
Black	44	61	victimization rates than whites or persons
Other	28	52	of other races.
Ethnicity			
Hispanic	36	59	Hispanics have somewhat higher violent
Non-Hispanic	31	61	victimization rates than non-Hispanics, but
			there is little difference between theft rates
			for the two groups.
Marital status by sex			
Males			
Never married	80	97	Those who never married have the highest
Divorced/separated	44	95	rates of both violent crimes and personal
Married	19	43	thefts, while persons who are divorced or
Widowed	*	23	separated have the second highest.
Females			Widowed persons have the lowest rates for
Never married	43	90	these crimes.
Divorced/Separated	45	74	
Married	11	44	
Widowed	6	22	
Family Income			
Less than $7,500	59	62	Victims with higher incomes have lower
$7,500–$9,999	42	61	violent victimization rates.
$10,000–$14,999	43	60	
$15,000–$24,999	31	57	Theft rates vary much less than violent
$25,000–$29,999	32	57	victimization rates across income
$30,000–$49,999	25	60	categories. However, members of families
$50,000 or more	20	66	earning $15,000 to $29,999 have lower
			theft rates than members of families earn-
			ing more than $50,000.

	Rate per 1,000 Persons Age 12 or Over	
	Violence	*Theft*
Education		
0–4 years	18	16
5–7 years	45	67
8 years	28	49
9–11 years	49	62
High school graduate	28	49
1–3 years college	36	83
College graduate	18	68
Residence		
Central city	44	75
1,000,000 or more	39	76
500,000–999,999	50	80
250,000–499,999	54	70
50,000–249,999	38	74
Suburban	26	61
Rural	25	44

City dwellers are more likely to be the victims of both violent and theft crimes than are suburban and rural residents.

*Based on 10 or fewer cases.

WHAT KINDS OF HOUSEHOLDS ARE THE VICTIMS OF CRIME?

	Rate per 1,000 Households		
	Household Burglary	*Larceny*	*Motor Vehicle Theft*
Age of household head			
12–19	194	206	46
20–34	73	114	26
35–49	59	100	26
50–64	39	75	23
65 and older	27	45	8
Race of household head			
White	50	87	19
Black	75	96	37
Other	52	85	34
Ethnicity of Household Head			
Hispanic	75	123	42
Non-Hispanic	51	85	20

Household victimizations are more likely in households headed by younger persons.

Households headed by blacks have the highest rates of household crimes.

For each household crime measured by the NCVS, Hispanics have higher rates than non-Hispanics.

Rate per 1,000 Households

	Household Burglary	Larceny	Motor Vehicle Theft	
Income				
Less than $7,500	81	96	10	As household income rises,
$7,500–$9,999	69	86	19	burglary rates fall.
$10,000–$14,999	65	92	19	
$15,000–$24,999	49	97	22	Households earning more than
$25,000–$29,999	45	76	16	$30,000 a year are generally
$30,000–$49,999	44	87	24	more likely than households in
$50,000 or more	41	80	28	most other income categories to
				be victims of motor vehicle
				theft.
Number of persons in household				
One	44	52	12	The more people in the
2–3	52	86	22	household, the higher the crime
4–5	62	122	30	rate. Households with 6 or more
6 or more	88	186	45	members have the highest
				household crime rates.
Form of tenure				
Home owned or being bought	42	77	18	Renters are more likely to be
Home rented	73	107	29	victims of household crimes
				than owners.
Place of residence				
Central city	70	117	37	Households in central cities are
1,000,000 or more	65	109	51	more likely to experience a
500,000–999,999	75	131	43	household crime than
250,000–499,999	80	114	36	households in suburban or rural
50,000–249,999	64	119	16	areas.
Suburban	45	78	21	
Rural	47	69	6	

WHO ARE THE OFFENDERS IN VIOLENT CRIMES?

Many Victims of Violent Crime Can Describe the Offender

The NCVS asks crime victims their perceptions of the age, sex, and race of the offenders in confrontational crimes like rape, robbery, and assault. Offender descriptions are not available from NCVS on those crimes where the victim and the offender do not confront one another, such as household larcenies. In general, NCVS data on offenders are consistent with other sources such as arrest data.

NUMBER OF OFFENDERS   Of violent incidents, 70% are committed by a lone offender. Rapes are more likely to involve only one offender than assaults or robberies. Robberies are more likely to involve multiple offenders than the other violent crimes.

AGE   Most violent crime victims describe the offender as young. Of violent victimizations committed by a lone offender, the offender was perceived to be—

- under age 14 in nearly 9% of the victimizations.
- between the ages of 15 and 17 in nearly 11%.
- between the ages of 18 and 20 in nearly 15%.
- between 21 and 29 years of age in 33%.
- age 30 and over in 33%.

When more than one offender committed a crime, victims perceived that the offenders were most often teenagers (between the ages of 12 and 20.)

SEX   The victim perceived the offender to be male in 85% of the single-offender victimizations including over 95% of the rapes and 92% of the robberies. Victims are more likely to be confronted by a female offender in an assault than in a rape or robbery. When more than one offender was involved, victims report that all the offenders were male in 83% of the victimizations, they were both male and female in 10%, and all were female in about 5%.

RACE   Violent crime victims reported that the offender was white in 64% of the victimizations by lone offenders, black in 28%, of other races in 7%. In 58% of the single-offender robberies, victims perceived that the offender was black.

Comparatively, victims described the offender as white in—

- 77% of rapes.
- 70% of simple assaults.
- 64% of aggravated assaults.

Of all multiple-offender victimizations, victims perceived that in—

- 38% all of the offenders were black.
- 35% they all were white.
- 16% they were mixed.
- 8% they were all of other races.

In Four-fifths of All Violent Crimes, the Victims and Offenders Are of the Same Race

Of all single-offender crimes of violence, 80% are intraracial including—

- 69% where the victim and offender are white.
- 11% where the victim and offender are black.

For the 20% of violent crimes that are interracial

- 15% involve white victims and black offenders.

- 3% involve white victims and other-race offenders.
- 2% involve black victims and white offenders.

Robbery is the most interracial crime; 37% involved victims and offenders of different races. Of all single-offender robberies—

- 31% involved white victims and black offenders.
- 4% involved white victims and other-race offenders.
- 2% involved black victims and white offenders.

How Many Offenders Were under the Influence of Drugs or Alcohol?

In 54% of violent victimizations, the victim reported on the offender's drug or alcohol use. When reported, the offender was perceived to be under the influence of drugs or alcohol in 61% of violent victimizations including—

- both drugs and alcohol in 10%.
- alcohol alone in 40%.
- drugs alone in 8%.

Robbery victims are less likely to report that the offender was under the influence of drugs or alcohol than are rape or assault victims.

ARE MOST CRIMES REPORTED TO THE POLICE?

In 1992, 39% of the Crimes Included in the NCVS Were Reported to the Police

Victims reported the crime to the police in—

- 50% of the violent victimizations.
- 41% of all household crimes.
- 30% of the personal thefts.

The proportion of reported crimes is highest for completed motor vehicle thefts; 92% were reported to the police. The lowest proportion of reported crime is for personal larceny without contact that resulted in a loss of less than $50; 15% were reported.

Except for thefts, completed crimes are more often reported than attempted crimes.

QUESTIONS FOR THOUGHT AND DISCUSSION

1. How is victimization data different from the *Uniform Crime Report*'s data?
2. Using what we learned from the National Crime Victimization Survey, what are some ways we can avoid being victimized?
3. According to data from the National Crime Victimization Survey, has the overall rate of crime been going up or down? What types of crime have been changing the most?

Crimes involving injury are more often reported than those without injury

Property crimes involving large losses are more often reported

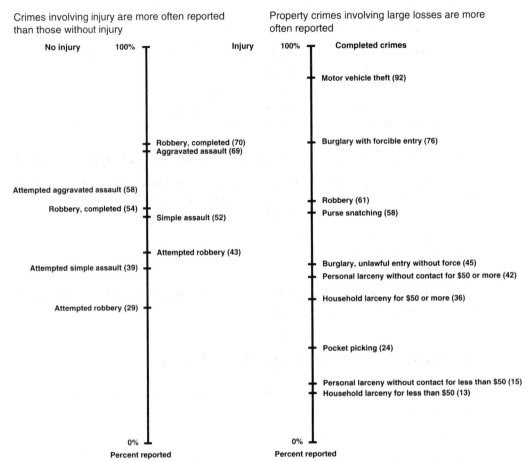

No injury   100%   Injury   100%   Completed crimes

                                                          Motor vehicle theft (92)

Robbery, completed (70)
Aggravated assault (69)   Burglary with forcible entry (76)

Attempted aggravated assault (58)   Robbery (61)
Robbery, completed (54)   Purse snatching (58)
Simple assault (52)

Attempted robbery (43)

Attempted simple assault (39)   Burglary, unlawful entry without force (45)
                                                          Personal larceny without contact for $50 or more (42)

Attempted robbery (29)   Household larceny for $50 or more (36)

                                                          Pocket picking (24)

                                                          Personal larceny without contact for less than $50 (15)
                                                          Household larceny for less than $50 (13)

0%   0%
Percent reported   Percent reported

Note: For some types of violent crime, 1992 reporting percentages were not available by whether or not the victim was injured. By definition, attempted assaults are without injury. In 1992, 53% of all rapes were reported to the police.

Various factors affect whether a crime is reported

Racism in the Criminal Justice System:

Two Sides of a Controversy

The Myth of a Racist Criminal Justice System*

William Wilbanks

White and black Americans differ sharply over whether their criminal justice system is racist. The vast majority of blacks appear to believe that the police and courts do discriminate against blacks, whereas a majority of whites reject this charge. A sizable minority of whites even believe that the justice system actually discriminates for blacks in "leaning over backward" for them in reaction to charges of racism from the black community and the media.

The contrasting views of blacks and whites as to the fairness of the criminal justice system are of more than academic interest as research indicates that the higher level of offending by blacks may be due in part to the belief that "the system" is unfair. The belief produces a "justification for no obligation" or the attitude that "I don't respect a system that is racist, and so I don't feel obliged to abide by the laws of that system." This view in the collective has led to riots in Miami and other cities. Furthermore, the hostility to police generated by the belief has led to a mutual expectation of violence between police and blacks that has produced more violence as part of a self-fulfilling prophesy. Finally, the white backlash to affirmative action programs may be due in part to the perception that blacks complain about racism in a society that actually practices reverse discrimination (favoritism toward blacks).

THE THESIS

I take the position that the perception of the criminal justice system as racist is a myth. This overall thesis should not be misinterpreted. I do believe that there is a racial prejudice and

*This is a summary of the book by the same name.

Coramae Richey Mann and William Wilbanks, "Racism in the Criminal Justice System: Two Sides of a Controversy," *Criminal Justice Research Bulletin*, Vol 3(5), 1987, 5 pp. Copyright © 1987 Sam Houston State University. Reprinted by permission of The Criminal Justice Center, Sam Houston State University, Huntsville, Texas.

discrimination *within* the criminal justice system, in that there are individuals, both white and black, who make decisions, at least in part, on the basis of race. I do not believe that *the system* is characterized by racial prejudice or discrimination *against* blacks. At every point from arrest to parole there is little or no evidence of an overall racial effect, in that the percentage outcomes for blacks and whites are not very different. There is evidence, however, that some individual decision makers (e.g., police officers, judges) are more likely to give "breaks" to whites than to blacks. However, there appears to be an *equal* tendency for other individual decision makers to favor blacks over whites. This "canceling-out effect" results in studies that find no *overall* racial effect.

The assertion that the criminal justice system is not racist does not address the reasons why blacks appear to offend at higher rates than whites before coming into contact with the criminal justice system. It may be that racial discrimination in American society has been responsible for conditions (e.g., discrimination in employment, housing, and education) that lead to higher rates of offending by blacks, but that possibility does not bear on the question of whether the criminal justice system discriminates against blacks. Also, the thesis that racism is not systematic and pervasive in the criminal justice system does not deny that racial prejudice and discrimination have existed or even been the dominant force in the design and operation of the criminal justice system in the past.

DEFINING RACISM

One of the main barriers in the discussion and resolution of the issue of racism in the criminal justice system involves the multiple uses and meanings of the term "racism." Definitions of this term range from a conscious attitude by an individual to an unconscious act by an institution or even to the domination of society by white culture. I have suggested that the term "racism" be abandoned in favor of the terms "racial prejudice" (an attitude) and "racial discrimination" (an act).

Any discussion of the pervasiveness of racism in the justice system is clouded by the tendency of Accusers (e.g., those who claim the system is racist) to use a double standard in that the term is used only to apply to whites. For example, it is often pointed out that 50% of the victims of police killings are black and that this fact alone presents a prima facie case of racism. But it is seldom pointed out that 50% of the police officers who are killed are victimized by blacks. If the first fact indicates racism by white police officers, why does not the second fact indicate racism by black killers of police?

At times the use of the term racism appears to constitute a "non-falsifiable thesis" in that any result is defined as racist. For example, in *McCleskey* v. *Georgia* (a case before the U.S. Supreme Court this term) the petitioner claims that he received the death penalty because he (a black) killed a white whereas those who kill blacks seldom receive the death penalty. Thus lenient treatment given to black killers (or those who kill black victims) is defined as racism. But if black killers had been more likely to be sentenced to death, that result would also be (and has been) viewed as racist. Thus the term is defined so that any result is indicative of racism (i.e., a non-falsifiable thesis). The double standard of racism is also seen in this case in that the death penalty statistics actually indicate harsher treatment of white than black killers, but this result is not seen as racism (against whites).

In a similar fashion a lower percentage of blacks (than whites) being convicted has been interpreted by Accusers as racist in that this result indicates that charges against blacks were often without substance. On the other hand, if more blacks were convicted, this result would also be viewed by Accusers as being indicative of racism since black defendants were treated more harshly.

THE DATA

The book (from which this chapter is taken) was undertaken to explain why blacks in the U.S. are 8 times more likely, on a per capita basis, to be in prison than are whites. The major point of the book is that the approximate 8:1 per capita ratio of blacks to whites in prison is the result of an approximately 8:1 black to white level at offending and not the result of racial selectivity by the police and the courts. In other words, the 8:1 black to white ratio at offending is not increased as offenders are brought into and processed by the criminal justice system.

Some original data are presented in an appendix to the book on the black vs. white gap from arrest to incarceration in prison for two states—California and Pennsylvania. In 1980 felony cases, blacks in California were arrested 5.2 times as often as whites. This black/white gap increased to 6.2 at incarceration. Thus the black/white "gap" increased by 20% from arrest to prison. However, the reverse occurred in Pennsylvania where the 8.1 gap at arrest decreased to 7.4 at incarceration (a decline of 9%). Overall, it would appear that the black/white gap does not increase from arrest to prison. Thus there is no evidence overall that black offenders processed by the criminal justice system fare worse than white offenders.

But perhaps the black/white gap at arrest is a product of racial bias by the police in that the police are more likely to select and arrest black than white offenders. The best evidence on this question comes from the National Crime Survey which interviews 130,000 Americans each year about crime victimization. Those who are victimized by violent crime are asked to describe the offenders (who were not necessarily caught by the police) as to age, sex, and race. The percentage of offenders described by victims as being black is generally consistent with the percentage of offenders who are black according to arrest figures. For example, approximately 60% of (uncaught) robbers described by victims were black and approximately 60% of those arrested for robbery in the U.S. are black. This would not be the case if the police were "picking on" black robbers and ignoring white robbers.

Given the above figures, those who claim that racism is systematic and pervasive in the criminal justice system should explain why the black/white gap does not cumulatively increase from arrest to prison. Furthermore, those who claim racism is pervasive should be asked to specify the number of black offenders who are thought to receive harsher treatment (e.g., whether 10%, 50%, or 100%) and the extent of that "extra" harshness in cases where "it" is given. For example, at sentencing do those mistreated black offenders receive on the average 10%, 50%, or 100% harsher sentence?

There is a large body of research on the alleged existence of racial discrimination at such points as arrest, conviction, and sentencing. The bibliography of my book lists over 80 sentencing studies which examined the impact of race on outcome. A number of scholars have examined this large body of research and concluded that there is no evidence of systematic racial discrimination. James Q. Wilson, the most prominent American criminologist, asserts that the claim of discrimination is not supported by the evidence as did a three-volume study of the sentencing literature by the National Academy of Sciences.

METHODOLOGICAL PROBLEMS

However, some studies do claim to have found evidence of racial discrimination. However, as Wilson and others have pointed out, most of these studies are marked by flaws in design or interpretation. One chapter of *The Myth of a Racist Criminal Justice System* is devoted to seven models of design and/or interpretation which have been utilized in studies of the possible existence of racial discrimination utilized a model of analysis that ensured such a result.

But many readers will be thinking at this point that "one can prove anything with statistics" and thus that the validity of the claim for a racist criminal justice system should be determined by what one knows by personal experience or observation. However, the layperson's confidence in and reliance upon "common sense" in rejecting the statistical approach to knowledge in favor of what one knows by personal experience and observation is misplaced. The layperson does not take into account the impact of bias (and in some cases racial prejudice) in personal experience and observation.

Let us take, for example, the question as to whether there is racial discrimination in the use of force by the police. Those who reject studies of large numbers of "use of force" incidents which do not show evidence of racial discrimination by race of victim suggest that "unbiased" observation will reveal racism. But suppose that several people see a white police officer hit a black youth. There are a multitude of explanations (e.g., the youth hit the officer first, the youth resisted authority, the officer was the macho type who would hit any victim who was not properly deferential, the officer was a racist) for such an act. The tendency is for those with a particular bias to select that explanation which is consistent with their bias. For example, other police officers or white citizens might select the explanation which is consistent with their bias. For example, other police officers or white citizens might select the explanation that the youth resisted authority while black citizens might select the explanation that the officer was a racist. In either case the observer simply infers the explanation that is most consistent with his/her bias and thus knowledge via observation is anything but unbiased. Large scale statistical studies allow one to control for factors (other than race) which might impact on a decision or act. Without such studies those who disagree on the impact of racism will simply be trading anecdotes. ("I know a case where…") to "prove" their case.

CONCLUSION

Racial prejudice, in my view, is the process by which people assign negative traits and motives to "them" (the other race). Blacks tend to see the beating of a black youth by a white police officer as being indicative of racism (an evil motive or trait attributed to the "out-group") while whites (or police officers) tend to see the beating as being the result of some improper action by the black youth. The white view is also influenced by the assigning of evil motives or traits to the out-group (to the black youth). In both cases the observers, whether black or white, have been influenced by racial prejudice in their assigning of blame or cause for the incident.

My basic position is that both the black and white views on the extent of racism in the criminal justice system are "ignorant" in that personal knowledge is gained primarily via observation and experience—methods which are heavily influenced by bias and racial prejudice. In other words, racial prejudice keeps the races polarized on this issue since each race sees the "facts" which "prove" its thesis. Statistical studies of large numbers of blacks and whites subjected to a particular decision (e.g., the use of force) are a safeguard against personal bias and are far more valid as a means to "truth" than personal observation and experience. It is my view that an examination of those studies available at various points in the criminal justice system fails to support the view that racial discrimination is pervasive. It is in this sense that the belief in a racist criminal justice system is a myth.

The Reality of a Racist Criminal Justice System
Coramae Richey Mann

I first heard of Bill Wilbanks' *The Myth of a Racist Criminal Justice System* at the Academy of Criminal Justice Sciences' annual meeting in Orlando during a panel discussion of urban crime in Black communities where the book rapidly became the focus of attention and outrage expressed by the panel and participants. The discussion clearly suggested that *The Myth* was the antithesis of the book I am writing, *Minorities, Crime and Public Policy*. Two subsequent readings of Wilbanks' book confirmed my original impression; therefore, when Editor Frank Williams invited me to present an alternative view to *The Myth*, I strongly agreed that another perspective was demanded.

In the two years that I have taught my undergraduate course on race and crime, the classes were fraught with anxiety and frustration in the face of the students' personal misconceptions, ignorance about American minorities, and reliance on racial stereotypes, particularly as applied to crime. There clearly was a need for a text which could present the "minority" side. With the arrival of *The Myth*, the need increased for a more balanced presentation of the topic.

As I view it, there are two major issues involved which must be definitively addressed. First, that Wilbanks is mistaken and that there *is* racial prejudice and discrimination in the criminal justice system (and throughout the United States' social system) which is *rooted* in racism. And second, the linchpin of his thesis not only relies on a simplistic and rather naive view of what takes place in the "real world" of criminal justice— out in the trenches so to speak—but also Wilbanks' complete dependence on quantitative data for his "proof" results in his dismissal of the rich qualitative available which he erroneously describes as "anecdotal" or as reported by "lay persons." It is this latter elitism that is most problematic.

DEFINITIONS

Despite the use of the eye-catching and inflammatory term *racist* in the title of his book, Wilbanks quickly and inexplicably abandons the term *racism* and substitutes *racial prejudice* and *racial discrimination* in its stead. It is my contention that all terms are applicable when the plight of minorities in the criminal justice system is examined. Although Wilbanks limited his thesis to Blacks, in this alternative view, I refer to all racial minorities, since racial prejudice, racial discrimination, and racism are directed at non-whites in this country.

Wilbanks cited, but glossed over, the impressive, in-depth, objective national assessment of the impact of the criminal justice system on minorities by the National Minority Advisory Council on Criminal Justice (1980:1) which used five study methods (literature review, public hearings, commissioned specific issue studies, field studies, and critical analyses of criminal justice programs and policies) to reach the conclusion that "...for minorities all over the nation, the issues, above all others, are political and economic exploitation and *racism*, the basic causes of conflict and disorder in the American criminal justice system." (Emphasis added.) Racism connotes power, thus, by definition, in only very few limited instances can a minority person have a quantum of power; and since they lack institutional power, it is definitionally impossible for American minorities to be identified as racist.

An Afro-American does not need to go to Brighton Beach (New York) to find out about racial prejudice and violence, an American Vietnamese need not travel to Boston or Florida to be insulted and violently attacked, nor does a Mexican American have to go to Los Angeles or a Native American (Indian) anywhere in the continental United States to experience differential treatment simply because of their color. All any of these persons have to do to face racial prejudice and discrimination is to be non-white in America today. As a minority who for a lifetime has experienced prejudicial treatment because of my race (and gender) I totally disagree with Wilbanks' contention that racial prejudice against minorities "appears to be declining" (p. 146). More in accord with our urbane times, racial prejudice has not declined but has simply "gone underground" and become much more subtle. That is, it has become institutionalized—the process that "institutionalized racism" connotes.

THE REALITY: AN ALTERNATIVE VIEW

Aside from the observation that Wilbanks often contradicts his own thesis throughout the book and adopts a chauvinistic approach by consistently reporting research to substantiate his position and skimming over contrary views (particularly qualitative studies), such detailed critique is left to book reviewers. The focus of this alternative view is therefore best served through analyses and comments that respond to Wilbanks' challenges to the discrimination thesis, or DT as he calls it, which is contrasted with NDT or a non-discrimination thesis (pp. 144–147).

1. After repeatedly stating that the research is "sparse," Wilbanks is chagrined that with or without controls, "a sizable race effect" cannot be demonstrated at decision points throughout the criminal justice system. Aside from not defining "sizable," "substantial," or even "race effect," Wilbanks uses his aggregate study in two states (California and Pennsylvania) for one year (1980) as the exemplar. This is curious, since in his later recommendations for future research, Wilbanks states that aggregate studies of decision making should be abandoned in favor of studies concentrating on individual decision makers (a point I strongly endorse), since research "attempting to validate the DT or the NDT has been seriously deficient" (p. 147). Thus we find that aggregate studies should not be used, yet such studies are an integral part of Wilbanks' thesis; notably his own California/Pennsylvania aggregate data (Appendix). Interestingly, in California Wilbanks' data revealed a 19 percent increase in the black/white "gap" from arrest to incarceration; whereas Pennsylvania showed a slight decrease in the black/white gap (p. 145). Nonetheless, the "gaps" continued to exist which is the major concern of a DT position. Unfortunately, the value of this effort is diminished since Wilbanks did not use any controls in the study. Wilbanks comments that "no study has examined the racial gap for all the decision points from arrest to incarceration" (p. 151). However, Petersilia (1983) reports such a study and the same has been reported for women felons (Mann, 1984). Petersilia (1983:93) found that minorities were "less likely to be given probation, more likely to receive prison sentences, more likely to get longer sentences, and more likely to serve a longer time in prison than whites after controlling for offense seriousness, prior record and prison violence."

2. A perplexing tactic that Wilbanks uses throughout *The Myth*, in addition to the "blaming the victim" approach, is the frequent use of an "apples and oranges" argument by the constant introduction of reverse sexism and reverse racism. The theoretical debate on whether female offenders are treated more leniently or more harshly by the criminal justice system is about as divided as that on race discrimination, but it is not the issue the book purports to address. Thus, the constant reference to "sexism" and "white discrimination" in *The Myth* tends to detract from the major thesis.

3. Wilbanks wonders why there is an over-representation of blacks in both arrests and incarcerations and the racial gap does not increase cumulatively. Again, he bases this interpretation of the black/white gap on his two-state study where in one state, it *did* increase. It should also be noted that an examination of the *Uniform Crime Reports* (UCR) for the past seven years (1979–1985) indicates that there is also an overrepresentation of arrests of Hispanic Americans, Asian Americans, and Native Americans disproportionate to their numbers in the population (Mann forthcoming). Also, contrary to Wilbanks' incitive and untrue statement that according to the UCR, 50 percent of those arrested in 1984 for sex offenses were black, for the period 1979–1985, black arrests for sex offenses showed little variation from 1979 (20.2 percent) to 1985 which was also 20.2 percent (U.S. Department of Justice, 1980; Table 25; 1986; Table 38).

4. A point stressed throughout the book is that the dropping of charges against blacks by the police or prosecutor, and less convictions, are interpreted as "more lenient treatment" than that received by whites, although harsher treatment is realized by blacks at the "back end" of the system. As Joan Petersilia's (1983:92) highly respected study of racial disparity in the criminal justice system clearly notes: minority suspects were more likely to be released after arrest because the police did not have strong cases! This is not more lenient treatment, but contrarily, could be viewed as discriminatory treatment since they were arrested without sufficient evidence in the first place.

5. Similar to other questionable figures cited throughout the book, Wilbanks challenges the DT by offering 1979 figures alleging that the southern (prejudiced) states (e.g., Mississippi) have the lowest black/white incarceration gap while those less racially prejudiced states (Minnesota, Wisconsin, Iowa, New Hampshire) have higher gaps (p. 146). However, it appears that the interpretation is in error since this would be the expected finding to support a discrimination thesis. Furthermore, according to *Prisoners in State and Federal Institutions* (U.S. Department of Justice, 1980; Table 6, p. 18), totalling *all* known incarcerated minorities yields the following minority/white percentages by race: Mississippi (54.5.27.1) or 2:1, Minnesota (26.7/72.3) or 1:2.7, Iowa (19.9/80) or 1:4, Wisconsin (42.9/58.8) or 1:1.4, New Hampshire (4.9/95.1) or 1:19.4 which are not as dramatic as the figures reported by Wilbanks for these same states a year earlier.

6. As with the erroneous charges of disproportionate black sex offense arrests (see #3 above), Wilbanks asserts that blacks are more likely to choose white victims to attack, rape, and rob, than black victims. The 1983 Bureau of Justice Statistics publication (1985:5) he cites supports all other victimization findings that violent crime is predominantly *intraracial* by stating:

> Violent crime had intraracial as well as interracial aspects. On the other hand, most violent crimes against whites were committed by white offenders (78%); most violent crimes against blacks were committed by black offenders (87%); and most violent crimes committed by white offenders were against white victims (98%). On the other hand, 55% of the violent crimes committed by black offenders were against white victims.

It is the last sentence that concerns Wilbanks and leads to his charge of black racism, when he emphasizes "choice" of victim. Two possible explanations come to mind with this statistic. First, victimization surveys which report *perceived* offenders have specific limitations where blacks are concerned. With rape, for example, white rape victims tend to report black offenders more than white rape offenders (Hindelang, 1978), while conversely, black rape victims have a tendency to under-report white male rapists (Weis and Borges, 1973); rapists of Spanish heritage are often reported as black; other racial characteristics and stereotypes may influence the victims' accounts (Hindelang, 1978); false accusations based on discovery with a black lover (Baughman, 1966) or racial prejudice (see Mann, forthcoming).

Second, the issue is not necessarily "choice" of a white victim, but availability. Whites have little hesitancy to enter segregated minority communities to undertake business and/or socialize with non-whites. On the other hand, a minority, particularly a black, is not only conspicuous in an all-white community, but is rarely welcomed and more frequently subject to attack. In sum, more "integration" in minority communities yields disproportionately more potential white victims than there are available black victims in white areas.

7. In his Conclusion Wilbanks states, "My basic position is that both black and white views on the extent of racism in the criminal justice system are 'ignorant' in that personal knowledge is gained primarily via observation and experience—methods which are heavily influenced by bias and racial prejudice." Such a statement is an affront to careful researchers who use observational methods and practitioners who rely upon the report their experience in the field. The accusation that they cannot be objective demonstrates a bias as well as a paucity of knowledge about qualitative research methods.

Clearly, one method is insufficient to explore such a sensitive issue as racism in the criminal justice system. As Wilbanks suggests, future research on this question should concentrate on individual decision makers (p. 147). This cannot be fully accomplished without qualitative methods such as observation, interviews, biographical, analyses, testing, card sorts, and similar techniques. It is the melding of the micro and macro levels of data gathering and analysis where we will hopefully come together for meaningful answers to the provocative questions Wilbanks raises. *The Myth of a Racist Criminal Justice System* introduces more questions than it provides answers, which makes it a long overdue catalyst for all social scientists interested in racial injustice.

REFERENCES

BAUGHMAN, LAURANCE E. ALAN 1966. Southern Rape Complex: One Hundred Years of Psychosis. Atlanta: Pendulum Books.

HINDELANG, MICHAEL J. 1978. "Race and involvement in common law personal crimes." American Sociological Review 43:93–109.

MANN, CORAMAE R. Forthcoming. Minorities, Crime, and Public Policy.

NATIONAL MINORITY ADVISORY COUNCIL ON CRIMINAL JUSTICE. 1980. The Inequality of Justice: A Report on Crime and the Administration of Justice. Washington, D.C.: U.S. Government Printing Office.

QUESTIONS FOR THOUGHT AND DISCUSSION

1. Make an argument that the criminal justice system is racist.
2. Make an argument that racism in the criminal justice system is a myth.
3. Which aspects of the criminal justice process most lend themselves to racism? How can racism in the system by prevented?

DRUGS, CRIME, AND THE JUSTICE SYSTEM

Bureau of Justice Statistics

WHAT RELATIONSHIPS EXIST BETWEEN DRUG USE AND CRIME?

The Link Between Drug Use and Crime Is Complex

In many ways drugs and crime are problems closely related to each other. Using or distributing some drugs is illegal, and violators are subject to criminal sanctions. Some crimes that do not involve drugs are a result of illegal drug use or distribution. For example—

- some users steal to support their drug use.
- prostitution is sometimes engaged in to support drug use.
- violence in drug markets is used to gain competitive advantage.

Being involved in drug use and crime are sometimes common features of a deviant lifestyle. Some individuals are inclined to be involved in multiple kinds of deviance, including drug use and criminal behavior.[1] Associations between drug users and contacts of users at drug markets when they buy drugs also strengthen the connection between drug use and crime. Such contacts can present opportunities to learn about the techniques and benefits of committing crime.

A wide range of psychological, social, and economic incentives can combine to produce serious drug use and crime patterns that become firmly established in some individuals. In such cases viewing drug use as a simple cause of crime oversimplifies their relationship. The two activities reinforce one another.

Understanding the Drug-crime Relationships Requires Specifying the Kinds of Drug Use and Crime

Some drugs, due to their power to induce compulsive use, are more likely to precipitate criminal activity than others. Cocaine and heroin are especially notable for their addictive power. Frequency of drug use is also a factor. A person who uses drugs several times a day is at higher risk of involvement in crime than is an irregular drug user.

From Bureau of Justice Statistics, *Drugs, Crime, and the Justice System*, Washington, D.C.: United States Department of Justice, December, 1992.

HOW ARE DRUGS AND CRIME RELATED?

Drugs and Crime Relationship	Definition	Examples
Drug-defined offenses	Violations of laws prohibiting or regulating the possession, use, distribution, or manufacture of illegal drugs.	Drug possession or use. Marijuana cultivation. Methamphetamine production. Cocaine, heroin, or marijuana sales.
Drug-related offenses	Offenses in which a drug's pharmacologic effects contribute; offenses motivated by the user's need for money to support continued use; and offenses connected with drug distribution itself.	Violent behavior resulting from drug effects. Stealing to get money to buy drugs. Violence against rival drug dealers.
Interactional circumstances	Drug use and crime are common aspects of a deviant lifestyle. The likelihood and frequency of involvement in illegal activity is increased because drug users and offenders are exposed to situations that encourage crime.	A life orientation with an emphasis on short-term goals supported by illegal activities. Opportunities to offend resulting from contacts with offenders and illegal markets. Criminal skills learned from other offenders.

There Is Extensive Evidence of the Strong Relationship Between Drug Use and Crime

A recent review of the evidence summarized the drug-crime relationship.:

- Drug users report greater involvement in crime and are more likely than nonusers to have criminal records.
- Persons with criminal records are much more likely than ones without criminal records to report being drug users.
- Crimes rise in number as drug use increases.[2]

Although some drug users do not commit property or violent crimes such as burglary and robbery, many drug users are heavily involved in crime. High levels of criminal activity are strongly related to the frequent use of drugs and the use of multiple drugs. Criminal activity is perhaps two to three times higher among frequent users of heroin or cocaine than among irregular users or nonusers of drugs.

Elimination of Illegal Drugs Would Not Eliminate All Crimes Committed by Drug Users

For some individuals drug use is independent of their involvement in crime. These people may continue to commit crimes even if drugs were unavailable. The illegal drug business is profitable for many who are involved in it. If this changed, some of those involved in the drug business might choose to pursue profits in other criminal enterprises.

HOW STRONG IS THE DRUG USE AND CRIME RELATIONSHIP?

What Sources Provide Information about the Relationship Between Drug Use and Crime?

The most important sources of information about drug use and crime are:

- urine testing of arrestees to determine their recent drug use.
- surveys of offender populations particularly jail and prison inmates that ask about their drug use.
- criminal justice and regulatory system records of arrests, convictions, incarcerations, and other sanctions of drug offenders.
- surveys of drug users particularly those in treatment that ask about their criminal activity.

What Proportion of Arrestees Recently Used Drugs?

The Drug Use Forecasting (DUF) program tests the urine of arrested persons in custody who submitted to voluntary testing. DUF tests for the presence of 10 drugs. In most cities, more than 50% of those tested were found to have used drugs recently.

In the 23 cities participating in 1990, the rate of males testing positive for drugs ranged from 30% to 78%. For females, the lowest rate in 21 participating cities was 39% and the highest was 76%. In eight of the cities, 70% or more of the female arrestees tested positive. About 20% of both male and female arrestees tested positive for two or more drugs.

In 1989 and 1990, the DUF program found cocaine in the urine of both male and female arrestees more often than any other drug. Chapters III and IV include more information about drug testing.

Inmates Report Very High Rates of Drug Use

More than 3 out of 4 jail inmates surveyed in 1989 by BJS reported some drug use in their lifetime. More than 40% had used drugs in the month before their offense with 27% under the influence of drugs at the time of their offense.

The 1989 survey of convicted jail inmates showed 13% committed their current offense to get money to buy drugs. Cocaine or crack users were 3 times more likely than other drug users to have committed their current offense to obtain money for drugs—39% said they were trying to get money for drugs when they committed their crime.

About 2 out of 3 State prison inmates reported they had used drugs as frequently as once a week or more for a period of at least a month at some time. More than a third reported having used heroin, methadone, cocaine, LSD, PCP, or being under the influence of drugs at the time of the current offense. Some of the methadone use may have been in connection with drug treatment.

Type of Drug Use	Percent of All State Prison Inmates	
	1979	1986
Under the influence of drugs		
at time of current offense	32%	35%
Ever used drugs regularly		
Any drug	63	62
A major drug	33	35
Used drugs daily in the month		
before the current offense		
Any drug	40	43
A major drug	14	19

Note: Major drugs include heroin, methadone, cocaine, LSD, and PCP. Regular use is once a week or more for at least a month in the past. Source: BJS, *Profile of State prison inmates, 1986*, Special report, NCJ-109926, January 1988, table 11, 6.

In 1987, more than 60% of juveniles and young adults in State-operated juvenile institutions reported using drugs once a week or more for at least a month some time in the past, and almost 40% reported being under the influence of drugs at the time of their offense.

Most People in Drug Treatment Report Involvement in Serious Crimes

Two national studies showed that most people in drug treatment had been arrested or incarcerated, or had admitted committing crimes for economic gain before entering treatment. The Drug Abuse Reporting Program (DARP) found that 87% had been arrested and 71% had been in jail or prison before entering treatment. The Treatment Outcome Prospective Study (TOPS) found that about 60% of those entering publicly funded residential treatment programs and about a third of those entering out-patient methadone or outpatient drug-free programs said they had committed one or more crimes for economic gain in the year before treatment. About a third of the clients in residential and outpatient drug-free programs were referred to treatment by the criminal justice system.

Crime Commission Rates for Individuals Rise and Fall with Involvement in Drug Use

A 1986 National Research Council panel report on criminal careers noted that active drug users commit offenses at high rates. A study of a national sample of youth found that offending rates rose with more serious drug involvement.

DRUG USE AT THE TIME OF OFFENDING HAS CHANGED OVER TIME

- The percentage of inmates committing their offense under the influence of drugs rose for State prison inmates from 1974 to 1986, but fell among jail inmates from 1983 to 1989.
- The proportion of offenders using cocaine at the time of their offense increased for both jail and prison inmates.

Offense Committed under the Influence of...	Percent of All Jail Inmates in		Percent of All State Prison Inmates in		
	1983	1989	1974	1979	1986
Any drug	30	27	25	32	35
Major drug					
Cocaine	6	14	1	5	11
Heroin	6	5	16	9	7
PCP	2	1	—	2	2
LSD	1	<1	—	2	2
Methadone	<1	<1	2	1	1
Other drugs					
Marijuana or hashish	17	9	10	18	19
Amphetamines	4	2	5	5	4
Barbiturates	3	1	6	6	3
Methaqualone	2	<1	—	—	2
Other drugs	2	<1	3	2	4

—Survey did not ask about the drug. Note: Individual drugs may not add to the "any drug" total because an inmate may have been under the influence of more than one drug.

Source: BJS, *Drug use and crime*, Special report, NCJ-111940, July 1988, table 1, 2; and BJS, *Profile of jail inmates, 1989*, Special report, NCJ-129097, April 1991, table 13, 8.

Studies of the number of crimes committed by heroin addicts during periods of addiction and nonaddiction in Baltimore and Southern California attest to the strength of the drug-crime relationship. For these addicts in the 1950s and 1960s—

- crime rates were four to six times higher and arrest rates were about twice as high during periods of addiction as during periods of nonaddiction.
- during periods of little or no drug use, crime rates were relatively low.

People in Drug Treatment Report Frequent Commission of Crime when They Are Using Drugs

Research on people in drug treatment shows less criminal activity when drug use is reduced. The DARP and TOPS studies of people in drug treatment show that decreases in drug use during and after treatment were associated with decreases in criminal activity. DARP followed people entering treatment from 1969 to 1972 for up to 12 years after treatment. Reported use of most drugs and criminal activity decreased after treatment, particularly during the first 6 years.

TOPS, which followed people who entered treatment from 1979 to 1981, showed that—

- the proportion of those who committed crimes for financial gain fell dramatically during treatment and remained well below pretreatment rates for up to 5 years after treatment.
- these decreases in criminal activity occurred along with substantial decreases in the prevalence and severity of drug use.

Interviews with 279 male heroin addicts admitted to methadone treatment in Southern California show a similar pattern of high offending rates during periods of addiction.

The Chronology of Initial Drug Use and Other Criminal Behavior Varies

Several studies have found that involvement in crime preceded drug use. An analysis of this relationship in a national survey of youth showed that—

- commission of less serious offenses preceded marijuana use and multiple drug use.
- less serious offenses preceded serious offenses.
- drinking preceded marijuana and multiple drug use.[3]

Other research confirms that findings that crime precedes drug use and suggests that the relationship between drugs and crime is developmental rather than causal, varies by the nature and intensity of drug use and criminal activity, and may change over time.

One recent study of drug use, drug trafficking, and other delinquency among inner-city adolescent males found—

- that drug users and sellers were more likely to commit offenses and at the highest rates.
- but that youths commit offenses for many reasons unrelated to drugs.[4]

A review of the research on the drug-crime relationship concluded that—

- many youth are involved in delinquent behavior before drug use.
- many youth who use drugs do not become involved in crime.
- drug use precedes crime for some people, but crime precedes drug use for others.
- involvement in minor crime usually occurs before involvement in serious crime.
- frequent use of multiple drugs generally follows involvement in property crime, and its onset may accelerate the development of a criminal career.[5]

Even though the onset of drug use and crime is not always easy to determine, it is clear that the two behaviors are highly correlated and probably reinforce each other.

State Prison Inmates Reported They Started Using Drugs Prior to Their First Arrest

Life Event	Median Age
Any drug use	
First use	15 years
First regular use	15
Major drug use	
First use	17
First regular use	18
Criminal justice contacts	
First arrest	17
First incarceration	19

Note: Major drugs include cocaine, heroin, PCP, LSD, and methadone.

Source: BJS, *Drug use and crime*, Special report, NCJ-111940, July 1988, table 7, 4.

HOW ARE DRUG USE AND THE ILLEGAL DRUG BUSINESS LINKED TO VIOLENT CRIME?

Drugs and Violence Are Linked in Multiple Ways

Some drugs can affect the user in ways that make violence more likely. At other times drug users commit violent acts to get money to buy drugs. Violence is common in drug trafficking as a result of disagreements about transactions and because traffickers sometime seek a competitive advantage over rival dealers through violent means.[6]

The Pharmacological Effects of Some Drugs May Lead to Violence

Legal drugs such as alcohol and illegal drugs such as cocaine, amphetamines, and PCP affect physiological function, cognitive ability, and mood. These effects can increase the likelihood that users will act violently.

Evidence of a pharmacologically based drugs-violence relationship is not strong, but many studies have found a link between alcohol use and violence. Many experts conclude that usually the effects of drugs and alcohol do not directly give rise to violence. Whether drug use leads to violence depends on a combination of direct and indirect factors such as the type of drug, personality characteristics, and situational and cultural factors.

In 1990, Victims Perceived that the Offender Was under the Influence of Drugs in More than 336,000 Crimes of Violence

Crimes of Violence	Number of Victimizations	Percent with Offender under the Influence of Drugs
All	6,008,790	5.6%
Rape	130,260	7.4*
Robbery	1,149,710	9.1
Assault	4,728,810	4.7
Aggravated	1,600,670	6.4
Simple	3,128,130	3.9

*Estimate is based on about 10 or fewer sample cases.

Source: BJS, *Criminal victimization in the United States 1990*, NCJ-134126, February 1992, table 42, 58.

These data probably underestimate drug use by violent offenders due to the victims' difficulty in assessing whether the offender was under the influence of drugs.

At the Time of the Offense Most Imprisoned Violent Offenders Were Drinking or Using Drugs

Among violent offenders in State prisons in 1986—

- more than half said they committed the offense under the influence of drugs or alcohol.
- drug use was more likely among offenders who victimized strangers and less likely among offenders who victimized a relative or family member.
- drugs or alcohol were most likely to be implicated in manslaughter cases (76% of offenders or victims were using either or both) and least likely to be implicated in sexual assault cases (50% of offenders or victims were using).

Whether Drug Use Is a Direct Factor in Family Violence Is Unclear

Alcohol use, along with other factors, is thought to contribute to family violence—especially male against female violence. Whether illegal drug use has a similar association to family violence has not received as much attention. A study of 1,243 female subjects from a prenatal clinic in Boston found that the drug use of a woman's partner was associated with violence against her. Another study of 234 men charged with assaulting their mates in Marion County, Indiana found that 32% of the men had a drug problem and 22% had dual drug and alcohol problems. A drug problem was associated with more severe domestic abuse.

Violence in Illegal Drug Networks Is Often Called Systemic

Systemic violence is the "traditionally aggressive patterns of interaction within the system of drug distribution and use."[7] ...violence is used to protect or expand markets, intimidate competitors, and retaliate against sellers or buyers who are suspected of cheating. To avoid being arrested and punished for trafficking, drug dealers commit violent crimes against police and threaten informants or witnesses. Some observers also believe that the illegal drug business attracts persons who are prone to violence.[8]

Violence Is Common in Illegal Drug Distribution

Situations in which violence can occur include—

- guarding drug-producing crops during harvest season.
- territorial disputes between rival drug dealers.
- enforcing normative codes within dealing hierarchies.
- robberies of drug dealers and their violent retaliation.
- elimination of drug informers.
- punishment for selling poor quality, adulterated, or phony drugs.
- punishment for failing to pay debts.
- punishment for stealing, tampering with, or not sharing drug supplies.
- retaliation for stealing, using without permission, or not sharing drug paraphernalia.

Because participants in the drug market want to avoid the police, much of this violence is not reported.

Many Homicides Are Related to Drug Trafficking

A study of 414 homicides in New York City in 1988 found that—

- in 53% of the cases, drugs or alcohol were judged to be an important cause of homicide.
- cocaine in any form (sometimes along with other drugs or alcohol) was involved in 84% of the drug-related homicides.
- in 32% of all homicides and 60% of the drug-related homicides, crack cocaine was present.
- most of the drug-related homicides were associated with trafficking.

Studies in three cities indicate that approximately a quarter to a half of homicides were drug related:

- 24% of New York City homicides were thought to be drug related in 1984.
- In Washington, D.C., from 1987 to 1991, the annual percentage of drug motivated homicides reached a peak of 53% in 1988 and declined to 35% in 1991.
- A study of homicide in Miami for the years 1978 to 1982 found 24% were drug related.

Some of the difference between these estimates is probably accounted for by differences in the definition of "drug related" among studies. For example, the Washington, D.C., definition includes homicides for which drug trafficking was judged to be a "direct cause." The New York City study of 1988 homicides counted as drug related those where

the killing was thought to have occurred as a result of the pharmacolo~
or where a victim was killed in the course of a robbery committed to
drugs, as well as those committed in connection with drug trafficking.

Of the 347 drug-related homicides reported in New York City in 19~
a drug location, usually at a site where drugs were sold. The police report~
these victims were drug traffickers. Similarly, in the District of Columbia, t~ ~avy concentration of homicides in common drug trafficking areas suggests that most of these drug-
related homicides occurred during or in relation to a drug transaction. One analysis suggests that homicide is relatively common among drug traffickers and users primarily
because of the fixed demand for drugs and the widespread availability of guns.[9]

Many Homicide Victims Have Drugs in Their System

Several studies of homicide victims had similar conclusions:

- A study of medical examiner cases from 1984 to 1987 in Wayne County,
  Michigan, found that half of all homicide victims had cocaine or cocaine metabo-
  lites in their body fluids at the time of death; this percentage had risen over the 4
  years of the study.
- A 1989 study of medical examiner cases found that 49% of the homicide victims
  in Fulton County, Georgia (Atlanta), had cocaine in their systems.
- In New York City in 1981, the blood tests of 27% of homicide victims indicated
  recent drug use.
- A National Institute of Justice (NIJ) report on homicide in eight cities in 1978 indicated 1% to 16% of victims had narcotics in their systems at the time of death.
  Oakland, California, had the highest rate.
- A 15-year followup of 78 New York heroin addicts found that 40% were homicide
  victims.
- A study in Philadelphia found that homicide was the leading cause of death among
  heroin addicts in 1972.

Victims and Assailants in Drug-related Homicides Are Often Hispanic or Black Males in Their 20s or 30s.

1978 to 1982 data on drug-related homicides in Dade County, Florida (Miami), showed
that 24% were drug-related. A comparison of the sociodemographic characteristics of the
Dade County and New York City victims found them to be similar:

- 89% of the Dade County victims were male.
- 38% were in their 20s.
- 31% were in their 30s.

Homicides not classified as drug related were more likely to involve female, white,
and older victims. A greater proportion of the Dade County than the New York City victims
were Hispanic, reflecting the greater proportion of Hispanics in the Dade County area.

Socio-demographic Characteristic	Drug-related Homicides in 1984 in New York City	
	Victims	Assailants
Age		
Under 21	14%	12%
21 to 30	48	31
31 to 40	24	18
Over 40	15	5
Unknown	—	35
Sex		
Male	90%	72%
Female	10	1
Unknown	—	27
Race/ethnicity		
Black	42%	37%
White	9	7
Hispanic	49	30
Other	0	0
Unknown	—	26
Number	347	403

Source: NIJ, Paul J. Goldstein and Henry H. Brownstein, *Drug-related crime analysis—Homicide.* A report to the NIJ Drugs, Alcohol, and Crime Program, July 1987, 52 and 54.

In Drug-related Homicides, Assailants Are Likely to Know Their Victims and to Use a Handgun

Assailants in drug-related homicides in New York City in 1984 were more likely to have known their victims and to use handguns to kill them than were assailants in homicides that were not drug related:

- Of the assailants in drug-related homicides, 79% knew their victims vs. 48% of the assailants in homicides that were not drug related.
- Of the victims in drug-related homicides, 80% were killed with a handgun vs. 47% of the victims in homicides that were not drug related.

An analysis of homicides in Dade County (Miami) between 1978 and 1982 reached similar findings: 85% of the drug-related homicides involved the use of guns vs. 71% of the homicides by gunshot that were not drug related.

A Fulton County, Georgia, study also found that homicide victims killed with a gun were more likely to have cocaine in their systems.

HOW IS DRUG USE LINKED TO INCOME-GENERATING CRIME?

Many Drug Users Commit Crimes to Support Their Drug Use

Many illegal drugs such as heroin and cocaine are both habit-forming and expensive. Some users commit property crimes to support their habits. Property crimes include burglary, larceny-theft, motor vehicle theft, forgery, fraud, arson, dealing in stolen property, and embezzlement. Robbery generates money but is usually considered a violent crime because of the use or threat of force.

Other crimes sometimes committed for income to support drug use are prostitution and drug trafficking. Disputes or extortion that can arise in the commission of these crimes may result in violence.

Is Drug Use Prevalent Among Arrestees Charged with Drug Sales or Possession, Burglary, Robbery, and Theft?

The DUF program reported that 60% or more of the males arrested in 1990 for the property crimes of burglary, larceny-theft, and stolen vehicles and for robbery who were voluntarily tested while in custody were found to be positive for drug use as were 50% or more of the females arrested for burglary, robbery, and stolen vehicles.

Arrest Charge	Positive for Any Drug	
	Male	Female
Drug sale/possession	79%	81%
Burglary	68	58
Robbery	66	66
Larceny-theft	64	59
Stolen vehicle	60	65
Stolen property	59	59
Homicide	52	49
Fraud/forgery	50	55
Prostitution	49	81
Assault	48	50

Note: The urinalysis results presented in this table were gathered from 19,883 male arrestees in 23 cities and 7,947 female arrestees in 21 cities. Drugs include cocaine, opiates, PCP, marijuana, amphetamines, methadone, methaqualone, benzodiazepines, barbiturates, and propoxyphene.

Source: NIJ, 1990, Drug Use Forecasting Program (DUF), unpublished data.

Jail Inmates Convicted of Property Offenses Were Often Influenced by Drugs

Nearly a third of 1989 jail inmates convicted of property offenses reported they were under the influence of drugs or drugs and alcohol at the time of their offenses. Almost 1 of 4 said the motive for their property offenses was to get money to buy drugs. Those convicted of burglary were more likely than other types of property offenders to have been under the influence of drugs at the time of the offense.

Property Offenders Are More Likely Than Violent Offenders to be Drug Users

The BJS State Prison Inmate Survey in 1986 showed that 35% of all inmates reported being under the influence of a drug at the time of their offense (including less than 1% who may have been taking a therapeutic dose of methadone). Those under the influence at the time of the offense included 43% of drug offenders, 39% of property offenders, and 33% of violent offenders (including 42% of robbers).

Forty-three percent reported daily use of any drug in the month before the conviction offense. This includes 51% of drug and 48% of property but only 39% of violent offenders (including 50% of robbers).

Prostitution Is Sometimes Used to Support Drug Use

One study of the relationship between drug use and prostitution maintains that although drug use does not necessarily lead to prostitution nor prostitution to drug use, users may resort to prostitution or increase their activity when drug-dealing activities are disrupted or drug prices rise.[10] A study of two samples of women in drug abuse treatment found that involvement in property crimes, drug dealing, and prostitution increased with the rise of narcotics use.[11]

Many prostitutes are heavily involved in drug use. In the 1990 DUF data, 81% of the females and 49% of the males arrested for prostitution and being held in jail who were voluntarily tested were found positive for drugs. A review of the drug-consensual crime relationship found that prostitutes were likely to be involved in drug dealing and property crimes.[12]

Drug users sometimes barter sex for drugs and may not consider it to be prostitution. Sex for crack exchanges seem especially frequent.

Daily Use of Heroin or Cocaine Is Highly Associated With Income-generating Crimes

The national TOPS study of people in drug abuse treatment in 1979–81 found that daily users of heroin or cocaine were more likely than other types of drug users to report income from crime. Daily heroin users had over $8,000 more in illegal income than nonusers of heroin, while daily cocaine users had over $7,000 more in illegal income than nonusers of cocaine.

A study of New York City's Harlem showed that heroin addicts had average incomes of about $10,000 per year from drug and nondrug crimes. Daily heroin users averaged about $15,000 in income from crime—about three times as much as irregular users.

Drug Users Support Themselves and Their Drug Use in Various Ways

Studies of frequent drug users show that most commit crimes for monetary gain. A study in Florida found that about half were also gainfully employed and about 1 in 5 received some form of public support. A recent RAND study in Washington, D.C., also found that about 2 in 3 arrested drug dealers reported being employed when they were arrested.

Many frequent drug users have dealt, sold, or distributed drugs, and most also are involved in a variety of other illegal activities and do not support themselves solely by dealing.

How Do Drug Using and Drug Selling Generate Crime?

Drug Use Can Attract Other Serious Crime to a Neighborhood

Drug users nodding in doorways and open use of marijuana in public places are examples of the public "signs of disorder" researchers have pointed to as early threats to informal community control and the communal life of apartment complexes and other neighborhoods.

Researchers summarizing results of their and others' work describe the sequence of events that can occur.[13]

- When neighborhood residents fear signs of disorder they do not challenge them, thinking that crime is on the rise.
- Disorder accumulates: a vacant building, litter in courtyards and streets, groups of teenagers hanging out, broken windows, prostitutes working openly on the streets.
- Familiar people move out, strangers move in.
- New households are less likely to be families and more likely to be single people or unrelated roommates.
- Fearful residents use the streets less and try not to "get involved" when they are out.

Such a decline in informal community control makes an area vulnerable to invasion by more serious crime. High rates of drug use may make an apartment complex or other neighborhood vulnerable to open selling of drugs on the street, associated violence, and predatory crime.

Participants in the Drug Market Are Often Attacked or Robbed

Those who buy or sell drugs are often attractive targets for predatory offenders because they are viewed as likely to have cash or drugs on their person. Because participants in the drug market are themselves involved in illegal behavior, offenders consider them less likely to report their victimization to the police—who find out about crimes mostly from victim reports.

The illegal character of the drug business accounts for some of the violence in another way. Laws and institutions that regulate legal transactions do not operate in illegal markets. As a result, the parties must rely on their own resources when disagreements arise. This often leads to violence and other forms of intimidation.

Drug Users Are Often Victimized

Heavily diluted drugs or counterfeit substances are often sold as high quality drugs. This results in the economic "victimization" of the buyer who may attempt to obtain redress—sometimes by violence.

Several other factors account for the elevated risks of victimization that face drug users and sellers:

- Drug use impairs cognition and judgment and the capacity to protect oneself.
- Simply being in the presence of drug offenders raises the risk of victimization given the rather high probability that drug offenders will commit predatory crimes against accessible targets.
- The 1989 BJS survey of local jail inmates indicated that 30% of convicted violent offenders thought one or more of their victims was using drugs, alcohol, or both at the time of their victimization.

Open Drug Marketing Can Devastate Neighborhood Life

Drug market violence often involves guns—sometimes automatic weapons that very rapidly fire many shots. Around the country deaths and injuries of innocent bystanders caught in the crossfire have been reported. The problem is acute in certain urban areas.

Open drug dealing poses two special threats for neighborhoods:

- Some area residents, particularly young people, may be drawn into illegal drug activities.
- Increased traffic associated with drug markets and the behavior of dealers and users are disruptive to communities and often escalate into predatory crimes and violence.

Residents of a Washington, D.C., apartment complex "notorious for its violent drug trade" described ways the drug market affected their lives:[14]

- Drug sellers were so bold: "They'd almost get in your car trying to sell you drugs."
- Residents feared for their children when drug sellers tried to recruit them as "foot soldiers" in the trade.
- Other parents described how they used to ask their children to run errands and allow them to play outside after dark but have changed the rules in recent years because of "that life-or-death fear for your children and yourself" brought about by nearby drug markets.[15]

People whose homes are not in the immediate vicinity of drug marketing locations also changed their routines. One woman said, "…here is your whole lifestyle being altered by this. You are afraid to go out at night… You never carry more than $20 on you… Sure it affects you."[16] And residents worried about what the crime and violence associated with drug markets will do to their neighborhood's image.

ENDNOTES

1. Eric D. Wish, "U.S. drug policy in the 1990s: Insights from new data from arrestees," *The International Journal of Addictions*, (1990–91), 25(3A):377–409, 393–395.

2. Jan M. Chaiken and Marcia R. Chaiken, "Drugs and predatory crime, " in *Drugs and crime*, Michael Tonry and James Q. Wilson, eds., volume 13, *Crime and Justice* (Chicago: University of Chicago Press, 1990), 203–239.

3. David H. Huizinga, Scott Menard, and Delbert S. Elliott, "Delinquency and drug use: Temporal and developmental patterns," *Justice Quarterly* (September 1989), 6(3):419–455.

4. David M. Altschuler and Paul J. Brounstein, "Patterns of drug use, drug trafficking and other delinquency among inner-city adolescent males in Washington, D.C." *Criminology* (1991), 29(4):589–622.

5. Jan M. Chaiken and Marcia R. Chaiken, "Drugs and predatory crime," in *Drugs and crime*, Michael Tonry and James Q. Wilson, eds. volume 13, *Crime and Justice* (Chicago: University of Chicago Press, 1990), 203–240.

6. Paul J. Goldstein, "The drugs/violence nexus: A tripartite conceptual framework," *Journal of Drug Issues* (Fall 1985), 15(4):497.

7. Paul J. Goldstein, "The drugs/violence nexus: A tripartite conceptual framework," *Journal of Drug Issues* (Fall 1985), 15(4):497.

8. M.H. Haller, "Bootlegging: The business and politics of violence" in *Violence in America*, Ted Robert Gurr, ed. (Newbury Park, CA: Sage, 1989), 146–162.

9. Margaret A. Zahn, "Homicide in the twentieth century United States," in *History and crime*, James A. Inciardi and Charles E. Faupel, eds. (Beverly Hills: Sage Publications, 1980), 11–132.

10. James A. Inciardi, "Hooker, whore, junkie, thief; dealer, doper, cocaine freak," in *The war on drugs: Heroin, cocaine, and public policy*, James A. Inciardi, ed. (Palo Alto, CA: Mayfield Publishing, 1986), 156–173.

11. M. Douglas Anglin and Yih-Ing Hser, "Addicted women and crime," *Criminology* (1987), 25(2):359–397.

12. Dana E. Hunt, "Drugs and consensual crimes: Drug dealing and prostitution," in *Drugs and crime*, Michael Tonry and James Q. Wilson, eds., volume 13, *Crime and Justice* (Chicago: The University of Chicago Press, 1990), 191–202.

13. James Q. Wilson and George L. Kelling, "Broken windows," *Atlantic Monthly* (March 1982), 29–38.

14. Lynne Duke, "Flurry of services, promises engulfs SE neighborhood," *The Washington Post*, December 4, 1989, D5.

15. Lynda Richardson, "NW family holds its ground amid the violence," *The Washington Post*, February 4, 1990, A1.

16. Michele L. Norris, "Life in P.G. changes in the face of fear," *The Washington Post*, November 6, 1989, A1.

17. Elijah Anderson, *Streetwise: Race, class, and change in an urban community* (Chicago: The University of Chicago Press, 1990), 134–137.

18. "The need for treatment," in *Treating drug problems*, D.R. Gerstein and H.J. Harwood, eds. (Washington: National Academy Press, 1990), 85; D.S. Gomby and P.H. Shiono, "Estimating the number of substance-exposed infants," *The future of children* (1991), 1:17–25, 22–23, cited in Ira J. Chasnoff, "Drugs, alcohol, pregnancy, and the neonate: Pay now or pay later," *Journal of the American Medical Association* (1991), 266(11):1567–1568.

19. Robert E. Hurley, Deborah A. Freund, and Donald E. Taylor, "Emergency room use and primary health care case management: Evidence from four Medicaid demonstration programs," *American Journal of Public Health* (1989), 79(7):843–846.

20. Craig Zwerling, James Ryan, and Endel John Orav, "The efficacy of preemployment drug screening for marijuana and cocaine in predicting employment outcome," *Journal of the American Medical Association* (November 1990), 264(20):2639–2643.

QUESTIONS FOR THOUGHT AND DISCUSSION

1. What is the relationship between illegal drug use and crime? How can we use this information to devise more effective crime control policies?
2. In what ways can drug use attract serious crime into a neighborhood and ruin neighborhood life?
3. Can we be effective in the fight against crime without addressing illegal drug use? Why or why not?

SUGGESTIONS FOR FURTHER READING

JAY BRANEGAN, "Is Singapore a Model for the West?," New York, NY: *Time*, January 18, 1993, pp. 36–37.

MARCIA CHAIKEN AND BRUCE JOHNSON, "Characteristics of Different Types of Drug-Involved Offenders," *Issues and Practices in Criminal Justice*, Washington, D.C.: National Institute of Justice, February 1988.

PAUL CROMWELL, *Breaking and Entering: An Ethnographic Analysis of Burglary*, Newbury Park, CA: Sage Publishing Company, 1991.

RICHARD LACAYO, "Lock 'em Up...," New York, NY: *Newsweek*, 142(6), February 7, 1994.

SAMUEL WALKER, *Sense and Nonsense about Crime and Drugs*, 3rd ed., Belmont CA: Wadsworth Publishing Company, 1994.

SECTION 2

The Police in America

INTRODUCTION

The police are on the front line in the fight against crime. They are by far the most likely of any officials in the criminal justice system to come into contact with citizens. In actual practice, they exercise rather broad discretionary power in this role. It is the individual officer who decides about what law to enforce, how much to enforce it, against whom it should be enforced, and under which circumstances. This fact alone places the police in a central position for determining how our justice system is viewed by the public, how effective it is in controlling various types of crime, how fairly it dispenses justice, and how our laws get translated into practice.

Most citizens do not realize the breath of the skills needed to be an effective police officer. Most citizens are well aware of the crime fighting activities of the police and the difficulty in performing these duties. However, many fail to realize that the majority of police work is best described as peacekeeping or order maintenance and that these activities require a completely different type of personal demeanor and skills than crime fighting. It is the vacillation between these divergent demands on the police officer that makes the police role so complex and difficult to fulfill. Section II focuses on the police, trends in policing, and some current issues.

In the first selection, "The Development of American Police" Craig Uchida examines the development of the police since 900 A.D. and then focuses on how the role of the police has changed in American society from colonial America to the present. This review of history illustrates how many present-day issues concerning the police have their roots in different epochs of American history. This selection then gives contextual meaning to many of the current problems and issues discussed in other selections.

Selection two, "The New Policing: Confronting Complexity" by law professor Herman Goldstein, outlines the importance of the relationship between the police and the public and the importance of engaging the citizenry in the overall task of policing. He examines the complexities involved in instituting community-based policing and outlines the extraordinary accomplishments being made.

"Policing and the Fear of Crime," written by Mark Moore and Robert C. Trojanowicz, is the third selection. The authors point out that often the largest and most enduring legacy of criminal victimization is fear and that fear of crime is an important problem in its own right. They explain how the fear then becomes contagious, spreading the injury throughout our communities. The authors identify aspects of fear, its causes and consequences, as well as police strategies that have been successful in reducing fear of crime.

Selection four, "Police Shootings: Myths and Realities," was written especially for this volume by Roger Dunham and Geoffery Alpert. The authors discuss what happens when police officers find it necessary to use their weapons to enforce the law. Drawing upon a ten-year shooting study of the Metro-Dade County (Florida) police and other studies, they uncover various patterns and trends concerning this most deadly use of force. While this issue is among the most controversial topics of policing, the image most citizens obtain from the media greatly overemphasizes the amount of police violence involved in typical police work, especially regarding the use of firearms.

In selection five, entitled "Dragons and Dinosaurs: The Plight of Patrol Women," Donna C. Hale and Stacey M. Wyland, a criminal justice professor and a female police officer, respectively, examine problems faced by women in policing, particularly those serving as patrol officers. While they recognize that needed changes will not take place overnight, they suggest a number of important changes that must be implemented to reduce the cultural resistance to female police officers.

Selection six includes the "Law Enforcement Code Of Ethics," and "The Police Code of Ethics" sponsored by the International Association of Chiefs of Police. Realizing that all law enforcement officers must be fully aware of the ethical responsibilities of their position, this professional organization outlines the fundamental duties of officers and the ethical standards of professional policing.

"Sexual Misconduct by Police Officers," the seventh selection, was written especially for this book by Allen D. Sapp. This author discusses an often hidden form of police misconduct: sexually motivated actions and behavior by police officers. He quotes from many lengthy interviews with police officers and supervisors in numerous large metropolitan police departments, as well as with many municipal and state officers. Seven categories of sexually motivated misconduct are outlined and discussed, followed by prescriptions for controlling sexual harassment.

Selection eight is entitled "Learning Police Ethics." It was written by Lawrence Sherman and is becoming a classic. He argues that ethics codes formally laid down by police departments are bound to fail. He demonstrates that the real "code" is acquired through socialization "on the job," which creates some problems. It is better to learn police ethics in a setting removed from the heat of the battle and the pressures of co-workers and supervisors. He concludes that ethically sound decision-making by police requires a special effort to counteract this informal socialization of recruits to the "old" way.

The ninth selection is an insider's description of police work written by William Wise to help guide college graduates in choosing a career in police work. It is entitled "The Frustrations of Police Work: The Idealism and Realism of Being a Police Officer." The author describes how his preconceived ideas about being a police officer were abruptly changed during the early weeks and months of the job as a state trooper in Michigan. He attributes many of his misperceptions about police work to media accounts of policing.

The final selection in this section, written by Professor Karen McElrath, reviews information vital for anyone planning a career in law enforcement. "Careers in Law Enforcement" includes information on trends in the job market, stages in an officer's career, qualifications, and job opportunities.

THE DEVELOPMENT OF THE AMERICAN POLICE

An Historical Overview

Craig D. Uchida

INTRODUCTION

During the past 20 years, scholars have become fascinated with the history of police. A plethora of studies have emerged as a result. Early writings were concerned primarily with descriptions of particular police agencies. Roger Lane (1967) and James F. Richardson (1970) broke new ground in describing the origins of policing in Boston and New York, respectively. Since that time, others have followed suit with narratives of police organizations in St. Louis (Maniha, 1970; Reichard, 1975), Denver (Rider, 1971), Washington, D.C. (Alfers, 1975), Richmond (Cei, 1975), and Detroit (Schneider, 1980).

Other authors have focused on issues in policing. Wilbur R. Miller (1977) examined the legitimation of the police in London and New York. Samuel Walker (1977) and Robert Fogelson (1977) concentrated on professionalism and reform of errant police in the 19th and 20th centuries. Eric Monkkonen (1981) took an entirely different approach by using quantitative methods to explain the development of policing in 23 cities from 1860 to 1920.[1]

Overall these histories illustrate the way in which police have developed over time. They point out the origins of concepts like crime prevention, authority, professionalism, and discretion. In addition, these historical analyses show the roots of problems in policing, such as corruption, brutality, and inefficiency.

The major purpose of this selection is to examine the development of the police since 900 A.D. and more specifically, to determine whether the role of the police has changed in American society over a period of about 300 years. This is not an easy task. The debate over the "true" or "proper" police function is an ongoing one and cannot itself be resolved in a selection such as this.[2] However, by describing the various roles, activities, and functions of law enforcement over time, we can at least acquire a glimpse of what the police do and how their activities have varied over time. To do so, we rely on a number of important contributions to the study of the history of police.

From Craig Uchida, "The Development of American Police" in *Critical Issues in Policing: Contemporary Readings*, 2nd ed., Roger Dunham and Geoffrey Alpert (eds.), Prospect Heights, IL: Waveland Press, Inc. 1993, pp. 16–32. All rights reserved. Reprinted by permission of Waveland Press, Inc.

The selection is divided into seven parts and basically covers the history of law enforcement and the role of the police from colonial America to the present. Part I examines the English heritage of law enforcement and its effect on colonial America. The colonists relied heavily on the mother country for their ideas regarding community involvement in law enforcement.

Part II examines the problems of urban centers in the 18th and 19th centuries and turns to the development of the full-time uniformed police in England and America. The preventive approach to law enforcement became central to the police role in both London and American cities. Part III is concerned with police activity in 19th century American cities. Patrol work and officer involvement in corruption are discussed.

In Part IV the reform movement of the Progressive Era is examined. From 1890 to 1920 reformers attempted to implement social, economic, and political change in the cities. As part of city government, police departments were targets of change as well.

In Part V we study a second reform era. From 1910 to 1960 chiefs became involved in a movement to professionalize the police. Part VI covers the riots and disorders of the 1960s and their immediate effect on policing across the country. Finally, in Part VII, we discuss the long-term legacy of the 1960s. That is, we examine the developments of the police since 1969 in terms of research and public policy.

COMMUNITIES, CONSTABLES, AND COLONISTS

Like much of America's common-law tradition, the origins of modern policing can be linked directly to its English heritage. Ideas concerning community policing, crime prevention, the posse, constables, and sheriffs developed from English law enforcement. Beginning at about 900 A.D., the role of law enforcement was placed in the hands of common, everyday citizens. Each citizen was held responsible for aiding neighbors who might be victims of outlaws and thieves. Because no police officers existed, individuals used state-sanctioned force to maintain social control. Charles Reith, a noted English historian, refers to this model of law enforcement as "kin police" (Reith, 1956). Individuals were considered responsible for their "kin" (relatives) and followed the adage, "I am my brother's keeper." Slowly this model developed into a more formalized "communitarian," or community-based police system.

After the Norman Conquest of 1066, a community model was established, which was called frankpledge. The frankpledge police system required that every male above the age of twelve form a group with nine of his neighbors called a tything. Each tything was sworn to apprehend and deliver to court any of its members who committed a crime. Each person was pledged to help protect fellow citizens and, in turn, would be protected. This system was "obligatory" in nature, in that tythingmen were not paid salaries for their work, but were required by law to carry out certain duties (Klockars, 1985:21). Tythingmen were required to hold suspects in custody while they were awaiting trial and to make regular appearances in court to present information on wrong-doing by members of their own or other tythings. If any member of the tything failed to perform his required duties, all members of the group would be levied severe fines.

Ten tythings were grouped into a hundred, directed by a constable (appointed by the local nobleman) who, in effect, became the first policeman. That is, the constable was the first official with law enforcement responsibility greater than simply helping one's neighbor. Just as the tythings were grouped into hundreds, the hundreds were grouped into shires, which are similar to counties today. The supervisor of each shire was the shire reeve (or sheriff), who was appointed by the king.

Frankpledge began to disintegrate by the 13th century. Inadequate supervision by the king and his appointees led to its downfall. As frankpledge slowly declined, the parish constable system emerged to take its place. The Statute of Winchester of 1285 placed more authority in the hands of the constable for law enforcement. One man from each parish served a one-year term as constable on a rotating basis. Though not paid for his work, the constable was responsible for organizing a group of watchmen who would guard the gates of the town at night. These watchmen were also unpaid and selected from the parish population. If a serious disturbance took place, the parish constable had the authority to raise the "hue and cry." This call to arms meant that all males in the parish were to drop what they were doing and come to the aid of the constable.

In the mid-1300s the office of justice of the peace was created to assist the shire reeve in controlling his territory. The local constable and the shire reeve became assistants to the justice of the peace and supervised the night watchmen, served warrants, and took prisoners into custody for appearance before justice of the peace courts.

The English system continued with relative success well into the 1700s. By the end of the 18th century, however, the growth of large cities, civil disorders and increased criminal activity led to changes in the system.

LAW ENFORCEMENT IN COLONIAL AMERICA

In colonial America (17th and 18th centuries), policing followed the English systems. The sheriff, constable, and watch were easily adapted to the colonies. The county sheriff, appointed by the governor, became the most important law enforcement agent particularly when the colonies remained small and primarily rural. The sheriff's duties included apprehending criminals, serving subpoenae, appearing in court, and collecting taxes. The sheriff was paid a fixed amount for each task he performed. Since sheriffs received higher fees based on the taxes they collected, apprehending criminals was not a primary concern. In fact, law enforcement was a low priority.

In the larger cities and towns, such as New York, Boston, and Philadelphia, constables and the night watch performed a wide variety of tasks. The night watch reported fires, raised the hue and cry, maintained street lamps, arrested or detained suspicious persons, and walked the rounds. Constables engaged in similarly broad tasks, such as taking suspects to court, eliminating health hazards, bringing witnesses to court, and so on.

For the most part, the activities of the constables and the night watch were "reactive" in nature. That is, these men responded to criminal behavior only when requested by victims or witnesses (Monkkonen, 1981). Rather than preventing crime, discovering criminal behavior, or acting in a "proactive" fashion, these individuals relied on others to define their work. Public health violations were the only types of activity that required the officers to exercise initiative.

PREVENTIVE POLICE: COPS AND BOBBIES

The development of a "new" police system has been carefully documented by a number of American and English historians. Sir Leon Radzinowicz (1948–1968), Charles Reith (1956), and T.A. Critchley (1967) are among the more notable English writers. Roger Lane (1967), James F. Richardson (1970), Wilbur R. Miller (1977), Samuel Walker (1977), and Eric Monkkonen (1981) represent a rather diverse group of American historians who describe and analyze a number of early police departments. Taken together these works present the key elements of the activities of the first English and American police systems that used the preventive model.

During the mid-to-late 1700s the growth of industry in England and in Europe led to rapid development in the cities. London, in particular, expanded at an unprecedented rate. From 1750 to 1820 the population nearly doubled (Miller, 1977) and the urban economy became more complex and specialized. The Industrial Revolution led to an increase in the number of factories, tenements, vehicles, and marketplaces. With industrial growth came a breakdown in social control, as crime, riots, disorder, and public health problems disrupted the city. Food riots, wage protests, poor sewage control, pickpockets, burglars, and vandals created difficulties for city dwellers. The upper and middle classes, concerned about these issues sought more protection and preventive measures. The constable-watch system of law enforcement could no longer deal successfully with the problems of the day, and alternative solutions were devised.

Some of the alternatives included using the militia; calling out the "yeomanry" or cavalry volunteers for assistance; swearing in more law-abiding citizens as constables; or employing the army to quell riot situations (Richardson, 1974:10). However, these were short-term solutions to a long-term problem.

Another proposal was to replace the constable-watch system with a stronger, more centralized police force. Henry and John Fielding (magistrates in the 1750s), Patrick Colquhoun (a magistrate from 1792 to 1818), and philosopher Jeremy Bentham and his followers advocated the creation of a police force whose principal object was the prevention of crime. A preventive police force would act as a deterrent to criminals and would be in the best interests of society. But the idea of a uniformed police officer was opposed by many citizens and politicians in England. An organized police too closely resembled a standing army, which gave government potentially despotic control over citizens and subjects. The proponents of a police force eventually won out, based primarily on the disorder and fear of crime experienced by London residents. After much debate in the early 1800s, the London Metropolitan Police Act was finally approved by Parliament in 1829 (see Critchley, 1967 and Reith, 1956).

The London Metropolitan Police Act established a full-time, uniformed police force with the primary purpose of patrolling the city. Sir Robert Peel, Britain's Home Secretary, is credited with the formation of the police. Peel synthesized the ideas of the Fieldings, Colquhoun, and Bentham into law, convinced Parliament of the need for the police, and guided the early development of the force.

Through Peel and his two police commissioners, Charles Rowan and Richard Mayne, the role of the London Police was formulated. Crime prevention was the primary function, but to enforce the laws and to exert its authority, the police had to first gain legitimacy in the eyes of the public. According to Wilbur R. Miller (1977) the legitimation of the London police was carefully orchestrated by Peel and his associates. These men recognized that in order to gain authority police officers had to act in a certain manner or the public would reject them. To gain acceptance in the eyes of the citizen, Peel and his associates selected men who were even-tempered and reserved; chose a uniform that was unassuming (navy blue rather than military red); insisted that officers be restrained and polite; meted out appropriate discipline; and did not allow officers to carry guns. Overall, the London police emphasized their legitimacy as based on *institutional* authority—that their power was grounded in the English Constitution and that their behavior was determined by rules of law. In essence, this meant that the power of the London "bobby" or "Peeler" was based on the institution of government.

American cities and towns encountered problems similar to those in England. Cities grew at phenomenal rates; civil disorders swept the nation, and crime was perceived to be increasing. New York, for example, sprouted from a population of 33,000 in 1790 to 150,000 in 1830. Foreign immigrants, particularly Irish and Germans, accounted for a large portion of the increase. Traveling to America in search of employment and better lifestyles, the immigrants competed with native-born Americans for skilled and unskilled positions. As a result, the American worker saw the Irishman and German as social and economic threats.

Other tensions existed in the city as well. The race question was an important one in the Northern cities as well as on the Southern plantations. In fact, historians have shown that hostility to blacks was just as high in the North as in the South (Litwack, 1961). Those opposed to slavery (the abolitionists) were often met by violence when they attempted to speak out against it.

Between the 1830s and 1870s, numerous conflicts occurred because of ethnic and racial differences, economic failures, moral questions, and during elections of public officials. In New York, 1834 was designated the "Year of the Riots" (Miller, 1977). The mayoral election and anti-abolitionist sentiment were the two main reasons for the disorders. Other cities faced similar problems. In Philadelphia, the Broad Street Riot of 1837 involved almost 15,000 residents. The incident occurred because native-born volunteer firemen returning from a fire could not get by an Irish funeral procession. In St. Louis in 1850, a mob destroyed the brothels in the city in an attempt to enforce standards of public decency. To quell most of these disturbances, the local militia was called in to suppress the violence, as the constables and the night watch were ineffectual.

At the same time that the riots occurred, citizens perceived that crime was increasing. Homicides, robberies, and thefts were thought to be on the rise. In addition, vagrancy, prostitution, gambling, and other vices were more observable on the streets. These types of criminal activities and the general deterioration of the city led to a sense of a loss of social control. But in spite of the apparent immediacy of these problems, replacements for the constable-watch police system did not appear overnight.

The political forces in the large industrial cities like New York, Philadelphia, Boston, and others precluded the immediate acceptance of a London-style police department. City councils, mayors, state legislatures, and governors debated and wrangled over a number of questions and could not come to an immediate agreement over the type of police they wanted. In New York City, for example, although problems emerged in 1834, the movement to form a preventive police department did not begin until 1841; it was officially created in 1845, but officers did not begin wearing uniforms until 1853.

While the first American police departments modeled themselves after the London Metropolitan Police, they borrowed selectively rather than exactly. The most notable carryover was the adoption of the preventive patrol idea. A police presence would alter the behavior of individuals and would be available to maintain order in an efficient manner. Differences, however, between the London and American police abounded. Miller (1977), in his comparative study of New York and London police, shows the drastic differences between the two agencies.

The London Metropolitan Police was a highly centralized agency. An extension of the national government, the police department was purposely removed from the direct political influence of the people. Furthermore, as noted above, Sir Robert Peel recruited individuals who fit a certain mold. Peel insisted that a polite, aloof officer who was trained and disciplined according to strict guidelines would be best suited for the function of crime prevention. In addition, the bobbies were encouraged to look upon police work as a career in professional civil service.

Unlike the London police, American police systems followed the style of local and municipal governments. City governments, created in the era of the "common man" and democratic participation, were highly decentralized. Mayors were largely figureheads; real power lay in the wards and neighborhoods. City councilmen or aldermen ran the government and used political patronage freely. The police departments shared this style of participation and decentralization. The police were an extension of different political factions, rather than an extension of city government. Police officers were recruited and selected by political leaders in a particular ward or precinct.

As a result of the democratic nature of government, legal intervention by the police was limited. Unlike the London police, which relied on formal institutional power, the American police relied on informal control or individual authority. That is, instead of drawing on institutional legitimacy (i.e., parliamentary laws), each police officer had to establish his own authority among the citizens he patrolled. The personal, informal police officer could win the respect of the citizenry by knowing local standards and expectations. This meant that different police behavior would occur in different neighborhoods. In New York, for example, the cop was free to act as he chose within the context of broad public expectations. He was less limited by institutional and legal restraints than was his London counterpart, entrusted with less formal power, but given broader personal discretion.

POLICE ACTIVITY IN THE 19TH CENTURY

American police systems began to appear almost overnight from 1860 to 1890 (Monkkonen, 1981). Once large cities like New York, Philadelphia, Boston, and Cincinnati had adopted the English model, the new version of policing spread from larger to smaller cities rather quickly. Where New York had debated for almost ten years before formally adopting the London-style, Cleveland, Buffalo, Detroit, and other cities readily accepted the innovation. Monkkonen explains that the police were a part of a growing range of services provided by urban administrations. Sanitation, fire, and health services were also adopted during this period and the police were simply a part of that natural growth.

Across these departments, however, differences flourished. Police activity varied depending upon the local government and political factions in power. Standards for officer selection (if any), training procedures, rules and regulations, levels of enforcement of laws, and police-citizen relationships differed across the United States. At the same time, however, there were some striking similarities.

Patrol Officers

The 19th century patrolman was basically a political operative rather than a London-style professional committed to public service (Walker, 1977). Primarily selected for his political service, the police officer owed his allegiance to the ward boss and police captain that chose him.

Police officers were paid well but had poor job security. Police salaries compared favorably with other occupations. On average in 1880, most major cities paid policemen in the neighborhood of $900 a year. Walker (1977) reports that a skilled tradesman in the building industry earned about $770 a year, while those in manufacturing could expect about $450 a year. A major drawback, however, was that job security was poor, as their employment relied on election day events. In Cincinnati, for example, in 1880, 219 of the 295 members of the force were dismissed, while another 20 resigned because of a political change in the municipal government. Other departments had similar turnover rates.

New officers were sent out on patrol with no training and few instructions beyond their rule books. Proper arrest procedures, rules of law, and so on were unknown to the officers. Left to themselves, they developed their own strategies for coping with life in the streets.

Police Work

Police officers walked a beat in all types of weather for two to six hours of a 12-hour day. The remaining time was spent at the station house on reserve. During actual patrol duty, police officers were required to maintain order and make arrests, but they often circumvented their responsibilities. Supervision was extremely limited once an officer was beyond the station house. Sergeants and captains had no way of contacting their men while they were on the beat, as communications technology was limited. Telegraph lines linked district stations to headquarters in the 1850s, but call boxes on the beat were not introduced until late in the 19th century, and radio and motorized communications did not appear until the 1900s (Lane, 1980). Police officers, then, acted alone and used their own initiative.

Unfortunately, little is known about ordinary patrol work or routine interactions with the public. However, historians have pieced together trends in police work based on arrest statistics. While these data have their limitations, they nonetheless provide a view of police activity.

Monkkonen's work (1981) found that from 1860 to 1920 arrests declined in 23 of the largest cities in the United States. In particular, crimes without victims, such as vice, disturbances, drunkenness, and other public order offenses, fell dramatically. Overall, Monkkonen estimated that arrests declined by more than 33% during the 60-year period. This trend runs contrary to "common sense notions about crime and the growth of industrial cities, immigration and social conflict" (p. 75). Further analysis showed that the decline occurred because the police role shifted from one of controlling the "dangerous class" to one of controlling criminal behavior only. From 1860 to 1890, Monkkonen argues, the police were involved in assisting the poor, taking in overnight lodgers, and returning lost children to their parents or orphanages. In the period of 1890 to 1920, however, the police changed their role, structure, and behavior because of external demands upon them. As a result, victimless arrests declined, while assaults, thefts, and homicide arrests increased slightly. Overall, however, the crime trend showed a decrease.

Police Corruption and Lawlessness

One of the major themes in the study of 19th century policing is the large-scale corruption that occurred in numerous departments across the country. The lawlessness of the police—their systematic corruption and nonenforcement of the laws—was one of the paramount issues in municipal politics during the late 1800s.

Police corruption was part of a broader social and political problem. During this period, political machines ran municipal governments. That is, political parties (Democrats and Republicans) controlled the mayor's office, the city councils, and local wards. Municipal agencies (fire departments, sanitation services, school districts, the courts, etc.) were also under the aegis of political parties. As part of this system, political patronage was rampant. Employment in exchange for votes or money was a common procedure. Police departments in New York, Chicago, Philadelphia, Kansas City, San Francisco, and Los Angeles were filled with political appointees as police officers. To insure their employment, officers followed the norms of the political party, often protecting illicit activities conducted by party favorites.

Corrupt practices extended from the chief's office down to the patrol officer. In New York City, for example, Chief William Devery (1898–1901) protected gambling dens and illegal prize fighting because his friend, Tim Sullivan (a major political figure on the Lower East Side) had interests in those areas. Police captains like Alexander "Clubber" Williams and Timothy Creeden acquired extensive wealth from protecting prostitutes, saloonkeepers, and gamblers. Williams, a brutal officer (hence, the nickname Clubber), was said to have a 53-foot yacht and residences in New York and the Connecticut suburbs. Since a captain's salary was about $3,000 a year in the 1890s, Williams had to collect from illegal enterprises in order to maintain his investments.

Because police officers worked alone or in small groups, there were ample opportunities to shake down peddlers and small businesses. Detectives allowed con men, pickpockets, and thieves to go about their business in return for a share of the proceeds. Captains often established regular payment schedules for houses of prostitution depending upon the number of girls in the house and the rates charged by them. The monthly total for police protection ranged between $25 and $75 per house plus $500 to open or re-open after being raided (Richardson, 1970).

Officers who did not go along with the nonenforcement of laws or did not approve of the graft and corruption of others found themselves transferred to less-than-desirable areas. Promotions were also denied; they were reserved for the politically-astute and wealthy officer (promotions could cost $10,000 to $15,000).

These types of problems were endemic to most urban police agencies throughout the country. They led to inefficiency and inequality of police services.

REFORM, REJECTION, AND REVISION

A broad reform effort began to emerge toward the end of the 19th century. Stimulated mainly by a group known as the Progressives, attempts were made to create a truly professional police force. The Progressives were upper-middle class, educated Protestants who opposed the political machines, sought improvements in government, and desired a change in American morality. They believed that by eliminating machine politics from government, all facets of social services, including the police, would improve.

These reformers found that the police were without discipline, strong leadership, and qualified personnel. To improve conditions, the progressives recommended three changes: (1) the departments should be centralized; (2) personnel should be upgraded; and (3) the police function should be narrowed (Fogelson, 1977). Centralization of the police meant that more power and authority should be placed in the hands of the chief. Autonomy from politicians was crucial to centralization. Upgrading the rank-and-file meant better training, discipline, and selection. Finally, the reformers urged that police give up all activities unrelated to crime. Police had run the ambulances, handled licensing of businesses, and sheltered the poor. By concentrating on fighting crime, the police would be removed from their service orientation and their ties to political parties would be severed.

From 1890 to 1920 the Progressive reformers struggled to implement their reform ideology in cities across the country. Some inroads were made during this period, including the establishment of police commissions, the use of civil service exams, and legislative reforms.

The immediate responses to charges of corruption were to create police administrative boards. The reformers attempted to take law enforcement appointments out of the hands of mayors and city councilmen and place control in the hands of oversight committees. The Progressives believed that politics would be eliminated from policing by using this maneuver. In New York, for example, the Lexow Committee, which investigated the corrupt practices of the department, recommended the formation of a bipartisan Board of Police Commissioners in 1895. Theodore Roosevelt became a member of this board, but to his dismay found that the commissioners were powerless to improve the state of policing. The bipartisan nature of the board (two Democrats and two Republicans) meant that consensus could not be reached on important issues. As a result, by 1900 the New York City police were again under the influence of party politics. In the following year the board of commissioners was abolished and the department was placed under the responsibility of a single commissioner (Walker, 1977). Other cities had similar experiences with the police commission approach. Cincinnati, Kansas City, St. Louis, and Baltimore were among those that adopted the commission, but found it to be short-lived. The major problem was still political—the police were viewed as an instrument of the political machine at the neighborhood level and reformers could not counter the effects of the Democratic or Republican parties.

Civil service was one answer to upgrading personnel. Officers would be selected and promoted based on merit, as measured by a competitive exam. Moreover, the officer would be subject to review by his superiors and removal from the force could take place if there was sufficient cause. Civil service met with some resistance by officers and reformers alike. The problem was that in guarding against the effects of patronage and favoritism, civil service became a rigid, almost inflexible procedure. Because it measured abstract knowledge rather than the qualities required for day-to-day work, civil service procedures were viewed as problematic. Eventually, the program did help to eliminate the more blatant forms of political patronage in almost all of the large police departments (Walker, 1977).

During this 30-year period, the efforts of the Progressive reformers did not change urban departments drastically. The reform movement resulted, in part, in the elimination of the widespread graft and corruption of the 1890s, but substantive changes in policing did not take place. Chiefs continued to lack power and authority, many officers had little or no education, training was limited, and the police role continued to include a wide variety of tasks.

Robert Fogelson (1977) suggests several reasons for the failure of reform. First, political machines were too difficult to break. Despite the efforts by the Progressives, politicians could still count on individual supporters to undermine the reforms. Second, police officers themselves resented the Progressives' interventions. Reformers were viewed by the police as individuals who knew little about police work and officers saw their proposals for change as ill-conceived. Finally, the reforms failed because the idea of policing could not be divorced from politics. That is, the character of the big-city police was interconnected with policymaking agencies that helped to decide which laws were enforced, which public was served, and whose peace was kept (Fogelson, 1977). Separating the police completely from politics could not take place.

THE EMERGENCE OF POLICE PROFESSIONALISM

A second reform effort emerged in the wake of the failure of the Progressives. Within police circles, a small cadre of chiefs sought and implemented a variety of innovations that would improve policing generally. From about 1910 to 1960 police chiefs carried on another reform movement, advocating that police adopt the professional model.

The professional department embodied a number of characteristics. First, the officers were experts; they applied knowledge to their tasks and were the only ones qualified to do the job. Second, the department was autonomous from external influences, such as political parties. This also meant that the department made its own rules and regulated its personnel. Finally, the department was administratively efficient, in that it carried out its mandate to enforce the law through modern technology and businesslike practices. These reforms were similar to those of the Progressives, but because they came from within police organizations themselves, they met with more success.

Leadership and technology assisted the movement to professionalize the police. Chiefs like Richard Sylvester, August Vollmer, and O.W. Wilson emphasized the use of innovative methods in police work. Samuel Walker (1977) notes that Sylvester, the chief of the Washington, D.C. police, helped to establish the idea of professionalism among police chiefs. As president of the International Association of Chiefs of Police (IACP), Sylvester inculcated the spirit of reform into the organization. He stressed acceptance of technological innovations, raised the level of discussion among chiefs to include crime control ideas, and promoted professionalism generally.

The major innovator among the chiefs was August Vollmer, chief of the Berkeley, California police. Vollmer was known for his pioneering work in developing college-level police education programs, bicycle and automobile patrols, and scientific crime detection aids. His department was the first to use forensic science in solving crimes.

Vollmer's emphasis on the quality of police personnel was tied closely to the idea of the professional officer. Becoming an expert in policing meant having the requisite credentials. Vollmer initiated intelligence, psychiatric, and neurological tests by which to select applicants. He was the first police chief to actively recruit college students. In addition, he was instrumental in linking the police department with the University of California at Berkeley. Another concern of Vollmer's dealt with the efficient delivery of police services. His department became the first in the nation to use automobiles and the first to hire a full-time forensic scientist to help solve crimes (Douthit, 1975).

O.W. Wilson, Vollmer's student, followed in his mentor's footsteps by advocating efficiency within the police bureaucracy through scientific techniques. As chief in Wichita, Kansas, Wilson conducted the first systematic study of one-officer squad cars. He argued that one-officer cars were efficient, effective, and economical. Despite arguments from patrol officers that their safety was at risk, Wilson claimed that the public received better service with single-officer cars.

Wilson's other contributions include his classic textbook, *Police Administration*, which lays out specific ideas regarding the use of one-man patrol cars, deployment of personnel on the streets, disciplinary measures, and organizational structure. Later in his career, Wilson accepted a professorship at the University of California at Berkeley where he taught and trained law enforcement officers. In 1947 he founded the first professional school of criminology.

Other chiefs contributed to the professional movement as well. William Parker changed the Los Angeles Police Department (LAPD) from a corrupt, traditional agency to an innovative, professional organization. From 1950 to his death in 1966, Parker served as chief. He was known for his careful planning, emphasis on efficiency, and his rigorous personnel selection and training procedures. His public relations campaigns and adept political maneuvers enabled him to gain the respect of the media and community. As a result, the LAPD became a model for reform across the country.

Technological changes also enabled the police to move toward professionalism. The patrol car, two-way radio, and telephone altered the way in which the police operated and the manner in which citizens made use of the police. Motorized patrol meant more efficient coverage of the city and quicker response to calls for service. The two-way radio dramatically increased the supervisory capacity of the police; continuous contact between sergeant and patrol officer could be maintained. Finally, the telephone provided the link between the public and the police. Though not a new invention, its use in conjunction with the car and two-way radio meant that efficient response to calls for service could be realized.

Overall, the second reform movement met with more success than the Progressive attempt, though it did not achieve its goal of professionalism. Walker (1977) and Fogelson (1977) agree that the quality of police officers greatly improved during this period. Police departments turned away the ill-educated individual, but at the same time failed to draw college graduates to their ranks. In terms of autonomy, police reformers and others were able to reduce the influence of political parties in departmental affairs. Chiefs obtained more power and authority in their management abilities, but continued to receive input from political leaders. In fact, most chiefs remained political appointees. In terms of efficiency, the police moved forward in serving the public more quickly and competently. Technological innovations clearly assisted the police in this area, as did streamlining the organizations themselves. However, the innovations also created problems. Citizens came to expect more from the police—faster response times, more arrests, and less overall crime. These expectations, as well as other difficulties, led to trying times for the police in the 1960s.

RIOTS AND RENEWAL

Policing in America encountered its most serious crisis in the 1960s. The rise in crime, the civil rights movement, anti-war sentiment, and riots in the cities brought the police into the center of a maelstrom.

During the decade of the 1960s crime increased at a phenomenal rate. Between 1960 and 1970 the crime rate per 100,000 persons doubled. Most troubling was the increase in violent crime—the robbery rate almost tripled during these ten years. As crime increased, so did the demands for its reduction. The police, in emphasizing its crime fighting ability, had given the public a false expectation that crime and violence could be reduced. But with the added responsibility of more crime, the police were unable to live up to the expectation they had created. As a result, the public image of the police was tarnished.

The civil rights movement created additional demands for the police. The movement, which began in the 1950s, sought equality for black Americans in all facets of life. Sit-ins at segregated lunch counters, boycotts of bus services, attempts at integrating schools, and demonstrations in the streets led to direct confrontations with law enforcement officers. The police became the symbol of a society that denied blacks equal justice under the law.

Eventually, the frustrations of black Americans erupted into violence in northern and southern cities. Riots engulfed almost every major city between 1964 and 1968. Most of the disorders were initiated by a routine incident involving the police. The spark that ignited the riots occurred on July 16, 1964, when a white New York City police officer shot and killed a black teenager. Black leaders in the Harlem ghetto organized protests demanding disciplinary action against the officer. Two days later, the demonstrators marched on precinct headquarters, where rock-throwing began. Eventually, looting and burning erupted during the night and lasted for two full days. When the riot was brought under control one person was dead, more than 100 injured, almost 500 arrested, and millions of dollars worth of property destroyed. In the following year, the Watts riot in Los Angeles led to more devastation. Thirty-four persons died, a thousand were injured, and 4,000 arrested. By 1966, 43 more riots broke out across the country and in 1967 violence in Newark and Detroit exceeded the 1965 Watts riot. Disorders engulfed Newark for five days, leaving 23 dead, while the Detroit riot a week later lasted nearly seven days and resulted in 43 deaths with $40 million in property damages.

On the final day of the Detroit riot, President Lyndon Johnson appointed a special commission to investigate the problem of civil disorder. The National Advisory Commission on Civil Disorders (The Kerner Commission) identified institutional racism as the underlying cause of the rioting. Unemployment, discrimination in jobs and housing, inadequate social services, and unequal justice at the hands of the law were among the problems cited by the commission.

Police actions were also cited as contributing to the disorders. Direct police intervention had sparked the riots in Harlem, Watts, Newark, and Detroit. In Watts and Newark the riots were set off by routine traffic stops. In Detroit a police raid on an after-hours bar in the ghetto touched off the disorders there. The police, thus, became the focus of national attention.

The Kerner Commission and other investigations found several problems in police departments. First, police conduct included brutality, harassment, and abuse of power. Second, training and supervision was inadequate. Third, police-community relations were poor. Fourth, the employment of black officers lagged far behind the growth of the black population.

As a means of coping with these problems in policing (and other agencies of the criminal justice system) President Johnson created a crime commission and Congress authorized federal assistance to criminal justice. The President's crime commission produced a final report that emphasized the need for more research, higher qualifications of criminal justice personnel, and greater coordination of the national crime-control effort. The federal aid program to justice agencies resulted in the Office of Law Enforcement Assistance, a forerunner of the Law Enforcement Assistance Administration (LEAA).

THE LEGACY OF THE 60S

The events of the 1960s forced the police, politicians, and policymakers to re-assess the state of law enforcement in the United States. For the first time, academicians rushed to study the police in an effort to explain their problems and crises. With federal funding from LEAA and private organizations, researchers began to study the police from a number of perspectives. Sociologists, political scientists, psychologists, and historians began to scrutinize different aspects of policing. Traditional methods of patrol deployment, officer selection, and training were questioned. Racial discrimination in employment practices, in arrests, and in the use of deadly force were among the issues closely examined.

In addition, the professional movement itself came into question. As Walker notes, the legacy of professionalization was "ambiguous" (Walker, 1977:167). On one hand, the police made improvements in their level of service, training, recruitment, and efficiency.

On the other hand, a number of problems remained and a number of new ones emerged. Corruption scandals continued to present problems. In New York, Chicago, and Denver systematic corruption was discovered. Political parties persisted in their links to policing.

The professional movement had two unintended consequences. The first involved the development of a police subculture. The second was the problem of police-community relations. In terms of the subculture, police officers began to feel alienated from administrators, the media, and the public and turned inward as a result. Patrol officers began to resent the police hierarchy because of the emphasis on following orders and regulations. While this established uniformity in performance and eliminated some abuses of power, it also stifled creativity and the talents of many officers. Rather than thinking for themselves (as professionals would) patrol officers followed orders given by sergeants, lieutenants, or other ranking officers. This led to morale problems and criticism of police administrators by the rank and file.

Patrol officers saw the media and the public as foes because of the criticism and disrespect cast their way. As the crime rate increased, newspaper accounts criticized the police for their inability to curtail it. As the riots persisted, some citizens cried for more order, while others demanded less oppression by the police on the streets. The conflicting messages given to the patrol officers by these groups led to distrust, alienation, and frustration. Only by standing together did officers feel comfortable in their working environment.

The second unintended consequence of professionalism was the problems it generated for police-community relations. Modern technology, like the patrol car, removed the officer from the street and eliminated routine contact with citizens. The impersonal style of professionalism often exacerbated police-community problems. Tactics such as aggressive patrol in black neighborhoods, designed to suppress crime efficiently, created more racial tensions.

These problems called into question the need for and effectiveness of professionalism. Some police administrators suggested abandoning the movement. Others sought to continue the effort while adjusting for and solving the difficulties. For the most part, the goal of professionalization remains operative. In the 1970s and 1980s, progressive police chiefs and organizations continue to press for innovations in policing. As a result, social science research has become an important part of policymaking decisions. By linking research to issues like domestic violence, repeat offenders, use of deadly force, training techniques, and selection procedures, police executives increase their ability to make effective decisions.

CONCLUDING REMARKS

This chapter has examined the history of American police systems from the English heritage through the 20th century. Major emphasis has been placed on the police role, though important events that shaped the development of the police have also been discussed. As can be seen through this review, a number of present-day issues have their roots in different epochs of American history. For example, the idea of community policing can be traced to the colonial period and to medieval England. Preventive patrol, legitimacy, authority, and professionalism are 18th and 19th century concepts. Riots, disorders, and corruption are not new to American policing; similar events occurred in the 19th century. Thus, by virtue of studying history, we can give contextual meaning to current police problems, ideas, and situations. By looking at the past, present-day events can be better understood.

ENDNOTES

1. This list of police histories is by no means a comprehensive one. A vast number of journal articles, books, and dissertations have been written since the 1960s.
2. A number of scholars have examined the "police function," particularly in the last 20 or so years. Among the most well-known are Wilson (1968), Skolnick (1966), Bittner (1971), and Goldstein (1977). Each of these authors prescribes to a different view of what the police should and should not do.

REFERENCES

ALFERS, KENNETH G. 1975. "The Washington Police: A History, 1800–1886." Ph.D. Dissertation. George Washington University.

BITTNER, EGON. 1970. *The Functions of the Police in Modern Society*. Chevy Chase, Maryland: National Institute of Mental Health.

CEI, LOUIS B. 1975. "Law Enforcement in Richmond: A History of Police Community Relations, 1737–1974." Ph.D. Dissertation. Florida State University.

CRITCHLEY, T.A. 1967. *A History of Police in England and Wales*. Montclair, New Jersey: Patterson Smith.

DOUTHIT, NATHAN. 1975. "August Vollmer: Berkeley's First Chief of Police and the Emergence of Police Professionalism." *California Historical Quarterly* 54 Spring: 101–124.

FOGELSON, ROBERT. 1977. *Big-City Police*. Cambridge: Harvard University Press.

GOLDSTEIN, HERMAN. 1977. *Policing a Free Society*. Cambridge: Ballinger Press.

KLOCKARS, CARL. 1985. *The Idea of Police*. Beverly Hills: Sage Publications.

LANE, ROGER. 1967. *Policing the City: Boston, 1822–1885*. Cambridge: Harvard University Press.

———. 1980. "Urban Police and Crime in Nineteenth-Century America," in Michael Tonry and Norval Morris (eds.), *Crime and Justice: An Annual Review of Research, Volume 2*. Chicago: University of Chicago Press.

LITWACK, LEON. 1961. *North of Slavery*. Chicago: University of Chicago Press.

MANIHA, JOHN K. 1970. "The Mobility of Elites in a Bureaucratizing Organization: The St. Louis Police Department, 1861–1961." Ph.D. Dissertation. University of Michigan.

MILLER, WILBUR R. 1977. *Cops and Bobbies: Police Authority in New York and London, 1830–1870*. Chicago: University of Chicago Press.

MONKKONEN, ERIC H. 1981. *Police in Urban America, 1860–1920*. Cambridge: Cambridge University Press.

RADZINOWICZ, LEON. 1948–1968. *History of the English Criminal Law, Volumes 1–4*. New York: MacMillan.

REICHARD, MAXIMILIAN I. 1975. "The Origins of Urban Police: Freedom and Order in Antebellum St. Louis." Ph.D. Dissertation. Washington University.

REITH, CHARLES. 1956. *A New Study of Police History*. Edinburgh.

RICHARDSON, JAMES F. 1970. *The New York Police: Colonial Times to 1901*. New York: Oxford University Press.

———. 1974. *Urban Police in the United States*. Port Washington, New York: Kennikat Press.

RIDER, EUGENE F. 1971. "The Denver Police Department: An Administrative, Organizational, and Operational History, 1858–1905." Ph.D. Dissertation. University of Denver.

SCHNEIDER, JOHN C. 1980. *Detroit and the Problems of Order, 1830–1880*. Lincoln: University of Nebraska Press.

SKOLNICK, JEROME, 1966. *Justice Without Trial: Law Enforcement in Democratic Society*. New York: John Wiley and Sons.

WALKER, SAMUEL. 1977. *A Critical History of Police Reform: The Emergence of Professionalism*. Lexington, Massachusetts: D.C. Heath and Company.

WILSON, JAMES Q. 1968. *Varieties of Police Behavior: The Management of Law and Order in Eight Communities*. Cambridge: Harvard University Press.

QUESTIONS FOR THOUGHT AND DISCUSSION

1. What are some current issues in policing that have their roots in earlier epochs of policing history? Are we making any progress in those areas?
2. How is the concept of community policing traced to the colonial period and to medieval England?
3. What problems within police departments were discovered by President Johnson's Kerner Commission?

THE NEW POLICING

Confronting Complexity

Herman Goldstein

Community policing is well on its way to becoming a common term in households across the Nation. That is a satisfying development for many, but causes some anxiety and discomfort for others. What accounts for the mixed reactions?

Under the rubric of community policing, progressive police administrators and interested citizens have been working hard for more than a decade to design and implement a form of policing that better meets the extraordinary demands on the police in the 1990s. Within these circles the term "community policing" has been used to embrace and intricately web together initiatives that have long been advocated for modern-day policing. These efforts have stimulated more productive thought and experimentation than has occurred at any previous time in the history of policing in this country. They have also created a new feeling of excitement and optimism in a field that has desperately needed both. It is understandable, therefore, why the current wave of popular support for community policing is so welcome in many quarters. It gives a tremendous impetus to these new initiatives.

The downside of this new-found popularity is that "community policing" is widely used without any regard for its substance. Political leaders and, unfortunately, many police leaders latch onto the label for the positive images it evokes but do not invest in the concept itself. Some police personnel resist community policing initiatives because of the belief that they constitute an effort to placate an overly demanding and critical segment of the community that is intent on exercising more control over police operations.

Indeed, the popularity of the term has resulted in its being used to encompass practically all innovations in policing, from the most ambitious to the most mundane; from the most carefully thought through to the most casual. The label is being used in ways that increase public expectations of the police and create the impression that community policing will provide an instant solution not only for the problems of crime, disorder, and racial tension, but for many of the other acute problems that plague our urban areas as well.

With such varied meanings and such broad expectations, the use of "community policing" creates enormous problems for those seriously interested in bringing about

From National Institute of Justice, *Research in Brief*, Washington, D.C.: United States Department of Justice, December, 1993.

meaningful change in the American police. Carefully developed initiatives bearing the community policing label, fragile by their very nature, are endangered because superficial programs are so vulnerable to attack.

One reaction to this dilemma is to press for definition and simplification, to seek agreement on a pure model of community policing. This pressure for simplification is joined by well-intentioned practitioners who, understandably, want to know—in specific detail—what they are supposed to do. *Oversimplification*, however, can be a deadly enemy to progress in policing. The field already suffers because so much in policing is oversimplified.

Crime, violence, and disorder, for example, are simple, convenient terms, but they disguise amorphous, complex problems. Their common and indiscriminate use, especially in defining the responsibilities of the police, places a heavy burden on the police and complicates the police task. The police respond with law enforcement and patrol—equally simple terms commonly used by the public without any awareness of the methods they embrace and their value. If community policing takes its place alongside law enforcement or patrol as just another generic response to a simplistic characterization of the police function, not much will have been gained and the concept will quickly lose its credibility.

RETHINKING THE POLICE ROLE

The policing of a free, diverse, and vibrant society is an awesome and complex task. The police are called upon to deal with a wide array of quite different behavioral problems, each perplexing in its own way. The police have tremendous power—to deny freedom and to use force, even to take a life. Individual officers exercise enormous discretion in using their authority and in making decisions that affect our lives. The very quality of life in this country and the equilibrium of our cities depend on the way in which the police function is carried out.

Given the awesome and complex nature of the police function, it follows that designing the arrangements and the organization to carry it out is equally complex. We are now in a period in which more attention is being given to the police function than at any prior time, a period in which we are rethinking, in all of its multiple dimensions, the arrangement for the policing of our society. We should not, therefore, lose patience because we have not yet come up with the perfect model; we should not get stalled trying to simplify change just to give uniform meaning to a single, catchy, and politically attractive term. We need to open up explorations rather than close them down. We need to better understand the complicated rather than search for the simple.

Some of the most common changes associated with community policing are already being implemented; for example, the permanent assignment of officers to specific beats with a mandate to get to know and relate to the community. There is now growing and persuasive support for decentralization, permanent assignments, and the development of "partnerships" between the police and the community. But these changes represent only a fragment of the larger picture.

Policing in the United States is much like a large, intricate, complex apparatus with many parts. Change of any one part requires changes in many others and in the way the parts fit and work together. For example, altering the way officers are assigned and how they patrol may be easy. But to gain full value from such changes, and to sustain them, changes are also necessary in the organization and leadership of the police department—in its staffing, supervision, training, and recruitment; and in its internal working environment. Thus, a change in direction requires more than tinkering. It requires, if it is to be effective, simultaneous changes in many areas affecting the enterprise. This, in turn, requires careful planning and coordination. And perhaps most important, it requires time, patience, and learning from experience.

Moreover, to succeed in improving policing, we need to move beyond the exclusive focus on the police *agency*. There is an urgent need to alter the public's expectations of the police. And we need to revise the fundamental provisions that we as a society make for carrying out the police function. For example:

- Refine the authority granted the police (curtail it in some areas and expand it in others).
- Recognize the discretion exercised by the police and provide a means for its review and control.
- Provide the police with the resources that will enable them to get their job done.

We need, in other words, without compromising our commitment to democratic values, to being expectations and capacity more into harmony so that a job increasingly labeled as "impossible" can be carried out.

THE NATURE OF CHANGE

To illustrate, in some detail, the complexity of change in policing, it is helpful to examine five spheres in which change is now occurring. What types of issues arise? And what is the interrelationship and interdependence among the factors involved in these changes?

Refining the Police Function and Public Expectations

The new forms of policing expand the police function from crime fighting, without any abdication of that role, to include maintaining order, dealing with quality-of-life offenses, and fixing the "broken windows"—all now recognized as being much more important than previously believed. The police have become more proactive, committed to preventing incidents rather than simply *reacting* to them. These shifts in emphasis appear to have gained widespread support.

But we need to be aware of the avalanche of business that this expansion of the police function invites lest it constitute a serious self-inflicted wound. The volume and nature of the miscellaneous tasks that accrue to the police are many. Cutbacks in other government services only add to their number. In areas that are starved for social services, the slightest improvement in police response increases the demand on the police. As water seeks its own level, the vast array of problems that surface in a large urban area inevitably find their way to the agency most willing to accept them.

For example, consider the officer assigned to a specific neighborhood with a broad mandate to improve service. Within a very short period of time, that officer will be over-whelmed by the need for services that—despite the greatest creativity and resourceful-ness—far exceeds his or her capacity to deliver.

Very often the police *can* do more to satisfy citizen needs. They can identify prob-lems and take actions that result in mitigating or solving them when they are given the time and license to do so. But in the larger scheme of things the need to reduce public expecta-tions is every bit as important as the need to broaden the police function—not simply to make limited resources fit the demand, but for more complex reasons. Many of the most troublesome aspects of policing stem from the pressure that has been exerted on the police to appear omnipotent, to do more than they are authorized, trained, and equipped to do.

Police tend to like challenges. But the challenge to fill needs, to live up to expecta-tions, can lead to the taking of shortcuts, the stretching of authority and, as a consequence, the potential for abuse of that authority. It is demoralizing to the thoughtful, dedicated offi-cer to create the expectation that he or she can do more than take the edge off some of the more intractable problems that the police confront.

The new policing seeks to make the police job more achievable by realigning what the police do and do not do by giving higher priority to some tasks and lower priority to others, by reducing public expectations and leveling with the public about police capaci-ty, by engaging the public in taking steps to help themselves, and by connecting with other agencies and the private sector in ways that ensure that citizens referred to them will be helped. There is a need to invest much more, in our individual communities, in working through the questions that arise in trying to achieve this better alignment.

Getting Involved in the Substance of Policing

A common theme in initiatives under the community policing umbrella is the emphasis on improving relationships with the citizenry. Such improvement is vital in order to reduce tensions, develop mutual trust, promote the free exchange of information, and acquaint officers with the culture and lifestyle of those being policed.

Improved relationships are important. They would constitute a major advance in some cities. But many would argue that they merely lay a groundwork and create an envi-ronment in which to strive for more. When citizens ask if community policing works, they are not so much interested in knowing if the community likes the police or if the police are getting along with the community. Rather, they usually want to know if the community policing initiative has had an impact on the problems of concern to them: their fear of using the streets, the abandoned cars in the neighborhood, the gang that has been intimi-dating them. If the initiatives that have been taken do not go beyond improving relation-ships, there is a risk that community policing will become just another means by which police operate without having a significant, demonstrable impact on the problems the police are expected to handle.

This tendency in policing to become preoccupied with means over ends is obvi-ously not new. It was this concern that gave rise to the work on problem-oriented polic-ing. The police must give more substance to community policing by getting more involved in analyzing and responding to the specific problems citizens bring to their attention. This calls for a much heavier investment by the police in understanding the varied pieces of their business, just as the medical field invests in understanding different diseases. It means that police, more than anyone else, should have a detailed understanding of such varied problems as homicides involving teenage victims, drive-by shootings, and carjackings. And it means that a beat officer should have indepth knowledge about the corner drug house, the rowdy teenage gang that assembles at the convenience store on Friday night, and the panhandler who harasses passersby on a given street corner. Analyzing each of these quite different problems in depth leads to the realization that what may work for one will not work for the other, that each may require a different combination of different responses. That is the beginning of wisdom in policing: One size clearly does not fit all.

Problem-solving is being integrated into community policing initiatives in many jurisdictions. It dominates the commitment to change in some jurisdictions. Conference and training sessions for police have, with increased frequency, focused on such problems as the homeless, family violence, high-risk youth, child abuse, and school violence.

More of the momentum associated with community policing must be focused on these and similar problems. Smarter policing in this country requires a sustained effort within policing to research substantive problems, to make use of the mass of information and data on specific problems accumulated by individual police agencies, to experiment with different alternative responses, to evaluate these efforts, and to share the results of these evaluations with police across the Nation. It would be useful to do more to reorient the work of research and development units in police departments, and to entice some of the best minds in the field of criminology and related specialties to assist in these efforts. The police should not only make greater use of research done by others; they should themselves be engaged in research.

Rethinking the Relationship Between the Police and the Criminal Justice System

Buried in all of the rhetoric relating to community policing is the fact that, with little notice and in subtle ways, the longstanding relationship between the police and the criminal justice system is being redefined. This is a radical change, but it is given scant attention in the literature on community policing. And the full consequences of the changes—and their relationship to some of the developments most commonly associated with community policing—have not been adequately explored.

The enforcement of criminal law is inherent in the police role. The great emphasis on enforcement affects the shape of their organizations, the attitudes and priorities of their personnel, and their relationship with the community. Significantly, police officers are referred to as "law enforcement officers." The felt need for objectivity and neutrality in law enforcement often results in the police being characterized as having no discretion. And the commitment to enforcement encourages the police to act in ways designed to inflate the public's impression of their capacity to enforce the law in the hope that their image alone will reduce crime and disorder.

Advanced forms of community policing reject many of the characteristics stemming from the emphasis on enforcement. A neighborhood police officer, for example, is expected to have a much broader interest than simply enforcing the criminal law, to exhaust a wide range of alternatives before resorting to arrest for minor offenses, to exercise broad discretion, and to depend more on resourcefulness, persuasion, or cajoling than on coercion, image, or bluff.

Reconciling these different perspectives has always been difficult. Some would even argue the two postures are incompatible. Simplistically, they are often distinguished as the "hard" and "soft" approaches in policing. But as a result of a sequence of developments in the past decade the difference between the two approaches has been diminished.

What has happened? So long as the police were intricately intertwined with the criminal justice system, they came to depend more heavily on the system. Thus, as violence and, especially, crimes associated with drugs increased, the police made more and more arrests of serious offenders. And to deal with disorder on the streets they arrested thousands of minor offenders as well, often stretching their authority somewhat (as police are pressured to do) in order to restore order. Predictably, the criminal justice systems in most large urban areas, and many smaller ones as well, have been overwhelmed to the point that it is no longer possible for the system to accept some serious offenders, let along minor offenders.

The consequences of recognizing that the capacity of the criminal justice system has limits are more far-reaching than is commonly recognized. Police can no longer use arrest, as they so freely did in the past, to deal with a wide variety of ambiguous situations. Moreover, the aura of authority on which the police have so heavily depended for getting so much of their job done, rooted in the capacity to arrest, has been greatly diminished. Police officers today simply do not appear as powerful and threatening to those who most frequently come in contact with them because they can no longer use the criminal justice system as they once did.

What does this mean for some of the central themes under the community policing umbrella? It means that there are new, pragmatic reasons for searching intensively for alternatives to the criminal justice system as the way in which to get the police job done.

It also means that there is now an added incentive to cultivate positive relationships with the community. The police need to replace the amorphous authority that they previously derived from the criminal justice system and on which they depended so heavily in the past. What better way to do this than arm themselves with what Robert Peel characterized in 1829 as that most powerful form of authority, the "public approval of their existence, actions, and behavior."

The congested state of affairs in the criminal justice system means, too, that the police must conserve their use of that system for those situations in which it is most appropriate and potentially most effective. This latter need should lead the police and others committed to community policing to join Attorney General Janet Reno in speaking out for a more sensible national criminal justice policy that curbs the indiscriminate overuse of a system that will, if not checked, draw scarce funds away from the police and away from preventive programs where those funds can do more good.

Searching for Alternatives

The diversification of policing—the move from primary dependence on the criminal law to the use of a wide range of different responses—is among the most significant changes under the community policing umbrella. It enables the police to move away from having to "use a hammer (the criminal justice system) to catch a fly"; it enables them to fine-tune their responses. It gives them a range of options (or tools) that in number and variety come closer to matching the number and variety of problems they are expected to handle. These may include informal, common sense responses used in the past but never formally authorized.

The primary and most immediate objective in authorizing the police to use a greater range of alternatives is to improve police effectiveness. Quite simply, mediating a dispute, abating a nuisance, or arranging to have some physical barrier removed—without resorting to arrest—may be the best way to solve a problem.

But there are additional benefits in giving police officers a larger repertoire of responses. Currently, for example, one of the greatest impediments to improvement in policing is the strength of the police subculture. That subculture draws much of its strength from a secret shared among police: that they are compelled to bend the law and take shortcuts in order to get their job done. Providing the police with legitimate, clear-cut means to carry out their functions enables them to operate more honestly and openly and, therefore, has the potential for reducing the strength and, as a consequence, the negative influence of the police subculture.

The diversification of options is also responsive to one of the many complexities in the staffing of police agencies. It recognizes, forthrightly, the important role of the individual police officer as a decision-maker—a role the officer has always had but one that has rarely been acknowledged. Acknowledging and providing alternatives contribute toward redefining the job of a police officer by placing a value on thinking, on creativity, and on decisionmaking. It credits the officer with having the ability to analyze incidents and problems and gives the officer the freedom to choose among various appropriate responses.

Changing to a system in which so much responsibility is invested in the lowest level employee, one who already operates with much independence on the streets, will not occur quickly or easily. And absent sufficient preparation, the results may be troublesome. This is especially so if officers, in their enthusiasm, blend together community support and their desire to please the community to justify using methods that are either illegal or improper. And implementation in a department that has a record of abuse or corruption is obviously much more problematic. Those concerned about control, however, must recognize that the controls on which we currently depend are much less effective than they are often thought to be. Preparations for the empowerment of officers requires changes in recruitment standards and training, establishing guidelines for the exercise of discretion, and inculcating values in officers that, in the absence of specific directions, guides their decisionmaking. Meeting these needs in turn connects with the fifth and final dimension of change.

Changing the Working Environment in a Police Agency

If new forms of policing are to take hold, the working environment within police agencies must change. Much has been written about new management styles supportive of community policing. But with a few remarkable exceptions relatively little has actually been achieved. And where modest changes have been made they are often lost when a change in administration occurs or when the handling of a single incident brings embarrassment, resulting in a reversion to the old style of control.

"Working environment" means simply the atmosphere and expectations that superiors set in relating to their subordinates. In a tradition-bound department, managers, supported by voluminous, detailed rules, tend to exercise a tight, paramilitary, top-down form of control—perhaps reflecting the way in which they have historically sought to achieve control in the community.

The initiatives associated with community policing cannot survive in a police agency managed in traditional ways. If changes are not made, the agency sets itself up for failure. Officers will not be creative and will not take initiatives if a high value continues to be placed on conformity. They will not be thoughtful if they are required to adhere to regulations that are thoughtless. And they will not aspire to act as mature, responsible adults if their superiors treat them as immature children.

But properly trained and motivated officers, given the freedom to make decisions and act independently, will respond with enthusiasm. They will grasp the concept, appreciate its many dimensions, and skillfully fill their new roles. These officers will solve problems, motivate citizens to join together to do things for themselves, and create a feeling of security and goodwill. Equally important, the officers will find their work demanding but very satisfying. In rank and file officers, there exists an enormous supply of talent, energy, and commitment that, under quality leadership, could rapidly transform American policing.

The major impediment to tapping this wellspring has been a failure to engage and elicit a commitment from those having management and supervisory responsibilities. It is disheartening to witness a meeting of the senior staff of a police agency in which those in attendance are disconnected and often openly hostile to changes initiated by the chief executive and supported by a substantial proportion of the rank and file. It is equally disheartening to talk with police officers on the street and officers of lower supervisory rank who cite their *superior officer* as their major problem, rather than the complexity of their job.

Because the problem is of such magnitude, perhaps, some bold—even radical—steps by legislative bodies and municipal chief executives may be necessary. Perhaps early retirement should be made more attractive for police executives who resist change. Perhaps consideration should be given to proposals recently made in England that call for the elimination of unnecessary ranks, and for making continuation in rank conditional on periodic review.

But before one can expect support for such measures, the public will need to be satisfied that police executives have exhausted whatever means are available to them for turning the situation around. When one looks at what has been done, it is troubling to find that a department's investment in the reorientation of management and supervisory personnel often consisted of no more than "a day at the academy"—and sometimes not even that. How much of the frustration in eliciting support from management and supervision stems from the fact that agencies have simply not invested enough in engaging senior officers, in explaining why change is necessary, and in giving these supervisors and managers the freedom required for them to act in their new role.

Some efforts to deal with the problem have been encouraging. The adoption of "Total Quality Management" in policing has demonstrated very positive results and holds much promise. It ought to be encouraged. An important lesson can be learned from experiences with TQM. Training to support changes of the magnitude now being advocated in policing requires more than a one-shot effort consisting of a few classroom lectures. It requires a substantial commitment of time in different settings spread over a long period, a special curriculum, the best facilitators, and the development of problems, case studies, and exercises that engage the participants. It requires the development of teamwork in which subordinates contribute as much as superiors. And it requires that the major dimension of the training take the form of conscious change in the day-to-day interaction of personnel—not in a training setting, but on the job.

CONCLUSION

Dwelling on complexity is risky, for it can be overwhelming and intimidating. It is difficult. It turns many people off. But for those who get involved, the results can be very rewarding.

There have been extraordinary accomplishments in policing in the past two decades by police agencies that have taken on some of these difficult tasks. There is an enormous reservoir of ability and commitment in police agencies, especially among rank and file officers, and a willingness on the part of individual citizens and community groups at the grass roots level to engage with the police and support change. Viewed collectively, these achievements should be a source of optimism and confidence. By building on past progress and capitalizing on current momentum, change that is deeper and more lasting can be achieved.

But there is an even more compelling overriding incentive to struggle with these complexities. We are being challenged today to commit ourselves anew to our unique character as a democracy, to the high value we as a nation place on diversity, ensuring equality, protecting individual rights, and guaranteeing that all citizens can move about freely and enjoy tranquil lives. The social problems that threaten the character of the Nation are increasing, not decreasing. It will take major changes—apart from those in the police—to reduce these problems. In this turbulent period it is more important than ever that we have a police capacity that is sensitive, effective, and responsive to the country's unique needs, and that, above all else, is committed to protecting and extending democratic values. That is a high calling indeed.

QUESTIONS FOR THOUGHT AND DISCUSSION

1. Why is it so important to involve the community in policing? What are some accomplishments being made in this area?
2. What are some of the changes being made in defining the police function and public expectations?
3. What is diversification of policing? What are some benefits and problems of diversification?

POLICING
AND THE FEAR OF CRIME

Mark H. Moore
Robert C. Trojanowicz

When crimes occur—when a ghetto teenager is shot to death in a gang war, when an elderly woman is mugged for her social security check, when a nurse is raped in a hospital parking lot, when one driver is punched by another in a dispute over a parking place, when a black family's new home is vandalized—society's attention is naturally focused on the victims and their material losses. Their wounds, bruises, lost property, and inconvenience can be seen, touched, and counted. These are the concrete signs of criminal victimization.

Behind the immediate, concrete losses of crime victims, however, is a different, more abstract crime problem—that of fear. For victims, fear is often the largest and most enduring legacy of their victimization. The raped nurse will feel vulnerable long after her cuts and bruises heal. The harassed black family suffers far more from the fear of neighborhood hostility than the inconvenience of repairing their property.

For the rest of us—the not-recently, or not-yet victimized–fear becomes a contagious agent spreading the injuriousness of criminal victimization. The gang member's death makes parents despair of their children's future. The mugging of the elderly woman teaches elderly residents to fear the streets and the teenagers who roam them. The fight over the parking place confirms the general fear of strangers. The harassment of the black family makes other minorities reluctant to claim their rights. In these ways, fear extends the damage of criminal victimization.

Of course, fear is not totally unproductive. It prompts caution among citizens and thereby reduces criminal opportunities. Too, it motivates citizens to shoulder some of the burdens of crime control by buying locks and dogs, thereby adding to general deterrence. And fear kindles enthusiasm for publicly supported crime control measures. Thus, reasonable fears, channeled in constructive directions, prepare society to deal with crime. It is only when fear is unreasonable, or generates counterproductive responses, that it becomes a social problem.

This paper explores fear as a problem to be addressed by the police. It examines current levels and recent trends in the fear of crime; analyzes how fear is linked to criminal victimization; considers the extent to which fear is a distinct problem that invites separate

From *Perspectives on Policing*, a publication of the National Institute of Justice and the Program in Criminal Justice and Policy Management, John F. Kennedy School of Government, Harvard University. Washington, D.C.: United States Department of Justice, June 1988.

control strategies; and assesses the positive and negative social consequences of fear. It then turns to what is known about the efficacy of police strategies for managing fear; i.e., for reducing fear when it is irrational and destructive, and for channeling fear along constructive paths when it is reasonable and helpful in controlling crime.

THE FEAR OF CRIME

Society does not yet systematically collect data on fear. Consequently, our map of fear—its levels, trends, and social location—is sketchy. Nonetheless, its main features are easily identified.

First, fear is widespread. The broadest impact was registered by "The Figgie Report on Fear of Crime" released in 1980. Two-fifths of Americans surveyed reported that they were "highly fearful" they would become victims of violent crime.[1] Similar results were reported by the Harris poll of 1975, which found that 55 percent of all adults said they felt "uneasy" walking their own streets.[2] The Gallup poll of 1977 found that about 45 percent of the population (61 percent of the women and 28 percent of the men) were afraid to walk alone at night.[3] An eight-city victimization survey published in 1977 found that 45 percent of all respondents limited their activities because of fear of crime.[4] A statewide study in Michigan reported that 66 percent of respondents avoided certain places because of fear of crime.[5] Interviews with a random sample of Texans in 1978 found that more than half said that they feared becoming a serious crime victim within a year.[6]

Second, fear of crime increased from the late 1960s to the mid-1970s, then began decreasing during the mid-1970s. According to the 1968 Gallup poll, 44 percent of the women and 16 percent of the men said that they were afraid to walk alone at night. In 1977, when a similar question was asked, 61 percent of the women and 28 percent of the men reported they were afraid to walk alone at night—and increase of 17 percent for women and 12 percent for men.[7] In 1975, a Harris poll found that 55 percent of all adults felt "uneasy" walking their own streets. In 1985, this number had fallen to 32 percent—a significant decline.[8]

Third, fear is not evenly distributed across the population. Predictably, those who feel themselves most vulnerable are also the most fearful. Looking at the distribution of fear across age and sex categories, the greatest levels of fear are reported by elderly women. The next most frightened group seems to be all other women. The least afraid are young men. Looking at race, class, and residence variables, blacks are more afraid of crime than whites, the poor more afraid than the middle class or wealthy, and inner-city dwellers more afraid than suburbanites.[9]

Indeed, while the current national trend may show a decline in fear, anecdotal evidence suggests that this trend has not yet reached America's ghettos. There, fear has become a condition of life. Claude Brown describes Harlem's problem in 1985:

> ...In any Harlem building,...every door has at least three locks on it. Nobody opens a door without first finding out who's there. In the early evening,...you see people...lingering outside nice apartment houses, peeking in the lobbies. They seem to be casing the joint. They are actually trying to figure out who is in the lobby of *their* building. "Is this someone waiting to mug me? Should I risk going in, or should I wait for someone else to come?"

> If you live in Harlem, USA, you don't park your automobile two blocks from your apartment house because that gives potential muggers an opportunity to get a fix on you. You'd better find a parking space within a block of your house, because if you have to walk two blocks you're not going to make it....
>
> In Harlem, elderly people walking their dogs in the morning cross the street when they see some young people coming....And what those elderly men and women have in the paper bags they're carrying is not just a pooper scooper—it's a gun. And if those youngsters cross the street, somebody's going to get hurt.[10]

These findings suggest that one of the most important privileges one acquires as one gains wealth and status in American society is the opportunity to leave the fear of crime behind. The unjust irony is that "criminals walk city streets, while fear virtually imprisons groups like women and the elderly in their homes."[11] James K. Stewart, Director of the National Institute of Justice, traces the important long-run consequence of this uneven distribution of fear for the economic development of our cities: if the inner-city populations are afraid of crime, then commerce and investment essentially disappear, and with them, the chance for upward social mobility.[12] If Hobbes is correct in asserting that the most fundamental purpose of civil government is to establish order and protect citizens from the fear of criminal attack that made life "nasty, brutish and short" in the "state of nature," then the current level and distribution of fear indicate an important governmental failure.[13]

THE CAUSES OF FEAR

In the past, fear was viewed as primarily caused by criminal victimization. Hence, the principal strategy for controlling crime was reducing criminal victimization. More recently, we have learned that while fear of crime is associated with criminal victimization, the relationship is less close than originally assumed.[14]

The association between victimization and fear is seen most closely in the aggregate patterns across time and space. Those who live in areas with high crime rates are more afraid and take more preventive action than people living in areas where the risk of victimization is lower.[15] The trends in levels of fear seem to mirror (perhaps with a lag) trends in levels of crime.

Yet, the groups that are most fearful are not necessarily those with the highest victimization rates; indeed, the order is exactly reversed. Elderly women, who are most afraid, are the least frequently victimized. Young men, who are least afraid, are most often victimized.[16] Even more surprisingly, past victimization has only a small impact on levels of fear; people who have heard about others' victimizations are almost as fearful as those who have actually been victimized.[17] And when citizens are asked about the things that frighten them, there is little talk about "real crimes" such as robbery, rape, and murder. More often there is talk about other signs of physical decay and social disorganization such as "junk and trash in vacant lots, boarded-up buildings, stripped and abandoned cars, bands of teenagers congregating on street corners, street prostitution, panhandling, public drinking, verbal harassment of women, open gambling and drug use, and other incivilities."[18]

In accounting for levels of fear in communities, Wesley Skogan divides the contributing causes into five broad categories: (1) actual criminal victimization; (2) second-hand information about criminal victimization distributed through social networks; (3) physical deterioration and social disorder; (4) the characteristics of the built environment (i.e., the physical composition of the housing stock); and (5) group conflict.[19] He finds the strongest effects on fear arising from physical deterioration, social disorder, and group conflict.[20] The impact of the built environment is hard to detect once one has subtracted the effects of other variables influencing levels of fear. A review article by Charles Murray also found little evidence of a separate effect of the built environment on fear. The only exception to this general conclusion is evidence indicating that improved street lighting can sometimes produce significant fear reductions.[21]

The important implication of these research results is that fear might be attacked by strategies other than those that directly reduce criminal victimization. Fear might be reduced even without changes in levels of victimization by using the communications within social networks to provide accurate information about risks of criminal victimization and advice about constructive responses to the risk of crime; by eliminating the external signs of physical decay and social disorder; and by more effectively regulating group conflict between young and old, whites and minority groups, rich and poor. The more intriguing possibility, however, is that if fear could be rationalized and constructively channeled, not only would fear and its adverse consequences be ameliorated, but also real levels of victimization reduced. In this sense, the conventional understanding of this problem would be reversed: instead of controlling victimization to control fear, we would manage fear to reduce victimization. To understand this possibility, we must explore the consequences of fear—not only as ends in themselves, but also as means for helping society deal with crime.

THE ECONOMIC AND SOCIETAL CONSEQUENCES OF FEAR: COSTS AND BENEFITS

Fear is a more or less rational response to crime. It produces social consequences through two different mechanisms. First, people are uncomfortable emotionally. Instead of luxuriating in the peace and safety of their homes, they feel vulnerable and isolated. Instead of enjoying the camaraderie of trips to school, grocery stores, and work, they feel anxious and afraid. Since these are less happy conditions than feeling secure, fear produces an immediate loss in personal well-being.

Second, fear motivates people to invest time and money in defensive measures to reduce their vulnerability. They stay indoors more than they would wish, avoid certain places, buy extra locks, and ask for special protection to make bank deposits. Since this time, effort, and money could presumably be spent on other things that make people happier, such expenditures must also be counted as personal costs which, in turn, become social costs as they are aggregated.

These are far from trivial issues. The fact that two-fifths of the population is afraid and that the Nation continues to nominate crime as one of its greatest concerns means that society is living less securely and happily than is desirable. And if 45 percent of the population restricts its daily behavior to minimize vulnerability, and the Nation spends more than $20 billion on private security protection, then private expenditures on reducing fear constitute a significant component of the national economy.[22] All this is in addition to the $40 billion that society spends publicly on crime control efforts.[23] In short, fear of crime claims a noticeable share of the Nation's welfare and resources.

Fear has a further effect. Individual responses to fear aggregate in a way that erodes the overall quality of community life and, paradoxically, the overall capacity of society to deal with crime.[24] This occurs when the defensive reactions of individuals essentially compromise community life, or when they exacerbate the disparities between rich and poor by relying too much on private rather than public security.

Skogan has described in detail the mechanisms that erode community life:

> Fear...can work in conjunction with other factors to stimulate more rapid neighborhood decline. Together, the spread of fear and other local problems provide a form of positive feedback that can further increase levels of crime. These feedback processes include (1) physical and psychological withdrawal from community life; (2) a weakening of the informal social control processes that inhibit crime and disorder; (3) a decline in the organizational life and mobilization capacity of the neighborhood; (4) deteriorating business conditions; (5) the importation and domestic production of delinquency and deviance; and (6) further dramatic changes in the composition of the population. At the end lies a stage characterized by demographic collapse.[25]

Even if fear does not destroy neighborhood life, it can damage it by prompting responses which protect some citizens at the expense of others, thereby leading to greater social disparities between rich and poor, resourceful and dependent, well-organized and anomic communities. For example, when individuals retreat behind closed doors and shuttered windows, they make their own homes safer. But they make the streets more dangerous, for there are fewer people watching and intervening on the streets. Or, when individuals invest in burglar alarms or private security guards rather than spending more on public police forces, they may make themselves safer, but leave others worse off because crime is deflected onto others.

Similarly, neighborhood patrols can make residents feel safe. But they may threaten and injure other law-abiding citizens who want to use the public thoroughfares. Private security guards sometimes bring guns and violence to situations that would otherwise be more peaceably settled. Private efforts may transform our cities from communities now linked to one another through transportation, commerce, and recreation, to collections of isolated armed camps, shocking not only for their apparent indifference to one another, but also ultimately for their failure to control crime and reduce fear. In fact, such constant reminders of potential threats may actually increase fear.

Whether fear produces these results or not depends a great deal on how citizens respond to their fears. If they adopt defensive, individualistic solutions, then the risks of neighborhood collapse and injustice are increased. If they adopt constructive, community-based responses, then the community will be strengthened not only in terms of its ability to defend itself, but also as an image of civilized society. Societies built on communal crime control efforts have more order, justice, and freedom than those based on individualistic responses. Indeed, it is for these reasons that social control and the administration of justice became public rather than private functions.

POLICE STRATEGIES FOR REDUCING FEAR

If it is true that fear is a problem in its own right, then it is important to evaluate the effectiveness of police strategies not only in terms of their capacity to control crime, but also in terms of their capacity to reduce fear. And if fear is affected by more factors than just criminal victimization, then there might be some special police strategies other than controlling victimization that could be effective in controlling the fear of crime.

Over the last 30 years, the dominant police strategy has emphasized three operational components: motorized patrol, rapid response to calls for service, and retrospective investigation of crimes.[26] The principal aim has been to solve crimes and capture criminals rather than reduce fear. The assumption has been that if victimization could be reduced, fear would decrease as well. Insofar as fear was considered a separate problem, police strategists assumed that motorized patrol and rapid response would provide a reassuring police omnipresence.[27]

To the extent that the police thought about managing citizens' individual responses to crime, they visualized a relationship in which citizens detected crime and mobilized the police to deal with it—not one in which the citizens played an important crime control role. The police advised shopkeepers and citizens about self-defense. They created 911 telephone systems to insure that citizens could reach them easily. And they encouraged citizens to mark their property to aid the police in recovering stolen property. But their primary objective was to make themselves society's principal response to crime. Everything else was seen as auxiliary.

As near monopolists in supplying enhanced security and crime control, police managers and union leaders were ambivalent about the issue of fear. On the one hand, as those responsible for security, they felt some obligation to enhance security and reduce fear. That was by far the predominant view. On the other hand, if citizens were afraid of crime and the police were the solution, the police department would benefit in the fight for scarce municipal funds. This fact has tempted some police executives and some unions to emphasize the risks of crime.[28]

The strategy that emphasized motorized patrol, rapid response, and retrospective investigations of crimes was not designed to reduce fear other than by a reduction in crime. Indeed, insofar as the principal objective of this strategy was to reduce crime, and insofar as citizens were viewed as operational auxiliaries of the police, the police could increase citizens' vigilance by warning of the risks of crime. Nevertheless, to the extent that reduced fear was considered an important objective, it was assumed that the presence and availability of police through motorized patrols and response to calls would achieve that objective.

The anticipated effects of this strategy on levels of fear have not materialized. There have been some occasions, of course, when effective police action against a serial murderer or rapist has reassured a terrorized community. Under ordinary circumstances, however, success of the police in calming fears has been hard to show. The Kansas City experiment showed that citizens were unaware of the level of patrol that occurred in their area. Consequently, they were neither reassured by increased patrolling nor frightened by reduced levels of patrol.[29] Subsequent work on response times revealed that fast responses did not necessarily reassure victims. Before victims even called the police, they often sought assistance and comfort from friends or relatives. Once they called, their satisfaction was related more to their expectations of when the police would arrive than to actual response time. Response time alone was not a significant factor in citizen satisfaction.[30] Thus, the dominant strategy of policing has not performed particularly well in reducing or channeling citizens' fear.

In contrast to the Kansas City study of *motorized* patrol, two field experiments have now shown that citizens are aware of increases or decreases in levels of *foot* patrol, and that increased foot patrol reduces citizens' fears. After reviewing surveys of citizens' assessments of crime problems in neighborhoods that had enhanced, constant, or reduced levels of foot patrol, the authors of *The Newark Foot Patrol Experiment* concluded:

> ...persons living in areas where foot patrol was created perceived a notable decrease in the severity of crime-related problems.[31]

And:

> Consistently, residents in beats where foot patrol was added see the severity of crime problems diminishing in their neighborhoods at levels greater than the other two [kinds of] areas.[32]

Similarly, a foot patrol experiment in Flint, Michigan, found the following:

> Almost 70 percent of the citizens interviewed during the final year of the study felt safer because of the Foot Patrol Program. Moreover, many qualified their response by saying that they felt especially safe when the foot patrol office was well known and highly visible.[33]

Whether foot patrol can work in less dense cities, and whether it is worth the cost, remain arguable questions. But the experimental evidence clearly supports the hypothesis that fear is reduced among citizens exposed to foot patrol.

Even more significantly, complex experiments in Newark and Houston with a varied mix of fear reduction programs showed that at least some programs could successfully reduce citizens' fears. In Houston, the principal program elements included:

1. a police community newsletter designed to give accurate crime information to citizens;
2. a community organizing response team designed to build a community organization in an area where none had existed;
3. a citizen contact program that kept the same officer patrolling in a particular area of the city and directed him to make individual contacts with citizens in the area;
4. a program directing officers to re-contact victims of crime in the days following their victimization to reassure them of the police presence; and
5. establishing a police community contact center staffed by two patrol officers, a civilian coordinator, and three police aids, within which a school program aimed at reducing truancy and a park program designed to reduce vandalism and increase use of a local park were discussed, designed, and operated.[34]

In Newark, some program elements were similar, but some were unique. Newark's programs included the following:

1. a police community newsletter;

2. a coordinated community policing program that included a directed police citizen contact program, a neighborhood community police center, neighborhood cleanup activities, and intensified law enforcement and order maintenance;

3. a program to reduce the signs of crime that included: (a) a directed patrol task force committed to foot patrol, radar checks on busy roads, bus checks to enforce city ordinances on buses, and enforcement of disorderly conduct laws; and (b) a neighborhood cleanup effort that used police auspices to pressure city service agencies to clean up neighborhoods, and to establish a community work program for juveniles that made their labor available for cleanup details.[35]

Evaluations of these different program elements revealed that programs "designed to increase the quantity and improve the quality of contacts between citizens and police" were generally successful in reducing citizens' fears.[36] This meant that the Houston Citizen Contact Patrol, the Houston Community Organizing Response Team, the Houston Police Community Station, and the Newark Coordinated Community Policing Program were all successful in reducing fear.

Other approaches which encouraged close contact, such as newsletters, the victim re-contact program, and the signs-of-crime program, did not produce clear evidence of fear reduction in these experiments. The reasons that these programs did not work, however, may have been specific to the particular situations rather than inherent in the programs themselves. The victim re-contact program ran into severe operating problems in trans-mitting information about victimization from the reporting officers to the beat patrol offi-cers responsible for the re-contacts. As a result, the contacts came far too long after the vic-timization. Newsletters might be valuable if they were published and distributed in the context of ongoing conversations with the community about crime problems. And efforts to eliminate the signs of crime through order maintenance and neighborhood cleanup might succeed if the programs were aimed at problems identified by the community. So, the initial failures of these particular program elements need not condemn them forever.

The one clear implication of both the foot patrol and fear reduction experiments is that closer contact between citizens and police officer reduces fear. As James Q. Wilson concludes in his foreword to the summary report of the fear reduction experiment:

> In Houston,...opening a neighborhood police station, contacting the citizens about their prob-lems, and stimulating the formation of neighborhood organizations where none had existed can help reduce the fear of crime and even reduce the actual level of victimization.[37]

In Newark, many of the same steps—including opening a storefront police office and directing the police to make contacts with the citizens in their homes—also had ben-eficial effects.

The success of these police tactics in reducing fear, along with the observation that fear is a separate and important problem, suggests a new area in which police can make a substantial contribution to the quality of life in the Nation's cities. However, it seems like-ly that programs like those tried in Flint, Newark, and Houston will not be tried elsewhere unless mayors and police administrators begin to take fear seriously as a separate problem. Such programs are expensive and take patrol resources and managerial attention away from the traditional functions of patrol and retrospective investigation of crimes. Unless their effects are valued, they will disappear as expensive luxuries.

On the other hand, mayors and police executives could view fear as a problem in its own right and as something that inhibits rather than aids effective crime control by forcing people off the streets and narrowing their sense of control and responsibility. If that were the case, not only would these special tactics become important, but the overall strategy of the department might change. That idea has led to wider and more sustained attacks on fear in Baltimore County and Newport News.

In Baltimore County, a substantial portion of the police department was committed to the Citizen Oriented Police Enforcement (COPE) unit—a program designed to improve the quantity and quality of contacts between citizens and the police and to work on problems of concern to citizens.[38] A major objective was to reduce fear. The effort succeeded. Measured levels of fear dropped an average of 10 percent for the various projects during a 6 month period.[39] In Newport News, the entire department shifted to a style of policing that emphasized problem-solving over traditional reactive methods.[40] This approach, like COPE, took citizens' fears and concerns seriously, as well as serious crime and calls for service.

These examples illustrate the security-enhancing potential of problem-solving and community approaches to policing. By incorporating fear reduction as an important objective of policing, by changing the activities of the police to include more frequent, more sustained contacts with citizens, and by consultation and joint planning, police departments seem to be able not only to reduce fear, but to transform it into something that helps to build strong social institutions. That is the promise of these approaches.

CONCLUSION

Fear of crime is an important problem in its own right. Although levels of fear are related to levels of criminal victimization, fear is influenced by other factors, such as a general sense of vulnerability, signs of physical and social decay, and inter-group conflict. Consequently, there is both a reason for fear and an opportunity to work directly on that fear, rather than indirectly through attempts to reduce criminal victimization.

The current police strategy, which relies on motorized patrol, rapid responses to calls for service, and retrospective investigations of crime, seems to produce little reassurance to frightened citizens, except in unusual circumstances when the police arrest a violent offender in the middle of a crime spree. Moreover, a focus on controlling crime rather than increasing security (analogous to the medical profession's focus on curing disease rather than promoting health) leads the police to miss opportunities to take steps that would reduce fear independently of reducing crime. Consequently, the current strategy of policing does not result in reduced fear. Nor does it leave much room for fear reduction programs in the police department.

This is unfortunate, because some fear reduction programs have succeeded in reducing citizens' fears. Two field experiments showed that foot patrol can reduce fear and promote security. Programs which enhance the quantity and quality of police contacts with citizens through neighborhood police stations and through required regular contacts between citizens and police have been successful in reducing fear in Houston and Newark.

The success of these particular programs points to the potential of a more general change in the strategy of policing that (1) would make fear reduction an important objective and (2) would concentrate on improving the quantity and quality of contacts between citizens and police at all levels of the department. The success of these approaches has been demonstrated in Baltimore County and Newport News.

Based on this discussion, it is apparent that a shift in strategy would probably be successful in reducing fear, and that that would be an important accomplishment. What is more speculative (but quite plausible) is that community policing would also be successful in channeling the remaining fear along constructive rather than destructive paths. Criminal victimization would be reduced, and the overall quality of community life enhanced beyond the mere reduction in fear.

ENDNOTES

1. *The Figgie Report on Fear of Crime: America Afraid, Part I: The General Public* (Research and Forecasts, Inc., Sponsored by A-T-O, Inc., Willoughby, Ohio, 1980), p. 29.
2. Louis Harris, "Crime Rates: Personal Uneasiness in Neighborhoods," *Chicago Tribune*, 6 June 1975.
3. *Gallup Poll Public Opinion*, Vol. 5: 1977 (New York: Random House, 1977), pp. 1240–41.
4. James Garofalo, *Public Opinion About Crime: The Attitudes of Victims and Non-Victims in Selected Cities* (Washington, D.C.: U.S. Government Printing Office, 1977).
5. "The Michigan Public Speaks Out on Crime" (Detroit, Michigan: Market Opinion Research, 1977).
6. R.H.C. Teske, Jr., and N.L. Powell, "Texas Crime Poll—Spring 1978," *Survey* (Huntsville, Texas: Sam Houston State University Criminal Justice Center, 1978), p. 19.
7. *Gallup Poll Public Opinion*, Vol. 3: 1935–1971 (New York: Random House, 1972), pp. 2164–65. *Gallup Poll Public Opinion*, Vol. 5: 1977 (New York: Random House, 1977), pp. 1240–41.
8. Louis Harris, "Crime Rates: Personal Uneasiness in Neighborhoods," *Chicago Tribune*, 6 June 1975. Louis Harris, "Crime Fears Decreasing," *Harris Survey* (Orlando, Florida: Tribune Media Services, Inc., 21 March 1985).
9. Wesley G. Skogan and Michael G. Maxfield, *Coping With Crime: Individual and Neighborhood Reactions*, Vol. 124 (Beverly Hills, California: Sage Publications, 1981), pp. 74–77.
10. Claude Brown in "Images of Fear," *Harper's*, Vol. 270, No. 1620 (May 1985), p. 44.
11. Robert C. Trojanowicz et al., "Fear of Crime: A Critical Issue in Community Policing" (Unpublished paper, Program in Criminal Justice Policy and Management, John F. Kennedy School of Government, Harvard University, Cambridge, 29 September 1987), p. 1.
12. James K. Stewart, "The Urban Strangler: How Crime Causes Poverty in the Inner City," *Policy Review*, No. 37 (Summer 1986), pp. 6–10.
13. Thomas Hobbes, *Leviathan* (New York: Penguin Publishing, 1981).
14. Wesley Skogan, "Fear of Crime and Neighborhood Change," in Albert J. Reiss, Jr., and Michael Tonry, *Communities and Crime*, Vol. 8 of *Crime and Justice: A Review of Research* (Chicago: The University of Chicago Press, 1986), p. 210.
15. Skogan and Maxfield, *Coping with Crime*, pp. 194–98.
16. Skogan and Maxfield, *Coping with Crime*, Chapter 5.
17. Skogan, "Fear of Crime and Neighborhood Change," p. 211.
18. Ibid., p. 212.
19. Ibid., pp. 210–15.

20. Ibid., p. 222.
21. Charles A. Murray, "The Physical Environment and Community Control of Crime," in James Q. Wilson, ed., *Crime and Public Policy* (San Francisco: Institute for Contemporary Studies, 1983), p. 115.
22. William C. Cunningham and Todd Taylor, *The Hallcrest Report: Private Security and Police in America* (Portland, Oregon: Chancellor Press, 1985).
23. National Institute of Justice, *Crime and Protection in America: A Study of Private Security and Law Enforcement Resources and Relationships* (Washington, D.C.: U.S. Department of Justice, May 1985).
24. For a discussion of the importance of "eyes on the street," see Jane Jacobs, *The Death and Life of Great American Cities* (New York: Random House, 1961).
25. Skogan, "Fear of Crime and Neighborhood Change," p. 215.
26. George L. Kelling and Mark H. Moore, "From Political to Reform to Community: The Evolving Strategy of Police," Working Paper #87-05-08 (Program in Criminal Justice Policy and Management, John F. Kennedy School of Government, Harvard University, Cambridge, October 1987).
27. O.W. Wilson, *Distribution of Police Patrol Forces* (Chicago: Public Administration Service, 1941).
28. For an example of the use of fear to build support for the police, see the discussion of the "fear city" campaign in *The Newark Foot Patrol Experiment* (Washington, D.C.: Police Foundation, 1981), pp. 120–21.
29. Kelling et al., *Kansas City Preventive Patrol Experiment.*
30. Antony Pate et al., *Police Response Time: Its Determinants and Effects* (Washington, D.C.: Police Foundation, 1987).
31. *The Newark Foot Patrol Experiment*, p. 72.
32. Ibid., p. 123.
33. Robert Trojanowicz, *An Evaluation of the Neighborhood Foot Patrol Program in Flint, Michigan* (East Lansing: Michigan State University, 1982), p. 86.
34. Antony Pate et al., *Reducing Fear of Crime in Houston and Newark*, pp. 7–10.
35. Ibid., pp. 10–18.
36. Ibid., p. 35.
37. James Q. Wilson, in Pate et al., *Reducing Fear of Crime in Houston and Newark*, p. ii.
38. Philip B. Taft, Jr., "Fighting Fear: The Baltimore County COPE Project" (Washington, D.C.: Police Executive Research Forum, February 1986).
39. Ibid., p. 20
40. John E. Eck and William Spelman, "Solving Problems: Problem-Oriented Policing in Newport News" (Washington, D.C.: Police Executive Research Forum, January 1987).

QUESTIONS FOR THOUGHT AND DISCUSSION

1. Has the fear of crime been increasing or decreasing since the 1960s? Which groups have the highest levels of fear?
2. What are the economic and social consequences of the fear of crime?
3. What are some police strategies that have been successful in reducing the public's fear of crime? What are some other ways the police could reduce the fear of crime?

POLICE SHOOTINGS

Myths and Realities

Roger G. Dunham
Geoffrey P. Alpert

Police use of deadly force has been a controversial topic for members of the public and police administrators since the beginning of policing. Misuse of force has dominated our concerns about the police because the consequences of deadly force in general and firearms specifically are so serious and irrevocable. In today's world, we readily accept the officers' right to use force to protect lives, control crime, and keep the peace. At the same time, however, citizens must maintain control over police use of force and sometimes restrict how that force is used (Alpert and Smith, 1994a).

The most prevalent examples of excessive force are those in which officers act too quickly or inappropriately against a perceived threat. That is, an officer may react to a suspect without knowing the situation or he may place himself in a situation where deadly force is used in self-defense (See Geller and Scott, 1992 and Note, 1988). Other, less frequent but more outrageous examples include the use of force to suppress a minority group, to express hatred for an individual, or to maintain the illegitimate interests of the powerful (United States Commission on Civil Rights, 1981).

The natural tension between the need to authorize the legitimate use of force for policing and the fear of abuse of that right has created a great dilemma. How can we as citizens authorize the police to use force in order to protest lives and maintain control in our neighborhoods and communities, and at the same time regulate that authority so that it is not used inappropriately or repressively against us? This dilemma is manifest whenever the police use any type of force, but becomes especially troublesome when the police use deadly force with a firearm, which is viewed as the ultimate use of force.

POLICE USE OF DEADLY FORCE: DISPELLING A FEW MYTHS

Critical questions concerning police use of firearms include: (1) how often do the police shoot citizens; (2) under what conditions do the police find it necessary to fire their weapons; (3) how often do the police hit their intended target; (4) how often do they hit innocent bystanders, someone's property, or another police officer; and (5) what are the

Roger G. Dunham and Geoffrey P. Alpert. Prepared especially for this volume–1996.

rules for when to shoot and when not to shoot? These questions, among others, have been the focus of several studies on police shootings. The purpose of this chapter is not to review all the information available on police shootings, but to use some general information on the use of firearms to answer these questions and then to describe findings from a recent study conducted in a major metropolitan police department over a ten-year period. First, we will address briefly several myths of policing and the amount of force used in a normal tour of duty.

Most of us get our ideas of what police officers do during a normal tour of duty from the mass media. We read about police activities in the newspapers and magazines, and we see depictions of the police on television and in the movies. These portrayals generally show the police in action-packed confrontations with dangerous criminals, constantly firing their weapons, fighting with offenders in difficult take-downs, and shooting at suspects in high-speed vehicle chases. In some cases, the confrontations that are presented in the electronic media include multiple officers and multiple suspects in massive shootouts. This, of course, makes exciting entertainment but creates an unrealistic view of police work. This type of high adventure seldom occurs in real-life situations. In fact, most police officers complete an entire career in police work without involvement in these types of confrontations with offenders. Even when such encounters occur, they seldom are of the type depicted in the media. In many cases, these portrayals would be good examples of what police officers should **not** do. A professional analysis of many of these accounts would reveal numerous laws and policies being broken by the police.

If potential recruits are interested in police work mainly for the crime-fighter image and envision themselves spending most of their time apprehending and arresting dangerous criminals, they will be greatly disappointed when they finally get on the job. Most of their time will be spent in peace-keeping or order-maintenance activities (and report writing) that have no contact with dangerous criminals. They will find that their image of police work greatly overemphasizes the amount of police violence, especially the use of firearms.

POLICE USE OF DEADLY FORCE: SOME EMPIRICAL FINDINGS

Having addressed some of the myths of police work concerning the use of force, the next step is to look at some of the facts and figures from studies of police discharge of weapons. Our design is to introduce an area of concern, create a general understanding of the issue with some information from other studies, and then report specific information from a recent ten-year study of the Metro-Dade Police Department in South Florida. The decision to focus on data from one agency over time rather than to report information from a variety of departments of different sizes that operate in different environments is to create an understanding of one agency's experiences (Alpert and Dunham, 1995). Metro-Dade police officers are required to fill out a special report each time they discharge a weapon. This includes all discharges except those occurring at the shooting range. Accidental discharges, shooting at animals that were threatening an officer or citizens, and shots that hit nothing at all are included. The figures presented here are generated from these reports.

It is important to recognize that the Metro-Dade Police Department is a large agency that has approximately 2,700 sworn officers today, but operated with a sworn force of less than 2,000 when the study began in 1984. Also, the department operates in a very high crime area with one of the most liberal gun laws in the country. It is hard to imagine any area of the country with greater danger to police officers performing their duties. The area is a major conduit for illegal drugs coming into the country. It suffers from serious immigration problems and experiences continual ethnic conflict, which occasionally erupts into race riots. The following statistics truly represent one of the most extreme social contexts for the use of force by police officers. While we would expect a great amount of force in such an atmosphere, it is surprising how little deadly force is actually used.

How Many Shootings?

The first thing we learn from agency statistics is how infrequently officers fire their weapons, and when they do, how infrequently they hit their intended target! Police officers actually killing a suspect is even less frequent. Larry Sherman and his associates compiled statistics for U.S. cities with over 250,000 people (Sherman, et al., 1986: I). They concluded:

> Police in all cities kill rarely, but at widely varying rates. The average Jacksonville police officer would have to work 139 years before killing anyone. In New York City, the wait would be 694 years. It would be 1,299 in Milwaukee and 7,692 years in Honolulu, all based on 1980–84 rates of killing.

They also found that the rates declined over the years they studied. While every incident is tragic, this picture is very different from the media portrayals.

In the Metro-Dade County (Florida) study there were 511 discharge of firearm incidents during the 10-1/2 year period studied (see Table 2–1).

Table 2–1   Overview of Weapon Discharges (Metro-Dade Police Department, 1984–1994)

Total Discharges	511	
Purposeful, involving suspects	240	47%
Purposeful, involving animals	155	30%
Accidental	104	20%
Miscellaneous, not involving suspects	012	02%

This is far fewer than one would expect from reading about the crime rate, the riots that occurred in Miami, and watching television shows such as *Miami Vice*. In fact, only 240 or 47% of the firearm discharge incidents were purposeful shootings involving suspects. This figure reveals that, on average, there were slightly less than twenty-three incidents per year. One hundred and fifty five of the other discharges were at animals, usually dogs threatening an officer or a citizen. One hundred and four were accidental discharges, and the remaining twelve incidents were officers shooting out lights and discharging their weapons for other, miscellaneous reasons. It is obvious then that shooting at a suspect is not nearly as frequent as most people imagine. In this large metropolitan department, which serves in a high-crime environment, officers shoot at suspects on the average less than TWICE per month. If this rate of shooting at suspects appears high to some, and if one is fearful that this contributes to a dangerous environment, one need only to look at the hit and fatality rates to feel a little more comfortable.

HIT RATES AND FATALITY RATES

To give a more current description of the details of shooting incidents from the Metro-Dade Study we will use the most recent data (over a 7-1/2 year period) as reported in the final report entitled *Metro-Dade Police Department Discharge of Firearm Study 1988–1994*. This data not only is the most current, but is more complete than the earlier data.

Most officers (64%) who did fire their weapons fired only one or two shots per incident, and very few fired more than four shots per incident (18%). Most of the time officers *did not* hit their intended target (68%). In only 41 of the 146 purposeful shootings during this time period, or 28% of the time, did the officer hit a suspect. Twenty-five of these suspects died. On the average, then, between six and seven suspects were shot by an officer per year, and between three and four died per year. This confirms the study cited earlier and the information presented that it is very unusual for an officer to shoot a suspect and even less likely to kill one. Of course, this is not meant to trivialize the shootings or to infer that police should not try to minimize the use of deadly force in enforcing the law. It does, however, give us a very different picture of police work than what we learn from the media.

ACCIDENTS: POLICE SHOOTING POLICE

An ironic finding of this study and other studies of police shootings is the frequency with which police personnel unintentionally shoot themselves or other officers. Several studies conducted in New York City and Chicago revealed that an alarming proportion of the police officers who were shot were shot either by themselves (accidental discharges or suicides) or by other police officers (accidental discharges or accidentally hitting another officer) (Geller and Scott, 1991). Over a ten-year period, 43% of the officers who were shot were shot by themselves or by other officers. The researchers conclude that "It is the armed robber and, paradoxically, the armed policeman who are the threats to the life of the police" (1991: 453). In our study, almost as many officers were shot in accidental discharges as were shot by offenders. According to the *Sourcebook of Criminal Justice Statistics—1993*, (pp. 401 and 405) during the period between 1984 and 1992 a total of 1,260 law enforcement officers (including federal, state, and local) were killed in the United States and its territories. Exactly 50% were killed feloniously and 50% accidentally. Most of the accidental deaths involved motor vehicles (86%), while only 8% involved accidental shootings. These data indicate that it is about as dangerous for officers to be on the road as it is to face dangerous criminals.

REASONS FOR SHOOTINGS

The most frequent circumstances precipitating a purposeful shooting incident involved the police stopping someone for committing a felony (35%), stopping someone who was suspicious or driving a suspicious car (29%), or trying to arrest someone in the midst of committing a felony (19%). The remainder involved drug-related arrests (7%), traffic stops (5%), domestic calls (3%), and activities of the Special Response Teams (2%). In almost all cases, there was resistance by the suspect (97%), and most of the time the suspect had a weapon of some type (89%). About half of the suspects had a gun. In a little more than one-third (34%) of the cases, the suspect actually shot at the police. Suspects verbally threatened to use the weapon on the police in 46% of the cases, and the remainder (20%) involved pushing, hitting, or grabbing the police officer.

It is obvious that in nearly all of these incidents, officers shoot because they are themselves threatened by a suspect. In fact, this was supported in several studies questioning whether officers discriminate against African-Americans and other minorities (see Dempsey, 1994; 253). The data indicate that almost 80% of police killings involve minority suspects, which seems to imply discrimination. In fact, several studies reveal that when the police shoot unarmed suspects, African-Americans are greatly overrepresented. Other studies, though, indicate that it is when the suspect engages in violent crime or violent confrontations with the police that police are most likely to shoot. The disparity between black and white shooting victims disappeared when participation in violent crime was considered. Police officers are most likely to shoot suspects who are armed and engage in violent confrontations with the police. When these factors are considered, racial differences in the police use of deadly force become insignificant (see Dempsey, 1994). This is not to say that specific instances of extreme racial and ethnic bias do not happen. Obviously they do, and they are of tremendous concern. In general, however, precipitating events tend to account for most racial disparities in police shooting incidents. This conclusion is supported by the Metro-Dade Police Study. Discharging a weapon at the police was more likely to be a precipitating incident in police shooting at African-American suspects (43%) than when compared to Anglo (32%) or Hispanic (35%) suspects. This was true whether the officer discharging the weapon was Anglo, Hispanic, or African-American.

CHARACTERISTICS OF OFFICERS

Officers involved in purposeful shooting incidents are mostly male (93%) and young. Females comprise 20% of the sworn officers and only 7% of the shootings. The average age of officers discharging their weapons was 33 years. The majority of the officers involved in shootings are on uniform patrol (54%) and plain clothes patrol (15%), with an average of 8 years on the force.

Fifty-two percent of the shootings involved Anglo officers, 34% Hispanic officers, and 14% African-American officers. This is just about identical to the ethnic breakdown of the sworn officers in the department. However, African-American officers are slightly underrepresented in the shooting incidents, and Hispanic officers are a little over represented. It is informative to analyze the ethnic matches between the officers and suspects involved in shooting incidents. In Table 2–2, an analysis of the ethnicity of the officer and of the suspect illustrates an almost complete absence of African-American officers shooting Anglo or Hispanic suspects. African-American officers shot only 3 non-black suspects over a 6-1/2 year period. It is hard to interpret this finding because it is impossible to estimate exactly how many situations there were in which African-American officers encountered threatening non-black suspects. Also, it is true that African-American officers are more likely to be assigned in African-American neighborhoods. However, in spite of this, it is striking how unlikely it is for an African-American officer to shoot non-black suspects. We asked a high-ranking African-American officer who had been in the police department for 35 years to help us interpret these findings. He was not surprised by the findings and gave two explanations for them. First, he reminded us of how relatively recent it has been that African-Americans were permitted to join the police department, and that initially African-American officers were not given the authority to arrest whites. When these laws changed, there was still an unwritten rule that African-Americans do not use force against white suspects. He said that much of the enforcement of these unwritten rules was by other African-American officers. If they were aware of an African-American officer using force against a white, they would pull him aside and straighten him out because such incidents would make life harder for all of them. Even though all this happened some time ago, today some of these informal norms still linger, making African-Americans less likely to use force against whites. He said that African-American officers will find other options to make an arrest.

Another reason the African-American administrator gave for African-American officers being underrepresented in shootings is that they are more likely to come from lower income, high-crime neighborhoods, which has given them more exposure to and experience with the types of conflict officers encounter. He thought the African-American officers, on the average, feel less threatened by these types of situations and are less likely to overrespond and use excessive force. They are more likely than other officers to find ways to deal with confrontations without using force.

TABLE 2–2 ETHNIC BACKGROUND OF OFFICERS AND SUSPECTS IN SHOOTING INCIDENTS (METRO-DADE POLICE DEPARTMENT, 1988–1994)

| Officer Ethnicity | Suspect Ethnicity | | | |
	Anglo	African-American	Hispanic	Total
Anglo	18	44	10	72
Total Percent	13	32	7	53
African-American	2	13	1	16
Total Percent	1	10	>1	12
Hispanic	10	29	9	48
Total Percent	7	21	7	35

CHARACTERISTICS OF SUSPECTS

Suspects at whom the police shoot are almost all males (97%) and tend to be young. The mean age of suspects in the Metro-Dade study is 27 years. Also in the Metro-Dade study, 60% of the suspects the police shot were African-American; 22% were Anglos; 14% Hispanic; and, 4% ethnicity was unknown. Most of the suspects had criminal histories. Sixty-two percent had criminal histories involving felonies, 6% had misdemeanor or traffic offenses, and 11% had no criminal history. In the remainder of the cases, the criminal history was unknown. Almost all of the suspects resisted the police in some manner (97%). In one well-regarded study, it was concluded that despite some diversity in findings, most studies over the past three decades support the following broad generalization: "The most common type of incident in which police and civilians shoot one another in urban America involves an on-duty, uniformed, white, male officer and an armed black, male civilian between the ages of 17 and 30 in a public location within a high-crime precinct at night in connection with a suspected armed robbery or a 'man with a gun' call" (Geller and Scott, 1991:.453).

LAWS AND POLICE POLICY REGARDING DISCHARGE OF WEAPONS

There are two fundamental authorities that guide the appropriate use of deadly force by the police. These are laws and policies. First and foremost, the United States Supreme Court in *Tennessee* v. *Garner*, 471 U.S. 1(1985) established the minimum legal standard: Deadly force cannot be used against a non-dangerous fleeing felon. That is, the Supreme Court created the standard that police agencies and officers cannot violate. Of course, police agencies can create policies that are more restrictive than what the Supreme Court requires and can limit officers from using deadly force except under very specific conditions. These policies establish the second authority by which police officers can use deadly force.

The *Garner* decision has become a very important decision for the police. First, it ruled that police shootings must be evaluated as seizures under the Fourth Amendment of the U.S. Constitution. Under this type of analysis, all purposeful shootings by police that hit the target are considered seizures. Seizures that are reasonable do not violate anyone's Constitutional rights but seizures that are unreasonable are illegal. Determining the reasonableness of a shooting is a difficult task. The Court in *Graham* v. *Conner* (490 U.S. 386, 396 [1989]) acknowledged that:

> the test of reasonableness under the Fourth Amendment is not capable of precise definition or mechanical application, however, its proper application requires careful attention to the facts and circumstances of each particular case, including the severity of the crime at issue, whether the suspect poses an immediate threat to the safety of officers or others, and whether he is actively resisting or attempting to evade arrest by flight...The reasonableness of a particular use of force must be judged from the perspective of a reasonable officer on the scene, rather by 20/20 hindsight (citations omitted).

The Court has left the understanding of an appropriate use of force application to the "reasonable officer," or stated in a different way, would a reasonable officer believe the force used was necessary? Unfortunately, what is reasonable and what is necessary are terms that were not defined precisely and were left open for interpretation (Alpert and Smith, 1994b).

To assist officers in understanding the limits of the application of deadly force, police departments promulgate their policies based upon the information presented in *Garner*. A wide range of policies exist, and some agencies adopt language taken directly from *Garner* without any definition or explanation, while others provide specific direction to their officers. This range of policies includes what is referred to as: (1) *Garner* or forcible felony policies; (2) defense of life policies; and (3) protection of life policies. These three types of policies differ on the type of shooting that is permitted. For example, under the *Garner*, or forcible felony, policies, shootings are justified if there is a substantial risk that a person who is escaping will cause death or serious bodily harm to someone if his arrest is delayed. This is the policy with the fewest restrictions and departments that adopt it will have the greatest number of shootings (Geller and Scott, 1992). A middle ground policy is what is known as a defense-of-life policy. Agencies operating under this type of policy limit the use of deadly force to situations where someone's life is in imminent peril. The defense-of-life policies include components that require officers to "plan ahead and consider alternatives" to the use of deadly force and to use deadly force "only as a last resort." Agencies operating under this type of policy will have the fewest number of shootings (Alpert and Fridell, 1992).

POLICE USE OF DEADLY FORCE: A CONCLUDING COMMENT

Police use of deadly force is a controversial topic that needs serious attention by law enforcement professionals and members of the public. The reform movements of the 1970s and 1980s have resulted in a change of philosophy within law enforcement. The authority for police officers to take the life of any felon who would not stop at the officer's command is over. However, departments operate under a wide variety of rules and regulations, some asking officers to use their discretion and some restricting the use of firearms to very specific situations. The data presented here, that of the Metro-Dade Police Department in Miami, reveal the nature and extent of discharges in one large metropolitan area. As demonstrated, police shootings do not resemble what is portrayed by the media. In real life, a shooting is a traumatic event for all concerned. Most officers go through a career without having taken a life or firing a weapon at a suspect. Hopefully, this trend will continue to improve and police officers will not be the judge, jury, and executioner of those they attempt to apprehend.

REFERENCES

ALPERT, GEOFFREY AND ROGER DUNHAM, *Metro-Dade Police Department Discharge of Firearm Study 1988–1994*. Final report prepared for Dade County, Florida, March 1995.

ALPERT, GEOFFREY AND LORIE FRIDELL, *Police Vehicles and Firearms: Instruments of Deadly Force*. Prospect Heights, IL: Waveland Press, 1992.

ALPERT, GEOFFREY AND WILLIAM SMITH, "Developing Police Policy: An Evaluation of the Control Principle." *American Journal of Police* 13: 1–20 (1994a).

ALPERT, GEOFFREY AND WILLIAM SMITH, "How Reasonable Is the Reasonable Man: Police and Excessive Force." *Journal of Criminal Law and Criminology* 85: 481–501 (1994b).

BUREAU OF JUSTICE STATISTICS, *Sourcebook of Criminal Justice Statistics–1993.* U.S. Department of Justice, Washington, D.C.: U.S. Government Printing Office, 1994.

DEMPSEY, JOHN S. *Policing: An Introduction of Law Enforcement.* St. Paul, MN: West Publishing Company, 1994.

GELLER, WILLIAM A. AND MICHAEL S. SCOTT, *Deadly Force: What We Know.* Washington, D.C.: Police Executive Research Forum, 1992.

GELLER, WILLIAM A. AND MICHAEL S. SCOTT, "Deadly Force: What We Know." In *Thinking About Police: Contemporary Readings.* edited by Carl B. Klockers and Stephen D. Mastrofski, 2nd ed., New York: McGraw-Hill, 1991.

Note, "Police Liability for Creating the Need to Use Deadly Force in Self-Defense." Michigan Law Review 86: 1982–2009 (1988).

SHERMAN, LAWRENCE W., ELLEN G. COHEN, PATRICK R. GRATIN, EDWIN E. HAMILTON, and DENNIS P. ROAD, *Citizens Killed by Big City Police, 1970–1984.* Washington, D.C.: Crime Control Institute, 1986.

UNITED STATES CIVIL RIGHTS COMMISSION, *Who Is Guarding the Guardians?* Washington, D.C.: United States Civil Rights Commission, 1981.

QUESTIONS FOR THOUGHT AND DISCUSSION

1. Why do most citizens have an exaggerated view of the amount of police violence involved in typical police work?
2. What are the three types of policies regarding police shooting at suspects?
3. What are some things that can be done to reduce the number of inappropriate shootings by the police?

DRAGONS AND DINOSAURS

The Plight of Patrol Women

Donna C. Hale
Stacey M. Wyland

Traveling in the male world is like going to a foreign country. Women have to learn the language, study maps and read guidebooks, and figure out the best way to get from place to place. We aren't surprised that we often feel frustrated, frightened, and lonely. We know we women have come from one tradition and that these people came from another. We may continue to think that our culture is better than theirs but also if we keep hanging in there someday we may enjoy the foreign culture. (Henning and Jardin, 1977: 214–215).

This analogy for prospective women managers is also appropriate for women on patrol who for the past twenty years have been struggling for acceptance and recognition by their male peers and supervisors. Little did women in policing imagine that the videotape of Rodney King's beating by four Los Angeles Police officers would result in the Los Angeles City Council recommending that more women patrol officers be hired. Unfortunately, it is often these serendipitous events that lead to the discovery of what we already knew in this case, that women are effective as patrol officers. The Christopher Commission's role in investigating the Rodney King incident was extremely important to the status of women on patrol because it resulted in illuminating the performance evaluation studies of the late 1970s that overall concluded that women are effective on patrol (Bloch and Anderson, 1974; Bloch, Anderson, and Gervais, 1973; Craig, 1976; Milton, Abramowitz, Crites, Gates, Mintz, and Sandler, 1974; Sichel, Friedman, Quint, and Smith, 1978). These findings, however, did not result in the acceptance of women on patrol. The organizational culture of policing as man's work has been entrenched since the nineteenth century and is very evident today in the attitudes of male peers and supervisors.

What *Time* reporter Jeanne McDowell describes (February 17, 1992) regarding the effective performance of women on patrol is not surprising. This information was reported at the time the performance evaluation studies were conducted fifteen years ago. It is ironic that the police organization has not accommodated the entry of women on patrol. Although the Equal Employment Opportunity Act and Commission have been in existence to ensure women's entry into patrol work, the organization has effectively kept the percentage of

From Donna Hale and Stacey Wyland, "Dragons and Dinosaurs: The Plight of Patrol Women," *Police Forum* 3:(2): 1–6. Reprinted with permission of the Academy of Criminal Justice Sciences.

women on patrol below ten percent. The time has arrived to acknowledge that women can do patrol, and that they should not have to continually prove that they can do so.

The Christopher Commission "unearthed" these findings that women on patrol communicate effectively without using physical force. This discovery resulted in the city council of Los Angeles recommending that its police department increase female sworn officers to forty-three percent within the next seven years (*Time*, 1992:72). In order to accomplish this feat, the police department needs to develop strategies to recruit and retain women as patrol officers.

Before discussing strategies to recruit and retain women in policing, it is important to examine the research that supports the fact that women can do patrol work. Consequently, the first section of this article is referred to as "old wine in new bottles" because most of the information presented in the recent *Time* article is based on the performance evaluation studies of the 1970s. It is evident from this reexamination of the performance evaluations that the problem is not that women cannot do patrol work; the problem is the resistance that male police officers either as peers or supervisors hold against women doing what is considered "men's work" (Balkin, 1988; Bell, 1982; Milton, 1975; Golden, 1981; Charles, 1982; Lord, 1986; Martin, 1990; Price, 1985; Remmington, 1983; Jones, 1986). It is unfortunate that it takes the brutality of the Rodney King videotaped beating to trigger a resurgence of the research substantiating that women can do patrol.

OLD WINE IN NEW BOTTLES: ARE WOMEN BETTER COPS?

Since the early 1970s, patrol women have struggled to be accepted as equals in what has traditionally been a male bastion patrol. The resistance and hostility towards women is primarily based on stereotypes and myths regarding the ability of women to do what is considered a man's job (Bell, 1982). The literature on women in policing is replete with conclusions that women as patrol officers are not accepted by their male peers and supervisors. If women decide to remain in patrol, they experience and endure sexual harassment and discrimination. If they stay, women must find ways of coping or adjusting to the culture. Susan Martin (1979) has written extensively on the ways women have "adjusted" to the male world of policing. Perhaps her best known work is her description of the POLICEwoman and the policeWOMAN. Women have also resorted to litigation to secure their positions in policing (Hale and Menniti, 1993).

The aftermath of King's assault resulted in the establishment of the Christopher Commission. This is not new. A cursory examination of any introductory text on policing refreshes our memories of earlier studies conducted as a result of police misconduct. For example, the Wickersham and Lenox Commissions reports from the early 1900s; the Knapp Commission investigation of corruption in the New York City Police Department; and, the Kerner Commission that investigated reasons for rioting and destruction in American cities during the summer of 1967 (Inciardi, 1990:302). Furthermore, it is interesting that although the Commission concluded that "there were numerous causes [of the rioting and destruction], it specified "aggressive preventive patrol, combined with police misconduct in the forms of brutality, unwarranted use of deadly force, harassment, verbal abuse, and discourtesy" as stimuli for the disruptions" (Inciardi, 1990: 302).

During the Christopher Commission's investigation experts testified that women are successful on patrol. Many of these experts' research substantiates the findings of the earlier performance evaluation studies of women on patrol that women could indeed accomplish the requisite duties of patrol.

The most significant contribution of *Time* reporter Jeanne McDowell was that her article reminded us what we already knew: women are effective at communication and calming volatile and potential violent situations. This information is a given: we have research that supports women are capable of patrol; what we need to do now is to keep these very capable women on the job. As McDowell (1972: 70) reported "...women constitute only 9% of the nation's 523,262 police officers...." After twenty years of meeting resistance by police departments, it is now time to examine the organizational culture of police departments and change the environment so women can be accepted as patrol officers.

Based on McDowell's report and the twenty-year-old research we know that: (1) women are better than men in talking people out of violence; (2) police work is not predominately violent; and (3) physical size is irrelevant because violence is so little a part of police work. These same conclusions from the Washington, D.C. study are substantiated by those reported in *Time* (May 27, 1974) once again from a study in the nation's capital, there was little difference in the abilities of men and women to deal with violent, or potentially violent situations. Women were similar or equal to men in the percentage of arrests made that resulted in conviction, their attitude toward the public, the number of incidents they were involved in that required back-up support from other officers, the number of injuries they sustained on the job, and even the number of driving accidents they had."

And twenty years ago in 1972, *Time* (May 1:60) reported that many police departments were assigning women patrol officers to do what was traditionally considered men's work—handling domestic disputes. The reason for this change was that women appeared to be more successful at calming disputes. Over the years research by Kennedy and Homant (1983) indicated that victims of domestic violence believed female officers were more patient and took more time to deal with the conflict. These studies reported that female officers were more tactful and subtle, stayed longer, and were concerned about root causes of conflict. Women were described as having "a soothing and calming effect."

Also in 1972, *Newsweek* (October 23: 117) reported that the major objections to the entry of women on patrol in Washington, D.C., Boston, Miami, and New York were: (1) women were presumed incapable of dealing with violent situations; (2) the chivalry factor; and (3) physical size. Effectiveness of women patrol officers was reported in handling family disputes, juvenile delinquency, shoplifting, and drugs. Therefore, comparing these early articles regarding the effectiveness of women on patrol with McDowell's (1992) report twenty years later, it is clear that the conclusions regarding the effectiveness of women on patrol have not changed. Interestingly, however, in both articles the dissatisfaction with the uniform women were required to wear is similar. McDowell reports "[I]n most places it means wearing an uncomfortable uniform designed for a man, including bulletproof vests that have not been adapted to women's figures." The 1972 article discusses women on patrol wearing skirts and carrying their guns in their purses.

Before we leave this section, it is important to examine a classic article published in 1981 by Van Wormer and to briefly update her advantages and disadvantages of using men on patrol. Her first advantage was superior physical strength combined with stamina to subdue a suspect. Research now substantiates that although women do not have the same upper body strength of their male counterparts they can be trained to compensate for lack of strength (Charles 1981, 1982). Earlier, Talney (1969: 50) pointed out that

> ...it is not unreasonable...to suggest that well-trained women officers could counter many kinds of disturbances and disorders which equally well-trained men could not....male officers are assaulted because...they represent a male authority figure which within the value system of many criminals makes them fair game...particularly if the encounter takes place in the presence of their peer group where such values are shared.

Talney (1969: 50) continues that female officers could avoid assaults because it is unheroic to assault a female...even a female police officer. "Furthermore, the public image of women facing unruly crowds could do much to swing public support to the side of proper police authority."

Van Wormer's second advantage was that men can handle long hours, nights, and rotating shifts. This is one area that women have difficulty with especially if they are single parents. In general, men do not encounter these problems because they have a spouse at home who is the primary caretaker of home and children.

The third advantage focuses on aggressiveness of men. Dranov (1985:174–175) indicates that some male officers are unsure about the reliability of a woman partner to back them up. Lewis Sherman (1975:435) found that although females were less aggressive and tend to make fewer arrests than men, they were effective on patrol.

The final advantage is that males have related job experience, primarily military experience. This may have been true in the 1970s, but it would be interesting to examine this in 1993 to see if recruits are coming from the military, college campuses, or other blue-collar occupations? This is important for recruitment practices because it is necessary to learn just what the military experience has in common with police work. It may be that a college education is more beneficial, since officers spend the majority of their time providing services to the community. Finally, individuals may be attracted to police work because it does not require a college degree, but pays a higher salary than many other blue-collar occupations.

According to Van Wormer, there are more complaints against men on patrol. The article by McDowell (1992) verifies that when the Christopher Commission investigated the Los Angeles Police Department after the King beating, it found "that the 120 officers with the most use-of-force reports were all men. Civilian complaints against women are also consistently lower. In San Francisco....female officers account for only 5% of complaints although they make up 10% of the 1,839-person force."

Van Wormer points out that male officers provoke violence and are more physically brutal. This has been supported by the performance evaluation research that reported women on patrol as more effective in dealing with conflict because they rely on mediation and intervention techniques. Dranov's (1985: 213) response that "the ability to subdue someone is not as important as the ability to communicate intelligently reflects the overall consensus of the research that women are effective." But, the comment by a deputy sheriff in southern California probably reflects many male's attitudes that physical size is more important than communication styles. The deputy sheriff stated "I don't care if a dame is Calamity Jane and can shoot a button off my vest. My biggest weapons are that I'm tall and pretty intimidating. These gals could only intimidate my little sister"

(*Newsweek*, October 23, 1972: 117). As Katherine Perkins, Detroit police officer, pointed out "Any <u>fool</u> can shoot a gun. What you really need is intelligence and sensitivity—and that's what women bring to the job" (Dreifus, 1981: 58). This is similar to Elizabeth Watson's statement in the McDowell article that "intelligence, communication, compassion, and diplomacy" (1992: 70) is required in policing.

Van Wormer stresses that women have a disarming affect and are better at public relations. Male officers often have poor reputations. Furthermore, male officers are not effective at questioning rape victims. Rape is a painful experience for female victims to report rape to male officers; and, male officers may either be insensitive or feel uncomfortable with this type of case, similar to child abuse investigations. Historically, female officers were hired to deal with women as offender and victims because of their gender. It was believed that women would be more sympathetic/empathetic in these situations. It is interesting to note, however, that the English police woman Lilian Wyles reported in her autobiographical account of her experience at Scotland Yard that male officers tried to shield policewomen from investigations regarding sexual offenses. The reason cited was the belief that middle class women should be protected from these type of situations that they may either sully or embarrass them.

Van Wormer's comments that male officers are reluctant to accept women on patrol and may overprotect them. This chivalry is a result of both stereotypes and socialization. Also, Van Wormer points out that historically, women in policing have had more education than men. This is well documented in the early literature of policewomen in America. Men were hired because of their physical size; women were required to have higher education for their positions. In the early 1970s Perlstein (1972:46) found that 35.3 percent of the women police in his study had higher educational levels. He concluded that more education results in less police authoritarism.

To conclude this section on the effectiveness of women on patrol, it should be noted that in 1980 the Los Angeles Police Department doubled the number of its female officers. Commander Ken Hickman used this opportunity to complete his dissertation research by comparing the records of sixty-eight female cops hired to go out on patrol after 1980 with those of male officers hired at the same time. In an examination of 6,000 daily field activity reports he found that male-female teams were just as productive in initiating potentially hazardous calls as were male-male teams and the individual top initiators of potentially hazardous activities were female. He also found that recruit training officers rated men lower than women in tactics, initiative and self-confidence, writing and communication, and public contacts. Also, the I.Q.s of the female recruits were higher and academically the women surpassed their male classmates in the police academy. Assessing physical fitness and height, Hickman found that these correlated with success in the field for only four percent of all police officers. Women officers got significantly more commendations from the public. He found that both men and women had similar numbers of complaints by the public. Productivity levels were high for the police women in the crime-ridden South Bureau. He also found that the females' communication skills were better and this was an advantage for them in domestic violence situations (Elias, 1984:17).

It is evident from this examination of the performance evaluation research on women on patrol that women can handle patrol work. It is no longer necessary to debate or discuss the effectiveness of women on patrol. It is time, however, to address the greater issue of how women can unconditionally be accepted by their peers and supervisors. Twenty years ago, Lewis Sherman (1973:384, 393) reported the benefits of hiring women patrol officers as:

1. a reduction in the incidence of violence between police officers and citizens;
2. increasing quality of police service because women accentuate the service role of police work more than men;
3. improved police community relations because women are more visible than men, make more contacts, and citizens will assist police women upon request;
4. police men can learn from the police women that an officer can be efficient without using force;
5. police women are more effective than police men in settling problems reported by women from low-income neighborhoods;
6. a police department becomes more democratic and responsive to the community by hiring personnel who are more representative of the community's population; and,
7. lawsuits charging sex discrimination could be avoided by the police department that develops and implements job-related selection, recruitment and promotional standards and tests.

Lewis Sherman's (1975: 438) conclusion that "the question of whether women could perform general patrol duties was primarily political rather than scientific [was evident] from the very beginning." He points out that "in many respects, the enormous efforts that have gone into evaluating the performance of women have been a diversion from what has always been the most genuinely important question in police research—what kind of person makes a good police officer? As he stated:

> Gender is not a relevant characteristic of that person. It is only a reflection of our prejudiced and conservative views that we should ever have thought it might be. The unassailable fact is that some women are good police officers and some women are not, just like men. Our quest still remains to define and measure a good cop, man, or women.

In the next section, a discussion of recruitment and retention is presented. The major problem for police departments is not recruiting women—the problem is retention because many police departments are locked in a "time-warp" that perpetuates the myth that only men can do patrol. Although research clearly substantiates that patrol is primarily service, and women can handle any physical problems requiring strength by using "karate, twist locks, or a baton instead of their fists" (McDowell, 1992), their male counterparts cannot accept reality. Men still perceive police work as a man's domain where women will only get in the way, cannot be depended upon for backup, or may get hurt. The expression "old habits die hard" is evident. The nineteenth century machismo legacy is slow to die in the police organizational culture.

RECOMMENDATIONS FOR RECRUITMENT AND RETENTION

The major problems facing the recruitment and retention of women as patrol officers are the political, cultural, and structural systems of the police organization. Therefore, in order to change the milieu of policing that is vested in traditions of machoism and sexism, it requires a leader who takes the responsibility of slaying the dragons and replacing the dinosaurs who keep the old traditions alive and well. These changes require a "transformational" leader who will work to change both the political and cultural systems of the police department. To begin the change the leader first must develop a vision of women as patrol officers; next, mobilize the department to work toward achieving the new vision and lastly, institutionalizing the changes over time (Tichy and Ulrich, 1984: 344).

Tichy and Ulrich (1984: 345) state that before an organization will change there must be a "trigger" that indicates change is needed. Although for the past twenty years we have known that women are capable of performing patrol, it takes a horrific incident like the Rodney King beating to recognize the effectiveness of women on patrol. As discussed earlier, this incident led to the Los Angeles City Council's recommendation that the percentage of female patrol officers be increased to forty-three percent in the next seven years. The new police chief of the Los Angeles Police Department, Willie Williams, must create an agenda that requires improving police community relations in addition to hiring more female and minority police officers. He will need to rely on effective recruitment and retention strategies to change the organizational culture.

One area that must be addressed in hiring more female officers is how to retain them on the force once they are hired. In general, women are kept out of male-dominated occupations by hostility, sexual harassment, and male attitudes (Jacobs, 1989). The presence of women in a traditionally male domain is threatening and they are perceived and treated as outsiders. They are treated paternalistically and prevented from learning tasks that will later help with promotions, or with hostility, or both (Padavic and Reskin, 1990). Furthermore, Cockburn (1985), Dreifus (1980), and Hunt (1990) report the presence of women in traditionally blue-collar male occupations may challenge the men's "culturally-granted gender power" (Cockburn, 1985 in Padavic and Reskin, 1990: 617).

The Christopher Commission did not address how to deal with the resistance by the dinosaurs who believe women have no place on patrol. This resistance is based on three interrelated systems: technical, political, and cultural. For example, technical resistance includes the uniforms that women wear. Even twenty years after the performance evaluation studies, improper fit of uniforms and bullet proof vests and size of handguns for women is still a problem. Another example of the technical aspects is the emphasis in the training academies on the physical testing as well as firearms training.

The political resistance in police departments is based on entrenched rules of patrol work established and maintained by the older male officers and supervisors. Especially evident in police departments are policies, or lack of policies regarding pregnancy and disability leaves for patrol women as well as flex shifts for women who have child care responsibilities. These policies also reflect the cultural aspect of the organization that resists changing the culture to accommodate the entry of women on patrol. Anecdotal information reveals that men become upset when women get special consideration because they are pregnant, or have child care responsibilities. Because of these responsibilities, women often move into administrative positions to have the more conventional shift of 8 a.m. to 5 p.m. Unfortunately, this removes the patrol women from the street where their visibility is important. Gender neutral shifts, flex shifts, child care programs, and paternity leaves would improve the organizational culture for both male and female officers.

An examination of the litigation regarding sexual harassment and discrimination toward women on patrol reveals the hostility women have encountered. Simply stated, men do not want women on patrol (Hale and Menniti, 1993). In order for women to remain on patrol, the police leader must change the environment emphasizing that harassment and discrimination will not be tolerated. It must be clearly communicated that women will be hired in police departments and that if these policies are violated, recriminations will follow. The leader must make sure that all members of the department are trained regarding sexual harassment and sexual discrimination.

During the recruitment stage it is crucial to explain what the duties of a patrol officer are as well as preparing women for the resistance they will encounter. Timmins and Hainsworth (1989: 204) found that women police officers believed that although admission requirements were usually clear, many of the women were uncertain about why they were hired, what sex roles they should play as women cops; what problems they were likely to encounter; and what the police academy experience was supposed to do for them.

During the recruitment process police departments need to include female police officers as recruiters. Advertisements should depict women officers conducting patrol work as well as describing the department's policy of hiring, paying, and deploying women the same as men (Sulton and Townsey, 1981). Once women are recruited, special workshop courses should be included in the police recruit training for both male and female recruits describing the stress of the job as well as explaining to both men and women officers that the evaluation research supports that women can do patrol. Also, in the recruit academy as well as later in-service training, time must be allocated to describing and discussing ethics and police work. Officers need to address issues of police violence and corruption through both presentation and discussion groups. In addition, training should include policies on sexual harassment and discrimination and explaining that these policies will be enforced. All these activities support the commitment that the police organization has to improving the organizational climate for both male and female officers.

Lastly, the changes regarding recruitment and retention of women on patrol must institutionalize the opportunity for promotion of qualified officers. This means that the existing performance evaluations/appraisal must be redesigned to reflect what patrol work is. It is also important that women patrol officers be trained by women patrol officers, or by men who are aware that women can do patrol work effectively.

These changes in the police organization will not take place overnight. They involve a major commitment by both the department's leadership and the local form of government to establish a police department that represents the community. Women as patrol officers should not have to encounter resistance by the peers and supervisors. Although dragons and dinosaurs die slowly; change must begin now. As Betty Freidan once said "A girl [sic] should not expect special privileges because of her sex but neither should she adjust to prejudice and discrimination" (Warner, 1992: 312). The evaluation research reveals that women did not expect special privileges as patrol officers—they just wanted the opportunity to do the job. The role of the police leader is to change the technical, political, and cultural resistance in the police department.

REFERENCES

BALKIN, JOSEPH. (1988). "Why Policemen Don't Like Policewomen." *Journal of Police Science and Administration*, 16(1): 29–38.

BELL, DANIEL J. (1982). "Policewomen: Myths and Reality." *Journal of Police Science and Administration*, 10(1): 112–120.

BLOCH, PETER B. AND DEBORAH ANDERSON. (1974). *Policewomen on Patrol: Final Report.* Washington, D.C.: Police Foundation.

BLOCH, PETER, DEBORAH ANDERSON, AND PAMELA GERVAIS. (1973). *Policewomen on Patrol—Major Findings: Final Report, Volume 1.* Washington, D.C.: Police Foundation.

CHARLES, MICHAEL T. (1981). "The Performance and Socialization of Female Recruits in the Michigan State Police Training Academy." *Journal of Police Science and Administration*, 9(2): 209–223.

CHARLES, MICHAEL T. (1980). "Policewomen and the Physical Aspects of Policing." *Law and Order,* 28(9): 83–89.

COCKBURN, CYNTHIA. (1985). *Machinery of Dominance.* London: Pluto.

CRAIG, G.B. (1976). *Women Traffic Officer Project: Final Report.* Sacramento, California: Department of California Highway Patrol.

DRANOV, PAULA. (1985). "The Lady is a Cop." *Cosmopolitan*, 199: 174–177, 213.

DREIFUS, CLAUDIA. (1981). "Why Two Women Cops Were Convicted of Cowardice." *Ms.,* 9(4): 57–58, 63–64.

DREIFUS, CLAUDIA. (1980). "People Are Always Asking Me What I'm Trying to Prove…" *Police Magazine*:18–25.

ELIAS, M.K. (1984). "The Urban Cop: A Job for a Woman." *Ms.*, 12: 17.

NONE CITED. (1972). "Female Fuzz." *Newsweek,* 80: 117.

GOLDEN, KATHRYN. (1981). "Women as Patrol Officers: A Study of Attitudes." *Police Studies*, 4:29–33.

HALE, DONNA C. AND DANIEL J. MENNITI. (1993). "Discrimination and Harassment: Litigation by Women in Policing," in *It's a Crime: A Critical Look at Women's Issues in Criminal Justice.* Edited by Roslyn Muraskin and Ted Alleman. Needham Heights, Massachusetts: Regents/Prentice-Hall.

HENNIG, MARGARET AND ANNE JARDIM. (1977). *The Managerial Woman.* New York, New York: Pocket Books.

HUNT, JENNIFER C. (1985). "The Logic of Sexism Among Police." *Women & Criminal Justice*, 1(2): 3–30.

INCIARDI, JAMES A. (1990). *Criminal Justice,* 3rd ed. New York, New York: Harcourt Brace Jovanovich, Publishers.

JACOBS, JERRY. (1989). *Revolving Doors.* Stanford, California: Stanford University Press.

JONES, SANDRA. (1986). "Women Police: Caught In The Act." *Policing*, 2(2): 129–140.

KENNEDY, DANIEL B. AND ROBERT J. HOMANT. (1983). "Attitudes of Abused Women Toward Male and Female Police Officers." *Criminal Justice and Behavior*, 10(4): 391–405.

LORD, LESLI KAY. (1989). "Policewomen," in *The Encyclopedia of Police Science*. Edited by William G. Bailey. New York, New York: Garland Publishing, Inc., 491–502.

LUNNEBORG, PATRICIA. (1990). *Women Changing Work*. New York, New York: Bergin and Garvey Publishers.

MARTIN, SUSAN E. (1979). "*Police*women and Police*women*: Occupational Role Dilemmas and Choices for Female Officers." *Journal of Police Science and Administration*, 7(3): 314–323.

MARTIN, SUSAN E. (1989). "Women on the Move?: A Report on the Status of Women in Policing." *Women & Criminal Justice*, 1(1): 21–40.

MCDOWELL, JEANNE. (1992). "Are Women Better Cops?" *Time*, 139(7): 70–72.

MILTON, CATHERINE HIGGS, AVA ABRAMOWITZ, LAURA CRITES, MARGARET GATES, ELLEN MINTZ, AND GEORGETTE SANDLER. (1974). *Women in Policing: A Manual*. Washington, D.C.: Police Foundation.

PADAVIC, IRENE AND BARBARA F. RESKIN. (1990). "Men's Behavior and Women's Interest in Blue-Collar Jobs." *Social Problems*, 37(4): 613–627.

PERLSTEIN, GARY R. (1972). "Policewomen and Policemen: A Comparative Look." *Police Chief*, 39(3): 72–74, 83.

THE PRESIDENT'S COMMISSION ON LAW ENFORCEMENT AND ADMINISTRATION OF JUSTICE. (1967). *Task Force Report: The Police*. Washington, D.C.: The U.S. Government Printing Office.

REMMINGTON, PATRICIA WEISER. (1983). "Women in the Police: Integration or Separation?" *Qualitative Sociology*, 6(2): 118–135.

Report of the National Advisory Commission on Civil Disorders. (1968). New York, New York: E.P. Dutton.

RESKIN, BARBARA F. (1988). "Bringing the Men Back In: Sex Differentiation and the Devaluation of Women's Work." *Gender and Society*, 2: 58–81.

SHERMAN, LEWIS J. (1973). "A Psychological View of Women in Policing." *Journal of Police Science and Administration*, 1(4):383–394.

SHERMAN, LEWIS J. (1975). "An Evaluation of Policewomen on Patrol in a Suburban Police Department." *Journal of Police Science and Administration*, 3(4):434–438.

SICHEL, JOYCE L., LUCY N. FRIEDMAN, JANET C. QUINT, AND MICHAEL E. SMITH. (January, 1978). *Women on Patrol: A Pilot Study of Police Performance in New York City*. Washington, D.C.: National Institute of Law Enforcement and Criminal Justice, Law Enforcement Assistance Administration, U.S. Department of Justice.

SULTON, CYNTHIA G. AND ROI D. TOWNSEY. (1981). *A Progress Report on Women in Policing*. Washington, D.C.: Police Foundation.

TALNEY, RONALD G. (1969). "Women in Law Enforcement: An Expanded Role." *Police*, 14:49–51.

TICHY, NOEL M. AND DAVID O. ULRICH. (Fall, 1984). "The Leadership Challenge—A Call for the Transformational Leader." *Sloan Management Review*, 59–68. Reprinted in *Classic Readings in Organizational Behavior*. Edited by J. Steven Ott. Belmont, California: Wadsworth, Inc. 1989, 344–355.

TIMMINS, WILLIAM M. AND BRAD E. HAINSWORTH. (1989). "Attracting and Retaining Females in Law Enforcement: Sex-Based Problems of Women Cops in 1988." *International Journal of Offender Therapy and Comparative Criminology*, 33(3): 197–205.

VAN WORMER, KATHERINE. (1981). "Are Males Suited to Police Patrol Work?" *Police Studies*, 3(4): 41–44.

WARNER, CAROLYN. (1992). *The Last Word: A Treasury of Women's Quotes*. Englewood Cliffs, New Jersey: Prentice-Hall.

NONE CITED. (1980). "Women Cops on the Beat." *Time*, 115:58.

NONE CITED. (1972). "The Women in Blue." *Time*, 99: 60.

WYLES, LILIAN. (1952). *A Woman at Scotland Yard*. London: Faber and Faber, Limited.

QUESTIONS FOR THOUGHT AND DISCUSSION

1. What are some ways that police departments can reduce the cultural resistance to female police officers?
2. In what ways are women officers more effective than male officers?
3. What are some of the benefits to police departments when they hire women patrol officers?

LAW ENFORCEMENT CODE OF ETHICS

As a law enforcement officer, my fundamental duty is to serve the community; to safeguard lives and property; to protect the innocent against deception, the weak against oppression or intimidation and the peaceful against violence or disorder; and to respect the constitutional rights of all to liberty, equality, and justice. I will keep my private life unsullied as an example to all and will behave in a manner that does not bring discredit to me or to my agency. I will maintain courageous calm in the face of danger, scorn, or ridicule; develop self-restraint; and be constantly mindful of the welfare of others. Honest in thought and deed both in my personal and official life, I will be exemplary in obeying the law and the regulations of my department. Whatever I see or hear of a confidential nature or that is confided to me in my official capacity will be kept ever secret unless revelation is necessary in the performance of my duty.

I will never act officiously or permit personal feelings, prejudices, political beliefs, aspirations, animosities, or friendships to influence my decisions. With no compromise for crime and with relentless prosecution of criminals, I will enforce the law courteously and appropriately without fear or favor, malice or ill will, never employing unnecessary force or violence and never accepting gratuities.

I recognize the badge of my office as a symbol of public faith, and I accept it as a public trust to be held so long as I am true to the ethics of police service. I will never engage in acts of corruption or bribery, nor will I condone such acts by other police officers. I will cooperate with all legally authorized agencies and their representatives in the pursuit of justice.

I know that I alone am responsible for my own standard of professional performance and will take every reasonable opportunity to enhance and improve my level of knowledge and competence.

I will constantly strive to achieve these objectives and ideals, dedicating myself before God to my chosen profession…law enforcement

POLICE CODE OF CONDUCT

All law enforcement officers must be fully aware of the ethical responsibilities of their position and must strive constantly to live up to the highest possible standards of professional policing.

The International Association of Chiefs of Police believes it important that police officers have clear advice and counsel available to assist them in performing their duties consistent with these standards, and has adopted the following ethical mandates as guidelines to meet these ends.

Primary Responsibilities of a Police Officer

A police officer acts as an official representative of government who is required and trusted to work within the law. The officer's powers and duties are conferred by statute. The fundamental duties of a police officer include serving the community, safeguarding lives and property, protecting the innocent, keeping the peace, and ensuring the rights of all to liberty, equality, and justice.

Performance of the Duties of a Police Officer

A police officer shall perform all duties impartially, without favor or affection or ill will and without regard to status, sex, race, religion, political belief, or aspiration. All citizens will be treated equally with courtesy, consideration, and dignity.

Officers will never allow personal feelings, animosities, or friendships to influence official conduct. Laws will be enforced appropriately and courteously and, in carrying out their responsibilities, officers will strive to obtain maximum cooperation from the public. They will conduct themselves in appearance and deportment in such a manner as to inspire confidence and respect for the position of public trust they hold.

Discretion

A police officer will use responsibly the discretion vested in his position and exercise it within the law. The principle of reasonableness will guide the officer's determinations, and the officer will consider all surrounding circumstances in determining whether any legal action shall be taken.

Consistent and wise use of discretion, based on professional policing competence, will do much to preserve good relationships and retain the confidence of the public. There can be difficulty in choosing between conflicting courses of action. It is important to remember that a timely word of advice rather than arrest—which may be correct in appropriate circumstances—can be a more effective means of achieving a desired end.

Use of Force

A police officer will never employ unnecessary force or violence and will use only such force in the discharge of duty as is reasonable in all circumstances.

The use of force should be used only with the greatest restraint and only after discussion, negotiation, and persuasion have been found to be inappropriate and ineffective. While the use of force is occasionally unavoidable, every police officer will refrain from unnecessary infliction of pain or suffering and will never engage in cruel, degrading, or inhuman treatment of any person.

Confidentiality

Whatever a police officer sees, hears, or learns of that is of a confidential nature will be kept secret unless the performance of duty or legal provision requires otherwise.

Members of the public have a right to security and privacy, and information obtained about them must not be improperly divulged.

Integrity

A police officer will not engage in acts of corruption or bribery, nor will an officer condone such acts by other police officers.

The public demands that the integrity of police officers be above reproach. Police officers must, therefore, avoid any conduct that might compromise integrity and thus undercut the public confidence in a law enforcement agency. Officers will refuse to accept any gifts, presents, subscriptions, favors, gratuities, or promises that could be interpreted as seeking to cause the officer to refrain from performing official responsibilities honestly and within the law. Police officers must not receive private or special advantage from their official status. Respect from the public cannot be bought; it can only be earned and cultivated.

Cooperation with Other Police Officers and Agencies

Police officers will cooperate with all legally authorized agencies and their representatives in the pursuit of justice.

An officer or agency may be one among many organizations that may provide law enforcement services to a jurisdiction. It is imperative that a police officer assist colleagues fully and completely with respect and consideration at all times.

Personal-Professional Capabilities

Police officers will be responsible for their own standard of professional performance and will take every reasonable opportunity to enhance and improve their level of knowledge and competence.

Through study and experience, a police officer can acquire the high level of knowledge and competence that is essential for the efficient and effective performance of duty. The acquisition of knowledge is a never-ending process of personal and professional development that should be pursued constantly.

Private Life

Police officers will behave in a manner that does not bring discredit to their agencies or themselves.

A police officer's character and conduct while off duty must always be exemplary, thus maintaining a position of respect in the community in which he or she lives and serves. The officer's personal behavior must be beyond reproach.

QUESTIONS FOR THOUGHT AND DISCUSSION

1. What ethical principles direct the police officers' use of force?
2. How does the Police Code of Conduct address the officer's behavior while off duty? Do you agree with these principles?
3. What are the fundamental duties of police officers according to the Law Enforcement Code of Ethics?

POLICE OFFICER SEXUAL MISCONDUCT

*A Field Research Study**

Allen D. Sapp

INTRODUCTION

Police officer misconduct is a complex phenomenon that varies widely in scope, intensity, duration, and incidence (Barker & Carter, 1994; Cooksey, 1992; Holden, 1992; Kevlin, 1986; Lundman, 1980; Myron, 1992; Simpson, 1977, among others). Much of the literature on police misconduct has focused on graft and corruption (see, for example, Barker and Roebuck, 1974; Goldstein, 1975; Lundman, 1980; Meyer, 1976; Sherman, 1974, among others). More recently, additional areas of officer misconduct have been studied. Barker and Carter (1990) focused on police lying and evidence tampering as a form of police misconduct. Carter reported on police brutality (1985) and offered a typology of police drug-related corruption (1990). Drug-related corruption has been the focus of a number of studies (Carter, 1990; Kraska & Kappeler, 1988; Police ethics, 1991; Sechrest & Burns, 1992, among others).

Shering (1981) studied police misconduct from an organizational perspective and identified a number of areas of organizational deviance and misconduct. Others have focused on sexual misconduct (Sapp, 1994), police and prostitutes (Kevlin, 1985), professional courtesies as misconduct (Kleinig & Gorman, 1992), and departmental rules violations (Sapp, Kappeler, & Carter, 1992).

Concern for control of police misconduct continues to be evident in the literature. Almost all of the studies cited above include some form of prescriptive recommendations to control or reduce police misconduct. Williams (1986) argues that effective maintenance of police integrity requires strong leadership by the chief of the law enforcement agency, coupled with significant changes in the organizational structure, procedures, and environment. He also suggests that changes are needed in the way police officers are selected and socialized. Goldman and Puro (1987) suggest that decertification of police officers and a national exchange of information about decertified officers would help to control corruption and other forms of police misconduct. Sykes (1985) argued that reforms that attempt to subordinate police officer discretion to bureaucratic due process were unsuccessful and

---

*Allen D. Sapp. Prepared expressly for this publication.

produced an appearance of change without any change in the fundamental status of police misconduct.

RESEARCH METHODOLOGY

This report presents preliminary findings from a research project intended to make some sense of an area of human behavior that is not easily quantified or understood. The nature of the problem of police sexual misconduct cannot easily be studied through survey or experimental research. In an attempt to gain an understanding of the behavior, field research methods were used. In the fourteen years since the project began, hundreds of discussions, interviews, and conversations with law enforcement officers at all levels, from municipal to federal, have been held. Many of the discussions and interviews took place in patrol cars, while others were in the home or office of the officers. Still others took place during coffee breaks or meals during duty hours of the officers.

The conversations were not initially directed to the subject of sexual misconduct but efforts were made to direct the interview into that area of discussion. Often, data collection was simply a matter of listening and watching officers at work and noting the behaviors evidenced and discussed. Whenever possible, the anecdotal material was verified through other sources. The overall methodology followed the model suggested by Polsky (1967) for collection and analysis of field data. Similarities, differences, and norms of behavior were identified and modified throughout the process.

Ultimately, this study began to focus on the deviations from the norm. In turn, those deviations from the norm were classified into a listing of types of behavior. The reported behaviors then were added to the classification of closest proximity. That listing then became the basis for the typology offered in this report. Typologies may be the best mechanism for understanding the behavior of groups and members of groups (Weber, 1947). By using ideal typologies, a form of working hypotheses for further investigation are created.

A TYPOLOGY OF SEXUAL MISCONDUCT BY POLICE

It is likely that no other occupation or profession offers the opportunities for sexual misconduct like the police occupation. Police officers frequently work alone, usually without direct supervision, in activities that involve frequent contact with citizens. When those contacts are made, usually in relative isolation, the police officer may use his authority inappropriately. The combination of the authority of the officer and isolated contacts with female citizens creates an opportunity for inappropriate sexually motivated behaviors by the officer.

It is evident that many police officers do not engage in such behaviors, but it is also evident that many do. The problem seems to be pervasive in police departments from the smallest to the largest, in all areas of the United States, and at all levels of law enforcement, from federal to local. Since the problem is widely distributed, it is worthy of study. While the opportunity for female officers to commit similar behavior does exist (see, for example, Female deputy, 1992), occurrences are much fewer and much less likely to occur. It also is possible for same sex activities to take place, but such occurrences are likely to be few in number. In this study, the focus is solely on male police officers who commit inappropriate sexual behaviors with female citizens.

The typology of sexually motivated behaviors by police officers offered below is preliminary. Eight categories of sexually motivated behaviors are suggested:

1. sexually motivated nonsexual contacts
2. voyeuristic contacts
3. crime victims contacts
4. offender contacts
5. juvenile female contacts
6. citizen-initiated sexual contacts
7. sexual shakedowns
8. sex crimes by police officers

The eight types are discussed below.

SEXUALLY MOTIVATED NONSEXUAL CONTACTS

This type of sexual misconduct involves officer-initiated contacts with female citizens without probable cause or any legal basis. The behavior is sexually motivated but does not involve direct sexual actions or even inferences of sexual motivation or actions. The impropriety of the officer's action usually is not recognized by the female citizen nor is she likely to understand the motivations behind the officer's actions.

A subtle form of sexual misconduct involves computer license checks of female drivers for the purpose of obtaining names and addresses for possible later contacts by the officer. In many police departments, dispatchers note that certain officers have a habit of running license checks on cars driven by females much more often than those with male drivers.

In a large municipal police department, a one-month review of license numbers checked without an accompanying traffic stop was conducted. Of the forty-two male traffic officers, six had more than 80 percent returns on female drivers. One dispatcher noted that some officers almost never ran license checks on cars driven by males. When the officers ran a license and it came back to a male, they often followed up with a traffic stop and a driver's license check of the female driver.

> Well, when you see a young chick driving a car, it is usually her own car and registered in her name, and if it isn't, then you know she's probably married or her old man loaned her a car. If you really want to know who she is, then you pull her over and check her license. It's also okay to ask her who owns the car and that way you learn whether she's married and all that. (Interview: Patrolman, Medium Municipal Police Department.)

In a medium-size sheriff's department, a dispatcher/computer operator offered odds on certain deputies running a woman's license on their next license check. In one medium-size police department, one officer ran license checks on women drivers 83 percent of the time with only 3 percent of those checks followed by a traffic stop. In the 17 percent of checks that reflected a male owner of the car, traffic stops followed 74 percent of the time. However, over 50 percent of the subsequent driver's license checks from those stops reflected female drivers. After the review of the records, the officer was transferred to non-traffic duties.

Another variation of this type of sexual misconduct is the traffic stop made without a valid reason. Officers may also stop a female pedestrian to initiate a conversation or to get her identification with similar motivations. It is rare for a citizen to complain about these incidents since they received no citation and the sexual motivation is not obvious. However, when a female citizen is stopped repeatedly for no apparent reason, she may complain and the resultant complaint reveal the officer's motives. A recent disciplinary case involved an officer whose chief received several complaints about his repeated traffic stops of female drivers. The officer was disciplined when his only reason given was "to look them over."

> You can stop almost any female and she will be so shook up that she doesn't even question whatever you tell her. I usually say that the turn signal didn't work or the brake lights are out and they buy that. It gives me a chance to check out the driver and any passenger. A lot of times they are so glad that I just give them a warning that they invite me to a party or to call them sometimes. Other times I see them somewhere and they remember me and that leads to something. Usually, to tell you the truth it is just another traffic stop and that's all it is but those other times have been pretty good as far as picking up women. (Interview: Traffic Officer, Large Municipal Police Department.)

VOYEURISTIC CONTACTS WITH CITIZENS

Some officers spend time engaged in voyeuristic behavior while on duty. The officers seek opportunities to view unsuspecting women partially clad or nude. Other officers seek out parked cars on "lovers lane" in hopes of observing sexual activities by the occupants of the cars.

> I'll never forget my first night on the street after the Academy. I was all fired up to go out and fight crime. I was assigned to a twelve-year veteran for on the street training. As soon as we left the station, he drove over to a side street behind the college dorms and parked in the middle of the block. He even had a pocket-type telescope in his briefcase and proceeded to check out the dorm windows while telling me all about the college girls he had seen. He pointed out two windows that were usually "good hunting." After checking the dorms for 15–20 minutes, he drove over into a residential area to show me three houses where "on a good night, you'll get an eyeful." Around two o'clock, he drove into another patrol district and into a parking lot to check the windows in an apartment building where "several barmaids and go-go dancers live." He said it was a "waste of time to get there before two o'clock because they don't get home before then." I rode with him for two months and he spent most of every shift looking for women undressing in front of window. (Interview: Patrolman, Patrol Division, Large Municipal Department.)

Officers who spend their time looking for women to view are rarely noted by the citizens who may be the target of their peeping. Women who discover a patrol car on the street are likely to blame themselves for leaving the curtains open or the blinds undrawn rather than to complain. As long as the officer responds to his service calls and does not leave the patrol vehicle to carry out his voyeuristic activities, he is unlikely to be caught and reported. Even if the officer is caught in a yard or behind a house, he can always claim to be checking out a call about a prowler.

More overt voyeurism is practiced by some officers who leave their cars and walk quietly to check parked cars in lovers' lane areas. These officers seek to observe and interrupt couples engaged in sexual activities in the parked automobiles.

> Joe and I used to hit the local parking places where the high school and college kids go to make out every weekend. Friday and Saturday nights were the best. Lots of times we sneaked up and watched the kids. You wouldn't believe some of the things we saw! [Several sexually graphic examples deleted.] Some of the girls would just really take their time getting their clothes back on like they enjoyed having us watch them. We never took anybody in—just made them get dressed while we watched and moved them on. We did arrest a couple of [homosexual males] once when we caught them. (Interview: Sergeant, Patrol Division, Large Municipal Department.)

Officers engaged in overt voyeuristic activities similar to those discussed above are rarely the subject of a complaint since the citizens being harassed are engaged in illicit activities and would likely be embarrassed to file a complaint. Unless other officers complain or unless the officer goes beyond voyeurism, the offending officer usually is not detected.

The first two classifications dealt with citizen-police contact with police initiation of the contact. The next category is one where the potential victim of sexual harassment contacts the police. The authority of the police becomes a major factor in such contacts.

CONTACTS WITH CRIME VICTIMS

Victims of crime are particularly susceptible to sexual harassment by police officers. The victims are often emotionally upset and turn to the police for support and assistance. The officer is at the scene at the request of the citizen, who is fully aware of the authority of the police officer. A wide variety of sexually motivated misbehavior may occur. Unnecessary callbacks to the residence of female victims are one of the common forms of police misconduct.

> When you drop in a few times to check on the victim or to tell her that you are still working on her case, you kind of establish a connection there. She will offer a cup of coffee or a drink. When one of them offers a drink, I usually tell them I can't drink on duty but I'll take a rain check. I get invited back a lot after hours and that sometimes leads to something. You can't do this with everyone, but if you pick them carefully, it gets me a lot of action. (Interview: Detective, Burglary Squad, Large Municipal Department.)

Sex crime victims are also susceptible to sexual harassment by officers. Some of the harassment is unintentional and results from a lack of sensitivity and knowledge on the part of the officer. Victims of sex crimes should be interviewed by well-trained officers who are knowledgeable of the psychological needs of sex crime victims. When an officer questions victims of sex offenses beyond the depth of details needed for investigation purposes, the questioning becomes a form of sexual harassment.

Many victims of rape and sexual assault have complained of being raped again by the criminal justice system. This "second rape" often starts with questioning by insensitive officers who insist on graphic details and who ask judgmental questions. Some officers have insisted on examining the victim for signs of physical injury that may involve partial disrobing by the victim. Such forms of questioning and examination are unnecessary and constitute a form of sexual harassment.

Two officers were fired by a sheriff's department in a southern state for unnecessary bodily contact with accident victims. The officers were accused of fondling or touching the breasts and genitals of accident victims on two separate occasions. Behavior of this type is likely to be reported unless the victim is unconscious. Other officers who observe such behavior may also be a source of reporting.

CONTACTS WITH OFFENDERS

Police officers have relatively frequent opportunities for sexual harassment and sexual contact with offenders. Offenders are not only aware of the authority of the officer but are also in a position where their complaints may be disregarded or played down.

> You bet I get (sex) once in a while by some broad who I arrest. Lots of times you can just hint that if you are taken care of, you could forget about what they did. One of the department stores here doesn't like to prosecute, but they always call us when they catch a shoplifter. Usually, we just talk to them and warn them and let them go. If it's a decent looking woman, sometimes I'll offer to take her home and make my pitch. Some of the snooty, high class broads turn on real quick if they think their friends and the old man doesn't have to find out about their shoplifting. I never mess around with any of the kids, but I know a couple of guys who made out with a couple of high school girls they caught on a B and E. (Detective, Theft Squad. Large Municipal Department.)

In addition to sexual demands placed on offenders, officers may also sexually harass female offenders by conducting body searches, frisks, and pat-downs. Although departmental rules and regulations require the female suspects be frisked and searched by female officers or jail matrons, officers in the field often feel justified in making a pat-down for weapons. Offenders who resist arrest may also become involved in unnecessary bodily contact. One state police officer stated: "Whenever a female starts to hassle or fight me, I just grab a [breast] and twist. That quiets them down quick."

Officials of a large metropolitan county in a midwestern state have been the subject of a civil rights suit over body searches and strip searches by officers of a different sex than the offenders. Although mostly all of the cases cited have involved female officers strip searching offenders returning from work-release programs, apparently there is a possibility for male officers to conduct similar searches for female offenders. As a result, the county has agreed to avoid opposite sex strip searches whenever possible. Interestingly, the county justified its actions by reference to a previous civil suit that resulted in a court order requiring the county to assign identical duties to male and female corrections officers.

Offenders who are in detention are in a position where sexual harassment behaviors can take place with relative impunity. Most jails are not constructed to provide privacy for inmates. Female inmates often can be seen in their cells, showers, toilets, or during searches by jail matrons. Some officers apparently seek out opportunities to observe females in various degrees of undress.

> Look at the women? Hell, you can't help but look at the women in here. The showers don't have any doors on them and you can't always wait until the showers are empty to go into the cell block. Some of the women try to show their bodies off to you, too. We don't have air conditioning and when the weather is hot, they lay around their cells with just underwear or even buck naked most of the time. I see so many naked women that after a while you just don't even notice it anymore. Now once in a while, we get a really built one in and the guys will make it a point to catch her in the shower or dressing, but most of those we get are really pigs, not worth looking at. (Sheriff's Detention Officer, Large Sheriff's Department.)

Female inmates in smaller jails particularly are sometimes exposed to sexual demands by their guardians. In many small jails, only one or two officers are on duty during the evening hours and their behavior is largely unsupervised.

> Over in a county west of here, they tell that a sheriff will sometimes grab a hooker working one of the truck stops or the rest areas on the Interstate (highway) over there and keep her in jail over the weekend. He works out some kind of a deal where he turns them loose without any charges or anything and they put out for the sheriff and the deputies that might be interested. I've heard this from several officers and I believe it's true. Now I don't go for that kind of stuff at all. Seems to me that the sheriff over there is really asking for trouble over this kind of thing. It is different if some woman in the jail wants to have a party or whatever with some of the deputies or the sheriff but to go out and arrest one and then make the deal is too much. (Patrolman, Working as Jailer at Medium Municipal Jail.)

CONTACT WITH JUVENILE OFFENDERS

Younger females may also be the subject of sexual harassment by police officers. Runaways, truants, and delinquents are in a position similar to that of adult offenders in relation to police authority and lack of credibility. Juvenile females may be highly impressionable and easily influenced by the police officer. They are much less likely to be "street wise" and to understand the limits of police authority and proper police behavior. A former juvenile squad sergeant in Louisiana was the subject of a recent television program after he failed to appear for trial on charges that he sexually molested a 12-year-old girl that he was "counseling" after earlier abuse by someone else.

Several of the officers interviewed for this chapter were aware of sexual contact between officers and underage females but all declined to discuss details or to have their comments recorded. In a Texas city, an officer assigned to a junior high school as a school liaison officer was fired after disclosure of his sexual involvement with several female students.

> I tell you, it takes a really crazy guy to go after the San Quentin quails. Some of the juvenile girls look like 21 and some act like 35 but it just ain't worth the trouble if you get caught. Some of the girls fall in love or think they are in love if you [have sex with] them and they can really cause trouble calling you and writing notes and all that teenage stuff. I knew a guy

that chased after the young girls all the time and he claims he got a lot of action, and he probably did because they were always calling him. He was single and I guess that helped him not get caught but it is really not worth it. (Patrol Officer in Large Municipal Police Department.)

Of the officers interviewed for this study, none admitted to having such contact themselves. This may be the rarest of the various forms of sexual misconduct because of the possible penalties.

SEXUAL SHAKEDOWNS

Demanding sexual service from prostitutes, homosexuals, or other citizens involved in illegal or illicit activities is one of the more severe forms of sexual harassment. Actual sexual activities are involved with an unwilling citizen who yields solely on the basis of the police authority to arrest and prosecute.

I know several dozen guys who have worked vice in the ten years I've been assigned to the vice squad. I believe everyone of them has gone beyond the rules on sex with prostitutes. You see, when you are assigned to the prostitute detail, you have to get the female subject to offer specific sexual acts and then state a price for those sex acts. Once you have that, you have a case and are supposed to identify and arrest. Sometimes the officer goes ahead and has sex and then makes the arrest and files a report saying he followed the procedures. If the whore claims otherwise, no one believes her anyway since they think she is just trying to get her case tossed out. Have I ever done that? Well, I'm not saying I did but I've been in this business ten years so you draw your own conclusion. Everyone I know does it at one time or another. The prostitute squad isn't the only way vice officers get action. I've been offered, and I'm not saying I took up the offers, understand, but I've been offered sexual services from barmaids, gamblers, narcotic addicts, and dealers, and damn near every other kind of case you run into. Most of those cases are just between you and the suspect and they will do almost anything to avoid the arrest. Guys that would never even consider taking money will take (oral sex or intercourse) from a good looking woman. I don't know if the guys who are oversexed get assigned to vice or if being exposed to so much of it makes the vice squad oversexed, but it seems to me there is more going on in vice than anywhere else. (Vice Squad Sergeant, Large Municipal Department.)

Police officers who exchange preferential treatment for sexual favors are not limited to those with the vice squad. Officers on traffic details, patrol, or other investigative squads may also offer differential treatment in exchange for sexual services.

When I first went on patrol, I was surprised to hear some of the other officers talking about the sex they got on duty or as a result of on-duty calls. Seems like everyone talked about it. I really didn't have any offers or even really think about it until I was assigned to a one-man car and one night I stopped a female subject for running a traffic light. She was really first class and the way she acted I just kind of hinted that maybe we could reach an understanding and she picked right up on it. Well, she had enough moving violations that another one could take her license and I guess she didn't want that to happen. Anyway, I met her later that night and had a wild session. I called her again a few days later and she wouldn't even talk to me. Yeah, I've had a few similar type experiences since but I'm real careful. It really isn't worth it if you get caught. There is plenty of opportunities without pressuring someone or taking a chance on someone filing on you. (Patrol Officer, Patrol Division, Medium Municipal Department.)

I worked traffic for a couple of years in (another city) before I quit and came here. I tell you, it was a rare night when I didn't get the batted eyes and tears and the "officer, I'll do anything" routine. My zone was close to the college and lots of the college girls were afraid that their old man would take their cars away, I guess, if they got tickets. We used to refer to traffic duty around the college as "fox hunting." It was quite an experience but after a while you get tired of it. Some of them would really give you a come-on and then later when it got right down to the nitty-gritty they wanted to back out or play kid games. You know, petting and no serious sex. One guy was supposed to meet one girl after the shift and when he showed up, her boyfriend came along. Man, that kind of stuff is weird and too risky. Naw, I didn't take up very many of them on the offers. I guess you could say that a couple of times I let it be known that maybe we could negotiate, but most always they made the offers. (Former Traffic Officer, Medium Municipal Department.)

Officers engaged in various forms of sexual shakedowns are engaged in activities that clearly are illegal and subject to severe penalties. While sexual shakedowns of prostitutes may be less risky, shakedowns of other citizens could easily become the subject of complaints.

CITIZEN-INITIATED SEXUAL CONTACTS

Some sexual contacts between law enforcement officers and female citizens are initiated by citizens rather than by the police officer. It is a rare police department that does not have stories about "police groupies," females, often young, who are attracted sexually to the uniform, weapons, or power of the police officer. Officers in many departments have been disciplined and/or dismissed for participating in sexual activities with "groupies."

Another form of citizen-initiated sexual contact is the call from lonely or mentally disturbed women who seek attention and affection from an officer. Most law enforcement officers are familiar with these service calls when a citizen calls for an officer and has no real reason for doing so other than to have someone with whom to talk. Some women offer sex in exchange for the officer's time and attention. Officers who take the offered sexual services often are dealing with a person who needs other forms of professional attention. These citizens may become well-known throughout the department.

We have several of the women who will call once or twice a week, always late at night to report a prowler or an attempted break-in or some other reason. We have to dispatch an officer when we get calls like that but everyone knows the addresses now and we warn our officers to avoid any situation where they would be compromised. We have orders to the dispatchers to always send a two-man unit or else send two units. These women are sick in my opinion because all they want when the officers get there is to talk and have the officers stay for a while. Some of them will offer sex or money or whatever just to keep the officers around for a while. I don't think we have any of our troops engaging in sex with any of these that we know about. Everyone knows what is going on when we get a call from them. I'm sure they aren't the only ones around and maybe there are others I don't know about. I guess some of the officers might not recognize that these subjects are sick but I don't know. (Captain, Patrol Division, Large Municipal Department.)

> There are three or maybe four addresses here in town that everyone knows when a car is dispatched that it's another call from one of the "lonely hearts" club. Everyone laughs but no one really wants the call because every time you make one of those runs everyone kids about whether you took care of the lady and so forth. You know, some guys never seem to know when an old joke is enough. You know what I mean? They just keep it up and no one is going to mess around with those women even though one of them is pretty young and fairly good-looking. She always answers the door in a nightgown that is nearly see-through and is scared or pretends to be so scared that she wants you to stay for a while. I answered one call, not one of the known addresses, and the woman just had a towel around her and she claimed someone was trying to get into her window while she was taking a shower. Well, when we looked the place over, the bathroom wasn't wet, the bed had been slept in and this was three o'clock in the morning. She just got lonely and wanted a man. I'll admit, she looked pretty good in that towel and she wasn't real careful, you know, about keeping it closed up and all. If I was there by myself I might of been tempted. My partner and I laughed about it but I'm sure other calls like that happen. The brass really stresses the known addresses and we have all been warned about them. They don't know about others though. (Patrolman in Captain's Division—see above.)

A third type of sexual contact initiated by the citizen is the offer of sexual services in return for favors, preferential treatment, or additional protection. This form of sexual contact is differentiated from officer-initiated contacts by the citizen making the offer without any prior indication from the officer that such an offer might be considered. Obviously, law enforcement officers who accept such offers in exchange for favors or preferential treatment are engaged in illegal use of police authority.

> I answered a call one day about a suspicious person out in one of the better neighborhoods. When I got there the woman, she was really a fox, about 35, and anyway, she wanted to know if it would be possible for me to come by her house several times a shift because her old man and her had split and he was harassing her by coming by and pounding on the door and such. I told her she would have to file a complaint and then she said that she was willing to "take care of me" if I would just watch her house when I could. She said that she would "screw my brains out" if I would just drive by a few times. It was tempting but I figured it would probably cause me trouble if I went for the deal so I hadda turn her down. Sure hated to but you know how it is. (Deputy Sheriff, Patrol Division, Medium County Sheriff's Department.)

Even though most police officers do not misuse their authority or take advantage of the numerous opportunities for sexual harassment of female citizens, some do and the result is that exploitation of citizens by law enforcement officers lessens the respect for the department involved and all other law enforcement agencies and officers. Control of officers who sexually harass citizens is extremely difficult to achieve but is a task that should receive attention from police administrators.

SEX CRIMES BY POLICE OFFICERS

A number of cases of sexual assaults on jail inmates have been documented in recent years. Recently, a former sheriff in a border state was indicted on fifteen counts of rape and sodomy where the victims were inmates in his jail. At the time of the latest indictments, he was serving a sentence in a federal prison for earlier conviction based on similar behavior.

A patrol officer was convicted in a major southern city after his arrest and subsequent rape of a citizen. Other jurisdictions have had similar cases where police officers on duty committed a serious sex crime. While a number of officers interviewed for the study indicated they were aware of such things happening, none were willing to admit to such activities.

SUMMARY AND CONCLUSIONS

The sample size and the limitations of the field research methods (Babbie, 1992) preclude conclusions that the observed behavior represents the universe of police sexual misconduct. The use of anecdotal data included cases where officers related stories about other officer behavior. Self-reports are also subject to exaggeration and embellishment. The results cannot be generalized beyond the officers studied. Therefore, the typology is offered as a heuristic finding that may aid further research to the topic.

Sexual harassment and sexual misconduct as part of law enforcement must not be acceptable in any law enforcement agency. This problem is similar to many others; by accepting some level of misconduct, the department invites such conduct. Only when administrators and supervisors make it clear to every member of the department that sexual misconduct and sexual harassment will not be tolerated in any form or any degree is the behavior likely to decrease. Police officers should be educated about sexual misconduct and its effect upon the department and the public. Sexual misconduct and sexual harassment of female citizens by male law enforcement officers can be reduced or eliminated only by a concerted effort of police administrators and supervisors. Apathy towards sexual misconduct and harassment must be reduced, both on the part of police officials and the general public. As long as the "boys will be boys" attitude prevails, sexual harassment will not receive the attention it deserves.

The secrecy surrounding sexual harassment and other forms of police misconduct must be removed. As long as misconduct of any type is hidden and thus largely invisible, the misconduct will continue. If the general public and the police officers are fully aware of the appropriate limits on police contacts with female citizens, the shroud of secrecy is torn and the misconduct is identified. Once police misconduct involving sexual harassment or sexually motivated behavior and activities is identified, appropriate disciplinary action must be taken. The disciplinary action should be fair, firm, and appropriate for the degree and type of misconduct. Dismissal and/or criminal charges are certainly within the range of appropriate responses to some of the more serious forms of sexual harassment and misconduct. On a broader scale, sexual misconduct in all occupations will not be eliminated until such time as we make basic changes in society and in our views of sex roles.

REFERENCES

BABBIE, E. (1992). *The Practice of Social Research*, 6th ed. Belmont, CA: Wadsworth Publishing Company.

BARKER, T. & ROEBUCK, J.B. (1974). *An Empirical Typology of Police Corruption: A Study in Organizational Deviance*. Springfield, IL: Charles C. Thomas, Publisher.

BARKER, T. (1978). "An Empirical Study of Police Deviance Other than Corruption," *Journal of Police Science and Administration,* 6(3), 264–272.

BARKER, T. & CARTER, D.L., EDS. (1994). *Police Deviance,* 3d ed. Cincinnati: Anderson Publishing Company.

BARKER, T. & CARTER, D.L. (1990). "Fluffing Up the Evidence and Covering Your Ass: Some Conceptual Notes on Police Lying." *Deviant Behavior,* 11(1) 61–75.

BRADY, D.H. (1992). "Police Corruption and Community Actions: Community Policing," *Police Studies,* 15(4), 178–183.

CARTER, D.L. (1990). "Drug-related Corruption of Police Officers: A Contemporary Typology," *Journal of Criminal Justice,* 18(2) 85–98.

CARTER, D.L. (1985). "Police Brutality: A Model for Definition, Perspective, and Control," in A. Blumberg & E. Niederhoffer, eds., *The Ambivalent Force: Perspectives on the Police,* 3rd ed. New York: Holt, Rinehart & Winston.

COOKSEY, O.E. (1992). "Corruption: A Continuing Challenge for Law Enforcement," *FBI Law Enforcement Bulletin,* 60(9), 5–9.

"Female Deputy Fired for Sexually Harassing Males." (December 15, 1992). *Law Enforcement News,* 18, 3.

GOLDMAN, R. & PURO, S. (1987). "Decertification of Police: An Alternative to Traditional Remedies for Police Misconduct," *Hastings Constitutional Law Quarterly,* 15(1) 45–80.

GOLDSTEIN, H. (1975). *Police Corruption: A Perspective on Its Nature and Control.* Washington, D.C.: Police Foundation.

"Harassment in the Workplace: A Proactive Approach." (1991). *The Police Chief,* 58(12), 29–30.

HOLDEN, R.N. (1992). *Law Enforcement: An Introduction.* Englewood Cliffs, NJ: Prentice-Hall.

KEVLIN, T.A. (1986). "Police Corruption and Prostitution in the United States: The Historical Background," *Journal of Police and Criminal Psychology,* 2(2), 24–38.

KLEINIG, J. AND GORMAN, A.J. (1992). "Professional Courtesies: To Ticket or Not to Ticket," *American Journal of Police,* 11(4), 97–113.

KRASKA, P.B. & KAPPELER, V.E. (1988). "Police on Duty Drug Use: A Theoretical and Descriptive Examination," *American Journal of Police,* 7(1), 1–28.

LUNDMAN, R.J., ED. (1980). *Police Behavior.* New York: Oxford University Press.

MEYER, J.C., JR. (1976). "Definitional and Etiological Issues in Police Corruption: Assessment and Synthesis of Competing Perspectives," *Journal of Police Science and Administration,* 4(1), 46–55.

MYRON, P. (1992). "Crooks or Cops: We Can't be Both," *The Police Chief,* 59(1) 23–25.

"Police Ethics: Building Integrity and Reducing Drug Corruption." (1991). *The Police Chief,* 58(1), 1.

POLSKY, N. (1967). *Hustlers, Beats, and Others.* Chicago, IL: Aldine Publishing.

SAPP, A.D. (1994). "Sexual Misconduct by Police Officers," in T. Barker & D.L. Carter, eds. *Police Deviance*, 3rd ed. Cincinnati: Anderson Publishing Company.

SAPP, A.D., KAPPELER, V.E. & CARTER, D.L. "Police Officer Higher Education, Citizen Complaints, and Departmental Rule Violations," *American Journal of Police,* 11(2), 37–54.

SECHREST, D.K. & BURNS, P. "Police Corruption: The Miami Case," *Criminal Justice & Behavior,* 19(3), 294–313.

SHEARING, C.D., ED. (1981). *Organizational Police Deviance: Its Structure and Control.* Toronto, Canada: Butterworth & Company.

SHERMAN, L.W., ED. (1974). *Police Corruption: A Sociological Perspective.* New York: Doubleday and Company.

SIMPSON, A.E. (1977). *The Literature of Police Corruption.* Volume 1. New York: John Jay Press.

SYKES, G.W. (1985). "The Myth of Reform: The Functional Limits of Police Accountability in a Liberal Society," *Justice Quarterly,* 2(1), 51–65.

WEBER, M. (1947). *The Theory of Social and Economic Organization.* New York: Oxford University Press.

WILLIAMS, H. (1986). "Maintaining Police Integrity: Municipal Policing in the United States," *Police Studies,* 9(1), 27–31.

QUESTIONS FOR THOUGHT AND DISCUSSION

1. What are some of the types of sexual misconduct regarding the police? What aspects of the police role facilitate each type of misconduct?
2. Can departments control this type of misconduct? If so, what can they do to control it?

LEARNING POLICE ETHICS

Lawrence Sherman

There are two ways to learn police ethics. One way is to learn on the job, to make your moral decisions in haste under the time pressures of police work. This is by far the most common method of learning police ethics, the way virtually all of the half million police officers in the United States decide what ethical principles they will follow in their work. These decisions are strongly influenced by peer group pressures, by personal self-interest, by passions and emotions in the heat of difficult situations.

There is another way. It may even be a better way. You can learn police ethics in a setting removed from the heat of battle, from the opinions of co-workers, and from the pressures of supervisors. You can think things through with a more objective perspective on the issues. You should be able to make up your mind about many difficult choices before you actually have to make them. And you can take the time to weigh all sides of an issue carefully, rather than making a snap judgment.

The purpose of this article is to provide a basis for this other, less common way of learning police ethics by making the alternative—the usual way of learning police ethics—as clear as possible. This portrait of the on-the-job method is not attractive, but it would be no more attractive if we were to paint the same picture for doctors, lawyers, judges, or college professors. The generalizations we make are not true of all police officers, but they do reflect a common pattern, just as similar patterns are found in all occupations.

Learning New Jobs

Every occupation has a learning process (usually called "socialization") to which its new members are subjected. The socialization process functions to make most "rookies" in the occupation adopt the prevailing rules, values, and attitudes of their senior colleagues in the occupation. Very often, some of the existing informal rules and attitudes are at odds with the formal rules and attitudes society as a whole expects members of the occupation to follow. This puts rookies in a moral dilemma: should the rookies follow the formal rules of society or the informal rules of their senior colleagues?

From Lawrence Sherman, "Learning Police Ethics," *Criminal Justice Ethics*, Vol. 1, No. 1, Winter/Spring 1982, pp. 10–19.

These dilemmas vary in their seriousness from one occupation and one organization to the next. Young college professors may find that older professors expect them to devote most of their time to research and writing, while the general public (and their students) expects them to devote most of their time to teaching. With some luck, and a lot of work, they can do both.

Police officers usually face much tougher dilemmas. Like waiters, longshoreman, and retail clerks, they may be taught very early how to steal—at the scene of a burglary, from the body of a dead person, or in other opportunities police confront. They may be taught how to commit perjury in court to insure that their arrests lead to conviction, or how to lie in disciplinary investigations to protect their colleagues. They may be taught how to shake people down, or how to beat people up. Or they may be fortunate enough to go to work in an agency, or with a group of older officers, in which none of these violations of official rules is ever suggested to them.

Whether or not rookie police officers decide to act in ways the wider society might view as unethical, they are all subjected to a similar process of being taught certain standards of behavior. Their reactions to that learning as the years pass by can be described as their *moral careers*: the changes in the morality and ethics of their behavior. But the moral career is closely connected to the *occupational career*: the stages of growth and development in becoming a police officer.

This article examines the process of learning a new job as the context for learning police ethics. It then describes the content of the ethical and moral values in many police department "cultures" that are conveyed to new police officers, as well as the rising conflict within police agencies over what those values should be. Finally, it describes the moral career of police officers, including many of the major ethical choices officers make.

BECOMING A POLICE OFFICER

There are four major stages in the career of anyone joining a new occupation:[1]

- the *choice* of occupation
- the *introduction* to the occupation
- the first *encounter* with doing the occupation's work
- the *metamorphosis* into a full-fledged member of the occupation

Police officers go through these stages, just as doctors and bankers do. But the transformation of the police officer's identity and self-image may be more radical than in many other fields. The process can be overwhelming, changing even the strongest of personalities.

Choice

There are three aspects of the choice to become a police officer. One is the *kind of person* who makes that choice. Another is the *reason* the choice is made, the motivations for doing police work. The third is the *methods* people must use as police officers. None of these aspects of choice appears to predispose police officers to be more or less likely to perform their work ethically.

Many people toy with the idea of doing police work, and in the past decade the applicants for policing have become increasingly diverse. Once a predominantly white male occupation, policing has accepted many more minority group members and attracted many more women. More college-educated people have sought out police work, but this may just reflect the higher rate of college graduates in the total population.

What has not changed, apparently, is the socio-economic background of people who become police. The limited evidence suggests police work attracts the sons and daughters of successful tradespeople, foremen, and civil servants—especially police. For many of them, the good salary (relative to the educational requirements), job security, and prestige of police work represent a good step up in the world, an improvement on their parents' position in life.

The motivation to become a police officer flows naturally from the social position of the people who choose policing. People do not seem to choose policing out of an irrational lust for power or because they have an "authoritarian personality"; the best study on this question showed that New York City police recruits even had a *lower* level of authoritarian attitudes than the general public (although their attitudes become more authoritarian as they become adapted to police work, rising to the general public's level of authoritarian attitudes).[2] Police applicants tend to see police work as an adventure, as a chance to do work out of doors without being cooped up in an office, as a chance to do work that is important for the good of society, and not as a chance to be the "toughest guy on the block." Nothing in the motivation to apply for a police position seems to predispose police officers towards unethical behavior.

Nor do the methods of selecting police officers seem to affect their long-term moral careers. There was a time when getting on the force was a matter of bribery or political favors for local politicians, or at least a matter of knowing the right people involved in grading the entrance examinations and sitting on the selection committees. But in the 1980s the selection process appears to be highly bureaucratic, with impersonal multiple-choice tests scored by computers playing the most important role in the process.

To be sure, there are still subjective background investigations, personal interviews, and other methods that allow biases to intrude upon the selection process. But these biases, if anything, work in the direction of selecting people who have backgrounds of unquestioned integrity. Combined with the high failure rate among all applicants—sometimes less than one in twenty is hired, which makes some police departments more selective in quantitative terms than the Harvard Law School—the selection process probably makes successful applicants feel that they have been welcomed into an elite group of highly qualified people of very high integrity.

Introduction

But this sense of high ideals about police work may not last for long. The introduction to policing provided by most police academies begins to convey folklore that shows the impossibility of doing things "by the book" and the frequent necessity of "bending the rules."

Police recruit training has changed substantially over the past thirty years. Once highly militaristic, it has recently taken on more of the atmosphere of the college classroom. The endurance test-stress environment approach, in which trainees may be punished for yawning or looking out the window, may still be found in some cities, but it seems to be dying out. Dull lectures on the technical aspects of police work (such as how to fill out arrest reports) and the rules and regulations of the department are now often supplemented by guest lectures on theories of crime and the cultures of various ethnic groups.

But the central method of *moral* instruction does not appear to have changed. The "war story" still remains the most effective device for communicating the history and values of the department. When the instructor tells a "war story," or an anecdote about police work, the class discipline is relaxed somewhat, the interest and attention of the class increase, and an atmosphere of camaraderie between the class and the instructor is established. The content of the war story makes a deep impression on the trainees.

The war stories not only introduce police work as it is experienced by police officers—rather than as an abstract ideal—they also introduce the ethics of police work as something different from what the public, or at least the law and the press, might expect. Van Maanen recounts one excerpt from a police academy criminal law lecture that, while not a "story," indicates the way in which the hidden values of police work are conveyed:

> I suppose you guys have heard of Lucky Baldwin? If not, you sure will when you hit the street. Baldwin happens to be the biggest burglar still operating in this town. Every guy in this department from patrolman to chief would love to get him and make it stick. We've busted him about ten times so far, but he's got an asshole lawyer and money so he always beats the rap....If I ever get a chance to pinch the SOB, I'll do it my way with my thirty-eight and spare the city the cost of a trial.[3]

Whether the instructor would actually shoot the burglary suspect is open to question, although he could do so legally in most states if the suspect attempted to flee from being arrested.* More important is the fact that the rookies spend many hours outside the classroom debating and analyzing the implications of the war stories. These discussions do help them decide how they would act in similar circumstances. But the decisions they reach in these informal bull sessions are probably more attributable to peer pressure and the desire to "fit in" to the culture of the department than to careful reflection on moral principle.

Encounter

After they leave the academy, the rookies are usually handed over to Field Training Officers (FTOs). In the classic version of the first day on patrol with the rookie, the FTO says, "Forget everything they taught you in the academy, kid; I'll show you how police work is really done." And show they do. The rookie becomes an observer of the FTO as he or she actually does police work. Suddenly the war stories come alive, and all the questions about how to handle tough situations get answered very quickly and clearly, as one police veteran recalls:

> On this job, your first partner is everything. He tells you how to survive on the job...how to walk, how to stand, and how to speak and how to think and what to say and see.[4]

The encounter with the FTO is only part of the rookie's "reality shock" about police work. Perhaps even more important are the rookie's encounters with the public. By putting

---

* Editor's note: The U.S. Supreme Court in *Garner* v. *Tennessee* (1985) severely limited the officer's right to shoot a fleeing felon.

on the uniform, the rookie becomes part of a visible minority group. The self-consciousness about the new appearance is heightened by the nasty taunts and comments the uniform attracts from teenagers and others.[5] The uniform and gun, as symbols of power, attract challenges to that power simply because they are there.[6] Other people seek out the uniform to manipulate the rookie to use the power on behalf of their personal interests. Caught frequently in the cross fire of equally unreasonable citizen demands, the rookie naturally reacts by blaming the public. The spontaneous reaction is reinforced by one of the central values of the police culture: the public as enemy.[7]

This is no different from the way many doctors view their patients, particularly patients with a penchant for malpractice suits. Nor is it different from the view many professors have of their students as unreasonable and thick-headed, particularly those who argue about grades. Like police officers, doctors and professors wield power that affects other people's lives, and that power is always subject to counterattack. Once again, Van Maanen captures the experience of the rookie:

> [My FTO] was always telling me to be forceful, to not back down and to never try to explain the law or what we are doing to a civilian. I really didn't know what he was talking about until I tried to tell some kid why we have laws about speeding. Well, the more I tried to tell him about traffic safety, the angrier he got. I was lucky just to get his John Hancock on the citation. When I came back to the patrol car, [the FTO] explains to me just where I'd gone wrong. You really can't talk to those people out there, they just won't listen to reason.[8]

It is the public that transforms the rookie's self-conception, teaching him or her the pains of exercising power. The FTO then helps to interpret the encounters with the public in the light of the values of the police culture, perhaps leading the rookie even further away from the values of family and friends about how police should act.

The FTO often gives "tests" as he or she teaches. In many departments, the tests are as minor as seeing if the rookie will wait patiently outside while the FTO visits a friend. In other departments, the test may include getting the rookie involved in drinking or having sex on duty, a seriously brutal slugfest against an arrestee, or taking bribes for nonenforcement. The seriousness of the violations may vary, but the central purpose of the test does not: seeing if the rookie can keep his or her mouth shut and not report the violations to the supervisors. A rookie who is found to be untrustworthy can be, literally, hounded and harassed from the department.

Finally, in the encounter stage, the rookie gets the major reality shock in the entire process of becoming a police officer. The rookie discovers that police work is more social work than crime fighting, more arbitration of minor disputes than investigations of major crimes, more patching of holes in the social fabric than weaving of webs to catch the big-time crooks. The rookie's usual response is to define most of the assignments received as "garbage calls," not *real* police work. Not quite sure whom to blame for the fact that he or she was hired to do police work but was assigned everything else, the rookie blames the police executive, the mayor and city council, and even previous U.S. presidents (for raising public expectations). But most of all the rookie blames the public, especially the poor, for being so stupid as to have all these problems, or so smart as to take advantage of welfare and other social programs.

Metamorphosis

The result of those encounters is usually a complete change, a total adaptation of the new role and self-conception as a "cop." And with that transformation comes a stark awareness of the interdependence cops share with all other cops. For all the independence police have in making decisions about how to deal with citizens, they are totally and utterly dependent on other police to save their lives, to respond to a call of an officer in trouble or need of assistance, and to lie on their behalf to supervisors to cover up minor infractions of the many rules the department has. This total change in perspective usually means that police accept several new assumptions about the nature of the world:

- loyalty to colleagues is essential for survival
- the public, or most of it, is the enemy
- police administrators are also the enemy
- any discrepancy between these views and the views of family and friends is due simply to the ignorance of those who have not actually done police work themselves

These are their new assumptions about the *facts* of life in police work, the realities which limit their options for many things, including the kinds of moral principles they can afford to have and still "survive," to keep the job, pay the mortgage, raise the kids, and vest the pension. This conception of the facts opens new police officers to learning and accepting what may be a new set of values and ethical principles. By the time the metamorphosis has been accomplished, in fact, most of these new values have been learned.

CONTENT OF POLICE VALUES TEACHING

Through the war stories of the academy instructor, the actions and stories of the FTO, the bull sessions with other rookies and veterans, and the new officer's encounters with the public, a fairly consistent set of values emerges. Whether the officer accepts these values is another question. Most students of police work seem to agree that these are the values (or some of them) that are taught:

1. Discretion A: *Decisions about whether to enforce the law, in any but the most serious cases, should be guided by both what the law says and who the suspect is.* Attitude, demeanor, cooperativeness, and even race, age, and social class are all important considerations in deciding how to treat people generally, and whether or not to arrest suspects in particular.
2. Discretion B: *Disrespect for police authority is a serious offense that should always be punished with an arrest or the use of force.* The "offense" known as "contempt of cop" or P.O.P.O. (pissing off a police officer) cannot be ignored. Even when the party has committed no violation of the law, a police officer should find a safe way to impose punishment, including an arrest on fake charges.
3. Force: *Police officers should never hesitate to use physical or deadly force against people who "deserve it," or where it can be an effective way of solving a crime.*

Only the potential punishments by superior officers, civil litigation, citizen complaints, and so forth should limit the use of force when the situation calls for it.
When you can get away with it, use all the force that society should use on people
like that—force and punishment which bleeding-heart judges are too soft to impose.

4. Due Process: *Due process is only a means of protecting criminals at the expense of
the law-abiding and should be ignored whenever it is safe to do so.* Illegal searches and wiretaps, interrogation without advising suspects of their Miranda rights,
and if need be (as in the much-admired movie, *Dirty Harry*), even physical pain to
coerce a confession are all acceptable methods for accomplishing the goal the public wants the police to accomplish: fighting crime. The rules against doing those
things merely handcuff the police, making it more difficult for them to do their
job.

5. Truth: *Lying and deception are an essential part of the police job, and even perjury should be used if it is necessary to protect yourself or get a conviction on a
"bad guy."* Violations of due process cannot be admitted to prosecutors or in court,
so perjury (in the serious five percent of cases that ever go to trial) is necessary
and therefore proper. Lying to drug pushers about wanting to buy drugs, to prostitutes about wanting to buy sex, or to congressmen about wanting to buy influence
is the only way, and therefore a proper way, to investigate these crimes without
victims. Deceiving muggers into thinking you are an easy mark and deceiving burglars into thinking you are a fence are proper because there are not many other
ways of catching predatory criminals in the act.

6. Time: *You cannot go fast enough to chase a car thief or traffic violator, nor slow
enough to get a "garbage" call; and when there are no calls for service, your time
is your own.* Hot pursuits are necessary because anyone who tries to escape from
the police is challenging police authority, no matter how trivial the initial offense.
But calls to nonserious or social-work problems like domestic disputes or kids
making noise are unimportant, so you can stop to get coffee on the way or even
stop at the cleaner's if you like. And when there are no calls, you can sleep, visit
friends, study, or do anything else you can get away with, especially on the midnight shift, when you can get away with a lot.

7. Rewards: *Police do very dangerous work for low wages, so it is proper to take any
extra rewards the public wants to give them, like free meals, Christmas gifts, or
even regular monthly payments (in some cities) for special treatment.* The general
rule is: take any reward that doesn't change what you would do anyway, such as
eating a meal, but don't take money that would affect your job, like not giving
traffic tickets. In many cities, however, especially in the recent past, the rule has
been to take even those rewards that do affect your decisions, as long as they are
related only to minor offenses—traffic, gambling, prostitution, but not murder.

8. Loyalty: *The paramount duty is to protect your fellow officers at all costs, as they
would protect you, even though you may have to risk your own career or your own
life to do it.* If your colleagues make a mistake, take a bribe, seriously hurt somebody illegally, or get into other kinds of trouble, you should do everything you can
to protect them in the ensuing investigation. If your colleagues are routinely break-

ing the rules, you should never tell supervisors, reporters, or outside investigators about it. If you don't like it, quit—or get transferred to the police academy. But never, ever, blow the whistle.

THE RISING VALUE CONFLICTS

None of these values is as strongly or widely held as in the past. Several factors may account for the breakdown in traditional police values that has paralleled the breakdown of traditional values in the wider society. One is the increasing diversity of the kinds of people who join police departments: more women, minorities, and college graduates. Another is the rising power of the police unions which defend individual officers who get into trouble—sometimes even those who challenge the traditional values. A third factor is the rise of investigative journalism and the romantic aura given to the "bucking the system" by such movies as *Serpico*. Watergate and other recent exposés of corruption in high places—especially the attitude of being "above the law"—have probably made all public officials more conscious of the ethics of their behavior. Last but not least, police administrators have increasingly taken a very stern disciplinary posture towards some of these traditional police values and gone to extraordinary lengths to try to counteract them.

Consider the paramount value of loyalty. Police reformer August Vollmer described it in 1931 as the "blue curtain of secrecy" that descends whenever a police officer does something wrong, making it impossible to investigate misconduct. Yet in the past decade, police officers in Cincinnati, Indianapolis, New York, and elsewhere have given reporters and grand juries evidence about widespread police misconduct. In New York, police officers have even given evidence against their colleagues for homicide, leading to the first conviction there (that anyone can recall) of a police officer for murder in the line of duty. The code of silence may be far from breaking down, but it certainly has a few cracks in it.

The ethics of rewards have certainly changed in many departments over the past decade. In the wake of corruption scandals, some police executives have taken advantage of the breakdown in loyalty to assign spies, or "field associates," to corruption-prone units in order to detect bribe-taking. These officers are often recruited for this work at the police academy, where they are identified only to one or two contacts and are generally treated like any other police officer. These spies are universally hated by other officers, but they are very hard to identify. The result of this approach, along with other anti-corruption strategies, has been an apparent decline in organized corruption.[9]

The ethics of force are also changing. In the wake of well-publicized federal prosecutions of police beatings, community outrage over police shootings, and an explosion in civil litigation that has threatened to bankrupt some cities, the behavior and possibly the attitude of the police in their use of force have generally become more restrained. In Los Angeles, Kansas City, Atlanta, New York, Chicago, and elsewhere, the number of killings of citizens by police has declined sharply.[10] Some officers now claim that they risk their lives by hesitating to use force out of fear of being punished for using it. Even if excessive use of force has not been entirely eliminated, the days of unrestrained shooting or use of the "third degree" are clearly gone in many cities.

The increasing external pressures to conform to legal and societal values, rather than to traditional police values, have generated increasing conflict among police officers themselves. The divide-and-conquer effect may be seen in police officers' unwillingness to bear the risks of covering up for their colleagues, now that the risks are much greater than they have been. Racial conflicts among police officers often center on these values. At the national level, for example, the National Organization of Black Law Enforcement Executives (NOBLE) has been battling with the International Association of Chiefs of Police (IACP) since at least 1979 over the question of how restrictive police department firearms policies should be.

These conflicts should not be over-emphasized, however. The learning of police ethics still takes place in the context of very strong communication of traditional police values. The rising conflicts are still only a minor force. But they are at least one more contingency affecting the moral choices police officers face as they progress through their careers, deciding which values to adopt and which ethical standards to live by.

THE POLICE OFFICER'S MORAL CAREER

There are four major aspects of moral careers in general that are directly relevant to police officers.[11] One is the *contingencies* the officer confronts. Another is the *moral experiences* undergone in confronting these contingencies. A third is the *apologia*, the explanation officers develop for changing the ethical principles they live by. The fourth and most visible aspect of the moral careers of police officers is the *stages* of moral change they go through.

Contingencies

The contingencies shaping police moral careers include all the social pressures officers face to behave one way rather than another. Police departments vary, for example, in the frequency and seriousness of the rule-breaking that goes on. They also vary in the openness of such rule-breaking, and in the degree of teaching of the *skills* of such rule-breaking. It is no small art, for example, to coax a bribe offer out of a traffic violator without directly asking for it. Even in a department in which such bribes are regularly accepted, a new officer may be unlikely to adopt the practice if an older officer does not teach him or her how. In a department in which older officers explicitly teach the techniques, the same officer might be more likely to adopt the practice. The difference in the officer's career is thus shaped by the difference in the contingencies he or she confronts.

The list of all possible contingencies is obviously endless, but these are some of the more commonly reported ones:

- the values the FTO teaches
- the values the first sergeant teaches
- the kind of citizens confronted in the first patrol assignment
- the level of danger on patrol
- whether officers work in a one-officer or two-officer car (after the training period)
- whether officers are assigned to undercover or vice work

- whether there are conflicts among police officers over ethical issues in the department
- the ethical "messages" sent out by the police executive
- the power of the police union to protect officers from being punished
- the general climate of civic integrity (or lack of it)
- the level of public pressure to control police behavior

Contingencies alone, of course, do not shape our behavior. If we were entirely the products of our environment, with no freedom of moral choice, there would be little point in writing (or reading) books on ethics. What contingencies like these do is push us in one direction or another, much like the waves in the ocean. Whether we choose to swim against the tide or flow with the waves is up to each of us.

Moral Experiences

The moral experience is a major turning point in a moral career. It can be an agonizing decision about which principles to follow or it can be a shock of recognition as you finally understand the moral principles implicit in how other people are behaving. Like the person asleep on a raft drifting out to sea, the police officer who has a moral experience suddenly discovers where he or she is and what the choices are.

Some officers have had moral experiences when they found out the system they worked for was corrupt: when the judge dismissed the charges against the son of a powerful business executive, or when a sergeant ordered the officer not to make arrests at an illegal after-hours bar. One leading police executive apparently went through a moral experience when he was first assigned to the vice squad and saw all the money that his colleagues were taking from gamblers. Shocked and disgusted, he sought and obtained a transfer to a less corrupt unit within a few weeks.

Other officers have had moral experiences in reaction to particular incidents. One Houston police rookie was out of the academy for only several weeks when he witnessed a group of his senior colleagues beat up a Mexican-American, Joe Campos Torres, after he resisted arrest in a bar. Torres drowned after jumping or being pushed from a great height into a bayou, and no one knew how he had died when his body was found floating nearby. The officer discussed the incident with his father, also a Houston police officer, and the father marched the young officer right into the Internal Affairs Division to give a statement. His testimony became the basis of a federal prosecution of the other officers.

Other officers may have a moral experience when they see their ethics presented in public, outside of the police culture. New York City police captain Max Schmittberger, for example, who had been a bagman collecting graft for his superiors in New York's Tenderlion district, was greatly moved by the testimony of prostitutes he heard at the hearings of the Lexow Committee investigating police corruption in 1893. He told muckraking reporter Lincoln Steffens that the parade of witnesses opened his eyes to the reality of the corruption, so he decided to get on the witness stand himself to reveal even more details of the corruption.

No matter, what contingencies occur to prompt a moral experience, the police officer faces relatively few choices about how to react. One option is to drift with the tide, letting things go on as they have been. Another option is to seek an escape route, such as a transfer, that removes the moral dilemma that may prompt the moral experience. A third option is to leave police work altogether, although the financial resources of police officers are not usually great enough to allow the luxury of resigning on principle. The fourth and most difficult option is to fight back somehow, either by blowing the whistle to the public or initiating a behind-the-scenes counterattack.

Not all moral experiences are prompted by criminal acts or even by violations of rules and regulations. Racist jokes or language, ethnic favoritism by commanders, or other issues can also prompt moral experiences. With some officers, though, nothing may ever prompt a moral experience; they may drift out to sea or back to shore, sound asleep and unaware of what is happening to them.

Apologia

For those officers with enough moral consciousness to suffer a moral experience, a failure to "do the right thing" could be quite painful to live with. "Even a bent policeman has a conscience," as a British police official who resigned on principle (inadequate police corruption investigations in London) once observed.[12] In order to resolve the conflict between what they think they should have done and what they actually did, officers often invent or adopt an acceptable explanation for their conduct. The explanation negates the principle they may have wished they actually had followed, or somehow makes their behavior consistent with that principle.

Perhaps the most famous apologia is the concept of "clean graft": bribes paid to avoid enforcement of laws against crimes that don't hurt people. Gambling and prostitution bribes were traditionally labeled as "clean graft," while bribes from narcotics pushers were labeled "dirty graft." (As narcotics traffic grew more lucrative, however, narcotics bribes were more often labeled "clean.")

The apologia for beating a handicapped prisoner in a moment of anger may draw on the police value system of maintaining respect for authority and meting out punishment because the courts will not. The apologia for stopping black suspects more often than white suspects may be the assumption that blacks are more likely to be guilty. No matter what a police officer does, he or she is apt to find *situationally justified* reasons for doing it. The reasons are things only the officer can understand because only the officer knows the full story, all the facts of the *situation*. The claim of situational expertise, of course, conveniently avoids any attempt to apply a general moral principle to conduct. The avoidance is just as effective in the officer's own mind as it would be if the apologia were discussed with the officer's spouse, clergyman, or parents.

Perhaps the most important effect of the apologia is that it allows the officer to live with a certain moral standard of behavior, to become comfortable with it. This creates the potential for further apologias about further changes in moral standards. The process can clearly become habit-forming, and it does. The progression from one apologia to the next makes up the stages of moral change.

Stages

The stages of moral change are points on a moral continuum, the different levels of moral improvement or of the "slippery slope" of moral degeneration. Such descriptions sound trite and old-fashioned, but they are commonly used by officers who get into serious trouble—such as being convicted for burglary—to account for their behavior.

The officers caught in the Denver police burglary ring in 1961, for example, appear to have progressed through many stages in their moral careers before forming an organized burglary ring:

1. First they suffered moral experiences that showed them that the laws were not impartially enforced and that judges were corrupt.
2. Then they learned that other police officers were dishonest, including those who engaged in "shopping," i.e., stealing goods at the scene of a nighttime commercial burglary, with the goods stolen by the police thus indistinguishable from the goods stolen by others.
3. They joined in the shopping themselves and constructed an apologia for it ("the insurance pays for it all anyway").
4. The apologia provided a rationale for a planned burglary in which they were burglars ("the insurance still pays for it").
5. The final stage was to commit planned burglaries on a regular basis.

These stages are logically available to all police officers. Many, perhaps most, officers progress to Stage 3 and go no further, just as most professors steal paper clips and photocopying from their universities, but not books or furniture. Why some people move into the further stages and others do not is a problem for the sociology of deviance, not ethics. The fact is that some officers do move into the more serious stages of unethical conduct after most officers have established the custom in the less serious, but still unethical, stages.

Each aspect of police ethics, from force to time to due process, has different sets of stages. Taken together, the officer's movement across all the stages on all the ethical issues makes up his or her moral career in police work. The process is not just one way; officers can move back closer to legal principles as well as away from them. But the process is probably quite connected across different issues. Your moral stage on stealing may parallel your moral stage on force.

LEARNING ETHICS DIFFERENTLY

This article has treated morality as if it were black and white, i.e., as if it consisted of clear-cut principles to be obeyed or disobeyed. Many issues in police ethics are in fact clear-cut, and hold little room for serious philosophical analysis. One would have a hard time making a rational defense of police officers stealing, for example.

But what may be wrong with the way police ethics is now taught and learned is just that assumption: that all police ethical issues are as clear-cut as stealing. They are not. The issues of force, time, discretion, loyalty, and others are all very complex, with many shades of gray. To deny this complexity, as the formal approaches of police academies and police rule books often do, many simply encourage unethical behavior. A list of "dos" and "don'ts" that officers must follow because they are ordered to is a virtual challenge to their ingenuity: catch me if you can. And in the face of a police culture that has already established values quite contrary to many of the official rules, the black-and-white approach to ethics may be naive.

As indicated above, an alternative approach may be preferred. This would consider both clear-cut and complex ethical issues in the same fashion: examining police problems in the light of basic moral principles and from the moral point of view. While there may be weaknesses in this alternative approach, it may well be the sounder road to ethical sensitivity in the context of individual responsibility.

ENDNOTES

1. See John Van Maanen, "On Becoming a Policeman," in *Policing: A View from the Street*, Peter Manning and John Van Maanen, eds. (Santa Monica, Calif.: Goodyear, 1978).
2. See John McNamara, "Uncertainties in Police Work: The Relevance of Recruits' Backgrounds and Training," in *The Police: Six Sociological Studies*, ed. David J. Bordua (New York: Wiley, 1967).
3. Van Maanen, "On Becoming a Policeman," p. 298.
4. Ibid., p. 301.
5. See William Westley, *Violence and the Police* (Cambridge, Mass.: M.I.T. Press, 1970), pp. 159–60.
6. See William Ker Muir, Jr., *Police: Streetcorner Politicians* (Chicago: University of Chicago Press, 1977).
7. See Westley, *Violence*, pp. 48–108.
8. Van Maanen, "On Becoming a Policeman," p. 302.
9. See Lawrence Sherman, "Reducing Police Gun Use" (Paper presented at the International Conference on the Management and Control of the Police Organizations, Breukelen, the Netherlands, 1980).
10. Ibid.
11. Cf. Erving Goffman, "The Moral Career of the Mental Patient," in *Asylum: Essays on the Social Situation of Mental Patients and Other Inmates* (Garden City, N.Y.: Anchor Books, 1961), pp. 127–69.
12. See Sherman, "Reducing Police Gun Use."

QUESTIONS FOR THOUGHT AND DISCUSSION

1. How does the police value of loyalty to each other conflict with living up to the code of ethics?
2. According to Sherman, what are the two main ways of teaching police ethics? Which one do you think is the most effective?
3. How can we be more effective in ensuring that police officers abide by the Code of Ethics?

THE FRUSTRATIONS OF POLICE WORK

The Idealism and Realism of Being a Police Officer

William C. Wise

I decided to become a police officer in my junior year at Michigan State University while studying for my bachelor's in sociology. As part of that program I began taking criminal justice courses which piqued my interest.

I was attracted to police work for a number of reasons. Like many who become police officers, I am somewhat altruistic. I wanted to provide a service and to see that justice was done. I wanted to protect people and their values and to make the world a safer place. I was willing to put my life on the line so that innocent, law-abiding people could live and move about without fear.

At the time I had high ideals. I felt that police work was a noble profession. I enjoyed the idea that I would be admired and trusted by others. I felt I would be doing something worthwhile and rewarding, to which society would respond favorably. I expected support from the majority of people.

I enjoyed being outdoors, moving about, meeting different people and encountering new challenges every day. The excitement of the job, the uniform, and the market patrol car made for an attractive prospect. I envisioned myself as a "crime fighter" engaged in street fights, shootouts, and high speed chases. Police work promised to provide all these things. This was Hollywood and the popular media's influence on my decision to become a police officer.

Upon graduation from Michigan State with my bachelor's in sociology I applied for the entry-level position of police patrol officer with a number of large cities in Michigan, Ohio, Indiana, and Illinois. I also applied to become a State Trooper. I possessed all the necessary qualifications: a high school diploma, good health and physical condition, and good character. I passed the background check, was a U.S. citizen, and had no prior arrests. My choices were quickly narrowed to a handful of departments due to local residency requirements and my eyesight. Most departments require eyesight to be no less than 20/40 correctable to 20/20. Mine was 20/100 correctable to 20/20. The Ann Arbor Police Department had rather liberal eye requirements and accepted applicants with eyesight correctable to 20/20. After passing an oral and written exam, I was hired by the city of Ann Arbor. I was sent to a 440-hour police academy administered by the Michigan Law Enforcement Officers Training Council (MLEOTC), followed by a 160-hour training academy at the Ann Arbor Police Department (AAPD). I was assigned to uniform patrol duty in September 1972, three months after being hired, and remained in uniform patrol for thirteen years until 1985 when I left to head the criminal justice program at Siena Heights College. During the eight years from 1977–1985, I was trained and served as an advanced accident investigator.

Although I knew police work would be difficult, I felt the day-to-day decision making processes with the public and the offender would be easy. Conduct is either legal or illegal. A person is either right or wrong. There would be no gray area, no room for interpretation and, most important, no politics or special favors. I would be able to enforce the law equally for everyone. These ideals were reinforced in my classes and again by the police academy.

I was to learn early in my career that things are rarely black and white but mostly gray, and politics is very much a part of law enforcement. As a new recruit I failed to see this. I also had a media-distorted view of the duties of a police officer. Any posted job description for an officer will include a range of activities such as: protecting life and property, preserving the peace, detecting and preventing crime and maintaining order through the application of the law. The officer's duties might be listed as: patrolling, crime prevention, making arrests, investigating, inspecting, issuing tickets, writing reports, reporting hazards, and appearing in court. Certainly these duties are a part of the job and, to the outsider or even the new recruit, they might be seen as the totality of the job. But these descriptions leave out the crucial social service function of police work which consumes as much as eighty to ninety percent of the officer's time!

I found that problem solving and social service networking were used far more frequently than the power of arrest and other means of official disposition, such as tickets or code violations. Officers' abilities to mediate situations and to provide alternative solutions for family, neighborhood, and personal problems are far more important and frequently used than their knowledge of the penal code. Often police are called in to handle situations that could be more appropriately handled by another social service agency. The officers must know which agencies are best suited to intervene and then be able to work and communicate with agency professionals. I was not prepared for this. It was not emphasized in the criminal justice classes nor in the police academy. Empathy and communication skills to deal with all types of people outside the context of official action are also very important. For example, I would have benefitted enormously from having taken courses in counselling, family therapy, interviewing and social work services, as well as having had practical experience working with problem populations. Officers must also be socially aware and respect cultural differences. Training that emphasizes the cultural diversity of American society would be enormously valuable in enabling police officers to more effectively perform their duties.

My preconceived ideas on the police use of technology were also seriously revised. Official job descriptions for police officers include the stipulation that they master the use of firearms, handcuffs, motorcycles, radios, radar, nightsticks, rescue and emergency equipment. These are very important tools of the profession and much emphasis is placed on proper training in their use. However, during my thirteen years as an officer I came to realize that other, more abstract "tools" are of equal importance. For instance, the ability to reason with people, the ability to empathize and the ability to negotiate are extremely important. A police officer's job revolves around people and human situations. Because of this much emphasis must be placed on training officers to manage people in different situations. Officers need to know effective ways of dealing with difficult people, violent people, angry people, frightened people, and grief stricken people. For example, in the course of my career I had to deliver many death messages to relatives and respond to many ambulance requests in which people died. Beyond providing various ways of telling a person that a loved one had died, the academy provided no direction. There was no training on how to deal with the survivor or how to assist the survivor in beginning the process of making arrangements or how to deal with your own emotions in these circumstances. Situations such as these are regularly faced by police officers, yet very little time is spent on training an officer to deal with such incidents. Of the six hundred hours of initial officer training, only twelve hours focussed on these issues.

Another underemphasized tool that I discovered to be invaluable was the ability to write with detail, clarity, and organization. Not only does writing ability help officers make and prove cases to judges, juries, and attorneys, but if officers can logically and clearly state their reasons for action in writing, to justify and argue the case, this serves as a protection against the increasingly encountered possibility of criminal and civil litigation.

A practical example of how good writing skills might help is in the use of affidavits for search warrants. Here a clearly articulated, logical narrative will easily show a judge the probable cause for requesting the warrant and the officer's expertise in the area being discussed. All too often warrants can be denied where good cause is present because of an officer's inability to argue the case. Good writing skills will also help the officer to document all the events leading up to an arrest, thus making it easier to obtain arrest warrant authorization from the prosecutor.

As I have said, many reasons, hopes, and expectations accompanied my decision to become a police officer. I think every one of my expectations was somewhat modified as I worked in the field. I wanted to provide a service, see justice was done, and help everyone feel safe. It was soon obvious that these ideals were not achievable from my role as an officer. I could not make a significant difference to the conditions in Ann Arbor, much less the world! I was forced to move from a global set of ideals to a more localized, personally focussed set of goals. Instead of changing the whole system, I had to focus on the specific incidents in which I became involved, and to do the best I could to solve problems and correct the wrongs in specific situations. I was forced to realize that I could only impact situations over a narrow time frame: from the point at which I became involved to when I had to turn the case over to someone else. There was little I could do to prevent situations from occurring and I had no control over dispositions, criminal or otherwise, once they were passed on to the next stage of the process. Police officers often become disenchanted with their jobs when they feel they are individually responsible for the entire criminal justice process. Yet no one had trained us how to detach our emotions and to let go. In order to survive I learned to rationalize: "It is only possible to influence people and events in a small way, and I should not despair about the large issues over which I have no control."

Nor was the decision-making system as easy and clear cut as I had imagined. Even though procedural law and department policy mandated uniform, consistent enforcement, the criminal law was not equally enforced towards all people, at all times. There were more gray issues than black or white ones, more ambiguity and circumstantial considerations than could ever be imagined. Individual officer discretion was a far greater determinant of who was arrested and of what laws were enforced. Arrests were made, tickets issued, and alternative actions were taken based more on career considerations of individual officers than on legal mandates. Police action or inaction was influenced most by pressure groups and powerful individuals. Community sentiment influenced the types of laws enforced, not what was written in the penal code. What is more, any action taken by police was open to a vast amount of interpretation and scrutiny by the public, the courts, and other police officers. Making decisions became one of the **most** difficult components of the job.

Regarding public "support," I found to my great surprise that the most vocal comments came from people who did not approve of police actions. Moreover, this negative view was carried over and reinforced by the police administration, who were quick to respond to a complaint against an officer, assuming the officer guilty until proven otherwise. In contrast, most of the people who were satisfied with police services said nothing. Commendations from citizens for officers were few and were not handled with the same degree of zeal as complaints. This distorted exposure to the negative gave me the feeling that there was little support from the public and that most people did not understand police officers, their job or their frustrations. Once thing that I really had to work on was the idea that the public **did** support the police even though this support was typically silent.

Finally, the hectic, action-packed *Starsky and Hutch* image of police work is largely a myth for the typical middle-America police officer. Even the recently popular realistic police shows like *Cops* and *American Detective* and *FBI—The Untold Stories* are distortions since they are incident-driven, otherwise they would make poor television. Actual police work, the day-to-day kind, can be very routine and boring with long periods of uneventful patrol. Many menial tasks such as writing parking tickets, handling noise complaints, and transporting prisoners, serve to frustrate officers, especially those who anticipate bigger, faster, and more exciting things. Working overtime was a common and unexpected occurrence and the resulting fatigue of working fifteen hour shifts was not something that I had anticipated. Just as waiters and waitresses cannot go home until all their "side-work" is completed, so it is with police officers who can't go home until all the reports are written and the evidence is logged. This is especially a problem if a major crime occurs near the end of an 8 or 10-hour shift. The officer may have to stay 8 to 10 more hours to finish the reports! This can have an unanticipated and destructive effect on family life and social relationships.

Then there are systemic problems of the organization of police work. In fact my greatest disappointment came with the officer evaluation system instituted by the Ann

Arbor Police Department. This was a productivity-based system that measured officer performance by the number of tickets issued, traffic stops, arrests made, and incidents investigated. On the surface it might seem appropriate to measure the number of tickets and arrests each officer makes as a gauge of his effectiveness. However, in Ann Arbor this became the **sole** basis for evaluation upon which depended whether an officer would receive promotion and special duty assignments. As a result officers began competing with one another. Quantity was valued over quality. Many marginal tickets were written and questionable arrests were made. The teamwork so necessary for successful law enforcement was compromised as officers refused to cooperate with one another in attempts to hoard arrests. Moreover, the easier traffic arrests would sometimes take precedence over the serious felony. Not without justification, the public saw the police as primarily traffic enforcers and not surprisingly, police/community relations suffered. The problem-solving, social networking approach, which is necessary to community vitality, became nonexistent. In fact it was precisely my frustration with the numbers-oriented police evaluation system that led to my career change in 1985.

In spite of these disappointments there was considerable satisfaction in some aspects of the profession. I enjoyed my job the most when I was investigating a complicated case. It was especially enjoyable to start with very little information and to put the pieces of the puzzle together to develop a case on suspects. During my career I was awarded a number of professional excellence citations for developing a case, writing a complete report, and bringing the case forward for successful prosecution. It was also very rewarding and exciting to make an apprehension on an in-progress felony or to render first-aid or CPR to save a life.

I think anyone entering law enforcement today needs to be flexible, open-minded, and tolerant of alternative lifestyles. Certainly one must be thoughtful and have the ability to empathize with others. A college education is a must, increasingly with a bachelor's degree as a minimum starting point. The apparent classroom redundancy of learning various aspects of social and societal relations, learning about families and about social problems will prove enormously valuable later in the job. It might be compared to learning to read and write, only here you are learning to read and write people and society. I am sure that many people will eventually find, as I did, that a master's degree is desirable and may eventually become the standard as police work becomes more specialized and more professionalized. Perhaps one of the most misunderstood aspects of police work is that it requires using one's intellectual capacity and not physical power.

I don't think I would have played my career any differently, although I could have been better prepared. I was an independent thinker who often questioned department policy and procedure. I believe that the paramilitary structure, common in many police departments, serves to stifle individual thought in favor of strict adherence to sometimes inflexible and unworkable rules and regulations. To be successful in a paramilitary police agency and to advance through the ranks, one must compromise; one must sell one's soul to the police administration. I had to put the police department above family, friends, and personal life. This served to further alienate me, as a police officer, from the community I served. Hopefully, this will begin to change as the criminal justice system realizes the need for greater involvement between the police and community.

QUESTIONS FOR THOUGHT AND DISCUSSION

1. In which ways are the day-to-day duties of police officers different from what many people expect? How can these misperceptions affect the morale of the new recruit?

2. What are some ways that potential recruits can better prepare themselves for the actual day-to-day duties of police officers?

CAREERS IN LAW ENFORCEMENT

Karen McElrath

Many students enrolled in criminal justice classes are considering a career in law enforcement. Experience has shown, however, that few undergraduate students know about the range of law enforcement opportunities available to them, and very few know how to go about narrowing down their search for the appropriate agency and how to apply for a position. This chapter describes law enforcement positions at the local, state, and federal levels of government. Job requirements, salaries and benefits, and career stages are discussed. A list of federal law enforcement agencies and addresses is included at the end of the chapter.

Importance of Planning

Students who seek law enforcement employment should plan carefully. The application and hiring phases are lengthy, and interested persons should apply six to nine months before graduation. Students should consider all available options by applying to several agencies simultaneously. If a person's goal is to work for a federal agency, he or she may find it easier to seek employment with a local department first; applicants are generally viewed more favorably if they have experience and education. Before considering the career options, interested applicants should speak with friends and acquaintances who are veteran law enforcement officers. Ask them to describe the advantages and disadvantages of their work. Student internships are an excellent way to learn more about law enforcement and to establish contacts within the field. If a college program does not offer internships with police agencies, contact the agency of interest and inquire about volunteering.

Image versus Reality

The image of police work is influenced greatly by the popular media. For example, television, news reports, and books of fiction about crime tend to portray violent crime out of proportion to its actual incidence. Most crimes are property or economic crimes that occur without violence. Television and movies portray police work as exciting and violent, with shoot-outs a common occurrence. In reality, few police officers ever draw their gun during their whole career and even fewer fire their gun at another person. Police investigators

Karen McElrath. Written especially for this publication.

are depicted in the media using brilliant deductive powers and scientific crime detection to solve cases, when in reality most crimes are solved because witnesses or informants provide the information necessary for apprehending the offender. And, although police work can be exciting, fulfilling, and rewarding, a considerable amount of police activity is spent completing paperwork, e.g., arrest reports, evidence reports, warrants, and citations.

LOCAL, STATE, AND FEDERAL AGENCIES

Local Law Enforcement

Local law enforcement includes city and county police agencies and sheriff's departments. The smallest local agencies might employ one officer only, while cities such as New York, Los Angeles, and Chicago, and sheriff's departments such as Los Angeles County employ thousands of officers and deputies. A few jurisdictions, such as Dade County, Florida, have abolished the office of sheriff opting instead for a county police department headed by an appointed director.

State Law Enforcement

In some states two agencies provide law enforcement at the state level. One agency is charged with traffic enforcement and a second agency conducts criminal investigations. In Florida, for example, the Florida Highway Patrol, while having statewide police authority, is primarily concerned with traffic offenses on state roadways. The Florida Department of Law Enforcement investigates criminal offenses and provides support for local police agencies. In other states, such as New York, Texas, and Kentucky, one state police agency conducts criminal investigations and patrols the roadways.

Federal Law Enforcement

Several federal agencies offer careers in law enforcement. The Department of Justice includes the Federal Bureau of Investigation (FBI), the Drug Enforcement Administration (DEA), the United States Marshal's office, and the Border Patrol. FBI special agents investigate white-collar crime, organized crime, and to a lesser degree, drug trafficking. The DEA also employs special agents whose primary role is to investigate drug trafficking. Deputy marshals with the United States Marshal's Office offer protection for federal witnesses, provide security for federal judges and in federal courtrooms, transport federal prisoners, and locate federal fugitives. Border patrol agents operate under the Immigration and Naturalization Service (INS). Their primary duty is to prevent illegal immigration at United States borders, primarily the border between Mexico and the United States.

The Department of Treasury operates the Secret Service, United States Customs, Alcohol, Tobacco, and Firearms (ATF), and the Internal Revenue Service (IRS). Secret Service agents provide protection for the President, Vice-President and their families, former Presidents and their spouses, visiting dignitaries, and major Presidential and Vice-Presidential candidates. Secret Service Agents also have jurisdiction over counterfeiting, stolen U.S. government checks and bonds, and major cases of credit card and ATM fraud, computer fraud, and other crimes involving the electronic transfer of bank funds. The uniformed branch of the Secret Service is assigned protective duties at the White House and other federal buildings. United States Customs agents work largely at ports of entry in the United States where they investigate smuggling. Agents employed with ATF today work largely with criminal cases involving firearms or explosives. IRS agents investigate tax evasion and tax fraud. These agencies are among the better known federal agencies, however, the Departments of Justice and Treasury operate several other law enforcement agencies. For example, the United States Mint (Department of Treasury) employs federal law enforcement officers in four cities. Further, other branches of the federal government also maintain law enforcement positions. A list of these agencies appears at the end of this chapter.

RECRUITMENT QUALIFICATIONS

Education

Most local and state enforcement agencies require a high-school diploma or the equivalent. Only a few departments require a college degree, although a significant number provide incentives and support for officers who seek to continue their education (Carter and Sapp, 1990).

Most federal agencies require a bachelor's degree; however, some agencies will allow law enforcement experience to substitute for college education. A degree in criminal justice or a related field is preferred for most positions, although most baccalaureate degrees are accepted for qualification. For federal agencies requiring a college degree, new hires are often expected to have achieved a grade point average of 3.00 or more (on a 4.00 scale). Note that these requirements are the minimum, and in many instances applicants whose educational backgrounds exceed the minimum are viewed favorably. A college degree is, of course, viewed favorably in promotion decisions (Carter and Sapp, 1988), and in many departments a college education results in higher salaries.

Residency and Relocation

Some local departments require officers to live in the area served by the police department for which the officer works. Other departments have no residency requirement. Federal agencies have no residency requirement but some agencies require agents to work in more than one city during their career. Entry level site placement for state and federal recruits is the decision of the agency, and there is no guarantee that an officer or an agent who wishes to transfer to another area will be granted the request.

Gender and Minority Status

At present, women and minority applicants who meet the minimum requirements are often given hiring preference over white nonHispanic males. This procedure resulted from federal legislation that requires opportunity for equal employment. For several years police departments were comprised largely of white, nonHispanic males and recent data suggest that most local and state police departments remain over 90 percent male (Martin, 1993; Stinchcomb, 1992:44) and over 80 percent white nonHispanic (Sullivan, 1989). The degree of ethnic diversity in a police department affects police-community relations, particularly in urban areas. Further, women officers generally manifest a different style of policing than men officers, and several reports have recommended that departments actively recruit women because their work styles have proved favorable in reducing the number of potentially violent interactions with citizens (see Hale and Wyland, 1993, for a review of research findings relating to gender and police performance).

Age

Most local and state departments require applicants to be at least 21 years of age. Some federal agencies, such as the FBI, require applicants to be 23 years old before applying. Also, some agencies will not accept new hires who are older than 35.

Physical Requirements

Today, most departments do not have height and weight restrictions although generally weight must be proportionate to height. Routine medical examinations are conducted and might include vision and hearing tests, blood tests, and urinalysis for drug screening.

Criminal Record

In the late 1970s most departments rejected applicants who had been convicted of a felony offense if the offense occurred as a juvenile (Griesinger et al., 1979). Today, a felony record is grounds for rejection although some departments might consider the age at which the offense occurred and the nature of the offense. Convictions for drug sales or possession nearly always result in rejection. Similarly, a felony or misdemeanor conviction for driving while intoxicated or under the influence of alcohol is likely to result in rejection.

Prior Illicit Drug Use

Students often ask whether they should admit on an application that they have experimented with illegal drugs. This question rests on ethical and moral principles, and applicants must decide for themselves. Law enforcement officials understand that many persons have experimented with marijuana but are far less tolerant of cocaine, amphetamines, and heroin and other "hard drugs." Experimentation means using once or twice, and applicants who admit to using illicit drugs will be questioned about the dates and the context of use. The age at which drug use occurred and the number of years since the applicant used drugs are likely to be considered in the screening process. Even if an applicant conceals a past drug use, misrepresentation is often revealed through a polygraph examination or from a background investigation (see below).

The Application Process

To apply with local agencies, candidates should contact the agency personnel office to determine the procedures for applying. These office telephone numbers appear in the local government section of the telephone directory. To apply with state agencies, applicants should also check the telephone directory, although, generally, applicants will be advised to contact the state agency's central office, typically located in the state capital. For federal positions, applicants must complete the SF-171, Application for Federal Employment. This form is lengthy and applicants might wish to photocopy the completed form before submitting it (omit the position of interest, the date, and the signature before photocopying).

During the initial application process, candidates will undergo a number of screening procedures, including a written examination, a formal interview, and psychological and medical screening. If these screening procedures produce favorable results, the agency will begin its background investigation. The background check often takes several months to complete, particularly for applicants who have lived in various places or who have an extensive work history. Typically, the FBI conducts background investigations on federal law enforcement applicants and then forwards the results of the investigation to the agency to which the individual applied. These investigations are quite detailed and might include criminal record checks on all immediate family members and lengthy interviews with friends, neighbors (past and present), employers, and co-workers (past and present). At times an applicant is rejected because of information obtained from the background check. Through the Freedom of Information Act, the applicant should request the written results from the background investigation. This review is important because the results might affect whether the applicant should continue to apply for federal law enforcement positions.

Academy Training

Once hired, the applicant enters the training academy where he or she undergoes training in the areas of criminal and constitutional law, courtroom testimony, patrol duties, criminal and crime scene investigation procedures, weaponry, dispute mediation, report writing, traffic control, defensive driving, and physical strength and agility. In some areas, applicants reside at the academy for several months, and in other areas, academies are nonresidential, operating during day hours only. State guidelines dictate the number of training hours that applicants must receive. During the 1990s, 400 hours is expected to be the modal number of academy training hours for local police (Stinchcomb, 1992). Many federal law enforcement agencies utilize the training site at Glynco, Georgia, although the FBI and the DEA train recruits at Quantico, Virginia. During the final phase of training, federal recruits are informed of the city of their first appointment.

Career Progression

At the local and state levels, upon graduation from the academy a candidate works with a field training officer. This probationary period continues for several months. For state and local officers, career progression is often a slow process. Many departments make promotion decisions with the aid of the assessment center tool, in which officers who apply for promotion are asked to role-play, decide critical issues, and prioritize decision-making. The results of this testing, coupled with interviews and experience, determine the list of persons to be promoted. Generally, the list becomes obsolete within a specified period of time. If a person is not promoted within this time period, he or she must undergo the process again.

SALARIES AND BENEFITS

Law enforcement salaries vary across agencies but generally minimum and maximum salaries are specified and hiring salary within the range is determined by education and experience. The average starting salary of police officers serving cities of 10,000 persons or more usually ranges from $20,000 to $28,000 per year. State police salaries vary considerably and in some areas are lower on average than local police salaries. Federal agencies follow the General Schedule (GS) pay scale and many entry level law enforcement positions are paid at the GS-5, GS-7, or the GS-9 level. Within this level, employees can progress through "steps" so that salary increases are frequent. For 1995, the GS-9 level ranged from $29,405 to $38,228 per year.

Salaries at local, state, and federal levels are base salaries and do not include other job-related income. Officers in many agencies earn hazardous duty pay, which is calculated as a percentage of the base salary. In some departments, officers who work the evening or night shift are paid more than officers who work the day shift. Overtime pay can be a considerable amount and can result from court appearances, depositions, and other assignments. An important benefit for law enforcement officers is that in many departments, one can retire after 20 years.

CONCLUSION

Availability of law enforcement positions is expected to continue for some time (Bureau of Labor Statistics, 1992), largely because of the perceived increase in the crime rate and legislative initiatives to control crime. Department of Labor data, however, also show that occupational growth in corrections is expected to exceed the growth in policing (Bureau of Labor Statistics, 1992:72,81). Therefore, competition for law enforcement positions is expected to be great. The information provided in this chapter is designed to assist law enforcement applicants in maximizing their hiring potential.

FEDERAL LAW ENFORCEMENT—ADDRESSES

Use the addresses below if the agency does not have a field office in your area.

1. Bureau of Alcohol, Tobacco, and
   Firearms
   Personnel Staffing Specialist
   Personnel Division, Room 1215
   1200 Pennsylvania Avenue, NW
   Washington, DC 20226

   Positions: Special Agent; Inspector

2. Department of Commerce
   Office of the Inspector General
   ATTN: Personnel Office

   14th Street and Constitution Avenue,
   NW, H7713
   Washington, DC 20230

   Position: Criminal Investigator

3. Department of Defense
   Defense Investigative Service
   Personnel Operations Division
   1900 Half Street, NW
   Washington, DC 20324

   Position: Special Agent/Investigator

4. Department of Health and Human
    Services
    200 Independence Avenue, SW
    Washington, DC 20201

    Position: Criminal Investigator

5. Department of State
    Bureau of Diplomatic Security
    2121 Virginia Avenue, NW
    Washington, DC 20522

    Positions: Special Agent; Security
    Officer

6. Department of the Interior
    National Park Service
    18th and C Streets, NW
    Washington, DC 20013

    Position: Park Police Officer

7. Department of the Interior
    Bureau of Indian Affairs
    Division of Personnel Management
    1951 Constitution Avenue, NW
    Washington, DC 20240

    Position: Criminal Investigator

8. Drug Enforcement Administration
    Office of Personnel
    600–700 Army-Navy Drive
    Arlington, VA 22202

    Position: Special Agent

9. Federal Bureau of Investigation
    9th Street and Pennsylvania, NW
    Washington, DC 20535

    Position: Special Agent

10. Immigration and Naturalization
    Service
    Personnel Division
    425 Eye Street, NW, Room 6032
    Washington, DC 20536

    Positions: Border Patrol Agent;
    Special Agent; Immigration
    Inspector

11. Internal Revenue Service
    1111 Constitution Avenue, NW
    Washington, DC 20224

    Positions: Special Agent; Security
    Inspector

12. United States Marshals Service
    600 Army-Navy Drive
    Arlington, VA 22202

    Position: Deputy U.S. Marshal

13. United States Coast Guard
    2100 Second Street, SW
    Washington, DC 20590

    Position: Maritime Law Enforcement
    Officer

14. United States Customs
    Office of Human Resources
    Servicewide Special Emphasis
        Program Coordinator
    2120 L Street, Room 7402
    Washington, DC 20229

    Positions: Inspector; Criminal
    Investigator; Customs Investigator;
    Special Agent; Intelligence
    Research Officer

15. United States Postal Service
    475 L'Enfant Plaza West, SW
    Washington, DC 20260

    Position: Postal Inspector

16. United States Secret Service
    1800 G Street, NW
    Washington, DC 20223

    Position: Special Agent; Uniformed
    Division

To learn of job openings in law enforcement subscribe to one of the following:

1. Word of Mouth Advantage
   Attn: Shane L. Williams
   1920 S. Ranney Road
   East Jordan, Michigan 49727

   Telephone: 800-880-9018

   Rates (1995): $49.95 for 13 monthly issues; $29.95 for 7 monthly issues; $18.95 for 4 monthly issues

2. National Employment Listing Service
   Criminal Justice Center
   Sam Houston State University
   Huntsville, Texas 77341-1692

   Telephone: 409-294-1653

   Rates (1993): $30.00 for 12 monthly issues; $17.50 for 6 monthly issues

For suggestions on completing the SF-171 (federal application), see Armstrong, Gordon and Frank Schmalleger (1994). *Career Paths: A Guide to Jobs in Federal Law Enforcement.* Englewood Cliffs, NJ: Regents/ Prentice Hall.

REFERENCES

BUREAU OF LABOR STATISTICS, United States Department of Labor. (1992). *Outlook: 1990–2005.* Bulletin 2402 (May). Washington, D.C.: United States Government Printing Office.

CARTER, DAVID L. AND ALLEN D. SAPP. (1990). "The Evolution of Higher Education in Law Enforcement: Preliminary Findings from a National Study," *Journal of Criminal Justice Education* 1:59–85.

———. (1988). "The State of Police Education: Critical Findings," *Police Executive Research Forum* 20:3–8.

GRIESINGER, GEORGE W. (1979). *Civil Service Systems: Their Impact on Police Administration.* Washington, D.C.: United States Government Printing Office.

HALE, DONNA C. AND STACEY M. WYLAND. (1993). "Dragons and Dinosaurs: The Plight of Patrol Women," *Police forum* April:1–6.

MARTIN, SUSAN E. (1989). "Female Officers on the Move. A Report on Women in Policing," in *Critical Issues in Policing: Contemporary Readings*, 2nd ed., Roger G. Dunham and Geoffrey P. Alpert, eds., pp. 327–347. Prospect Heights, IL: Waveland.

STINCHOMB, JAMES. (1992). *Opportunity in Law Enforcement and Criminal Justice Careers.* Lincolnwood, IL: VGM Career Horizons.

SULLIVAN, PEGGY S. (1989). "Minority Officers: Current Issues," in *Critical Issues in Policing: Contemporary Readings*, Roger G. Dunham and Geoffrey P. Alpert, eds., pp. 331–345. Prospect Heights, IL: Waveland.

QUESTIONS FOR THOUGHT AND DISCUSSION

1. What is the recruitment and application process that one must go through to obtain a law enforcement job? Discuss how long this process is and how an applicant might prepare himself or herself for it.
2. What are the general qualifications needed to obtain a law enforcement job? Why is advanced planning so important?

SUGGESTIONS FOR FURTHER READING

ROBERT DELUCIA AND THOMAS DOYLE, *Career Planning in Criminal Justice*, 2nd ed., Cincinnati, OH: Anderson Publications, Inc., 1994.

ROGER DUNHAM AND GEOFFREY ALPERT, *Critical Issues in Policing*. Prospect Heights, IL: Waveland Press, 1993.

J. SCOTT HARR AND KAREN HESS, *Seeking Employment in Law Enforcement, Private Security, and Related Fields*. St. Paul, MN: West Publishing Company, 1992.

GEORGE KELLING, *"Police and Communities: The Quiet Revolution," Perspectives on Policing*. Washington D.C.: National Institute of Justice. June, 1988.

ELLEN SCRIVNER, *"Controlling Police Use of Excessive Force: The Role of the Police Psychologist," Research in Brief*. Washington D.C.: National Institute of Justice. October, 1994.

SAMUEL WALKER, *Police in America*, 2nd ed., New York, New York: McGraw-Hill, 1992.

SECTION 3

Adjudication and Sentencing

INTRODUCTION

The courts are at the core of the criminal justice system. They are among the most controversial, most powerful, and perhaps the least understood and least studied components of the criminal justice system. In this section, we examine the roles of some of the key players in the judiciary process and analyze some of the major issues.

In selection one, "The Judicial Process: Prosecutors and Courts," an overview of the court and its role in the criminal justice system is presented. In addition, the functions of the prosecutor, the defense attorney, and the grand jury are discussed.

Selection two, "Why Prosecutors Misbehave," analyzes the issue of misconduct by prosecutors. The authors argue that the temptation to cross over the allowable ethical limit must often seem irresistible in that it provides a distinct advantage in assisting the prosecutor in winning his or her case. This reading is important because the prosecutor's role provides the link between the law enforcement and adjudicatory processes.

In selection three, "The Criminal Lawyer's "Different Mission": Reflections on the Right to Present a False Case," Harry I. Subin, writing in the *Georgetown Journal of Legal Ethics*, discusses dilemmas encountered in his representation of a client in a rape case. Ethical and practical issues are raised with reference to just how far a defense attorney should go in representing a client. This reading raises a fundamental issue for defense attorneys concerning the role that "truth" should play in a defense strategy.

In selection four, entitled "Sentencing," law professor Richard Singer describes the recent history of sentencing in America, gives an overview of recent changes in sentencing laws and practices, and provides a summary of the arguments made by opponents and proponents of those recent changes. The author debates the ethics of indeterminent sentences, the purposes of sentencing, and whether sentences should be influenced by the size of the prison population.

The right to a trial by jury is one of the most sacred rights of American citizens. Selection five, "Trial by Jury in the United States," is derived from a report of a young French lawyer, Alexis de Tocqueville, who arrived in the United States in 1831 with an official mission to study American prisons. His personal mission was to satisfy his curiosity about this new experiment in democracy. In this selection from his report to the French government, he provides a view of the complexity of the American jury system as a political institution.

New York *Daily News* writer Sheila Anne Feeney examines how lawyers choose a sympathetic jury in selection six, entitled "Twelve Good Reasons." She draws upon interviews with lawyers, judges, and jury-selection consultants to illustrate how stereotypes, generalizations, and sometimes racist assumptions are used to exclude prospective jurors. She raises a serious question concerning the effectiveness of excluding prospective jurors.

The seventh reading, "Ethics in the Courts," written by Joycelyn M. Pollock, addresses a vital issue concerning the courts today: a formal code of ethics for judges and lawyers. Many times we wonder if the justice system is really just and if lawyers and judges actually follow ethical principles. Highly publicized trials, such as Watergate and the O.J. Simpson trial, seem to expose an unethical side of the justice system and its officers. Joycelyn Pollock discusses the low level of confidence the public has in the justice system, a formal code of ethics for lawyers and judges, and some of the ethical dilemmas faced by officers of the court. While all officers of the court are sworn to uphold the highest principles of the law, day-to-day operations, politics, and bureaucracy all regularly come into conflict with ethical principles.

Selection eight, "Careers in the Courts" by Robert C. Delucia and Thomas J. Doyle, describes career opportunities in the court system, including duties and qualifications for positions of attorneys, judges, court clerks, victim-witness counselors, court stenographers, and bailiffs, among others.

THE JUDICIAL PROCESS

Prosecutors and Courts

Bureau of Justice Statistics

The Courts Have Several Functions in Addition to Deciding Whether Laws Have Been Violated

The courts—

- settle disputes between legal entities (persons, corporations, etc.).
- invoke sanctions against law violations.
- decide whether acts of the legislative and executive branches are constitutional.

In deciding about violations of the law the courts must apply the law to the facts of each case. The courts affect policy in deciding individual cases by handing down decisions about how the laws should be interpreted and carried out. Decisions of the appellate courts are the ones most likely to have policy impact.

Using an Arm of the State to Settle Disputes Is a Relatively New Concept

Until the Middle Ages disputes between individuals, clans, and families, including those involving criminal acts, were handled privately. Over time, acts such as murder, rape, robbery, larceny, and fraud came to be regarded as crimes against the entire community, and the State intervened on its behalf. Today in the United States the courts handle both civil actions (disputes between individuals or organizations) and criminal actions.

An Independent Judiciary Is a Basic Concept of the U.S. System of Government

To establish its independence and impartiality, the judiciary was created as a separate branch of government co-equal to the executive and the legislative branches. Insulation of the courts from political pressure is attempted through—

From *Report to the Nation on Crime and Justice*, Bureau of Justice Statistics, U.S. Department of Justice, March 1988, pp. 81–82, 71–72, 74–75.

- the separation of powers doctrine.
- established tenure for judges.
- legislative safeguards.
- the canons of legal ethics.

Courts are without the power of enforcement. The executive branch must enforce their decisions. Furthermore, the courts must request that the legislature provide them with the resources needed to conduct their business.

Each State Has a System of Trial and Appeals Courts

Generally, State court systems are organized according to three basic levels of jurisdiction:

- **Courts of limited and special jurisdiction** are authorized to hear only less serious cases (misdemeanors and/or civil suits that involve small amounts of money) or to hear special types of cases such as divorce or probate suits. Such courts include traffic courts, municipal courts, family courts, small claims courts, magistrate courts, and probate courts.
- **Courts of general jurisdiction**, also called major trial courts, are unlimited in the civil or criminal cases they are authorized to hear. Almost all cases originate in the courts of limited or special jurisdiction. Most serious criminal cases are handled by courts of general jurisdiction.
- **Appellate courts** are divided into two groups, intermediate appeals courts, which hear some or all appeals that are subject to review by the court of last resort, and courts of last resort, which have jurisdiction over final appeals from courts of original jurisdiction, intermediate appeals courts, or administrative agencies. As of 1985, 36 States had intermediate appellate courts, but all States had courts of last resort.

The U.S. Constitution Created the U.S. Supreme Court and Authorized the Congress to Establish Lower Courts as Needed

The Federal court system now consists of various special courts. U.S. district courts (general jurisdiction courts), U.S. courts of appeals (intermediate appellate courts that receive appeals from the district courts and Federal administrative agencies), and the U.S. Supreme Court (the court of last resort). Organized on a regional basis are U.S. courts of appeals for each of 11 circuits and the District of Columbia. In Federal trial courts (the 94 U.S. district courts) more than 300,000 cases were filed in 1985; there was one criminal case for every seven civil cases. In 1985 more than half the criminal cases in district courts were for embezzlement, fraud, forgery and counterfeiting, traffic, or drug offenses.

Court Organization Varies Greatly Among the States

State courts of general jurisdiction are organized by districts, counties, dual districts, or a combination of counties and districts. In some States the courts established by the State are funded and controlled locally. In others the court of last resort may have some budgetary or administrative oversight over the entire State court system. Even within States there is considerable lack of uniformity in the roles, organization, and procedures of the courts. This has led to significant momentum among States to form "unified" court systems to provide in varying degrees, for uniform administration of the courts, and, in many cases, for the consolidation of diverse courts of limited and special jurisdiction.

Most Felony Cases Are Brought in State and Local Courts

The traditional criminal offenses under the English common law have been adopted, in one form or another, in the criminal laws of each of the States. Most cases involving "common law" crimes are brought to trial in State or local courts. Persons charged with misdemeanors are usually tried in courts of limited jurisdiction. Those charged with felonies (more serious crimes) are tried in courts of general jurisdiction.

In all States criminal defendants may appeal most decisions of criminal courts of limited jurisdiction; the avenue of appeal usually ends with the State supreme court. However, the U.S. Supreme Court may elect to hear the case if the appeal is based on an alleged violation of the Constitutional rights of the defendant.

State Courts Process a Large Volume of Cases, Many of Them Minor

In 1983, 46 States and the District of Columbia reported more than 80 million cases filed in State and local courts. About 70% were traffic-related cases, 16% were civil cases (torts, contracts, small claims, etc.), 13% were criminal cases, and 1% were juvenile cases. Civil and criminal cases both appear to be increasing. Of 39 States that reported civil filings for 1978 and 1983, 32 had increases. Of the 36 States that reported criminal filings for both years, 33 showed an increase in the volume of criminal filings.

In the 24 States that could report, felony filings comprised from 5% to 32% of total criminal filings with a median of 9%.

Victims and Witnesses Are Taking a More Significant Part in the Prosecution of Felons

Recent attention to crime victims has spurred the development of legislation and services that are more responsive to victims.

- Some States have raised witness fees from $5–10 per day in trial to $20–30 per day, established procedures for victim and witness notification of court proceedings, and guaranteed the right to speedy disposition of cases.
- 9 States and the Federal Government have comprehensive bills of rights for victims.
- 39 States and the Federal Government have laws or guidelines requiring that victims and witnesses be notified of the scheduling and cancellation of criminal proceedings.
- 33 States and the Federal Government allow victims to participate in criminal proceedings via oral or written testimony.

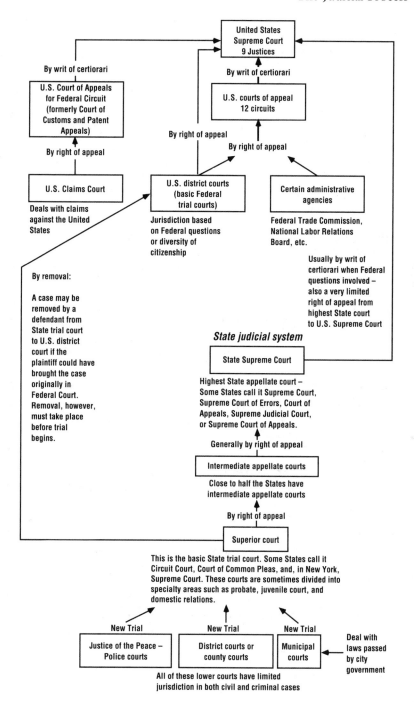

United States
Supreme Court
9 Justices

By writ of certiorari

U.S. Court of Appeals
for Federal Circuit
(formerly Court of
Customs and Patent
Appeals)

By writ of certiorari

U.S. courts of appeal
12 circuits

By right of appeal

By right of appeal

By right of appeal

U.S. Claims Court

U.S. district courts
(basic Federal
trial courts)

Certain administrative
agencies

Deals with claims
against the United
States

Jurisdiction based
on Federal questions
or diversity of
citizenship

Federal Trade Commission,
National Labor Relations
Board, etc.

Usually by writ of
certiorari when Federal
questions involved –
also a very limited
right of appeal from
highest State court
to U.S. Supreme Court

By removal:

A case may be
removed by a
defendant from
State trial court
to U.S. district
court if the
plaintiff could have
brought the case
originally in
Federal Court.
Removal, however,
must take place
before trial
begins.

State judicial system

State Supreme Court

Highest State appellate court –
Some States call it Supreme Court,
Supreme Court of Errors, Court of
Appeals, Supreme Judicial Court,
or Supreme Court of Appeals.

Generally by right of appeal

Intermediate appellate courts

Close to half the States have
intermediate appellate courts

By right of appeal

Superior court

This is the basic State trial court. Some States call it
Circuit Court, Court of Common Pleas, and, in New York,
Supreme Court. These courts are sometimes divided into
specialty areas such as probate, juvenile court, and
domestic relations.

New Trial

New Trial

New Trial

Justice of the Peace –
Police courts

District courts or
county courts

Municipal
courts

Deal with
laws passed
by city
government

All of these lower courts have limited
jurisdiction in both civil and criminal cases

Courts at various levels of government interact in many ways

Differences in how prosecutors handle felony cases can be seen in 4 jurisdictions

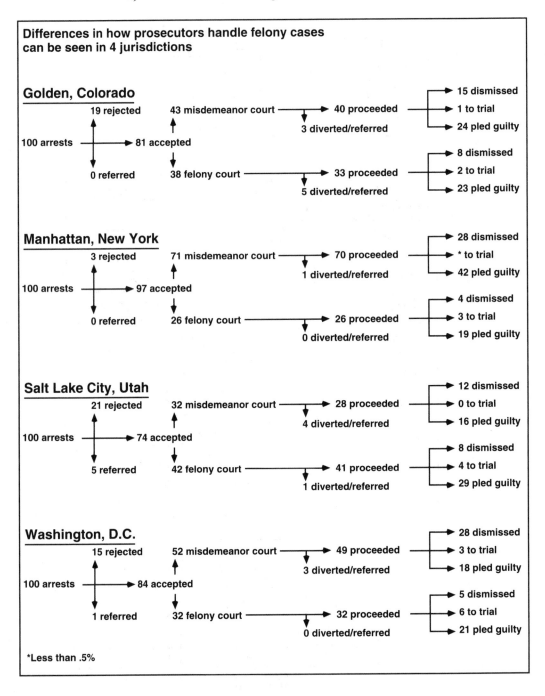

Golden, Colorado

100 arrests → 81 accepted

19 rejected

0 referred

43 misdemeanor court → 40 proceeded
3 diverted/referred
- 15 dismissed
- 1 to trial
- 24 pled guilty

38 felony court → 33 proceeded
5 diverted/referred
- 8 dismissed
- 2 to trial
- 23 pled guilty

Manhattan, New York

100 arrests → 97 accepted

3 rejected

0 referred

71 misdemeanor court → 70 proceeded
1 diverted/referred
- 28 dismissed
- * to trial
- 42 pled guilty

26 felony court → 26 proceeded
0 diverted/referred
- 4 dismissed
- 3 to trial
- 19 pled guilty

Salt Lake City, Utah

100 arrests → 74 accepted

21 rejected

5 referred

32 misdemeanor court → 28 proceeded
4 diverted/referred
- 12 dismissed
- 0 to trial
- 16 pled guilty

42 felony court → 41 proceeded
1 diverted/referred
- 8 dismissed
- 4 to trial
- 29 pled guilty

Washington, D.C.

100 arrests → 84 accepted

15 rejected

1 referred

52 misdemeanor court → 49 proceeded
3 diverted/referred
- 28 dismissed
- 3 to trial
- 18 pled guilty

32 felony court → 32 proceeded
0 diverted/referred
- 5 dismissed
- 6 to trial
- 21 pled guilty

*Less than .5%

THE PROSECUTOR PROVIDES THE LINK BETWEEN THE LAW ENFORCEMENT AND ADJUDICATORY PROCESSES

The Separate System of Justice for Juveniles Often Operates Within the Existing Court Organization

Jurisdiction over juvenile delinquency, dependent or neglected children, and related matters is vested in various types of courts. In many States the juvenile court is a division of the court of general jurisdiction. A few States have statewide systems of juvenile or family courts. Juvenile jurisdiction is vested in the courts of general jurisdiction in some counties and in separate juvenile courts or courts of limited jurisdiction in others.

The American Prosecutor Is Unique in the World

First, the American prosecutor is a public prosecutor representing the people in matters of criminal law. Historically, European societies viewed crimes as wrongs against an individual whose claims could be pressed through private prosecution. Second, the American prosecutor is usually a local official, reflecting the development of autonomous local governments in the colonies. Finally, as an elected official, the local American prosecutor is responsible to the voters.

Prosecution Is the Function of Representing the People in Criminal Cases

After the police arrest a suspect, the prosecutor coordinates the government's response to crime—from the initial screening, when the prosecutor decides whether or not to press charges, through trial. In some instances, it continues through sentencing with the presentation of sentencing recommendations.

Prosecutors have been accorded much discretion in carrying out their responsibilities. They make many of the decisions that determine whether a case will proceed through the criminal justice process.

Prosecution Is Predominantly a State and Local Function

Prosecuting officials include State, district, county, prosecuting, and commonwealth attorneys; corporation counsels; circuit solicitors; attorneys general; and U.S. attorneys. Prosecution is carried out by more than 8,000 State, county, municipal, and township prosecution agencies. In all but five States, local prosecutors are elected officials. Many small jurisdictions engage a part-time prosecutor who also maintains a private law practice. In some areas police share the charging responsibility of local prosecutors. Prosecutors in urban jurisdictions often have offices staffed by many full-time assistants. Each State has an office of the attorney general, which has jurisdiction over all matters involving State law but generally, unless specifically requested, is not involved in local prosecution. Federal prosecution is the responsibility of 93 U.S. attorneys who are appointed by the President subject to confirmation by the Senate.

The Decision to Charge Is Generally a Function of the Prosecutor

Results of a 1981 survey of police and prosecution agencies in localities of over 100,000 indicate that police file initial charges in half the jurisdictions surveyed. This arrangement, sometimes referred to as the police court, is not commonly found in the larger urban areas that account for most of the UCR Index crime. Usually, once an arrest is made and the case is referred to the prosecutor, most prosecutors screen cases to see if they merit prosecution. The prosecutor can refuse to prosecute, for example, because of insufficient evidence. The decision to charge is not usually reviewable by any other branch of government.

Some Prosecutors Accept Almost All Cases for Prosecution; Others Screen Out Many Cases

Some prosecutors have screening units designed to reject cases at the earliest possible point. Others tend to accept most arrests, more of which are dismissed by judges later in the adjudication process. Most prosecutor offices fall somewhere between these two extremes.

Arrest deposition patterns in 16 jurisdictions range from 0 to 47% of arrests rejected for prosecution. Jurisdictions with high rejection rates generally were found to have lower rates of dismissal at later stages of the criminal process. Conversely, jurisdictions that accepted most or all arrests usually had high dismissal rates.

Prosecutorial Screening Practices Are of Several Distinct Types

Several studies conclude that screening decisions consider—

- evidentiary factors.
- the views of the prosecutor on key criminal justice issues.
- the political and social environment in which the prosecutor functions.
- the resource constraints and organization of prosecutorial operations.

Jacoby's study confirmed the presence of at least three policies that affect the screening decision:

- Legal sufficiency—an arrest is accepted for prosecution if, on routine review of the arrest, the minimum legal elements of a case are present.
- System efficiency—arrests are disposed as quickly as possible by the fastest means possible, which are rejections, dismissals, and pleas.
- Trial sufficiency—the prosecutor accepts only those arrests for which, in his or her view, there is sufficient evidence to convict in court.

The Official Accusation in Felony Cases Is a Grand Jury Indictment or a Prosecutor's Bill of Information

According to Jacoby, the accusatory process usually follows one of four paths:
- arrest to preliminary hearing for bindover to grand jury for indictment
- arrest to grand jury for indictment

- arrest to preliminary hearing to a bill of information
- a combination of the above at the prosecutor's discretion

Whatever the method of accusation, the State must demonstrate only that there is probable cause to support the charge.

The Preliminary Hearing Is Used in Some Jurisdictions to Determine Probable Cause

The purpose of the hearing is to see if there is probable cause to believe a crime has been committed and that the defendant committed it. Evidence may be presented by both the prosecution and the defense. On a finding of probable cause the defendant is held to answer in the next stage of a felony proceeding.

The Grand Jury Emerged From the American Revolution as the People's Protection Against Oppressive Prosecution by the State

Today, the grand jury is a group of ordinary citizens, usually no more than 23, which has both accusatory and investigative functions. The jury's proceedings are secret and not adversarial so that most rules of evidence for trials do not apply. Usually, evidence is presented by the prosecutor who brings a case to the grand jury's attention. However, in some States the grand jury is used primarily to investigate issues of public corruption and organized crime.

Some States Do Not Require a Grand Jury Indictment to Initiate Prosecutions

Grand Jury Indictment Required	Grand Jury Indictment Optional
All Crimes	Arizona
New Jersey	Arkansas
South Carolina	California
Tennessee	Colorado
Virginia	Idaho
	Illinois
All Felonies	Indiana
Alabama	Iowa
Alaska	Kansas
Delaware	Maryland
District of Columbia	Michigan
Georgia	Missouri
Hawaii	Montana
Kentucky	Nebraska
Maine	Nevada
Mississippi	New Mexico

Grand Jury Indictment Required	Grand Jury Indictment Optional
New Hampshire	North Dakota
New York	Oklahoma
North Carolina	Oregon
Ohio	South Dakota
Texas	Utah
West Virginia	Vermont
	Washington
Capital Crimes Only	Wisconsin
Connecticut	Wyoming
Florida	
Louisiana	***Grand Jury Lacks Authority to Indict***
Massachusetts	Pennsylvania
Minnesota	
Rhode Island	

Note: With the exception of capital cases a defendant can always waive the right to an indictment. Thus, the requirement for an indictment to initiate prosecution exists only in the absence of a waiver.

Source: Deborah Day Emerson, *Grand jury reform: A review of key issues*, National Institute of Justice, U.S. Department of Justice, January 1983.

The Secrecy of the Grand Jury Is a Matter of Controversy

Critics of the grand jury process suggest it denies due process and equal protection under the law and exists only to serve the prosecutor. Recent criticisms have fostered a number of reforms requiring due process protections for persons under investigation and for witnesses; requiring improvements in the quality and quantity of evidence presented; and opening the proceeding to outside review. While there is much variation in the nature and implementation of reforms, 15 States have enacted laws affording the right to counsel, and 10 States require evidentiary standards approaching the requirements imposed at trial.

The Defense Attorney's Function Is to Protect the Defendant's Legal Rights and to be the Defendant's Advocate in the Adversary Process

Defendants have the right to defend themselves, but most prefer to be represented by a specialist in the law. Relatively few members of the legal profession specialize in criminal law, but lawyers who normally handle other types of legal matters may take criminal cases.

The Right to the Assistance of Counsel Is More Than the Right to Hire a Lawyer

Supreme Court decisions in *Gideon* v. *Wainwright* (1963) and *Argersinger* v. *Hamlin* (1972) established that the right to an attorney may not be frustrated by lack of means. For both felonies and misdemeanors for which jail or prison can be the penalty, the State must provide an attorney to any accused person who is indigent.

The institutional response to this Constitutional mandate is still evolving as States experiment with various ways to provide legal counsel for indigent defendants.

QUESTIONS FOR THOUGHT AND DISCUSSION

1. What are some of the functions of the courts, other than deciding whether laws have been violated? Are the courts the most effective way of performing these functions?
2. How are victims and witnesses today playing a more significant role in the prosecution of felons?
3. What is the role of the grand jury in the judicial process?

WHY PROSECUTORS MISBEHAVE

Bennett L. Gershman

The duties of the prosecuting attorney were well-stated in the classic opinion of Justice Sutherland fifty years ago.[1] The interest of the prosecutor, he wrote, "is not that he shall win a case, but that justice shall be done. As such, he is in a peculiar and very definite sense the servant of the law, the twofold aim of which is that guilt shall not escape or innocence suffer. He may prosecute with earnestness and vigor—indeed, he should do so. But, while he may strike hard blows, he is not at liberty to strike foul ones."[2]

Despite this admonition, prosecutors continue to strike "foul blows," perpetuating a disease which began long before Justice Sutherland's oft-quoted opinion. Indeed, instances of prosecutorial misconduct were reported at least as far back as 1897,[3] and as recently as the latest volume of the *Supreme Court Reporter*.[4] The span between these cases is replete with innumerable instances of improper conduct of the prosecutor, much of which defies belief.

One of the leading examples of outrageous conduct by a prosecutor is *Miller* v. *Pate*,[5] where the prosecutor concealed from the jury in a murder case the fact that a pair of undershorts with red stains on it, a crucial piece of evidence, were stained not by blood but by paint. Equally startling is *United States* v. *Perry*,[6] where the prosecutor, in his summation, commented on the fact that the "defendants and their counsel are completely unable to explain away their guilt."[7] Similarly, in *Dubose* v. *State*,[8] the prosecutor argued to the jury: "Now, not one sentence, not one scintilla of evidence, not one word in any way did this defendant or these attorneys challenge the credibility of the complaining witness."[9] At a time when it should be clear that constitutional and ethical standards prevent prosecutors from behaving this way,[10] we ought to question why prosecutors so frequently engage in such conduct.

Much of the above misconduct occurs in a courtroom. The terms "courtroom" or "forensic misconduct" have never been precisely defined. One commentator describes courtroom misconduct as those "types of misconduct which involve efforts to influence the jury through various sorts of inadmissible evidence."[11] Another commentator suggests

From Bennett Gershman, "Why Prosecutors Misbehave," in M. Braswell, B.R. McCarthy, and B.J. McCarthy, *Justice, Crime, and Ethics*. Cincinnati, OH: Anderson Publishing Company, 1991. Used with permission of the publisher.

that forensic misconduct "may be generally defined as any activity by the prosecutor which tends to divert the jury from making its determination of guilt or innocence by weighing the legally admitted evidence in the manner prescribed by law."[12] For purposes of this analysis, the latter definition applies, as it encompasses a broader array of behavior which can be classed as misconduct. As will be seen, prosecutorial misconduct can occur even without the use of inadmissible evidence.

This article will address two aspects of the problem of courtroom misconduct. First, it will discuss why prosecutors engage in courtroom misconduct, and then why our present system offers little incentive to a prosecutor to change his behavior.

WHY MISCONDUCT OCCURS

Intuition tells us that the reason so much courtroom misconduct by the prosecutor[13] occurs is quite simple: it works. From my ten years of experience as a prosecutor, I would hypothesize that most prosecutors deny that misconduct is helpful in winning a case. Indeed, there is a strong philosophical argument that prosecutorial misconduct corrupts the judicial system, thereby robbing it of its legitimacy. In this regard, one would probably be hard pressed to find a prosecutor who would even mention that he would consider the thought of some form of misconduct.

Nonetheless, all of this talk is merely academic, because, as we know, if only from the thousands of cases in the reports, courtroom misconduct does occur. If the prosecutor did not believe it would be effective to stretch his argument to the ethical limit and then risk going beyond that ethical limit, he would not take the risk.

Intuition aside, however, several studies have shown the importance of oral advocacy in the courtroom, as well as the effect produced by such conduct. For example, the student of trial advocacy often is told of the importance of the opening statement. Prosecutors would undoubtedly agree that the opening statement is indeed crucial. In a University of Kansas study,[14] the importance of the opening statement was confirmed. From this study, the authors concluded that, in the course of any given trial,[15] the jurors were affected most by the first strong presentation which they saw. This finding leads to the conclusion that if a prosecutor were to present a particularly strong opening argument, the jury would favor the prosecution throughout the trial. Alternatively, if the prosecutor were to provide a weak opening statement, followed by a strong opening statement by the defense, then, according to the authors, the jury would favor the defense during the trial. It thus becomes evident that the prosecutor will be best served by making the strongest opening argument possible, and thereby assist the jury in gaining a better insight into what they are about to hear and see. The opportunity for the prosecutor to influence the jury at this point in the trial is considerable, and virtually all prosecutors would probably attempt to use this opportunity to their advantage, even if the circumstances do not call for lengthy or dramatic opening remarks.[16]

An additional aspect of the prosecutor's power over the jury is suggested in a University of North Carolina study.[17] This study found that the more arguments counsel raises with respect to the different substantive arguments offered, the more the jury will believe in that party's case. Moreover, this study found that there is not necessarily a correlation between the amount of objective information in the communication and the persuasiveness of the presentation.

For the trial attorney, then, this study clearly points to the advantage of raising as many issues as possible at trial. For the prosecutor, the two studies taken together would dictate an "action packed" opening statement, containing as many arguments that can be mustered, even those which might be irrelevant or unnecessary to convince the jury of the defendant's guilt. The second study would also dictate the same strategy for the closing argument. Consequently, a prosecutor who, through use of these techniques, attempts to assure that the jury knows his case may, despite violating ethical standards to seek justice,[18] be "rewarded" with a guilty verdict. Thus, one begins to perceive the incentive that leads the prosecutor to misbehave in the courtroom.[19]

Similar incentives can be seen with respect to the complex problem of controlling evidence to which they jury may have access. It is common knowledge that, in the course of any trial, statements frequently are made by the attorneys or witnesses, despite the fact these statements may not be admissible as evidence. Following such a statement, the trial judge may, at the request of the opposing counsel, instruct the jury to disregard what they have heard. Most trial lawyers, if they are candid, will agree that it is virtually impossible for jurors realistically to disregard these inadmissible statements. Studies here again demonstrate that our intuition is correct and that this evidence often is considered by jurors in reaching a verdict.

For example, an interesting study conducted at the University of Washington[20] tested the effects of inadmissible evidence on the decisions of jurors. The authors of the test designed a variety of scenarios whereby some jurors heard about an incriminating piece of evidence while other jurors did not. The study found that the effect of the inadmissible evidence was directly correlated to the strength of the prosecutor's case. The authors of the study reported that when the prosecutor presented a weak case, the inadmissible evidence did in fact prejudice the jurors. Furthermore, the judge's admonition to the jurors to disregard certain evidence did not have the same effect as when the evidence had not been mentioned at all. It had a prejudicial impact anyway.

However, the study also indicated that when there was a strong prosecution case, the inadmissible evidence had little, if any, effect.[21] Nonetheless, the most significant conclusion from the study is that inadmissible evidence had its most prejudicial impact when there was little other evidence on which the jury could base a decision. In this situation, "the controversial evidence becomes quite salient in the jurors' minds."[22]

Finally, with respect to inadmissible evidence and stricken testimony, even if one were to reject all of the studies discussed, it is still clear that although "stricken testimony may tend to be rejected in open discussion, it does have an impact, perhaps even an unconscious one, on the individual juror's judgment."[23] As with previously discussed points, this factor—the unconscious effect of stricken testimony or evidence—will generally not be lost on the prosecutor who is in tune with the psychology of the jury.

The applicability of these studies to this analysis, then, is quite clear. Faced with a difficult case in which there may be a problem of proof, a prosecutor might be tempted to sway the jury by adverting to a matter which might be highly prejudicial. In this connection, another study[24] has suggested that the jury will more likely consider inadmissible evidence that favors the defendant rather than inadmissible evidence that favors conviction.[25]

Despite this factor of "defense favoritism," it is again evident that a prosecutor may find it rewarding to misconduct himself in the courtroom. Of course, a prosecutor who adopts the unethical norm and improperly allows jurors to hear inadmissible proof runs the risk of jeopardizing any resulting conviction. In a situation where the prosecutor feels there is a weak case, however, a subsequent reversal is not a particularly effective sanction when a conviction might have been difficult to achieve in the first place. Consequently, an unethical courtroom "trick" can be a very attractive idea to the prosecutor who feels he must win.[26] Additionally, there is always the possibility of another conviction even after an appellate reversal. Indeed, while a large number of cases are dismissed following remand by an appellate court, nearly one half of reversals still result in some type of conviction.[27] Therefore, a prosecutor can still succeed in obtaining a conviction even after his misconduct led to a reversal.

An additional problem in the area of prosecutor-jury interaction is the prosecutor's prestige; since the prosecutor represents the "government," jurors are more likely to believe him.[28] Put simply, prosecutors "are the good guys of the legal system,"[29] and because they have such glamour, they often may be tempted to use this advantage in an unethical manner. This presents a problem for the prosecutor in that the "average citizen may often forgive, yea urge prosecutors on in ethical indiscretions, for the end, convictions of criminals, certainly justifies in the public eye any means necessary."[30] Consequently, unless the prosecutor is a person of high integrity and is able to uphold the highest moral standards, the problem of courtroom misconduct inevitably will be tolerated by the public.

Moreover, when considering the problems facing the prosecutor, one also must consider the tremendous stress under which the prosecutor labors on a daily basis. Besides the stressful conditions faced by the ordinary courtroom litigator,[31] prosecuting attorneys, particularly those in large metropolitan areas, are faced with huge and very demanding case loads. As a result of case volume and time demands, prosecutors may not be able to take advantage of opportunities to relax and recover from the constant onslaught their emotions face every day in the courtroom."[32]

Under these highly stressful conditions, it is understandable that a prosecutor occasionally may find it difficult to face these everyday pressures and to resist temptations to behave unethically. It is not unreasonable to suggest that the conditions under which the prosecutor works can have a profound effect on his attempt to maintain high moral and ethical standards. Having established this hypothesis, one can see yet another reason why courtroom misconduct may occur.

WHY MISCONDUCT CONTINUES

Having demonstrated that courtroom misconduct may in many instances be highly effective, the question arises as to why such practices continue in our judicial system. A number of reasons may account for this phenomenon. Perhaps the most significant reason for the continued presence of prosecutorial misconduct is the harmless error doctrine. Under this doctrine, an appellate court can affirm a conviction despite the presence of serious misconduct during the trial. As Justice Traynor once stated, the "practical objective of tests of harmless error is to conserve judicial resources by enabling appellate courts to cleanse the judicial process of prejudicial error without becoming mired in harmless error."[33]

Although the definition advanced by Justice Traynor portrays the harmless error doctrine as having a more desirable consequence, this desirability is undermined when the prosecutor is able to misconduct himself without fear of sanction. Additionally, since every case is different, what constitutes harmless error in one case may be reversible error in another. Consequently, harmless error determinations do not offer any significant precedents by which prosecutors can judge the status of their behavior.

By way of illustration, consider two cases in which the prosecutor implicitly told the jury of his personal belief in the defendant's guilt. In one case, the prosecutor stated, "I have never tried a case where the evidence was so clear and convincing."[34] In the other case, the prosecutor told the jury that he did not try cases unless he was sure of them.[35] In the first case the conviction was affirmed, while in the second case the conviction was reversed. Interestingly, the court in the first case affirmed the conviction despite its belief that the "prosecutor's remarks were totally out of order."[36] Accordingly, despite making comments which were "totally out of order," the prosecutor did not suffer any penalty.

Contrasting these two cases presents clear evidence of what is perhaps the worst derivative effect of the harmless error rule. The problem is that the stronger the prosecutor's case, the more misconduct he can commit without being reversed. Indeed, in the *Shields* case, the court stated that "the guilt of the defendant was clearly established not only beyond a reasonable doubt, but well beyond any conceivable doubt."[37] For purposes of our analysis, it is clear that by deciding as they do, courts often provide little discouragement to a prosecutor who believes, and rightly so, that he does not have to be as careful about his conduct when he has a strong case. The relation of this factor to the amount of courtroom misconduct cannot be ignored.

Neither can one ignore the essential absurdity of a harmless error determination. To apply the harmless error rule, appellate judges attempt to evaluate how various evidentiary items or instances or prosecutorial misconduct may have affected the jury's verdict. Although it may be relatively simple in some cases to determine whether improper conduct during a trial was harmless, there are many instances when such an analysis cannot properly be made but nevertheless is made. For example, consider the situation when an appellate court is divided on whether or not a given error was harmless. In *United States v. Antonelli Fireworks Co.*,[38] two judges (including Judge Learned Hand) believed that the prosecutor's error was harmless. Yet, Judge Frank, the third judge sitting in the case, completely disagreed, writing a scathing dissent nearly three times the length of the majority opinion. One wonders how harmless error can be fairly applied when there is such a significant difference of opinion among highly respected members of a court as to the extent of harmfulness of trial errors. Perhaps even more interesting is the Supreme Court's reversal of the Court of Appeals for the Second Circuit's unanimous finding of harmless error in *United States v. Berger*.[39] As noted, *Berger* now represents the classic statement of the scope of the prosecutor's duties. Yet, in his majority opinion for the Second Circuit, Judge Learned Hand found the prosecutor's misconduct harmless.

The implications of these contradictory decisions are significant, for they demonstrate the utter failure of appellate courts to provide incentives for the prosecutor to control his behavior. If misconduct can be excused even when reasonable judges differ as to the extent of harm caused by such misbehavior, then very little guidance is given to a prosecutor to assist him in determining the propriety of his actions. Clearly, without such guidance, the potential for misconduct significantly increases.

The *Shields* case presents yet another factor which suggests why the prosecutor has only a limited incentive to avoid misconduct. In *Shields*, the court refused to review certain "potentially inflammatory statements" made by the prosecutor because of the failure of the defense to object.[40] Although this approach has not been uniformly applied by all courts, the implications of this technique to reject a defendant's claim are considerable. Most important, it encourages prosecutors to make remarks that they know are objectionable in the hope that defense counsel will not object. This situation recalls the previous discussion, which dealt with the effect of inadmissible evidence on jurors. Defense counsel here is in a difficult predicament. If he does not object, he ordinarily waives any appealable issue in the event of conviction. If he does object, he highlights to the jury the fact that the prosecutor has just done something which some jurors may feel is so damaging to the defendant that the defense does not want it brought out.

The dilemma of the defense attorney in this situation is confirmed by a Duke University study.[41] In that study, jurors learned of various pieces of evidence which were ruled inadmissible. The study found that when the judge admonished the jury to disregard the evidence, the bias created by that evidence was not significantly reduced.[42] Consequently, when a prejudicial remark is made by the prosecutor, defense counsel must act carefully to avoid damaging his client's case. In short, the prosecutor has yet another weapon, in this instance an arguably unfair aspect of the appellate process, which requires preservation of an appealable issue.[43]

A final point when analyzing why prosecutorial misconduct persists is the unavailability or inadequacy of penalties visited upon the prosecutor personally in the event of misconduct. Punishment in our legal system comes in varying degrees. An appellate court can punish a prosecutor by simply cautioning him not to act in the same manner again, reversing his case, or, in some cases, identifying by name the prosecutor who misconducted himself.[44] Even these punishments, however, may not be sufficient to dissuade prosecutors from acting improperly. One noteworthy case[45] describes a prosecutor who appeared before the appellate court on a misconduct issue for the third time, each instance in a different case.

Perhaps the ultimate reason for the ineffectiveness of the judicial system in curbing prosecutorial misconduct is that prosecutors are not personally liable for their misconduct. In *Imbler* v. *Pachtman*,[46] the Supreme Court held that "in initiating a prosecution and in presenting the state's case, the prosecutor is immune from a civil suit for damages under Section 1983."[47] Furthermore, prosecutors have absolute rather than a more limited, qualified, immunity. Thus, during the course of a trial, the prosecutor is absolutely shielded from any civil liability which might arise due to his misconduct, even if that misconduct was performed with malice.

There is clearly a need for some level of immunity to be accorded all government officials. Without such immunity, much of what is normally done by officials in authority might not be performed out of fear that their practices are later deemed harmful or improper. Granting prosecutors a certain level of immunity is reasonable. Allowing prosecutors to be completely shielded from civil liability in the event of misconduct, however, provides no deterrent to courtroom misconduct.

CONCLUSION

This analysis was undertaken to determine why the issue of misconduct seems so prevalent in the criminal trial. For the prosecutor, the temptation to cross over the allowable ethical limit must often be irresistible because of the distinct advantages that such misconduct creates in assisting the prosecutor to win his case by effectively influencing the jury. Most prosecutors must inevitably be subject to this temptation. It takes a constant effort on the part of every prosecutor to maintain the high moral standards which are necessary to avoid such temptations.

Despite the frequent occurrences of courtroom misconduct, appellate courts have not provided significant incentives to the prosecutor to avoid misconduct. It is not until the courts decide to take a stricter, more consistent approach to this problem that inroads will be made in the effort to end it. One solution might be to impose civil liability on the prosecutor who misconducts himself with malice. Although this will not solve the problem, it might be a step in the right direction.

ENDNOTES

1. *Berger* v.*United States*, 295 U.S. 78 (1935).
2. Id. of 88.
3. See *Dunlop* v. *United States*, 165 U.S. 486 (1897), where the prosecutor, in an obscenity case, argued to the jury "I do not believe that there are twelve men that could be gathered by the venire of this court..., except where they were bought and perjured in advance, whose verdict I would not be willing to take..." Id. at 498. Following this remark defense counsel objected, and the court held that statement to be improper.
4. See *Caldwell* v. *Mississippi*, 105 S. Ct. 2633 (1985) (improper argument to capital sentencing jury): *United States* v. *Young*, 105 S. Ct. 1038 (improper argument but not plain error).
5. 386 U.S. 1 (1967). In this case, the Supreme Court overturned the defendant's conviction after the Court of Appeals for the Seventh Circuit had upheld it. The Court noted that the prosecutor "deliberately misrepresented the truth" and that such behavior would not be tolerated under the Fourteenth Amendment. Id. at 67.
6. 643 F.2d 38 (2d Cir. 1981).
7. Id. at 51.
8. 531 S.W.2d 330 (Texas 1975)
9. Id. at 331. The court noted that the argument was clearly a comment on the failure of the defendant to testify at trial.
10. See *Griffin* v. *California*, 380 U.S. 609 (1965), where the Supreme Court applied the Fifth Amendment to the states under the Fourteenth Amendment.
11. Alschuler, "Courtroom Misconduct by Prosecutors and Trial Judges," 50 Tex. L. Rev. 627, 633 (1972).

12. Note, "The Nature and Function of Forensic Misconduct in the Prosecution of a Criminal Case," 54 Col. L. Rev. 946, 949 (1954).

13. Of course, there is also a significant amount of defense misconduct which takes place. In this respect, for an interesting article which takes a different approach than this article, see Kamm. "The Case for the Prosecutor," 13 U. Tol. L. Rev. 331 (1982), where the author notes that "courts carefully nurture the defendant's rights while cavalierly ignoring the rights of the people."

14. Pyszczynski, "The Effects of Opening Statement on Mock Jurors' Verdicts in a Simulated Criminal Trial," II *Journal of Applied Soc. Psychology* 301 (1981).

15. All of the cited studies include within the report a caveat about the value of the study when applied to a "real world" case. Nonetheless, they are still worthwhile for the purpose of this analysis.

16. In some jurisdictions, attorneys may often use the voir dire to accomplish the goal of early influence of the jury.

17. Calder, "The Relation of Cognitive and Memorial Processes to Persuasion in a Simulated Jury Trial," 4 *Journal of Applied Soc. Psychology* 62 (1974).

18. See *Model Code of Professional Responsibility* EC 7-13 (1980) ("The duty of the prosecutor is to seek justice.")

19. Of course, this may apply to other attorneys as well.

20. Sue, S., R.E. Smith, and C. Caldwell, "The Effects of Inadmissible Evidence on the Decisions of Simulated Jurors—A Moral Dilemma," 3 *Journal of Applied Soc. Psychology* 345 (1973).

21. Perhaps lending validity to application of the harmless error doctrine, which will be discussed later in this article.

22. Sue, note 20 *supra* at 351.

23. Hastie, *Inside the Jury* 232 (1983).

24. Thompson, "Inadmissible Evidence and Jury Verdicts," 40 *Journal of Personality & Soc. Psychology* 453 (1981).

25. The author did note that the defendant in the test case was very sympathetic and that the results may have been different with a less sympathetic defendant.

26. Of course, this begs the question: "Is there a prosecutor who would take a case to trial and then feel that he didn't have to win?" It is hoped that, in such a situation, trial would never be an option. Rather, one would hope for an early dismissal of the charges.

27. Roper, "Does Procedural Due Process Make a Difference?" 65 *Judicature 136* (1981). This article suggests that the rate of nearly 50 percent of acquittals following reversal is proof that due process is a viable means for legitimatizing the judiciary. While this is true, the fact remains that there is still a 50 percent conviction rate after reversal, thereby giving many prosecutors a second chance to convict after their original misconduct.

28. See *People* v. *McCoy*, 220 N.W.2d 456 (Mich. 1974), where the prosecutor, in attempt to bolster his case, told the jury that "the Detroit Police Department, the detectives in the Homicide Bureau, these detectives you see in court today, and myself from the prosecutor's office, we don't bring cases unless we're sure, unless we're positive." Id. at 460.

29. Emmons, "Morality and Ethics—A Prosecutor's View," *Advanced Criminal Trial Tactics* 393–407 (P.L.I. 1977).

30. Id.

31. For an interesting article on the topic, see Zimmerman, "Stress and the Trial Lawyer," 9 *Litigation 4*, 37–42 (1983).

32. For example, the Zimmerman article suggests time off from work and "celebration" with family and friends in order to effectively induce relaxation.

33. R. Traynor, *The Riddle of Harmless Error,* 81 (1970).

34. *People* v. *Shields*, 58 A.D.2d 94, 96 (N.Y.), aff'd, 46 N.Y.2d 764 (1977).

35. *People* v. *McCoy*, 220 N.W.2d 456 (Mich. 1974).

36. *Shields*, 58 A.D.2d at 97.

37. Id. at 99.

38. 155 F.2d 631 (2d Cir. 1946).

39. 73 F.2d 278 (1934), rev'd, 295 U.S. 78 (1935).

40. *Shields*, 58 A.D.2d at 97.

41. Wolf, "Effects of Inadmissible Evidence and Level of Judicial Admonishment to Disregard on the Judgments of Mock Jurors," 7 J. *Applied Soc. Psychology* 205 (1977).

42. Additionally of note is the fact that if the judge rules the evidence and did not admonish the jury, then the biasing effect of the evidence was eliminated. The authors of the study concluded that by being told not to consider certain evidence, the jurors felt a loss of freedom and that in order to retain their freedom, they considered it anyway. The psychological term for this effect is called reactance.

43. Of course, this does not mean that appeals should always be allowed, even in the absence of an appealable issue. Rather, one should confine the availability of these appeals to the narrow circumstances discussed.

44. See *United* v. *Burse*, 531 F.2d 1151 (2d Cir. 1976), where the Court named the prosecutor in the body of its opinion.

45. *United States* v. *Drummond*, 481 F.2d 62 (2d Cir. 1973).

46. 424 U.S. 409 (1976).

47. Id. at 431. 42 U.S.C. § 1983 authorizes civil actions against state officials who violate civil rights "under color of state law."

QUESTIONS FOR THOUGHT AND DISCUSSION

1. In what ways can prosecutors gain distinct advantages for winning cases by crossing over ethical limits?

2. Which aspects of the prosecutor role create the most temptation to act unethically?

3. What are some ways to curb the misconduct of prosecutors?

THE CRIMINAL LAWYER'S "DIFFERENT MISSION"

Reflections on the "Right" to Present a False Case

Harry I. Subin

About fifteen years ago I represented a man charged with rape and robbery. The victim's account was as follows: Returning from work in the early morning hours, she was accosted by a man who pointed a gun at her and took a watch from her wrist. He told her to go with him to a nearby lot, where he ordered her to lie down on the ground and disrobe. When she complained that the ground was hurting her, he took her to his apartment, located across the street. During the next hour there, he had intercourse with her. Ultimately, he said that they had to leave to avoid being discovered by the woman with whom he lived. The complainant responded that since he had gotten what he wanted, he should give her back her watch. He said that he would.

As the two left the apartment, he said he was going to get a car. Before leaving the building, however, he went to the apartment next door, leaving her to wait in the hallway. When asked why she waited, she said that she was still hoping for the return of her watch, which was a valued gift, apparently from her boyfriend.

She never did get the watch. When they left the building, the man told her to wait on the street while he got the car. At that point she went to a nearby police precinct and reported the incident. She gave a full description of the assailant that matched my client. She also accurately described the inside of his apartment. Later, in response to a note left at his apartment by the police, my client came to the precinct, and the complainant identified him. My client was released at that time but was arrested soon thereafter at his apartment, where a gun was found.[1] No watch was recovered.

My client was formally charged, at which point I entered the case. At our initial interview and those that followed it, he insisted that he had nothing whatever to do with the crime and had never even seen the woman before.[2] He stated that he had been in several places during the night in question: visiting his aunt earlier in the evening, then traveling to a bar in New Jersey, where he was during the critical hours. He gave the name of

From Harry Subin, "The Criminal Lawyer's "Different Mission": Reflections on the "Right" to Present a False Case, *Journal of Legal Ethics*, Volume 1 (1987), pp. 125–136. Reprinted with permission of the publisher, © 1988 Georgetown Journal of Legal Ethics & Georgetown University.

a man there who would corroborate this. He said that he arrived home early the next morning and met a friend. He stated that he had no idea how this woman had come to know things about him such as what the apartment looked like, that he lived with a woman, and that he was a musician, or how she could identify him. He said that he had no reason to rape anyone, since he already had a woman, and that in any event he was recovering from surgery for an old gun shot wound and could not engage in intercourse. He said he would not be so stupid as to bring a woman he had robbed and was going to rape into his own apartment.

I felt there was some strength to these arguments, and that there were questionable aspects to the complainant's story. In particular, it seemed strange that a man intending rape would be as solicitous of the victim's comfort as the woman said her assailant was at the playground. It also seemed that a person who had just been raped would flee when she had the chance to, and in any case would not be primarily concerned with the return of her watch. On balance, however, I suspected that my client was not telling me the truth. I thought the complaining witness could not possibly have known what she knew about him and his apartment, if she had not had any contact with him. True, someone else could have posed as him, and used his apartment. My client, however, could suggest no one who could have done so.[3] Moreover, that hypothesis did not explain the complainant's accurate description of him to the police. Although the identification procedure used by the police, a one person "show up," was suggestive, the woman had ample opportunity to observe her assailant during the extended incident. I could not believe that the complainant had selected my client randomly to accuse falsely of rape. By both her and my client's admission, the two had not had any previous association.

That my client was probably lying to me had two possible explanations. First, he might have been lying because he was guilty and did not see any particular advantage to himself in admitting it to me. It is embarrassing to admit that one has committed a crime, particularly one of this nature. Moreover, my client might well have feared to tell me the truth. He might have believed that I would tell others what he said, or, at the very least, that I might not be enthusiastic about representing him.

He also might have lied not because he was guilty of the offense, but because he thought the concocted story was the best one under the circumstances. The sexual encounter may have taken place voluntarily, but the woman complained to the police because she was very angry at my client for refusing to return the valued wrist watch, perhaps not stolen, but left, in my client's apartment. My client may not have been able to admit this, because he had other needs that took precedence over the particular legal one that brought him to me. For example, the client might have felt compelled to deny any involvement in the incident because to admit to having had a sexual encounter might have jeopardized his relationship with the woman with whom he lived. Likewise, he might have decided to "play lawyer," and put forward what he believed to be his best defense. Not understanding the heavy burden of proof on the state in criminal cases, he might have thought that any version of the facts that showed that he had contact with the woman would be fatal because it would simply be a case of her word against his.

I discussed all of these matters with the client on several occasions. Judging him a man of intelligence, with no signs of mental abnormality, I became convinced that he understood both the seriousness of his situation, and that his exculpation did not depend upon maintaining his initial story. In ensuring that he did understand that, in fact, I came close enough to suggesting the "right" answers to make me a little nervous about the line between subornation of perjury and careful witness preparation, known in the trade as "horseshedding." In the end, however, he held to his original account.

At this point the case was in equipoise for me. I had my suspicions about both the complainant's and the client's version of what had occurred, and I supposed a jury would as well. That problem was theirs, however, not mine. All I had to do was present my client's version of what occurred in the best way that I could.

Or was that all that was required? Committed to the adversarial spirit…, I decided that it was not. The "different mission" took me beyond the task of presenting my client's position in a legally correct and persuasive manner, to trying to untrack the state's case in any lawful way that occurred to me, regardless of the facts.

With that mission in mind, I concluded that it would be too risky to have the defendant simply take the stand and tell his story, even if it were true. Unless we could create an iron-clad alibi, which seemed unlikely given the strength of the complainant's identification, I thought it was much safer to attack the complainant's story, even if it were true. I felt, however, that since my client had persisted in his original story I was obligated to investigate the alibi defense, although I was fairly certain that I would not use it. My students and I therefore interviewed everyone he mentioned, traveled and timed the route he said he had followed, and attempted to find witnesses who may have seen someone else at the apartment. We discovered nothing helpful. The witness my client identified as being at the bar in New Jersey could not corroborate the client's presence there. The times the client gave were consistent with his presence at the place of the crime when the victim claimed it took place. The client's aunt verified that he had been with her, but much earlier in the evening.

Because the alibi defense was apparently hopeless, I returned to the original strategy of attempting to undermine the complainant's version of the facts. I demanded a preliminary hearing, in which the complainant would have to testify under oath to the events in question. Her version as precisely as I have described it, and she told it in an objective manner that, far from seeming contrived, convinced me that she was telling the truth. She seemed a person who, if not at home with the meanness of the streets, was resigned to it. To me that explained why she was able to react in what I perceived to be a nonstereotypical manner to the ugly events in which she had been involved.

I explained to my client that we had failed to corroborate his alibi, and that the complainant appeared to be a credible witness. I said that in my view the jury would not believe the alibi, and that if we could not obtain any other information, it might be appropriate to think about a guilty plea, which would at least limit his exposure to punishment. The case, then in the middle of the aimless drift towards resolution that typifies New York's criminal justice system, was left at that.

Some time later, however, my client called me and told me that he had new evidence; his aunt, he said, would testify that he had been with her at the time in question. I was incredulous. I reminded him that at no time during our earlier conversations had he indicated what was plainly a crucial piece of information, despite my not too subtle explanation of the elements of an alibi defense. I told him that when the aunt was initially interviewed with great care on this point, she stated that he was not with her at the time of the crime. Ultimately, I told him that I thought he was lying, and that in my view even if the jury heard the aunt's testimony, they would not believe it.

Whether it was during that session or later that the client admitted his guilt I do not recall. I do recall wondering whether, now that I knew the truth, that should make a difference in the way in which the case was handled. I certainly wished that I did not know it and began to understand, psychologically if not ethically, lawyers who do not want to know their clients' stories.

I did not pause very long to ponder the problem, however, because I concluded that knowing the truth in fact did not make a difference to my defense strategy, other than to put me on notice as to when I might be suborning perjury. Because the mission of the defense attorney was to defeat the prosecution's case, what I knew actually happened was not important otherwise. What did matter was whether a version of the "facts" could be presented that would make a jury doubt the client's guilt.

Viewed in this way, my problem was not that my client's story was false, but that it was not credible, and could not be made to appear so by legal means. To win, we would therefore have to come up with a better theory than the alibi, avoiding perjury in the process. Thus, the defense would have to be made out without the client testifying, since it would be a crime for him to assert a fabricated exculpatory theory under oath. This was not a serious problem, however, because it would not only be possible to prevail without the defendant's testimony, but it would probably be easier to do so. Not everyone is capable of lying successfully on the witness stand, and I did not have the sense that my client would be very good at it.

There were two possible defenses that could be fabricated. The first was mistaken identity. We could argue that the opportunity of the victim to observe the defendant at the time of the original encounter was limited, since it had occurred on a dark street. The woman could be made out to have been in great emotional distress during the incident.[4] Expert testimony would have to be adduced to show the hazards of eyewitness identification. We could demonstrate that an unreliable identification procedure had been used at the precinct. On the other hand, given that the complainant had spent considerable time with the assailant and had led the police back to the defendant's apartment, it seemed doubtful that the mistaken identification ploy would be successful

The second alternative, consent, was clearly preferable. It would negate the charge of rape and undermine the robbery case.[5] To prevail, all we would have to do would be to raise a reasonable doubt as to whether he had compelled the woman to have sex with him. The doubt would be based on the scenario that the woman and the defendant met, and she voluntarily returned to his apartment. Her watch, the object of the alleged robbery, was either left there by mistake or, perhaps better, was never there at all.

The consent defense could be made out entirely through cross-examination of the complainant, coupled with arguments to the jury about her lack of credibility on the issue of force. I could emphasize the parts of her story that sounded the most curious, such as the defendant's solicitude in taking his victim back to his apartment, and her waiting for her watch when she could have gone immediately to the nearby precinct that she went to later. I could point to her inability to identify the gun she claimed was used (although it was the one actually used), that the allegedly stolen watch was never found, there was no sign of physical violence, and no one heard screaming or any other signs of a struggle. I could also argue as my client had that even if he were reckless enough to rob and rape a woman across the street from his apartment, he would not be so foolish as to bring the victim there. I considered investigating the complainant's background, to take advantage of the right, unencumbered at the time, to impeach her on the basis of her prior unchastity.[6] I did not pursue this, however, because to me this device, although lawful, was fundamentally wrong. No doubt in that respect I lacked zeal, perhaps punishably so.

Even without assassinating this woman's character, however, I could argue that this was simply a case of a casual tryst that went awry. The defendant would not have to prove whether the complainant made the false charge to account for her whereabouts that evening, or to explain what happened to her missing watch. If the jury had reason to doubt the complainant's charges it would be bound to acquit the defendant.

How all of this would have played out at trial cannot be known. Predictably, the case dragged on so long that the prosecutor was forced to offer the unrefusable plea of possession of a gun. As I look back, however, I wonder how I could justify doing what I was planning to do had the case been tried. I was prepared to stand before the jury posing as an officer of the court in search of the truth, while trying to fool the jurors into believing a wholly fabricated story, i.e., that the woman had consented, when in fact she had been forced at gunpoint to have sex with the defendant. I was also prepared to demand an acquittal because the state had not met its burden of proof when, if it had not, it would have been because I made the truth look like a lie. If there is any redeeming social value in permitting an attorney to do such things, I frankly cannot discern it.

Others have discerned it, however, and while they have been criticized, they seem clearly to represent the majority view. They rely on either of two theories. The first is that the lawyer cannot possibly be sufficiently certain of the truth to impose his or her view of it on the client's case. The second is that the defense attorney need not be concerned with the truth even if he or she does know it. Both are misguided.

ENDNOTES

1. The woman was not able to make a positive identification of the gun as the weapon used in the incident.
2. A student working on the case with me photographed the complainant on the street. My client stated that he could not identify her.
3. The woman had indicated that her assailant opened the door with a key. There was no evidence of a forced entry.
4. This would be one of those safe areas in cross-examination, where the witness was damned no matter what she answered. If she testified that she was distressed, it would make my point that she was making an unreliable identification; if she testified that she was calm, no one would believe her....
5. Consent is a defense to a charge of rape. *e.g.*, N.Y. Penal Law § 130.05 (McKinney 1975 & Supp. 1987). While consent is not a defense to a robbery charge, N.Y. Penal Law § 160.00-.15 (McKinney 1975 & Supp. 1987), if the complainant could be made out to be a liar about

the rape, there was a good chance that the jury would not believe her about the stolen watch either.

6. When this case arose it was common practice to impeach the complainant in rape cases by eliciting details of her prior sexual activities. Subsequently the rules of evidence were amended to require a specific showing of relevance to the facts of the case. *N.Y. Crim. Proc. Law* § 60.42 (McKinney 1981 & Supp. 1987).

QUESTIONS FOR THOUGHT AND DISCUSSION

1. How far should defense attorneys go in presenting a false case to represent a client, and when have they gone too far?
2. What are the arguments used to debate the "truth" theory versus the "fight" theory? With which do you agree?

SENTENCING

Richard Singer

HISTORICAL BACKGROUND

Sentencing is the process by which judges impose punishment on persons convicted of crimes. The punishments imposed may range from probation without conditions to the death penalty and also include fines, community service, probation with conditions, and incarceration in jail or prison.

For most of the 20th century, all American jurisdictions had "indeterminate" sentencing systems. Criminal statutes generally authorized judges to impose a sentence from within a wide range. Probation to 5 years was a common range; probation to 25 years was not unknown. The judge's decision was usually final; appellate courts seldom considered appeals from sentencing decisions.

For defendants sentenced to prison, the judge's sentence set the outer limits, but a parole board would decide when the offender was released. The judge might have imposed a "3-to-10-year sentence," but the parole boards often had authority to release after 1 year, or after the offender had served a designated fraction (often one-third) of the sentence. Thus, whether the offender served 1 year in prison, or 3, or 5, was generally up to the parole board.

This system was called indeterminate because the prisoner's actual time in prison would not be known, or determined, until final release by the parole board. The system of indeterminate sentencing could be justified on a number of bases, but its primary theoretical rationale was that it permitted sentencing and parole release decisions to be individualized, often on the basis of the offender's rehabilitative progress or prospects.

Criminologists long accepted the view that an offender's criminal misbehavior could be analogized to a disease, which could be cured if properly treated in a proper institution. Cure became a major goal of both sentencing and incarceration; when released, the offender would enjoy a more satisfying, productive, and lawful life; he would not commit additional crimes and everyone's interests would be served. This medical model of disease

From *Crime File*, a videotape series produced by the National Institute of Justice and WETACOM through a grant from the Police Foundation. This material written by Richard Singer for the study guide to the videotape, "Sentencing." n.d.

and cure required that offenders be returned to the free world when professionals judged that they were "cured."

Treatment programs were seen as essential, and both vocational and psychological training programs were introduced into prisons. This rehabilitative outlook shaped even the vocabulary of criminal punishment. Prisons were often called "correctional" institutions; those for young adults were often called "reformatories." Indeterminate sentencing survived for so long because it could be many things to different people. For those not enamored of rehabilitation, its capacity for individualizing punishment meant that offenders seen as dangerous could be held for lengthy periods and thereby be *incapacitated*. For those concerned with *retribution*, indeterminate sentencing allowed sentences to be individualized on the basis of an assessment of each offender's unique circumstances and degree of moral guilt. Finally, the threat and possibilities of severe sentences could be seen as a deterrent to crime.

The discretions of judges and parole boards were exercised without legislative direction as to which sentencing goals were primary, or which factors should be considered in setting sentences or determining parole release. Different judges in the same courthouse could consider the same factor as either mitigating or aggravating the defendant's culpability. Thus, for example, while one judge might consider drug addiction as a mitigating factor that justified reducing the offender's sentence, another judge or parole board member might consider such information an indicator of future criminality and a reason to increase the sentence.

RECENT CHANGES IN SENTENCING

By 1970, indeterminate sentencing had come under attack. Some critics claimed that the wide, unreviewable discretions of judges and parole boards resulted in discrimination against minorities and the poor. Some were concerned about unwarranted sentencing disparities. Because sentences could not be appealed, there was nothing a prisoner could do about a disparately severe sentence. A considerable body of research demonstrated the existence of unwarranted sentencing disparities and many believed them to be inherent in indeterminate sentencing. In addition, highly publicized reviews of research on treatment programs concluded that their effectiveness could not be demonstrated; the resulting skepticism about rehabilitative programs undermined one of indeterminate sentencing's foundations.

None of these critiques of indeterminate sentencing was uncontroverted. Supporters of treatment programs argued that such programs could and do succeed, or that the evaluation research was flawed, or that programs failed because they were poorly managed, or underfunded, or targeted on the wrong categories of offenders. Judges, but not only judges, argued that sentencing disparities were not as great a problem as critics contended. First, because judges were able to consider all factors characterizing the offender, the offense, and the offender's prior criminal record, many judges argued that most sentences were soundly based and only appeared disparate. Second, because individual judges inevitably hold different opinions and values, and have different beliefs about the purpose of punishment, their sentences properly might reflect those differences.

The critics of indeterminate sentencing have successfully attacked it in many jurisdictions. Changes in sentencing laws have swept the country. Many new systems are "determinate" in that parole release has been eliminated and the duration of a prison sentence can be determined at the time of sentencing. States as different and dispersed as Maine and California, or Florida and Washington, have instituted major changes. These include the abolition of parole, the establishment of various systems of "presumptive" sentencing. A number of jurisdictions have established new administrative agencies called "sentencing commissions" and delegated authority to them to develop guidelines for sentencing.

Parole Reforms—Abolition and Guidelines

The attacks upon indeterminate sentencing moved several States to limit or eliminate the discretion of parole boards. A dozen States, including Pennsylvania, Connecticut, Maine, California, and Washington, have recently abolished their parole boards. While this has effectively eliminated the indeterminate aspect of sentencing, it has not necessarily affected the wide discretion held by judges. In the early 1970s, Maine eliminated the parole board but allowed judges to impose any sentence from within a very wide range authorized by law (e.g., probation to 15 years). The legislature provided no guidance as to the "appropriate" sentence within that range. At the other extreme, States like California abolished parole releases, but adopted detailed standards for judges' sentencing decisions. Some jurisdictions retained parole release but adopted parole guidelines. The Oregon parole board and the United States Parole Commission, among others, voluntarily adopted strict guidelines to standardize their release decisions. This reduced both the unpredictability of sentences and the *ad hoc* discretionary aspect of parole release that had bothered many critics.

Sentencing Commissions

In several States, including Minnesota, Pennsylvania, and Washington, sentencing commissions have developed comprehensive "sentencing guidelines" which attempt to standardize sentences, primarily on the basis of the offender's crime and his past criminal record. Of course, even where the legislature delegates the task of setting sentencing guidelines to a commission, it retains the right to ratify or reject the commission's proposals. The details of the guidelines systems vary substantially, as have their impacts. In Minnesota, it appears that judges have generally followed the guidelines and that sentencing disparities have been reduced. In 1984, Congress established a Federal sentencing commission to develop sentencing guidelines for the Federal system.

Presumptive Sentencing

Some of the new determinate sentencing systems provide a range within which the judge should impose sentences in ordinary cases. Others, such as North Carolina, New Jersey, and California, have established a single presumptive sentence. In California the "presumptive" sentence for a number of crimes is 3 years, but a judge may sentence an offender for either 2 or 4 years and still remain within the range authorized by the statute. In an example from Minnesota...the presumptive sentence is 49 months, but the judge may impose sentences between 45 and 53 months without leaving the range. In other States, however, that range may be much wider—20 to 50 years in Indiana for Class A felonies. If the range is too wide, one of the main reasons for removing indeterminacy—the effort to reduce disparities—may not have been achieved at all.

Not even the most restrictive of these schemes totally precludes the judge from imposing any sentence, so long as it is within the statutory minimum or maximum sentence. Even under sentencing guidelines, a judge may sentence outside the guidelines if a written statement of reasons is provided. Some States provide lists of aggravating and mitigating circumstances that may be considered in departing from the guideline sentence or range.

If the sentencing rules restrict discretion only for sentences of imprisonment but do not affect the judge's decision to imprison or not (the "in-out" decision), one purpose of the reform may be substantially frustrated. In California, for example, while the percentage of persons convicted of burglary who were sentenced to prison rose after new sentencing legislation was enacted, from 27 percent to 35 percent, nearly two-thirds of persons convicted of burglary received no prison sentence, while one-third received a prison term within relatively strict guidelines. In Minnesota, judges follow the in-out guideline in 91 to 94 percent of the cases, thereby establishing some consistency in these decisions. It could be argued that the decision whether to imprison is more important, at least in terms of disparity, than the decision of how long to imprison.

Voluntary Guidelines

Finally, many jurisdictions, such as Michigan and Denver, have experimented with "voluntary" sentencing guidelines, which provide judges with information on the "usual" sentence for the offense and the offender; the judge is not obligated to follow these guidelines. Voluntary guidelines have generally been developed by judges or by advisory committees appointed by the State's chief justice. Some judges favor voluntary guidelines, even though they believe judges should retain full discretion over each individual sentence.

ARGUMENTS AND COUNTER-ARGUMENTS

Recent changes in sentencing laws and practices have not gone unchallenged. Some, as noted above, question the premises for change and the critiques of indeterminate sentencing.

Other critics argue that retribution or "just deserts," the primary purpose of many modern sentencing laws, is philosophically unacceptable in the late 20th century, and that sentencing grids which substantially constrain judicial discretion are unfair because they forbid judges to consider mitigating factors and to act mercifully. Some also argue that the endorsement of retribution (albeit "equal" retribution) as a proper goal of sentencing has led to severely increased sentences, which these critics see as undesirable.

Another concern about the new sentencing laws is that the perceived rigidity of the statutes or guidelines enhances the discretion of the prosecutor, particularly during plea bargain negotiations. Judicial discretion at least is exercised in the open, while prosecutorial discretion is generally exercised behind closed doors.

There is another concern…If determinate sentencing systems retain "good time" (time off for good behavior) to reduce sentences, prison guards and other prison personnel may effectively become sentencers. Minnesota and most other States that have adopted determinate sentencing still provide for substantial good time; California recently enlarged the amount of good time a prisoner can earn off his determinate sentence and has therefore enlarged the discretionary power of prison officials to affect the actual duration of confinement.

Yet another criticism of sentencing reform is that it has contributed to recent increases in prison crowding, first by causing the sentencing to prison of many offenders who previously would have received probation, and second by removing the "safety valve" of early release on parole in the event of overcrowding. This problem was avoided in Minnesota, where the legislature specifically instructed the sentencing commission to take prison capacity into account when it developed the guidelines. Minnesota has entrusted to the commission the job of realigning the guidelines to avoid overcrowding if it arises. A similar provision is contained in newly enacted Federal legislation. The provision should be emulated by any State considering changes in the sentencing system unless, of course, the State's citizens are wiling to bear the financial burden of building more prisons.

The controversy over indeterminate and determinate sentencing reflects deeper arguments over the purposes of the criminal law. For the past century, those who argued for uncertainty and indeterminacy sought to use the criminal sentence as a means of crime control. They sought to frighten the potential offender, to rehabilitate the "treatable" offender, and to incapacitate the incorrigible in order to reduce victimization in society. Recent sentencing changes, while partly based on empirical disillusionment with these goals, also draw upon the retributive notion of a fair, certain, and equal punishment for all those who inflict the same harm upon society. The dispute over the purposes of criminal sanctions has persisted for centuries, and the recent changes are unlikely to resolve that dispute.

REFERENCES

AMERICAN FRIENDS SERVICE COMMITTEE. (1971.) *Struggle for Justice: A Report on Crime and Punishment in America*. New York: Hill and Wang.

BLUMSTEIN, ALFRED, JACQUELINE COHEN, SUSAN E. MARTIN, AND MICHAEL H. TONRY, eds. (1983.) *Research on Sentencing: The Search for Reform*. Washington, D.C.: National Academy Press.

FRANKEL, MARVIN. (1973.) *Criminal Sentences: Law Without Order*. New York: Hill and Wang.

ROTHMAN, DAVID. (1980.) *Conscience and Convenience: The Asylum and Its Alternatives in Progressive America*. Boston: Little, Brown.

SINGER, RICHARD G. (1979.) *Just Deserts: Sentencing Based on Equality and Desert*. Cambridge, Massachusetts: Ballinger.

TONRY, MICHAEL H., AND FRANKLIN E. ZIMRING, EDS. (1983.) *Reform and Punishment: Essays on Criminal Sentencing*. Chicago: The University of Chicago Press.

VON HIRSCH, ANDREW. (1976.) *Doing Justice: The Choice of Punishments*. New York: Hill and Wang.

QUESTIONS FOR THOUGHT AND DISCUSSION

1. What should be the purpose of sentencing—rehabilitation, deterrence, incapacitation, or retribution?
2. What is an indeterminate sentencing system, and what are the criticisms leveled against it?
3. Should sentencing decisions be influenced by the size of the prison population?

TRIAL BY JURY IN THE UNITED STATES

Alexis de Tocqueville

Since my subject has led me to speak of the administration of justice in the United States, I will not pass over it without referring to the institution of the jury. Trial by jury may be considered in two separate points of view: as a judicial, and as a political institution. If it was my purpose to inquire how far trial by jury, especially in civil cases, ensures a good administration of justice, I admit that its utility might be contested. As the jury was first established when society was in its infancy and when courts of justice merely decided simple questions of fact, it is not an easy task to adapt it to the wants of a highly civilized community when the mutual relations of men are multiplied to a surprising extent and have assumed an enlightened and intellectual character.

My present purpose is to consider the jury as a political institution; any other course would divert me from my subject. Of trial by jury considered as a judicial institution I shall here say but little. When the English adopted trial by jury, they were a semi-barbarous people; they have since become one of the most enlightened nations of the earth, and their attachment to this institution seems to have increased with their increasing cultivation. They have emigrated and colonized every part of the habitable globe; some have formed colonies, others independent states; the mother country has maintained its monarchical constitution; many of its offspring have founded powerful republics; but everywhere they have boasted of the privilege of trial by jury. They have established it, or hastened to re-establish it, in all their settlements. A judicial institution which thus obtains the suffrages of a great people for so long a series of ages, which is zealously reproduced at every stage of civilization, in all the climates of the earth, and under every form of human government, cannot be contrary to the spirit of justice.[1]

But to leave this part of the subject. It would be a very narrow view to look upon the jury as a mere judicial institution; for however great its influence may be upon the decisions of the courts, it is still greater on the destinies of society at large. The jury is, above all, a political institution, and it must be regarded in this light in order to be duly appreciated.

By the jury I mean a certain number of citizens chosen by lot and invested with a temporary right of judging. Trial by jury, as applied to the repression of crime, appears to me an eminently republican element in the government, for the following reasons.

The institution of the jury may be aristocratic or democratic, according to the class from which the jurors are taken; but it always preserves its republican character, in that it places the real direction of society in the hands of the governed, or of a portion of the governed, and not in that of the government. Force is never more than a transient element of success, and after force comes the notion of right. A government able to reach its enemies only upon a field of battle would soon be destroyed. The true sanction of political laws is to be found in penal legislation; and if that sanction is wanting, the law will sooner or later lose its cogency. He who punishes the criminal is therefore the real master of society. Now, the institution of the jury raises the people itself, or at least a class of citizens, to the bench of judges. The institution of the jury consequently invests the people, or that class of citizens, with the direction of society.

In England the jury is selected from the aristocratic portion of the nation; the aristocracy makes the laws, applies the laws, and punishes infractions of the laws; everything is established upon a consistent footing, and England may with truth be said to constitute an aristocratic republic. In the United States the same system is applied to the whole people. Every American citizen is both an eligible and a legally qualified voter. The jury system as it is understood in America appears to me to be as direct and as extreme a consequence of the sovereignty of the people as universal suffrage. They are two instruments of equal power, which contribute to the supremacy of the majority. All the sovereigns who have chosen to govern by they own authority, and to direct society instead of obeying its directions, have destroyed or enfeebled the institution of the jury. The Tudor monarchs sent to prison jurors who refused to convict, and Napoleon caused them to be selected by his agents.

However clear most of these truths may seem to be, they do not command universal assent; and in France, at least, trial by jury is still but imperfectly understood. If the question arises as to the proper qualification of jurors, it is confined to a discussion of the intelligence and knowledge of the citizens who may be returned, as if the jury was merely a judicial institution. This appears to me the least important part of the subject. The jury is pre-eminently a political institution; it should be regarded as one form of the sovereignty of the people: when that sovereignty is repudiated, it must be rejected, or it must be adapted to the laws by which that sovereignty is established. The jury is that portion of the nation to which the execution of the laws is entrusted, as the legislature is that part of the nation which makes the laws; and in order that society may be governed in a fixed and uniform manner, the list of citizens qualified to serve on juries must increase and diminish with the list of electors. This I hold to be the point of view most worthy of the attention of the legislator; all that remains is merely accessory.

I am so entirely convinced that the jury is preeminently a political institution that I still consider it in this light when it is applied in civil causes. Laws are always unstable unless they are founded upon the customs of a nation: customs are the only durable and resisting power in a people. When the jury is reserved for criminal offenses, the people witness only its occasional action in particular cases; they become accustomed to do without it in the ordinary course of life, and it is considered as an instrument, but not as the only instrument, of obtaining justice.

When, on the contrary, the jury acts also on civil causes, its application is constantly visible; it affects all the interests of the community; everyone co-operates in its work: it thus penetrates into all the usages of life, it fashions the human mind to its peculiar forms, and is gradually associated with the idea of justice itself.

The institution of the jury, if confined to criminal causes, is always in danger; but when once it is introduced into civil proceedings, it defies the aggressions of time and man. If it had been as easy to remove the jury from the customs as from the laws of England, it would have perished under the Tudors; and the civil jury did in reality at that period save the liberties of England. In whatever manner the jury be applied, it cannot fail to exercise a powerful influence upon the national character; but this influence is prodigiously increased when it is introduced into civil causes. The jury, and more especially the civil jury, serves to communicate the spirit of the judges to the minds of all the citizens; and this spirit, with the habits which attend it, is the soundest preparation for free institutions. It imbues all classes with a respect for the thing judged and with the notion of right. If these two elements be removed, the love of independence becomes a mere destructive passion. It teaches men to practice equity; every man learns to judge his neighbor as he would himself be judged. And this is especially true of the jury in civil causes; for while the number of persons who have reason to apprehend a criminal prosecution is small, everyone is liable to have a lawsuit. The jury teaches every man not to recoil before the responsibility of his own actions and impresses him with that manly confidence without which no political virtue can exist. It invests each citizen with a kind of magistracy; it makes them all feel the duties which they are bound to discharge toward society and the part which they take in its government. By obliging men to turn their attention to other affairs than their own, it rubs off that private selfishness which is the rust of society.

The jury contributes powerfully to form the judgment and to increase the natural intelligence of a people; and this, in my opinion, is its greatest advantage. It may be regarded as a gratuitous public school, ever open, in which every juror learns his rights, enters into daily communication with the most learned and enlightened members of the upper classes, and becomes practically acquainted with the laws, which are brought within the reach of his capacity by the efforts of the bar, the advice of the judge, and even the passions of the parties. I think that the practical intelligence and political good sense of the Americans are mainly attributable to the long use that they have made of the jury in civil causes.

I do not know whether the jury is useful to those who have lawsuits, but I am certain it is highly beneficial to those who judge them; and I look upon it as one of the most efficacious means for the education of the people which society can employ.

What I have said applies to all nations, but the remark I am about to make is peculiar to the Americans and to democratic communities. I have already observed that in democracies the members of the legal profession and the judicial magistrates constitute the only aristocratic body which can moderate the movements of the people. This aristocracy is invested with no physical power; it exercises its conservative influence upon the minds of men; and the most abundant source of its authority is the institution of the civil jury. In criminal causes, when society is contending against a single man, the jury is apt to look upon the judge as the passive instrument of social power and to mistrust his advice. Moreover, criminal causes turn entirely upon simple facts, which common sense can readily appreciate; upon his ground the judge and the jury are equal. Such is not the case, however, in civil causes; then the judge appears as a disinterested arbiter between the conflicting passions of the parties. The jurors look up to him with confidence and listen to him with respect, for in this instance, his intellect entirely governs theirs. It is the judge who sums up the various arguments which have wearied their memory, and who guides them through the devious course of the proceedings; he points their attention to the exact question of fact that they are called upon to decide and tells them how to answer the question of law. His influence over them is almost unlimited.

If I am called upon to explain why I am but little moved by the arguments derived from the ignorance of jurors in civil causes, I reply that in these proceedings, whenever the question to be solved is not a mere question of fact, the jury has only the semblance of a judicial body. The jury only sanctions the decision of the judge; they sanction this decision by the authority of society which they represent, and he by that of reason and of law.

In England and in America the judges exercise an influence upon criminal trials that the French judges have never possessed. The reason for this difference may easily be discovered; the English and American magistrates have established their authority in civil causes and only transfer it afterwards to tribunals of another kind, where it was not first acquired. In some cases, and they are frequently the most important ones, the American judges have the right of deciding causes alone. On these occasions they are accidentally placed in the position that the French judges habitually occupy, but their moral power is much greater; they are still surrounded by the recollection of the jury, and their judgment has almost as much authority as the voice of the community represented by that institution. Their influence extends far beyond the limits of the courts; in the recreations of private life, as well as in the turmoil of public business, in public, and in the legislative assemblies, the American judge is constantly surrounded by men who are accustomed to regard his intelligence as superior to their own; and after having exercised his power in the decision of causes, he continues to influence the habits of thought, and even the characters, of those who acted with him in his official capacity.

The jury, then, which seems to restrict the rights of the judiciary, does in reality consolidate its power; and in no country are the judges so powerful as where the people share their privileges. It is especially by means of the jury in civil causes that the American magistrates imbue even the lower classes of society with the spirit of their profession. Thus the jury, which is the most energetic means of making the people rule, is also the most efficacious means of teaching it how to rule well.

ENDNOTES

1. If it were our object to establish the utility of the jury as a judicial institution, many arguments might be brought forward, and among others the following:

   In proportion as you introduce the jury into the business of the courts, you are enabled to diminish the number of judges, which is a great advantage. When judges are very numerous, death is perpetually thinning the ranks of the judicial functionaries and leaving places vacant for newcomers. The ambition of the magistrates is therefore continually excited, and they are naturally made dependent upon the majority or the person who nominates to vacant offices; the officers of the courts then advance as do the officers of an army. This state of things is entirely contrary to the sound administration of justice and to the intentions of the legislator. The office of a judge is made inalienable in order that he may remain independent; but of what advantage is it that his independence should be protected if he be tempted to sacrifice it of his own accord? When judges are very numerous, many of them must necessarily be incapable; for a great magistrate is a man of no common powers: I do not know if a half-enlightened tribunal is not the worst of all combinations for attaining those ends which underlie the establishment of courts of justice. For my own part, I had rather submit the decision of a case to ignorant jurors directed by a skillful judge than to judges a majority of whom are imperfectly acquainted with jurisprudence and with the laws.

QUESTIONS FOR THOUGHT AND DISCUSSION

1. How did Alexis de Tocqueville assess the American jury system? Do you agree or disagree with his assessments?
2. What does the author mean by saying the jury is a political institution rather than a judicial institution?

Twelve Good Reasons

How Lawyers Judge Potential Jurors

Sheila Anne Feeney

"If a Presbyterian enters the jury box, carefully rolls up his umbrella, and calmly and critically sits down, let him go. He is cold as the grave. The Baptists are more hopeless than the Presbyterians....You do not want them on the jury, and the sooner they leave, the better."

Fifty-seven years ago, the famed criminal defense attorney Clarence Darrow wrote an *Esquire* magazine essay on the art of picking a jury. Defense lawyers would be "guilty of malpractice" for not giving the nod to an Irishman—certain to identify with an accused criminal, Darrow wrote. Similarly, he urged colleagues to pack the jury box with Jews and agnostics.

Offensive? Sure. Nonetheless, jury selection and behavior have vexed attorneys, beguiled court buffs, and miffed potential jurors since the first court gavel descended, generating not only studies and papers, but also a folklore rife with stereotypes, mythology, and superstitions.

Picking a sympathetic jury is so crucial to winning a case that sometimes lawyers hire consultants. Cathy Bennett, one of the best-known jury-selection consultants before her death last year, helped pick the Florida panel that acquitted William Kennedy Smith of rape charges. Bennett believed that asking potential jurors about definitive life experiences, about whom they admire, and then analyzing body language as they replied, was more revealing than generalizations about appearance, ethnicity, and occupation.

"We spend our lives trying to read their minds and no matter how hard we try, we just can't" sighs Mark A. Longo, a Brooklyn attorney who specializes in civil litigation. When representing a defendant in a personal injury case, Longo concedes to a weakness for middle-aged women with children ("they're skeptical people"), scientific types, engineers, and homeowners. Of the last grouping, he says, "They pay insurance premiums. And although you're absolutely not allowed to mention that fact, everyone is sophisticated enough to know" that premiums are linked to payouts.

From *New York Live*, July 25, 1993, pp.4–5. © 1993 by New York *Daily News*, L.P., reprinted with permission.

Generalizations about race, religion, relatives, and reading materials continue to be routine during *voir dire* (jury selection). "If your last name is Slotnick and your husband is a criminal defense attorney, you will never be picked as a juror."

"Ask my wife. It makes her very angry," says Barry Slotnick, who won Bernhard Goetz an acquittal on attempted murder charges.

Slotnick is the first to admit: "I'm not looking for a fair juror, I'm looking for someone who will acquit."

According to conventional wisdom, people with science backgrounds are thought to be good for the prosecution, social workers and artistic types are supposedly sympathetic to the defense.

Slotnick says he is less influenced by race and occupation that by apparel, body language, and professed habits: "People who read the *National Review* are more conservative. In the Goetz case, I would want *National Review* readers. In most others, I would not."

"I very often look for jurors who run against type," muses David Lewis, who defended Carolyn Warmus against murder charges in her first trial, which ended in a hung jury. (Warmus was later convicted in a second trial.) When Lewis represented a man accused of killing his gay lover, his lead juror was a "devout Baptist who said homosexuality was an abomination unto God." He picked her because he believed she would take her oath not to hold her prejudice against the defendant "more seriously than any other juror." His client was acquitted.

Older homemakers in traditional marriages tend to judge date-rape victims more harshly than younger women or men, and are particularly harsh if the victim has "a nontraditional lifestyle," notes Manhattan sex crimes prosecutor Linda Fairstein. It's dangerous to rely on "overgeneralizations" during *voir dire*, says Fairstein, but schools and seminars teach prosecutors to exclude people by occupation. "They tell you to pick Con Ed and phone workers—people in stable jobs for a long time."

Former Brooklyn judge and prosecutor Alan Broomer contends that race is a factor: "People who are discriminated against—be they black, obese, or physically disabled—tend to identify with the defendant." People of color in poor neighborhoods often have a "tremendous prejudice" against the police, Broomer adds.

The Supreme Court has repeatedly ruled that potential jurors may not be excluded simply because of their race, but that does not stop some attorneys from making racist assumptions. The Supreme Court has yet to render an opinion on excluding jurors by gender.

Residency is also used to form assumptions about a juror's predisposition, hence the expression "Bronx jury"—describing the borough where, it is believed, record punitive damages are handed down and accused criminals may have a better chance of acquittal. Likewise, you have "Simi Valley" juries, where police are thought to have an advantage.

Even Broomer revises his stereotype that "prejudice by blacks, for blacks" benefits criminal defendants when it comes to stereotyping Staten Island. In Richmond County, says Broomer, who served there for six months, "The blacks and Puerto Ricans are just as conservative as the whites—even more so."

Hard as it may be to believe, some people lie so they can get on a jury. But they are less likely to fib about their life experiences, however, which is why folks are so often asked about their background.

Cathy Bennett had a remarkable gift for paying attention to "verbal and nonverbal cues lawyers don't hear or see," notes Lewis, who consulted her on his cases.

"Some of us thought she was a witch." He recalls questioning a Bensonhurst woman of Italian descent on a case involving an accused gunrunner for the Irish Republican Army. "I fought like hell to keep her off on the theory that the Italians and the Irish don't get along. Everything about her—based on stereotypic thinking—was bad to me." Yet Bennett demanded he clear the woman for the jury.

Lo and behold, "the woman goes ahead and leads the jury to an acquittal. Her boyfriend gave her the book 'Trinity' to read during the trial and her boyfriend's name turns out to be Sean Cronin," marvels Lewis, laughing at the lesson he learned. His bias-busting schooling was not over yet. Several months after the trial, Sean Cronin visited Lewis because he needed a lawyer. "Sean Cronin," says Lewis, "turned out to be black."

QUESTIONS FOR THOUGHT AND DISCUSSION

1. Do you agree or disagree with our system of excluding prospective jurors? Explain why.
2. How accurately can attorneys assess the influence a juror may have on a verdict?
3. What are some of the personal characteristics used to dismiss prospective jurors? Which characteristics are appropriate and which are inappropriate?

ETHICS AND THE COURTS

Joycelyn M. Pollock

Many people refer to the criminal justice system as the criminal *injustice* system because of a perception that practices in this nation's courtrooms do not necessarily conform to ideals of justice. As mentioned in previous chapters, justice is a goal that may not necessarily be achieved by a legal system. Moreover, sometimes the day-to-day practices of the system may even be inconsistent with or violate the principles of law, further removing practice from the ideal. The basic elements of a justice system are an impartial fact-finding process and a fair and equitable resolution, with protection against error. Those who work in the justice system have ethical and moral duties to fulfill to protect this concept of justice.

Common perceptions of lawyers indicate that the public has little confidence in their ability to live up to the ideals of justice. In a Gallup survey reported in *U.S. News and World Report*, lawyers were rated as less ethical and less honest than police officers, doctors, television reporters, and funeral directors, among others. Only building contractors, politicians, and car salespeople had lower ratings than lawyers (Kelly, 1982, 29). The public's opinion of attorneys was said to have reached a new low when it was disclosed that almost all the Watergate figures were lawyers (Davis and Elliston, 1986, 43, 115). This perception of the lawyer as an amoral "hired gun" is in sharp contrast to the ideal of the lawyer as an officer of the court, sworn to uphold the ideals of justice declared sacrosanct under our system of law. Which is closer to the truth?

History indicates that the ethics of those associated with the legal process have always been suspect. Plato and Aristotle condemned the advocate because of his ability to make the truth appear false and the guilty appear innocent. This early distrust has continued throughout history; early colonial lawyers were distrusted and even punished for practicing law. For many years lawyers could not charge a fee for their services because the mercenary aspects of the profession was condemned (Papke, 1986, 32). Gradually lawyers and the profession itself were accepted, but suspicion and controversy continued in the area of fees and qualifications. Partly to counteract public antipathy, lawyers formed their own organization, the American Bar Association (ABA), in 1878. Shortly afterward, this professional organization established the first ethical guidelines for lawyers.

From Joycelyn M. Pollock, *Ethics in Crime and Justice Decisions*, Belmont, CA: Wadsworth Publishing Co. pp. 136–160, 1989. Used by permission of the publisher.

PERCEPTIONS OF JUDICIAL PROCESSING

As mentioned before, the ideal of the justice system is that two advocates of equal ability will each engage in a pursuit of truth, guided by a neutral fact finder, with the truth emerging from the contest. Actual practices in our justice system are very different. Various descriptions profess to offer a more realistic picture of the system. One approach is to use game theory to describe judicial processing. The movement of an offender from arrest to conviction is, in some respects, played like a game. Each player has a certain role to perform, with rules and responsibilities. Also, hidden agendas (covert motivations and goals) exist. The adversarial system pits the defense attorney against the prosecutor, and the judge may be considered the umpire in this contest. The judge sets down the rules and, unless there is a jury, decides who wins the contest. The rationale for the system is that the best person wins, obviously an optimistic view. If a powerful and rich defendant is able to hire the best criminal lawyer in the country complete with several assistants and investigators, the prosecuting attorney, a public servant who may have many other cases to deal with simultaneously, is faced with stiff competition. This is the exception, of course; more commonly, a defendant must rely on an overworked public defender, a young, inexperienced attorney just starting out, or an attorney who can only make criminal law profitable through high caseloads and quick turnover. In any of these cases, the defense is matched against a public office that has greater access to evidence and some investigative assistance.

A variation on game theory is offered by Blumberg (1969), who refers to the practice of law as a confidence game because both prosecutor and defense attorney conspire to appear as something they are not—adversaries in a do-or-die situation. What is more commonly the case is that the prosecutor and the defense attorney will still be working together when the client is gone; thus their primary allegiance is not to the client, but to themselves. For defense attorneys this may involve either making the case appear more difficult than it is to justify their fee or, if the client has no resources, arbitrarily concluding a case that has merit. Attorneys may use their power for reasons other than the client's interest; in the following example cited by Blumberg (1969, 329), where all actors cooperate in the conspiracy against the client:

> [Judges] will adjourn the case of an accused in jail awaiting plea or sentence if the attorney requests such action. While explicitly this may be done for some innocuous and seemingly valid reason, the tacit purpose is that pressure is being applied by the attorney for the collection of his fee, which he knows will probably not be forthcoming if the case is concluded.

The game here is to make the client believe that the advocacy system is working for him or her while in reality it is being used against him or her. Other stories are told of attorneys asking for continuances because of a missing witness, "Mr. Green" (referring to money owed to the attorney by the client). For this charade to be successful, all players in the system must cooperate; evidently in many situations they do. Great shows of anger and emotion in the courtroom help clients believe they are getting something for their money, but such performances are belied by the jocular relationship sometimes apparent between the defense attorney and the prosecutor shortly after trial or between courtroom sessions. In fact, many defense attorneys are ex-prosecutors. This is, in some respects, helpful to their clients because they know the way the prosecutor's office works and what a reasonable plea offer would be. But one also must assume that their prosecutorial experience has shaped their perceptions of clients and what would be considered fair punishments. Moreover, their continuing relationships with prosecutors overlap into their social and personal lives and, thus, it is not surprising that allegiances are more often all lawyers against civilians, rather than defense versus prosecution.

Other authors have also used the analogy of a confidence game to describe the interaction among prosecutor, defense attorney, and client. For example, Scheingold (1984, 155) writes:

> The practice of defense law is all too often a "confidence game" in which the lawyers are "double agents" who give the appearance of assiduous defense of their clients but whose real loyalty is to the criminal courts. The defendant, from this perspective, is only an episode in the attorney's enduring relationships with the prosecutors and judges whose goodwill is essential to a successful career in the defense bar.

Another perspective describes our courts as administering *bureaucratic justice*. Each individual case is seen only as one of many for the professionals who work in the system. The goal of the system—namely, bureaucratic efficiency—becomes more important than the original goal of justice. Also, because each case is part of a workload, decision making takes on a more complicated nature. For instance, a defense lawyer may be less inclined to fight very hard for a "loser" client if he or she wants a favor for another client later in the week. The prosecutor may decide not to charge a guilty person in order to get him or her to testify against someone else. In this sense, each case is not separately tried and judged, but is linked to others and processed as part of a workload. The bureaucratic system of justice is seen as developing procedures and policies that although not intentionally discriminatory, may contribute to a perception of unfairness. For instance, a major element in bureaucratic justice is the presumption of guilt, while the ideal of our justice system is a presumption of innocence. District attorneys, judges, and even defense attorneys approach each case presuming guilt and place a priority on achieving the most expeditious resolution of the case. This is the basic rationale behind plea bargaining, whether it is recognized or not; the defendant is assumed to be guilty and the negotiation is to achieve a guilty plea while bargaining for the best possible sentence—the lowest possible is the goal of the defense while the highest possible is the goal of the prosecutor. Plea bargaining is consistent with the bureaucratic value system because it is the most efficient way of getting maximum punishment for minimum work.

Descriptions of bureaucratic justice such as the following (Scheingold, 1984, 158) allow for the fact that efficiency is tempered with other values and priorities:

> The concept of bureaucratic justice…provides the most persuasive account of how the participants in criminal process reconcile legal and bureaucratic forces. "Bureaucratic justice unites the presumption of guilt with the operational morality of fairness."…All participants in the criminal process behave as if a person who is arrested is probably guilty. Nevertheless, the coercive thrust of the presumption of guilt is softened somewhat by the operational morality of fairness that leads the participants to make certain that defendants get neither more nor less than is coming to them—that defendants, in other words, get their due.

Scheingold is referring to the practice of judges, prosecutors, and defense attorneys who adapt the system to their personal standards of justice. This is exemplified by a judge who determines that an individual offender is a threat to society and so overlooks errors during trial to make sure that the individual ends up in prison. In the same way, a person who is legally guilty may get a break because it is determined that he is a decent guy who made a mistake rather than a "bad character." Moreover, in almost all cases, there may be general consensus on both sides as to what is fair punishment for any given offender. Defense attorneys who argue for unrealistically low sentences do so in a desultory and uncommitted fashion, knowing that the prosecutor would not and could not offer such a sentence. Prosecutors put up very little argument when defense attorneys ask for sentences that fit office guidelines. Instead of describing the justice system as a system that practices the presumption of innocence and takes careful steps to determine guilt, what may be more realistic is to characterize it as a system wherein all participants assume guilt, take superficial steps to arrive at the punishment phase, and operate under a value system that allocates punishment and mercy to offenders according to an informal operating standard of fairness.

One other perception of the criminal justice system is that of Samuel Walker's "wedding cake" illustration based on a model proposed by Lawrence Friedman and Robert Percival. In this scheme, the largest portion of criminal cases are presented as the bottom layers of the cake and the few serious cases as forming the top layer. The courtroom work group is believed to share definitions of seriousness and operates as a unit to keep the dynamics of the courtroom static, despite changes that are forced upon it. Changes such as the exclusionary rule, determinate sentencing, and other legislation have surprisingly little impact on court outcomes because of a shared perception of serious crime and appropriate punishment. The vast majority of crime, however, is considered trivial, and the processing of these cases involves very little energy or attention from system actors (Walker, 1985).

FORMAL ETHICS FOR LAWYERS AND JUDGES

A profession, as defined earlier, involves a specialized body of knowledge, commitment to the social good, ability to regulate itself, and high social status (Davis and Elliston, 1986, 13). The presence of ethical standards is essential to the definition of a profession. Formal ethical standards for lawyers and judges were originally promulgated by the ABA in the Model Code of Professional Responsibility. The original canons, adapted from the Alabama Bar Association Code of 1887, were adopted by the ABA in 1908 and have been revised frequently since then (American Bar Association, 1979). Several years ago, the ABA switched its endorsement of the Model Code as the general guide for ethical behavior to the Model Rules of Professional Responsibility....

Today's Model Rules cover many aspects of the lawyer's profession, including such areas as client-lawyer relationships, the lawyer as counselor, the lawyer as advocate, transactions with others, public service, and maintaining the integrity of the profession. Ethical issues in criminal law may involve courtroom behavior, suborning perjury, conflicts of interest, use of the media, investigation efforts, use of immunity, discovery and the sharing of evidence, relationships with opposing attorneys, and plea bargaining (Douglass, 1981).

To enforce these ethical rules, the ABA has a standing committee on ethical responsibility to offer formal and informal opinions when charges of impropriety have been made. Also, each state bar association has the power to sanction offending attorneys by private or public censure or recommending suspension of their privilege to practice law. The bar associations also have the power to grant entry into the profession, since one must ordinarily belong to the bar association of a particular state to practice law there. Bar associations judge competence by testing the applicant's knowledge, but they also judge moral worthiness by background checks of the individual. The purpose of these restrictive admission procedures is to protect the public image of the legal profession by rejecting unscrupulous or dishonest individuals or those unfit to practice for other reasons. Many feel, however, that if bar associations were serious about protecting the profession, they would continue to monitor the behavior and moral standing of current members with the same care they seem to take in the initial decision regarding entry (Elliston, 1986, 53).

Law schools have been criticized for being singularly uninterested in fostering any type of moral conscience in graduating students. Several writers have condemned the law school practice of reshaping law students so that when they emerge "thinking like a lawyer," they have mastered a type of thinking that is concerned with detail and logical analysis but gives little regard to morality and larger social issues.

Gerry Spence, for instance, a flamboyant defense attorney, brags of receiving low grades in law school—an indication, he believes, that he did not "sell out" to the mindset of bottom-line winning and profit above all else that is representative of law school indoctrination (Spence, 1989). Stover (1989) writes how public interest values decline during law school. The reason for this decline seemingly has to do with the low value placed on public interest issues by the law school curriculum, which also treats ethical and normative concerns as irrelevant or trivial compared to the "bar courses" such as contract law and torts. Morality and ethics are often made light of, even in professional responsibility courses where there are more stories (humorous and otherwise) of how to get around the ethical mandates than stories of how to resolve dilemmas and maintain a sense of personal integrity.

A practicing attorney is investigated only when complaints have been lodged against him or her. The investigative bodies have been described as decentralized, informal, and secret. They do little for dissatisfied clients since typical client complaints involve competence—a vague and ill-defined term (Marks and Cathcart, 1986, 72). Another study of client satisfaction found that the biggest complaint against attorneys was that too little time was given the client by the lawyer or that the lawyer was inaccessible (Arafat and McCahery, 1978, 205). Neither of these complaints is likely to receive a disciplinary ruling by an ethics committee.

Many of the Model Rules involve the special relationship the attorney has with the client. The separation of professional and personal responsibility poses difficult issues. Many lawyers feel that loyalty to the client is paramount to their duties as a professional. This loyalty surpasses and eclipses individual and private decisions, and the special relationship said to exist between lawyer and client justifies decisions when the client's interests are at stake that might otherwise be deemed unacceptable. An extreme position is that the attorney is no more than the legal agent of the client. The lawyer is neither immoral nor moral, but merely a legal tool. This position is represented by the statement "I am a lawyer, first and foremost." A more moderate position is that the loyalty to the client presents a special relationship between client and lawyer, similar to that between mother and child or trusted friends. This protected relationship justifies fewer actions than the one described above. Utilitarianism supports the special relationship in that it benefits us all to have these relationships available (Fried, 1986, 136). The ethics of care may also be used to support this position since the focus on the special relationship with and needs of the client is consistent with this ethical system. Many people reject this perspective and regard lawyers as individuals who must take personal responsibility for their decisions. They are perceived as the legal *and* moral agents of their clients, rather than merely the legal agent. Their personal responsibility to avoid wrongdoing precludes involving themselves in their clients' wrongdoing (Postema, 1986, 168). This position is represented by the statement "I am a person first, lawyer second."

Elliott Cohen (1991), an advocate of the "moral agent" position, believes that to be purely a legal advocate is inconsistent with being a morally good person in several ways. For instance, the virtue of justice would be inconsistent with a zealous advocate who would maximize the chance of his or her client's winning, regardless of the fairness of the outcome. A pure legal agent would sacrifice values of truthfulness, moral courage, benevolence, trustworthiness, and moral autonomy. Only if the attorney is a moral agent, as well as a legal advocate, can there be any possibility of the attorney's maintaining individual morality. Cohen (1991, 135–36) suggests some principles attorneys must follow to be consistent with both goals:

1. Treat others as ends in themselves and not as mere means to winning cases.
2. Treat clients and other professional relations who are relatively similar in a similar fashion.
3. Do not deliberately engage in behavior apt to deceive the court as to the truth.
4. Be willing, if necessary, to make reasonable personal sacrifices—of time, money, popularity, and so on—for what you justifiably believe to be a morally good cause.
5. Do not give money to, or accept money from, clients for wrongful purposes or in wrongful amounts.
6. Avoid harming others in the process of representing your client.
7. Be loyal to your client and do not betray his confidences.
8. Make your own moral decisions to the best of your ability and act consistently upon them.

The rationale for these principles seems to be an amalgamation of ethical formalism, utilitarianism, and other ethical frameworks. Some may seem impossible to uphold; for instance, it may be difficult to avoid harming others when representing a client in an adversary role. There are losers and winners in civil contests, as well as in criminal law, and lawyers must accept responsibility for the fact that sometimes the loser is harmed in financial or emotional ways.

The Model Code of Professional Responsibility for attorneys dictated that they should "be temperate and dignified" and "refrain from all illegal and morally reprehensible conduct." The Model Rules expect that "a lawyer's conduct should conform to the requirements of the law, both in professional service to clients and in the lawyer's business and personal affairs." These are similar prescriptions to those found in the Law Enforcement Code of Ethics. Both groups of professionals are expected to uphold a higher standard of behavior than the general public. They provide protection and help enforce the rules of behavior for the rest of us. Since both professions have a special place in society's attempt to control individual behavior, it is not inconsistent to expect a higher standard of behavior to apply.

USE OF DISCRETION

Although the issues of force and authority do not arise with legal professionals in the same manner as they do with law enforcement and correctional professionals, the power of discretion is shared. Discretion exists at every stage of the criminal justice system; professionals at each stage have the power to use their discretion wisely and ethically, or for self-interest and other unethical purposes. In the courts, prosecutors have discretion to charge and pursue prosecution, defense attorneys have discretion to accept or refuse cases and choose trial tactics, and judges have discretion to make rulings on evidence and other trial procedures, as well as convictions and sentences.

One view of law is that it is neutral and objective. Law and the formal rules of law are the focal points of decision making (Pinkele and Louthan, 1985, 9). The reality is that lawmakers, law enforcers, and lawgivers have a great deal of discretion in making and interpreting the law. Law is political in that it is responsive to power interests. Far from being absolute or objective, the law is a dynamic, ever-changing symbol of political will. Just as lawmaking and interpretation are influenced by political will and power groups, individual lawgivers and those who work in the system also have a great deal of discretion in interpreting and enforcing the law. For instance, the Supreme Court interprets constitutional or legislative intent, and these interpretations are far from being neutral or inviolate. This is not to say that discretion exists unfettered or operates in unsystematic ways. Louthan (1985, 14) offers the following observation:

> For some, discretion is "law without order," the authority to make decisions according to one's own judgment...," the "departure from legal rules"; in short, "normlessness." Others, though, would contend that while discretion may refer to a procedural context of decisions reached informally, it does not necessarily imply that decisions are made on an ad hoc basis, without order, and without reference to some kind of directional norm. Indeed, it can be argued that discretionary behavior itself becomes routine, that the environment of decision is one in which the actor thinks as much (maybe simultaneously, maybe first) about the norms or folkways of discretion and its related currencies of informal exchange as he does about what may be required by the rule of law.

If we accept that discretion is an operating reality in the justice system, then we must ask in what ways legal professionals use this discretion. If individual value systems replace absolute rules of laws, then these individual value systems may be ethical or unethical. For instance, even if we decided that discretion is morally acceptable, there might be problems with how it is used. Judges might base their decisions on a concept of fairness, or they might instead base their decisions on a prejudiced perception that blacks are always more criminal so they deserve longer sentences or that women are not dangerous so should get probation. In these examples, the discretion is misused because prejudicial values take the place of the concept of fairness. Judges' rulings on objections are supposed to be based on rules of evidence, but sometimes there is room for interpretation and individual discretion. Some judges use this discretion appropriately and make decisions in a best effort to conform to the rules, but other judges use arbitrary or unfair criteria, such as personal dislike of an attorney, or in the case of one particular judge, awarding favorable rulings to each attorney by turns regardless of the merit of the objection.

In our legal system, discretionary decisions at the trial level can be reexamined through the process of appeal. Appeals are part of due process in that they serve as a check on the decision making of trial judges. Any gross errors will be corrected; any extremely unethical actions will result in a retrial. However, appeals are not conducted in all cases, and even in cases that are appealed, many errors go unnoticed and uncorrected. Courtroom behavior, for instance, is seldom noticed or corrected unless it extremely and blatantly violates constitutional rights.

The remainder of this chapter will explore the use of discretion in the courts by looking at the role responsibilities of the major actors in the system—namely, the defense attorney, the prosecutor, and the judge. Obviously, these actors work with a criminal code that is handed down to them by the legislature. The formation of laws, and the factors and compromises that go into a law's creation or revision, is a subject unto itself. We will address the ethical questions that arise in the implementation, rather than the creation, of law.

ETHICAL ISSUES FOR DEFENSE ATTORNEYS

The role of the defense attorney is to protect the due process rights of the defendant. Due process is supposed to minimize mistakes in judicial proceedings that might result in a deprivation of life, liberty, or property. Due process rights, including notice, neutral fact finders, cross-examination, presentation of evidence and witnesses, and so on, are supposed to minimize the risk of error. The defense attorney is present to ensure that these rights are protected—for instance, during interrogation to make sure no coercion is used; at lineup to make sure it is fair and unbiased; and during trial to ensure adequate defense and cross-examination. The pure role of advocate is contradictory to the reality that the defense attorney must, if he or she is to work with the other actors in the court system, accommodate their needs as well as those of clients.

Defense attorneys have a fairly negative reputation in the legal community, as well as with the general public. They are seen as incompetent and/or unable to compete on the higher rungs of the status ladder of law, those higher rungs beings corporate, tax, and international law. Alternatively or additionally, they are seen as "shady" or "money grubbers" who get the guilty off by sleazy tactics. In fiction, defense attorneys are presented as either fearless crusaders who always manage to defend innocent clients (usually against unethical prosecutors); or as sleazy dealmakers who are either too burned out or egoistic to care about their clients. The reality fits neither of these portrayals. Kittel (1990) finds that the majority of defense attorneys would not change their career given an opportunity to do so and most chose their career because they were interested in the trial work it offered or for public policy reasons, as opposed to the common myth that criminal defense attorneys enter that field because they couldn't make it anywhere else.

As mentioned earlier, the system tends to operate under a presumption of guilt. Indeed, defense attorneys are often in the position of defending clients they know are guilty. The rationale for defending a guilty person is, of course, that a person deserves due process before a finding of guilt and punishment. Before punishment can be morally imposed, a fair procedure must ensure the punishment is appropriate. To ensure appropriate punishment, a set of fact-finding procedures is necessary, and the defense attorney's role is to make sure the rules are followed. If defense attorneys are doing their job, then we can all be comfortable with a conviction. If they do not do their job, then we have no system of justice, and none of us is safe from wrongful prosecution. Due process protects us all by making the criminal justice system prove wrongdoing fairly; the person who makes sure no shortcuts are taken is the defense attorney.

Responsibility to the Client

> The basic duty defense counsel owes to the administration of justice and as an officer of the court is to serve as the accused's counselor and advocate with courage and devotion and to render effective, quality representation. (Standard 4–1.2[b])

Defense attorneys are always in the position of balancing the rights of the individual client against overall effectiveness. Extreme attempts to protect these rights will reduce the defense attorney's effectiveness for other clients. Furthermore, defense attorneys must balance the needs and problems of the client against their ethical responsibilities to the system and profession.

A lawyer is supposed to provide legal assistance to clients without regard for personal preference or interest. A lawyer is not allowed to withdraw from a case simply because he or she no longer wishes to represent the client; only if the legal action is for harassment or malicious purposes, if continued employment will result in a violation of a disciplinary rule, if discharged by a client, or if a mental or physical condition renders effective counsel impossible can a lawyer be mandatorily withdrawn. In other cases, a judge may grant permission to withdraw when the client insists upon illegal or unethical actions, is uncooperative and does not follow the attorney's advice, or otherwise makes effective counsel difficult. Legal ethics mandate that people with unpopular causes and individuals who are obviously guilty still deserve counsel, and it is the ethical duty of an attorney to provide such counsel. In fact, although many people condemn attorneys and especially the American Civil Liberties Union for defending such groups as the American Nazi Party or the Ku Klux Klan or such individuals as Charles Manson or notorious drug dealers, clearly they could not do otherwise under their own ethical principles.

Some lawyers have no problem at all with defending "unworthy" clients. Drug cases are becoming well known as lawyers' pork barrels. Many lawyers have made millions of dollars defending major drug smugglers and dealers, sometimes on a retainer. In effect, they share in the wealth generated by illegal drugs. Is it ethical to take any client able to pay large and continuing bills? It is commonly believed that anytime a criminal defendant can and will pay, a lawyer can always be found to take the case to trial and conduct innumerable appeals, no matter what the likelihood of winning.

Recently, the government has started using provisions under the Racketeer Influenced and Corrupt Organizations Statute (18 U.S.C. Sections 1961–68—, usually referred to as RICO, to confiscate drug money, including fees already paid to attorneys. Defense attorneys object to this practice, protesting that it endangers fair representation for drug defendants because attorneys may be less willing to defend these clients when there is a possibility that their fees will be confiscated. Some prosecutors, it should be noted, have gone a step further and are starting to prosecute attorneys themselves if there is evidence that an attorney is engaged in a continuing conspiracy to further a criminal enterprise by his or he association with the client. This use of the RICO statute is extremely controversial, as are other uses of it that will be discussed later.

Many people are firmly convinced that the quality of legal representation is directly related to the thickness of the defendant's wallet. When people can make bail and afford private attorneys, do they receive better justice? Do defense attorneys exert more effort for clients who pay well than they do for court-appointed clients? Obviously, professional ethics would dictate equal consideration, but individual values also affect behavior. If an attorney felt confident that his or her court-appointed clients received at least adequate representation, then could one not justify a more zealous defense for a paying client? Where adequate representation is vaguely and poorly defined, this question is even more problematic.

Confidentiality

> Defense counsel should not reveal information relating to representation of a client unless the client consents after consultation, except for disclosures that are impliedly authorized in order to carry out the representation and except that defense counsel may reveal such information to the extent he or she reasonably believes necessary to prevent the client from committing a criminal act that defense counsel believes is likely to result in imminent death or substantial bodily harm. (Standard 4–3.7[d])

Attorney-client privileges refers to the confidentiality that exists in the communication between the two. The confidentiality protection is said to be inherent in the fiduciary relationship between the client and the attorney, but more important is that the client must be able to expect and receive the full and complete assistance of his or her lawyer. If a client feels compelled to withhold negative and incriminatory information, he or she will not be able to receive such assistance; thus, the lawyer must be perceived as a completely confidential agent of the client. Parallels to the attorney-client relationship are relationships between spouses and the priest-penitent relationship. In these cases the relationship creates a legal entity that approximates a single interest rather than two, and a break in confidentiality would violate the Fifth Amendment protection against self-incrimination (Schoeman, 1982, 260).

The only situations wherein a lawyer can ethically reveal confidences of a client are when the client consents, when disclosure is required by law or court order, when the intention of the client is to commit a crime and the information is necessary to prevent the crime, or when one needs to defend oneself or employees against an accusation of wrongful conduct. In the following situation described by Harris (1986, 116), none of these factors applied; therefore, the lawyers felt ethically bound to withhold the location of two bodies from the families of the victims.

> In July 1973, Robert Garrow, a 38-year-old mechanic from Syracuse, New York, killed four persons, apparently at random. The four were camping in the Adirondack Mountains. In early August, following a vigorous manhunt, he was captured by state police and indicted for the murder of a student from Schenectady. At the time of the arrest, no evidence connected Garrow to the other deaths....The court appointed two Syracuse lawyers, Francis R. Belge and Frank H. Armani, to defend Garrow.
>
> Some weeks later, during discussions with his two lawyers, Garrow told them that he had raped and killed a woman in a mine shaft. Belge and Armani located the mine shaft and the body of the Illinois woman but did not take their discovery to the police. The body was finally discovered four months later by two children playing in the mine. In September, the lawyers found the second body by following Garrow's directions. This discovery, too, went unreported; the girl's body was uncovered by a student in December.
>
> Belge and Armani maintained their silence until the following June. Then, to try to show that he was insane, Garrow made statements from the witness stand that implicated him in the other three murders. At a press conference the next day, Belge and Armani outlined for the first time the sequence of events.
>
> The local community was outraged. The lawyers, however, believed they had honored the letter and spirit of their professional duty in a tough case. "We both, knowing how the parents feel, wanted to advise them where the bodies were," Belge said, "but since it was a privileged communication, we could not reveal any information that was given to us in confidence."
>
> Their silence was based on the legal code that admonishes the lawyer to "preserve the confidence and secrets of a client." The lawyer-client "privilege" against disclosure of confidences is one of the oldest and most ironclad in the law. If the defendant has no duty to confess his guilt or complicity in a crime, it can make no sense to assert that his lawyer has such a duty. Otherwise, the argument goes, the accused will tell his lawyer at best a deficient version of the facts, and the lawyer cannot as effectively defend the client. This argument frequently seems unconvincing; it certainly did to the people of Syracuse.

The author goes on to evaluate the actions of the two lawyers under the utilitarian ethical framework and decides that they did the right things since it would be ethically acceptable for lawyers to break client confidentiality only in cases in which a death or crime could be prevented by disclosure. This formulation is, as always, based on the greatest utility for society, and it is believed that society benefits in the long run from attorney-client confidence. Therefore, it should be sacrificed only when the confidence endangers a life.

Religious ethics might condemn the attorneys' actions since lying to the parents who sought information was a form of deception. On the other hand, in the Catholic religion, a similar ethical dilemma might arise because of the confidentiality of the priest-penitent relationship. In that example, it would be impossible for the priest to betray a confession no matter what the circumstances. Ethical formalism also is difficult to reconcile with the lawyers' actions. First of all, under the categorical imperative, the lawyers' actions must be such that we would be willing for all others to engage in similar behavior under like circumstances. Could one will that it become universal law for attorneys to keep such information secret? What if you were the parents who did not know the whereabouts of their daughter or even if she was alive or dead? It is hard to imagine that they would be willing to agree with this universal law. On the other hand, ethical formalism is also concerned with duty, and it is the duty of the attorney to protect his or her client. There may be a formulation of the confidentiality rule that could pass the universalism principle. The ethical rule that allows confidentiality to be breached to prevent future crime is consistent with both utilitarianism and ethical formalism principles.

The ethics of care would be concerned with the needs of both the client and the parents in the case described. It would perhaps resolve the issue in a less absolutist fashion than the other rationales. For instance, when discussing this case in a college classroom, many students immediately decide that they would call in the location of the bodies anonymously, thereby relieving the parents' anxiety and also protecting to some extent the confidential communication. While this compromise is unsupported by an absolute view of confidentiality since it endangers the client (he would not even be charged with the crimes if the bodies were never found), it protects the relationship of the attorney and the client and still meets the needs of the parents.

A defense attorney's ethics may also be compromised when a client insists on taking the stand to commit perjury. Disciplinary rules specifically forbid the lawyer from allowing perjury to take place; if it happens before the attorney realizes the intent of the client, the defense must not use or refer to the perjured testimony (Freedman, 1986; Kleinig, 1986). But if the attorney appears to disbelieve or discredit his or her client, then this behavior violates the ethical mandate of zealous defense. Pellicciotti (1990) contends that the attorney must take an active stand against perjured testimony when he or she knows that it is untruthful by trying to dissuade the client from lying if the attorney knows in advance what is contemplated, by informing the court, by withdrawing from the case, or by another means. If the attorney merely suspects the information is perjured, then Pellicciotti instructs that ethics requires the attorney to proceed and give the defendant the best defense possible, even though the attorney may himself or herself have doubts. Of course, this then raises the question as to whether it is ethical for attorneys to tell their clients, "Before you say anything, I need to tell you that I cannot participate in perjury and if I know for a fact that you plan to lie, I cannot put you on the stand." Defense attorneys often explain that they don't bother to inquire as to guilt or innocence in the first place because their clients more often than not lie to them, so they proceed with the defense wanting to know only pertinent information rather than an admission of guilt. The approach of defending someone without regard to guilt or innocence and without wanting to know may be problematic in itself.

Conflicts of Interest

> Defense counsel should not permit his or her professional judgment or obligations to be affected by his or her own political, business, property, or personal interests. (Standard 4–3.5[a])

Attorneys are specifically prohibited from engaging in representations that would compromise their loyalty to their clients. Specifically, attorneys must not represent clients who may have interests that conflict with those of the attorney—for instance, a client who owns a company that is a rival to one in which the attorney has an interest. The attorney also must not represent two clients who may have opposing interests—for instance, codefendants in a criminal case, since very often one will testify against the other. The attorney would find it impossible in such a situation to represent each individual fairly. Disciplinary rules even prohibit two lawyers from a single firm from representing clients with conflicting interests. In some informal and formal decisions from ethics committees, this rule has even been used to prohibit legal aid or public defender offices from defending codefendants (American Bar Association, 1986).

Although attorneys may not ethically accept clients with conflicting interests, there is no guidance on the more abstract problem that all criminal clients in a caseload have conflicting interests in that their cases are often looked upon as part of a workload rather than considered separately. Many defense attorneys make a living by taking cases from people with very modest means or taking court-appointed cases where the fee is set by the court. The defense attorney then becomes a fast food lawyer, depending on volume and speed to make a profit. What happens here, of course, is that quality may get sacrificed along they way. When lawyers pick up clients in the hallways of courtrooms and from bail bondsmen referrals, the goal is to arrange bail, get a plea bargain, and move on to the next case. Guilt or innocence has very little to do with this operation and rarely does the case come to trial.

About 90 percent of the cases in the criminal justice system are settled by a plea bargain (Senna and Siegel, 1987, 310). The defense attorney's goal in plea bargaining is to get the best possible deal for the client—namely, probation or the shortest prison sentence the prosecutor is willing to give for a guilty plea. The defense attorney also has to be aware that he or she cannot push to the limit in every case, since usually the prosecutor and defense attorney have an ongoing relationship. A courtroom appearance may be an isolated event for the client, but for the defense attorney and prosecutor, it is an ongoing, weekly ritual—only the names change. Because of the nature of the continuing relationship, the defense attorney must weigh present needs against future gains. If the defense becomes known as unwilling to play ball, reduced effectiveness may hurt future clients.

Most conclude that plea bargaining, even if not exactly "right," is certainly efficient and probably inevitable. Even in those jurisdictions that have moved to determinate sentencing, what has happened is that plea bargaining has become charge bargaining instead of sentence bargaining. Should we measure the morality of an action by its efficiency? This efficiency argument is similar to that used to defend some deceptive investigative practices of police. The goals of the system—crime control or bureaucratic efficiency—may be contrary to individual rights. Obviously, plea bargaining would fail under the categorical imperative, since the individual is treated as a means in the argument that plea bargaining is good for the system. Utilitarian theory may or may not be used to justify plea bargaining, depending on how one calculates the long-term effects it has on society's views toward the justice system. It is possible that plea bargaining undermines society's sense of justice and thus cannot be justified even under utilitarianism.

Even if we do approve of plea bargaining because of its benefits to the system, what about practices that take place within plea bargaining, such as trading cases, or "train justice"? When a defense attorney has several cases to bargains, he or she may trade off on some to get better deals for others. Can any ethical system justify this practice? Clearly, conflicts of interest may exist even when clients are not related or associated in any way.

Another conflict of interest may occur if the attorney desires to represent the client's interests in selling literary or media rights. Standard 4-3.4 specifically forbids entering into such agreements before the case is complete. The temptations are obvious—if the attorney hopes to acquire financial rewards from a share of profits, his or her professional judgment on how best to defend the client may be clouded. Whether putting off signing such an agreement until the case is complete removes the possibility of unethical decisions is debatable.

Zealous Defense

> Defense counsel, in common with all members of the bar, is subject to standards of conduct stated in statutes, rules, decisions of courts, and codes, canons, or other standards of professional conduct. Defense counsel has no duty to execute any directive of the accused which does not comport with law or such standards. Defense counsel is the professional representative of the accused, not the accused's alter ego. (Standard 4–1.2[e])

Few would challenge the idea that all people deserve to have their due process rights protected. What many people find unsettling, however, is the zeal with which some defense attorneys approach the courtroom contest. For instance, how diligent should the defense be in protecting the defendant's rights? An inconsistency may arise between providing an effective defense and maintaining professional ethics and individual morality. Lawyers should represent clients zealously within the bounds of the law, but the law is sometimes vague and difficult to determine. Some actions are simply forbidden. The lawyer may not engage in motions or actions to intentionally and maliciously harm others, knowingly advance unwarranted claims or defenses, conceal or fail to disclose that which he or she is required by law to reveal, knowingly use perjured testimony or false evidence, knowingly make a false statement of law or fact, participate in the creation or preservation of evidence when he or she knows or it is obvious that the evidence is false, counsel the client in conduct that is illegal, or engage in other illegal conduct. The attorney is also expected to maintain a professional and courteous relationship with the opposing attorneys, litigants, and witnesses and to refrain from disparaging statements or badgering conduct. The defense attorney must not intimidate or otherwise influence the jury or trier of fact or use the media for these purposes.

Despite these ethical rules, practices such as withholding evidence, manufacturing evidence, witness badgering, and defamation of victims' characters are commonly used tactics in the defense arsenal. For instance, the sexual history of rape victims has been brought out purely to cast doubt on the character of the rape victim and persuade the jury to believe she deserved or asked for her rape. It may be the case that the evidence against a client is so overwhelming the only thing left for the defense attorney is to try and attack the credibility of witnesses. In some cases defense attorneys go to extreme lengths to change the course of testimony, for example, by bribing witnesses or not stopping the client from intimidating the witness. These cases are rare, of course, but they are not unheard of.

Defense attorneys may sacrifice their integrity for the sake of a case. For instance, in one trial, the defense attorney and prosecutor were getting ready to try a barroom murder case. The prosecutor was able to present only one eyewitness to the shooting—the bartender. No one else in the bar was willing to testify that they saw anything. The prosecutor had other circumstantial evidence of the defendant's guilt, but the eyewitness was crucial. Unfortunately, the bartender had a ten-year-old murder conviction—a fact that would reduce his credibility in the jury's eyes. This fact could be brought out by the defense under the rules of evidence; however, the prosecutor could petition the court to have the fact suppressed and had a good chance of succeeding since it bore no relevance to the case and would be prejudicial, but she did not file the appropriate motion. Just before the trial was about to start, the prosecutor asked the defense attorney if he was going to bring out this fact on his cross-examination of the bartender. If he planned to do so, the prosecutor would have asked for a continuance and filed a motion to have it suppressed, or at least brought it out herself on direct to reduce its impact. He told her specifically and clearly that he had no intention of using that information or questioning the witness about it since it was so long ago and irrelevant to the case. When the direct examination of this witness was over and the defense attorney started his cross-examination, his first question was "Isn't it true that you were convicted of murder in 19—?" While the prosecutor may have committed an error in judgment by trusting the defense attorney, the defense attorney deliberately misled the prosecutor as to his intentions—he lied. If a defense attorney makes a practice of such tactics, he or she will quickly develop a reputation as untrustworthy and find that prosecutors will not cooperate with his requests for continuances or other favors. Zealous defense is a weak rationale for lying. When asked about his actions, the defense attorney explained that it "just slipped out" and complained that the prosecutor took these things "too seriously." This behavior is an example of an unethical decision used for short-term gain, an egoistic rationalization, and a view of due process as a game since when an opponent is offended by a lie, she is taking things "too seriously."

A recent innovation in trial tactics is the development of "scientific" jury selection. Attorneys often contend that a trial has already been won or lost once the jury has been selected. Whether or not this is true, attorneys are becoming increasingly sophisticated in their methods of choosing which members of a jury panel would make good jurors. A good juror is defined not as one who is unbiased and fair, but as someone who is predisposed to be sympathetic to that attorney's case. The ability to use these methods is limited only by a budget. Some lawyers, such as the famed "Racehorse" Haynes in Houston, have used methods such as surveying a large sample of the population in the community where the case is to be tried to discover how certain demographic groups feel about issues relevant to the case so that these findings can be used when the jury is selected. Other attorneys hire jury experts, psychologists who sit with the attorney and through a combination of nonverbal and verbal clues, identify those jury panel members who are predisposed to believe the case presented by the attorney. Another method uses a "shadow jury"—a panel of people selected by the defense attorney to represent the actual jury that sits through the trial and provides feedback to the attorney on the evidence being presented during the trial. This allows the attorney to adjust his or her trial tactics in response. Some of these methods were used in the William Kennedy Smith rape trial in Florida, which resulted in an acquittal. While attorneys have always used intuition and less sophisticated means to decide which jury members to exclude, these tactics are questioned by some as too contrary to the basic idea that a trial is supposed to start with an unbiased jury (Smith and Meyer, 1987).

While bribery and suppression of evidence are not difficult to identify as unethical practices, it is more difficult to determine when a defense attorney's treatment of a witness is badgering as opposed to energetic cross-examination or when exploring a witness's background is character assassination as opposed to a careful examination of credibility. Other trial tactics include putting the opposing attorney at a disadvantage by aggressive personal attacks or allegations of incompetence. Female attorneys have reported that male opponents use paternalism in an effort to infantilize or feminize the female attorney to reduce her credibility with the jury. The line where zealous defense stops and unethical practices begin is difficult to determine.

ETHICAL ISSUES FOR PROSECUTORS

As the second line of decision makers in the system, prosecutors have extremely broad powers of discretion. The prosecutor acts like a strainer—he or she collects some cases for formal prosecution while eliminating a great many others. Because of limited resources, full enforcement of the law is impossible. Also, the severity of the criminal law may be inappropriate to some situations; thus, there is a need for discretion so that these cases may be diverted.

To guide discretion, there are ethical standards relating specifically to the role of the prosecutor. Chapter 3 of the ABA Standards for Criminal Justice covers the prosecution function. These standards cover topics similar to those for defense attorneys, but they also make special note of the unique role of the prosecutor as a representative of the court system and the state, rather than a pure advocate.

Use of Discretion

> A prosecutor should not institute, or cause to be instituted, or permit the continued pendency of criminal charges when the prosecutor knows that the charges are not supported by probable cause. A prosecutor should not institute, cause to be instituted, or permit the continued pendency of criminal charges in the absence of sufficient admissible evidence to support a conviction. (Standard 3–3.9[a])

The prosecutor must seek justice, not merely a conviction. Toward this end, prosecutors must share evidence, use restraint in the use of their power, represent the public interest, and give the accused the benefit of reasonable doubt. Disciplinary rules are more specific: they specifically forbid the prosecutor from pursuing charges when there is no probable cause and mandate timely disclosure to defense counsel of evidence, especially exculpatory evidence that might mitigate guilt or reduce the punishment.

One court has described the prosecutor's functions in the following way (*State* v. *Moynahan*, 164 Conn. 560, 325 A.2d 199, 206; cert. denied, 414 U.S. 976 [1973]):

As a representative of the people of the state, [the prosecutor] is under a duty not solely to obtain convictions but, more importantly, (1) to determine that there is reasonable ground to proceed with a criminal charge [citation omitted]; (2) to see that impartial justice is done the guilty as well as the innocent; and (3) to ensure that all evidence tending to aid in the ascertaining of the truth be laid before the court, whether it be consistent with the contention of the prosecution that the accused is guilty.

Despite these ideals of prosecutorial duty, an individual factor in prosecutorial discretion is that prosecutors want to and must win; therefore, their choice of cases is influenced by this value, whether it is ethically acceptable or not. Law enforcement considerations also influence prosecutorial action. If there is a bargain to be struck with an informant, if a lesser charge will result in testifying or uncovering information that could lead to further convictions, then this is considered in decision making. Finally, the pressure of public opinion is a factor to consider. Prosecutors may pursue cases they might otherwise have dropped if there is a great deal of public interest in the case.

Prosecutors can elect to charge or not; their discretion is influenced by political pressures, the chance for conviction, the severity of the crime, prison population, a "gut feeling" of guilt or innocence, and the weight of evidence. The prosecutorial role is to seek justice, but justice doesn't mean the same thing to everyone and certainly does not entail prosecuting everyone to the fullest extent of the law. Whether to charge or not is one of the most important decisions of the criminal justice process. The decision should be fair, neutral, and guided by due process, but this is an ideal; often many other considerations enter into the decision. Prosecutors don't usually use their charging power for intimidation or harassment, but personal factors may be involved in charging, such as a particular interest in a type of crime, such as child abuse, or public pressure over a particular crime that impels the prosecutor to charge somebody quickly, as in serial rape or murder. As in charging, the decision not to charge is open to ethical questions. To give one person who participated in a brutal crime immunity to gain testimony against others is efficient, but is it consistent with justice? Should such an individual escape punishment for betraying his or her friends? To not charge businesspeople with blue law violations because they are good citizens is questionable if other businesses are prosecuted for other ordinances.

Various studies have attempted to describe prosecutor decision making; one cites office policy as an important influence. *Legal sufficiency* is an office policy that weeds out those cases where the evidence is not strong enough to support further action. *System efficiency* is an office policy with goals of efficiency and accountability; all decisions are made with these goals in mind, so many cases result in dismissals. Another policy is *defendant rehabilitation*, which emphasizes diversion and other rehabilitation tools rather than punitive goals. Finally, *trial sufficiency* is an office policy that encourages a permanent definition of the charge to stick with through trial (Jaccoby, Mellon, and Smith, 1980).

Another study looks at the prosecutor as operating in an exchange system. The relationship between the prosecutor and the police is described as one of give-and-take. Prosecutors balance police needs or wishes against their own vulnerability. The prosecutor makes personal judgments as to which police officers can be trusted. Exchange also takes place between the prosecutor's office and the courts. When jails become over-crowded, deferred adjudication and probation may be recommended more often; when dockets become impossible, charges may be dropped. Finally, exchange takes place between defense attorneys and prosecutors, especially since many defense attorneys have previously served as prosecutors and may be personally familiar with the procedures and even the personalities in the prosecutor's office (Cole, 1970).

Discretion is considered essential to the prosecutorial function of promoting indi-vidualized justice and softening the impersonal effects of the law. On the other hand, dis-cretion is the key element in perceptions of the legal system as unfair and biased toward certain groups of people or individuals. Solutions to the problem of prosecutorial discre-tion may include regulation or internal guidelines. For instance, an office policy might include a procedure for providing written reasons for dropping charges; this procedure would respond to charges of unbridled discretion.

Conflicts of Interest

> A prosecutor should avoid a conflict of interest with respect to his or her official duties. (Standard 3.1–3[a])

Part-time prosecutors present a host of ethical issues. A Bureau of Justice Statistics 1992 bulletin reported that 47 percent of prosecutors held their jobs as a part-time occu-pation. Obviously there is the possibility of a conflict of interest. It may happen that a part-time prosecutor has a private practice, and situations may occur where the duty to a pri-vate client runs counter to the prosecutor's duty to the public. In some cases, it may be that a client becomes a defendant, necessitating the prosecutor to either hire a special prosecu-tor or step aside as counsel. Even when no direct conflicts of interest exist, time is always a problem for part-time prosecutors. The division of time is between the private practice, where income is correlated with hard work, and prosecutorial cases, where income is fixed no matter how many hours are spent. Obviously, this may result in a less energetic prose-cutorial function than one might wish.

It is well known that the prosecutor's job is a good stepping-stone to politics, and many use it as such. In these cases, one has to wonder whether cases are taken on the basis of merit or on their ability to place the prosecutor in the public eye and help his or her career. Winning becomes more important also. The prosecutor's relationship with the press is important. The media can be enemy or friend depending on how charismatic or forth-coming the prosecutor is in interviews. Sometimes cases are said to be tried in the newspa-pers—the defense attorney and the prosecutor stage verbal sparring matches for public con-sumption. Prosecutors may react to cases and judges' decisions in the newspapers, criticiz-ing the decision or the sentence and in the process denigrating the dignity of the system.

The RICO statute has increasingly been used as a tool to confiscate property and money associated with organized criminal activity. Once this tactic was approved by the courts, a veritable flood of prosecutions began that were designed, it seems, primarily to obtain cash, boats, houses, and other property of drug dealers. Making decisions based on the potential for what can be confiscated rather than other factors is a very real and dan-gerous development in this type of prosecution.

Plea Bargaining

> A prosecutor should not knowingly make false statements or representations as to fact or law in the course of plea discussions with defense counsel or the accused. (Standard 3–4.1[c])

Arguments given in defense of plea bargaining include heavy caseloads, limited resources, legislative overcriminalization, individualized justice, and legal problems of cases (legal errors that would result in mistrials or dropped charges if the client did not plead) (Knudten, 1978, 275). If we concede that plea bargaining is an acceptable element of judicial processing, there are ethical guidelines for its use. Prosecutors may over-charge—that is, charge at a higher degree of severity or press more charges than could possibly be sustained by the evidence—so that they can bargain down. Prosecutors may even mislead defense attorneys about the amount of evidence or the kind of evidence they have or about the sentence they can offer to obtain a guilty plea. Only 36 percent of chief prosecutors reported that explicit criteria for plea bargains were in place in 1990 (Bureau of Justice Statistics, 1992). Guidelines providing a range of years for certain types of charges would help the individual prosecutors maintain some level of consistency in a particular jurisdiction.

Zealous Prosecution

> The duty of the prosecutor is to seek justice, not merely to convict. (Standard 3–1.2[c])

Just as the defense attorney is at times overly zealous in defense of clients, prosecutors may be overly ambitious to attain a conviction. Often one hears of appeals based on overlooked or ignored witnesses or other evidence. When prosecutors are preparing a case, they are putting a puzzle together and any piece of evidence that doesn't fit the puzzle is sometimes conveniently ignored. Witnesses with less than credible reasons for testifying are used if they help a case. Moreover, witness preparation by both defense attorneys and prosecutors is not necessarily unethical; however, it does tend to confuse the jury by having witnesses appear with false images. Dress, behavior, and response to questions are all carefully orchestrated to present the information in the most favorable light. Witnesses are not supposed to be paid, but their expenses can be reimbursed, and this may be incentive enough to say what they think the prosecutor wants to hear.

There are very few controls on the behavior of prosecutors in the courtroom. Voters have some control over who becomes a prosecutor, but once in office most prosecutors stay in the good graces of a voting public unless there is a major scandal or an energetic competitor. In cities, most work is conducted by assistant prosecutors who are hired rather than elected. Misconduct in the courtroom is sometimes verbally sanctioned by trial judges, and perhaps an appellate decision may overturn a conviction, but these events are rare. Gershman (1991) writes that prosecutors misbehave because it works and they can get away with it. Because misconduct is only scrutinized when the defense attorney makes an objection and then files an appeal, and even then the appellate court may rule that it was a harmless error, there is a great deal of incentive to use improper tactics in the courtroom. Although some misconduct may result in a case being overturned, very seldom does the individual prosecutor face any personal penalties.

Ordinarily, then, prosecutors' misbehavior is unchecked; it may take the form of persistent reference to illegal evidence, leading witnesses, nondisclosure of evidence to the defense, appeals to emotions, and so on. One prosecutor admitted that early in his career he sometimes made faces at the defendant while his back was to the jury and the defense attorney wasn't looking. The jury saw the defendant glowering and looking angry for no discernible reason, which led to a negative perception of his sanity, temper, or both. Of course, the defense attorney may be engaged in other unethical actions as well, so the contest between them becomes one of effectiveness of methods rather than an attempt to abide by the strictures of law or ethical considerations.

Expert Witnesses

> A prosecutor who engages an expert for an opinion should respect the independence of the expert and should not seek to dictate the formation of the expert's opinion on the subject. (Standard 3–3.3[a])

Expert witnesses, who can receive a fee, are often accused of compromising their integrity for money or notoriety. The use of expert witnesses has risen in recent years. Psychiatrists often testify as to the mental competency or legal insanity of an accused. Forensic experts have for many years testified regarding factual issues of evidence. Today, criminologists and other social scientists may be asked to testify on such topics as victimization in prison, statistical evidence of sentencing discrimination, the effectiveness of predictive instruments for riots and other disturbances, risk assessment for individual offenders, mental health services in prison, patterns of criminality, the battered woman syndrome, and so on. When the expert is honest in his or her presentation as to the limitations and potential bias of the material, no ethical issues arise. However, expert witnesses may testify in a realm beyond fact or make testimony appear factual when some questions are not clearly answerable. Because of the *halo effect*—essentially, when a person with expertise or status in one area is given deference in all areas—an expert witness may endow a statement or conclusion with more legitimacy than it may warrant. When expert witnesses are used, they run the risk of having their credibility attacked by the opposing side; credibility is obviously much easier to attack when a witness has attempted to present theory or supposition as fact or conclusion, either for ideological reasons or because of pressure from zealous attorneys. Those who always appear on either one side or the other may also lose their credibility. For instance, a doctor who is used often by prosecutors in one jurisdiction during capital sentencing hearings has become known as "Dr. Death" because he always determines that the defendant poses a future risk to society, which is one of the necessary elements for the death penalty. While he is well known to both prosecutors and defense attorneys by reputation, juries would not be expected to know of his predilection for finding future dangerousness and would take his testimony at face value unless the defense attorney bring this information out on cross-examination.

Competing expert witnesses who present entirely different "facts" to the jury create an atmosphere of cynicism and distrust. Expert witnesses can and do provide valuable contributions to the trial process. Ethical dilemmas can be avoided by clearly presenting the limits and biases of the information offered.

Turning to attorneys' actions, the use of expert witnesses can present ethical problems when the witness is used in a dishonest fashion. To pay an expert for time is not unethical, but to shop for experts until one is found who benefits the case may be, since the credibility of the witness is suspect. Experts are used to prove the truth of facts in essentially the same manner as eyewitnesses are used to prove facts. When eyewitnesses differ as to what they have seen, the explanation is that someone is either wrong or lying. It is no different with expert witnesses; however, since they profess to have extensive knowledge in the area, it is more difficult to conclude they are mistaken. Another difficulty is presented when one side obtains an expert who develops a conclusion or set of findings that would help the other side. Ethics do not prohibit a civil attorney from merely disregarding the information, without notice to the opponent of information that could benefit his or her case. However, prosecutors operate under a special set of ethics since their goal is justice, not pure advocacy. Any exculpatory information is supposed to be shared with the defense; this obviously includes test results and may also include expert witness findings.

Some ethical issues prosecutors are faced with are similar to those of defense attorneys, since they are, in a way, opposite players in the same game. However, they have a qualitatively different role because of their discretionary power in the decision-making process. Their discretion to charge dramatically affects defendants' lives. Their role as an officer of the court puts them in a very powerful position and, as such, results in different ethical standards for the prosecutor.

ETHICAL ISSUES FOR JUDGES

Perhaps the most popular symbol of justice is the judge in his or her black robe. Judges are expected to be impartial, knowledgeable, and authoritative. They guide the prosecutor, defense attorney, and all the other actors in the trial process from beginning to end, helping to maintain the integrity of the proceeding. This is the ideal, but judges are human, with human failings.

Ethical Guidelines

To help guide judges in their duties, a Code of Judicial Conduct was developed by the American Bar Association. This code identifies the special ethical considerations unique to judges. The primary theme of judicial ethics is impartiality. If we trust the judge to give objective rulings, then we must be confident that his or her objectivity isn't marred by any type of bias.

Judges may let their personal prejudices influence their decisions. To head off this possibility, the ABA's ethical guidelines specify that each judge should try to avoid all appearance of bias, as well as actual bias. Judges must be careful to avoid financial involvements or personal relationships that may threaten objectivity. We expect judges, like police officers, to conform to higher standards of behavior than the rest of us. Therefore, any hint of scandal in their private lives calls into question their professional ethics also. The obvious rationale is that judges who have less than admirable personal values cannot judge others objectively, and those judges who are less than honest in their financial dealings do not have a right to sit in judgment on others.

There are a number of problematic issues in the perceived objectivity of judges. For instance, in those states where judges are elected, the judges must solicit campaign contributions. These monies are most often obtained from attorneys, and it is not at all unusual for judges to accept money from attorneys who practice before them. Does this not provide at least the appearance of impropriety? This is exacerbated in jurisdictions that use court appointments as the method for indigent representation. In these jurisdictions, judges hand out appointments to the very same attorneys who give money back in the form of campaign contributions. Obviously, the appearance, if not the actuality, of bias is present in these jurisdictions.

Use of Discretion

Judges' discretion occurs in two major areas. The first area is in the interpretation of the law in court cases. For instance, a judge may be called upon to assess the legality of evidence and make rulings on the various objections raised by both the prosecutors and the defense attorneys. A judge also writes instructions to the jury, which set up the legal questions and definitions of the case. The second area of judicial discretion is in sentencing decisions.

Judges must rule on the legality of evidence; they may make a decision to exclude a confession or a piece of evidence because of the way it was obtained and by so doing may allow the guilty to go free. The exclusionary rule has generated a storm of controversy since it may result in a guilty party avoiding punishment because of an error committed by the police. The basis for the exclusionary rule is that one cannot accept a conviction on tainted evidence. The ideals of justice reject such a conviction because accepting tainted evidence, even if obtained against a guilty party, is a short step away from accepting any type of evidence, no matter how illegal, and thus poses a threat to the whole concept of due process. The conviction is so violative of due process that it is ruled void. A more practical argument for the exclusionary rule is that if we want police officers to behave in a legal manner, we must have heavy sanctions against illegalities. If convictions are lost due to illegal evidence collection, police may reform their behavior. Actual practice provides little support for this argument, though. Police have learned how to get around the exclusionary rule, and in any event, cases on appeal are so far removed from the day-to-day decision making of the police that they have little effect on police behavior. Recent court decisions have created several exceptions to the exclusionary rule…. Judges who decide to exclude evidence and set aside convictions do so by disregarding short-term effects for more abstract principles—specifically, the protection of due process.

Ethical frameworks may or may not provide a rationale for the implementation of the exclusionary rule in a particular case. Religious ethics don't give us much help unless we decide that this ethical system would support vengeance and thus would permit the judge to ignore the exclusionary rule in order to punish a criminal. On the other hand, religious ethics might also support letting the criminal go free to answer to an ultimate higher authority, since human judgment was in this case imperfect. The categorical imperative would probably support the exclusionary rule since one would not want a universal law of accepting all tainted evidence. On the other hand, one would have to agree to retrying all criminals, regardless of the severity of the crime, whenever the evidence was tainted despite the possibility of further crime or harm to individuals. Act utilitarianism would support ignoring the exclusionary rule if the crime was especially serious or if there were a good chance that the offender would not be retried successfully. The utility derived from ignoring the rule would outweigh the good. However, rule utilitarianism could be used to support the exclusionary rule, since the long-term effect of allowing illegal police behavior would be more serious than letting one criminal go free.

The judge is called upon to decide many and various questions throughout a trial. He or she, of course, has the law and legal precedent as guidance, but in most cases each decision involves a substantial element of subjectivity. Judges have the power to make it difficult for either the prosecutor or the defense attorney through their pattern of rulings on objections, evidence admitted, and even personal attitude toward the attorney, which is always noted by the jury and is influential in their decision.

The second area of judicial discretion is in sentencing. The following makes clear the small amount of training judges receive for this awesome responsibility (Johnson, 1982, 20):

> Few judges have the benefit of judicial training sessions prior to embarking upon the often bewildering and frequently frustrating task of pursuing that vague, if not indefinable, entity so commonly known as justice....Thus, it is not uncommon for the new judge, relying upon a philosophy often formulated hastily, to be placed in the unenviable position of pronouncing a sentence upon another human being without any special preparation.

Judges' decisions are scrutinized by public watchdog groups and appellate-level courts. One wonders, in fact, if judges aren't overly influenced by the current clamor for strict punishments. On the other hand, if judges are supposed to enact community sentiment, perhaps it is proper for them to reflect its influence. Is there one just punishment for a certain type of offender, or does the definition of what is just depend on community opinion of the crime, the criminal, and the time?

Evidence indicates that the decision making of judges actually is based on personal standards, since no consistency seems to appear between the decisions of individual judges in the same community. One study found that two judges in Louisiana had remarkably different records on numbers of convictions. The two also differed in their patterns of sentencing (Pinkele and Louthan, 1985, 58). It must be noted that others have found a general consistency among sentencing practices, and the system provides a basic, if rough, fairness in sentencing.

CONCLUSION

According to the basic tenets of our law, the accused is innocent until conviction. Prosecutors, judges, and defense attorneys are all officers of the court and as such are sworn to uphold the highest principles of our law, including the basic assumption of innocence. However, in the day-to-day operations of courthouse politics and bureaucracy, the rights of individuals may compete with the goal of efficient processing.

The presence and use of discretion in the criminal justice system is pervasive; however, discretion requires decision makers to depend on individual values and ethics rather than structured laws and rules.

ETHICAL DILEMMAS

Please read and respond to the following situations. Be prepared to discuss your ideas.

Situation 1

You are deputy prosecutor and have to decide whether or not to charge Joe Crum with possession and sale of a controlled substance. You know you have a good case because the guy sold to the local junior high school and many of the kids are willing to testify. The police are pressuring you to make a deal because he has promised to inform on other dealers in the area if you don't prosecute. What should you do?

Situation 2

Your first big case is a multiple murder. As defense attorney for Sy Kopath you have come to the realization that he really did break into a couple's home and torture and kill them in the course of robbing them of jewelry and other valuables. He has even confessed to you that he did it. You are also aware, however, that the police did not read him his Miranda warning and he was coerced into giving a confession without your presence. What should you do? Would your answer be different if you believed he was innocent or didn't know for sure either way?

Situation 3

You are a judge who must sentence two defendants. One insisted on a jury trial and, through his defense attorney, dragged the case on for months with delays and motions. He was finally convicted by a jury. The other individual was his codefendant and pleaded guilty. They were apparently equally responsible for the burglary. How would you sentence them?

Situation 4

You are a member of a jury. The case is a child molestation case where the defendant is accused of a series of molestations in his neighborhood. You have been advised by the judge not to discuss the case with anyone outside the courtroom and especially not to talk to anyone on either side of the case. Going down in the elevator after the fourth day of the trial, you overhear the prosecutor talking to one of the police officer witnesses. They are discussing the fact that the man has a previous arrest for child molestation but it has not been allowed in by the judge as too prejudicial to the jury. You were pretty sure the guy was guilty before, but now you definitely believe he is guilty. You also know that if you tell the judge what you have heard, it will probably result in a mistrial. What would you do?

QUESTIONS FOR THOUGHT AND DISCUSSION

1. Why do you think the public has such low levels of confidence in the criminal justice system?
2. What are the advantages and problems with plea bargaining?
3. Should defense attorneys shop for lenient judges, prepare witnesses, and engage in other actions designed to get the defendant the best chance of an acquittal?

CAREERS IN THE COURTS

Robert C. DeLucia
Thomas J. Doyle

All virtue is summed up in dealing justly.

—Aristotle

In the previous chapter, law enforcement careers were described as the first step in the administration of the criminal justice system. Law enforcement was defined as the prevention and investigation of crime, with the arrest and bringing to trial of those who break the law. Careers in the courts play a significant role in this process.

The main responsibility of those who work in the courts can be defined as the administration of justice in a swift, fair, and efficient manner. While most are familiar with such high-profile positions as judge and attorney, and have a basic knowledge of the organization of the American judiciary, they may not be aware of some of the relatively low-profile, yet critical, professional opportunities that exist in the court system. Included in this section are some well-known and lesser-known career positions that work to facilitate the efficient operation of the judicial system.

Opportunities within the court system are ever-changing and growing, as there is a continual call for court-related reform and reorganization. As this general change in our judicial system takes place, the personnel staffing needs of the federal, state, and local court administrations will require educated and able people with diverse skills and abilities to contribute and be a part of this task.

ATTORNEY/LAWYER

- Interpret laws, serve as advocates/advisers
- Conduct research and write legal briefs
- Represent clients in civil or criminal court
- Can serve to prosecute, regulate, and enforce laws

Robert DeLucia and T. Doyle, "Careers in the Courts," in *Career Planning in Criminal Justice*, 2nd ed., Cincinnati, OH: Anderson Publishing Company, 1994. Used with permission of the publisher.

- Must have Juris Doctor degree
- Entrance into law school extremely competitive

The system of laws in a democratic form of government is extremely important yet complicated. Laws affect every aspect of our lives. They regulate relationships among individuals, citizens, groups, businesses, and governments. They define our rights and restrictions, protect and defend our freedom, and insure our safety as individual citizens and as a society.

Lawyers are the professional experts who connect our system of laws to society by developing, interpreting, and regulating them. Lawyers generally work as advocates or as advisers. As advocates, lawyers represent parties in criminal and civil court trials to resolve disputes. As advisers they inform their clients as to their legal rights. In either case, a lawyer must be extremely familiar with the laws and their application to each specific situation or case.

As a lawyer you can expect to be involved in active and in-depth research and report writing to clearly substantiate a particular position. Much of your work will be in an office or law library. You should not expect that court appearances will be a frequent responsibility unless you are a trial attorney.

Although many lawyers serve as generalists, a substantial number of lawyers specialize in a particular branch of the law, i.e., international law, family law, business law, probate law, civil law, environmental law, entertainment law, to name a few. Most lawyers, approximately 75 percent, are in private practice working either in law firms or in solo practices. Others are employed by private business and others work for non-profit organizations, i.e., legal aide societies, and public interest law.

A substantial number of lawyers are employed in various levels of government. Lawyers who work in government service represent an integral part of the criminal justice system. At the federal level each department or agency employs lawyers whose function is to prosecute, regulate, and enforce laws. For example, at the federal level, you may investigate cases for the Department of Justice, the Federal Bureau of Investigation (FBI), or the Treasury Department. Each state may have administrative or regulatory agencies staffed with lawyers that work for the State Attorney General's office, a prosecutor, or a public defender. At the county or municipal level, a lawyer might work as district attorney representing the prosecution in criminal cases or handling post-conviction matters (motions for a new trial) at the trial court level. If you are a lawyer in government service you are likely to work less hours than those in private practice, although the pay is generally lower.

Your preparation for a career in law should begin as early as the first year of college. Although there is no recommended pre-law major, certain courses and activities are considered more helpful than others. For example, courses that help you develop your writing skills, communicate verbally, and help you to analyze and think logically are most important. Pre-law advisers often suggest enrolling in courses such as English, history, government, law, and philosophy. To be eligible to attend law school you must demonstrate an aptitude to study law, usually evidenced by the grades you obtained in college. Law schools will also look at your Law School Admissions Test (LSAT) score, as well as recommendations from professors, and a personal statement is also given consideration. Law schools vary in the weight they attach to each of the above. Graduates of law school receive a Juris Doctor (J.D.) degree. All lawyers must pass the bar exam in the state in which they wish to practice. To qualify for this exam, a candidate must graduate from a law school approved by the American Bar Association or the state authorities.

Large national and regional law firms will continue to be selective in hiring new lawyers for associate positions that offer the potential for partnership status. Graduates of prestigious law schools and those who rank high in their classes should have the best opportunities for such positions. Graduates of less prominent schools and those with lower scholastic ratings may experience difficulty in securing associate positions with partnership potential but should experience an easing of competition for positions with smaller law firms. Due to competition for jobs, a law graduate's geographic mobility and work experience assume greater importance. The willingness to relocate may be an advantage in getting a job, but to be licensed in a new state, a lawyer may have to take an additional state bar examination. Establishing a new practice probably will continue to be easiest in small towns and expanding suburban areas. Nevertheless, starting a new practice will remain an expensive and risky undertaking that should be weighed carefully. Most salaried positions will remain in urban areas where government agencies, law firms, and large corporations are concentrated.

BAILIFF (COURT OFFICER)

- Uniformed law enforcement; provides courtroom security
- Assists judge
- Escorts prisoners, jury members
- Requires high school diploma and passing grade on Civil Service Examination

Similar to the Deputy U.S. Marshal, who provides courtroom security and protection during federal court cases, the bailiff or court officer retains similar responsibilities in the courts on the state and local levels.

Essentially, the bailiff is the uniformed law enforcement person present at trials and hearings in the court. The bailiff assumes the responsibility of the protection of judges and courtroom participants. Working under the direction of the judge, bailiffs perform daily courtroom searches and reports. They remain on guard to take corrective action on any security violations or to respond to potentially dangerous situations that may arise. Bailiffs often escort and take charge of prisoners and jury members in and out of the courtroom.

In typical courtroom procedures, bailiffs call defendants and witnesses to the stand and generally act as a liaison between the jurors and the court. Bailiffs are responsible for a variety of routine assignments. Each day they inspect and prepare the courtroom to assure that all necessary equipment is in operable condition. They may perform a variety of clerical and/or administrative tasks including report writing, screening visitors, answering the telephone, making appointments, and generally being available to service the needs of the judge.

Becoming a bailiff requires graduation from high school, with college preferred and required in some areas. In most cases applicants will be required to pass a written test as well as an oral exam. Since the position entails constantly dealing with attorneys, witnesses, prisoners, jurors, and others, candidates will be examined for their ability to exercise tact, good judgment, and courtesy. Experience involving extensive contact with the public in a court system or in an agency providing administrative support services to the court system is helpful and may be substituted in lieu of education requirements.

COURT ADMINISTRATOR

- Perform administrative and management functions within the court
- Assist judge with court calendar, case flow, personnel management, research, and evaluation
- Maintain court facilities
- BA/BS in public administration
- Administrative court experience
- Knowledge of law important

The primary function of the court administrator is to assist the chief judge with the overall operation of the court to which they are assigned. The person in this position can oversee a wide variety of areas as they relate to the administrative support areas of the day-to-day workings of the judicial system.

At minimum, the education for a court administrator requires graduation from an accredited college with a specialization in judicial studies, business, public administration, or management. Applicants should have at least five years of progressively responsible experience in a staff or administrative capacity with a criminal justice agency. Ideally, the court administrator holds a graduate or professional degree in the above-mentioned fields and should have extensive knowledge of calendar management techniques, case law and procedures, and human management skills and abilities.

The court administrator establishes policies and procedures for the centralized control and coordination of all court calendars and programs; directs the evaluation, development, and direction of activities pertaining to the automation of calendar operations; coordinates the court's data processing activity with other criminal justice agencies; directs the preparation of reports, statistical studies, and other documents pertaining to calendar matters; evaluates and modifies existing calendar procedures; initiates and oversees the preparation of procedural manuals; has responsibility for reports showing the arraignment, detention, adjudication calendars, including original department designations and transfers of cases; meets with the chief judge, judges, attorneys, and other related personnel to assure the proper assignment, transfer, and disposition of cases; holds chief responsibility for the coordination and planning of court security facilities and activities; and could attend meetings as a representative of the chief judge or serve as a member on various internal and external committees concerned with the judicial system.

COURT CLERK

- Clerical assistant with a variety of administrative responsibilities
- Record and maintain case records

- Prepare statistical reports
- Prepare and receive court documents
- Explain court procedures to parties involved in court cases
- High school diploma required
- BS/BA degree or business school training a plus

The court administrator oversees a number of professionals who help to insure the efficient daily operations of the court calendar. Court clerks are excellent examples of this type of support personnel.

Generally, court clerks are considered clerical assistants who host a variety of administrative responsibilities. Two titles from the U.S. District Court and the U.S. District Court of Appeals provide an example of the responsibilities of this position.

A case processing clerk is responsible for the maintenance of the official case records in both civil and criminal cases for the court. This person also provides pertinent information, either in person, by telephone or by correspondence to the public. Other case-processing tasks are performed by this person as assigned.

A docket clerk reports to the director of courtroom services and is responsible for maintaining the official case records in both civil and criminal cases. This person prepares statistical reports on cases commenced and closed, furnishing information, either in person, by telephone, or by correspondence, as to the status of cases.

To attain a job as a court clerk, individuals should have at least a high school diploma, combined with some form of clerical work experience. Training at a business school is often viewed favorably, particularly if the job applicant has typing skills. A college degree is also helpful. All court clerks are required to have knowledge of the law, court procedures and policies, and a general understanding of court operations. As in the case of most court careers, the ability to communicate effectively is considered a prerequisite. There is room for advancement if the clerk is a concerned and competent employee.

COURT LIAISON COUNSELOR

- Assist and counsel defendants charged with crimes
- Evaluate and initiate treatment plans
- Make referrals to support agencies
- BA/BS in social work/counseling
- A desire to be helpful to others required

There are a number of specialized pretrial intervention projects or alternatives to detention programs throughout our nation's courts. Many of these projects employ the court liaison counselor.

The basic responsibility of this counselor is short-term counseling of the program participants. The participants are defendants charged with criminal and penal offenses who have been released by the court into the project's supervision before entering their plea. In addition to counseling, the court liaison counselor is responsible for referring the participants to appropriate community agencies, maintaining case files, evaluating client's motivation for help, determining problems that clients have, and formulating and implementing the treatment/counseling plan to prevent conditions that could lead to recidivism or rearrest.

One of the most important qualifications for this job is that the court liaison counselor possess strong human relations skills. He or she must show the ability to express thoughts on paper in a concise and organized manner and also must be able to assess the client's situation and formulate a counseling plan from this assessment. Interpersonal skills are also important because the court liaison officer will be interacting with professionals such as social workers, probation officers, and other staff members. Finally, the counselor should be able to accept supervision, make use of community resources and be able to work with program participants whose lifestyles may differ significantly from their own.

Counseling/correctional-type experience for two to three years in the above areas, when combined with a BA/BS in criminal justice, social work, counseling, or psychology provides the required background for application to this position.

COURT REPORTER (SHORT-HAND REPORTER)

- Record all trial proceedings with the use of a stenographic machine
- Must pass certifying exam as court reporter
- Knowledge of legal vocabulary essential

The court reporter is a "specialized" stenographer who records all statements made at trials and hearings, then presents their recording as the official transcript of the court. The position requires the utmost in skill, accuracy, and speed. Only the most experienced and highly trained reporters are recruited for court recording work.

In the recruitment of court reporters there is a preference for reporters who possess the ability to use a stenographic machine, which prints symbols as certain keys are pressed. They must also be knowledgeable in the vocabulary of the legal profession.

As mentioned previously, only the most highly skilled stenographers are employed with the courts. In many states, a court reporter must be certified through the passing of the certified shorthand reporter (CSR) test, which is administered by a board of examiners. The mark of excellence in this profession is to earn the designation of registered professional reporter. This is accomplished through further education and testing.

While employment in the stenographic field is expected to decline, the demand for skilled court reporters is expected to remain strong as federal and state court systems expand to handle the rising number of cases being brought to the court.

Students interested in this field should consult colleges and business schools that specialize in this area.

COURT REPRESENTATIVE

- Ascertain eligibility for alternative to detention sentences
- Heavy interaction with defendant population
- Requires some related experience and education for appointment

Another position in the area of alternative-to-detention programs is the court representative, who is responsible for reviewing court papers in order to identify and compile a daily list of defendants whose arraignment charge, criminal history, residence and disposition make them "paper-eligible" for a community service sentence. These defendants have already been convicted of a property crime but instead of serving a jail term they serve a community sentence based on a court representative's finding.

Once these "paper-eligible" defendants are identified, the court representative then conducts interviews with them and keeps a record of the defendant's sentence. Finally, the court representative conducts participant-orientation interviews with the defendant as well.

The court representative must have the ability effectively to interact not only with court personnel, but also with the defendant population. Generally speaking, this position requires at least one year of work experience in the criminal justice system or a college degree, or a combination of education and related experience.

DOMESTIC VIOLENCE COUNSELOR

- Assist/counsel victims of domestic violence
- Possess strong human relations skills
- Administrative/organizational skills vital
- Varied work hours

Many family courts throughout the country operate domestic violence units in which victims of domestic disputes are assisted. These counselors provide court advocacy, crisis intervention, short-term counseling, and assist victims in the petition room for filing for Orders of Protection, and concrete services and referrals as needed. There are a number of duties associated with this position. In the actual courtroom setting they may provide the victims with an orientation to the family court and escort the clients to court when necessary. They can assist their clients with other direct services such as placement into shelters, relocation, transportation, public assistance, or other assistance when necessary. Finally as in most every position within the criminal justice system, they are responsible for and must maintain accurate case records and statistics.

Domestic violence counselors must have strong interviewing and interpersonal skills, good organizational ability, the ability to work day/night shifts, and an understanding of the issues of domestic violence. A degree in criminal justice and prior experience or internship background in the social services would usually qualify candidates for an entry-level position in this field. In some areas of the nation, bilingual ability would be considered an advantage.

JUDGE

- Oversee legal process in courts of law
- Safeguard rights, determine legal positions, instruct jury
- Many judges appointed/elected thus part of political process

- Determine sentences, set bail, award damages
- Most judges hold the Juris Doctor degree

The job responsibilities of a judge may vary according to his/her jurisdictions and powers. In general, a judge oversees the legal process in courts of law. They insure that trials and hearings are conducted fairly and that the legal rights of all parties are safeguarded. They insure that rules and procedures are strictly adhered to with respect to such items as the admissibility of evidence and methods of conducting testimony. In the initial phase of a trial called a "pretrial," a judge will listen to allegations to determine whether a particular case has enough merit to warrant a trial. In criminal cases, a judge may decide whether a person should be remanded to jail prior to trial or decide whether, and in what amount, bail will be set in order to release the accused. In civil cases, a judge may determine specific conditions to be upheld by opposing parties until the trial.

A judge may decide the outcome of a case when laws do not require a jury trial. In cases requiring a jury trial, a judge will instruct the jury on applicable laws and direct them to deduce the facts from the evidence presented to determine a verdict. In a criminal case, a judge may determine the sentence, and in a civil case, award compensation for the litigants.

There are different types of judges whose responsibilities vary according to jurisdiction. Trial court judges of the federal and state court system generally try civil cases that transcend the jurisdiction of lower courts and all cases involving felony offenses. Federal and state appellate court judges have the greatest power and prestige. They review cases handled by lower courts to support or nullify the verdict of the lower court. The majority of state court judges preside in courts whose jurisdiction is limited by law to certain types of cases. For example, traffic violations, small claims, misdemeanors, and pretrial hearings constitute the bulk of the work. Administrative judges or hearing officers are employed by government agencies to rule on appeals of agency administrative decisions regarding such issues as: workers' compensation, and enforcement of health and safety regulations.

Judges do most of their work in offices, courtrooms, and law libraries, and generally work a 40-hour week. Much of a judge's time is spent preparing for trial, researching the law, and preparing rulings and judgments for trial. Judges held approximately 40,000 jobs in 1988 with about one-half working at the state level.

In most cases, to become a judge you must first be a lawyer. All federal judges are appointed by the President with the consent of the Senate. About one-half of state judges are appointed while the remainder are elected in partisan or nonpartisan elections. The prestige associated with serving as a judge should insure continued intense competition for openings on the bench.

PARALEGAL/LEGAL ASSISTANT

- Perform clerical and administrative duties for lawyers
- Research and prepare cases
- Obtain and draft legal documents
- Interview defendants and witnesses
- BA in legal or paralegal studies, certificate desired

In effect, paralegals function in very much the same way that lawyers do, except that they do not give legal advice or represent clients in court. They assist in all phases of case preparation. Duties include collecting evidence, drafting legal documentation, and researching and summarizing information about laws pertinent to cases, as well as those tasks which are relatively routine in nature (i.e., clerical responsibilities). Paralegals commonly attend and schedule hearings, interview defendants, witnesses or citizens, and obtain legal documents such as sworn affidavits.

At the present time, no standardization exists for employment or certification of paralegals. Those employed in this field have qualifications that range from high school graduation with work experience to those who hold college degrees emphasizing courses in criminal justice and law.

There has been a growing trend towards meeting specific educational and/or training requirements. Today there are a number of educational institutions such as business schools, colleges, and paralegal training institutions that provide specific legal education training and experience vital to obtaining a position in this field. Students should evaluate the variety of these programs for their educational content and job placement success before enrolling but, by all means should seek additional educational expertise, as the trend to hire students with some formal training is expected to rise.

In addition to acquiring knowledge about legal forms, procedures, and terminology, students must be able to write clear and concise reports. Good English and legal vocabularies are essential. It is also important for paralegals to be able to work effectively with people as they meet and communicate regularly with a variety of other professionals in the course of the their job.

PRETRIAL SERVICES OFFICER, U.S. DISTRICT COURTS

- Investigation and supervision specialist
- Advises court on pretrial release and detention, release condition supervision, monitoring, pretrial diversion, and public safety
- Duties may be similar to probation officer
- Requires a college degree, and specialized experience for appointment at Judicial Salary Plan level 7/9

The pretrial services officer has duties and responsibilities similar to those of a probation officer on the federal level. He or she will conduct background investigations of those alleged to have violated federal statutes and refer these investigations to the courts, will recommend release or detention after the investigation, and will supervise those defendants who are released.

The officer is also responsible for notifying the courts of violations of pretrial release, assisting persons under supervision with social service referrals, monitoring pretrial release reports for the U.S. Attorney, and maintaining effective interagency liaisons when required.

The pretrial services officer is expected to participate in ongoing personal training and education, cooperate with community agencies and, if deemed necessary by the court, carry firearms.

To qualify for a position as a pretrial services officer, a person must be a college graduate from an accredited college or university with a degree in a social science or in a field appropriate to the subject matter of the position and must have a minimum of one year of specialized experience. Specialized experience for this title can be defined as progressively responsible experience in the investigation, counseling and guidance of offenders in community correction or pretrial programs, or in closely allied fields such as education guidance counselor, social worker, case-worker, psychologist, substance abuse treatment specialist, or correctional researcher. A person interested in such a position may apply to the Federal Court District Office of Pretrial Services in which he or she desires to work.

RELEASE-ON-OWN-RECOGNIZANCE (ROR) INTERVIEWER

- Interviews and collects background information on defendants
- Makes release recommendations to judge
- Frequent court appearances
- BA/BS degree required

A position found in some areas of the country, and one that is relatively new, is that of the release-on-own-recognizance (ROR) interviewer. The ROR interviewer emerged as an offshoot of judicial reform that attempted to enhance the efficiency and fairness of the pretrial process in two ways. The first was an effort to decrease the number of days spent in detention by defendants who could safely be released to the community while awaiting trial. The second was to reduce the rate of nonappearance in court by defendants released from detention and awaiting trial.

The ROR interviewer's main task is the interviewing of defendants to verify information regarding their background and community ties to determine whether they could qualify for release on their own recognizance. In this position, the ROR interviewer interviews the defendant shortly after his/her arrest, usually at central booking. Information on the defendant's residential, employment, and family status is collected, and attempts are then made to verify this information by telephone. Additional information from police department arrest reports, prior convictions, and outstanding warrants are added to all that has been collected. Upon completion of this process, the ROR interviewer makes a release recommendation based on the strength of the community ties, and the likelihood of voluntary return to court. This information and recommendation is forwarded to the judge, who in turn examines this data, and in conjunction with other factors in the case, arrives at a bail or release-on-own-recognizance decision.

Other typical tasks may involve appearing in court and responding to questions relating to defendant's eligibility for ROR or interpreting information for the judge, district attorney and defense attorney. The ROR interviewer might also assist defendants in following directions to ensure that they appear in court, maintain contact with defendants and provide them with any information necessary to successfully complete court appearances, and contact defendants for whom warrants have been issued to make arrangements for a voluntary return.

The basic qualifications for this position include at least two full years of college and two years of full-time work experience in some form of court contact (interviewing, counseling, job placement referrals) in a social service or criminal justice agency. In some cases, a bachelor's degree from an accredited university is a substitute for the experience.

RESEARCH ANALYST/STATISTICIAN

- Prepare and evaluate statistical research reports designed to improve effectiveness and operation of agency or department
- BA/BS minimum requirement, master's degree preferred
- Strong math and computer skills essential

Research analysts perform a vital function within the overall administrative and management systems of the courts. Usually working under the direction of the chief judge's designee or the court administrator's deputy, research analysts prepare and evaluate statistical research and management reports designed to improve the structure and flow of court services, programs, and procedures. Analysts concern themselves with the improvement of existing programs and help to create and implement new ones.

Common areas for research include case flow through the courts, cost control, probation and parole services, grant writing, court procedures, space and equipment management, and other vital services.

A BA/BS degree is the minimum educational requirement for an entry-level position. In most cases, a research position in the courts requires, at minimum, a master's degree in criminal justice, public administration, business administration, or statistics. A strong background in math, statistical theory, research techniques, and computers is essential. Depending on the jurisdiction, applications for this position are made directly to the clerk of the court or by taking an appropriate Civil Service Examination.

SUPPORT SERVICES COORDINATOR

- Assist nonviolent misdemeanant in alternative sentencing programs with social service needs
- Requires knowledge of social service programs
- Ability to work with hard-to-employ population
- Experience in counseling
- Excellent entry-level position for correctional counseling

The support services coordinator is responsible for assisting nonviolent misdemeanants in alternative sentencing programs in finding employment, education, housing, health, or other necessary services that these clients might require. In order to perform this duty, a support services coordinator must first evaluate a client's needs by conducting assessment interviews and administrating basic educational exams such as math and English. The support services coordinator also must develop a network of social and health agencies which could provide the required resources for the client. The coordinator also provides employment counseling and accompanies the client to interviews. Finally, the support services coordinator is responsible for collecting data and writing reports on the services provided for each client, as well as enforcing the client's sentence.

Since the participants are considered difficult to employ, experience working with and a desire to assist this group is paramount. Further qualifications for this type of position include extensive contacts with and knowledge of referral agencies, effective communication skills, ability to work well in a small group setting, and possession of a valid driver's license. Educational requirements can vary with each jurisdiction.

SITE SUPERVISOR

- Supervise defendants in community service sentencing projects
- Possess handyman skills and motivational abilities
- Good entry-level position for social service, corrections, alternative-to-detention field

In some court jurisdictions, an alternative to detention sentence might involve assigning the defendants to rehabilitation of public property. Site supervisors are responsible for the supervision of the defendants involved in this community service. This supervision involves teaching proper work techniques in cleaning out buildings, painting and plastering interiors, and other forms of restorative construction.

The site supervisors are also responsible for continuous on-site inspections in order to observe not only the level of work being done, but to ensure that a high level of safety and productivity is being maintained. Site supervisors also write reports on each worker and on the progress of the work being done, and distribute stipends to the workers. Finally, the site supervisors are expected to maintain effective communication and constructive ties with the community and community groups.

This position requires experience in manual labor, good interpersonal and motivational skills, supervisory experience, ability to handle pressure and familiarity with the problems of ex-offenders.

VICTIM SERVICES PERSONNEL

- Provide assistance to crime victims
- Will be exposed to crisis situations oftentimes unpleasant
- Must work well under pressure
- Provide counseling service and casework
- College degree usually required
- Background in social work/counseling
- Mature, calm, and caring personality needed

Victim services personnel provide supportive assistance to victims of crime and their families. In certain regions, these professionals find employment in municipally sponsored victim services agencies; however, more than likely, opportunities will be found in private not-for-profit agencies affiliated with local police departments, district attorney offices, hospitals, and through the courts.

Victim Services Specialist

The duties of the victim services specialist generally fall into two particular areas of the judicial process: complaint and arraignment. In the complaint room, the victim services specialist interviews victims to determine service needs; provides orientation to central booking, complaint room and arraignment proceedings; collects notification information for possible future court appearances; screens cases for restitution; advocates for victim needs in the District Attorney's complaint room; and assists with property releases and affidavits. Ability to accurately record information and a high level of organizational ability are required. A college degree is required, and prior work or internship experience helpful.

Child and Youth Counselor

There is a compelling need for child and youth counselors. To meet the problems confronted when children are victims of crimes, the victim services agencies have developed a number of programs where child and youth counselors can help children and parents overcome the trauma of the crime as well as the possible criminal proceedings that follow.

In many areas, victim services agencies operate children's centers, which provide structured day care for child victims and children whose parents are involved in court proceedings. For child victims who must testify in court, child and youth counselors explain the process and accompany the child to meetings with lawyers and into the courtroom. These counselors help court officials understand the child's cognitive abilities and emotional state before the case proceeds. Child and youth counselors also help children express and dispel fears resulting from the crime. They prepare them for dealing with such threatening situations as what to do when they see the defendant in the neighborhood or courtroom, or how to tell friends about their experiences.

Child preventive services programs are programs which are designed to protect children from abuse. In these programs, child and youth counselors assist families with a history of violence, where children are at risk of abuse or neglect.

A third program in which the child and youth counselor is involved in aiding child victims is in the child victim unit. This project helps child victims and their families deal with the family court system and cope with the crime. The child and youth counselor accompanies the child to court and acts as a liaison between the attorney and the victim's family. The child and youth counselor also helps the child deal with the emotional consequences of the crime.

The child and youth counselor also assists in school victim assistance programs, which provide individual and family counseling for students who have witnessed violence themselves or between victims of crime at school, at home, or in the street.

Finally, a child and youth counselor may assist in group counseling for children who have experienced or witnessed violence at home, and in support groups for the brothers and sisters of murder victims, where these youths can discuss their feelings and help one another cope with the trauma of their losses.

The basic qualifications to work as a child/youth counselor include an advanced degree in social work and/or counseling, or in some cases a bachelor's degree in a relevant field combined with some social service work experience. Preferably, such work should be with children and families. Sensitivity and concern for others is necessary, and working knowledge of the courts and criminal justice system is helpful.

Crisis Counselor

The responsibilities of crisis counselors basically consist of providing services to victims of domestic violence, incest, rape, or runaway youths, and youths contemplating running away. A crisis counselor provides services such as crisis intervention, short-term counseling, and concrete services and information and referral for victims and their families. They also assess victims' needs and formulate treatment plans for victims.

In addition, crisis counselors coordinate and conduct educational programs and develop support groups for victims and their families. They also assist in establishing and maintaining service linkages with other social services and community agencies, and assist in staff training. Finally, a crisis counselor maintains case records and statistics on services provided, and performs other related tasks as assigned.

The qualifications needed to become a crisis counselor are an advanced degree in social work or a related field, or a BA and two years of relevant experience, or an equivalent combination of relevant course work and experience. Other important qualifications include telephone counseling experience, knowledge of the police and the criminal justice system, and being able to work with others as a team.

Runaway Counselor

The job of the runaway counselor is to assist runaway children by discussing with them the dangers of the streets and the options for improving the situation at home through counseling, family mediation, and peer support groups. Runaway counselors also assist parents of runaways by giving support and advice on how to search for their children or how to respond should their child call or return home. In addition, runaway counselors counsel parents whose children are at risk of running away about the warning signs and how to cope with them.

Runaway counselors usually work via a hotline number that is given out by the police, churches, hospitals, and city agencies. Runaway counselors may also reach out to young people who are involved or who are at risk of becoming involved in juvenile prostitution by taking to the streets. The counselors may go to a specific area in the afternoons and evenings and try to identify and establish contact with teenagers on the streets.

Once the runaway counselor has gained the confidence of the young people, he or she can provide them with support, guidance, and information. The counselor also offers food and clothing and arranges for emergency medical care, shelter, and transportation.

Qualifications for runaway counselors include a combination of education and experience, preferably in the area of counseling, peer counseling, or human services.

QUESTIONS FOR THOUGHT AND DISCUSSION

1. What are the primary functions of a court administrator?
2. What are the duties of a paralegal or legal assistant?
3. What is the role of victim services personnel?

SUGGESTIONS FOR FURTHER READING

ROBERT DeLUCIA AND THOMAS DOYLE, *Career Planning in Criminal Justice*, 2nd ed., Cincinnati, OH: Anderson Publications, Inc., 1994.

FRED FRIENDLY AND MARTHA ELIOT, "A Knock at the Door: How the Supreme Court Created a Rule to Enforce the Fourth Amendment," *The Constitution: That Delicate Balance*, New York, NY: McGraw-Hill, Inc. 1984.

BENNETT GERSHMAN, "Abuse of Power in the Prosecutor's Office," in *The World and I*, Washington, D.C.: The Washington Times Corp., June 1991.

LISA McINTYRE, "But How Can You Sleep at Night," in *The Public Defender: The Practice of Law in the Shadows of Repute*, Chicago, IL: University of Chicago Press, 1987.

JOYCELYN POLLOCK, "Ethics and the Courts," in *Ethics in Crime and Justice: Dilemmas and Decisions*, 2nd ed., Belmont, CA: Wadsworth Publishing Company, 1994.

JILL SMOLOWE, "The Trials of the Public Defender," in *Time*. New York, NY: Time, Inc., March 29, 1993.

SEYMOUR WISHMAN, *The Anatomy of a Jury*, New York, NY: Penguin Books, 1986.

SECTION 4

Jails, Prisons, and Community-Based Corrections

INTRODUCTION

By the 1990s the number of adults under some form of correctional control in the United States had reached an all-time high of 4.3 million—one out of every 43 Americans—in jail, prison, or under some form of community-based correctional supervision. The system, overcrowded and seemingly ineffective, has been subject to a great deal of controversy, beginning with the Quaker-inspired prisons in Pennsylvania over 200 years ago and continuing today. This section analyzes the major components of the correctional system, examines the issues, and reviews alternatives to traditional prison and community-based correctional modalities.

In the first selection, "Jail Overcrowding: Social Sanitation and Warehousing of the Urban Underclass," Rutgers professor, Michael Welch reports that 30 percent of America's large city jails are under court order to reduce overcrowding. He provides a comprehensive analysis of court-ordered reforms, and changes in institutional conditions and policy alternatives. He recommends carefully weighing alternatives and developing optimal policy plans based on a well-coordinated approach to problem analysis and design. This reading is especially relevant today due to the pervasive overcrowding of jails.

In selection two, "The Dirty Secret of Cellblock 6: A Report From the Inside," *New York Magazine* staff writer, Craig Horowitz, provides a view of New York City's main jail, Rikers Island, from the perspectives of both inmates and correctional staff. In this engrossing account of life inside the jail, Horowitz suggests that it is "only a matter of time before the world's largest penal colony explodes."

Doris Layton MacKenzie reviews and evaluates the currently popular boot camp programs in selection three. She finds that some of the goals are being achieved while others are not. She identifies strategies for overcoming difficulties in designing boot camp programs in her article, entitled "Boot Camp Prisons." A day in the life of a boot camp inmate is depicted.

In selection four, "Women in Prison," Tracy L. Snell reports results of the most comprehensive survey of women confined in state prisons ever undertaken. The study found that women inmates resemble male inmates in terms of race, ethnic background, and age. However, women are more likely than men to be serving time for a drug offense and less likely to be serving time for a violent crime. Nearly 60 percent grew up in a single-parent household and about one-half reported that an immediate family member had also served time. More than 40 percent reported prior physical or sexual abuse.

Selection five, "Private Prisons" by John J. Dilulio, discusses the private sector involvement in prison construction and management. Princeton professor Dilulio sets out the major issues and controversies related to private prisons. The idea of privatization of prisons is especially important today due to prison overcrowding.

Drawn from a Distinguished Faculty Lecture at American University entitled, "This Man Has Expired," selection six, by Robert Johnson, presents a view of the death penalty never before revealed, as he describes the work of executioners as they prepare for and conduct an execution. The author raises a controversial question during a time when executions have been rapidly increasing.

In selection seven, "Parole: Past and Present," Paul Cromwell reviews the history of the issues and problems associated with the use of parole, and argues that, despite a history of controversy, parole remains viable and a necessary adjunct to other correctional modalities. The author also outlines a new role for parole.

Selection eight, "Romancing the Stone or Stoning the Romance: Ethics of Community-Based Corrections," provides an examination of an oft-ignored topic, criminal justice ethics. Sam Houston State University professor Sam Souryal considers the cases for and against community-based corrections with particular reference to the issues of severity, proportionality, restrictions against humiliation and degradation, privacy, and other ethical choices.

Selection nine enumerates the "American Correctional Association's Code of Ethics," a guide for all correctional employees. These principles remind correctional employees of their commitment to professional and compassionate service.

What is work in the criminal justice system really like? This is a common concern of criminal justice and criminology students. In selection ten, "An Officer of the Court: Working in Probation," probation officer Linda Peck describes the frustration and satisfaction of the work of a probation officer in a district court in a medium-sized city. It is important to get an inside view of criminal justice jobs before selecting a career. Many times the actual job is very different from what we expect, since our expectations are usually based on popular media accounts or other sources that tend to romanticize the job.

Selection eleven, "Careers in Correction," written by Robert Delucia and Thomas Doyle, provides a more comprehensive overview of the types of jobs in the correctional system. Jobs are described briefly in the general areas of detention, rehabilitation, and administration. The correctional field is experiencing the greatest growth rate for jobs among all the criminal justice fields.

Jail Overcrowding

Social Sanitation and the Warehousing of the Urban Underclass

Michael Welch

On Being Warehoused in an Overcrowded Jail

Immediately after being arrested and booked on drug charges or any similar offense, most white, middle-class persons are detained only as long as it takes for a family member to arrive with the cash needed to secure their release. In cases such as these, bail may be set at $1,000: high enough to ensure the defendant's court appearance, but certainly not high enough to prevent his or her release from jail.

But for an unemployed person from the lower class facing similar charges, the same $1,000 bail might readily prevent his release. Therefore he will remain in jail until his court appearance, a wait that may last weeks or even months.

During this wait he will experience the horrific aspects of pretrial detention, which are exacerbated by jail overcrowding. For instance, every day for the next number of weeks or months, he will wait in line to use the telephone for nearly one hour before he can call his family, as well as his court-appointed lawyer whom he will not actually meet until moments before he appears before the judge. In fact, because most pretrial detainees have such difficulty calling their family and reaching their attorney, they eventually realize that waiting in line for the telephone is a waste of time.

Due to overcrowded jail conditions, a pretrial detainee may have to sleep on the floor for several days or weeks before a bed becomes available. However, the actuality of being able to sleep should not be taken for granted. Loud voices of other inmates can be heard at all hours of the day and night. Thoughts of release become an obsession, especially when it is painfully clear that being held in jail means being denied even the most basic elements of outside living.

Pretrial detention also means eating cold institutional food, wearing dirty clothes reeking of body odor, and having to shower and go to the bathroom without privacy. In overcrowded jails, the plumbing cannot keep pace with the demands placed on the toilets; hence clogged toilets and flooding create an unbearable stench. These nauseating odors are worsened by the summer heat, which generates a permanent stench of urine that permeates the living units. As one develops a heightened sense of vigilance, the insufferable condi-

Reprinted with permission of the author. An earlier version of this paper appeared in *Critical Issues in Crime and Justice*, Albert P. Roberts (ed.). Sage Publications, 1994.

tions eventually fade into the background. One continually maintains close surveillance over the other inmates to ward off any potential threats of physical and sexual assault.

Understandably, pretrial detention in an overcrowded jail is a punishing experience. And this form of punishment raises two serious issues. First, being forced to undergo this punishment *before* trial violates the "innocent until proven guilty" principle of criminal justice. Second, this form of pretrial punishment is often reserved for those who cannot financially secure their release by meeting the bail. In other words, even at the early stages of determining one's guilt or innocence, the criminal justice system treats persons differently on the basis of their social class. Upper- and middle-class persons are more likely to spend time in the community while awaiting trial, whereas those who are poor face months of detention in an overcrowded jail.

An Introduction to Jails

During the summer of 1989, the election campaign for mayor of New York City was heating up. At this point, most of the political rhetoric had mirrored national political strategies by targeting street crime as society's most pressing issue. Most mayoral candidates in New York City spent several months exaggerating their "tough on crime" promises. Candidate Ronald S. Lauder amplified his disdain for street crime by visiting Rikers Island, the largest penal colony in the world, located off the banks of New York City.

Lauder was outraged at what he saw at Rikers Island: Inmates were allowed to watch television and had access to recreational facilities. Lauder proclaimed that he would remove televisions and close the recreational facilities, which he believed helped criminals strengthen their bodies for their return to the streets. Regarding jails, Lauder quipped, "It says that, hey, it is not so bad. If it were up to me, I would have them breaking stones to pebbles" (Barbanel, 1989, p. B1).

Although Lauder's condemnation of the jail system may have earned him some votes from those equally fed up with street crime, it is clear that Lauder himself did not know the fundamental differences between jails and prisons. What he failed to realize is that Rikers Island is a jail complex in which 65% of the population are pretrial detainees. Moreover, according to the Correctional Association of New York (1989), most of these pretrial detainees are held there because they are too poor to meet their bail, which is sometimes as low as $250 to $500.

Corrections officials at Rikers Island responded to Lauder's misinformed remarks by pointing out that exercise and television are essential to managing the inmate population by easing tensions and relieving stress. Furthermore, the policy at Rikers Island that grants inmates 1 hour of recreation per day is consistent with the minimum standards of incarceration that are also observed by federal penitentiaries (Barbanel, 1989).

Even though we might expect politicians to be aware of the basic differences between jails and prisons, Lauder's level of confusion is common among many persons who are uneducated about the various components of the criminal justice system. In brief, although jails and prisons differ in numerous ways, the distinction has traditionally been drawn along the lines of the legal status of their inmates. For example, whereas prisons house convicted felons (those serving sentences for 1 year or more), jails hold pretrial detainees, convicted misdemeanants (those serving sentences of less than 1 year), and convicted felons who are awaiting transfer to their assigned prison. Furthermore, jails are usually local and county institutions, whereas prisons are governed by state or federal authorities. Due to these basic differences, jails and prisons are destined to remain distinct institutions that face problems unique to their respective roles in the criminal justice system (Welch, 1992a).

The purpose of this chapter is to promote a heightened awareness of how jails differ from prisons. As we explore the use of jails, particularly in major urban settings, we will learn that jails also serve a distinct function in society known as *social sanitation*. Moreover, we will examine jail overcrowding in light of correctional *warehousing*: the practice of incarcerating massive numbers of inmates with the sole institutional goal of securing custody. Human storage, not rehabilitation or reform, is the primary objective in warehousing, and it is society's *urban underclass* who are most likely to undergo this form of incarceration. In this chapter, we will focus on the problems associated with jail overcrowding and proposed solutions, and because urban jails have the highest concentration of inmates, particular attention will be paid to the jail systems in New York City, Chicago, Los Angeles, Houston, and Miami.

CORRECTIONAL OVERCROWDING: THE SCOPE OF THE PROBLEM

The United States is the world's leader in the number of persons it holds in prisons and jails, and its lead continues to widen over second-place South Africa and third-place Soviet Union. At an annual cost of $20 billion, taxpayers have inherited the burden of incarcerating more than 1 million Americans in prisons and jails. This massive warehousing effort in the United States is almost 4 times the incarceration rate of most European and Asian nations (Mauer, 1992a).

During the 1980s the prison and jail population more than doubled, and although considerable deliberation has focused on the crisis of prison overcrowding, less attention has been placed on jails, whose population increased by 77% between 1983 and 1989 (Bureau of Justice Statistics, 1989). While state prisons continue to absorb more inmates than they can reasonably manage, large urban jails take on a proportionately higher influx of admissions. New York State's prison population has jumped 160% over the past 12 years. By comparison, the inmate population in New York City jails has tripled during the same period (Mauer, 1992b).

Perhaps the most disturbing contradiction in this pattern of warehousing is that crime rates increased by only 2% in the period 1979–1988 (Mauer, 1992a). For those suggesting that Americans are soft on crime, it must be pointed out that our nation has "become more punitive than at any other time in our history" (Austin & Irwin, 1990, p. 2).

JAIL OVERCROWDING

Overcrowding is considered the most pressing problem facing jails; in fact, in a widely cited survey, Guynes (1988) found that jail overcrowding poses a more serious problem than prison overcrowding. The "War on Drugs" has contributed to booming populations in both prisons and jails, and the unique role of the jail within the criminal justice system adds to the perennial problem of having to admit more inmates than there is space (see Klofas, Stojkovic, & Kalinich, 1992; Welsh, Leone, Kinkade, & Pontell, 1991).

The jail has been viewed as a "strange correctional hybrid" because it is used as a detention center for suspects, a correctional facility for misdemeanants, and a refuge to hold social misfits (Clear & Cole, 1990, p. 205). Throughout history, the poor have disproportionately occupied jails. Hence jails live up to their reputation as being the "poorhouses of the twentieth century," the "ultimate ghettos," and "storage bins for humans," as well as social "garbage cans" used to discard society's "rabble" (Clear & Cole, 1990; Goldfarb, 1975; Glaser, 1979; Irwin, 1985; Moynahan & Stewart, 1980; Welch, 1991a). Much like the persons detained there, jails are the most neglected institutions within the criminal justice system.

As of June 1990, the average daily jail population in the United States was 408,075, which constitutes a 5.5% increase from 1989. (This figure is significantly lower than the increase recorded between 1988 and 1989, which reached 15%). Overall, the number of inmates exceeded available space in jails: occupancy was 104% of the rated capacity (Bureau of Justice Statistics, 1991a).

Unlike their prison counterparts, which hold a relatively stable population in terms of admissions and releases, the jail operates more like a "people-processing station" distinguished by a constant flow of traffic with around the clock activity. From June 1989 to June 1990, there were nearly 20 million jail admissions and releases; clearly, jails have more contact with the general population than do prisons.

WHO GOES TO JAIL?

Unlike the board game Monopoly, one does not end up in jail by mere chance; there is a clear pattern of detention. The jail population does *not* represent a cross-section of the general population; rather, its inmates are disproportionately black, Hispanic, and most significantly, poor, uneducated, and unemployed. According to the Bureau of Justice Statistics, the percentages of black and Hispanic jail inmates increased substantially between 1983 and 1989. "With the increase in drug offenders, the jail population was generally older, less likely to have been incarcerated in the past, and less likely to be serving time for a violent offense in 1989 than in 1983" (Bureau of Justice Statistics, 1989).

In an attempt to help answer the question "Who goes to jail?" let us examine the following findings from the most recent (1989) profile survey on jail inmates (Bureau of Justice Statistics, 1991b, pp. 1–2).

- In 1989 nearly 1 in every 4 jail inmates was in jail for a drug offense, compared to 1 in every 10 in 1983.
- More than a third of all Hispanic inmates and a quarter of black non-Hispanic inmates were in jail for a drug violation, compared to less than a sixth of the white non-Hispanic inmates.
- During the month before their offense, more than 4 of every 10 convicted inmates had used a drug, and at least 1 of every 4 was a current user of a major drug.

- More than half of all jail inmates said they were under the influence of drugs or alcohol at the time of their current offense—12.1% under the influence of both drugs and alcohol, 15.4% under the influence of only drugs, and 29.2% under the influence of only alcohol.
- More than three quarters of the jail inmates had a prior sentence to probation or incarceration. At least a third were in jail for a violent offense or had a prior sentence for a violent offense.
- Among those inmates sentenced to jail, half had received a sentence of 6 months or less. The median time that the inmates sentenced to jail would serve before release was 4.8 months.
- Approximately 39.1% of all jail inmates had grown up in a single parent household, and an additional 10.5% lived in a household without either parent.

CHARACTERISTICS OF JAIL INMATES

To further our understanding of who goes to jail, it is important to consider additional research findings. We have already established that jail inmates are disproportionately young (age 18 to 34) black men from the inner city with a history of drug abuse. But looking at Tables 4.1 and 4.2 we can identify additional characteristics of jail inmates. For example, more than half (53.8%) of the jail inmates have not completed high school: 38.2% report having some high school education and 15.6% have achieved an eighth grade education or less. Another 33.1% are high school graduates and 13.1% report some college.

Prearrest employment status figures in Table 4.2 shed additional light on the population characteristics of jail inmates. At the time of arrest, 53.1% of jail inmates were employed full time, 11.4% were employed part time, and 35.5% were unemployed and either looking or not looking for work.

Prearrest income among those jail inmates who were free for at least 1 year prior to arrest is provided in Table 4.2. More than one fourth (26.5%) of the jail inmates reported annual incomes of less than $3,000 per year. Even more alarmingly, though, about 78% of all jail inmates earned less than $15,000 a year.

Perhaps the most accurate interpretation of the education, employment, and income figures is that jail inmates generally represent two segments of the lower class: They are either members of the working poor or permanent members of the underclass. Moreover, if one considers their educational background, it is clear that many of them have limited means to survive economically.

We have already established that those who are charged with drug offenses now make up 1 in 4 jail inmates. Table 4.3 presents the other changes in current offense data. As indicated by the data, those in jail for a violent offense (e.g., murder, rape, robbery, assault) decreased from 30.7% in 1983 to 22.5% in 1989. It is important to note that this decrease is expressed as a percentage: The total number of inmates charged with a violent offense actually increased from an estimated 67,439 in 1983 to 85,532 in 1989, an increase of 26.8%. In other words, there has been an overall increase in violent offenders, but their percentage drops because of an increase in two other offense categories. In addition to an

TABLE 4.1   SELECTED CHARACTERISTICS OF JAIL INMATES, BY CONVICTION
STATUS, 1989 AND 1983

| Characteristics | Percentage of Jail Inmates in 1989 | | | 1983 |
	Convicted	Unconvicted	Total	Total
Sex				
Male	90.0	91.5	90.5	92.9
Female	10.0	8.5	9.5	7.1
Race/Hispanic origin				
White non-Hispanic	42.5	33.5	38.6	48.4
Black non-Hispanic	37.1	48.2	41.7	37.5
Hispanic	17.5	16.7	17.4	14.3
Other[a]	2.9	1.6	2.3	1.8
Age				
17 or younger	1.1	2.0	1.5	1.3
18–24	30.9	35.1	32.6	40.4
25–34	44.0	41.2	42.9	38.6
35–44	17.0	16.5	16.7	12.4
45–54	5.0	4.0	4.6	4.9
55 or older	2.0	1.2	1.7	2.4
Marital status				
Married	20.1	17.3	19.0	21.0
Widowed	1.2	.7	1.0	1.4
Divorced	15.8	14.2	15.1	15.7
Separated	8.2	8.4	8.2	7.9
Never married	54.8	59.4	56.7	54.1
Education				
8th grade or less	16.0	15.1	15.6	17.7
Some high school	38.1	39.0	38.2	41.3
High school graduate	32.2	34.3	33.1	29.2
Some college or more	13.7	11.7	13.1	11.8
Military service				
Veterans	15.7	15.2	15.5	21.2
Vietnam era	3.2	3.3	3.2	9.2
Other	12.5	11.9	12.3	12.0
Nonveterans	84.3	84.8	84.5	78.8
Number of jail inmates	218,797	162,441	395,554	223,552

Source: *Profile of Jail Inmates*, 1989, by the Bureau of Justice Statistics, 1991, Washington, DC:
Government Printing Office.
Notes: Total includes jail inmates with an unknown conviction status or no offense. Data were missing for
marital status on 0.2% of the inmates; for education, on 1.7% of the inmates; and for military service, on
1.2% of the inmates.
[a]Includes Asians, Pacific Islanders, American Indians, Aleuts, Eskimos, and other racial groups.

TABLE **4.2**   PREARREST EMPLOYMENT AND INCOME FOR JAIL INMATES, 1989 AND 1983

| | *Percentage of Jail Inmates* | |
	1989	*1983*
Prearrest employment	100.0	100.0
Employed	64.5	53.2
Full time	53.1	40.9
Part time	11.4	12.3
Not employed	35.5	46.8
Looking for work	21.4	32.9
Not looking	14.1	13.9
Prearrest income		
Annual income[a]		
(Free at least 1 year)	100.0	100.0
Less than $3,000[b]	26.5	33.1
$3,000–$4,999	12.2	13.7
$5,000–$9,999	23.3	24.2
$10,000–$14,999	15.5	13.7
$15,000–or more	22.4	15.3
Number of jail inmates	285,599	170,393
Monthly income[c]		
(Free less than 1 year)	100.0	100.0
Less than $300[b]	22.4	36.3
$300–$499	15.5	17.1
$500–$999	25.3	28.0
$1,000–$1,449	17.4	8.4
$1,500 or more	19.4	10.2
Number of jail inmates	65,677	38,566

Source: *Profile of Jail Inmates*, 1989 by the Bureau of Justice Statistics, 1991, Washington, DC: U.S. Government Printing Office.

Notes: Prearrest employment data were available for approximately 99% of jail inmates in 1989 and 1983. Income data were available for 89% of the inmates in 1989 and 93% in 1983.

[a.]Annual income figures based on inmates who reported being free at least 1 year prior to the offense for which they were sent to jail.

[b.]Includes inmates reporting no income.

[c.]Monthly income figures for inmates who were free less than 1 year prior to the offense for which they were sent to jail.

increase of the percentage of drug offenses (from 9.3% in 1983 to 23% in 1989), there was also an increase of those charged with public order offenses (from 20.6% in 1983 to 22.8% in 1989). Yet those charged with driving while intoxicated account for almost all of the change in this category. Finally, the percentage of property offenses (e.g., burglary, larceny/theft, fraud) also decreased, from 38.6% in 1983 to 30% in 1989.

The Jail: Managing the Underclass in American Society

The aforementioned research findings on the profile of jail inmates provide us with ample evidence indicating that jail populations are disproportionately poor, young, black, Hispanic, uneducated, and unemployed persons who have drug abuse problems and reside in the lower class neighborhoods of our nation's major cities. Considering these socioeconomic characteristics, the issue of social class is simply too important to ignore. As mentioned, those in jail occupy one of two segments of the lower class: the working poor and the underclass. Whereas the jail experience adversely affects both groups, those who are considered the working poor appear to be less disrupted because, at the very least, they possess some skills and the opportunity to survive economically upon their release. In contrast, the underclass, by its very definition, are those who have limited means to survive: They are uneducated, possess virtually no job skills, and have little or no work experience. For them, the jail experience reinforces their inability to lead a productive and economically independent life (Gibbs, 1982; Weisheit and Klofas, 1989; Welch, 1989, 1991b; Wilson, 1987).

John Irwin has greatly contributed to the discourse of the social function of jails and the underclass in his book entitled *The Jail: Managing the Underclass in American Society* (1985). Irwin contends that jails are used in American society to manage the underclass. In his analysis of jails, he has identified a specific economically subordinate social group that he classifies as the *rabble*. The rabble are socially detached (not belonging to any conventional social network), disorganized, disorderly, and viewed by the conventional world as *offensive* to their middle-class sensibilities. Irwin claims that most persons who occupy jails (the rabble) are detained for minor offenses and do not fit the stereotype of the dangerous and threatening criminal. Whereas one might believe that jail inmates are detained for the purpose of protecting society while they await trial, Irwin found that many jail inmates represent various types of "disreputables" such as petty hustlers, derelicts, and junkies. These "disreputables" are generally detained for nonviolent and minor offenses (for example, drug possession) and are simply too poor to meet their bail. Moreover, by the very nature of their economic standing, the rabble are unable to adequately defend themselves legally. Therefore, from the moment of arrest, they are at the mercy of the police, the jail staff, their court-appointed attorney, and the courts.

In light of the issues surrounding social class, Irwin places his findings in a larger social context. He concludes that the jail functions as an extension of the welfare state and become a means by which society manages and controls the underclass. Similar arguments have been developed by other researchers, such as Piven and Cloward in *Regulating the Poor: The Functions of Public Welfare* (1971). In their work, Piven and Cloward assert

TABLE 4.3   MOST SERIOUS OFFENSE OF JAIL INMATES BY CONVICTION STATUS, 1989 AND 1983

| Most Serious Offense | *Percentage of Jail Inmates in 1989* | | | *1983* |
	Convicted	*Unconvicted*	*Total*	*Total*
Violent offenses	16.6	30.4	22.5	30.7
Murder	1.2	5.1	2.8	4.1
Negligent manslaughter	0.7	0.3	0.5	0.6
Kidnapping	0.3	1.5	0.8	1.3
Rape	0.7	1.0	0.8	1.5
Other sexual assault	2.7	2.4	2.6	2.0
Robbery	5.0	9.1	6.7	11.2
Assault	5.1	10.0	7.2	8.6
Other violent	1.0	1.2	1.1	1.3
Property offenses	29.2	31.2	30.0	38.6
Burglary	9.8	12.0	10.7	14.3
Larceny/theft	8.5	7.1	7.9	11.7
Motor vehicle theft	2.8	2.9	2.8	2.3
Arson	0.5	0.9	0.7	0.8
Fraud	4.2	3.6	4.0	5.0
Stolen property	2.2	2.6	2.4	2.5
Other property	1.2	2.1	1.6	1.9
Drug offenses	22.5	23.8	23.0	9.3
Possession	10.7	8.4	9.7	4.7
Trafficking	10.7	13.7	12.0	4.0
Other/unspecified	1.0	1.6	1.3	0.6
Public-order offenses	30.2	12.9	22.8	20.6
Weapons	2.2	1.5	1.9	2.3
Obstruction of justice	2.4	3.4	2.8	2.0
Traffic	4.1	0.9	2.7	2.2
Driving while intoxicated	13.8	2.0	8.8	7.0
Drunkenness/morals	2.0	1.3	1.7	3.4
Violation of parole/probation	3.7	2.1	3.0	2.3
Other public-order	2.0	1.6	1.8	1.6
Other	1.4	1.8	1.6	0.8
Number of jail inmates	218,303	161,858	380,160	219,573

Source: *Profile of Jail Inmates, 1989,* by the Bureau of Justice Statistics, 1991, Washington, DC: Government Printing Office.

that throughout contemporary history, welfare has been used to reduce social unrest and reinforce the poor's social position in a class society.

According to Irwin, criminal justice resources are likely to continue placing disproportionate emphasis on managing the underclass instead of pursuing more serious offenders. Such forms of law enforcement, he asserts, serve as a "political diversion" that draws attention from the apparent lack of success in dealing with the serious offenders (Irwin, 1985, p. 112). Although critics argue that Irwin overstates his case by "claiming that jailed persons are less involved in serious criminality than is the case," there is agreement with him "regarding the broader issues of public policy toward members of the rabble class who get caught up in lawbreaking, and in many cases, who get sent to jails" (Backstand, Gibbons, & Jones, 1992, p. 228). (Also refer to Table 4.3 for current offense date.)

In taking a closer look at the jail experience, Irwin learned that the rabble undergo a distinct form of socialization by which they are stigmatized and kept constrained within the underclass. Inspired by the work of Erving Goffman in *Asylums* (1961), Irwin outlined various passages of the jail experience that comprise four stages: disintegration, disorientation, degradation, and preparation.

Disintegration

Unlike white, employed, middle-class persons, who are perceived as being reputable and thus generally released on their own recognizance or are able to meet bail, disreputable persons (the rabble) are detained. This denotes the outset of the disintegration stage because it tends to destroy the few social ties the rabble might have. Simply being denied convenient access to telephones makes it difficult to contact one's family, friends, and court-appointed attorney. Moreover, being detained prevents one from "taking care of business," such as calling one's employer or paying bills.

Although having convenient access to telephones while in jail is often rare, sometimes there are circumstances that make this problem worse. For example, in New York City's Rikers Island jail complex, there are reports that black inmates monopolize one telephone while the Hispanic inmates dominate the other, leaving white inmates (who represent only 5% of the pretrial detainee population) without regular access to telephones.

Obviously, without regular contact with family, friends, and lawyers, jail inmates undergo considerable disintegration. Upon release inmates have the stressful task of "picking up the pieces." Irwin notes.

> Unlike released convicts and mental patients, they [jail inmates] have received no official preparation for their release. And when they do get out, city, county, and private agencies rarely offer them any help in coping with the problems of reentering society. In trying to pick up the pieces of their shattered lives, most of them will be working alone, with virtually no resources and many handicaps. (1985, p. 52; see also Weisheit & Klofas, 1989).

Disorientation

Among the psychological effects of being arrested and detained is a profound sense of internal disorganization and demoralization. Subsequent to months of detention, released inmates understandably reenter society in a state of confusion similar to "being in a fog." This degree of disorientation is compounded by the replacement of one's personal routine by the institution's. For example, one eats according to a schedule organized by the staff, and assuming one can actually sleep, that too is dictated by the institution. Eventually, one's sense of independence is replaced by feelings of powerlessness, which are further compounded by the humiliation inherent to being in jail. Moreover, Irwin reminds us that in jail one eats, urinates, defecates, washes, changes clothes, and bathes without privacy. Inmates are continuously subjected to stares, comments, insults, and threats.

"Persons who are arrested and thrown in jail experience a sudden blow that hurls them outside society. It not only unravels their social ties; it stuns them and reduces their capacity and their resolve to make the journey back into society" (Irwin, 1985, p. 66). Irwin concedes that being detained once or twice does not lead to permanent social isolation, but because many inmates are rabble who are detained rather frequently, their ability to "bounce back" is strained. "The jail is not the only expelling process, of course; economic misfortune and drug abuse are others" (p. 66).

Degradation

As might be expected, the jail experience also involves relentless humiliation as inmates are continuously stripped of their dignity. Inmates are met with unyielding hostility from police officers, deputies, guards, and other detainees. Under routine surveillance by the staff, inmates are subjected to frisks, strip searches, and body cavity examinations. Irwin provides us with a glimpse of the humiliation one feels during a "kiester search" as described by a deputy:

> "Now bend over and spread your cheeks," I ordered. The kid bent over and grabbed his buttocks, pulling them apart. The plastic bag [of narcotics] inserted into his rectum had broken. The red pills had partially melted from his body heat, and his anus was a flaming scarlet color. The intestinal pressure had forced some of the pills out through his sphincter where they remained matted in his anal hair. We began to laugh with black humor at the grotesque sight. When the cops became bored with the game, the kid was ordered to dig the narcotics out of his rectum. (1985, p. 77)

In some jails, inmates are required to wear orange jump suits instead of their own clothes, which might help preserve whatever sense of personal identity that can be salvaged. Additional aspects of the degradation process are the loss of privacy and being forced to live in an environment where the human density is intolerable; indeed, inmates are literally *warehoused*.

While in jail, inmates also endure a barrage of insults. They are routinely called slime balls, dirt balls, pukes, scum, kronks, and the most popular reference, assholes. Following months of detention, their outward appearances are likely to change: Because shaving is not always easy, many inmates grow beards, and their hair becomes long and straggly. Not only is this an extension of degradation, but at their court appearance, inmates are judged not solely or even primarily in terms of crimes, but rather for their character, which is generally assessed by their physical appearance (Irwin, 1985).

Preparation

Irwin points out that a great majority of those arrested and those detained are not sentenced to serve a jail or prison term. Considering the humiliation and degradation experienced at the hands of the criminal justice system, however, all those arrested are subjected to some form of punishment, even those whose charges are dismissed. Indeed, one way to view this pattern of social disgrace it to recognize it as "process as punishment."

Whereas reputable persons are likely to "pick up the pieces" and move forward with their lives, the rabble are less likely to do so. With limited means to survive and few resources and economic opportunities at their disposal, the rabble fall victim to the self-fulfilling prophecy constructed by the criminal justice system. For many, accepting the labels of "loser" or "asshole" and dropping out of society becomes the inevitable option. Considering this, the rabble become even more defeated and more socially disintegrated or marginalized, and, as Irwin asserts, "The jail experience prepares them for an acceptance of the rabble life" (1985, p. 84).

Social Sanitation

So why is the jail in the business of locking up poor and disreputable persons? What larger social purpose is served by warehousing the rabble, especially when it is clear that these persons are *not* dangerous and do *not* pose an imminent threat to the community? One objective is *social sanitation*, the process by which police remove socially offensive (disreputable) persons from specific urban zones, thereby creating the illusion that certain sections of a city are indeed reputable.

Every medium to large city in the nation has a so-called "good" section and a so-called "seedy" section. Among the many tasks expected of city police is to keep the "good" section free of "riffraff" or disreputable persons: those who offend the middle-class sensibilities of the conventional world, such as street-walking prostitutes, the homeless, bums, junkies, and drug peddlers. Again, it is important to emphasize that the rabble are not regarded by the police as dangerous, but rather as offensive to society at large. Whereas the truly dangerous go to prison, the merely offensive are sent to jail for a temporary stay (Irwin, 1985, p. 3; also see Klofas, 1987; McCarthy, 1990; Spitzer, 1975). In this sense, social sanitation is a form of *social control* more than it is a form of *crime control* because it emphasizes sweeping the urban streets of those persons deemed offensive but not necessarily dangerous.

Therefore the jail should always be contextualized within the concept of social sanitation. As mentioned, the role of the jail in social sanitation has historical precedents. As early as the 16th century in Europe, as feudalism was unraveling and more vagabonds, beggars, prostitutes, "gonophs" (petty thieves), and peasants were drifting into the urban centers, jails were constructed for the purpose of social sanitation (Chesney, 1972).

The Effects of Jail Overcrowding

Not only is overcrowding itself a problem, but it becomes a source of other institutional problems as well. For example, it places enormous strain on classification, sorting, housing assignments, food, medical services (especially in light of AIDS and TB), security, and various programs, such as substance abuse counseling. Overcrowding also disrupts the daily routine of the facility and places additional pressure on budgetary institutional operations by affecting both inmates and staff. The social psychological effects of overcrowding can be traced primarily to the stress it creates, resulting in anger, hostility, violence, anxiety, and depression. Jails are by their very nature stressful environments; overcrowding merely compounds pre-existing problems that result from warehousing too many persons in too little space.

More specifically, recent studies have documented the effects of overcrowding on staff in terms of increased sick call and disciplinary violation rates, as well as higher mortality rates (Werner & Keys, 1988; see also Leger, 1988; Paulus, Cox, McCain, & Chandler, 1975). This places additional stress not only on the staff and inmates, but also on the jail as an institution, which must respond to the requirements of health care, security, and maintaining internal order.

The degree of disruption caused by overcrowding is far greater in jails than in prisons owing to a number of factors. First, because jails are designed for short-term confinement, there is little emphasis on long-range routines for inmates. Consequently, there are few programs and services available that can occupy and pacify the inmates. In fact, many violent incidents can be traced directly to inmates' resorting to fist fights to relieve the boredom caused by idleness. Again, this is a feature of warehousing, whereby inmates are merely tossed into jails until their court appearances. Additionally, the inmates' relatively short stay in jail makes it difficult for staff to keep sorting out the troublemakers who are responsible for aggravating the already volatile conditions. Moreover, corrections officers have the ominous task of ensuring the fist fights do not escalate to large-scale disturbances and riots (see Sechrest, 1989).

CIVIL SUITS AND COURT ORDERS

As noted in *Cook* v. *City of New York* (1984), inmates do not forfeit all of their constitutional rights when they are incarcerated, even though the facility may limit some inmate rights in order to meet reasonable institutional needs (*U.S.* v. *Lewis*, 1975). Yet among the numerous consequences of overcrowding are civil and class-action suits filed by attorneys representing jail inmates against the jail administrators (see Champion, 1991; Embert, 1986). Figures from the latest Bureau of Justice Statistics (1991a) survey show that in 1990, 508 jurisdictions were under court order to reduce population or to improve conditions of confinement. More specifically, 28% of the jurisdictions had at least one jail under court order to limit population, and 30% were under court order to improve one or more conditions of confinement.

In 1979, a landmark case known as *Bell* v. *Wolfish* was filed in federal court. This case challenged the double-bunking practices of the Metropolitan Correctional Center (also known as the MCC), which serves as a federal jail in New York. The doublebunking policy was initiated when the pretrial detainee population dramatically increased, thus inducing the Federal Bureau of Prisons to assign sentenced and unsentenced inmates to single-occupancy accommodations. The class-action suit alleged violations of constitutional rights (such as undue length of confinement, improper searches, and inadequate employment, recreational, and educational opportunities). The U.S. Supreme Court rejected the allegations that these conditions violated inmates' constitutional rights. More important, because nearly all pretrial detainees were released within 60 days, double-bunking was not regarded as unconstitutional.

Despite the *Bell* v. *Wolfish* ruling, sheriffs and jail wardens remain alert because the courts are capable of holding them personally liable for damages in cases filed by inmates who allege violations of their constitutional rights. Even if the courts rule in favor of the jail administrators, the time and effort involved in litigation become a major distraction to jail management. In light of these developments, many of the large urban jails, which are described in the next section, face similar law suits and court orders.

SOLUTIONS AND REMEDIES: HOW FIVE MAJOR CITY JAILS COPE WITH OVERCROWDING

Due to the possibility of litigation, jail administrators stay continuously aware of their jail's conditions, especially if their facility is under court order to limit population. As we have mentioned throughout this chapter, the highest concentrations of inmates are held in large urban jails. Moreover, the nation's largest cities also have the highest concentrations of the underclass (the rabble), many of whom also come into contact with the criminal justice system. As mentioned, the majority of inmates held in these large jails are disproportionately young, black or Hispanic, of low socioeconomic status, poorly educated, and unemployed, report polysubstance-abuse problems, and are arrested for nonviolent offenses such as drug violations (possession and/or sales) as well as property offenses that often relate to drug violations. Considering this, it is instructive to examine how the following jail systems cope with overcrowding: New York City, Chicago, Los Angeles, Houston, and Miami. It should be noted that the selection of these cities is intended to target some of the nation's largest cities and to feature different geographic regions: the Northeast, Midwest, West, Southwest, and Southeast, respectively.

New York City

The jail system in New York City consists of 18 facilities, including the Rikers Island jail complex and the borough jails. As of May 1992, the inmate population was more than 21,690, and the operating budget had increased from approximately $100 million a year to nearly $800 million. Approximately 65% of the city's jail population consists of pretrial detainees, most of whom are confined not because they have been judged dangerous but because they are too poor to make the relatively low bails (sometimes as low as $500 or even $250) that have been set for them (Correctional Association of New York, 1989).

It should be pointed out that New York City's jail population is further bloated by the number of convicted felons who are awaiting transfer to state prisons, which do not expedite transfer because of overcrowding there as well. In fact, this is a national problem that jails are continuously forced to deal with: Of the 37,965 jail inmates nationwide held for other authorities in 1990, 24,238 were being held because of overcrowding elsewhere, especially in state prisons (Bureau of Justice Statistics, 1991a).

Though many jail systems nationwide have experimented with makeshift jails—the conversion of existing structures such as old buildings for correctional purposes—New York City has introduced jail barges, which constitute one of the most unique and controversial applications of makeshift jails. Jail barges are literally floating jails, and a small fleet of them is located at the river banks surrounding the city. Two of these barges in particular have an interesting history. Known as the Bibby Resolution and the Bibby Venture, they were purchased from England for the purposes of alleviating overcrowding at Rikers Island, but years before they had several troop barracks for the British navy during the Falklands Island War with Argentina (Welch, 1991a).

After their conversion to jails, the Bibby Venture and Bibby Resolution also known as the "Love Boats" by the inmates, were moored on the banks of the Hudson and East Rivers to house minimum security, low-risk nonviolent inmates who were enrolled in substance abuse treatment and work release programs. Because they were docked next to middle-class neighborhoods, residents engaged in a "not in my backyard" dispute with the city, forcing the barges to be moved to other locations, where similar protests also occurred (Welch, 1991a).

The Bibby Venture formerly held inmates involved in work-release and substance abuse programs (380 capacity), but it has been temporarily vacated due to increased capacity in other facilities within the system. However, as of May 1992, the Bibby Resolution houses 280 work-release inmates (capacity is also set at 380). The third barge in this fleet of floating jails is the Vernon Bain, currently being prepared for operations, whose capacity is set at 800.

To appreciate the extent to which the city has gone to create additional capacity, it should be noted that two refurbished Staten Island ferries holding 162 inmates each, are also moored at Rikers Island. Furthermore a series of *sprungs* have been installed to Rikers to house 1,900 inmates (50 beds per unit). Sprungs are another form of makeshift jails that resemble large bubble-like structures commonly used elsewhere as indoor tennis courts. At Rikers, the sprungs are used as dormitories for inmates from the general population and inmates enrolled in substance abuse and shock incarceration programs. Soon a few sprungs will be converted into medical units for inmates suffering from contagious diseases.

Another strategy designed to alleviate overcrowding at Rikers Island is the shock incarceration program, quasimilitary boot camp regiment for young first-offenders. The primary institutional benefit of the shock incarceration program is that it imposes a shorter, although more intense sentence, thereby making more beds available sooner.

In addition to a number of substance abuse programs, the city also has a proposed plan to introduce electronic monitoring. According to James Bennett of the Board of Correction for the City of New York (a correctional watchdog group), the strategy to deal with jail overcrowding in the 1990s is fundamentally different from that of the 1980s. During the 1980s, the city attempted to "build their way out of the crisis" by constructing more facilities. The lesson learned was that officials had subsequently placed themselves on the "correctional treadmill," meaning that construction did not keep pace with increased admissions. By contrast, in the 1990s, the city is placing renewed emphasis on programs and other alternatives to incarceration.

Finally, many of the administrative policies dealing with overcrowding are monitored by the federal courts in an effort to comply with court orders. In 1989, Judge Morris E. Lasker of the Federal District Court in Manhattan handed down a court order that specified that each new inmate be assigned a bed and given a medical examination within 24 hours of being taken into the department's custody. In 1990, a fine for noncompliance was established in which inmates who were not assigned a bed would be paid $150. To complicate matters, in May 1992, 21 jail supervisors and officers were charged with falsifying records to conceal such violations. The city's investigator claimed that the department falsified or made errors in the records of about 650 inmates (Raab, 1992).

Chicago/Cook County

Chicago's Cook County Jail is the largest single-site detention facility in the nation. The jail, which was designed to house 6,217 inmates, was in fact holding approximately 9,000 inmates as of May 1992. The jail employs more than 2,700 corrections officers, administrators, and staff members, and its annual operating budget is in excess of $98 million. The jail complex is made up of eight divisions, and the oldest division was built in 1929 (Sheriff's Office of Cook County, Illinois).

To better understand the overcrowding problem in the Cook County Jail, it is important to address its contemporary history in the context of inmate litigation. In 1974, pretrial detainees filed a class-action suit protesting the conditions of confinement, citing them as a violation of their constitutional rights. The suit, *Duran* v. *Elrod*, led to a consent decree handed down in 1982 that stated that each pretrial detainee is entitled to a permanent bed in a cell. But less than 1 year later, jail officials were charged with violating that consent decree by allowing inmates to sleep on the floors. Following numerous debates about which government branches should be responsible for decision making and inmate management, the court ordered that inmates with the lowest bail amounts who had been incarcerated the longest be released on their own recognizance.

This practice led to the formal introduction of Administrative Mandatory Furlough (AMF), which has since functioned as one of the primary mechanisms of dealing with overcrowding. It should be pointed out, however, that overcrowding and the practice of allowing inmates to sleep on floors, in dayrooms, and under stairwells remained a problem. According to the John Howard Association (a prison reform, advocacy, and watchdog organization), in September 1989 the jail was in violation of the consent decree, resulting in fines exceeding $270,000 paid by the county officials to the Inmate Welfare Fund (expended for goods directly benefiting inmates).

Because pretrial detainees represent about 95% of the inmate population, various measures installed to deal with overcrowding were designed with this in mind. For example, the specific strategies now in place include AMF, work furlough program (periodic imprisonment), and electronic monitoring. The electronic monitoring program began in 1989 and currently involves more than 1,100 detainees. The idea is to keep detainees under virtual house arrest by strapping a tamperproof bracelet to them, allowing the authorities to monitor them in their residences. In some cases, detainees are allowed to leave their homes to attend school, receive job training, or continue their regular employment; hence the program sets out to avoid expensive incarceration while maintaining nonviolent detainees as productive members of society.

Los Angeles County

The city/county jail system in Los Angeles is the largest in the nation. As of April 1992, the inmate population exceeded 22,790, which placed the jail complex of 10 facilities 136% over capacity. Consequently, city and county officials have cooperated with the Sheriff's Department and the Countywide Criminal Justice Coordination Committee to develop a series of mechanisms and programs to alleviate overcrowding. Such efforts have led to the implementation of nearly 50 mechanisms and programs countywide. The following are brief descriptions of a few of these criminal justice strategies, presented in the *1990 Programs Affecting Courts and Jails Report* published by the Countrywide Criminal Justice Coordination Committee (1990).

> Early Release Program
>
> The Sheriff's Department under the authority of a May 1988 federal court order, instituted this program in June 1988. Eligible inmates qualifying for this program include all sentenced inmates with a County jail sentence. The inmates are released after a discretionary number of days and are credited to the original sentence by the Sheriff. (p. 95)
>
> Pretrial Supervised Release Program
>
> This Program is partially funded by a grant through the Bureau of Justice Assistance (BJA). The remainder is funded through the County. The program is offered by the Pretrial Services Division of the Superior Court and is aimed at providing an alternative release mechanism for the courts that, in turn, positively impacts jail overcrowding. All defendants are supervised and may be involved in the following additional components:

- Drug Testing
- Treatment Referral
- Electronic Monitoring (p. 103)

> Regimented Inmate Diversion
>
> Also known as RID or BOOT CAMP, this program includes youthful nonviolent offenders who are given reduced sentences for participation in a rigid military style basic training program. The goals of the program are to reduce jail overcrowding, cut costs, deter recidivism, and improve control. (p. 105)

Other programs and mechanism include Own Recognizance, Community Service Sentencing, Bail Deviation Program, Weekend Commitment to Local Jails, Work Furlough, and Work Release.

Houston/Harris County

As of May 1992 the jail system in the city of Houston and Harris County held more than 13,000 inmates. In contrast to Chicago, the overcrowding problem in Houston is not caused by an excess number of pretrial detainees, but rather by an excess number of state-ready felons. That is, Houston's jail population is bloated by the enormous number of convicted felons awaiting transfer to the state prison system—again, a problem facing jails nationwide.

To understand how the Houston jail system inherited this problem of housing inmates who belong to the state prison system, we turn to the recent correctional history of the state of Texas. In 1972, a landmark lawsuit known as *Ruiz* v. *Estelle* filed by inmates against the state prison system led to sweeping changes on how the state prison system would manage inmates. Among the numerous modifications affecting the prison system was the agreement that the state prisons would not exceed 95% capacity. Consequently, the county jails throughout Texas were forced to hold state-ready inmates until there were openings in the state prisons. The jail system in Houston, much like the jail systems in Dallas, Fort Worth, and San Antonio, found itself confronting overcrowding effected by the state prison system. In this case, prisons overcrowding creates a *hydraulic effect*: "when pressure is alleviated at one point in the correctional system, it is increased at another" (Champion, 1991, p. 214).

Fortunately, the jail system in Houston does a fairly good job detaining only those inmates who really belong in the system. This is achieved by a number of screening mechanisms that keep many pretrial detainees out of the system while awaiting trial. Yet the degree of overcrowding has forced the jail system to look elsewhere for additional jail space. At this time, 1,600 inmates who belong to the Houston/Harris County jail system are held at neighboring county jails on a contract basis. This strategy, also known as "farming out," is supported by the state of Texas which compensates the participating county's expenditures. Nevertheless, due to the problems stemming from overcrowding in the state prisons, contracting has emerged as a costly and logistically awkward procedure.

Finally, the city of Houston and Harris County offer additional programs to deal with jail overcrowding. For example, adult probation services help alleviate jail crowding by supervising more than 49,000 probationers, and at this time there are more than 380 inmates enrolled in their Boot Camp Program.

Miami/Dade County

The Miami jail complex in Dade County comprises seven facilities holding more than 6,200 inmates as of May 1992. The problem in the Miami system also features litigation, in that the jail currently operates under a state lawsuit limiting overcrowding. The conditions of this court order have led to the construction of an additional 1,000 beds, which have allowed the jail system to discontinue use of makeshift jails (a series of trailers housing as many as 400 inmates).

In addition to the construction of a new facility, the Miami system utilizes such programs as Release on Own Recognizance (for nonviolent detainees), Pretrial Release and Diversion, and Work Furloughs. Overall, the Miami/Dade County jail complex resembles many other jail systems throughout the nation. It is generally a well-functioning system despite being enormously overburdened. Again, a major problem with jail overcrowding is that it generates other institutional problems by placing undue stress on resources and staff (see Kalinich, 1986; Thompson and Mays, 1991).

In sum, the strategies, mechanisms, and programs implemented to alleviate jail overcrowding can be classified into two policy categories: those accommodating social sanitation and those resisting social sanitation. Strategies designed to reduce overcrowding by constructing additional jails (building new facilities or renovating old facilities) accommodate social sanitation by expanding capacity needed to warehouse the underclass. However, those strategies developed to return the inmate into the community run counter to, or resist, social sanitation.

Large urban jails experience similar difficulties, especially problems related to poverty and substance abuse. These problems are further exacerbated when we take into consideration that jails are also dealing with problems previously handled by other human service agencies and mental health systems (Jerrell & Komisaruk, 1991; Kalinich, Embert, & Senese, 1991; Lawrence, 1989). For instance, today jails have to deal more with the homeless mentally ill than ever before (Abram, 1990; Belcher, 1988). Therefore strategies that merely alleviate jail crowding by releasing detainees do not necessarily address the underlying social problems, and it is these social problems that contribute to larger numbers of persons being processed by the criminal justice system.

CONCLUSIONS

In this chapter, we have examined jail overcrowding in a larger social context by drawing attention to the urban underclass and social sanitation. By exploring the various ways in which large city jails cope with overcrowding, we have learned that jail policy tends to swim against the tide of complex social problems such as poverty, unemployment, homelessness, substance abuse, inadequate education, and inaccessible health care, each of which directly or indirectly contributes to street crime and jail overcrowding (Welch, 1992b).

In light of the interconnection between jail policy and social forces, it is important that we expand our awareness of social problems facing our cities and demand more ambitious social policies. For example, we have noted throughout this chapter that drug arrests account for the latest surge in jail populations. As mentioned, it makes more sense to treat drug abuse as a public health problem than as a criminal justice problem. Clearly, treatment upon demand is more cost effective and goal oriented than mere warehousing.

Other areas of social policy requiring additional development are employment and educational programs. Indeed, serious investment in such programs is actually a crime control strategy. According to Mauer, "Studies of the Head Start program, for example, have shown that every $1 invested in early intervention resulted in savings of $4.75 in remedial education, welfare, and crime costs" (1992b, p. 82; see also Currie, 1985). Such educational and employment programs are particularly relevant in light of the problems facing the urban underclass. Moreover, such interventions also cut to the root of the problem instead of relying on warehousing as a form of social sanitation.

Finally, Irwin (1985) argues that social reforms must be addressed before jail reform "because no progress at all can be made on reforming the jail until we begin to reform our fundamental societal arrangements. Until we do, the police will continue to sweep the streets of the rabble and dump them in the jails" (p. 118).

REFERENCES

ABRAM, K.M. (1990). "The Problem of Co-occuring Disorders among Jail Detainees: Antisocial Disorder, Alcoholism, Drug Abuse, and Depression, in *Law and Human Behavior, 14*, 333–344.

AUSTIN, J., & IRWIN, J. (1990). *Who Goes to Prison*. San Francisco: National Council on Crime and Delinquency.

BACKSTAND, J.A., GIBBONS, D., & JONES, J.F. (1992). "Who Is in Jail? An Examination of the Rabble Hypothesis," *Crime Delinquency, 38*, 219–229.

BARBANEL, J. (1989, June 15). "Lauder Likes TV but at Rikers Jail It's an 'Outrage.'" *New York Times*, p. B-1.

BELCHER, J.R. (1988). "Are Jails Replacing the Homeless Health System for the Homeless Mentally Ill?" in *Community Mental Health Journal, 24*(3), 185–194.

BELL V. WOLFISH, 441 U.S. 520 (1979).

BUREAU OF JUSTICE STATISTICS. (1989). *1989 Survey of Inmates in Local Jails*. Washington, DC: Government Printing Office.

BUREAU OF JUSTICE STATISTICS. (1991a). *Jail Inmates, 1990*. Washington, DC: Government Printing Office.

BUREAU OF JUSTICE STATISTICS. (1991b). *Profile of Jail Inmates, 1989*. Washington, DC: Government Printing Office.

CHAMPION, DEAN J. (1991). "Jail Inmate Litigation in the 1990s," in J.A. Thompson & G.L. Mays (Eds.), *American Jails: Public Policy Issues*, pp. 197–215. Chicago: Nelson-Hall.

CHESNEY, K. (1972). *The Victorian Underworld*. New York: Schocken.

CLEAR, T., & COLE, G.F. (1990). *Introduction to Corrections*, 2nd ed. Monterey, CA: Brooks/Cole.

COOK V. CITY OF NEW YORK, 578 F. Supp. 179 (1984).

CORRECTIONAL ASSOCIATION OF NEW YORK. (1989). *Basic Prison and Jail Fact Sheet*. New York: Author.

COUNTYWIDE CRIMINAL JUSTICE COORDINATION COMMITTEE (1990). *1990 Programs Affecting Courts and Jails*. Subcommittee on Court Process. County of Los Angeles, California.

CURRIE, E. (1985). *Confronting Crime: An American Challenge*. New York: Pantheon.

DURAN V. ELROD, 74 C. 2949 (1974).

EMBERT, P.S. (1986). "Correctional Law and Jails," in D.B. Kalinich & J. Klofas, eds., *Sneaking Inmates Down the Alley: Problems and Prospects in Jail Management*, pp. 63–84. Springfield, IL: Charles C. Thomas.

GIBBS, J.J. (1982). "The First Cut Is the Deepest: Psychological Breakdown and Survival in the Detention Setting," in R. Johnson & H. Toch, eds., *The Pains of Imprisonment*, pp. 97–114. Prospect Heights, IL: Waveland.

GLASER, D. (1979). "Some Notes on Urban Jails," in D. Glaser, ed., *Crime in the City*. New York: Harper & Row.

GOFFMAN, E. (1961). *Asylums*. Garden City, NY: Doubleday.

GOLDFARB, R. (1975). *Jails: The Ultimate Ghetto*. Garden City, NY: Doubleday.

GUYNES, R. (1988). *Nation's Jail Managers Assess Their Problems*. Rockville, MD: National Institute of Justice.

IRWIN, J. (1985). *The Jail: Managing the Underclass in American Society*. Berkeley: University of California Press.

JERRELL, J., & KOMISARUK, R. (1991). "Public Policy Issues in the Delivery of Mental Health Services in a Jail Setting," in J.A. Thompson & G.L. Mays, eds., *American Jails: Public Policy Issues* (pp. 100–115). Chicago: Nelson-Hall.

KALINICH, D. (1986). "Overcrowding and the Jail Budget: Addressing Dilemmas of Population Control," in D.B. Kalinich & J. Klofas, eds., *Sneaking Inmates Down the Alley: Problems and Prospects in Jail Management*, pp. 85–100. Springfield, IL: Charles C. Thomas.

Kalinich, D., Embert, P., & Senese, J. (1991). "Mental Health Services for Jail Inmates: Imprecise Standards, Traditional Philosophies, and the Need for Change, in J.A. Thompson & G.L. Mays, eds., *American Jails: Public Policy Issues*, pp. 79–99. Chicago: Nelson-Hall.

KLOFAS, J. (1987). "Patterns of Jail Use," *Journal of Criminal Justice, 15*, 403–411.

KLOFAS, J., STOJKOVIC, S., & KALINICH, D.A. (1992). "The Meaning of Correctional Crowding: Steps Toward an Index of Severity," *Crime and Delinquency, 38*(2), 171–187.

LAWRENCE, J.E. (1989). "Substance Abusers in Jail: Health Service Breakdown in Five New York Jails," *American Journal of Criminal Justice, 14*(1), 122–134.

LEGER, R. 91988). "Perception of Crowding, Racial Antagonism, and Aggression in a Custodial Prison," *Journal of Criminal Justice, 16*, 167–181.

MAUER, M. (1992a). *Americans Behind Bars: One Year Later*. Washington, DC: The Sentencing Project.

MAUER, M. (1992b, February 11). "Lock 'em up" is not key to crime control. *New York Newsday*, pp. 44, 82.

MCCARTHY, B.R. (1990). " A Micro-Level Analysis of Social Structure and Social Control Intrastate Use of Jail and Prison Confinement," *Justice Quarterly, 7*, 325–340.

MOYNAHAN, J.M., & STEWART, E.K. (1980). *The American Jail: Its Growth and Development*. Chicago: Nelson-Hall.

PAULUS, P.B., COX, C.V., MCCAIN, G., & CHANDLER, J. (1975). "Some Effects of Crowding in a Prison Environment," *Journal of Applied Social Psychology, 1*, 86–91.

PIVEN, F.F., & CLOWARD, R.A. (1971). *Regulating the Poor: The Functions of Public Welfare*. New York: Vintage.

RAAB, S. (1992, May 16). "Charges Filed in Crackdown at Corrections: Altered Inmate Records Prompt Hearings for 21," *New York Times*, pp. 25–26.

RUIZ v. *ESTELLE*, F. 2d 115 (5th Cir. 1982).

SECHREST, D.K., & COLLINS, W.C. (1989). *Jail Management and Liability Issues*. Miami: Coral Gables.

SPITZER, S. (1975). "Toward a Marxian Theory of Deviance," *Social Problems, 22,* 638–651.

THOMPSON, J.A., & MAYS, G.L. (1991). "Paying the Piper but Changing the Tune: Policy Changes and Initiatives for the American Jail," in J.A. Thompson & G.L. Mays, eds., *American Jails: Public Policy Issues,* pp. 240–246. Chicago: Nelson-Hall.

U.S. v. LEWIS, 400 F. Supp. 1046 (1975).

WEISHEIT, R.A., & KLOFAS, J.M. (1989). "The Impact of Jail on Collateral Costs and Affective Response," *Journal of Offender Counseling, Services and Rehabilitation, 14*(1), 51–66.

WELCH, M. (1989). "Social Junk, Social Dynamite and the Rabble: Persons with AIDS in Jail," *American Journal of Criminal Justice, 14,* 135–147.

WELCH, M. (1991a). "The Expansion of Jail Capacity: Makeshift Jails and Public Policy, J. A. Thompson & G.L. Mays, eds., *American Jails: Public Policy Issues,* pp. 148–162. Chicago: Nelson-Hall.

WELCH, M. (1991b). "Persons with AIDS in Prison: A Critical and Phenomenological Approach to Suffering," *Dialectical Anthropology, 16*(1), 51–61.

WELCH, M. (1992a, July/August). "How Are Jails Depicted by Corrections Textbooks? A Content Analysis Provides a Closer Look," *American Jails: The Magazine of the American Jail Association,* pp. 28–34.

WELCH, M. (1992b). "Social Class, Special Populations, and Other Unpopular Issues: Setting Jail Research Agenda for the 1990s," in G.L. Mays, ed., *Setting the Jail Research Agenda for the 1990s,* pp. 17–23. Washington, DC: National Institute of Corrections.

WELSH, W., Leone, M.C., Kinkade, P., & Pontell, H. (1991). "The Politics of Jail Overcrowding: Public Attitudes and Official Policies," in J.A. Thompson & G.L. Mays, eds., *American Jails: Public Policy Issues,* pp. 131–147. Chicago: Nelson-Hall.

WERNER, R.E., & KEYS, C. (1988). "The Effects of Changes in Jail Population Densities on Crowding, Sick Call, and Spatial Behavior," *Journal of Applied Social Psychology, 18*(10) 852–866.

WILSON, W.J. (1987). *The Truly Disadvantaged: Inner City, the Underclass and Public Policy.* Chicago: University of Chicago Press.

QUESTIONS FOR THOUGHT AND DISCUSSION

1. What are the alternatives available to reduce overcrowding in large city jails? Which do you think is the best approach in reducing jail overcrowding?
2. What are the arguments given to support the claim that our jails mainly exist to manage the underclass in American society?
3. Discuss the major negative effects of being in jail and of being jailed in an overcrowded facility.

WOMEN IN PRISON

Tracy L. Snell

The number of women in State prisons grew 75% from yearend 1986 to yearend 1991, reaching almost 39,000 by June 1991. At that time women were 5.2% of all prisoners, up from 4.7% in 1986.

Relying on responses to questions in interviews with a nationally representative sample of State inmates, this report describes those women. It provides details on offenses and criminal histories, and it also depicts the women's personal characteristics and backgrounds.

Most of the female State prison inmates were over age 30, at least high school graduates or holders of a GED, and members of a racial or ethnic minority. Large majorities were unmarried, mothers of children under age 18, and daughters who had grown up in homes without both parents present. Before entering prison a large percentage of the women had experienced physical or sexual abuse.

The following findings summarize some major points of the report:

CURRENT OFFENSES

The expanding population of women who served a sentence for a drug offense accounted for more than half of the total growth; violent offenders, a fifth.

- In 1991, 10% of female inmates were in prison for fraud (which includes forgery and embezzlement), down from 17% in 1986.

CRIMINAL HISTORIES

Nearly half of all women in prison were currently serving a sentence for a nonviolent offense and had been convicted in the past for only nonviolent offenses. Nearly two-thirds of all female inmates had two or fewer prior convictions.

From Tracy L. Snell, "Women in Prison," *Special Report*, Bureau of Justice Statistics, Washington, D.C.: United States Department of Justice, March 1994.

- About 71% of all State female prisoners had served a prior sentence to probation or incarceration, including 20% who had served a sentence as a juvenile.

VICTIMS OF VIOLENT INMATES

Nearly two-thirds of the women serving a sentence for a violent crime had victimized a relative, intimate, or someone else they knew.

FAMILY CHARACTERISTICS

Two-thirds of the women had at least one child younger than 18; altogether, they were mothers to more than 56,000 minor children.

- An estimated 46% of women with minor children said they talked with those children on the phone at least once a week; 45% had contact by mail at least once a week; and 9% were visited by their children.
- More than half reported their minor children were living with grandparents; a quarter, with the father.
- About 47% of the women reported having an immediate family member who had been in jail or prison. About 35% had brothers and 10% had sisters who had been incarcerated.

DRUG AND ALCOHOL USE

Almost half of the women in prison reported committing their offense under the influence of drugs or alcohol.

- More than half of women in prison in 1991 had used drugs in the month before their current offense. About two-fifths had used drugs daily.
- The percentage of women who had used cocaine or crack in the month before their offense increased from 23% in 1986 to 36% in 1991.

SURVEY OF INMATES OF STATE CORRECTIONAL FACILITIES, 1991

The Bureau of Justice Statistics conducted the 1991 Survey of Inmates of State Correctional Facilities in 277 prisons nationwide. At each facility, inmates were chosen systematically from the day's roster. Through personal interviews with 13,986 inmates, about 94% of those selected, data were collected on individual characteristics of State prison inmates, current offenses and sentences, characteristics of victims of violent inmates, criminal histories, prior drug and alcohol use and treatment, and health care services provided in prison. Similar surveys occurred in 1974, 1979, and 1986.

INCREASE IN NUMBER OF WOMEN IN PRISON

The State prison population grew 58% between 1986 and 1991. During the same period, the number of women in prison increased 75%, and the number of men, 53%.

| | State Prison Inmates | | Percent Change |
	1986	1991	
Female	22,777	39,917	75.2%
Male	464,603	728,246	52.9%

Note: Data are based on custody counts from the National Prisoner Statistics program.

Adult arrest statistics reflected similar changes. While the number of female arrests increased 24% between 1986 and 1991, the number of male arrests increased 13%. Women accounted for 19% of all adult arrests in 1991, up from 17% in 1986.

| | Adult Arrests | | Percent Change |
	1986	1991	
Female	1,805,422	2,230,417	23.5%
Male	8,582,422	9,667,402	12.6%

Note: The number of adult arrests was estimated by applying the sex and age distributions from reported arrests to the total estimated number of arrests. Adults are defined as persons age 18 or older.
Source: FBI, *Crime in the United States*.

CHARACTERISTICS OF WOMEN IN PRISON

Women in State prisons in 1991 were most likely to be black (46%), age 25 to 34 (50%), unemployed at the time of arrest (53%), high school graduates, holders of a GED, or with some college (58%), and never married (45%). Compared to 1986, the female prison population in 1991 had higher percentages of Hispanics, women older than 25, and women who had completed high school. There were lower percentages of non-Hispanic whites and of women under age 25.

Although the men in prison overall were older in 1991 than in 1986, they were younger on average than the women. From 1986 to 1991 the median age of men went from 29 to 30, and in 1991, 22% of the men were younger than age 25.

The percentage of women in prison who had never married increased from 42% in 1986 to 45% in 1991. About a third of female inmates in both years were either separated or divorced. More than half the male inmates in 1986 (54%) and in 1991 (56%) reported that they had never married.

Imprisoned women in 1991 had completed more years of education than women in 1986. An estimated 23% of female inmates had completed high school in 1991, up from 19% in 1986. Male inmates had a similar increase in high school graduates, from 18% to 22%. In the 1991 survey, a third of the women who had dropped out of school—about a fifth of all women in prison—had gotten a GED. Altogether, 43% of female inmates had a high school diploma or its equivalent as the highest level of education. As in 1986, women in prison in 1991 were more likely than men to have had some college education (16% compared to 12%).

Female inmates in 1991 were significantly less likely than male inmates to be employed at the time of their arrest. An estimated 47% of women in prison were working, compared to 68% of the men. More than a third of the women were unemployed and not looking for a job.

CURRENT OFFENSE

From 1986 to 1991 a large increase occurred in the percentage of women in prison for drug offenses, and this was matched by a decline in the percentage in prison for property offenses. Nearly 1 in 3 female inmates were serving a sentence for drug offenses in 1991, compared to 1 in 8 in 1986. This increase in sentenced drug offenders accounted for 55% of the increase in the female prison population between 1986 and 1991.

The percentage of women in prison for property offenses declined from 41% in 1986 to 29% in 1991. Sentences for fraud decreased more than for any other single offense type, dropping from 17% of the women in prison to 10%.

Women incarcerated for violent offenses included about 3 in 10 female inmates in 1991, down from 4 in 19 in 1986. Despite this decrease in the proportion of violent female inmates, the number of women sentenced for a violent offense rose from 8,045 to 12,400 during the 5-year period. Murder, the most prevalent violent offense among female inmates in 1991, accounted for just over a third of the women sentenced for a violent offense.

VIOLENT FEMALE INMATES AND THEIR VICTIMS

In 1991 nearly two-thirds of the women in prison for a violent offense had victimized a relative, intimate, or someone else they knew. Women serving a sentence for a violent offense were about twice as likely as their male counterparts to have committed their offense against someone close to them (36% versus 16%). Another third of the women, but half of the men, had victimized a stranger.

Women in prison for homicide were almost twice as likely to have killed an intimate (husband, ex-husband, or boyfriend) as a relative like a parent or sibling (32% versus 17%). Female inmates were more likely to have killed relatives or intimates (49%) than nonrelatives (30%) or strangers (21%).

Relationship of Victim to Offender	Percent of Females Serving a Sentence for Homicide*
Intimate	31.9%
Relative	17.0
Well known	14.3
Acquaintance	12.8
Known by sight only	2.7
Stranger	21.3

*Homicide includes murder, negligent manslaughter, and nonnegligent manslaughter.

CRIMINAL HISTORY

Female inmates generally had not been sentenced to incarceration or probation as often as male inmates, and their record of past convictions was generally less violent than that of male inmates About 28% of the women reported no previous sentences to incarceration or probation, compared to 19% of the men. Four in ten women had a history of violence, compared to more than 6 in 10 men.

Nearly half of all women in prison were currently serving a sentence for a nonviolent offense and had only nonviolent offenses for prior convictions. Among women with no prior sentences, more than half were serving a sentence for a violent offense. Among those women with a previous sentence, about a third were serving a sentence or had served a sentence for a violent offense.

Female inmates also had shorter criminal records than male inmates. An estimated 51% of all women in prison had one or no prior offenses, and 66% had two or fewer offenses, compared to 39% and 55% of the men, respectively. About 2 in 10 women had a criminal record as a juvenile, compared to 4 in 10 men. Half of all women in prison had criminal records as adults only.

SENTENCE LENGTH

Overall, female prisoners had shorter maximum sentences than men. Half of the women had a maximum sentence of 60 months of less, while half of the men had a sentence of 120 months or less. Excluding sentences to life or death, women in prison had received sentences that, on average, were 48 months shorter than those of men (mean sentences of 105 and 153 months, respectively). An estimated 7% of the women and 9% of the men received sentences to life or death.

The differences in sentence length are, partly, the result of variation in the distribution of offenses among female and male inmates. Women were more likely than men to be

| Maximum | Percent of Inmates | |
Sentence Length	Female	Male
Less than 36 months	24.2%	12.4%
36–59	18.7	15.0
60–119	20.5	22.3
120–179	11.9	13.2
180 or more	17.7	27.9
Life/death	7.0	9.2

in prison for drug and property offenses, which had shorter average sentences than violent offenses.

For each category of offense, women received shorter average maximum sentences than men. For property offenses, female prisoners had a mean sentence 42 months shorter than men; for drug offenses, 18 months shorter; and for violent offenses, 39 months shorter.

FAMILY BACKGROUND

More than half of the women in prison had grown up in a household without the presence of both parents. An estimated 42% had lived in a single-parent household—39% with their mothers and 3% with their fathers. An additional 16% had lived in a household with neither parent present.

Relative to the general population, female inmates were nearly twice as likely to have grown up in a single-parent household. In 1975—when most of the inmates in 1991 were between ages 10 and 18—80% of the 66.1 million children in the Nation's households were living with both parents.[1]

The composition of the childhood household differed among white, black, and Hispanic women in prison. More than half of white women and less than a third of black women grew up with both parents present. Black female inmates were the most likely to have grown up in a home with only their mothers (46%). Hispanic women were equally likely to have lived with both parents (40%) or their mothers only (41%).

Among female inmates of all races, about 17% had lived in a foster home, agency, or other institution at some time while they were growing up. White women were more likely than other women to have ever lived in such an alternative care facility when young.

Women in prison were more likely than the men to have had at least one member of their immediate family who had been incarcerated: 47% of female inmates and 37% of male inmates. About 35% of the women had a brother and 10% had a sister who had served a jail or prison sentence.

Higher percentages of black women than of white women had family members who had been in jail or prison. Among women 42% of black inmates, 36% of Hispanic inmates, and 26% of white inmates said a brother had been incarcerated. White women (11%) were more likely than black women (5%) to have had a father with jail or prison time.

A third of the female inmates and a quarter of the males said that a parent or guardian had abused drugs or alcohol while the inmate was growing up. Alcohol was more often cited than drugs. Thirty-two percent of the women had a parent who abused alcohol, and 7% had a parent who used drugs. Of white women in prison, 42% reported parental abuse of drugs or alcohol, compared to 33% of Hispanic women and 26% of black women.

PHYSICAL AND SEXUAL ABUSE OF PRISONERS

In 1991 survey participants responded to a series of questions about any abuse experienced and their age at the time of abuse. For the first time in a BJS inmate survey, inmates reported their relationship to their abusers, and female inmates indicated if sexual abuse involved rape.

More than 4 in every 10 women reported that they had been abused at least once before their current admission to prison. An estimated 34% of female inmates reported being physically abused, and 34% reported being sexually abused. About 32% said the abuse had occurred before age 18, and 24% said they had been abused since age 18.

Compared to men in prison, women were at least 3 times more likely to report any prior abuse and at least 6 times more likely to report sexual abuse or abuse since age 18.

Among inmates who reported prior abuse, women differed somewhat from men in their relationships to their abusers. An estimated 50% of women in prison who reported abuse said they had experienced abuse at the hands of an intimate, compared to 3% of men. While both female and male inmates were most likely to name a relative as an abuser, women were less likely than men to say that a parent had abused them (38% compared to 57%).

More than three-quarters of the female inmates who had a history of abuse reported being sexually abused. An estimated 56% of the abused women said that their abuse had involved a rape, and another 13% reported an attempted rape.

Among the women in prison, those who reported abuse had different types of offenses than those who did not. The victims of abuse were more likely to be in prison for a vio-

Type of Abuse	Percent of Female Inmates Who Were Abused
Physical only	21.2%
Sexual only	21.9
Both	56.9
Type of sexual abuse	
Total	78.8%
Completed Rape	55.8
Attempted rape	13.0
Other sexual abuse	10.0
Refusal	.8

lent offense (42% versus 25%) and less likely to be serving a sentence for a drug offense (25% versus 38%) or a property offense (25% versus 31%).

Most Serious Offense	Percent of Female Inmates Who Experienced Prior Abuse*	No Prior Abuse
Violent	41.7%	25.0%
Property	25.3	31.4
Drug	25.3	38.5
Public-order	6.9	4.6
Other	.7	.5
Number of inmates	16,385	21,439

*Includes those inmates who experienced physical or sexual abuse prior to

Half of the violent female inmates who had been abused were sentenced for homicide, compared to two-fifths of other violent female inmates.

Violent Offense	Percent of Violent Female Inmates Who Experienced Prior Abuse*	No Prior Abuse
Homicide	50.8%	41.9%
Sexual assault	6.1	3.9
Robbery	20.1	29.4
Assault	18.0	20.7
Other violent	5.0	4.2
Number of inmates	6,827	5,369

MOTHERS IN PRISON

More than three-quarters of all women in prison had children, and two-thirds of the women had children at the time of the survey. An estimated 25,700 female inmates had more than 56,000 children under age 18. Male inmates were slightly less likely to have children: 64% reported having any children and 56% had children under age 18.

Black (69%) and Hispanic (72%) female inmates were more likely than white (62%) women to have children under age 18. Black women were slightly more likely than other women to have lived with their young children before entering prison.

Among inmates with children under age 18, 25% of the women, but nearly 90% of the men, said that their children were living with the other parent. More than a third of white female inmates reported that one or more of their children were living with their fathers at the time of the interview, compared to a quarter of Hispanic women and less than a fifth of black women. Regardless of race, the children's grandparents were the most common single category of caregivers: 57% of black mothers, 55% of Hispanic mothers, and 41% of white mothers. Nearly 10% of the women reported that their children were in a foster home, agency, or other institution.

Among inmates with children, women were more likely than men to have had contact with their children since admission to prison, regardless of the children's ages. Nearly 90% of women with children under age 18 had contact with their children, compared to about 80% of men. An estimated 87% of women with only adult children, compared to 72% of men, had contact with those children during their incarceration.

Since entering prison, half of the women had been visited by their children, four-fifths had corresponded by mail, and three-quarters had talked with them on the phone.

An estimated 46% of women with minor children said they talked with those children on the phone at least once a week; 45% had contact by mail at least once a week; and 9% were visited by their children. Female inmates with children younger than 18 were more likely than those with only adult children to make daily telephone calls to their children (16% versus 11%).

DRUG USE HISTORY

Women in prison in 1991 used more drugs and used those drugs more frequently than men. About 54% of the women had used drugs in the month before their current offense, compared to 50% of the men. Female inmates were also more likely than male inmates to have used drugs regularly (65% versus 62%), to have used drugs daily in the month preceding their offense (41% versus 36%), and to have been under the influence at the time of the offense (36% versus 31%). Nearly 1 in 4 female inmates reported committing their offense to get money to buy drugs, compared to 1 in 6 males.

Compared to the women in prison in 1986, higher percentages of female inmates in 1991 reported that they had used drugs in the month before their offense (54% compared to 50%). Among women using a drug in the month before the offense, the percentage using cocaine or crack rose from 23% in 1986 to 36% in 1991. However, marijuana use during the same period declined from 30% of the women to 20%. The use of other types of drugs either declined or remained about the same during this period.

About the same percentage of women in both years said they were under the influence of drugs at the time of their offense. At the time of their offense, 23% of female inmates were using cocaine or crack in 1991, up from 12% in 1986. Marijuana use dropped from 8% to 5%. Use of heroin and other opiates remained about the same.

Among inmates, women were more likely than men to report having used a needle to inject illegal drugs: a third of female inmates, compared to a quarter of male inmates. An estimated 18% of the women and 12% of the men also said that they had shared a needle at least once in the past.

Prisoners	Ever Used a Needle	Ever Shared a Needle
Female*	34.0%	18.0%
White	41.6	25.0
Black	24.0	10.3
Hispanic	45.9	24.5
Male	24.3%	11.5%

*Includes Asians, Pacific Islanders, American Indians, Alaska Natives, and other racial groups.

Injecting drugs was more widespread among Hispanic and white women than among black women. About 46% of the Hispanic women, 42% of the white women, and 24% of the black women used a needle to inject illegal drugs before admission to prison. About a fourth of the Hispanic and white women and about a tenth of the black women had shared a needle for drugs.

Female inmates who used drugs differed from those who did not in the types of crimes they committed. Regardless of the measure of drug use, users were less likely than nonusers to be serving a sentence for a violent offense.

One in four of the women who had used drugs in the month before their offense and 2 in 5 of the nonusers were serving a sentence for a violent offense. Among women who had committed the offense under the influence of drugs, 24% were sentenced for a violent offense, and among those not under the influence, 37% were sentenced for a violent offense. Women who had not used drugs were about twice as likely as users to have committed homicide, but were less likely to have committed robbery.

Among women who said they committed their crimes to get money to buy drugs, 17% were serving a sentence for a violent offense and 43%, for a property offense. Female inmates who said that drug money was a motive for their crimes were about twice as likely as other inmates to be incarcerated for robbery, burglary, larceny, or fraud (54% versus 27%).

About half the women in prison in 1991 reported that they had never participated in a drug treatment or drug education program. Those prisoners reporting a more recent use of drugs were more likely to have been participants. Among female inmates who had ever used drugs, 64% had been in a clinic, therapy, self-help group, class, or some other treatment program. Of the women who had used drugs in the month before their offense, 71% had participated in a drug treatment program; 42% had been in treatment before admission. Twelve percent of the women using drugs in the month before their arrest were also in treatment at that time.

After admission to prison 38% of the women had participated in a drug treatment program. The most frequently used programs were group counseling (30%) and self-help treatment groups (21%). More than half of those who had used drugs in the month before their offense had participated since admission; nearly a third were enrolled in a program at the time of the survey.

Type of Treatment	Percent of Female Inmates in Drug Treatment Program After Admission to Prison
All types*	37.7%
Inpatient	8.6%
Counseling	
Group	30.2%
Individual	10.5
Peer/self-help	21.4
Drug education	10.7%

*Detail adds to more than total because inmates may have participated in more than one type of treatment program.

ALCOHOL USE

Although women in prison were more likely than men to have committed their offense under the influence of drugs (36% versus 30%), women were less likely to have been drinking alcohol (22% versus 32%). Nearly half of both women and men were under the influence of either drugs or alcohol at the time of the offense.

Female inmates generally drank less often than male inmates during the year before their current offense: 58% of women in prison reported any alcohol use, compared to 73% of men. About 2 in 10 women, compared to 3 in 10 men, drank every day during that year.

Among inmates, women had participated less than men in any alcohol treatment but were about as likely as men to have joined an alcohol-related group like Alcoholics Anonymous or Al-Anon after admission. Heavier drinkers, regardless of their sex, were more likely to participate in alcohol-related prison groups than those who drank less often before entering prison. However, for inmates who drank at least once a week before admission, the women (23%) were more likely than the men (18%) to participate. The same difference in participation levels between women and men existed for inmates who had committed their offense under the influence of alcohol.

PRISON HEALTH CARE FOR WOMEN

About 6% of women in prison in 1991 had entered prison pregnant. An estimated 6.7% of black women, 5.9% of Hispanic women, and 5.2% of white women were pregnant at admission. Most women who had been pregnant had received both routine gynecological exams and prenatal care.

White female inmates were more likely than other women to have received mental health care after admission. Twenty-nine percent of white women had participated in individual or group counseling for problems other than drug or alcohol abuse, compared to 21% of black women and 15% of Hispanic women. Before their current admission white female inmates (18%) were more likely than black (8%) or Hispanic (6%) females to have stayed overnight in a mental hospital or other mental health treatment program. Nearly 1 in 6 women had received medication prescribed by a psychiatrist or other doctor for an emotional or mental problem since admission to prison.

ENDNOTES

1. *Statistical Abstract of the United States, 1978*, U.S. Bureau of the Census, table 68.

QUESTIONS FOR THOUGHT AND DISCUSSION

1. How are female inmates different from male inmates? What do these differences tell us about female crime versus male crime and judicial processing of females and males?
2. What is the ratio of males to females in prison? Has this ratio changed in the past ten years?

THE DIRTY SECRET OF CELLBLOCK 6

Craig Horowitz

"Where's green eyes at, man? *Heeeey*, Listen up," yelled the captain, a big, exuberant black man with a luminous, toothy smile. "I'm looking for Green Eyes. Yo, brother, *brutha*. Yeah, you. Where he at? In the back? What about Leo? Go tell 'em to get out here. Tell 'em there's someone here wants to see 'em. Okay?"

It was 10:30 in the morning, and the captain, a correction officer, had just walked into Green Eyes and Leo's domain: Cellblock 6A in the James A. Thomas Center, a maximum-security jail on Rikers Island. Few of the 70-odd inmates bothered to look up. Most continued doing what they were doing, which was, essentially, nothing. Blank-faced, empty-eyed, they wandered aimlessly around the cramped space outside the cells, moving so slowly they looked like they were underwater. If the whole scene seemed *Dawn of the Dead* narcotized, that was just a tactic: indolence as survival.

"You wanna get a sense of what this place is like," the captain said, scanning the house with its three tiers of cells stacked on top of one another and its narrow catwalks, "you want it real, you talk to Green Eyes and Leo. They small, they don't look tough, but nobody fucks with them. They run this house."

The captain stood with his arms folded across his broad chest, oddly relaxed given the surroundings. Outside, the late-summer sun was so radiant that splinters of light weakly penetrated the prison's small, thickly crusted iron-mesh-covered windows.

"Hey, Captain, what's happening?" A shirtless Hispanic inmate had ambled over. It was Leo, a five-foot-five-inch 28-year-old drug dealer with a gold stud through his left nostril, a dark, sculpted beard that traced the outline of his jaw, and TIFFANY ANN tattooed on his bicep.

"Leo," the captain said happily, flashing his neon smile. "How you living?"

"You know, captain, jail is jail," said Leo, whose long criminal résumé is highlighted with serious violence. In addition to a half-dozen trips to Rikers—he's here for attempted murder—he has spent five years in "the mountains" (state prison) for "a body" (killing someone).

"C'mon, Leo, tell this gentleman here how you really living?" The captain was in Leo's face now, still smiling but leaning in close to make his point.

"Hey, man, this is the danger zone, know what I'm saying? We killing each other in here over the phone, the TV...anything. You got to stay to yourself. You show you're scared, you got real problems. Only the strong survive."

"Stop frontin', Leo. You jailin' too long for that. I asked you how *you're* living, okay? There ain't gonna be no paybacks. Just keep it real. Maybe we should go take a look inside your cell," the captain said more as a tease than with real conviction. "Take a look at that bodega you got goin' on back there...."

"C'mon, Captain. What you be talking all that shit for? We ain't got no—"

"I told you, Leo, keep it real. Otherwise maybe we go check out the current inventory, know what I'm saying? Whaddaya think? No? Bad idea? Then tell me again, Leo, and this time make it real. How you living?"

"Truth is, Captain, I be livin' lovely."

In Cellblock 6A, Green Eyes and Leo are in nearly complete control, and little happens without their approval. They operate with such impunity that they actually do run a store out of their cells: junk food, batteries, blankets, cigarettes. Anything can be bought from Leo and Green Eyes, as long as the inmate's willing to pay the vig—the markup is 100 percent. Take a carton of Kools, pay back with two. If payment is late, the price goes up and there's the promise of violence to ensure that everybody keeps his word. Green Eyes and Leo even trade in more serious commodities like weapons, drugs, and sex.

"You got the money, you can buy anything here. Okay?" said Cuba, a bulky man with dark circles under his eyes and a RAMBO tattoo on his arm who works for Leo and Green Eyes.

"Explain the sex part to me," I said. "Guys you control will have sex with someone if you order them to?"

"No, sex with *women*, man, with *women*," said Cuba, who has been to Rikers eight times for what he calls "everything." He's currently facing charges of armed robbery—the weapon was a baseball bat.

"Women? From where?"

"Look around, you see any women here?" asked Cuba with obvious exasperation.

"Only the officers." (About 28 percent of the correction officers are women.)

"There you go."

But aside from what may or may not be the occasional sale of sexual favors by uniformed staff—I heard this (unconfirmable) story in at least one other cellblock, where they also told me a (confirmed) story about an inmate with plenty of drug money who paid a C.O. $5,000 to bring in live lobsters for dinner—Green Eyes and Leo control what is, next to plain old racial hatred, the single greatest source of conflict in jail, the telephones. "I can go to any housing unit on Rikers," said the captain, "and figure out who's in charge just by seeing who has prime slot time—from, say, eight to eleven at night. But, man, if I was in jail, I'd *never* use the phone. Too dangerous."

When Green Eyes finally wandered over in a Perry Ellis T-shirt and big, baggy jeans, it was immediately clear where the lanky Hispanic kid got his name. He had alabaster skin and incandescent light-green eyes. Only 21 and charged with murder and armed robbery,

Green Eyes is facing 37 years if he "blows" (gets convicted). "It doesn't matter *where* you come from," he said, explaining why he has the respect of the other inmates, "it matters *how* you come. Real niggers recognize real niggers." Asked what it takes to run a cellblock filled with vicious, predatory inmates, he curled his right hand into a fist and pounded his chest. "You need it right here. You need heart."

"You know what he means?" asked the captain, suddenly serious. "When he says you got to have heart, he means you got to be able to stick a shank in somebody's eye and go on about your business. He means you got to be able to take a razor and slash somebody's face from his ear down to his mouth, giving him a scar he'll have for the rest of his life...and never give it a minute's thought. When he says you need heart, that's what he means." Green Eyes just looked at him, his face blank.

To the shock and dismay of surprisingly few people, the inmates are now running the asylum. As a result, conditions on Rikers Island have deteriorated to the point where, practically everyone who knows the place agrees, a full-scale riot is now only one dis, one argument, one short-tempered outburst away.

Violence has reached epidemic proportions: gangs operate openly and freely; the number of inmates is growing; the budget has been drastically cut, and is about to be cut more; officers are overworked, stressed out, and suffer from abysmally low morale. "It's just a matter of time," Officer Reggi White says about the possibility of a major blowup on Rikers. "Anything can set it off, and no one's doing anything to prevent it. It should be called the Department of Reactions instead of the Department of Corrections."

But while many people who work in the jails, like Reggi White, are willing to speak out about conditions, there seems to be an orchestrated silence at the top (as the city's budget crisis has worsened, the mayor and his staff have made it clear that they will not tolerate open dissent—anywhere). When Rikers warden Ali Al-Rahman who had 22 years' experience in the jails, warned over the summer that the current state of the jails "rivals the pre-riot conditions of 1990," the last time there was a major explosion on Rikers, he was forced out of the department.

"The whole thing is a goddamned mess," says Stan Israel, head of the correction-officers union. "The department is in crisis and there's no one who seems to know how to take control and restore stability. The jails are more dangerous and in worse shape than they've ever been before, and they're ignoring all the signals. The people who make policy are deaf and blind to the reality."

The anguished cries echo off the mustard-colored tile walls, and they are, at first, bone-chilling. *There are dead bodies in the yard...there are dead bodies in the yard,* the hollow-sounding voice yells over and over. No one pays attention. Perhaps that's because eight cells away, correction officers have just finished putting out a fire. An inmate had taken some toilet paper and held it to the naked lightbulb in his cell until it caught, and then he burned his mattress, the sheets, and the pillowcases. "The guy was pissed off," an officer says, "because he has a court date tomorrow and he says he didn't get a haircut."

This is the Central Punitive Segregation Unit, or as it is known by everyone in the jails, the Bing. On an island filled with thousands of murderers, rapists, armed robbers, drug dealers, arsonists, and muggers, the city's least reconstructible miscreants—350 to 475 of them—are held in several maximum-maximum-security cellblocks in the maximum-security Thomas Center. For the officers who volunteer to work in the Bing, it's like Vietnam—hazardous duty that entitles them, after eighteen months, to their choice of assignments. For the inmates, it is supposed to be hard time—they are not allowed to smoke, have radios, watch TV, or put pictures on the walls of their cells. And they are locked in for more than 21 hours a day. It was designed as a 30-to-90-day punishment for attacking an officer or another inmate, or engaging in some other form of uncontrollable behavior. But there are guys in the Bing who have racked up more than 1,000 days of this kind of confinement—sentences that they will never serve out. (Because Rikers is city-run, almost all the inmates on the island are detainees who are being held for trial or simply couldn't make bail. Though the average stay is 53 days, some inmates linger for months, hoping to outlast witnesses who might testify against them.)

A skinny 26-year old Jamaican named Michael, who has a scar that starts at the corner of his mouth and runs halfway across his face, has managed to accumulate an astonishing 1,500 days of Bing time for slashing other inmates. In addition to his other offenses, he now faces a smuggling rap. Someone mailed him a pair of Clark leather boots— "They give a good bump when you walk"—and concealed in the soles were twenty single-edged razors and two bags of marijuana. He's actually been on Rikers for nearly three years, without any resolution of the charges against him. "He's been stalling because he's trying to have all the witnesses against him knocked off," says one of the officers.

There are dead bodies in the yard. There are dead bodies in the yard. As an officer finally makes his way down the cellblock toward the screamer, a food tray comes flying out through the slot in the door of another cell. It doesn't miss the C.O. by much, and when it crashes against the wall, milk and juice and unidentifiable globs of food splatter everywhere. Deputy Warden Walter Johnson, who runs the Bing, calmly tries to talk to the inmate who threw the tray.

"Go ahead and write the ticket, man. I don't give a fuck about no infraction. You disrespected me," says a disoriented-looking black man with a gold front tooth and a huge, sixties-style Afro. In a modulated voice, Johnson tries to find out why the inmate believes he was disrespected. "I asked the man [another C.O.] for a shower and he didn't want to give me no razor. They they don't change my sheets. Fuck that, man, okay?"

While he continued his rant, another inmate was yelling, "Yo, I say yo, can I get some attention here?" A third inmate, his arms hanging out his cell door so he could follow us in the reflection of the glass face of his watch, was screaming, "I want to see that reporter. Make sure you bring him down here, know what I'm saying?" Richard Pryor used to joke that one visit to a prison was all it took to see why they have those places, and one trip to the Bing makes the same point. It is a place where the inmates throw urine and feces at the C.O.'s, where they masturbate in front of the female officers.

"Look," says Johnson wearily, "it doesn't take a rocket scientist to figure out that if you take all of the problems of the world and put them in one area you're not gonna create Shangri-la."

What has been created, however, satisfies no one—not the officers, the inmates, nor the prison-oversight agencies. The C.O.'s would like to see Bing inmates kept in their cells 24 hours a day. But because the courts have ruled that the inmates must be allowed out to recreate and go to the law library, they have the opportunity to pick up weapons and then cut someone. Oversight agencies, meanwhile, routinely charge that the officers use excessive force.

"I wouldn't let them go anywhere, anytime," says Johnson. "I'd make Bing time shorter, but I'd make it real time. If it was up to Legal Aid, we'd have patio furniture, umbrellas, and piña coladas. These guys'll take a razor, show it to the officer, and then stuff it back in their rectum. I don't have closets at home that can hold as much as they can get in their bodies."

This practice is known as slamming. The razor is wrapped in tissue paper, rubbed with vaseline, and then slammed. Officers know if they see an inmate with vaseline on his lips or behind his ears, he's getting ready to slam a weapon. "It's against their civil rights for me to go in their rectum and get it out," Johnson says.

He says that his primary concern is, naturally, for the safety and well-being of his officers. And as is the case now for all of the C.O.'s in all of the jails on Rikers, that concern is more acute than it has been at any time in recent memory. But Johnson also must help his officers cope with the daily indignities of working in the Bing. "You want to know what real intimidation is?" Johnson asks. "It's dropping a piece of paper out of your cell when an officer walks by that has his address on it."

Last year, there were more than 1,100 violent incidents in New York City jails, an increase of 9 percent over the previous year. During this past July and August, there were 176 slashings and stabbings just on Rikers Island, an average of nearly three a day and a rate 40 percent higher than that for the first six months of the year. But the problem is far more complex than just numbers. "There's been a change in the nature and quality of these violent incidents," says Richard Wolf, the executive director of the Board of Correction, a prison-oversight agency. "It used to be that the attacks were one-on-one, but now it's often four or five inmates attacking four or five other inmates, and these are much harder to bring under control, and more dangerous for the officers."

One week recently, a team of officers found 183 homemade weapons while conducting random searches. Included in this haul was a new and particularly grisly little toy. Inmates are now fond of splitting a razor blade in two. They heat up the end of a toothbrush and insert the blades into the soft plastic, both halves facing out the same way. When the plastic cools, they have a weapon that makes not one but two slashes. "This way, when they cut somebody," says Captain Mike Hourihane, "it can't be stitched. Because there's two deep cuts that run right next to each other, the doctor can't pull the skin together to sew it. This leaves a really ugly scar."

The proliferation of gangs has added immeasurably to the chaos. Predominantly Hispanic gangs like the Latin Kings and the Ñetas are everywhere, recruiting new members through intimidation, preying on the weak, and feuding with black-run gangs like the Bloods and the Crips. Five minutes standing in the hallway of any institution is all it takes to get a full-blown view of the gang influence: It seems as if three out of every four are flying the colors. Some gang members wear the identifying black, white, and red rosary beads of the Ñetas, others wear the black and yellow beads of the Latin Kings, and still others wear red do-rags to show their membership in the Bloods.

Then there's the sudden unplanned-for rise in the number of inmates. New York's prison population had been steadily falling from its peak of 22,600 in 1991. It is now back on the upswing, and in the meantime the city has sold or closed several jails. Just last week, the jails reached 100.6 percent of capacity with 19,423 inmates—15,989 of them on Rikers. (As recently as 1980, the average daily population in all of the city's jails was only 7,035.) Though there has been talk of opening closed jails, like the Brig in Brooklyn, the mayor has said this won't happen because of the budget crunch. Giuliani has instead begun talking about double-bunking inmates, an idea viewed as extremely dangerous by jail experts.

And as long as Mayor Giuliani continues to arrest more criminals, the number of inmates will keep climbing. They may be afraid to say it publicly, but many people in the correction department believe that the mayor is pushing the system to its red line. It's a sobering case study in urban policy: The problems are more and more intractable; the money less and less available. How can you fill the jails beyond their capacity, many are asking, while at the same time making deep cuts in the prison budget? Giuliani's fiscal-1995 budget calls for a 9 percent cut in correction-department funds, which will translate into the loss of 841 correction officers—there are currently 9,800 C.O.'s, down from 10,700 two years ago. "If the mayor is gonna lock up the world, it doesn't reconcile to cut the correction budget. It simply doesn't make sense," says one warden.

The official City Hall position is that other cities have higher inmate-to-officer ratios and what's needed in the department is better management. Spending time in the jails tells a different story. No one would dispute that the department could be run more efficiently, but there's no getting around certain basic realities of the system. Most of the housing units on Rikers, for example, are divided into an A and a B side, with 50 to 75 inmates and one correction officer in each. At the entrance to the unit is a command post, known as the bubble. It's about the size of a token booth and is manned round the clock by one officer.

Under the proposed personnel cuts, many would lose either the A or the B officer. I interviewed dozens of people who work in the jails, and without exception, everyone believed that cutting this post was ridiculous. The danger for the lone patrolling officer would simply be too great. Just imagine what 50 to 75 inmates could do, they all said, when left alone while the officer patrolled the other half of the housing unit. Cameras are viewed as at best an adjunct to staff and at worst a joke. Everyone remembers that the 1990 Rikers' riot began when inmates smeared mashed potatoes on a camera lens and then attacked an officer. Twenty C.O.'s and 142 inmates were hurt in the riot. "Cameras are a tool," says Warden Ralph McGrane. "They were never intended to replace staff, because they simply can't."

One long-time, highly placed correction official told me, "The feeling downtown is that something really awful will happen in the jails, some disaster in which one or more correction officers and maybe some inmates get seriously hurt, and then everyone will come to their senses and put the money back in the budget."

The other jailhouse verity that the mayor and Correction Commissioner Anthony Schembri seem intent on ignoring is overtime. Giuliani's budget set aside $50 million for overtime for the year, and for the first three months the bill is around $2.2 million a week—more than double the allocation. Officers routinely work three or four double shifts a week, whether they want to or not. Since a post in the jails cannot be left unmanned, C.O.'s are forced to work another shift if their replacement doesn't show up. Because of the low morale and the high incidence of injury, correction officers "bang in" (call to say they aren't showing up for work) with chronic regularity.

At a typical afternoon shift change recently in the Anna M. Kross Center, 194 officers were supposed to report to work for the 3-to-11-P.M. shift. This is known as the warrior tour, because it's when all the inmates are awake and locked out of their cells, and consequently when most of the trouble occurs. When the sea of blue lined up for roll call against a tile wall painted with the inscription SANITATION IS A WAY OF LIFE, there were 164 people—30 short. "This is a daily problem," a captain inspecting the officers told me, shaking his head. "Look at it this way," says a corrections expert, "if you had unlimited sick leave, would you go to work every day if you didn't feel safe?"

Acute concern for their own safety combined with the belief that no one cares about them has led some officers to close their eyes when the toughest inmates take control of a cellblock. Short term, this can in some perverse way make a few correction officers feel a little safer. After all, if a couple of thugs keep the lid on a cellblock, it means that the officer responsible for those 75 inmates never has to risk mixing it up to settle disputes. But the long-term impact is catastrophic.

All lines of authority break down, respect for the officers disintegrates, the inmates lose whatever small incentive they have to play by the rules, and the entire fabric of the system begins to come apart. There are officers who also actively participate in the prison black market. They both smuggle things in and look the other way when contraband is passed to inmates by visitors. (One way officers can tell if drugs have been passed during visiting hours is if they see an inmate drink shampoo—he is trying to regurgitate the drugs he swallowed earlier.) "There are a lot of drugs in the jails," says Legal Aid's John Boston, "and I find it very difficult to believe that most of that stuff is coming in without staff complicity. This is a major covert issue in the system."

Another factor that has contributed to the free-for-all on Rikers is simple arithmetic. Not only is the overall inmate population booming, but the individual jails have simply grown too big to be manageable. The Kross Center, which was built for 600 inmates, now houses just shy of 3,000. With the modular additions that have been grafted on over the years, the jail has 40 housing units spread over 40 acres. "A jail should not be this big," says McGrane. "No jail should be bigger than 500 beds."

There's a growing national movement to make prison time tougher by limiting or taking away television, radios, weights, and recreation. But McGrane, a small, powerfully built man whose shoes are polished military-style, is adamant that this hardheaded tough-guy stance could ultimately be disastrous—particularly at the jails on Rikers, where inmates are out of their cells every morning at seven and not locked in again until eleven at night.

"Servicing of prisoners is money well spent," the warden says—City Hall wants to cut funding here too. "The perception is we give them too much. But cutting services is always the first step toward increased inmate violence and disturbances. I'd like to work and exercise them to death. The more tired they are, the less energy they have to assault my people."

To the inmates, it's simply "The Rock," but to most New Yorkers, Rikers Island is some unspeakably wretched place that they'd rather not think about. Ever. Ask someone in the city where Rikers Island is and the response is usually a quick "Oh, it's in…it's near the…um…you can see it from the Triborough Bridge, right?…Well," they invariably say after a few moments, "I know it's in the river somewhere." It is, actually, a 415-acre island in the East River, just off the shoreline of Astoria and only about 100 feet from the end of Runway 22 at La Guardia. Most New Yorkers are equally surprised when told that Rikers has not one but ten separate jails, and is the largest penal colony in the world.

The island was once a green and leafy refuge that housed only one jail—built in 1933 and known today as the James A. Thomas Center—and it was actually possible for escaped inmates to hide in the thicket. Over the years, however, the island has been consumed by the seemingly endless demand for jail space.

Today, Rikers is an amalgam of old George Raft-style penitentiaries, modern prefab jails, modular units where the prisoners live in dormitory-style housing units, trailers, and tennis-bubble housing. Every day, in addition to the 15,989 inmates, there are 7,000 correction officers, 3,000 nonuniformed staff, and perhaps as many as 13,000 vehicles on the island, which is accessible only by a two-lane bridge. And there are all the requisite support services and facilities to run what has become a medium-size town: a huge power plant, a firehouse, a bakery big enough to make bread every day for more than 25,000 people (it's even baked without preservatives), a K-9 unit, a marine unit, an emergency-response unit, and a makeshift courthouse where prisoners can file the more than 200 writs a week that they bring against the system.

Though the complex business of locking up huge numbers of people is taken for granted as an integral part of modern urban life, it is worth considering just a few statistics to get a sense of the system's broad sweep. Since it is tough to wrap your mind around a number as big as $765 million, the city's corrections budget for last year, a look at some of the individual budget items is actually more enlightening. And shocking. The city spent almost $100 million last year, for example, to provide health care for the inmates—including fixing their teeth. How about $30 million to feed them? There is a choice of regular, Muslim, kosher, and medical meals (low sodium, low fat). A total of $3 million was spent for excess telephone charges last year. Since a court order requires that inmates have access to both English- and Spanish-language newspapers, the city laid out $200,000 last year to make sure they had something to read with their morning coffee.

The salient question raised by all these numbers is the one that's rarely asked. While the city spends $60,000 a year to house an inmate—more than eight times what is spent to educate a child—what exactly is this money buying? Little more than a temporary, secure—though not necessarily safe—lockup for an increasingly violent group of repeat offenders.

Last year, 111,000 inmates passed through Rikers Island, a little more than 10,000 of them women. Seven out of ten have been in jail before, almost eight out of ten are substance abusers, and perhaps as many as one in five are HIV-positive. More than 92 percent of the prison population is black and Hispanic—by rough estimate, about 7 percent of the city's black and Hispanic males between the ages of 18 and 29 pass through Rikers in a given year. It is unusual to see a white inmate. Racial battles take place almost exclusively between Hispanics and blacks, who are differentiated into Yankees and Jamaicans. Virtually every housing unit has a black phone and a Hispanic phone, and the Jim Crow-style rules are enforced by whoever's running the house.

"This causes a problem for the occasional white guy," says Warden McGrane, laughing. "The white guys have to keep a timid profile. If they try to stake out a piece of territory, they're gonna get stabbed. But the white guys are so outnumbered that it's really not much of a problem. They're simply last for everything. Anytime something's going on—barber shop, commissary, recreation, whatever—the white guy's gonna be last."

On a steamy morning in August, Commissioner Anthony Schembri's three-car minimotorcade pulled up in front of the George Motchan Detention Center, home to 2,500 inmates. It was the first stop on one of Schembri's much-publicized celebrity tours of Rikers Island. The star on this day was actor Ossie Davis, and the commissioner, a short, round, perky man, was so excited he looked like he was going to hyperventilate. A friendly, accomplished glad-hander, Schembri escorted Davis into the prison, where the actor and sometime activist would address a group of several hundred inmates, shaking the hands of as many officers as possible as he went. Once the entourage had cleared a series of metal detectors and iron gates just inside the front door of the jail, Schembri said to no one in particular, "If this isn't a morale booster, I don't know what is."

Several weeks later, sitting in his office on Hudson Street, the commissioner was no less pumped about the impact show-business personalities have on the jails. "I go out there and I say to those officers, 'How's your day doing? Meet Ossie Davis.' And they say, 'Jeez, my *day*, you made my year.' And you're gonna sit there and tell me I didn't do something about morale? No way. You can't tell me that, I felt very good about that day. I went home and I went like this," he says, raising both arms in the air and shaking his clenched fists in a show of triumph.

"I believe in having fun with the smallest guy, because they think I'm a big guy," says Schembri, whose tenure as police commissioner in the Westchester town of Rye, which has 36 officers, was the basis for the television series *The Commish* (hence the Hollywood connections). "I don't think I'm a big guy, but they go home and tell their wife, 'Guess what? I had a cup of coffee with the commissioner today.' It's no big deal to me, but it's a big deal to them. I smile when I talk to the officers, and I see their faces light up because it's important to them because they think I'm a big guy."

There's no denying the commish is a regular "dese," "dem," and "dose" Brooklyn guy. Nor is there any denying his uncanny ability to sound like Yogi Berra: "I'm a results-oriented guy, and if the results don't work, I go to something else." Or: "The officers are unhappy for a number of reasons and No. 1 is morale." But what is open to question is whether he has the experience and the skills to run the department during this time of crisis.

Schembri, who was appointed this past March, has been hammered for many of his ideas, among the most recent of which was a plan to make inmates found with weapons wear a big W (the plan was later modified). He has instituted a program to search a whole housing unit if one member is found with a weapon. He has also put up posters in the jails warning inmates they will be arrested and consecutively sentenced if they assault an officer. "In the real world," says Stan Israel, "if an inmate's facing murder or armed-robbery charges or some offense that's gonna get him ten to fifteen years, what's he gonna get for assaulting an officer? They don't care."

Schembri's harshest critics inside and outside the department say he simply doesn't get it. "He doesn't engender respect, and he doesn't understand corrections issues," says one longtime corrections expert. "He's very naïve." Some of the critics believe that he's unlikely to last out the year and that he was appointed by Giuliani because he was the only candidate who would make the budget cuts. Schembri bristles at the charge. "I was appointed to take a fresh look and a different approach," he says. "Like in *Dead Poets Society* when Robin Williams stood on top of the desk and got everybody to stand on top of the desk and look at things in a different way. I think that's what the mayor wants me to do."

"We have a commissioner," Stan Israel says, "who doesn't know about prisons, and he's being asked to run the department on vapors. Look, I don't envy his position. I don't know too many prison professionals who would do the job under these conditions. They'd walk away. At some point, he has to stand up and tell the mayor, 'I can't run the department this way.' If he doesn't, he will have to bear the responsibility for what happens."

Board of Correction member David Lenefsky was even more hyperbolic. "If there is blood," he has said, "it's going to coagulate on the mayor's desk."

When the commissioner and Ossie Davis left the Motchan Detention Center to continue their tour of the island, I walked the jail with Captain Jorge Ocasio. Like all of the jails, the Motchan Center is a dreadful place. The halls stink from disinfectant. The noise level is unbearable, with the inmates yelling; the officers screaming; gates, bars, and supply wagons clanging; planes roaring overhead; and music blaring. The hallways are dark and dreary and filled with groups of inmates grudgingly being herded along. The officers are constantly at them to stay within the lanes painted on the floor. They all seem to have bad skin, bad teeth, tattooed arms, and disdain for the officers.

"The police get treated like kings and queens," says Ocasio. "But us? We don't get any respect; the community doesn't know what we do. We're like prisoners ourselves." The soft-spoken Ocasio, like most correction officers, points to money and job security as the reasons he does the job. After eight weeks of training, C.O.'s start at $26,000 a year; as they get promoted, they can easily make, with overtime, $75,000 a year or more. Still, the daily exposure to the jails takes its toll. "I've seen guys get 150 stitches over a pair of sneakers. I saw a guy die over a game of dominoes. No matter where you're at, you have this place in you. I can be in a department store with my wife, and as soon as I hear an alarm…."

Ocasio was stabbed in 1990. He was working the day tour when an alarm was sounded. Until the alarm was over, he had to lock down the house. One inmate's cell door wasn't working, so Ocasio had to transfer him. The inmate wasn't happy about it, and he threatened Ocasio. "A couple of days later I was on a housing inspection and two inmates staged a fight. I went to break it up, and I felt two sharp stabs in my back. I saw the guy running away. He flushed the weapon, and since he was headed upstate anyway, he was never charged with the stabbing."

Ocasio believes the jails are more dangerous today. "We used to have a larger percentage of career criminals, and they realized Rikers was a part of their lives. So they behaved a certain way. Today, these guys are younger, more vicious, and they don't listen to nobody. And they make weapons out of anything—floor tiles, pieces of stripping from the dropped ceiling; they'll put a bar of soap in a sock and swing it….They're really ingenious." Warden McGrane agrees. "The jails," he says, "have just become an extension of the streets."

Even toilet paper can't be left out. A favorite prisoner ploy is to stuff up a toilet, make it overflow to create a distraction, and then attack someone. Overflowing toilets are also used to wet down the floors when an alarm is sounded. When the emergency-response team shows up, it has to deal with slippery floors that hamper its ability to secure the area.

But the greatest danger is the gangs. They extort money from other inmates and they force the family members of the weaker prisoners to deposit money in their commissary accounts. "You see special treatment for the gang leaders here," says Ocasio. "Some get a personal escort to and from their housing areas. They're allowed to set policy in some houses. They regularly disobey orders and say they're not doing what they're told until they speak to this or that captain. I had eight guys in the pen [the holding area for new inmates and those going to or from court recently]," Ocasio says, as if he still can't believe it, "and there were seven Latin Kings beating on this one guy. When I started yelling for them to stop, they continued beating him and saying, 'He disrespected us.'"

Schembri organized a gang task force several months ago, headed by warden McGrane. Schembri has had their report for at least a month but is unprepared to go public with his policy. One issue is whether to let gang members continue to wear their identifying beads. When I asked the commissioner about this, he seemed to be prepared to ban beads in the jails. Neither the officers nor the gang members I talked to believed this would have any real impact. Banning beads will no more stop gang activity on Rikers than banning ventless, double-breasted suits would wipe out the Mafia.

Gang members will simply wear some piece of clothing to show the colors, or they'll communicate with elaborate hand signals. They meet in the chapel, the library, the yard, ignoring the cameras installed to monitor them. "These beads stand for inmates' rights," a Ñeta named Luis tells me one afternoon at the Kross Center. It is a stock response.

"Our goal is to live in harmony with all our brothers. We want to stop the robbin' in here of sneakers, of gold, and we want to stop the abuse by the staff." Luis talks about the "25 norms" that make up the Ñetas' charter. They read like a gang version of the Ten Commandments—no killing, no stealing, no fighting, no provoking the police. In fact, if the "norms" were followed, none of the Ñetas would be in jail in the first place.

But Luis, who has a goatee and gold hoops through both ears, is facing charges that he robbed the courtesy desk at Barneys. He is 25 years old, and his case is more or less typical. He is innocent, of course, the victim of some kind of mixup. When I ask him if he's been to Rikers before, he says yes. He also tells me that he served five years in the mountains for manslaughter. He laughs when he says this. "What's so funny?" I risk asking him. We are standing toe-to-toe in the narrow space between a row of cells in a housing unit called Quad Lower 70.

"I'm laughing," he says, "because it sounds fucked up, right? Second-degree manslaughter. It sounds really bad, don't it? But it wasn't. What happened was I tied somebody up and they choked on the gag." Luis is joined by his friend Antonio, who was arrested with six pounds of coke, and they both have a good laugh at the story.

The darkest part of the Rikers picture, if only because of its long-term implications, is the quaintly named Adolescent Reception and Detention Center (ARDC). This is where young criminals, ages 16 to 18, are held, and it is by all estimates the most dangerous jail in America. Nearly a third of the stabbings and slashings on Rikers in July and August took place in ARDC. Even the staff in the other jails talk about it with a mixture of awe and amazement. "Adolescents simply don't give a fuck," says Kross warden McGrane, "they'll cut anybody, anybody—that's what it's all about over there."

It's about kids like Ressy, Sharief, and Demetrius: young, strong, violent, and uncontrollable. They are now part of something called the Winners program, which seeks to take the worst of the bad kids, isolate them, work with them, and get them to conform at least while they're in jail. Ressy is an 18-year-old drug dealer who was shot when he was 16 and is now charged with the murder of a rival dealer. While at ARDC, he stabbed another inmate and spent 180 days in the Bing. "This new kid says he has to get two hours on the phone, so I blasted [cut] him," says Ressy, waving his hands around for emphasis. "I used a razor I bought from another guy for $10."

Demetrius is also 18, has also done Bing time, and is charged with robbing a warehouse in Brooklyn with a gun. Sharief, who has a shaved head, is unlike the other two only in that he's already been sentenced. He stuck a gun in somebody's face on the subway during rush hour, stole their jewelry, and received fifteen years in the mountains. He is due to be shipped to state prison in a matter of days.

All of them seem so old and so surprisingly bright. "We been doing this so long, and we got nothing to show for it," Ressy said in a tired voice. "Niggers out there don't even remember us. Half the people I been here with went home and got killed. You know, you be thinking just cause I was ringing bells a couple of years ago it still matters. But it don't. It's different now: now everybody's got guns," he said, his voice trailing off. "I remember back in Brooklyn we be all souped up, talking all kind of shit about going to Rikers. But when they first bring me over the bridge, man I was mad scared. *Mad scared.* Nobody ever tells the truth about this."

Sharief talks to younger kids now, tries to get them to avoid his mistakes. He works to get them to understand that going to Rikers is no badge of honor, no symbol of manhood, no matter what they hear on the street. He stood up and slouched a little to one side, adopting his street posture, and acted out what he does for the kids. "Yeah, me and my man was there on the Rock, that's right, we be cool and shit." He shifted back to his regular voice. "But nobody ever told me how it really was, what a cold and awful place this is. I'm humble now."

This kind of attitude change remains an anomaly. Most of the inmates seem resigned to their fate, without hope, and without spirit. "What chance do I have?" a 29-year-old prisoner at the Motchan Center who has seven kids asked me. "I don't blame anyone for this, so let's be honest. Our life is in and out, and in and out, until we're in forever."

Last month, the reign of Leo and Green Eyes came to an end. But not at the hand of the administration. "Who knows exactly why," says the captain, "maybe the other inmates just felt they'd gotten too big. You know, in jail, you can think you got the power, but there's always someone wanting to take it away." Cuba, the henchman, had heard the Latin Kings wanted control of Cellblock 6A and had had himself immediately transferred.

Several new inmates, Latin Kings, distracted the on-duty officer and took Green Eyes to "the source," the back of the cellblock. After a brief knife fight, Green Eyes ran to the front gate, the captain says, "which means he lost." Leo was transferred. Green Eyes went to the Bing. "But he did some damage," the captain says with evident admiration, "and he still hasn't gotten cut. He still got the heart."

QUESTIONS FOR THOUGHT AND DISCUSSION

1. Why does the author of the article, "The Dirty Secret of Cellblock 6" expect this jail system to explode? How could this be prevented?
2. Discuss the types of violence that goes on in jails and the main causes of this violence.

BOOT CAMP PRISONS

Doris Layton MacKenzie

Boot camp programs, frequently called shock incarceration, require offenders to serve a short term in a prison or jail in a quasi-military program similar to military boot camps or basic training. Currently 30 States, 10 local jurisdictions, and the Federal Bureau of Prisons had boot camp programs (see Exhibit 1).[1] Another 8 programs have been designed solely for juveniles.[2] This report focuses on State boot camp programs for adults.

Most state programs target young adult offenders convicted of nonviolent crimes who are serving their first prison terms. Offenders accepted into the programs must serve between 90 and 180 days in the heavily regimented programs. Both the number of States with shock incarceration programs and the capacities of these programs have continued to increase during the 1990s. New York has the largest capacity with 1,500 beds, but programs in Georgia (800 beds), Oklahoma (400 beds), Michigan (600 beds), Texas (400 beds), and Maryland (440 beds) continue to grow in size (see Exhibit 2).

There are currently well over 7,000 beds devoted to boot camp programs. On average, offenders spend 107 days in the programs. Thus, more than 23,000 offenders could potentially complete programs in a 1-year period.

Offenders who successfully complete shock incarceration programs are released to community supervision. Forty-two percent of the States intensively supervise offenders who are released from boot camp; 50 percent vary the supervision depending upon evaluated risk; and the remaining 8 percent require moderate or standard supervision. In some States a fairly large percentage of the inmates are dismissed from the program for one reason or another. These offenders must serve their sentences in traditional prisons or return to court for resentencing.

A DAY IN BOOT CAMP

Upon arrival at the boot camp prison, male inmates have their heads shaved (females may be permitted short haircuts) and are informed of the strict program rules. At all times they

From *National Institute of Justice Journal*, National Institute of Justice, Washington, D.C.: United States Department of Justice. November 1993, pp. 21–29.

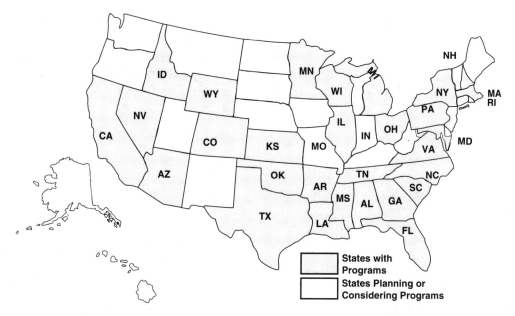

EXHIBIT 1.   Shock Incarceration Programs in the U.S., April 1993

are required to address staff as "Sir" or "Ma'am," must request permission to speak, and must refer to themselves as "this inmate." Punishments for even minor rule violations are summary and certain, frequently involving physical exercise such as push-ups or running in place. A major rule violation can result in dismissal from the program.

In a typical boot camp program for adult offenders, the 10- to 16-hour day begins with pre-dawn reveille. Inmates dress quickly and march to an exercise yard where they participate in an hour or two of physical training and drill. Following this they march to breakfast in a dining hall where they must stand at attention while waiting in line and move in a military manner when the line advances. Inmates are required to stand behind their chairs until commanded to sit and must eat without conversation. After breakfast they march to work sites where they participate in hard physical labor that frequently involves community service such as picking up litter in State parks or along highways. When the 6- to 8-hour work day is over, offenders return to the compound where they participate in more exercise and drill. Dinner is followed by evening programs that include counseling, life skills training, academic education, or drug education and treatment.

As their performance and time in the program warrants, shock incarceration inmates gradually earn more privileges and responsibility. A special hat or uniform may be the outward display of their new status. Those who successfully finish the program usually attend an elaborate graduation ceremony with visitors and family invited to attend. Awards are often presented to acknowledge progress made during the program, and the inmates may perform the drill routines they have practiced throughout their time in the boot camp.

EXHIBIT 2   GROWTH OF SHOCK INCARCERATION PROGRAMS FOR ADULTS

Date Began	State	Number of Programs in 1992 and 1993	Number of Participants/ Capacity in 1992 and 1993	Average Length of Stay[a]
1983	Georgia	5	800/800	90
	Oklahoma	4	415/438	90[b]
1984				
1985	Mississippi	1	223/263	120
1986				
1987	Florida	1	93/100	90
	Louisiana	1	64/136	120
	New York	5	1500/1500	180
	South Carolina	2	198/216	90
1988	Alabama	1	140/180	90
	Arizona	1	92/150	120
	Michigan	3	160/600	90
1989	Idaho	1	236/250	120
	North Carolina	1	82/90	92
	Tennessee	1	103/150	91
	Texas	2	329/400	80
1990	Illinois	1	215/230	120
	Maryland	1	332/448	168
	New Hampshire	1	32/65	120
	Wyoming	1	23/24	95
1991	Arkansas	1	150/150	105
	BOP-male	1	192/192	190
	Colorado	1	114/100	90
	Kansas	1	66/104	180
	Nevada	1	60/60	150
	Ohio	1	76/94	90
	Virginia	1	79/100	90
	Wisconsin	1	40/40	180
1992	BOP-female	1	119/120	180
	Massachusetts	1	95/256	120
	Minnesota	1	12/36	180
	Pennsylvania	1	45/50	180
1993	California	1	48/176	180[c]
Total		46	6133/7518	121
1993	Considering beginning programs: Indiana, Missouri, and Rhode Island.			

[a]Based upon graduates of the program
[b]Four programs, two 90-day programs and two 45-day programs
[c]The first phase is 120 days with a capacity of 176 and the second phase is 60 days with a capacity of 64.

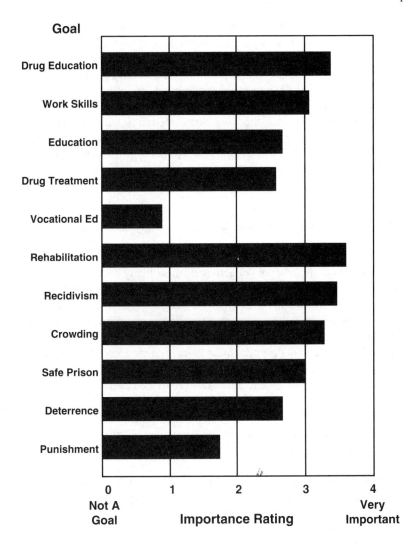

Goal

EXHIBIT 3. Importance of Shock Incarceration Goals

GOALS

A survey of the 26 programs in operation in early 1992 indicated that program officials considered rehabilitation and reducing recidivism as the most important goals. However, reducing crowding and providing a safe prison environment were still considered important. These results are consistent with the goals of most other intermediate sanctions—providing judges options beyond probation or prison, reducing prison crowding, and changing offenders' behavior patterns. The importance given to one goal over the other probably depends upon the individual who is doing the rating.

Judges may be particularly interested in programs that have an impact on the individual offender and that provide more control than traditional probation. In contrast, corrections administrators, seeking new programs and facing serious prison crowding, may emphasize the importance of using intermediate sanctions such as boot camp.

When different types of rehabilitation efforts were rated, the officials judged drug education and work skills as the most important rehabilitation aspects. Since "work" in most programs means hard physical labor, the work skills referred to are probably related to good work habits rather than vocational skills that might result in increased employment opportunities. Academic education and drug treatment were also considered by many to be important aspects of their programs. Vocational education was rated as unimportant or not a goal by most respondents.

DRUG TREATMENT AND EDUCATION

All programs operating in 1992 reported incorporating drug education or a combination of drug education and treatment in the schedule of activities, most likely because of the large number of drug-involved offenders entering the programs. However, the amount of time devoted to drug education or treatment varies greatly among programs. Some programs have as few as 15 days of treatment; in contrast, offenders in the New York program receive drug treatment every day of the 180-day program.

Programs also differ in the way drug treatment is incorporated into the schedule of activities. New York uses a therapeutic community model for its boot camp program, and all offenders receive the same drug treatment while they are in the program. The platoons form a small "community" and meet daily to solve problems and discuss their progress in the program. Inmates also spend time in substance abuse education classes and in group counseling. The counseling program is based on the Alcoholics Anonymous (AA) and Narcotics Anonymous (NA) model of abstinence and recovery. All inmates participate in the drug treatment programs regardless of their substance abuse history.

The Illinois program also targets substance abusers, but incorporates treatment in a very different manner from the New York model. In Illinois drug counselors evaluate offenders and match the education or treatment level to the severity of the offender's substance abuse problems. Inmates with no history of substance abuse receive only 2 weeks of drug education. Those who are identified as probable substance abusers receive 4 weeks of group counseling along with the drug education. Inmates who are classified as having drug addictions receive the drug education and 10 weeks of drug treatment.

In the Texas shock incarceration program, all participants receive approximately 5 weeks of drug education. Treatment is available after the education program ends, but offenders must volunteer for this treatment. They may also have individual counseling if requested, and they can attend 12-step fellowship meetings.

DEVELOPMENT AND CHANGE

Boot camp programs continue to develop and change. The first programs that were developed in Oklahoma and Georgia in 1983 emphasized the military atmosphere, physical training, and hard labor. Although these still play a significant role in shock incarceration, many boot camp programs have begun to allot an increasing amount of time to rehabilitation and education.

Also, many programs are developing innovative methods to help offenders make the transition from shock incarceration back to the community. Maryland is developing transitional housing for boot camp graduates who do not have acceptable housing available in the community. While in the boot camp program, the Maryland inmates are helping with the renovations needed for the transitional housing.

New York has an intensive "after-shock" program that incorporates work programs, employment counseling, drug counseling, and a continuation of the daily therapeutic community meetings that were part of the boot camp program.

In Illinois, offenders who graduate from the program are electronically monitored for the first 3 months of community supervision.

California's new boot camp prison at San Quentin will train convicts for 120 days. Following this, offenders will be required to live at a nearby naval air station for 60 days.[3] During this time, they may leave the base if they are employed or work on the base while they search for a job. Upon release from the base, they are intensively supervised in the community for an additional 4 months.

There has also been some interest in applying aspects of the boot camp model to other prison populations. As the Valdosta Correctional Institution, a close custody prison, the Georgia Department of Corrections is using a modified version of the boot camp approach in two programs for inmates who present special management problems. The Intensive Therapeutic Program for disruptive inmates, and the Mental Health Program for disruptive inmates who have been diagnosed as mentally ill.

The program for disruptive inmates involves strict discipline, regimented drills, adherence to a code of ethics, maintenance of personal living quarters, and high standards of personal hygiene. The program was designed to teach disruptive inmates acceptable ways to deal with frustration, anger, and fear and provides inmates a means of earning their way back into the general prison population.

The Mental Health Program at Valdosta is similar to the program for disruptive inmates, but was designed in consultation with mental health professionals as a treatment modality for seriously mentally ill inmates who are also disruptive. All inmates in the program are assigned to a mental health caseload after being referred by one of the diagnostic and classification centers, staff at another penal institution, or the Valdosta staff.

THE MULTISITE STUDY

Eight States are participating in the study of shock incarceration sponsored by the National Institute of Justice: Florida, Georgia, Illinois, Louisiana, New York, Oklahoma, South Carolina, and Texas. The programs represent very different models of the shock incarceration concept. The two most significant differences are (1) whether the court or the department of corrections makes placement decisions; and (2) whether the program's focus is on treatment and education (New York, Illinois, Louisiana) or the military discipline, physical training, and work (Georgia, Texas).[4]

Intensive interviews with program staff and a thorough examination of written materials from the programs revealed that all were designed in part to address the problems of prison crowding. In some States this was expected to be accomplished because prison-bound offenders would serve less time in the boot camp than if they served a full prison sentence. In New York, Louisiana, and Illinois, the department of corrections selects candidates for the programs, and offenders can earn their way out of prison in less time than if they serve their original sentences.

In other States, offenders are sent to the boot camp by the court, which maintains full control over the offenders. Those who are dismissed prior to completion and those who successfully complete the program must return to the court for final disposition. Texas and the original programs in Georgia and South Carolina were designed this way. However, South Carolina now operates its program through the department of corrections, and Georgia operates some programs through the court and some through corrections.

There were large differences among the eight sites in the number of offenders completing the shock incarceration program in a one-year period, largely as a result of differences in the numbers of beds devoted to the program, the length of the program, and the dismissal rates. Depending upon the prison, between 8 and 50 percent of the inmates fail to complete the program. For example, in 1989 Georgia graduated more offenders (849 graduates) than New York (743 graduates), yet New York had a 1,500 bed capacity while Georgia had only 250 beds. The difference resulted from the fact that Georgia's program lasted an average of 89 days with only a 9 percent dismissal rate while New York's lasted 180 days and had a 31 percent dismissal rate. Overall, the States with the lowest dismissal rates were those in which the judge had decision-making authority.

One phase of the multisite study was designed to examine the effect shock incarceration programs had on the attitudes of the participating offenders. Some critics of shock incarceration have argued that the programs might have a negative impact on the offenders, that offenders would leave the boot camp more alienated and antisocial than before they entered.

The programs in the multisite study differed greatly in daily schedules, the emphasis placed on therapeutic activities, the types of offenders participating, and dropout rates—all differences that would be expected to have an influence on the attitudes of the participants. In some programs most of the day was devoted to physical training, drill, and work, while others devoted a substantial amount of time to counseling, education, and treatment.

The researchers were interested in determining whether the inmates' attitudes toward their boot camp experience or their general antisocial attitudes changed as a result of the programs. Inmates' attitudes were measured once soon after they arrived and again near the end of the program. Despite the differences among the programs the results were surprisingly consistent. Boot camp inmates became more positive about their experience in the program and they became less antisocial. This was true of the programs that had a therapeutic emphasis and those that emphasized work and physical training.

The attitudes of the boot camp participants were also compared with the attitudes of similar prisoners in the general prison population and were found to be generally more positive. The general population inmates did not think their experience in prison had helped them to learn self-discipline, to learn about themselves, to change in a positive way, or to become more mature, while boot camp inmates were more apt to agree with these statements.

On the other hand, both the general population inmates and the boot camp inmates became less antisocial in their attitudes while incarcerated. They were more apt to accept responsibility for themselves and their actions instead of blaming the police or judges, they felt more positive about their relationships with others, and they held more socially acceptable opinions about behavior.

Thus, there was no evidence that shock incarceration had a negative impact on inmates' attitudes. Those nearing the end of their incarceration reported that the boot camp program had been a positive experience for them. Similar inmates in traditional prisons did not report that their experience was positive. However, both the boot camp inmates and prison comparison samples became less antisocial during their term in prison.

The researchers are now examining the performance of the offenders upon release from the shock incarceration programs in the eight sites. The positive activities and adjustment and the recidivism rates of the offenders released from boot camps will be compared to those of similar offenders who received different sentences.

These programs continue to evolve. The objective of this research is to inform program planners about the impact of the programs and to help them design programs to achieve the desired goals.

ENDNOTES

1. For information on county boot camps see Austin, J., M. Jones and M. Bolyard, *Assessing the Impact of a County Operated Boot Camp*, 1993.
2. For information on juvenile boot camps see Toby, J. and F.S. Pearson, "Juvenile Boot Camps, 1992" in *Boot Camps for Juvenile Offenders: Constructive Intervention and Early Support-Implementation Evaluation*, final report to NIJ, 1992.
3. Quinn, Michelle, correspondent, *San Francisco Chronicle*, Tuesday, January 19, 1993.
4. As has happened throughout the U.S. these boot camps programs continue to develop and change. The descriptions of these programs are based on conditions as they were at the time of the study.

QUESTIONS FOR THOUGHT AND DISCUSSION

1. Explain the goals of boot camp programs.
2. How effective are boot camp programs? Which goals are not being achieved?

PRIVATE PRISONS

John J. Dilulio, Jr.

RECENT DEVELOPMENTS

The quality of life inside America's prisons and jails continues to be a major public policy issue. By some definitions, most correctional facilities are crowded; by any definition, many of them are unpleasant, violent, and unproductive. In dozens of States, all or part of the correctional system is under court order to change and improve. Where new facilities are being built, often the aim is as much to improve conditions as to increase capacity. Meanwhile, the public has been paying more and more for corrections. In 1975, expenditures by State correctional agencies totaled around $2.2 billion. In 1987, spending will be about six times that amount.

Practitioners, activists, policymakers, and scholars have been searching for ways to relieve America's ailing correctional complex. In the 1960s and early 1970s, one popular answer was to stop building secure institutions and to deinstitutionalize offenders— "Tear down the walls!" In the 1980s, amid the ongoing search for meaningful alternatives to incarceration, proposals have been made to give the private sector a significant role in the administration, finance, and construction of correctional facilities and programs— "Sell the walls!"

By the beginning of 1987, three States had enacted laws authorizing privately operated State correctional facilities, while more than a dozen were actively considering the option. In 1985, Corrections Corporation of America (CCA), a leader among the 20 or so firms that have entered the "prison market," made a bid to take over the entire Tennessee prison system. Though this bid was unsuccessful, CCA now operates several correctional facilities, among them a Federal Bureau of Prisons halfway house, two Immigration and Naturalization Service facilities for the detention of illegal aliens, and a 370-bed maximum-security jail in Bay County, Florida. On January 6, 1986, U.S. Corrections Corporation opened what is currently the Nation's only private State prison, a 300-bed minimum-security facility in Marion, Kentucky, for inmates who are within 3 years of meeting the parole board.

From *Crime File*. A videotape series produced by the National Institute of Justice, Washington, D.C.: United States Department of Justice, Study Guide by John Dilulio, 1988.

More than three dozen States now contract with private firms for at least one correctional service or program.* The most frequent contracts involve medical and mental health services, community treatment centers, construction, remedial education, drug treatment, college courses, staff training, vocational training, and counseling.

The paramount question in the debate over the privatization of corrections is now whether private firms can succeed where public agencies have ostensibly faltered, but whether the privatization movement can last.

Many observers believe that the movement, though only 6 or 7 years old, is already running out of steam. They point to such things as the failure of CCA to win control of the Tennessee system, Pennsylvania's 1-year statutory moratorium on privatization initiatives, enacted in 1986, and the fact that private prison operations have not advanced much beyond the proposal stage in most jurisdictions.

Other observers, however, see privatization as a response to three main factors—soaring inmate populations and correctional caseloads, escalating costs, and the widespread perception that public corrections bureaucracies have failed to handle convicted criminals in ways that achieve public protection, deterrence, just punishment, and humane, cost-effective rehabilitation.

MAJOR ISSUES AND CONTROVERSIES

At least three sets of questions need to be considered about the privatization of corrections.

1. Can private corrections firms outperform public corrections agencies? Can they produce and deliver more and better for less? What present and potential costs and benefits, if any, are associated with the private administration, construction, and financing of correctional institutions and programs?
2. Should the authority to administer criminal justice programs and facilities be delegated to contractually deputized private individuals and groups, or ought it to remain fully in the hands of duly constituted public authorities? What, if any, moral dilemmas are posed by private-sector involvement in these areas?
3. Does privatization present a single "either-or" bundle of policy alternatives or does it pose multiple choices?

At this stage, it is impossible to answer empirical questions about the cost effectiveness and efficiency of private correctional programs. The necessary research simply has not been done, and relevant data remain scarce. Theoretical speculations, anecdotes, and raw statistics abound, but there is as yet little dependable information to tell us if or how privatization can work, or at what human and financial cost.

Much of the discussion of the morality of privatization has centered on the profit motive of the firms involved. It is not clear, however, that the moral dilemmas posed by privatization—if, indeed, any exist—are related primarily to the fact that CCA and its counterparts are out to make money. The philosophical waters surrounding the issue are deep and muddy.

* Editor's note: By 1993 there were 73 facilities with a rated capacity of 25,000 inmates under contract to private firms.

Conceptually at least, privatization is not an "either-or" issue. Corrections includes prisons and jails, probation and parole, and various community programs ranging from compulsory drug abuse treatment to fines and restitution. Most correctional programs include administrative, financial, and construction components. Any of these correctional program components may be public or private. Thus there are numerous possible permutations of private involvement in corrections, only some of which provoke substantial controversy.

THE DEBATE

Pro

Proponents of privatization claim that it can shave anywhere from 10 to 25 percent from the Nation's correctional budget. Unlike government bureaucracies, advocates argue, private firms are freed to a degree from politics, bureaucracy, and costly union contracts. Private companies must answer to their investors and satisfy the terms of their contract with the government or risk losing it.

As in any open market, the firms must compete with each other to maximize services while minimizing costs or go out of business. Thus, for example, the claim is made that private construction projects will be completed cheaply and on schedule, unlike public construction projects which often suffer costly overruns and meet with countless delays. While government agencies enjoy a virtual monopoly and need not strive to improve the quantity and quality of services, it is argued, private firms will have every incentive to economize and will be held accountable at every turn.

Further, privatization may engender a legislative climate more receptive to proposals to repeal laws that now limit or forbid production and sale of prison-made goods. Operators of private facilities have incentives to produce and sell inmate-made goods and might help persuade lawmakers to authorize prison industry as an effective cost-saving measure and thus to join the movement to transform prisons and jails into "factories within fences."

Finally, it is argued that private firms will be a source of technical and managerial innovations in a field in which most experts believe new methods are needed.

Con

Opponents of privatization claim that major cost cutting can be achieved only at the expense of humane treatment. Private firms, it is reasoned, have no incentive to reduce crowding (since they may be paid on a per-prisoner basis) or to foster less expensive (and to the private firm, less lucrative) alternatives to incarceration. Indeed, critics charge, since prisons have traditionally been financed through tax-exempt general obligation bonds, privatization encourages prison construction. Elected officials can pay for construction through lease arrangements that fall within government's regular appropriation process, thereby avoiding the political problems involved in raising debt ceilings or gaining voters' approval of bond issues. The firms' staffs, it is predicted, will be correctional versions of "rent-a-cops"—ill-trained, under-educated, poorly paid, and unprofessional.

In theory, concerns about staffing, compliance with correctional standards, use of force (lethal and nonlethal), strikes, fiscal accountability, and bankruptcy can be addressed through tightly drawn contracts. Opponents worry that, in practice, government regulation will prove inadequate and that the costs of regulation will more than consume any savings from privatization.

Finally, critics argue that privatization can neither minimize the liability of governmental units under Federal civil rights laws (under which most "conditions of confinement" litigation has been brought), nor relieve the government of its moral and constitutional duty to administer the criminal justice system.

THE CONTEXT

Historical, political, budgetary, administrative, and philosophical dimensions of "private prisons" ought to be considered as background for the debate.

History

State, Federal, and local governments in this country have long contracted for a wide range of goods and services, from solid waste disposal and moviemaking to weapons research and transportation. Indeed, for much of the 19th century and well into the 1960s, numerous States and localities contracted for penal services. In Texas, Michigan, California, Arkansas, and many other jurisdictions, all or part of the prison system has at one time or another been privately owned and operated.

The history of private-sector involvement in corrections is unrelievedly bleak, a well-documented tale of inmate abuse and political corruption. In many instances, private contractors worked inmates to death, beat or killed them for minor rule infractions, or failed to provide them with the quantity and quality of life's necessities (food, clothing, shelter) specified in often meticulously drafted contracts.

Is this history bound to repeat itself? Could such abuses occur today beneath the eyes of a watchful, activist judiciary and vigilant media? Has the corrections profession itself grown beyond the days when such situations were tolerated? To date, no private corrections firm has been found guilty of mistreating inmates or bribing officials, and most private facilities are accredited. What, if any, institutional "checks and balances" exist to ensure that this does not change as the industry matures and becomes more powerful politically?

Politics

Much of domestic politics in this country involves competition and struggle among two or more groups which seek to influence public policy. Correctional policy, however, is often made in the context of what political scientists like to call "subgovernments"—small groups of elected officials and other individuals who make most of the decisions in a given policy area. As the late penologist and correctional practitioner Richard A McGee observed, since the 1960s correctional policy has been affected by a larger than ever contingent of "coaches, customers, and critics," among them Federal judges. Still, the coaches are relatively few, the customers are virtually powerless, the critics are divided (liberals versus conservatives), and the institutions are normally hidden from public view (except in the immediate aftermath of a major disorder or scandal).

Will privatization perpetuate correctional subgovernments, or will it serve to break them up? If the former, is there a danger that private executives will enter into relationships with public officials that undermine the whole array of regulatory mechanisms, perhaps fostering a correctional version of the military-industrial complex? If the latter, will the quality of correctional activities necessarily improve (and the costs of these activities decrease) as a result?

Budget

Correctional spending has been rising rapidly. Relative to other categories of public expenditure, however, corrections ranks close to last. Less than three-quarters of a penny of every dollar of total government spending goes into corrections. Even if CCA and the other firms were willing to run every single facet of America's correctional complex for free, it would not produce significant relief in public expenditures. In the context of public spending generally, corrections is an unpromising place to try to save money.

Nevertheless, corrections represents the fastest growing part of the budget in dozens of States and local jurisdictions. The belief that privatization can cut costs without reducing services might prove true if the "prison market" develops into something akin to what economists have called "perfect competition" (many firms, few barriers to entering the industry, prices set according to marginal costs). It might also prove true if the firms are driven to introduce money-saving technologies and managerial innovations.

Right now, however, it is not clear whether, or how, these goals will be met. Corrections, especially the administration of secure institutions, is a labor-intensive "business." Roughly three-quarters of the corrections budget goes to personnel costs. The most expensive (and difficult) correctional activity is the management of higher custody prisons, but the private firms have shown little eagerness to take a crack at running the Nation's "Atticas" and "San Quentins." Thus far, they have engaged in what critics call "creaming"—getting contracts for correctional facilities and services in which offenders are not hardcore, facilities are new or recently renovated, and profits are more predictable and easier to generate. To avoid political headaches, the firms have for the most part steered clear of jurisdictions with strong public employee unions, but it is precisely in such jurisdictions that costs are highest. There is as yet no evidence to suggest that privatization can lead to the adoption of new and better correctional programs and practices or cheaper financing arrangements.

Administration

The practices and performance of public correctional agencies vary widely. In administering prisons, some jurisdictions have relied on paramilitary structures while others have employed more complex management systems. Some field services units have adopted computer technologies; others have not. Some prisons are orderly; others are riotous. Some jails are clean; others are filthy. Some agencies offer a rich menu of work and educational opportunities; others offer few or offer them only on paper. And some departments spend much money per prisoner and perform badly while others spend less and seem to do much better.

Whatever else it may suggest, the existence of such concrete differences in correctional practices and outcomes makes it impossible to accept that public correctional bureaucracies have failed. What are the administrative and related factors associated with better public correctional facilities and programs? Only after we have studied the enormous variation in the public sector experience does it make good sense to ask whether private firms can do better (and more consistently) than government bureaucracies. From an administrative perspective, the issue is not public versus private management, but under what conditions competent, cost-effective management can be institutionalized. On this and related questions about privatization, the jury is still out.

Philosophy

In weighing the morality of private prisons, the profit motive of the privatizers may be less important than is commonly supposed. The real issue may be instead whether the authority to deprive fellow citizens of their liberty, and to coerce (even kill) them in the course of this legally mandated deprivation, ought to be delegated to private, nongovernmental entities. Inescapably, corrections involves the discretionary exercise of coercive authority.

Even if the corporations were to offer their correctional services for free (as do a small number of foundations and other groups), and even if it were a certainty that the firms could reduce costs and improve services without realizing a single fear of their opponents, would privatization be justifiable? What is the proper scope of the government's authority? Where does its responsibility begin? Where does it end? Should the government's responsibility to govern end at the prison gates, or are not imprisonment (and other forms of correctional supervision) the most significant powers that the government must exercise, on a regular basis, over a large body of citizens?[1] All other things being equal, does it matter whether the patch on the correctional officer's sleeve reads "State of Tennessee" or "Corrections Corporation of America?"

Taken seriously, the moral issues surrounding private prisons are far and away the most interesting, challenging, and important problems the subject poses. In studying or debating this subject, we may be tempted to avoid philosophical questions entirely or (worse still!) to address them casually, to wrap them in polemics, or to "settle" them by making abrupt recourse to the name (or well-known maxim) of some famous, long-dead writers whose views appear to support our own. Let us resist.

ENDNOTES

1. In 1986, about 1 out of every 33 adult males in America was under some form of correctional supervision.

QUESTIONS FOR THOUGHT AND DISCUSSION

1. Do you think that private companies can better achieve the goals of prisons for less money than government has spent?
2. Do private prisons represent an improper or unethical delegation of authority?
3. Discuss the arguments against privatization of prisons.

'THIS MAN HAS EXPIRED'

Witness to an Execution

Robert Johnson

The death penalty has made a comeback in recent years. In the late sixties and through most of the seventies, such a thing seemed impossible. There was a moratorium on executions in the U.S., backed by the authority of the Supreme Court. The hiatus lasted roughly a decade. Coming on the heels of a gradual but persistent decline in the use of the death penalty in the Western world, it appeared to some that executions would pass from the American scene [cf. *Commonweal*, January 15, 1988]. Nothing could have been further from the truth.

Beginning with the execution of Gary Gilmore in 1977, over 100 people have been put to death, most of them in the last few years. Some 2,200 prisoners are presently confined to death rows across the nation. The majority of these prisoners have lived under sentence of death for years, in some cases a decade or more, and are running out of legal appeals. It is fair to say that the death penalty is alive and well in America, and that executions will be with us for the foreseeable future.

Gilmore's execution marked the resurrection of the modern death penalty and was big news. It was commemorated in a best-selling tome by Norman Mailer, *The Executioner's Song*. The title was deceptive. Like others who have examined the death penalty, Mailer told us a great deal about the condemned but very little about the executioners. Indeed, if we dwell on Mailer's account, the executioner's story is not only unsung; it is distorted.

Gilmore's execution was quite atypical. His was an instance of state-assisted suicide accompanied by an element of romance and played out against a backdrop of media fanfare. Unrepentant and unafraid, Gilmore refused to appeal his conviction. He dared the state of Utah to take his life, and the media repeated the challenge until it became a taunt that may well have goaded officials to action. A failed suicide pact with his lover staged only days before the execution, using drugs she delivered to him in a visit marked by unusual intimacy, added a hint of melodrama to the proceedings. Gilmore's final words, "Let's do it," seemed to invite the lethal hail of bullets from the firing squad. The nonchalant phrase, at once fatalistic and brazenly rebellious, became Gilmore's epitaph. It

From *Commonweal*, January 13, 1989, pp. 9–15. © 1989 by Commonweal Foundation. Reprinted by permission.

clinched his outlaw-hero image, and found its way onto tee shirts that confirmed his celebrity status.

Befitting a celebrity, Gilmore was treated with unusual leniency by prison officials during his confinement on death row. He was, for example, allowed to hold a party the night before his execution, during which he was free to eat, drink, and make merry with his guests until the early morning hours. This is not entirely unprecedented. Notorious English convicts of centuries past would throw farewell balls in prison on the eve of their executions. News accounts of such affairs sometimes included a commentary on the richness of the table and the quality of the dancing. For the record, Gilmore served Tang, Kool-Aid, cookies, and coffee, later supplemented by contraband pizza and an unidentified liquor. Periodically, he gobbled drugs obligingly provided by the prison pharmacy. He played a modest arrangement of rock music albums but refrained from dancing.

Gilmore's execution generally, like his parting fete, was decidedly out of step with the tenor of the modern death penalty. Most condemned prisoners fight to save their lives, not to have them taken. They do not see their fate in romantic terms; there are no farewell parties. Nor are they given medication to ease their anxiety or win their compliance. The subjects of typical executions remain anonymous to the public and even to their keepers. They are very much alone at the end.

In contrast to Mailer's account, the focus of the research I have conducted is on the executioners themselves as they carry out typical executions. In my experience executioners—not unlike Mailer himself—can be quite voluble, and sometimes quite moving, in expressing themselves. I shall draw upon their words to describe the death work they carry out in our name.

DEATH WORK AND DEATH WORKERS

Executioners are not a popular subject of social research, let alone conversation at the dinner table or cocktail party. We simply don't give the subject much thought. When we think of executioners at all, the imagery runs to individual men of disreputable, or at least questionable, character who work stealthily behind the scenes to carry out their grim labors. We picture hooded men hiding in the shadow of the gallows, or anonymous figures lurking out of sight behind electric chairs, gas chambers, firing blinds, or, more recently, hospital gurneys. We wonder who would do such grisly work and how they sleep at night.

This image of the executioner as a sinister and often solitary character is today misleading. To be sure, a few states hire free-lance executioners and traffic in macabre theatrics. Executioners may be picked up under cover of darkness and some may still wear black hoods. But today, executions are generally the work of a highly disciplined and efficient team of correctional officers.

Broadly speaking, the execution process as it is now practiced starts with the prisoner's confinement on death row, an oppressive prison-within-a-prison where the condemned are housed, sometimes for years, awaiting execution. Death work gains momentum when an execution date draws near and the prisoner is moved to the death house, a short walk from the death chamber. Finally, the process culminates in the death watch, a twenty-four-hour period that ends when the prisoner has been executed.

This final period, the death watch, is generally undertaken by correctional officers who work as a team and report directly to the prison warden. The warden or his representative, in turn, must by law preside over the execution. In many states, it is a member of the death watch or execution team, acting under the warden's authority, who in fact plays the formal role of executioner. Though this officer may technically work alone, his teammates view the execution as a shared responsibility. As one officer on the death watch told me in no uncertain terms: "We all take part in it; we all play 100 percent in it, too. That takes the load off this one individual [who pulls the switch]." The formal executioner concurred. "Everyone on the team can do it, and nobody will tell you I did it. I know my team." I found nothing in my research to dispute these claims.

The officers of these death watch teams are our modern executioners. As part of a larger study of the death work process, I studied one such group. This team, comprised of nine seasoned officers of varying ranks, had carried out five electrocutions at the time I began my research. I interviewed each officer on the team after the fifth execution, then served as an official witness at a sixth electrocution. Later, I served as a behind-the-scenes observer during their seventh execution. The results of this phase of my research form the substance of this essay.

THE DEATH WATCH TEAM

The death watch or execution team members refer to themselves, with evident pride, as simply "the team." This pride is shared by other correctional officials. The warden at the institution I was observing praised members of the team as solid citizens—in his words, country boys. These country boys, he assured me, could be counted on to do the job and do it well. As a fellow administrator put it, "an execution is something [that] needs to be done and good people, dedicated people who believe in the American system, should do it. And there's a certain amount of feeling, probably one to another, that they're part of that—that when they have to hang tough, they can do it, and they can do it right. And that it's just the right thing to do."

The official view is that an execution is a job that has to be done, and done right. The death penalty is, after all, the law of the land. In this context, the phrase "done right" means that an execution should be a proper, professional, dignified undertaking. In the words of a prison administrator, "We had to be sure that we did it properly, professionally, and [that] we gave as much dignity to the person as we possibly could in the process....If you've gotta do it, it might just as well be done the way it's supposed to be done—without any sensation."

In the language of the prison officials, "proper" refers to procedures that go off smoothly; "professional" means without personal feelings that intrude on the procedures in any way. The desire for executions that take place "without any sensation" no doubt refers to the absence of media sensationalism, particularly if there should be an embarrassing and undignified hitch in the procedures, for example, a prisoner who breaks down or becomes violent and must be forcibly placed in the electric chair as witnesses, some from the media, look on in horror. Still, I can't help but note that this may be a revealing slip of the tongue. For executions are indeed meant to go off without any human feeling, without any sensation. A profound absence of feeling would seem to capture the bureau-cratic ideal embodied in the modern execution.

The view of executions held by the execution team members parallels that of cor-rectional administrators but is somewhat more restrained. The officers of the team are clos-er to the killing and dying, and are less apt to wax abstract or eloquent in describing the process. Listen to one man's observations:

> It's a job. I don't take it personally. You know, I don't take it like I'm having a grudge against this person and this person has done something to me. I'm just carrying out a job, doing what I was asked to do....This man has been sentenced to death in the courts. This is the law and he broke this law, and he has to suffer the consequences. And one of the consequences is to put him to death.

I found that few members of the execution team support the death penalty outright or without reservation. Having seen executions close up, many of them have lingering doubts about the justice or wisdom of this sanction. As one officer put it:

> I'm not sure the death penalty is the right way. I don't know if there is a right answer. So I look at it like this: if it's gotta be done, at least it can be done in a humane way, if there is such a word for it…The only way it should be done, I feel, is the way we do it. It's done profession-ally; it's not no horseplaying. Everything is done by documentation. One time. By the book.

Arranging executions that occur "without any sensation" and that go "by the book" is no mean task, but it is a task that is undertaken in earnest by the execution team. The tone of the enterprise is set by a team leader, a man who takes a hard-boiled, no nonsense approach to correctional work in general and death work in particular. "My style," he says, "is this: if it's a job to do, get it done. Do it and that's it." He seeks out kindred spirits, men who see killing condemned prisoners as a job—a dirty job one does reluctantly, perhaps, but above all a job one carries out dispassionately and in the line of duty.

To make sure that line of duty is a straight and accurate one, the death watch team has been carefully drilled by the team leader in the mechanics of execution. The process has been broken down into simple, discrete tasks and practiced repeatedly. The team leader describes the division of labor in the following exchange:

> the execution team is a nine-officer team and each one has certain things to do. When I would train you, maybe you'd buckle a belt, that might be all you'd have to do…And you'd be expected to do one thing and that's all you'd be expected to do. And if everybody does what they were taught, or what they were trained to do, at the end the man would be put in the chair and everything would be complete. It's all come together now.

> So it's broken down into very small steps….*Very small*, yes. Each person has *one* thing to do. I see. What's the purpose of breaking it down into such small steps?

> So people won't get confused. I've learned it's kind of a tense time. When you're executin' a person, killing a person—you call it killin', executin', whatever you want—the man dies any-way. I find the less you got on your mind, why, the better you'll carry it out. So it's just very simple things. And so far, you know, it's all come together, we haven't had any problems.

This division of labor allows each man on the execution team to become a specialist, a technician with a sense of pride in his work. Said one man,

> My assignment is the leg piece. Right leg. I roll his pants leg up, place a piece [electrode] on his leg, strap his leg in…I've got all the moves down pat. We train from different posts; I can do any of them. But that's my main post.

The implication is not that the officers are incapable of performing multiple or complex tasks, but simply that it is more efficient to focus each officer's efforts on one easy task.

An essential part of the training is practice. Practice is meant to produce a confident group, capable of fast and accurate performance under pressure. The rewards of practice are reaped in improved performance. Executions take place with increasing efficiency, and eventually occur with precision. "The first one was grisly," a team member confided to me. He explained that there was a certain amount of fumbling, which made the execution seem interminable. There were technical problems as well: The generator was set too high so the body was badly burned. But that is the past, the officer assured me. "The ones now, we know what we're doing. It's just like clockwork."

THE DEATH WATCH

The death-watch team is deployed during the last twenty-four hours before an execution. In the state under study, the death watch starts at 11 o'clock the night before the execution and ends at 11 o'clock the next night when the execution takes place. At least two officers would be with the prisoner at any given time during that period. Their objective is to keep the prisoner alive and "on schedule." That is, to move him through a series of critical and cumulatively demoralizing junctures that begin with his last meal and end with his last walk. When the time comes, they must deliver the prisoner up for execution as quickly and unobtrusively as possible.

Broadly speaking, the job of the death watch officer, as one man put it, "is to sit and keep the inmate calm for the last twenty-four hours—and get the man ready to go." Keeping a condemned prisoner calm means, in part, serving his immediate needs. It seems paradoxical to think of the death watch officers as providing services to the condemned, but the logistics of the job make service a central obligation of the officers. Here's how one officer made this point:

> Well, you can't help but be involved with many of the things that he's involved with. Because if he wants to make a call to his family, well, you'll have to dial the number. And you keep records of whatever calls he makes. If he wants a cigarette, well he's not allowed to keep matches so you light it for him. You've got to pour his coffee, too. So you're aware what he's doing. It's not like you can just ignore him. You've gotta just be with him whether he wants it or not, and cater to his needs.

Officers cater to the condemned because contented inmates are easier to keep under control. To a man, the officers say this is so. But one can never trust even a contented, condemned prisoner.

The death-watch officers see condemned prisoners as men with explosive personalities. "You don't know what, what a man's gonna do," noted one officer. "He's liable to snap, he's liable to pass out. We watch him all the time to prevent him from committing suicide. You've got to be ready—he's liable to do anything." The prisoner is never out of at least one officer's sight. Thus surveillance is constant, and control, for all intents and purposes, is total.

Relations between the officers and their charges during the death watch can be quite intense. Watching and being watched are central to this enterprise, and these are always engaging activities, particularly when the stakes are life and death. These relations are, nevertheless, utterly impersonal; there are no grudges but neither is there compassion or fellow-feeling. Officers are civil but cool; they keep an emotional distance from the men they are about to kill. To do otherwise, they maintain, would make it harder to execute condemned prisoners. The attitude of the officers is that the prisoners arrive as strangers and are easier to kill if they stay that way.

During the last five or six hours, two specific team officers are assigned to guard the prisoner. Unlike their more taciturn and aloof colleagues on earlier shifts, these officers make a conscious effort to talk with the prisoner. In one officer's words, "We keep them right there and keep talking to them—about anything except the chair." The point of these conversations is not merely to pass time; it is to keep tabs on the prisoner's state of mind, and to steer him away from subjects that might depress, anger, or otherwise upset him. Sociability, in other words, quite explicitly serves as a source of social control. Relationships, such as they are, serve purely manipulative ends. This is impersonality at its worst, masquerading as concern for the strangers one hopes to execute with as little trouble as possible.

Generally speaking, as the execution moves closer, the mood becomes more somber and subdued. There is a last meal. Prisoners can order pretty much what they want, but most eat little or nothing at all. At this point, the prisoners may steadfastly maintain that their executions will be stayed. Such bravado is belied by their loss of appetite. "You can see them going down," said one officer. "Food is the last thing they got on their minds."

Next the prisoners must box their meager worldly goods. These are inventoried by the staff, recorded on a one-page checklist form, and marked for disposition to family or friends. Prisoners are visibly saddened, even moved to tears, by this procedure, which at once summarizes their lives and highlights the imminence of death. At this point, said one of the officers, "I really get into him; I watch him real close." The execution schedule, the officer pointed out, is "picking up momentum, and we don't want to lose control of the situation."

This momentum is not lost on the condemned prisoner. Critical milestones have been passed. The prisoner moves in a limbo existence devoid of food or possessions; he has seen the last of such things, unless he receives a stay of execution and rejoins the living. His identity is expropriated as well. The critical juncture in this regard is the shaving of the man's head (including facial hair) and right leg. Hair is shaved to facilitate the electrocution; it reduces physical resistance to electricity and minimizes singeing and burning. But the process has obvious psychological significance as well, adding greatly to the momentum of the execution.

The shaving procedure is quite public and intimidating. The condemned man is taken from his cell and seated in the middle of the tier. His hands and feet are cuffed, and he is dressed only in undershorts. The entire death watch team is assembled around him. They stay at a discrete distance, but it is obvious that they are there to maintain control should he resist in any way or make any untoward move. As a rule, the man is over-whelmed. As one officer told me in blunt terms, "Come eight o'clock, we've got a dead man. Eight o'clock is when we shave the man. We take his identity; it goes with the hair." This taking of identity is indeed a collective process—the team makes a forceful "we," the prisoner their helpless object. The staff is confident that the prisoner's capacity to resist is now compromised. What is left of the man erodes gradually and, according the officers, perceptibly over the remaining three hours before the execution.

After the prisoner has been shaved, he is then made to shower and don a fresh set of clothes for the execution. The clothes are unremarkable in appearance, except that velcro replaces buttons and zippers, to reduce the chance of burning the body. The main signifi-cance of the clothes is symbolic: they mark the prisoner as a man who is ready for execu-tion. Now physically "prepped," to quote one team member, the prisoner is placed in an empty tomblike cell, the death cell. All that is left is the wait. During this fateful period, the prisoner is more like an object "without any sensation" than like a flesh-and-blood per-son on the threshold of death.

For condemned prisoners, like Gilmore, who come to accept and even to relish their impending deaths, a genuine calm seems to prevail. It is as if they can transcend the dehu-manizing forces at work around them and go to their deaths in peace. For most condemned prisoners, however, numb resignation rather than peaceful acceptance is the norm. By the account of the death-watch officers, these more typical prisoners are beaten men. Listen to the officers' accounts:

> A lot of 'em die in their minds before they go to that chair. I've never known of one or heard of one putting up a fight....By the time they walk to the chair, they've completely faced it. Such a reality most people can't understand. Cause they don't fight it. They don't seem to have anything to say. It's just something like "Get it over with." They may be numb, sort of in a trance.

> They go through stages. And, at this stage, they're real humble. Humblest bunch of people I ever seen. Most all of 'em is real, real weak. Most of the time you'd only need one or two people to carry out an execution, as weak and as humble as they are.

These men seem barely human and alive to their keepers. They wait meekly to be escorted to their deaths. The people who come for them are the warden and the remainder of the death watch team, flanked by high-ranking correctional officials. The warden reads the court order, known popularly as a death warrant. This is, as one officer said, "the real deal," and nobody misses its significance. The condemned prisoners then go to their deaths compliantly, captives of the inexorable, irresistible momentum of the situation. As one officer put it, "There's no struggle....They just walk right on in there." So too, do the staff "just walk right on in there," following a routine they have come to know well. Both the condemned and the executioners, it would seem, find a relief of sorts in mindless mechan-ical conformity to the modern execution drill.

WITNESS TO AN EXECUTION

As the team and administrators prepare to commence the good fight, as they might say, another group, the official witnesses, are also preparing themselves for their role in the execution. Numbering between six and twelve for any given execution, the official witnesses are disinterested citizens in good standing drawn from a cross-section of the state's population. If you will, they are every good or decent person, called upon to represent the community and use their good offices to testify to the propriety of the execution. I served as an official witness at the execution of an inmate.

At eight in the evening, about the time the prisoner is shaved in preparation for the execution, the witnesses are assembled. Eleven in all, we included three newspaper and two television reporters, a state trooper, two police officers, a magistrate, a businessman, and myself. We were picked up in the parking lot behind the main office of the corrections department. There was nothing unusual or even memorable about any of this. Gothic touches were notable by their absence. It wasn't a dark and stormy night; no one emerged from the shadows to lead us to the prison gates.

Mundane consideration prevailed. The van sent for us was missing a few rows of seats so there wasn't enough room for all of us. Obliging prison officials volunteered their cars. Our rather ordinary cavalcade reached the prison but only after getting lost. Once within the prison's walls, we were sequestered for some two hours in a bare and almost shabby administrative conference room. A public information officer was assigned to accompany us and answer our questions. We grilled this official about the prisoner and the execution procedure he would undergo shortly, but little information was to be had. The man confessed ignorance on the most basic points. Disgruntled at this and increasingly anxious, we made small talk and drank coffee.

At 10:40 P.M., roughly two-and-a-half hours after we were assembled and only twenty minutes before the execution was scheduled to occur, the witnesses were taken to the basement of the prison's administrative building, frisked, then led down an alleyway that ran along the exterior of the building. We entered a neighboring cell block and were admitted to a vestibule adjoining the death chamber. Each of us signed a log, and was then led off to the witness area. To our left, around a corner some thirty feet away, the prisoner sat in the condemned cell. He couldn't see us, but I'm quite certain he could hear us. It occurred to me that our arrival was a fateful reminder for the prisoner. The next group would be led by the warden, and it would be coming for him.

We entered the witness area, a room within the death chamber, and took our seats. A picture window covering the front wall of the witness room offered a clear view of the electric chair, which was about twelve feet away from us and well illuminated. The chair, a large, high-back solid oak structure with imposing black straps, dominated the death chamber. Behind it, on the back wall, was an open panel full of coils and lights. Peeling paint hung from the ceiling and walls; water stains from persistent leaks were everywhere in evidence.

Two officers, one a hulking figure weighing some 400 pounds, stood alongside the electric chair. Each has his hands crossed at the lap and wore a forbidding, blank expression on his face. The witnesses gazed at them and the chair, most of us scribbling notes furiously. We did this, I suppose, as much to record the experience as to have a distraction from the growing tension. A correctional officer entered the witness room and announced that a trial run of the machinery would be undertaken. Seconds later, lights flashed on the control panel behind the chair indicating that the chair was in working order. A white curtain, opened for the test, separated the chair and the witness area. After the test, the curtain was drawn. More tests were performed behind the curtain. Afterwards, the curtain was reopened, and would be left open until the execution was over. Then it would be closed to allow the officers to remove the body.

A handful of high-level correctional officials were present in the death chamber, standing just outside the witness area. There were two regional administrators, the director of the Department of Corrections, and the prison warden. The prisoner's chaplain and lawyer were also present. Other than the chaplain's black religious garb, subdued grey pinstripes and bland correctional uniforms prevailed. All parties were quite solemn.

At 10:58 the prisoner entered the death chamber. He was, I knew from my research, a man with a checkered, tragic past. He had been grossly abused as a child, and went on to become grossly abusive of others. I was told he could not describe his life, from childhood on, without talking about confrontations in defense of a precarious sense of self—at home, in school, on the streets, in the prison yard. Belittled by life and choking with rage, he was hungry to be noticed. Paradoxically, he had found his moment in the spotlight, but it was a dim and unflattering light cast before a small and unappreciative audience. "He'd pose for cameras in the chair—for the attention," his counselor had told me earlier in the day. But the truth was that the prisoner wasn't smiling, and there were no cameras.

The prisoner walked quickly and silently toward the chair, an escort of officers in tow. His eyes were turned downward, his expression a bit glazed. Like many before him, the prisoner had threatened to stage a last stand. But that was lifetimes ago, on death row. In the death house, he joined the humble bunch and kept to the executioner's schedule. He appeared to have given up on life before he died in the chair.

En route to the chair, the prisoner stumbled slightly, as if the momentum of the event had overtaken him. Were he not held securely by two officers, one at each elbow, he might have fallen. Were the routine to be broken in this or indeed any other way, the officers believe, the prisoner might faint or panic or become violent, and have to be forcibly placed in the chair. Perhaps as a precaution, when the prisoner reached the chair he did not turn on his own but rather was turned, firmly but without malice, by the officers in his escort. These included the two men at his elbows, and four others who followed behind him. Once the prisoner was seated, again with help, the officers strapped him into the chair.

The execution team worked with machine precision. Like a disciplined swarm, they enveloped him. Arms, legs, stomach, chest, and head were secured in a matter of seconds. Electrodes were attached to the cap holding his head and to the strap holding his exposed right leg. A leather mask was placed over his face. The last officer mopped the prisoner's brow, then touched his hand in a gesture of farewell.

During the brief procession to the electric chair, the prisoner was attended by a chaplain. As the execution team worked feverishly to secure the condemned man's body, the chaplain, who appeared to be upset, leaned over him and placed his forehead in contact with the prisoner's, whispering urgently. The priest might have been praying, but I had the impression he was consoling the man, perhaps assuring him that a forgiving God awaited him in the next life. If he heard the chaplain, I doubt the man comprehended his message. He didn't seem comforted. Rather, he looked stricken and appeared to be in shock. Perhaps the priest's urgent ministrations betrayed his doubts that the prisoner could hold himself together. The chaplain then withdrew at the warden's request, allowing the officers to affix the death mask.

The strapped and masked figure sat before us, utterly alone, waiting to be killed. The cap and mask dominated his face. The cap was nothing more than a sponge encased in a leather shell with a metal piece at the top to accept an electrode. It looked decrepit and resembled a cheap, ill-fitting toupee. The mask, made entirely of leather, appeared soiled and worn. It had two parts, the bottom part covered the chin and mouth, the top the eyes and lower forehead. Only the nose was exposed. The effect of a rigidly restrained body, together with the bizarre cap and the protruding nose, was nothing short of grotesque. A faceless man breathed before us in a tragicomic trance, waiting for a blast of electricity that would extinguish his life. Endless seconds passed. His last act was to swallow, nervously, pathetically, with his Adam's apple bobbing. I was struck by that simple movement then, and can't forget it even now. It told me, as nothing else did, that in the prisoner's restrained body, behind that mask, lurked a fellow human being who, at some level, however primitive, knew or sensed himself to be moments from death.

The condemned man sat perfectly still for what seemed an eternity but was in fact no more than thirty seconds. Finally the electricity hit him. His body stiffened spasmodically, though only briefly. A thin swirl of smoke trailed away from his head and then dissipated quickly. The body remained taut, with the right foot raised slightly at the heel, seemingly frozen there. A brief pause, then another minute of shock. When it was over, the body was flaccid and inert.

Three minutes passed while the officials let the body cool. (Immediately after the execution, I'm told, the body would be too hot to touch and would blister anyone who did.) All eyes were riveted to the chair; I felt trapped in my witness seat, at once transfixed and yet eager for release. I can't recall any clear thoughts from that moment. One of the death watch officers later volunteered that he shared this experience of staring blankly at the execution scene. Had the prisoner's mind been mercifully blank before the end? I hoped so.

An officer walked up to the body, opened the shirt at chest level, then continued on to get the physician from an adjoining room. The physician listened for a heartbeat. Hearing none, he turned to the warden and said, "This man has expired." The warden, speaking to the director, solemnly intoned: "Mr. Director, the court order has been fulfilled." The curtain was then drawn and the witnesses filed out.

THE MORNING AFTER

As the team prepared the body for the morgue, the witnesses were led to the front door of the prison. On the way, we passed a number of cell blocks. We could hear the normal sounds of prison life, including the occasional catcall and lewd comment hurled at uninvited guests like ourselves. But no trouble came in the wake of the execution. Small protests were going on outside the walls, we were told, but we could not hear them. Soon the media would be gone; the protestors would disperse and head for their homes. The prisoners, already home, had been indifferent to the proceedings, as they always are unless the condemned prisoner had been a figure of some consequence in the convict community. Then there might be tension and maybe even a modest disturbance on a prison tier or two. But few convict luminaries are executed, and the dead man had not been one of them. Our escort officer offered a sad tribute to the prisoner: "The inmates, they didn't care about this guy."

I couldn't help but think they weren't alone in this. The executioners went home and set about their lives. Having taken life, they would savor a bit of life themselves. They showered, ate, made love, slept, then took a day or two off. For some, the prisoner's image would linger for that night. The men who strapped him in remembered what it was like to touch him; they showered as soon as they got home to wash off the feel and smell of death. One official sat up picturing how the prisoner looked at the end. (I had a few drinks myself that night with that same image for company.) There was some talk about delayed reactions to the stress of carrying out executions. Though such concerns seemed remote that evening, I learned later that problems would surface for some of the officers. But no one on the team, then or later, was haunted by the executed man's memory, nor would anyone grieve for him. "When I go home after one of these things," said one man, "I sleep like a rock." His may or may not be the sleep of the just, but one can marvel at such a thing, and perhaps envy such a man.

QUESTIONS FOR THOUGHT AND DISCUSSION

1. Has the rate of executions been going up or down over the past fifteen years?
2. Explain what the death watch team is and what are the goals of the team.

PAROLE

Past and Present

Paul Cromwell

The procedure known as parole was first tried in the United States over a century ago. During the years that have intervened since its first official sanction at Elmira reformatory in 1876, its use has been expanded into all parts of the country and today has become one of the primary methods by which offenders are released from prisons and correctional institutions.

The motives for the development and spread of parole were mixed. They were partly humanitarian, to offer some mitigation of lengthy sentences; partly to control in-prison behavior by holding out the possibility of early release; and partly rehabilitative, since supervised reintegration into the community is more effective and safer than simply opening the gates.

However, even after a century of use, there is much misapprehension and misunderstanding about parole, and much of this arises from a confusion in terminology. The public often considers parole to be based on clemency or leniency and seldom distinguishes parole from probation and pardon. These three terms are used indiscriminately, not only by the public, but even by officials, judges, and in some states, statutes. Because of the confusion in terminology and administration, parole is often charged with all the shortcomings of other release procedures, for which it is in no way responsible. It is evident, therefore, that the prerequisite for an analysis of parole is a clear definition of the term.

Parole is the conditional release of a convicted offender from a penal or correctional institution, under the continued custody of the state, to serve the remainder of his or her sentence in the community under supervision.

PAROLE DISTINGUISHED FROM PROBATION

Probation and parole are two different methods of dealing with offenders, although the two terms are often used interchangeably. While parole is a form of release granted to a prisoner who has served a portion of a sentence in a correctional institution, probation is grant-

Prepared especially for this volume. An earlier version appeared in Paul Cromwell and George G. Killinger, *Community-Based Corrections: Probation, Parole, and Intermediate Sanctions*, 3rd ed., St Paul, MN: West Publishing Company, 1994.

ed to an offender without requiring incarceration. Parole is an administrative act of the executive or an executive agency, while probation is a judicial act of the court. In recent years the distinction between probation and parole has been further blurred by the development of "split sentencing" schemes, such as shock probation, which mandates a brief period of incarceration followed by *probation* supervision.

PAROLE DISTINGUISHED FROM PARDON

One authoritative source distinguishes between pardon and parole as follows:

> Pardon involves forgiveness. Parole does not. Pardon is a remission of punishment. Parole is an extension of punishment. Pardoned prisoners are free. Parolees may be arrested and reimprisoned without a trial. Pardon is an executive act of grace; parole is an administrative expedient.[1]

In reality there is no similarity between pardon and parole, except that both involve release from an institution.

Parole has played a major role in the American correctional system. Once an offender is sentenced to prison, it is largely the parole authorities who determine when he or she will be released; under what conditions; and whether the offender's conduct after release warrants continued freedom.

PAROLE DECISIONMAKING

The decision to grant parole is a complicated one, and the consequences of the decision are of the gravest importance, both to society and for the inmate. A decision to grant parole results in conditional release prior to the expiration of the maximum term of imprisonment; a denial results in continued imprisonment. The parole release decision is often more important than the sentence of the court in determining how long prisoners actually spend incarcerated. In the absence of clear legislative or judicial guidelines for parole release decision making, vast responsibility has been placed upon parole boards. Parole decisions traditionally have been considered matters of special expertise, involving observation and treatment of offenders and release under supervision at a time that maximizes both the protection of the public and offenders' rehabilitation. This idealistic correctional aim of protecting society and rehabilitating the offender has served as an additional justification for the broad discretionary powers vested in parole authorities.[2]

Statutes have usually directed parole boards to make decisions based upon one or more of the following criteria: (a) the probability of recidivism, (b) the welfare of society, (c) the conduct of the offender while in the correctional institution, and (d) the sufficiency of the parole plan. Traditionally, the hearing stage of parole decisionmaking was thought to provide decision makers with an opportunity to speak with and observe the prospective parolee, to search for such intuitive signs of rehabilitation as repentance, willingness to accept responsibility, and self-understanding. Parole decisions were not based upon formally articulated criteria or policies, but on the discretionary judgments of the individual decision makers.[3] This broad discretion has brought criticism upon the paroling authority for arbitrary, capricious, and disparate decisionmaking. The lack of fundamental fairness of such situations led to a search for more empirically based predictors of risk of recidivism.

DEVELOPMENT OF PAROLE GUIDELINES

In 1973, the U.S. Board of Parole (now the U.S. Parole Commission) initiated a system of parole guidelines, which made explicit the primary factors considered in parole selection. In so doing, parole board provided judges, the public, and inmates with a clearer idea of the manner in which it intended to exercise its discretion.

Research had shown that decisions could be predicted by using specific variables. Three variables were identified as explaining a large number of the board's decisions. These variables were: (1) the seriousness of the offense, (2) the risk posed by the inmate (probability of recidivism), and (3) the institutional behavior of the inmate (a variable that was relatively less important than the first two). The researchers produced a chart that linked seriousness of offense and risk of recidivism to suggested terms of imprisonment. Based on this chart, the parole board constructed a matrix by plotting the two dimensions—seriousness of offense and risk of recidivism—on a graph. Range of sentence length was determined by the position of both dimensions on the graph. This actuarial device was continually validated and evaluated over ten years and went through several changes. Known as the Salient Factor Score, it provided explicit guidelines for release decisionmaking based upon a determination of the potential risk of parole violation.

Following the lead of the federal parole system, other states adopted guidelines for use in release decisionmaking. While some states adopted a *matrix* guideline system similar to the Salient Factors, others adopted different types of guidelines. Most often, these involve a list of factors to be considered in making a parole release decision.

Regardless of the form parole release guidelines take, their goal is to structure the exercise of discretion. Parole boards are free to deviate from their guidelines, but generally must give reasons for doing so. Parole authorities are guided in their decisionmaking, while retaining broad powers; deviations from these guides are checked by the possibility of appeal.

Research indicates that guidelines have performed one of their intended functions, which is to even out obvious disparities and make prison time more predictable.

CRITICISMS OF PAROLE

Although parole has drawn support from many sources and generally has a history of consensual acceptance, it has on occasion been subject to vigorous criticism and reexamination. In the early years of the twentieth century, particularly after World War I, parole administration came under attack. Critics claimed that parole was not fulfilling its promise. Anti-parole groups believed that parole release was used primarily as a means of controlling inmates and that it failed to encourage changes in their behavior and attitudes after their release from prison.

Other critics pointed out that release was granted after only a cursory review of the records of inmates and that paroling authorities had no criteria by which rehabilitation could be measured and upon which release decisions could be based.

These criticisms led to two major changes in parole administration and organization. First, increasing emphasis was placed upon postrelease supervision of parolees, with a corresponding increase in the number of parole conditions. Second, there was a shift away from giving parole authority to prison personnel and toward parole boards, with independent authority and statewide jurisdiction.

By the mid-1930s, the parole system was again being scrutinized as to its continuance as a viable part of the justice system. The Attorney General's Survey of Release Procedures, a monumental study of the correctional process, was essentially established to review the efficacy of parole. The survey stated:

> While there has never been a time when the functions and purpose of parole have been clearly understood, at no period has the entire institution been the object of so much controversy and attack or viewed with as much suspicion by the general public as it has been during the past four or five years.[4]

Mounting prison population and rising recidivism rates aggravated the general uneasiness concerning early release via parole. Questions regarding the value of rehabilitation itself were making themselves heard, and without the philosophical underpinnings of reform and rehabilitation as a purpose of punishment, parole had no meaning in the criminal justice system.

Both the concept of rehabilitation and the practice of parole survived the criticism, and in 1940, President Franklin D. Roosevelt declared, "We know from experience that parole, when it is honestly and expertly managed, provides better protection for society than does any other method of release from prison."[5]

The years between World War II and 1970 witnessed the development and evolution of the so-called "medical," or rehabilitative, model of corrections. The belief that criminals could be changed if given the opportunity and if sufficient skills, funds, and personnel were available, was the central philosophy of this approach to corrections. By 1967 (at the height of the rehabilitation era), a Harris Poll, using a nationwide sample, found that 77 percent of the population believed that prisons should be *mainly corrective*, while only 11 percent believed prisons should be *mainly punitive*.[6] In this social context, parole was considered a viable and necessary aspect of the American system of corrections. By 1977, nearly three-quarters of those released from prison were released via parole.[7]

A PHILOSOPHICAL CHANGE

By the middle 1970s, with a suddenness remarkable in social change, there was a dramatic turnabout. Individualism, rehabilitation, sentence indeterminacy, and parole all seemed, once again, to fall from grace and appeared to be on their way out.[8]

The failure of the correctional system to reduce the steadily increasing crime rate and the system's obvious inability to reduce recidivism, rehabilitate offenders, or make predicative judgments about offenders' future behavior brought about public disillusionment, disappointment, and resentment. The pendulum began to swing, and by the late 1970s seemed to have moved 180 degrees from the rehabilitative ideal to a "just deserts" approach to criminal correction.

In contrast to the rehabilitative ideal, the just deserts, or "justice model," denies the efficacy of rehabilitation and changes the focus of the system from the offender to the offense. The general aim of those favoring determinate sentencing was to abolish, or at least tightly control, discretion. This included the discretion of the prosecutor to choose charges and plea bargain; the discretion of judges to choose any sentence within a broad range of time; the discretion of prison administrators to decide what kind of treatment a prisoner needed to become law-abiding; and the discretion of parole boards to release or not release prisons without ever having to justify their decision or render their decisions consistent. Determinate sentencing was the reformers' answer to this problem.[9] The proposals of the mid-1970s called for clear, certain, uniform penalties for all crimes, either through legislative action or the promulgation of guidelines to which prosecutors, judges, and parole boards would be required to adhere.

The public attitude prevalent at the time seemed inevitably to point toward increasing determinacy in sentencing and, ultimately, abolishing parole as a release mechanism. Between 1976 and 1982, at least 15 states passed determinate sentencing legislation. Other states increased penalties, passed mandatory sentencing, and career criminal laws. One observer wrote, "Even though no model came to predominate, the impact on parole, especially discretionary parole release, was dramatic."[10] In some states both parole release and postrelease supervision were abandoned. In other states, parole release was abandoned but supervision was retained. In some jurisdictions, the legislature limited the releasing power of the parole board by requiring that prisoners serve a flat minimum or proportion of the maximum sentence before becoming eligible for parole. In other states parole guidelines were established to reduce and structure release decisionmaking.

A REPRIEVE AND A NEW ROLE FOR PAROLE

The abolition of discretionary parole release did not prove to be the panacea that some expected. During the 1970s and 1980s the nation's prison population grew dramatically—at least partly fueled by the reduction in parole discretion and the harsher sentences that came with determinate and mandatory sentencing. In 1970, there were 196,429 prisoners in state and federal prisons. The rate of incarceration was 96 per 100,000. By 1980 the rate of incarceration had risen to 139 per 100,000. By June 30, 1990, the U.S. prison population had reached 755,425; the rate of incarceration was 289 per 100,000, a 300 percent increase since 1970.[11]

In some jurisdictions the rapid increase in prison populations brought about a reappraisal of the abolition decision. Maine, which abolished parole in 1976, has had to build four new prisons to handle the increased population. Other jurisdictions have faced similar problems. The U.S. Parole Commission, scheduled to be phased out by 1992, was given an "extension" until 1997. In 1985, Colorado reinstated parole, six years after abolition. North Carolina, which had placed severe limitations on the use of parole, has since given it more discretion. Florida, which adopted sentencing guidelines in 1983 and abolished parole, returned the function under a new name, Controlled Release Authority."[12]

A New Role for Parole: Prison Population Control

Parole boards have always been the "back-door keeper" of America's prisons, often serving as a safety valve to relieve crowded institutions. While this practice is not consistent with the philosophy of parole as a tool of rehabilitation, and most paroling authorities do not believe that the management of prison populations should be a primary responsibility, prison [population] management has become a *de facto* function of parole in many jurisdictions.[13]

Recent years have witnessed an institutionalization of this function. Some states have given legislative authority and direction to their parole boards to control prison population. Others have done so through informal agreements between the governor, director of corrections, and the parole board. Increasingly, through a variety of formal and informal methods, parole boards are being utilized in an effort to reduce and maintain the prison population—with varying and arguable degrees of success.

However, most authorities agree that it is not feasible, in the long term, to control prison populations by parole board action. The reductions achieved are at best, temporary— and have often achieved those results to the detriment of effective postrelease supervision due to escalating caseloads. It has become apparent that where parole boards are used as the "back-door" for overcrowded prisons, the prison population crisis is often simply transferred from the institutional component of corrections to the community component.

SUMMARY

Although the 1990s finds the criminal justice system embroiled in controversy, engaged in self-examination, and subjected to scrutiny by the public and the courts, the issues involved—overcrowding of prisons, the efficacy of parole, sentencing disparity, parole release decisionmaking, and indeed, the continued existence of parole—are not new, and neither are the proposed solutions. The inertia of the criminal justice system is as great as is its failure to learn the lessons of history. These same issues have been studied, scrutinized, rejected, embraced, modified, codified, outlawed, and reincarnated under new labels for over a century. Presidential commissions have alternatively recommended the extension of parole and indeterminacy of sentencing and the outright abolition of the same. The answer is not yet at hand. History has taught us that all too often the unenvisioned and unintended consequences of reform have aggravated rather than mitigated the problems leading to their enactment. Prudence in reform efforts is advisable, and such lessons that can be learned from past efforts should be carefully assessed. Parole, as it functions today, is an integral part of the total correctional process. As such, it is a method of selectively releasing offenders from the institution and placing them under supervision in the community, whereby the community is afforded continuing protection while the offender is making adjustments and beginning to contribute to society.

ENDNOTES

1. Attorney General's Survey of Release Procedures, *Parole*, vol. 4. Washington, D.C.: Government Printing Office, 1939. p. 2.
2. William J. Genego, Peter D. Goldberger, and Vicki C. Jackson, "Parole Release Decision Making and the Sentencing Process," 84 *Yale Law Journal. 810*, 1975.
3. 84 *Yale Law Journal. 810*, 820.
4. U.S. Department of Justice, *Parole*, vol. 4 of *Attorney General's Survey of Release Procedures*, Washington, 1939.
5. Quoted by Sanford Bates in his speech, "The Next Hundred Years," at the Thirty-Fifth Annual Conference of the National Probation Association, Atlantic City, N.J., 1941.
6. Harris Poll, *Los Angeles Times*, Aug. 14, 1967.
7. Edward E. Rhine, William R. Smith, and Ronald W. Jackson, *Paroling Authorities: Recent History and Current Practice*. Laurel, MD: American Correctional Association, 1991, p. 26.
8. National Advisory Commission on Criminal Justice Standards and Goals, *A National Strategy to Reduce Crime* Washington: Law Enforcement Assistance Administration, 1973.
9. David B. Griswold and Michael D. Wiatrowski, "The Emergence of Determinate Sentencing," *Federal Probation*, June 1983.
10. Rhine, et al., supra, p. 25.
11. Id. at 26.
12. Id.
13. Id.

QUESTIONS FOR THOUGHT AND DISCUSSION

1. How is parole different from probation and pardon?
2. Discuss the major criticisms of parole. Do you think parole has an important role in the justice system or that it should be abolished?
3. Describe the new role for parole and give your opinion about its prospects for success.

ROMANCING THE STONE OR STONING THE ROMANCE

Ethics of Community-Based Corrections

Sam S. Souryal

In a recent Hollywood film, a couple of adventurers went to the Amazon jungle in search of a precious stone that had no equal in the entire world, but, after some dangerous encounters with native tribesmen, professional thieves, and, of course, a bout with exploding trucks and maneating crocodiles, they ended up destroying what they had fought for—the stone itself. In a sense, this illustrates how society today handles the jewel called community-based corrections.

In a less romantic scene, Americans can be seen as experts in building walls when the bricks are straight; if the bricks are not straight and the wall is warped, they pass it off to the next generation to fix. The nation has repeatedly done so with regard to the national debt, national health care, education, and may be doing the same today with corrections. While the goals of community-based corrections represent the admirable virtues of human dignity, self-realization, a utilitarian concern for the welfare of society—all under the canopy of social justice—the means of conducting probation and parole duties indicate a "comedy of errors" similar to that in policing and prisons. Once more, society fails to stand up to the ends-means dilemma: the seduction of accomplishing glorious things the wrong way.

Community-based corrections is a value-neutral concept; it is neither inherently good nor does it threaten unexpected harm. As such, the concept produces goodness only if applied ethically, and produces evil the rest of the time. However, like most other ideals of criminal justice, the concept of community-based corrections seems to have degenerated in a miasma of indifference wrapped in political propaganda. What some may view as the most moral punishment package ever invented, others may consider a social cop-out, disproportionate to the gravity of the crime, and unduly intrusive on either offenders' human dignity or the privacy of third parties (von Hirsh, 1990).

Proponents of community-based corrections justify its goodness on the basis of its apparent effectiveness and record of success—the lower rate of return to crime. Critics, on the other hand, argue that the system may only appear successful in a "corporate sense," yet it is qualitatively deficient, falling short of delivering the benefits it is billed to deliv-

Sam S. Souryal, "Romancing the Stone or Stoning the Romance: Ethics of Community-Based Corrections," in *Ethics in Criminal Justice: In Search of Truth*. Cincinnati, OH: Anderson Publishing Company. Used with permission of the publisher.

er. It is noteworthy however, that while supporters of community-based corrections focus invariably on its contribution to humanity as opposed to harsh treatment in prisons, detractors, while equally critical of prisons, raise a broader, rather contradictory, range of ethical issues. These include leniency of punishment, on one hand (the Morris and Tonry thesis) and severity (the von Hirsh thesis), on the other.

THE CASE FOR COMMUNITY-BASED CORRECTIONS

Advocates of community-based corrections argue that the practice is ethically superior to institutional corrections because it offers several distinct benefits; freedom from incarceration at the humanistic level; cost-effectiveness at the utilitarian level; and maintaining family relationships, at the socio-organic level. Nothing else is considered to be of greater moral significance. In sum, the case for community-based corrections seems to be artificially constructed as a convenient scheme to alleviate the adverse image and high cost of incarceration. A brief summary of the principal benefits of community-based corrections, from the prescriptive of its advocates, follows:

FREEDOM FROM INCARCERATION.   Even with the considerable advances in penological practices in this century, the perception of prisons as doing more harm than good lingers. Community-based corrections, on the other hand, maintains some semblance of the social qualities of free life. Community-based programs are not considered "total institutions" and penalties involved are not perceived as "real punishments." After all, they do not involve high walls, cell blocks, window bars, curfew requirements, and other degrading trappings of imprisonization. Furthermore, community-based programs make every effort to spare offenders the psychological damage of living under a totalitarian community created and administered to reinforce inferiority and debasement. Critics, as we will see, question this benefit, asserting that probation, despite any benevolent label given to it, is still punishment and at times, can be as cruel as imprisonment.

COST EFFECTIVENESS.   The cost of incarceration have escalated in recent years. At present, the estimated cost per bed is $70,000, often not including capital investment, costs of operation, food, medical services, and other invisible costs. Community-based programs, on the other hand, are operated at a small fraction of the cost of incarceration. Basically, what a program requires is office space. All other social services cost much less than prison (Newman and Anderson, 1989:449). Moreover, because the offender usually maintains employment while under supervision, the "invisible" costs do not accrue. Instead, the offender usually contributes to his or her upkeep through taxes, social security, family support, and, in some cases, restitution to victims. Thus, the general perception is that while prisons are financial liabilities, community-based corrections are assets. Critics refute this benefit by asserting that the idea of immediate savings as a result of substituting a prison sentence by probation is a false assumption. True savings, they assert, cannot accrue unless substantial numbers are taken out of prison so that a prison or a wing of the prison may be closed. That, critics add, does not seem an immediate likelihood in most American jurisdictions (Morris and Tonry, 1990:18).

FAMILY RELATIONSHIPS.   Newman and Anderson state, community-based corrections help avoid "social surgery"—that is, the severing of a person's family and community relationships. In contrast to prison, community-based corrections provide a local base where the offender continues to receive support from family members, friends, church members, and other sources. Furthermore, depending on the offender's needs, agencies such as Alcoholics Anonymous, drug treatment centers, marital and vocational counseling, as well as religious organizations can be all utilized toward the person's self realization. Such services tend to satisfy the offender's psychological needs, reinforce his self-esteem, and perhaps help purify his sinful soul. Critics, as we will also see, question this benefit, asserting that the punitiveness of probation may very well disturb family relations and further complicate one's self-esteem (von Hirsh, 1990:163).

From an ethical standpoint, the case for community-based corrections must be considered a worthy step on the road toward instilling humanity in the conduct of criminal justice. In contrast to the degradation of prison, this method of corrections signifies a moral concern for the individual, one that is consistent with the natural law ethics of "dignity of man," the constitutional ethics of individualized treatment, and *perhaps* the religious ethics of redemption. The offender in community-based corrections is treated as a responsible person, capable of upholding moral obligations toward self, family, and community, as well as making restitution for the offense committed. More important, however, is the common perception of community-based programs as a huge economic saving, regardless of whether they advance the objective of rehabilitation—the principal purpose behind its theory.

The Case Against Community-Based Corrections

Critics of community-based corrections do not question the movement's tendency to humanize the correctional process. Harsh as imprisonment is, its deprivations are manifest, and so is the need to limit its use. Critics, nevertheless, argue that this real—or contrived—focus on humanity may obscure more serious moral issues related to justice and equity, on one hand, or to the rights of offenders, on the other.

Two notable critics have examined the state of community-based corrections in considerable detail and forwarded adequate reasoning for criticism. Morris and Tonry in *Between Prison and Probation* (1990) argue that the practice of probation is essentially too lenient and should then be integrated into a more effective system of intermediate sanctions. On the other hand, in *The Ethics of Community-Based Corrections* (1990), von Hirsh argues that community-based corrections may be too severe and may violate significant ethical principles that must be addressed before the practice is considered an appropriate means for noncustodial penalties.

The Leniency View of Morris and Tonry

In their thesis, the authors point out that the correctional system in America is, in general, both too lenient, and too severe; too lenient, with many on probation who should be subject to tighter controls in the community, and too severe, with many in prison and jail who would present no serious threat to community safety if they were under control in the community (Morris and Tonry, 1990:3).

In reference to the current theory of corrections, the authors state most directly (1990:5) that:

> convicted criminals should not be spared punitive responses to their crimes; there is no point in imposing needless suffering, but effective sentencing will normally involve the curtailment of freedom, either behind walls or in the community, large measures of coercion, and enforced diminutions of freedom; this is entirely properly regarded as punishment. The language of treatment, reform, and rehabilitation has been corrupted by unenforced and uncritically evaluated good intentions. We fool ourselves—or worse, pretend—if we fail to acknowledge that the intrusions into people's lives that result from criminal punishment are unpleasant and painful.

Having explained their view of what punishment ought to be and justifying the need to restore "real punishment" to the correctional process, Morris and Tonry characterize the state of contemporary probation by stating:

> [Probation] in many cities has degenerated into ineffectiveness under the pressure of excessive caseloads and inadequate resources. For certain categories of offenders now on probation, some though not all could be better subjected to more intensive controls than probation now provides" (1990:6–10).

In their quest to propagate a system of *intermediate punishments* as a rational (and, presumably, more just) sentencing system, the authors proposed a hierarchy of sanctions, starting with capital punishment and ending with electronic monitoring. Intermediate levels include prison, fines, house arrest, probation, intermittent imprisonment, forfeiture, and restitution. Details of these punishments will not be discussed because they are fairly complex and are of lesser relevance to the discussion of ethics of probation. At the probation level, however, the authors particularly noted the propriety of intensive probation. The authors underscore intensive probation as "a mechanism by which reality can be brought to all intermediate punishments (Morris and Tonry, 1990:11). They further assert that intensive probation has the specific capacity of both controlling offenders in the community and facilitating their growth to crime-free lives" (Morris and Tonry, 1990:11). In the next segment we will discuss intensive probation, because of its significance to effective probation and electronic monitoring, two of the most attractive—yet perhaps ethically questionable—intermediate sentences.

Intensive Probation

Morris and Tonry characterize this method of probation as a more intensive withdrawal of autonomy than ordinary probation. While conditions of intensive probation may vary from state to state, the central feature, however, is that more control is exerted over the offender than the standard conditions of probation. These extra control mechanisms invariably involve restrictions on liberty of movement, coercion into treatment programs, employment obligations, or all three.

The intensive probation program in Georgia has been highly acclaimed as a model for other jurisdictions. The program is a judicially imposed package (as opposed to

Massachusetts, for instance, where the decision is administratively made by the probation department) the characteristics of which are: (a) small caseloads for team supervision, each team consisting of two officers (a probation officer and a surveillance officer); (b) each team supervises about 25 offenders; (c) each team is authorized to enforce a variety of conditions, including curfews, employment, community service, drug and alcohol monitoring; and (d) at least five face-to-face contacts each week; (e) offenders pay fees for service ranging from $10 to $50 per month, the amount being set by the sentencing judge.

From an ethical perspective, however, Morris and Tonry do not address the moral implications of intensive probation—namely, the *direction of intensification* in terms of any added capacity to promote rehabilitation. Little mention, if any, is made regarding visionary means by which the probationers' behavior can be modified or their relationships with society improved, i.e., intensified psychological or spiritual counseling, intensified academic or vocational schooling, or intensified means for locating gainful employment. If these directions are not the impetus for intensification, then what is being described as "intensive" is simply an intensified effort at individual deterrence—not to commit crime during the duration of probation. But, in the philosophy of probation, this goal must be considered secondary at best. All offenders would eventually be released from probation, whether intensive or standard, and unless a redeeming change away from crime could be started "within" the person, no real merit can be claimed by intensive programs over standard programs, except perhaps the negative merit of wasted cost. Furthermore, it is a rather peculiar reasoning to argue that a probationer who has been compelled to meet with her probation officer five times per week (as opposed to once or twice) and was forced to endure greater punitive restrictions, would turn out to be a better citizen than someone who was not, only for that reason.

Another ethical consideration can be raised pertaining to the requirement of paying service fees. Although most offenders will probably not object to such a condition because it is their exit tax out of prison, the requirement, in principle, is ethically questionable on at least four counts: (1) as the sovereign entity, the state has an obligatory interest to reform all of its "delinquent children" as a means of protecting society, and because the state governs the correctional system, it is then obliged by social arrangement, by legal tradition, or for that matter, by the absence of alternative means, to accommodate its "offenders" as long as it takes, free of charge. If that is not the case, then prison inmates should be required to pay for their cell space, meals, showers, medical services, and custodial costs. And because placing offenders on probation is a "greater interest" to society than keeping them in prison (where they remain idle, cost more, and pay anything), then requiring probation fees is both unreasonable and inequitable. While some may argue that the probationer has an option to accept or to refuse probation, given the "boogey man of prison," such an option does not amount to a fair choice. The requirement to pay service fees can, of course, be even more unjust if the individual cannot afford to pay or would be seriously harmed by diverting badly needed earnings to pay for probation purposes. While there are, of course, legal safeguards against revoking the probation of indigents, such provisions, in themselves, do not make the original issue of paying fees any more ethical; (2) to impose a probation sentence, but make it contingent upon paying service fees can be equally unjust because it could lead to the imprisonment of low-risk criminals who cannot afford to pay and the release on probation of more dangerous offenders who can; (3) since one of the prominent claims of probation is to create the opportunity for offenders to be gainfully employed so as to be able to pay their taxes, then requiring a service fee—without which one's opportunity to become gainfully employed may be seriously impaired—amounts to the imposition of a poll tax, a policy prohibited in all civilized laws; (4) if, hypothetically, all probationers decided not to pay service fees, the only alternative left for the state is to imprison them at a much greater cost to society than keeping them on probation at no cost. Would that be a rational or a desirable choice by the state, especially given the astronomical rise in prison costs today?

Electronic Monitoring

Contrary to popular belief, electronic monitoring is not a form of punishment—it is an enforcement mechanism for the practice of house arrest as a form of intermediate punishment. As a result, an industry has developed to market monitoring devices. Obviously, none of the systems in use are foolproof; each has its share of "bugs," false alarms, and unexpected costs. The presumption, however, is that these problems will be solved and the system will become reliable and affordable (Morris and Tonry, 1990:215).

At present, there are three main systems of electronic monitoring: active, passive, and tracking.

Active telecommunication systems consist of a small transmitter, strapped to the ankle or wrist of the offender, that emits a signal to a receiver-dialer unit connected by the offender's telephone to a centrally located computer. Provided that the offender remains within a 150- to 200-foot radius of the receiver-dialer, no interruption in the signal occurs. If there is an interruption, the receiver-dialer conveys this fact to the central computer. Such a signal is also transmitted if there is interference with the strap attaching the transmitter to the offender. This system provides constant monitoring.

Passive systems are slightly different but are still based on the technology of connecting a telephone and a centrally located computer. Tracking systems are considerably different because they are built on radio technology that has been used to track wild and domestic animals. A transmitter worn by the offender emits a constant radio signal to a portable receiver in the monitoring officer's car when he is sufficiently close to pick up the signal (at present, about a city block). The probation or parole officer can, at any time, locate the offender (Morris and Tonry, 1990:215).

Several ethical concerns, however, have been raised regarding electronic monitoring. These basically revolve around the issues of class bias and ability to pay for the service. The latter issue is similar to the requirement to pay probation fees, which has been discussed. The difficulty of paying service fees can, of course, be more severe in the case of electronic monitoring. Given the higher amortized cost for installing and maintaining such sophisticated equipment, not many offenders are in a position to meet such fees. This leaves us with the other major issue—class bias.

The issue of class bias stems from the fact that for offenders to qualify for electronic monitoring, they must first have a home and a telephone. But not every offender has either. This requirement unavoidably creates a tendency to apply house arrest and electronic monitoring to the more privileged and to deny it to the indigent. For example, all offenders, regardless of offense, who are homeless (living under bridges) or staying at public shelters or cheap motels are *prima facie* ineligible. This is a striking violation of the basic principle of equality under the premises of social justice theory; "inequalities can only be accepted if in such a manner that offers the greatest benefit to the least advantaged (Borchert and Steward, 1986:303).

Class bias is particularly worrisome because most electronic monitoring legislations do not define "a home." Without a clear definition, electronic monitoring programs may raise serious constitutional concerns related to the provision of equal protection under the law. The Kentucky house arrest program is one that has defined what a "home" is for the purposes of electronic monitoring. The Kentucky legislation defines a "home" to include hospitals, hospices, nursing centers, halfway houses, group homes, and residential treatment centers. The enabling act, however, does not include a single property in which more than one family, other than the offender's, reside (Morris and Tonry, 1990:2). While this omission may not sound alarming, the question, in principle, may lead to a wider variety of inequities that may not be easy to explain or justify.

Evidence of class bias has been apparent in the increased use of electronic monitoring for those convicted of driving under the influence of alcohol, a tendency resented by victim groups, such as Mothers Against Drunk Driving, who see it as both an insufficiently severe sanction and as a class-biased sanction (Morris and Tonry, 1990:218). Consider, for example, the 1988 case of John Zaccaro, Jr., the son of former vice presidential candidate Geraldine Ferraro. He was sentenced to four months of house arrest for selling cocaine. He spent his sentence, however, in his $1,500-a month luxury apartment in Vermont, with maid service, cable TV, and other expensive amenities. Zaccaro's prosecutor has reportedly observed, "This guy is a drug felon and he's living in conditions that 99.9 percent of the people of Vermont couldn't afford" (Schmalleger, 1991:394).

The Severity View of von Hirsh

This view is based on the assumption that community-based corrections—and probation in particular—may not be a benign, friendly, or ethical intermediate sentence, as is popularly thought. The punitive character of probation and parole is often less visible to those who espouse them. Because these sanctions are often packaged as more humane alternatives to the harsher sanction of imprisonment, the deviations they themselves cause are often overlooked. von Hirsh comments, "Because the offender no longer has to suffer the pains of confinement, why cavil at the pains the new program makes him or her suffer in the community?" (von Hirsh, 1990:163).

von Hirsh raises three specific issues pertaining to the severity of community-based sentences: (1) proportionality or desert, (2) restrictions against humiliation and degradation, and (3) concerns for the intrusive nature of punishment upon the privacy of third persons. In the enthusiasm for community-based sanctions, von Hirsh argues that such issues have been easily overlooked. The following is a brief discussion of von Hirsh's views.

Proportionality and Desert

According to von Hirsh, the proportionality of punishment (its level of severity or leniency) has been sacrificed in community-based corrections, because such programs have principally been evaluated in terms of their effectiveness, rather than fairness. If a program (i.e., an intensive supervision scheme) seems to "work" in the sense that its participants have a low rate of recidivism, then it is said to be a "good" program (von Hirsh, 1990:163). Part of the attraction of these programs has been that their more punitive character gives them greater public credibility.

But noncustodial measures, especially those pertaining to intensive supervision, home detention, and day-fines are also punishments that involve substantial deprivations, according to von Hirsh: intensive supervision and home detention curtail an offender's freedom of movement, a community-service program exacts enforced labor, and a day-fine may inflict substantial economic losses. Advocates of community-based corrections seem to overlook the fact that many offenses committed by those under supervision are not serious enough to make the sanctions proportional in response. In a sense, von Hirsh seems to imply a hypocritical streak—if not an outright deception—on the part of community-based enthusiasts. He states, "intensive supervision programs tend to be applied to offenders convicted of the least serious felonies because program organizers feel that such persons would be more likely to cooperate" (1990:164). Some sanctions, remarks von Hirsh, are nevertheless quite severe, given the low level of seriousness of the crime committed.

Restrictions Against Humiliation and Degradation

In his examination of what constitutes "dignified treatment" of offenders, von Hirsh reiterates several previously repeated themes in this chapter: (a) a punishment will be unjust if it is of such a nature as to be degrading or dehumanizing in terms of its intrusion on the individual under supervision; (b) intrusion depends not on technology but on the extent to which the practice affects the dignity and privacy of those intruded upon. For instance, frequent unannounced home visits may be much more disturbing than an electronic telephone monitor that verifies the offender's presence in the home but cannot see into it; (c) even legal intrusion (in accordance with constitutional provisions) does not meet the minimum obligations of community-based personnel to treat offenders with dignity. Convicted felons, adds von Hirsh, are still members of the moral community and should be treated as such; (d) enforcement sanctions that are grossly humiliating should be ruled out because justifying indignity on the basis of creating (or reinforcing) a noncustodial sanction with a "punitive bite" is ethically unjustifiable.

Implications Concerning the Privacy of Third Persons

Because community-based corrections reintroduces the offender into settings in which others live, the offender's punishment spills over into the lives of others. von Hirsh suggests that concern for the privacy of others has been grossly overlooked, For example, he points out that home visits may be potentially shaming to the offender in part because of the presence of unconvicted third-party witnesses, but the visits inevitably also affect those very witnesses, diminishing their own sense of privacy. von Hirsh subsequently proposes that community-based corrections personnel should be sensitive to such dangers and earnestly attempt to reduce their adverse impact. Toward that, he suggests that the impact on third persons should be a critical criterion in choosing among noncustodial penalties, and that the practitioner, in enforcing the penalty, should be considerate of the impact of the enforcement mechanism on the lives of third parties present (1990:171).

The very notions raised by von Hirsh bring us back to the imperative of ethics in the treatment of offenders whether in prison or in the community. This imperative should be universally accepted because: (a) regardless of how we view offenders, human beings should treat others with dignity—it is the law of nature that preceded human existence; (b) regardless of how we view offenders, equitable treatment is consistent with constitutional law and the spirit of laws; (c) regardless of how we view offenders, it is in the interest of a civilized society to treat people with decency, especially in light of the doctrine of "we are all doing time;" (d) regardless of how we view offenders, the ethical imperative can purify our souls and realize our yearning for a more peaceful society; and (e) regardless of how we view offenders, extending goodness to others can bring us more into God's grace.

WORK STRATEGIES OF PROBATION AND PAROLE PRACTITIONERS

Given their professional orientation, the complexity of their work environment, and their career challenges, probation and parole officers engage in and pursue numerous work strategies. Abadinsky (1991) cites a variety of such strategies. The following are among the more significant ones:

1. *Detection.* This strategy involves identifying when a client is at risk or when the community is at risk. It serves three basic objectives: (a) identifying the individuals who are experiencing difficulty or who are in danger of becoming a risk to the community; (b) identifying conditions in the community that may be contributing to personal problems of the client (i.e., lack of jobs, lack of training, availability of drugs); and (c) determining whether the community is at risk from the probationer or parolee and taking steps to protect the community.

2. *Brokering.* This strategy seeks to steer clients to existing services that can be beneficial to them. The essential benefit of this strategy is the physical hookup of the client with the source of help. Examples include locating a job or a training facility where a client can be educated or retrained.

3. *Advocating.* This strategy attempts to fight for the rights and dignity of clients who need help. The key assumption in this strategy is that there will be instances in which practices, regulations, and general conditions prevent clients from receiving services or obtaining assistance. Advocacy aims at removing the obstacles that prevent clients from exercising their rights and receiving available resources. Examples include advocacy on the part of the Parole Officers Association in New York to change restrictions on parolees who need to operate a motor vehicle in order to pursue legitimate employment needs.

4. *Mediating.* This strategy seeks to mediate between clients and resource systems. The key assumption is that problems do not exist within people nor within resource systems, but rather in the interaction between people, resource systems and between systems. As opposed to the advocate role, the mediator's stance is one of neutrality.

5. *Enabling.* This strategy seeks to provide support and facilitate change in the client's behavior patterns, habits, and perceptions. The key assumption is that problems may be alleviated and crises may be prevented by modifying, adding, or extinguishing discrete bits of behavior by increasing insights or by changing the client's values and attitudes.

6. *Educating.* This strategy involves conveying and imparting information and knowledge as well as developing various skills. A great deal of what has been called social casework or therapy is simple instruction.

7. *Community Planning.* This strategy entails participating in and assisting neighborhood planning groups, agencies, community agents, or governments in the development of community programs to assure that client needs are represented and met to the greatest extent feasible.

8. *Enforcing.* This strategy requires the officer to use the authority of his or her office to revoke the probationer/parolee's standing due to changes in status quo which involves heightened community or client risk outside the control of the officer.

ETHICAL CHOICES IN PROBATION/PAROLE OPERATIONS

Based on the strategies mentioned above, some ethical questions should be raised: "What are *professional* probation and parole officers supposed to do? Whom should they be serving? How can they maximize goodness and minimize social harm?" In answering these questions, four *ethical typologies* may be explored, each representing an ethical principle, or a cluster of principles. (Allen et al., as cited in Abadinsky, 1991:305).

These typologies, however, cannot be taken at face value—every practitioner fits one type or another. There are those who fit a combination of types, or none at all, without being considered unethical. Furthermore, practitioners within a given type may not practice uniformly; some may be more knowledgeable (Platonian), more compassionate (Epicurean), more duty-bound (Kantian), more religious (Augustinian), more democratic (Jeffersonian), or simply more gentlemanly (Aristotelian). The typology, nevertheless, has been widely recognized for its rationality and consistency.

The Punitive/Law Enforcement Practitioner

Practitioners of this type see the *summum bonum* of community corrections in serving the interests of the community. Any other interest can—and must be—sacrificed. This model underscores a dogmatic utilitarian view that seeks to maximize "goodness" through serving the largest number of beneficiaries—community members. Toward achieving that goal, anything goes, including the welfare of the probationer, her family, her career, and her destiny. In this model, *control* of the individual under supervision is viewed as the main purpose, and the strategy of *enforcement* is the chief tool. All rules and regulations are enforced, including surveillance, home and employment visits, checks for drug use, harassment, intimidation, and a detective-like enforcement style. The practitioner of this type is generally characterized by depersonalization and extreme detachment. Contacts with the individual are frequent, formal, short, and abrupt. Concerns for the personal and family welfare of the individual are deemed unimportant, and whether the individual "makes it" or returns to prison is irrelevant. A hedonistic streak may also appear in this type—an overemphasis on efficiency as a tool of securing a promotion or a career advancement. In this model, recognition of the "true" purpose of supervision, of the obligation to assist a fellow human being in distress, or of fidelity to the ethics of treatment are all but ignored.

The Welfare/Therapeutic Practitioner

Practitioners of this type see the *summum bonum* of community corrections as rehabilitating the individual under supervision. Of primary concern is the improved welfare of the individual, even if it contradicts the conditions of supervision or the popular interests of the community. Among work strategies, emphasis is placed on advocating, brokering, educating, enabling, and mediating. The practitioner recognizes the relationship with the individual as a "clientship," rehabilitation as a therapeutic treatment, and the client's needs as preeminent. Of paramount concern is providing the client with adequate employment, housing, and psychological assistance, among other support services. Clients are created with dignity, fairness, openness, and personal sympathy. A streak of religiosity may also pervade this type of practitioner, making his role rather missionary in nature. They may invite the individual into their homes or volunteer to pay for the cost of schooling his children. Obviously, this model may be hailed for its ethical overtones; nevertheless, it can be criticized for its lack of moderation—bias in favor of the client and neglect of the broader interests involved in community corrections. Another criticism is the practitioner's lack of knowledge of behavior modification methods; a situation that may lead overzealous practitioners to cause more psychological harm to the client than originally intended (Dietrich, as cited in Abadinsky, 1991:307). Finally, there is the danger of becoming too personally involved with the client, a situation that may lead to considerable disappointment and frustration on the part of the practitioner.

The Passive/Time Server Practitioner

Practitioners of this type see the *summum bonum* as inactivity and avoidance. They have minimal concern for both the welfare of community and the client. They adhere to the serviceable model of management and practice double bookkeeping when it is necessary. They see their work as meaningless and requiring no ethical attention. Many such practitioners are political opportunists who fail to see the truth of the community-service ideal, are burned-out employees who await retirement, or are simply amoral creatures.

The Combined Model Practitioner

Practitioners of this type see the *summum bonum* as the practice of moderation between the welfare of the individual under supervision and protection of the community. Focus in this model is placed on the provision of social and therapeutic services to the client, while also attending to control functions. Practitioners integrate their community protection role with their enforcement role, while maintaining the flexibility to use one more than the other in an individualized response to each case. They adapt work strategies that are useful, while sacrificing others, sometimes cynically, on the alter of reality (Abadinsky, 1991:306). Practitioners of this type are loyal to the humanitarian essence of community corrections. Their decisions are based on an intellectual view of the interests of "community" as equal to the interests of "corrections." They also are experts in a vast range of human problems far beyond the possibilities of ordinary competence. In essence, their role is primarily "Solomonian" (Solomon, a prophet in the Old Testament, threatened to cut a baby in half in order to decide who the child's mother should be). Practitioners of this type are also "Aristotelian" in thought because they are capable of being rational and consistent, yet practical. When gifted with the virtues of goodness and morality, endowed with an appreciation for social justice, and enveloped in good faith, such practitioners could be the most ethical yet (recall Maslow's profile of the ethical person).

Most probation and parole agencies would fall somewhere between the combined and the therapeutic models, with parole departments leaning toward the combined model and probation departments leaning toward the therapeutic model (Abadinsky, 1991:306). Ethical management, however, cannot overlook the damage incurred by practitioners of other types and still claim professionalism. Intensive but sincere efforts are essential for reclaiming such practitioners, and influence, motivation, education—or otherwise termination—should be exercised. Termination, however, should be reserved as a matter of the last resort. Cumbersome and undesirable as it may be, it might in the long range be the most ethical means for serving both community interests and the interests of clients.

QUESTIONS FOR THOUGHT AND DISCUSSION

1. What are the arguments for and against community-based corrections?
2. What is electronic monitoring? How many kinds are currently in use, and how do they differ?
3. Identify and explain five work strategies common in probation and parole practice.

CODE OF ETHICS

American Correctional Association

The American Correctional Association expects of its members unfailing honesty, respect for the dignity and individuality of human beings; and a commitment to professional and compassionate service. To this end we subscribe to the following principles:

RELATIONSHIPS WITH CLIENTS/COLLEAGUES/ OTHER PROFESSIONS/THE PUBLIC

- Members will respect and protect the civil and legal rights of all clients.
- Members will serve each case with appropriate concern for the client's welfare and with no purpose of personal gain.
- Relationships with colleagues will be of such character to promote mutual respect within the profession and improvement of its quality of service.
- Statements critical of colleagues or their agencies will be made only as these are verifiable and constructive in purpose.
- Members will respect the importance of all elements of the criminal justice system and cultivate a professional cooperation with each segment.
- Subject to the client's rights of privacy, members will respect the public's's right to know, and will share information with the public with openness and candor.
- Members will respect and protect the right of the public to be safeguarded from criminal activity.

PROFESSIONAL CONDUCT/PRACTICES

- No member will use his or her official position to secure special privileges or advantages.

Reprinted from the American Correctional Association's *Code of Ethics*, with permission of the American Correctional Association, Laurel, MD. Adopted August 1975 at the 105 Congress of Correction.

- No member, while acting in an official capacity, will allow personal interest to impair objectivity in the performance of duty.
- No member will use his or her official position to promote any partisan political purposes.
- No member will accept any gift or favor of such nature to imply an obligation that is inconsistent with the free and objective exercise of professional responsibilities.
- In any public statement, members will clearly distinguish between those that are personal views and those that are statements and positions on behalf of an agency.
- Members will be diligent in their responsibility to record and made available for review any and all case information which could contribute to sound decisions affecting a client or the public safety.
- Each member will report, without reservation, any corrupt or unethical behavior which could affect either a client or the integrity of the organization.
- Members will not discriminate against any client, employee, or prospective employee on the basis of race, sex, creed, or national origin.
- Members will maintain the integrity of private information; they will neither seek personal data beyond that needed to perform their responsibilities, nor reveal case information to anyone not having proper professional use for such.
- Any member who is responsible for agency personnel actions will make all appointments, promotions, or dismissals only on the basis of merit and not in furtherance of partisan political interests.

QUESTIONS FOR THOUGHT AND DISCUSSION

1. What is involved in a commitment to professional service? Give some examples of unprofessional behavior.
2. What does it mean to be committed to compassionate service? What aspects of correctional work might make it difficult, at times, to display compassion?

AN OFFICER OF THE COURT

Working in Probation for a District Court

Linda Peck

I decided to go back to college when I found that I couldn't support myself and my three sons on the kind of jobs available to someone with no more than a high school diploma. When I went through the colleges' choice of degree programs, I came across criminal justice. I looked over the required classes, many of which were sociology, psychology and law courses and decided I was interested in studying these areas. The more courses I took, the more they excited me.

I thought that in the criminal justice field I would be part of upholding the laws of the land. I believed there would be clear-cut rules of right and wrong. I saw the job as black and white; the good guys against the bad. Of course the law breakers were bad and the criminal justice system was good. It had to be. It was upholding the laws of the American people.

I had never been involved with the justice system personally. I relied only on outside images: book learning, media news, and the movies. While in college I interned for six months at the Probate-Juvenile Court as a juvenile intake worker and for six months at the 15th District Court as a probation officer with adults and misdemeanor offenders. I also worked as an auxiliary police officer for 10 months. Each of these positions gave me a different insider perspective on the criminal justice system. Fortunately I met and worked with some very good and dedicated people. They shared their knowledge and experiences with me. I also saw those who were burned out and discouraged with the system. My intern experiences helped me the most in deciding on my career choice as a probation officer. I liked the idea of working as a probation officer better than anything else I had tried or the other careers I had read about. I decided to work towards that goal when I finished college.

Besides a bachelor's degree in one of the social science fields, I found job experience and substance abuse training were required by most courts and probation departments. Maturity also ranked high as a requirement. I graduated in 1983 with a B.S. degree in criminal justice and with a minor in sociology. I then obtained a Michigan's apprentice

From Stuart Henry, ed., *Inside Jobs: A Realistic Guide to Criminal Justice Careers for College Graduates*, Salem, WI: Sheffield Publishing Co., pp. 137–142, Copyright (c) 1994. Reprinted with permission of the publisher, Sheffield Publishing Company.

Substance Abuse Counselor Certification credentials. I worked retail while watching for criminal justice openings in my area and then moved to the west coast.

While in California I worked as a counselor in juvenile residential homes for two years. The children in these homes and/or their parents had all been involved with the criminal justice system in some way. Most of them were wards of the court and state. Counseling them was often a difficult task. Some had lived through more bad experiences than most adults. The counseling experience, however, was valuable in preparing me for a successful interview for the position as a probation officer which I obtained when I moved back to Michigan.

I really felt I was going to make a difference. I believed our justice system was fair and that, as an officer of the court, I would help and counsel those in need and help to turn their lives around. I would assist the judge in obtaining background information and in preparing fair and equal sentencing recommendations. I was so excited. Here was a position in which I'd be respected and serve my fellow human beings. It was a position where I could do some good while upholding the laws of my state, where criminals would see the errors of their ways and change their ways or go to jail! I was naive.

I was not prepared for the numbers of clients. The number of clients each probation officer has on their case load far exceeds real manageability; it ranges from 250 to 350 clients per probation officer. The officer will do 6 to 10 new assessments and/or interviews per week and write full reports on each of them. She will get background information and verify information when needed for the written reports. She will see up to 25 clients a day who are reporting to her monthly or bi-monthly. While seeing these clients she will keep a written report of their visits and monitor all things that they are ordered to do by the court. She will also take daily telephone calls from clients, attorneys, family members, police officers, and counselors. In some courts the probation officer spends from half to one and a half days per week in court. She will read mail daily and monitor clients who are reporting by mail. She will notify other courts when she has a client who is on probation in another jurisdiction but now has a new case with her court. She checks her court's records and the state and federal criminal information system's records (Law Enforcement Information Network—LEIN) when seeing new clients. One to three days per week she may see the new clients out of court after their sentencing. She will go over their probation orders with them and set them up with their first appointments or put them on mail-in probation. She will interview defendants brought to her office from lock-up by a court officer when the judge needs their background information and a recommendation in a shorter period of time. On some occasions she will interview a defendant while they are locked up. This may be because the court officers are busy or because the defendant is a security risk and may be violent and endanger the lives of others if released. These "quick interviews," as we refer to them, are hand-written and delivered to the judge in court so that the defendant may be sentenced that same day. Two or three times per month we have "violations of probation" and "show cause" hearings. These may take a half or a whole day each. Each probation officer will see their clients prior to the client going before the judge in the court room. At that time the probation officer will try and work out with the client what is going to be done about the client's violations. It could be they have failed to pay court costs or it could be multiple other problems with their probation. If the defendant pleads guilty to the Violation of Probation, they will be sentenced that day. They may go to jail for one day or up to one year, whichever is the maximum penalty for the offense. Alternatively the client may incur more costs and/or more provisions for probation and that probation may continue or be extended but will not exceed a two year period (misdemeanor courts). If the defendant pleads not guilty, the Violation of Probation is set for a full hearing at a future date.

At the hearings the defendant can be represented by an attorney. At the second hearing the probation officer will again talk with the defendant before they go before the judge. They will then go into court. If the defendant pleads guilty, sentence is passed by the judge. If the plea is not guilty the client must prove that the charges brought by the probation officer are not true. I have never seen any defendants prove that they were innocent. The probation officer is there in court because she has documented the behavior of the defendant. The defendant is sentenced by the judge. If the clients/defendants fail to show, the probation officer asks the judge for a bench warrant to be issued for the defendant's arrest.

The probation officer works closely with other probation officers, the judges, court recorders, the court administrator, court clerks, police, and counselors. She also works closely with the department's secretary who is a very important part of any probation department. Courts vary in size, this being determined by the population served. Our city has a population of 72,000, so we have two judges and one magistrate/court administrator and two court officers. We are fortunate to have a new facility which houses the courts, clerks and probation department all in one building. We are also located beside the police department which is convenient. Many courts are in separate buildings from their probation departments which makes court operations much more difficult.

Probation officers put in a minimum of 40 hours per week. In some departments, one day a week they stay until 8:00 pm so they can see clients who work daytime hours. Probation officers' salaries are often lower than they should be for the job qualifications required and the duties of that job.

I am now the supervisor of the probation department. We have a full-time secretary and two full-time probation officers. The department takes interns from local colleges. We have them, usually two at the same time, for a period of 6 to 8 months for 16 hours per week. We also have 10 volunteer probation officers who give 3 to 12 hours per month of their time. They are assigned a case load and I supervise them. Some of our present volunteers have been with us for up to 8 years.

I look forward to going into work in the mornings and I feel the other probation officers I work with feel the same way. We are fortunate to have a good working relationship in our office. It is a job that can bring a lot of frustration and stress. We try to use humor to lighten up situations and not take client behaviors personally. In this field, burnout is a reality that we discuss in order to get things off our chest. We also ask each other for ideas, opinions, and advice.

The defendants are as diverse as the areas they come from and quite representative of this area's population. They are more often on the lower end of the income scale, with many making only minimum wage. They frequently have not completed high school and often have no real job skills or training. A small percent cannot read or write. In this jurisdiction they are mostly caucasians, with blue-collar and service jobs. A large percentage have moved here from the south, searching for work, either by themselves or with their parents or grandparents. Many come from families where education was not important.

Most are trying to do the best they can with what they have. Over 50% have a substance abuse problem with the majority having a problem with alcohol. Many of them do not see their problem or understand it. The majority do not have any health insurance. Around 50% made a bad choice and that's why they're in court. Most of them will not return. The one-time encounter will be enough to steer them clear of the courts. Some need counseling and assistance in other ways and, for the most part, it is given and they too will not return. The other approximately 40% will return. Some see nothing wrong with their behavior and actually like what they do until they get caught. Many are drug users and alcoholics who refuse to see their problem. Others come from backgrounds in which this behavior is the norm.

There are some very bad people on the streets who should not be anywhere but behind bars for the rest of their lives. They are habitual criminals that will never change their behavior and, in the course of their lifetime, they hurt and injure many people. Unfortunately, these people know the system as well as I do. They play it, use it and manipulate it. They make a probation officer's job frustrating and cost the taxpayers thousands of dollars. The ideals of justice being served increasingly go out the door with our overcrowded prisons. Probation officers and judges compromise because there's nowhere to put these criminals. Usually the judge and probation officer both want them in jail or prison but can't get them placed there for lack of space. If they go at all it is just for a short time and they're back on the streets again. Most of the time, a person on probation or parole for a felony can commit a new misdemeanor offense and not expect to be returned to prison. They know it. Occasionally we are able to put them in jail through the district courts. This is where the legislature and governor—politics—enter the picture. It is an enormous problem that will not be corrected overnight.

Most courts and probation departments are understaffed. Some probation departments are so overloaded that they aren't able to do much monitoring of clients at all. Taxpayers think more probation officers will cost them more money but the truth is that the court with its probation department pays for itself with revenue in excess of its expenditures.

After stating these frustrations of the criminal justice system it might seem that I am cynical about probation, but I still enjoy my job. There are always those clients who improve because you have been there for them. And on a few occasions you get a "Thank you." Like most of life you just know you are doing what one person can do and doing it well. I plan to finish my master's degree and move up administratively in the field. I also am working on making people aware of the prison system and campaigning to get new prisons opened and for more alternative sentencing programs. Things are more gray than they are black and white!

QUESTIONS FOR THOUGHT AND DISCUSSION

1. After reading this article, what aspect of probation work surprised you the most? Are you more or less inclined to choose a career in probation?
2. Which aspect of probation work do you think would be the most difficult to perform? How could you prepare yourself for this prior to becoming a probation officer?

CAREERS IN CORRECTIONS

Robert C. DeLucia
Thomas J. Doyle

> Humane treatment may raise up one in whom the divine image has
> long been obscured. It is with the unfortunate, above all, that
> humane conduct is necessary.
>
> —*Dostoevski*

Individuals in the field of corrections deal with incarcerated persons or those who obtain alternatives to incarceration. These professionals have a goal of rehabilitation and prevention of recidivism. Jobs are found in the general areas of detention, rehabilitation, and administration. Required for any aspect of this field is an ability of the candidate to be concerned about people in difficulty, and to have a desire sensitively to assist individuals who have experienced conflict with fellow human beings.

CORRECTIONAL TREATMENT SPECIALIST (FEDERAL PRISON)

- Provide guidance/support to inmate population
- Requires BA/BS plus graduate credit or experience
- Appointment at GS-9 level
- Work solely within prison confines

On the federal level correctional treatment specialists perform correctional casework in an institutional setting. They develop, evaluate, and analyze program needs and other data about the inmates; evaluate progress of individual offenders in the institution; coordinate and integrate inmate training programs; develop social histories; and evaluate positive and negative aspects in each case. Correctional treatment specialists also provide case reports to the U.S. Parole Commission; work with prisoners, their families, and interested persons in developing parole and release plans; and work with the U.S. Probation Officers and

From Robert C. DeLucia and Thomas J. Doyle, *Career Planning in Criminal Justice*, Cincinnati, OH: Anderson Publishing Co., 1994, pp. 73–86. Used with permission.

other social agencies in developing and implementing release plans of programs for selected individuals. The work may include individual and group interviews or discussions and extensive correspondence; and may involve contact and coordination with prisoners, relatives, interested persons, former and prospective employers, courts, social agencies, boards of parole, U.S. Probation Officers, and law enforcement agencies. Applicants for the correctional treatment specialist position must be U.S. citizens, less than 35 years old at time of appointment, and will be required to successfully complete an employment interview, physical examination, and full-field security investigation.

Additionally all candidates must have a bachelor's degree with at least 24 semester hours of social science. The applicant must also have two years of graduate study in social science or two years of graduate education and casework experience. Qualified applicants are appointed at the GS-9 level with promotion potential to GS-11 after one year. For further information applicants should contact the Federal Bureau of Prisons, Examining Section, Room 400, 320 First Street, N.W., Washington, DC 20534.

CORRECTIONS COUNSELOR

- Guide and counsel inmates during their incarceration
- Assess and develop appropriate rehabilitative programs for each inmate
- Conduct individual and group counseling sessions
- BA/BS and/or master's degree in counseling, social work, or psychology
- Strong interest in helping others

Corrections counselors (educational, guidance, vocational) are individuals with educational background and expertise in casework techniques. Along with other professionals in a correctional facility, they are involved in the selection of individual educational and vocational programs and treatment for inmates, in planning and coordinating inmate rehabilitation programs, and in intensive inmate counseling. Corrections counselors interview new inmates, study their case histories, review reports from various sources, summarize this material, and make program recommendations. Areas in which inmates receive counseling are family, institutional, educational, vocational, financial, parole, and disciplinary matters. Counselors may also participate in parole and disciplinary hearings.

These positions, depending on the jurisdiction, generally require a written examination to be considered for appointment. These exams are designed to test for knowledge, skills, and abilities in the areas of correctional counseling and preparing written material, with emphasis on clarity and organization.

Other important minimal experiential and educational requirements must also be met. A bachelor's degree is necessary, usually in a relevant discipline, in addition to three years of experience as a caseworker or groupworker in a recognized social service, correctional, criminal justice, community or human welfare agency, or in a position providing program services to incarcerated inmates. An alternative to this requirement would be a bachelor's degree in social work, sociology, criminal justice, psychology, probation and parole, or a closely related social services field. Some agencies permit holders of a master's degree in criminal justice, social work, or a related field to substitute this advanced education for up to two years of work experience. The experience should involve casework or program services that includes the establishment of an ongoing one-on-one relationships between counselor and clients. The groupwork experience must include responsibility for conducting group sessions designed to provide the participants with therapeutic services for significant social problems, such as alcohol and drug abuse, mental and emotional problems, family disturbance and delinquency.

CORRECTIONS OFFICER

- Guard, observe, and supervise inmates in correctional facility
- Ability to enforce rules and regulations
- College degree helpful but not required
- Sensitivity to people
- Rotating shifts
- Element of danger to be considered

A career as a corrections officer is a very demanding, yet potentially rewarding position for someone with a strong sense of authority, responsibility, and sensitivity towards others.

Corrections officers are primarily responsible for the safekeeping of prisoners either awaiting trial or previously sentenced to a federal, state, or municipal correctional facility. A correctional facility may be large, such as a penitentiary, or small, such as a jail or detention center. The level of security at these sites can range from minimum to maximum with each classification reflecting the relative level of supervision inmates receive. The major responsibility of corrections officers involves the continued observation and supervision of inmates. Corrections officers must be alert for signs of disorder, tension, and rule infractions by inmates, and be prepared to enforce these rules and regulations, should the situation arise. This involves settling disputes, administering discipline, and searching of inmates on a regular basis. The element of danger is considered part of the job, particularly when corrections officers respond to emergency situations involving riotous inmate behavior or escape. The use of firearms, chemical agents, or other emergency equipment may be required.

Corrections officers may be required to report orally and in writing regarding such matters as inmate conduct, their work habits, and progress. Therefore, good writing skills are helpful. Another common task is the inspection of prison cells and other facilities to ensure that proper health, safety, and security are maintained.

By virtue of their close and continued contact with the prison population, corrections officers are an integral part of the rehabilitation process of inmates. It is not uncommon for corrections officers to participate in a variety of programs with other professionals such as counselors, social workers, and psychologists, who work to help inmates adjust to prison life in the institution and in the process of preparing for life outside.

Because the custody and security of inmates is a 24-hour-a-day job, corrections officers may be required to work night shifts, holidays, weekends, and overtime during emergencies, working both indoors and outdoors and spending long periods of time on their feet.

In the coming years, employment prospects in this field are expected to rise. As inmate populations increase, more corrections officers will be needed.

Promotional opportunity in this field is generally good. Corrections officers may advance to corrections sergeant, lieutenant, captain, or assistant warden. With additional education, corrections officers may qualify for related jobs such as parole and probation officers, corrections counselors, and a variety of administrative positions within the institutions.

Most corrections departments have civil service regulations that require corrections officers to be at least 21 years of age, possess a high school diploma or its equivalent, and be in sound physical health. Strength, good judgment, and the ability to think and act quickly are assets. Some states may require candidates to pass a written examination. Others require candidates to have some experience in corrections or police work. In the federal prison system, college education can be substituted for general experience.

The Federal Bureau of Prisons provides two weeks of formalized training for all new employees. In some states, newly hired corrections officers are required to complete similar formal training programs. Most states and local governments use experienced officers to train new employees informally, on-the-job.

JUVENILE JUSTICE COUNSELOR

- Counsel juveniles assigned to state youth division
- Work with juveniles ranging from Persons in Need of Supervision (PINS) to more hard-core troubled adolescents
- Work frequently performed in an institutional setting
- Generally requires BA/BS degree (jurisdiction can require high school diploma plus experience)
- Requires compassion and sensitivity

Most states have a division for youth or similar agency which is designed to promote the physical, emotional, and social well-being of the state's youth. Its mandate is to provide a unified system of youth development and juvenile justice services which assist the youth to become productive, fully integrated members of society.

A major responsibility of a youth service division is the rehabilitation of youths found guilty of crimes against persons or property. These youths are placed with the division by the county and designated as juvenile delinquents or juvenile offenders, depending on the severity of their actions.

Juvenile justice counselors also work with persons in need of supervision (PINS), also referred to as "status offenders," who are placed with the division for youth by the family courts. Such youths include runaways, truants, and those who must be removed from their homes because of family difficulties. Often victims rather than offenders, PINS are now protected by federal statutes which prohibit their confinement in detention facilities or with youths who have been indicted for more serious offenses.

Juvenile justice counselors basically work under the jurisdiction of a program coordinator. Counselors can be expected to perform any or all of the following tasks: providing support and counseling to residents; participating in the development and execution of treatment plans; interacting with staff members regarding the needs of residents; participating in recreational and cultural activities; providing a safe and clean environment for residents; maintaining discipline and order among residents; providing safe transportation for residents; participating in ongoing meetings, conferences and training; maintaining records and case files; and preparing and presenting oral and written reports.

Minimum requirements for this position include a bachelor's degree with a major in psychology, criminal justice, social service or a related field, and preferably some related experience in the counseling or social service field. Information on application procedures can generally be found with the personnel office of the state division for youth or its equivalent.

PAROLE OFFICER

- Employed in correctional facility or private agency
- Guide inmates in their preparation for and adjustment to community life
- Investigate and take action for parole violations
- BA/BS degree required; master's degree helpful
- Training in firearms
- Social work and counseling background necessary

Parole is defined as a system of discretionary release of inmates from correctional facilities and jails prior to the maximum expiration of their sentences. Parole is also the community supervision of offenders who have been released to parole. Parole is usually implemented through an administrative body or board composed of members who are appointed by the governor of a state to serve a term, the length of which varies from state to state. The parole board is broken down into panels of perhaps three to four members who visit the correctional facilities to make parole decisions.

An inmate is eligible for parole consideration when he/she has served the minimum period of imprisonment as imposed by the court. The parole board conducts an in-depth personal interview in which it considers all of the available information concerning the inmate. Factors taken into account might include such factors as the crime, criminal history, adjustment while confined, and release plans.

In an institutional assignment, the parole officer guides and directs inmates during their incarceration to help them develop positive attitudes and behavior, to motivate their participation in appropriate programs of self-improvement, and to prepare inmates for hearings before the parole board and their eventual release to the community.

If assigned to the field, the parole officer guides and directs parolees during their period of adjustment from incarceration to community life. They Help them comply with the terms and conditions of parole, investigate, and take appropriate action concerning parole violations. As peace officers, parole officers are trained in the use of firearms and are required to apprehend and arrest parole violators.

While this career has been categorized under counseling or social service, parole work involves both social work and law enforcement responsibilities, requiring firearms training and knowledge of arrest procedures. In most parole agencies, all appointees will be required to participate in and satisfactorily complete a training program including classroom instruction in such areas as basic law, social work practice and case management, firearms training, and arrest procedures.

The applicant must pass a thorough character investigation, with a previous felony conviction barring appointment. Physical and medical standards include vision requirements in some parole departments, along with the ability to function effectively in possibly arduous and physically demanding field assignments. As travel to their field assignments is frequent, most parole agencies require possession of a valid driver's license at the time of appointment.

The parole officer title will minimally require a bachelor's degree with a major in the social sciences and one to three years of experience as a social caseworker or group worker in a recognized social services, correctional, criminal justice, or human welfare agency. Qualifying casework experience involves the establishment of ongoing one-on-one relationship between the caseworker and client, with the development of treatment plans and implementation of appropriate treatment services. Groupworker experience shows abilities in conducting group sessions designed to provide the participants with therapeutic services for significant social problems such as substance abuse, mental and emotional problems, family disturbance, and juvenile delinquency.

As a substitution for education and experience, many parole agencies will favorably consider a law degree or a master's degree in social work, probation and parole, sociology, criminal justice, or psychology.

For those who meet these requirements, many states require passing a written test designed to elicit knowledge, skills, and abilities in such areas as preparing written material, interviewing techniques, principles, and practices of casework, counseling in a correctional setting, and a knowledge and understanding of social issues relating to minorities, the poor and ethnic groups and cultures.

Contact the State Civil Service Commission, the State Correctional Services Department or the Division of Parole to receive applications for this position. On the federal level, the role of parole officer is incorporated with that of federal probation officer.

Finally, cities, counties, and other jurisdictions have their own parole programs, and the local criminal justice agencies for these areas should be contacted for employment information.

PRE-RELEASE PROGRAM CORRECTIONAL COUNSELOR

- Counsel clients
- Help in transition from custody to society
- Work is within confines of the facility
- Must be able to interact well with inmates
- May require BA/BS degree plus experience in social service field

Pre-release program correctional counselors work with residents of state prison pre-release centers. They assist in orienting residents to the facility and its procedures in order to provide emotional support. Pre-release program correctional counselors also provide individual and group counseling under the supervision of the center's administration.

Furthermore, the counselors accompany residents to job interviews, hospitals and assist the employment counselors in helping the resident to find meaningful employment. Finally, the pre-release counselors also assist in the general operation of the facility at the request of the administrators.

To qualify for employment as a pre-release center correctional counselor, one must have, at minimum, a bachelor's degree in addition to two years of social service related counseling experience. Resume and employment inquiries should be addressed to the personnel office of the state prison system.

Pre-Release Program Employment Counselor

- Provide vocational guidance for those soon to be released from incarceration
- Requires BA/BS and experience in career/vocational counseling
- Work entails placement of hard-to-employ clients
- Job site usually located within a detention center or halfway house
- Requires strong communication skills

Pre-release program employment counselors work with residents of state prisons by attempting to provide a range of vocational counseling. The duties of the employment counselor can vary, but usually involve interviewing and assessing prisoners; developing and maintaining job placement and training contacts; administering scoring, and interpreting vocational aptitude and standardized tests; maintaining written records; developing and coordinating a program of workshops on vocational issues and verifying the place of prisoners' employment through site visits and telephone contact with the employers.

Requirements for the employment counselor include a bachelor's degree plus two years of experience in the labor market or vocational counseling field. However, these qualifications can be substituted in some prison systems by a satisfactory combination of education and experience coupled with evidence of the knowledge, skills, and ability to perform these tasks well. Inquiry can be made at the state, county, or local correctional facilities administrative headquarters.

Pre-Release Program Halfway House Manager

- Similar to a corrections officer/prison administrator
- Residents will be easier to work with than those in prison
- Requires strong administrator skills
- Must be willing to work all shifts and weekends
- College degree or equivalent combination of education and experience preferred

Pre-release program halfway house managers can be employed in state-run pre-release programs. Additionally, they can also be employed as contract employees in federally financed probation programs designed to aid prisoners in their return to society.

Halfway house managers maintain custodial responsibility for the facility and are accountable for the whereabouts of the residents. They conduct personal searches and dispense supplies and medication. In addition, they can supervise daily clean-up duties and oversee all visitors entering and leaving the building on a daily basis. Finally, halfway house managers write reports on the prisoners along with census and population statistics.

This position usually requires a high school diploma. However, college credits or a bachelor's degree may be required, depending on the size of the halfway house program. Candidates must be wiling to work mornings, evenings, nights, and weekends, as 24-hour/seven-day coverage is required. The ability to work well with people and effectively deal with an inmate population is essential.

PROBATION OFFICER

- Conduct presentence reports and evaluations concerning release conditions
- Work to rehabilitate and supervise offender once released
- Counseling and referral to community agencies
- Some law enforcement background helpful
- BA/BS in social sciences; master's degree and/or work experience helpful
- Human relations skills a must

A probation officer provides supervision of offenders in the community instead of prison. Their task is to help protect the community by supervising adult and juvenile offenders and aiding them in leading a law-abiding life. Probation officers also service individuals and families with problems that may come to the attention of the family court.

Similarities do exist between probation and parole officers. Ideally, they have a dual role, that is, protection of the public while also helping the offender interact successfully in the community.

Probation officers can be employees of the federal, state, county, or city government. They are responsible for the delivery of professional probation services to clients and courts, and they perform a wide variety of duties related to court proceedings and to the delivery of correctional services to juveniles and adults.

These duties include intake evaluations, completion of reports and investigations, and the supervision of persons sentenced to probation. Peace officer status can be connected with the probation officer position, which may include some law enforcement responsibilities such as execution of warrants, searches and seizures, and making arrests. This work is usually performed under the supervision of a higher-level professional employee.

Probation officers should possess a genuine respect and concern for people. They should be able to communicate with all types of individuals. Since the job is stressful, the probation officer should be emotionally strong and able to cope with difficult situations. This requires strong leadership skills and the ability to be at times both gentle and firm.

The minimum qualification is a bachelor's degree, preferably in one of the social sciences. Many positions found on the city, state, or county level will probably require a written and oral examination designed to test the applicant's ability to provide client services. As the probation officer gains work experience and additional formal education, he or she can move to higher-level positions, usually in supervision or administration.

JUVENILE PROBATION OFFICER

- Provide intake, investigation, and supervising services to family court for juveniles
- Requires desire to work with youths and their families
- Generally requires BS degree in related field in addition to two years of casework or counseling-type experience
- Ability to manage heavy caseload and work effectively with an offender-type population

A juvenile probation officer, an employee of the probation department, provides intake, investigation and supervision services to the family court for juveniles generally up to the age of 16 who appear as the result of delinquent acts or as Persons in Need of Supervision (PINS).

In the intake process, the juvenile probation officer assesses the total situation of the petitioner when first making contact with the family court. The officer weighs the attitudes and strengths, and evaluates the risks of the petitioner. Based on these decisions, the juvenile probation officer may present an alternative plan that is consistent with protecting both the community and the needs of the petitioner. If the petitioner is a PINS project participant, the juvenile probation officer helps determine the eligibility and suitability of the PINS respondent as well as the needs of his family. The juvenile probation officer also has the possible alternative of referring the respondent to community service and ensuring that initial appointments are kept with the service provider.

This investigative process is intended to provide the court with a comprehensive picture of the offender and the offense. The investigative report reviews and analyzes social factors as well as the details of the current offense and the respondent's legal history. The juvenile probation officer then submits a recommendation to assist the court in reaching an appropriate disposition. Because of the special skills and knowledge of the resources needed to best meet the needs of juveniles, the juvenile probation officers also has responsibility for all presentence investigations on youthful offenders before higher courts.

In supervision services to the family court, the juvenile probation officer conducts interviews with the juvenile after he or she is placed on probation. The main purpose of this contact is to explain the conditions of probation as specified by the court and to establish a preliminary supervision plan. After placement on probation, the officer, probationer, and parents become involved in further developing the supervision treatment plan and defining goals for the probation. The juvenile probationer will also identify community services that are available and plans are made to utilize them if necessary.

Finally, the juvenile probation officer may make visits to the probationer's home if necessary, and if the probationer fails to comply with the conditions of probation, the juvenile probation officer may file a violation and explore other dispositional alternatives. In most jurisdictions a juvenile probation officer is required to have a bachelor's degree in a related field such as psychology, human services, social work, or criminal justice. Some probation departments also may require a master's degree in social work or counseling. Experience in paid casework-type counseling is also extremely important, with some jurisdictions asking that the applicant have at least two years of experience in this work. Other requirements include strong analytical abilities, excellent written and oral communication skills, ability to manage a sometimes heavy and stressful caseload, possession of a valid driver's license and, perhaps most importantly, a willingness and ability to interact effectively with an offender/ex-offender population.

WARDEN

- Overall supervision and administration of correctional facility
- Plan, direct, coordinate programs
- Responsible for all rehabilitative, security, disciplinary, and educational programs
- Oversee and supervise staff
- BA/BS degree, master's degree preferred
- Excellent managerial skills
- Knowledge of all phases of corrections operation

Wardens function to oversee all operations and programs that are a part of life within the correctional facility. However, they do not work alone, nor do they always have direct involvement in all phases of corrections operations. Because their job responsibilities are so all-encompassing, they must successfully delegate responsibilities to a host of administrative professionals who serve under their direct supervision. Through these subordinates, wardens direct, plan, and coordinate operations and correctional facility programs in such areas as security, discipline, education, rehabilitations, budget and fiscal management, staffing, and inmate care.

They meet regularly with the staff members to develop and establish policies and regulations, review inmate records and behavior, prepare written reports, gather statistics, and evaluate all components of a facility's operations.

Wardens must possess a complete knowledge and understanding of correctional programs and the operation of a correctional facility, including knowledge of the methods and techniques of inmate care, rehabilitation, and custody. In addition, wardens need to be good supervisors, administrators, and managers.

The position of warden, a senior-level position, is designed for someone who has gained experience through a working knowledge of the correctional system. A limited number of qualified individuals rise to this rank. Students striving toward this occupation should have, at minimum, a bachelor's degree, with a master's degree preferred. Coursework in sociology, psychology, criminology, and penology is recommended.

OTHER RELATED CORRECTIONS OCCUPATIONS

When considering that a correctional institution is in many ways like a small community, it is understandable that a wide variety of career specialists are employed to care for and rehabilitate the inmate population, as well as maintain the services of the correctional facility.

Within the institution a number of specialists are employed to help in the rehabilitative process.

Clinical psychologists work closely with inmates. Often as members of an interdisciplinary health care team, they participate in administering a wide variety of psychological assessment (intellectual, personality, aptitude, vocational, and educational), interpret results and prepare comprehensive reports. They are also involved in the development and organization of individual and group therapy and other rehabilitative programs for the treatment of prisoners with many kinds of problems. Specific emphasis may be geared toward vocational planning, so as to prepare the inmates for successful return to community life. Students interested in a career as a correctional psychologist should receive training in the area of criminal psychology. A doctoral degree is required, as well as the appropriate state licensing or certification.

Vocational counselors provide educational programs in vocational specialities. For example, they might teach a course in carpentry, automotive repair, electronics, or provide other career training through work programs that sell their products or services to federal agencies. Vocational instructors determine learning needs, abilities, and other facts about inmates. They may participate in discussion with other members of the treatment team and staff professionals to assess and aid in the overall rehabilitation of individuals.

Recreation counselors conduct and supervise the social activities of inmates such as team sports and games, hobbies, and dramatics, designed to promote the emotional, physical, and social well-being of inmates. Recreation leaders work with individuals of all ages and races. The ability to organize and motivate participation and interest through their own excitement and concern is a highly desirable personal quality.

Academic teachers are employed on all levels within a correctional facility. They might instruct in basic remedial courses designed to increase rudimentary English, reading or math abilities, or be employed to teach on a college level. In either case, a teacher within a correctional facility is a special kind of professional who must be able to communicate with inmates, convey knowledge, monitor and encourage progress, and adjust to the varied interests, abilities and personalities of this kind of population. Time is spent grading papers, preparing lesson plans, and attending meetings with other support staff.

Caseworkers/HIV specialists are increasingly in demand to provide support services to the growing number of residents of traditional and nontraditional correctional facilities who are testing positive for the HIV virus.

Caseworkers help HIV-infected inmates cope with their emotional and health-related concerns while incarcerated. They also work closely with inmates soon to be released to help make their transition to society more manageable. This usually involves helping to coordinate many community support services as well as regular home visits. Caseworkers/HIV specialists are often responsible for facilitating educational programs. It is essential that caseworkers be able to deal with HIV issues pertinent to men and women, mothers and fathers, minority communities, substance abusers, homosexual, heterosexual, and bisexual clients. Equally essential is that candidates possess a genuine concern/caring for others. A bachelor's degree and experience in social services are required.

Education counselors are responsible for providing counseling services to aid inmates in making an effective adjustment to the facility educational programs. Working with inmates and staff, they help to ensure that the inmate's choice of program is in relation to his or her long-term goals. They periodically evaluate the progress of inmates to provide suggestions and make recommendations for continued educational training and supportive services.

Substance abuse specialists can be found in correctional institutions, pre-release and other alternative detention programs. These professionals primarily function as substance and alcohol abuse education and prevention workers. Working with criminal offenders, parolees, and other high-risk groups and their family members, these professionals provide individual and group counseling that focuses on the issues and problems surrounding alcohol and/or drug abuse. These positions usually require a college degree, in addition to a familiarity with the addictive personality and withdrawal process. Some agencies and institutions require a C.A.C. (Certified Alcoholism Counselor) certificate or specific training in substance abuse.

On an administrative level, a variety of other career specialists are available to help plan, direct, research, and evaluate the many programs and activities found within a correctional facility.

Classification and treatment directors and other management coordinators apply the principles of management to the overall planning, coordination, and evaluation of correctional programs. They assign inmates to particular programs, review inmate case reports and consult with other staff members to recommend parole, educational or vocational training, medical treatment, and other services for the inmate. The ability to organize and direct the work of others is an essential requirement of this position. Additionally, they should be well informed about all phases of inmate care, custody, rehabilitation, and operations.

Inmate records coordinators supervise personnel with records and other correspondence. They maintain responsibility for receiving and transferring of inmates, prepare inmate reports and written work regarding such matters as court proceedings, legal affidavits, furloughs, leaves of absence, and escapes, to name a few.

Correctional facilities specialists engage in on-site visitation to local and state correctional facilities to determine that proper standards and regulations have been followed.

Facilities specialists investigate and report on complaints involving state and local correctional facilities referred by officials, organizations, residents, or other interested parties. They may also participate in the plans for the building or remodeling of a facility or to develop programs or policies that are seen as promoting the rehabilitation process.

Prisoner-classification interviewers interview new inmates and compile social and criminal histories. They collect such data as work histories; school, criminal, and medical records; evaluations from correctional staff; information from relatives; and data surrounding each offender's crime and criminal background. With this thorough background investigation, and after a personal interview with each offender, prisoner-classification interviewers construct profiles of each new inmate with a recommendation to work assignment and the degree of custody recommended.

In the field of corrections a variety of specialists are employed to help research and evaluate correctional programs, policies, the inmate population, and crime in general.

Penologists conduct research and study the control and prevention of crime, punishment for crime, management of correctional facilities, and rehabilitation of inmates, with an emphasis on treatment programs and parole procedures. These professionals work closely with other specialists such as economists, anthropologists, statisticians, physicians, social workers, and historians. Students who are interested in this kind of career should pursue master's-level training and education in the specialization of penology or sociology with an emphasis on research and design skills. Often a doctoral degree is required for directorships of major research projects or higher-level positions in this area.

Occupations within the field of corrections can be considered similar to nearly every kind of job found outside the system. There are positions that range from those requiring a high degree of formal education and experience to those that require more modest ability and education. Advancement within the system is possible with continued training and education.

QUESTIONS FOR THOUGHT AND DISCUSSION

1. What are the three general areas of corrections? Discuss the different types of work required for each of these areas.
2. What are the differences between a corrections treatment specialist, or corrections counselor, and a corrections officer?
3. What are the duties of the various prerelease staff positions?

SUGGESTIONS FOR FURTHER READING

CARROTHERS, HELEN, (1992) *The Effective Correctional Officer*, Laurel, MD: American Correctional Association.

CROMWELL, PAUL, AND KILLINGER, GEORGE, (1994) *Community-Based Corrections: Probation, Parole, and Intermediate Sanctions*, St. Paul, MN: West Publishing Company.

DeLUCIA, ROBERT, AND DOYLE, THOMAS, (1994) *Career Planning in Criminal Justice*, 2nd ed., Cinncinatti, OH: Anderson Publications, Inc.

HAAS, KENNETH, AND ALPERT, GEOFFREY, (1995) *The Dilemmas of Corrections*, 3rd ed., Prospect Heights, IL: Waveland Press.

IRWIN, JOHN, AND AUSTIN, JAMES, (1994) *Its About Time: America's Imprisonment Binge*, Belmont, CA: Wadsworth Publishing Company.

JOHNSON, ROBERT, (1987) *Hard Time: Understanding and Reforming the Prison*, Pacific Grove, CA: Brooks/Cole Publishing Company.

JOHNSON, ROBERT, "This Man Has Expired," *Commonweal*, January 13, 1989.

SILBERMAN, MATTHEW, (1995) "The Social Organization of Prison Life," *A World of Violence*, Belmont, CA: Wadsworth Publishing Company.

WENER, RICHARD, et al., "The New Jails: Psychologically Designed for Success," *Psychology Today* 21(4). June, 1987.

WHITEHEAD, JOHN, (1991) "Ethical Issues in Probation and Parole," *Justice, Crime, and Ethics*, Cinncinatti, OH: Anderson Publishing Company.

Looking Toward the 21st Century

INTRODUCTION

As we rapidly approach the end of the twentieth century and look toward the new millennium, we are conscious of the history of failure in the criminal justice system and aware of the challenges of the new century. What will America look like in twenty years—fifty years? What new problems will we face? What might technology offer in the way of amelioration of our myriad problems in crime and criminal justice?

In this first selection, "Peeking Over the Rim: What Lies Ahead?" University of Nevada criminal justice professor Ken Peak reviews challenges for the future in policing, courts, and corrections. He examines several methods for determining what the future will be like and then discusses forecasted changes in police technology to cope with crime, the courts, and corrections. Computers and AIDS play a role in these forecasts.

In selection two, "The Changing Face of America," Robert C. Trojanowicz and David L. Carter examine the changing demographic make-up of American society and forecast future shifts in age, income, race, and ethnicity of the population. They discuss how these changes may be responsible for higher levels of victimization, criminal behavior, and more problems for the police in the future.

Selection three, "Ophelia the C.C.W.: May 11, 2010" by Rutgers criminologist Todd R. Clear, explores the changing nature of probation and parole and uses a clever futuristic scenario to describe the future and how technology may directly affect the delivery of probation and parole services.

In the final selection, "Police: A Future of Utopia or Dystopia," William N. Holden and Allen D. Sapp review two possible future scenarios for policing and discuss the consequences of each. The first is a look at what a police organization would be like in a utopian society. This depiction is then compared with a police organization in a dystopian world. The authors conclude with a brief review of the factors that will ultimately shape the future of police organizations.

"PEEKING OVER THE RIM"

What Lies Ahead

Kenneth J. Peak

I like the dreams of the future better than the history of the past.

—*Patrick Henry*

The trouble with our times is that the future is not what it used to be.

—*Paul Valery*

INTRODUCTION

What will the future bring? In attempting to answer that impossible question, we all have probably wished at some time that we could gaze into a crystal ball and have what former President George Bush referred to as "the vision thing." It is important that today's criminal justice students listen to what the prognosticators tell us about the future and understand their methods; they could well be the administrators of justice in a mere decade. They, like current justice administrators, must take the time today to "peek over the rim" to anticipate and plan for the future.

This chapter opens by examining several methods by which futurists attempt to determine what the future holds—in short, tools for prediction. Using those best-guess methods, we then look at what appears imminent with respect to demographics and crime in the United States. We then view what the experts portend in terms of police technology to cope with crime, as well as forecasted changes in both courts (including possibilities for reform) and corrections (population growth and the need to build more prisons). We close with discussions of how computers have changed (and will continue to change) justice administration, and how AIDS has affected personnel, policy, and litigation, and clients of the justice system.

Kenneth J. Peak, *Justice Administration: Police, Courts, and Corrections Management*, (c) 1995, pp. 436–455. Reprinted by permission of Prentice-Hall, Inc., Englewood Cliffs, N.J.

How to Predict the Future

Many variables can affect predictions and trends, one of the most important being money. If you have unlimited funds, you do not need to be concerned with futures. Over the next 14 to 20 years, the driving force for major changes in law enforcement agencies will be the economy. In a phrase, "there is a lot of crime prevention in a T-bone steak." Unfortunately, with the volatile nature of the world's oil supplies, the value of the dollar, and many other related matters, our economy is in a delicate balance and our future is uncertain.

Contemporary futures research has two major aspects: environmental scanning and scenario writing. Environmental scanning is an effort to put a social problem under a microscope, with an eye toward the future. We may consult experts on their opinions, such as demographers, social scientists, technologists, and economists. A Delphi process may also assist, gathering experts, looking at all possible factors, and getting an idea of what will happen in the future. Thus environmental scanning permits us to identify, track, and assess changes in the environment.

Through scanning, we can examine the factors that seem likely to "drive" the environment. "Drivers" are factors or variables—economic conditions, demographic shifts, governmental policies, social attitudes, technological advances, and so on—that will have a bearing on future conditions. Three categories of drivers will serve to identify possible trends and impacts on the American criminal justice system by and beyond the year 2000: (1) social and economic conditions (e.g., size and age of the population, immigration patterns, nature of employment, and lifestyle characteristics); (2) shifts in the amounts and types of crimes (including the potential for new types of criminality and for technological advances that might be used for illegal behavior); and (3) possible developments in the criminal justice system itself (e.g., changes in the way the police, courts and corrections subsystems operate; important innovations).

Scenario writing is simply the application of drivers to three primary situations or elements: public tolerance for crime, amount of crime, and the capacity of the criminal justice system to deal with crime. An important consideration is whether each will occur in high or low degrees. For example, drivers may be analyzed in a scenario of *low* public tolerance for crime, a *high* amount of crime, and a *high* capacity of the criminal justice system to deal with crime. Conversely, a scenario may include a view of the future where there is a *high* tolerance for crime, a *low* amount of crime, and a *low* capacity for the system to cope with crime; and so on.

The Changing Face of America

In 1996 the first wave of "baby boomers" will turn 50; by 2010 one in every four Americans will be 55 or older. By the year 2000, an estimated 34.9 million elderly people will constitute 13 percent of the population. The minority population is increasing rapidly; by the year 2000 an estimated 34 percent of American children will be Hispanic, black, or Asian. More than 25 million women headed their own households in 1990, 28 percent of the nation's 91 million households. Two-thirds of black and Hispanic households are headed by women. And if present trends continue, one-half of all marriages occurring today will end in divorce within a decade.

In our "postindustrial" society, there are fewer blue-collar jobs and more white-collar jobs. Jobs that are declining in number are those that could be filled by those with fewer skills. The fastest-growing jobs are those requiring more language, math, and reasoning skills. For the next decade, 90 percent of all new jobs will be in the service sector—fields that often require high levels of education and skill. Ten years ago, 77 percent of all jobs required some type of generating, processing, retrieving, or distribution of information; by the year 2000, heavily computerized information processing will be involved in 95 percent of all jobs. Statistics indicate that America is becoming a bifurcated society with more wealth, poverty, and a shrinking middle class. The gap between the "haves" and "have nots" is widening. An underclass of people—those who are chronically poor and live outside of society's rules—is growing. Between 1970 and 1980 the underclass tripled.

The influence of immigration to America, and the growth of minority-group populations in general, cannot be overstated. America now accepts nearly a million newcomers per year, which equates to about 10 million new residents each decade (excluding their offspring) even if immigration rates do not rise. Shortly after the turn of the twenty-first century, Asians are expected to reach 10 million; today's 18 million legal and illegal Hispanics may well double by then. In less than 100 years we can expect white dominance of the United States to end, as the growing number of blacks, Hispanics, and Asians together become the new majority. History has shown that where newcomers cluster together in poor neighborhoods with high crime rates, the police are soon involved. And when these various minority groups are forced to compete for increasingly scarce, low-paying service jobs, intergroup relations sour and can even become combative, as has occurred recently in Los Angeles, Miami, and other cities.

In sum, today's economy is based on knowledge. Whereas employers in the past mostly wanted muscle, today more and more jobs presuppose skills, training, and education. Fewer jobs remain for those on the bottom rung; the results are clear in our inner cities.

A Changing Nature of Crime

Three important drivers contribute to the changing nature of crime in the West: (1) the advent of high technology in our society; (2) the distribution and use of narcotics; and (3) a declining population in the 15 to 24 age bracket.

The nature of crime is rapidly changing. The new crimes of data manipulation, software piracy, industrial espionage, bank card counterfeiting, and embezzlement by computer are here to stay. What will probably tend to decrease will be the traditionally illegal means of obtaining funds: robbery and burglary. These new crimes will require the development of new investigative techniques, specialized training for law enforcement investigators, and the employment of people with specialized, highly technological backgrounds.

The abuse of narcotics is spreading in numbers and throughout various social classes, continuing to demand an ever-increasing amount of law enforcement time and resources. The real solution to the drug problem is for people to stop demanding a supply. However, that is probably an impossible goal at this time.

The decline in the size of the 15 to 24 cohort, the crime-prone youth of our society, has significantly affected crime rates. We are witnessing a decline in several types of crime, although crimes of violence are increasing. As we see the increase in the "graying of America," however, the young criminals will increasingly prey on the elderly and flourish. The growing numbers of crime-prone youths in our metropolitan areas virtually ensures that high crime rates will continue in the inner city.

Future criminal justice recruiting efforts are implicated by the nation's shift in demographic makeup. A change toward older workers, fewer entry-level workers, and more women, minorities, and immigrants in the population will force criminal justice and private industry to become more flexible to compete for qualified applicants. With the aging of America, justice agencies that only recruit recent high school graduates will probably face a shortage of qualified workers. Agencies must devise new strategies to attract 21- to 35-year-olds. This age group will be at a premium over the next 10 years, and the trend will continue well into the middle of the next century. Criminal justice will also need to offer better wage and benefits packages to compete with private businesses, such as day care, flexible hours, and paid maternity leave.

By the year 2000 an estimated 75 percent of the labor force will need retraining; justice agencies will have to train existing personnel, both professional and clerical, and a major thrust will be toward communication with non-English-speaking communities.

POLICING AND TECHNOLOGY IN THE FUTURE

The high-speed technological revolution, which has barely begun, will introduce new weapons for criminals and the police alike. Some futurists feel that the old methods and equipment for doing police work will soon fall by the wayside, replaced, for example, by electric and methane-fueled scooters and bubble-topped tricycles for densely populated areas; steamwagons and diesel superchargers for police in the rural and suburban areas; and methane-filled helium dirigibles, equipped with infrared night goggles and sophisticated communications and lighting devices, for patrol and assistance in planning barricades to trap high-speed drivers and search and rescue operations.

Patrol officers in this scenario will be able to type in an analysis of how a crime was committed and receive a list of suspects. With a bit more analysis and data, the computer will also give a probability of various suspects committing that particular crime at that particular place. All homes and businesses will be linked to a central dispatch system in a police-approved, computer-based remote linkage system that will combine burglar and fire alarms. Community policing teams will be assigned by zone, the officers wearing blazers instead of paramilitary uniforms. Basic police training will last a minimum of 10 months and will be geared so that the lower one-third of the class will flunk out.

Others see the future of policing differently. The twenty-first-century cop may patrol by means of jet backpack flight equipment, and officers will be able to tie in to "language banks" of translators via their wrist radios. Holographic, or three-dimensional photography may be used for mug photos, and satellite photography will probably be used to assist in criminal investigations. Police vehicles will have all electronic equipment built in, and private vehicles will have a factory-installed "kill switch" that can be activated by depressing a button in a nearby patrol vehicle, thus preventing high-speed pursuits. Police officers may spend no time in court, instead transmitting their testimony by home computer/video systems.

Obviously, law enforcement needs to assign some of its best thinkers to the task of probing the future. What should be the agency's budget? How should police personnel be trained? What skills will be needed? What new technologies will the police face? How should forces be deployed?

An area of concern among futurists is law enforcement's organizational structure. Increasing numbers of law enforcement executives are beginning to question whether or not the "pyramid"-shaped police bureaucracy will be effective in the future. Communications within the pyramid structure are often broken down and frustrated by the levels of bureaucracy; perhaps the organizational structure, the argument goes, could be changed to a more horizontal design to facilitate the flow of information and ideas.

Personnel and labor/management problems will continue to loom large in the future. Opportunities for graft and corruption will not decline, so police administrators must be sure to develop personnel policies that will protect the integrity of the profession. Debate is currently underway regarding mandatory drug testing and the use of the polygraph to safeguard the organizations. Traditional police personnel problems are not anticipated to decline either. Such matters as age discrimination, employment misconduct, sexism, new employee attitudes, and poor work habits will not be resolved in the near future.

FUTURE ADAPTATIONS BY THE COURTS

Major Modification on the Horizon

Many people believe that the inability to think systematically about the future is particularly apparent in the court community. In 1990 the chairman of the board of directors of the State Justice Institute and former Chief Justice of the Supreme Court of Alabama noted with regret that "The common picture of an American court is that of an institution rooted in the past, resistant to change, and resigned to inefficiency." And in the early 1980s a futurist working with the Hawaii judiciary asked what were the most important long-term issues facing the courts; one reply was "how the parking spaces are allocated." The reasons for this short-term focus in the courts are several: the urgent pressure to attend to the present; judicial priorities set in annual or biannual legislative sessions; legal personnel being trained to apply the past (precedent-guiding decisions made in the present), the common law assumes the future will take care of itself; and judges, in particular, having an inherent preference for sensing the facts before them, not intuiting probable or possible future possibilities.

Looking at current trends, however, futurist Clement Bezold offered some court-related speculation for the early twenty-first century:

1. Rise of courts as a business: Efficiency and cost/benefit focuses will become more important. Private judging, arbitration, and mediation will increasingly compete with public-run courts for faster and fairer dispute resolution.

2. Death of the adversary system: The adversary system is slow, costly, and fraught with "unfairness." New, less confrontational, more humanistic ways to resolve disputes will arise, buttressed by the increase in technology.

3. The vast majority of judicial decision making (in such grass-roots areas as small claims, traffic, and status offenses) will be by nonlawyer, citizen pro-tempore judges. The need for quick decisions will lead more and more to this system for cases requiring little legal knowledge or training.

4. Courts will be depoliticized. Appointed professional managers will become the norm, and merit selection of judges will become more commonplace.

5. Technology will allow quick, easy synthesis of information and data for judicial decision making. This will provide a "quicker path to decision" and greater efficiency.

6. Courts will increasingly be called upon to resolve social problems involving drugs, poverty, and domestic violence—with little success.

7. Court programs will become increasingly decentralized. As courts become more service oriented, court programs will move closer to client groups.

8. Court organization structures will become more informal, with less reliance on hierarchical, bureaucratic structures, and shared leadership.

Suggestions for Reform

Suggestions for reform in the federal courts include adding additional judges to handle increasing federal calendars, geographic alignment to balance the court caseloads, delegating court management to professional managers, and diverting certain cases for arbitration. However, a major problem that permeates all of these reforms is the decentralized nature of the federal judiciary.

At the state court level, three major administrative reforms have been recommended by such groups as the American Bar Association and the American Judicature Society, all of which come under the heading of "court unification": structural unification, administrative centralization, and unified budgeting. *Structural unification* involves consolidating and simplifying existing trial courts and forming a single superior court on a county-wide basis; lower courts cease to exist. *Administrative centralization* would place statewide authority for court policy and administration in the supreme court or judicial council, with overall governance placed with the chief justice of the highest court or a chief administrative judge. Such an organization "provides the state's highest court with the power to make rules, appoint managerial personnel, assign judges nonjudicial staff, and prepare and execute a centralized, state-financed yearly budget." Under this system, a high degree of uniformity is achieved; judges can also be moved across counties on temporary assignments to reduce case backlogs.

Opponents of unification and centralization argue that such changes would lead to a large central bureaucracy which would be insensitive to local concerns; rigidity would be substituted for individual justice. *Unified budgeting* "means that the budget for the court system is prepared at the state level, regardless of the source of funds, and that the executive branch does not have the authority to modify the budget request" since this would encroach upon the separation of powers.

How to Approach Reform

In an excellent book entitled *Court Reform on Trial*, in which he examined reform with bail, pretrial diversion, sentence reform, and speedy trial rules, Malcolm Feeley provided several stages in the planned-change process for the courts; succinctly, they are: (1) diagnosis or conception (identifying problems and solutions); (2) initiation (new functions added or practices significantly altered); (3) implementation (staffing, clarifying goals, adapting to a new environment); (4) routinization (commitment to supply funding and a physical base of operations); and (5) evaluation (assessment should take place during the first three stages).

The courts, Feeley wrote, while staffed with trained professionals, are also enmeshed in a web of rules that can often be inimical to change. Because of rigid segmentation, broad perspectives, and systemwide thinking are discouraged and innovation is stifled. Segmentation in the adversary process inhibits communication, feeds distrust, and breeds antagonism. Finally, because of the large numbers of cases that courts must handle, courts are forced to emphasize efficiency; the greater this emphasis, the more likely that program change will be discouraged. When change *is* initiated, it often cannot be implemented. Because attempts to change encounter at least some of these problems, the successes are few and far between. Feeley concluded that "The courts do face real problems—and problems that have not been taken seriously enough. The question is: Can proponents of planned change adequately identify these problems, diagnose them accurately, and make improvements?"

THE FUTURE AND CORRECTIONS

Continuing the "Boom Industry"

Probably nowhere in the justice system is forecasting for the future more difficult and dismal than in corrections. The most ominous problems for the future of corrections will continue to be those we have concentrated upon already and which are the most difficult to predict—crowding and its related costs.

Attempts were made in the mid-1980s to estimate future state prison populations, using a mathematical model that extrapolated crime, incarceration, and demographic patterns to the year 2020. The conclusion was that prison populations would continue to rise into the early 1990s, and then that the "birth dearth" that followed World War II would begin to affect prison admissions, and the number of persons behind bars would decline slightly for about a decade. Around the turn of the century, levels were predicted to rise again and continue upward through 2020.

However, reality has a way of outstripping forecasts and mathematical models, especially in corrections. One estimate was that by 2020, prison populations would grow between 20 and 25 percent over 1983 levels. But between 1983 and 1986 alone, those populations grew 30 percent. The projections fell short partly because the forecasters could not anticipate changes in sentencing policy and partly because they did not capture adequately the subtle and possibly changing interactions among age, race, crime, and criminal justice processing. For example, the baby boom never really stopped in the black and Hispanic communities, and these groups will constitute an increasingly large proportion of the young male cohort in the coming decades. Because young black and Hispanic men have higher arrest and incarceration rates than whites, and because there is some evidence that those rates are increasing, the slowdown in prison populations that has been forecast may not come to pass.

Even more ominous is the prediction by corrections author and futurist Douglas McDonald that the U.S. prison population might double again in the next 10 years. The current rates of growth are pointing in that direction. If the prison population doubles, governments will rapidly have to construct as many cells as now exist to handle the demand, as well as replacing currently substandard facilities. The cost of this construction, based on a projected average of $51,000 per bed, will be approximately $26 billion in constant 1986 dollars. Jail populations have also been rising quickly and could also double in the next 10 years if past trends continue. Assuming an average construction cost of nearly $49,000 per bed, doubling the size of America's jail capacity would cost approximately $12 billion.

Pains will be more severe in those states having high incarceration rates, few alternative-to-incarceration programming planned, and higher levels of poverty (with, by extension, weaker tax bases). Most states in the south are so characterized. Local governments maintaining jails will fare even worse than state governments, because their revenue bases are narrower.

Another concern today is with correctional administrators being able to "find their way." As one corrections worker observed, "Correctional administrators"…tend to face inward toward their organizations…and are little in touch with the outside world…and seem to be isolated from organized efforts to advance and refine general understanding of administration, especially public administration." And as Alvin Cohn noted:

> Unfortunately, many correctional managers have learned that [their bosses have] as a motto, "Let sleeping dogs lie." More unfortunately, they have learned that "barking" or "attacking" dogs generally will not survive. This is not to argue that there cannot be change; we know that change is inevitable. The question is whether an executive chooses to be reactive or proactive…will simply ride the currents of change…or deliberately attempt to harness and control change. The former is crisis management, the latter is the kind of manager we should be training to assume mantles of leadership.

Prisons: To Reform or Not to Reform

Given the extent of corrections' responsibility and problems throughout its history, it is not surprising that many people have called for its reform. The story of penal reform in the United States is an old and discouraging one. From the development of the penitentiary in the late eighteenth and early nineteenth centuries, to the determinate sentencing movement of the last two decades, penal "reforms" in this country have led to few real improvements in the practice of punishment. Even if the reforms alleviated old problems, in so doing they often created new ones, requiring new reforms, which led to further problems, and so on. However, now that we are ending the current reform cycle, that of determinate sentencing, it is timely and perhaps even necessary to consider why reforms fail, and whether or not anything will work. According to Samuel Pillsbury, "Reform begins with the proposal of a scheme for penal improvement. In most instances it is suggested by an idealist who links the proposed penal reform to a view of the ideal society prominent at the time. The idealist promotes a penal ideology which emphasizes the rightness or goodness of the proposed change in terms of society's relation to the offender."

George Bernard Shaw warned against penal reform more than a half century ago. He urged the following upon persons interested in pursuing penal reform for benevolent purposes: "To put it down and go about some other business. It is just such reformers who have in the past made the neglect, oppression, corruption, and physical torture of the common goal the pretext for transforming it into that diabolical den of torment, mischief, and damnation, the modern prison."

There are many who have sought, both from within the system as well as from without, to make prisons better places. Internally initiated reform has from time to time involved inmate rioting; although this method is not the most effective tool for the expression of inmate grievances, it has focused attention on prison problems and helped pave the way for inmate councils, grievance procedures, conflict resolution, and the position of ombudsman. Changing the internal administration is another means of attempting internal reform. An example was Arkansas Governor Winthrop Rockefeller's hiring in the 1960s of Tom Murton to administer a prison system that had become corrupted and even lethal (Murton unearthed a number of scandals and even human skeletons at the prison). This attempt at reform was made famous by the 1980 movie "Brubaker," starring Robert Redford.

Murton was quite critical during his tenure, referring to the "facade of reform" and saying that the "reform of penal practices has often appeared to follow the motto, 'Do something, even if it proves to be wrong'." He added that "the reformer long ago came to realize that chief executives, prison boards, prison staffs, and most inmates are not willing to risk the consequences of seeking real reform."

Normally, internally initiated reform by the staff is short-lived; either the old routine returns or the reforms settle into a new but equally sterile routine. Unless real reform occurs at all levels, there is little incentive for initiating new programs. The most lasting reforms appear to be those that have been initiated by external sources or with the knowledge and support of the outside community and public leaders.

At the state level, externally induced reform is usually brought by legislative or executive action. A state's criminal code may be revised, allowing such benefits as educational and home furloughs. The executive branch of government can enact executive orders. At the federal level, the most active reformer has been the U.S. Supreme Court. A number of major court decisions have affected prisoners' rights. External pressure is also brought to bear by private organizations, such as the John Howard Association, the American Correctional Association, and the National Council on Crime and Delinquency. All seek reform through prison certification visits and suggestions to correctional administrators. Organizations of ex-offenders who work with prisoners, such as the Seventh Step Foundation, Man-to-Man, and the Fortune Society, also seek correctional reform.

An official of the California school system provided some food for thought for simple prison reform, saying:

You want to know where prison reform starts? I'll tell you. It's the third grade. We know the high risk groups who will drop out of school. We know individuals from these groups make up a disproportionate share of prison inmates. Give me part of the $20,000 a year we now spend on these kids as adults [in prison], give it to me now, and we can make sure they won't wind up in prison, costing the state money not only to lock them up, but for the crimes they've committed, and for the welfare payments if they have a family.

According to prison expert John Dilulio, Jr., three steps could be taken by prison officials to help create better prisons in the short and long terms:

1. Provide continuity in the commissioner's office (and, it should be added, in the warden's office; both have an average tenure that is often less than five years). The current situation of high turnover for the past 15 years fosters a power vacuum at many levels of management.
2. Adopt the practice of unit management as a means of reducing prison violence. In addition to its potential for calming the institution and its residents, there are fewer staff rotations, allowing management to measure performance better. Officers are given more authority, act more as professionals, and morale is boosted.
3. Allow products manufactured by inmates in state prisons to be sold to the federal government. This would eliminate the presently endless hours of idleness for inmates. The federal system has a large and ready market for its products.

Building More Prisons: Large, Small, or None at All?

No issue has brought criminal justice more to the forefront of public policy—and into the living rooms of America—than that of corrections cost. In fact, state spending for corrections throughout the nation grew by more than 50 percent during the 1980s—the greatest increase of any state-funded service. Furthermore, from 1975 to 1985, the cost of operating corrections in the country rose by nearly 240 percent. Americans now spend $13 billion each year to confine adult offenders.

Legal reforms have expanded the use of determinate and mandatory sentences and thus enlarged the correctional population. With the current annual cost of incarceration running as high as $50,000 per inmate, there is increasing concern over the cost of incarcerating such large numbers of offenders and crowding in general. As a result, a variety of proposals have surfaced to cope with the problem of population and save money. One purported cost-saving mechanism is privatization, discussed earlier in this chapter. Others include marginally credible ideas ranging from that of a New York City mayor, to make use of old tugboats to hold prisoners, to politically volatile solutions such as early-release programs, to electronic surveillance home-detention programs.

Although it is clear that the concern among legislators, correctional administrators, and the public over the cost of corrections is justified, the public is sending mixed messages. For example, legislative changes to penal codes in the late 1980s, in the form of mandatory prison terms for drunk drivers and for those who commit gun crimes, as well as calls for the abolition of parole boards, seemed to indicate a popular sentiment for more prison space. More recently, however, the public seems to be gradually reversing itself, balking at the prospect of spending $30 to 50 million every few years to construct a new prison for housing offenders (especially when schools, highways, health care, and social services are suffering). Thus we now see a movement beginning toward early release and other types of programs designed to reduce the overload and divert offenders away from incarceration.

Douglas McDonald determined that larger prisons were less expensive on a per-prisoner basis than smaller ones. In addition, the average per-capita cost of operating maximum-security prisons was lower than the cost of minimum-security camps, which in turn were less expensive than medium-security facilities. These cost differences resulted largely from variations in the way each type of facility was staffed. Maximum-security prisons were larger, on average, and had fewer staff persons per inmate than other facilities. *"As the staff/inmate ratio increased, so did cost."* [emphasis his].

All is not gloom and doom in the area of corrections costs, however. Construction and financing costs can make building prisons seem overwhelmingly expensive. However, according to the National Institute of Justice (NIJ), when these charges are amortized over the useful life of a facility, they become quite modest. But the NIJ also noted that there are other unintended costs of imprisonment for a community. Imprisonment of breadwinners may force their families into welfare dependency. There are other variables as well. For example, if an inmate was unemployed at the time of imprisonment, the state would actually gain by paying less unemployment compensation.

One estimate is that society lost an average of $408 in taxes and $84 in welfare payments per year of imprisonment. Assuming a total social loss of $5000 per year, the NIJ concluded that a year in prison implies confinement costs of roughly $20,000, for a total social cost of about $25,000. Carrying this analysis a bit further and adding new twist, by combining crime costs and offense rates, NIJ found that a typical inmate (found in a survey to commit 187 crimes per year) is responsible for $430,000 in crime costs. Sentencing 1000 more offenders to prison would obligate correctional systems to an additional $25 million per year, but about 187,000 felonies would be averted in the process of incapacitation. *These crimes represent about $430 million in social costs* [emphasis theirs].

In addition to being sensitive to the high cost of imprisonment and the political sensitivity of this issue, correctional administrators must be adept at determining the best approach to keeping abreast with the structural needs of their criminal population. Timing can be a hidden, yet important variable, as the public is not always amenable to new, normally expensive construction proposals. Also, legislative enactments (such as those concerning mandatory sentencing or early-release proposals) also weigh into the prison construction decision. Alternatives to imprisonment must also be considered.

Can Administrators "Reinvent" Criminal Justice?

Casting Off Old Ways

Reinventing Government, the book that recently swept the country and was on the bookshelves of many governors, city managers, and criminal justice administrators, provided ideas about how government can and should work as efficiently and productively as the best-run private businesses. It uses myriad examples of government agencies that have slashed red tape, begun focusing on the "customer," cut costs tremendously, revamped the budget-expenditure process to provide incentives for saving money, abandoned archaic civil-service systems, decentralized authority, and empowered their employees. It showed how these agencies can become more entrepreneurial and "steer" rather than "row," be driven by missions rather than by rules, encourage competition over monopoly, and invest in prevention rather than cure. Generally—and the reason for the book's widespread popularity—it demonstrated what can be accomplished when government leaders decided to "break the mold" and try new methods.

The authors of *Reinventing Government*, David Osborne and Ted Gaebler, went beyond the five principles of total quality management, espoused by W. Edwards Deming in 1950, which focused on results, customers, decentralization, prevention, and a market (or systems) approach. Osborne and Gaebler found that most entrepreneurial governments focused on promoting *competition* between service providers; they *empower* citizens by pushing control out of the bureaucracy and into the community; and they measure the performance of their agencies, focusing not on inputs but on *outcomes*. They are driven by their goals—their *missions*—rather than by rules and regulations. They redefine their clients as *customers* and offer them choices—between levels of involvement, training programs, and so on. They *prevent* problems before they emerge, rather than simply offering services afterward. They *decentralize* authority, embracing participatory management. They prefer *market* mechanisms to bureaucratic mechanisms. And they focus not simply on providing public services, but on *catalyzing* all sectors—public, private, and voluntary—into action to solve their community's problems.

Some Success Stories

Can some or all of these principles be applied in criminal justice agencies? Indeed, several principles are at the very heart of community-oriented policing problem solving. Perhaps a closer look at some justice-related examples will demonstrate how many of the Osborne and Gaebler principles can be implemented when administrators become determined to "reinvent" their organizations.

- The Visalia, California, Police Department pioneered a lease-purchase program for squad cars which allowed the city to cut its energy consumption by 30 percent. In a few years, the department had saved $20 million in cash, almost its entire operating budget.
- In Tulsa, Oklahoma, police studied arrest trends, school dropout statistics, drug treatment data, and the problems of the city's public housing developments. They concluded that teenagers from one section of town were creating most of the city's drug problems, so they began working with the community to attack the problem. They organized residents and together prosecuted and evicted residents who were dealing, they created an antidrug education program in the projects and established job placement and mentoring programs, they set up a youth camp for teenagers, and they worked with the schools to develop an antitruancy program.

- Sunnyvale, California, developed performance measures for all municipal depart-ments, defining the results it wanted. In each program area, the city articulated a set of "goals," a set of "community condition indicators," a set of "objectives," and a set of "performance indicators." Objectives set the specific targets for each unit of city government. For example, in public safety, one objective was to keep the city "within the lowest 25 percent of Part I crimes for cities of comparable size, at a cost of $74.37 per capita."
- Many police agencies now survey their communities—victims, witnesses, even offenders—regarding agency performance and ways to generate revenue. The Madison, Wisconsin, Police Department mailed surveys to every thirty-fifth person it encountered. It asked citizens to rate the police on seven factors: concern, help-fulness, fairness, knowledge, quality of service, professional conduct, how well they solved the problem, and whether they put the person at ease.
- The St. Louis County Police Department developed a system that allows officers to call in their reports; the department licensed the software to a private company and earns $25,000 each time the package is sold to another department.
- Paulding County, Georgia, built a 244-bed jail when it needed only 60 extra beds, so that it could charge other jurisdictions $35 a night to handle their overflow. In the first year of business, the jail brought in $1.4 million, $200,000 more than its operating costs.
- Some enterprising police departments in California are earning money renting out motel rooms as weekend jails. They reserve blocks of rooms at cheap motels, pay someone to sit outside to ensure that inmates stay in their rooms, and rent the rooms to convicted drunk drivers at $75 a night.

A Shift in Governance

These examples clearly demonstrate what can happen when administrators begin thinking like entrepreneurs rather than strict bureaucrats. Unfortunately, the great majority of our federal, state, and local government agencies do not so operate. They reward failure and enhance bureaucracies rather than creating, incentives to save money or serve customers. When the crime rates increase, justice agencies are given more money; if they continue to fail, they are given even more. As police departments professionalized, they began focus-ing on chasing crooks, not on solving community problems. This approach encourages agencies to ignore the root causes of crime, simply continue chasing criminals, and not consider possible solutions to problems.

What Osborne and Gaebler call for is nothing less than a shift in the basic model of governance used in America—a shift that is already under way, doubtless largely because of the recent recession and demands on government agencies to "do more with less." It is now essential that justice administrators engage in strategic planning, looking beyond tomorrow, and anticipating the future. Some police administrators began coping with recent revenue shortfalls in some new and unique—if not always popular—ways: charg-ing fees for traditionally free public services, such as accident investigations, unlocking vehicles, and response to false alarms.

It will become increasingly important for justice administrators to think of such revenue-enhancing possibilities and ways to save money. They must also listen more to one of their greatest resources—the rank and file—although a revamped or "inverted" pyramidal organization structure may be necessary for accomplishing this goal. Greater collaboration with the public is also needed: the police must insist that private citizens, institutions, and organizations within their communities shoulder greater responsibility for assisting in crime control. Some examples of excellent collaborative efforts are D.A.R.E., M.A.D.D., Neighborhood Watch, and Court Watch.

In sum, justice administrators and society must rethink its approach to crime. They must play a catalytic role, not just reduce services or, as in the past, throw more money and personnel at ongoing problems. They must steer rather than row, with a clear map in hand. In short, they need a new vision of government.

COMPUTER APPLICATIONS IN CRIMINAL JUSTICE

An Information Technology Revolution

Advances in computer technology have revolutionized many concepts of organizational management, altered the value of information, and affected the flow of information within organizations. Computer technology has changed our society, the processes of government, and the disposition of justice itself. We are witnessing an "information technology revolution."

When a police officer investigates a crime, a probation officer prepares a presentence report, a court schedules a case for trial, a victim calls the district attorney's office to learn the status of his case, or a parole board tracks an inmate's parole eligibility date, information is collected, analyzed, and stored for future use. Criminal justice agencies use many different types of files, including those of criminal information, case investigation, budgets, and personnel.

Computers also allow justice administrators to engage *planning* at a level never before possible. As shown earlier in this chapter, strategic planning and forecasting are essential for developing and implementing policy within the limitations of present knowledge and decision making within political and economic realities. Data bases that contain information specifically used by management in decision making (planning, budgeting, fiscal, personnel management, or inventory control information) are called *management information systems* (MISs). Data bases that are used in agency operations (investigations, crime trend analysis, social history information, and arrest information) are called *operations data bases* (ODB).

Mainframe computer systems are designed to store, retrieve, manipulate, and analyze massive amounts of information. There are three mainframe data bases in criminal justice: (1) the National Criminal Justice Information Center (NCIC), which contains detailed arrest and intelligence information on known and wanted offenders; (2) the *Uniform Crime Reports* (UCR), published annually by the FBI, which compiles, summarizes, and reports national crime data on a quarterly and annual basis; and (3) the

Sourcebook of Criminal Justice Statistics, published by the federal Bureau of Justice Statistics, U.S. Department of Justice, which publishes a comprehensive summary of justice activities across the country. Mainframe data-based management systems are also used extensively in criminal justice at all levels of government in functions ranging from psychological profiles of terrorists and kidnappers to automobile registration and construct descriptions and sketches of criminal subjects. Computers are also used as investigative tools in crime laboratories across the country.

Harnessing Computers in Justice Agencies

Courts use computers not only to schedule cases but also to monitor jail populations and ensure that prisoners scheduled for court appearances are brought to court on time. In San Diego, police use computers as memory banks for storing nicknames, scars and marks, and field investigations. In Dallas, the court uses a mainframe computer to issue subpoenas and summonses. Patrol cars in many jurisdictions come equipped with computers, linking officers with NCIC and other crime bases and allowing them to do reports in the field. Corrections agencies are able to use computers to manage inmate records, conduct presentence investigation, supervise offenders in the community, provide instruction to inmates, and train correctional personnel. Jail administrators, with computer assistance, receive daily reports on court schedules, inmate rosters, time served, statistical reports, maintenance costs, and other data.

The fiscal savings and overall accomplishments provided by microcomputers and mainframes is considerable. The St. Louis, Missouri, Police Department experienced a 53 percent reduction in time spent by investigators in writing and typing reports. San Diego's computerized investigations systems resulted in over 3000 arrests. In St. Petersburg, all emergency dispatching is computerized. In Chicago, computers coordinate field command communications. In Baton Rouge, drug investigators search out abusers and unethical doctors from among mountains of pharmaceutical prescriptions. Many police agencies use computer-aided instruction to train police officers. In Dallas, courts use computers to transmit subpoenas via electronic mail.

Clearly, criminal justice students as well as in-service practitioners need to become knowledgeable in basic computer operation. As strongly indicated earlier in this chapter, the future holds far greater growth and development in our information-processing society. Several questions and issues attend this development, however. Will justice agencies become overly dependent on computers? Will personnel forget how to write reports? Does efficiency and productivity mean a fairer justice system? Does computerization actually save time and eliminate unnecessary paperwork?

Administrators must be certain that the advent of high technology does not become a bane to their mission. Nonetheless, it is certain that "the future is now" in this regard.

ENDNOTES

1. Kenneth J. Peak, *Policing America: Methods, Issues, Challenges* (Englewood Cliffs, N.J.: Regents/Prentice Hall, 1993), p. 419.

2. Ibid.

3. Ibid., p. 423.

4. Ibid.

5. Ibid.

6. Ibid., pp. 424–425.

7. Rob McCord and Elaine Wicker, "Tomorrow's America: Law Enforcement's Coming Challenge," *FBI Law Enforcement Bulletin* 59 (January 1990):31.

8. Edward A. Thibault, "Proactive Police Futures," in Gene Stephens (ed.), *The Future of Criminal Justice* (Cincinnati, Ohio: Anderson, 1982), pp. 67–85.

9. Ibid., pp. 73-77.

10. Clyde L. Cronkhite, "21st Century Cop," *The National Centurion* (April 1984):26–29, 47–48.

11. Quoted in James A. Dator and Sharon J. Rodgers, *Alternatives for the State Courts of 2020* (Chicago: American Judicature Society, 1991), p. ix.

12. Clement Bezold, "On Futures Thinking and the Courts," *The Court Manager* 6 (Summer 1991):4–11.

13. J. Woolford Howard, Jr., *Courts of Appeal: A Study of the Second, Fifth, and District Of Columbia Circuits* (Princeton, N.J.: Princeton University Press, 1981).

14. Ronald Stout, "Planning for Unified Court Budgeting," *Judicature* 69 (December/January 1986):206.

15. Thomas A. Henderson, Cornelius M. Kerwin, Randall Guynes, Carl Baar, Neal Miller, Hildy Saizow, and Robert Grieser, *The Significance of Judicial Structure: The Effect of Unification on Trial Court Operations* (Washington, D.C.: U.S. Government Printing Office, 1984), p. 5.

16. Ronald Stout, "Planning for Unified Court Budgeting," p. 206.

17. Malcolm Feeley, *Court Reform on Trial* (New York: Basic Books, 1983).

18. Ibid., pp. 35-37.

19. For a thorough discussion of this subject, see Jerald Hage and Michael Aiken, *Social Change in Complex Organizations* (New York: Random House, 1970).

20. Malcolm Feeley, *Court Reform on Trial*, pp. 38-39.

21. Ibid., p. 32.

22. Thomas F. Rich and Arnold I. Barnett, "Model-Based U.S. Prison Population Projections," *Public Administration Review* 45 (November 1985):780–789.

23. U.S. Department of Justice, Bureau of Justice Statistics Bulletin, *Prisoners in 1985* (Washington, D.C.: Author, 1986), p. 1.

24. Douglas C. McDonald, "The Cost of Corrections: In Search of the Bottom Line," in Joan Petersilia (ed.), *Research in Corrections* (U.S. Department of Justice, National Institute of Corrections) 2 (February 1989):1–25.

25. Ibid., p. 23.

26. Ibid., pp. 23–24.

27. R. Sanfilippo, *Management Development: Key to Increased Correctional Effectiveness* (Washington, D.C.: Joint Commission on Correctional Manpower and Training, n.d.):5.

28. Alvin W. Cohn, "The Failure of Correctional Management Reviewed: Present and Future Dimensions," *Federal Probation* 56 (June 1991):12–16.

29. Samuel H. Pillsbury, "Understanding Penal Reform: The Dynamic of Change," *The Journal of Criminal Law and Criminology* 80 (1989):726–780.

30. Ibid., pp. 726-727.

31. George Bernard Shaw, *The Crime of Imprisonment* 13 (1922).

32. Tom Murton and Joe Hyans, *Accomplices to the Crime: The Arkansas Prison Scandal* (New York: Grove Press, 1967); Thomas O. Murton, *The Dilemma of Prison Reform* (New York: Holt, Rinehart and Winston, 1976), p. xii.

33. Ibid., p. 89.

34. Harry E. Allen and Clifford E. Simonsen, *Corrections in America: An Introduction* (5th ed.) (New York: Macmillan, 1989), p. 66.

35. Ibid., p. 71.

36. Quoted in Jim Bencivenga, "State Prisons: Crucibles for Justice," *The Christian Science Monitor* (July 28, 1988):14–15.

37. Quoted in Ibid.

38. National Institute of Corrections, *Research in Corrections* 2 (February 1989), Editor's Note.

39. Ibid., p. 1.

40. *New York Times* (October 14, 1986).

41. *Gainesville Sun* (June 16, 1987):3B, (April 21, 1988):3B.

42. Douglas C. McDonald, "The Cost of Corrections: In Search of the Bottom Line," p. 19.

43. U.S. Department of Justice, National Institute of Justice Research in Brief, *Making Confinement Decisions* (Washington, D.C.: Author, 1987), pp. 2–3.

44. Ibid., p. 4.

45. David Osborne and Ted Gaebler, *Reinventing Government: How the Entrepreneurial Spirit Is Transforming the Public Sector* (Reading, Mass.: Addison-Wesley, 1992), pp. 19–20.

46. Ibid., p. 4.

47. Ibid., p. 50.

48. Ibid., pp. 143–144.

49. Ibid., p. 173.

50. Ibid., p. 197.

51. Ibid., p. 197.

52. Ibid., p. 197.

53. William G. Archambeault and Betty J. Archambeault, *Computers in Criminal Justice Administration and Management: Introduction to Emerging Issues and Applications* (2nd ed.) (Cincinnati, Ohio: Anderson, 1989), pp. 1, 3.

54. William G. Archambeault and Betty J. Archambeault, *Correctional Supervisory Management: Principles of Organization, Policy, and Law* (Englewood Cliffs, NJ.: Prentice Hall), p. 10.

55. William G. Archambeault and Betty J. Archambeault, *Computers in Criminal Justice Administration and Management: Introduction to Emerging Issues and Applications* (2nd ed.), p. 61.

56. Ibid., p. 63.

57. Ibid., pp. 63–70.

58. Ibid., pp. 192–193.

QUESTIONS FOR THOUGHT AND DISCUSSION

1. What are the three important factors that will change the nature of crime in Western nations? How will each change the nature of crime?

2. What changes in police technology are forecasted to cope with the crime of the future? What possible problems could these changes cause?

3. How will the courts adapt to the changes in crime?

4. What are the major changes forecast for corrections?

THE CHANGING FACE OF AMERICA

Robert C. Trojanowicz
David L. Carter

In the next century America's population will change considerably. According to demographers, in less than 100 years, we can expect white dominance of the United States to end, as the growing number of blacks, Hispanics, and Asians together become the new majority.[1] As we approach the 21st century, we already see white America growing grayer. In the past decade, there has been an estimated 23-percent increase in the number of Americans 65 and older.[2] In fact, more people of retirement age live in the United States now than there were people alive in this country during the Civil War. But while the average age of all Americans is now 32, the average age of blacks is 27; Hispanics 23.[3] By 2010 more than one-third of all American children will be black, Hispanic, or Asian.[4]

These dramatic changes in the overall make-up of American society have profound implications for law enforcement, particularly because many of the legal and illegal immigrants flooding into this country are of different races, ethnic groups, religions, and cultures. Many do not have even a rudimentary knowledge of the English language.

To understand fully what such immigration will mean for policing in the 21st century requires exploring some crucial questions. Who are these new immigrants? How many are there? Why do they come here? What new demands will they place on law enforcement in the future? How can the police prepare today to meet these changing needs?

THE NEW IMMIGRANTS

For many of us, the word "immigrant" evokes two vivid images: (1) The wave after wave of Europeans flooding through Ellis Island, and (2) the metaphor of the "melting pot." These two memories often converge in a romanticized view of the past as a time when those "poor, hungry, huddled masses" from other countries required only a generation or two for their offspring to become full-fledged Americans. However, a closer look shows that many immigrant groups found the path to full assimilation difficult. For many this meant struggling to find ways to blend in without losing their unique cultural identities.

Robert C. Trojanowicz and David L. Carter, "The Changing Face of America," *FBI Law Enforcement Bulletin*, January 1990, pp. 7–12.

Our past experience should also forewarn us that race constitutes the biggest barrier to full participation in the American dream. In particular, the black experience has been unique from the beginning because most African Americans did not come here seeking freedom or greater opportunity, but were brought to this country as slaves. And the lingering problem of racism still plays an undeniable role in preventing blacks from achieving full participation in the economic and social life of this country.

De facto segregation persists in keeping many minorities trapped in decaying crime- and drug-riddled, inner-city neighborhoods. Though blacks constitute only 12 percent of the total U.S. population, as a result of "white flight," many of this country's major cities have minority majorities, while the suburbs that surround them remain virtually white.

The role of race as an obstacle to full assimilation and participation is of obvious concern since almost one-half of all legal immigrants over the past decade have been Asians—Chinese, Filipino, Indian, Korean, Vietnamese, and Kampucheans (Cambodians)—and slightly more than one-third have been from Latin America.[5] Though 9 of 10 Hispanics are counted as "white,"[6] there is no doubt that they face discrimination because of their Hispanic ethnicity. At the same time, only 12 percent of the immigrants since 1980 have been Europeans, whose experience would be likely to mirror more closely those of their counterparts in the past.[7]

Because minorities are expected to continue to exhibit higher birth rates than whites, demographers expect minorities to constitute an even larger percentage of young people in this country in the near future. By 2020 a majority of children in New Mexico, California, Texas, New York, Florida, and Louisiana will be minorities—blacks, Asians, and Hispanics.[8]

White males have traditionally dominated our society, in power and wealth as well as sheer numbers. Over the past few decades, both minorities and women have made significant gains, particularly in the business world. Yet, both groups still earn significantly less than their white male counterparts, and they have yet to attain leadership roles in the public and private sectors equal to their respective numbers in society.

Certain questions naturally arise. In the future, will the power and wealth of white males erode as their numbers decline? Will minorities band together as a new coalition or splinter apart into competing special interests? How will mainstream attitudes change along the way? Are we embarking on a new era of tolerance and cooperation or a new era of hostility, in which various groups will battle each other for status, dollars, and power?

THE NUMBERS

When we look at the number of legal immigrants arriving each year, their overall numbers appear deceptively small compared to the more than 255 million people who already live here. In fiscal year 1988, a total of 643,000 newcomers arrived,[9] but their potential impact becomes clearer if we remember that would mean roughly 6.5 million new residents in just the next decade, even if immigration rates did not rise. And the picture becomes clearer still when we consider that many immigrants often cluster in specific areas, which makes their combined impact on certain communities far greater than if they were dispersed evenly nationwide.

Shortly after the turn of the 21st century, Asians are expected to reach 10 million.[10] Today's 18 million Hispanics may well double by then.[11] Included in such totals, of course, are the illegal immigrants who find their way into America each year. While the actual numbers are unknown, the 1987 law that granted amnesty to those undocumented aliens and agricultural workers who qualified allowed roughly 3 million to stay.[12]

Another indicator is that the Border Patrol now apprehends roughly 900,000 people who try to enter illegally each year, down 800,000 from 1986, the year before the employer sanctions of the new Federal immigration legislation went into effect.[13] Again, we most often think first of undocumented aliens as being Mexican nationals and other Latin Americans who penetrate our southern borders; but these figures also include substantial numbers of people from the Pacific Rim and the Caribbean, as well as the Irish, Canadians, and Western Europeans who often come in as tourists and then decide to stay.

WHY THEY COME

Current U.S. immigration policy gives highest priority to reuniting families. Among the 265,000 legal immigrants in 1988 subject to limitations (quotas based on country of birth), almost 200,000 were admitted on the basis of "relative preference," that is, they were related to a permanent resident or citizen of the United States.[14] Immediate relatives (spouses, parents, and children) of U.S. citizens are exempt from restrictions, and in 1988, they constituted approximately 219,000 of the 379,000 in the exempt category.[15]

The next largest category of legal immigrants admitted is refugees and those seeking asylum, roughly 111,000 in 1988.[16] To qualify under these provisions, applicants must persuade the Immigration and Naturalization Service (INS) that they are fleeing persecution at home, not that they are simply escaping poverty. An article in the *Wall Street Journal* alleged that the INS routinely rejects applicants from Haiti and El Salvador and that it is also difficult for Nicaraguans, Ethiopians, Afghans, and Czechs to qualify.[17]

The fourth largest category of legal immigrants includes those given preference on the basis of their education and occupation, less than 54,000 in 1988—only 4 percent of that year's total.[18] Morton Kondracke in an article in *The New Republic* notes, "...this tiny number provided 52 percent of the mathematicians and computer scientists who came in and 38 percent of the college teachers."[19]

Chances are, however, that the immigration policy will not change dramatically in the near future, though efforts will be made to allow more people with preferred job skills to immigrate. The question is whether they should be admitted in addition to or instead of those scheduled to be reunited with their families. This also has racial implications, because shifting from family to occupational considerations would mean a shift from Asians and Latin Americans toward more Europeans.

THE LAW ENFORCEMENT CHALLENGE

All of these issues have obvious implications for law enforcement, but perhaps the first challenge is to remember that generalities tend to be false. Each immigrant, whether legal or illegal, arrives not only as part of a larger group but also as an individual with unique gifts—and faults.

Particularly where newcomers cluster together in poor neighborhoods with high crime rates, the police, perhaps even more so than the population at large, must guard against stereotyping. Some newcomers may be too timid to interact widely in their new communities; yet, they may contact the police. The police, therefore, have a tremendous responsibility because those first impressions matter, not just in terms of how new arrivals will see the police but how they view the entire society.

Imagine how much Asians and Latin Americans have to learn, especially if they are not proficient in English. Who will assure them that the public police do not use torture or keep files on their activities? Will they understand the difference between the public police and private police? Will they really believe we have no secret police? Many of today's arrivals come from places where the police are feared, not respected, and the last thing they would be likely to do is ask an officer for help or share any information. We have had our whole lives to understand the written and unwritten rules of this society, with all their nuances. It is unreasonable to expect immigrants to absorb these cultural characteristics in even a few years.

Police officers so often see people at their worst, not their best. And because police officers focus so much attention on crime, there is always the danger that they will have a distorted view of who the "bad guys" are and how many there are of them. This temptation to generalize from a few to the many is a particularly critical problem for the police in the case of immigrants.

A small fraction of the immigrants coming in will be career criminals, eager to ply their trades here. The police have had to battle Asian drug gangs and Jamaican posses, as well as the alleged hardened criminals that entered this country as part of the Mariel Boat Lift.

Moreover, there will always be the larger group that turns to crime when faced with economic hardship. Police departments must take steps to ensure that officers remain sensitive to the reality that the majority of the newcomers are law-abiding people, eager to build a new life.

Because police departments are a microcosm of a larger society, it would be naive to assume that everyone who wears the uniform is free of bias. In addition, the statistics verify that there is a link between race and crime, but the mistake lies in seeing this as cause and effect.

Studies show that blacks are arrested for violent crimes at rates four times higher than their overall numbers would justify; Hispanics at rates two and a half times what they should be, even though they are often poorer than blacks.[20] But we have only to look at the rates of violent crimes in the black-run nations of Africa, which are nowhere near as high as they are here, to see that our problems are not caused by their genes but by our culture. Perhaps the increasing minority numbers will help make this society more color blind.

Unfortunately, many of these new immigrants will become victims, particularly of violent crimes that disproportionately afflict minorities. Ignorance of our laws and customs can make them easy targets for all kinds of predators. Fear of the police will also work against them. And if they cannot speak the language, at least not well, it may be difficult for them to share information.

Toward a Solution: Community Policing

As even this cursory analysis shows, immigrants face all the problems, and more, that everyone in this culture faces. The primary challenge for law enforcement will be to find ways to meet their needs with special concern for their racial, ethnic, cultural, and religious diversity—and their specific vulnerabilities.

A community policing approach offers law enforcement officers unique flexibility in tailoring their response to meet local needs in ways that promote sensitivity and respect for minority concerns. This new philosophy and organizational strategy proposes that only be decentralizing and personalizing police service will law enforcement be able to meet the needs of an increasing diverse society.

Community policing rests on the belief that no technology can surpass what creative human beings can achieve together. It says that police departments must deploy their most innovative, self-disciplines, and self-motivated officers directly into the community as outreach specialists and community problem-solvers. Only be freeing these new community policing officers (CPOs) from the isolation of their patrol cars, so they can interact with people face-to-face in the same areas every day, can departments develop the rapport and trust necessary to encourage people to become active in the process of policing themselves.

In addition to serving as full-fledged law enforcement officers, CPOs would work to reduce fear of crime and the physical and social disorder and neighborhood decay that act as magnets for a host of social ills, including crime and drugs. They also can serve as the community's ombudsmen to city hall, to ensure prompt delivery of vital government services, and as the community's link to the public and private agencies that can help.

Particularly in the case of immigrants, community policing allows the department an opportunity for mutual input and enrichment. CPOs can help educate immigrants about our laws and customs and how to cope with our culture. Equally important, this grassroots, two-way information flow allows immigrants the opportunity to teach the department how to take their particular concerns into account, with dignity and respect for their cultural identities.

The Right People for the Job

One of the more difficult problems that police departments will continue to face is how to develop the capacity to speak to new immigrants in their native tongues. It is often easier in theory than in practice to recruit qualified bilingual candidates from immigrant populations, especially since many come from countries where police work may not be a respectable career.

This issue raises more questions than answers. How many officers should be bilingual? How proficient must they be? Should foreign language be a requirement for college degrees in criminal justice? What will it cost police departments to meet this need? Is this an opportunity to use civilian volunteers? Can a department develop the capacity to speak to all in their native tongues?

Such a changing society also will demand that the police remain sensitized to the issue of how to serve people who exhibit racial, ethnic, religious, and cultural diversity. This is a two-fold concern. First, it implies that departments must establish and enforce guidelines to ensure existing officers discharge their duties with care and concern. Second, it means that departments must recruit candidates who are the best capable to handle the increasing challenge posed by the future.

To recruit officers from minority populations is a logical response to this challenge. However, a study by the Center for Applied Urban Research on the Employment of Black and Hispanic Officers shows recent efforts aimed at minority recruiting have produced uneven results. Almost one-half of the big city police departments made significant progress in hiring black officers; yet, 17 percent reported a decline. Forty-two percent of the departments made gains in hiring Hispanics, but almost 11 percent reported a decline.[21] Part of the reason related to whether the departments pursued affirmative action plans, but there are also concerns that some minorities leave because of better career opportunities elsewhere, often because policing is perceived as falling short in providing meaningful career development. Overall, however, a 1989 study by the Police Executive Research Forum (PERF) found that in cities with a population of 50,000 or more, the number of black and Hispanic police officers were generally proportionate to the population.[22]

The PERF study also indicated that college-educated officers exhibit the greatest sensitivity to the diversity that will increasingly become the hallmark of this society. The study also verified that the officers with at least some college education are not only increasing in numbers in the rank and file but also in police management as well.[23] But again, retaining these officers can be difficult. Therefore, research supporting the widespread perception that community policing not only makes officers feel safer but also that it provides job enlargement and job enrichment, indicating that community policing may be a potent new way to keep the best people for the challenges that lie ahead.[24]

POLICE POLICY TOWARD ILLEGAL IMMIGRANTS

The obvious obstacle in building trust between the police department and immigrants who are here illegally stems from their fears that the police will inform INS officials about their status. One chief of police in a border city wrestled with this issue and decided that the police must serve the needs of *all* members of the community. The department's policy is that it will not inform INS about undocumented residents except, of course, in cases where the police arrest someone for a crime.

The chief based his decision on the argument that it is the job of the INS, not the police, to track down and deport illegals. He also believes that this policy has helped his department gain the trust of the entire community, so that people in the community are now far more willing to share the information that the police need to do their best job. This is a decision that more chiefs will face in the future, and they must weigh the best interests of the department and the community within the dictates of their individual consciences.

SERVING THE ENTIRE COMMUNITY

The successful assimilation of new immigrant groups, particularly those of different races, will depend on changing attitudes in mainstream society. This is of particular concern, because current trends portend a society in which the youngest members will increasingly consist of minority youths, while the ranks of the elderly will remain far whiter.

These trends also show that younger workers, many of whom will be minorities in low-paying service jobs, increasingly will be asked to pay for the needs of primarily white retirees, whose health care costs alone may prove staggering.

Adding to these generational tensions is the incendiary issue of crime, with its overlay of age and race considerations. The bulk of the crimes committed in this society are perpetrated by the young, at rates far beyond what other industrialized Western nations endure. Though the elderly exhibit lower-than-average rates of actual victimization, they rank among the groups with the greatest fear of crime. In some neighborhoods, we see the elderly becoming virtual prisoners of fear. Indeed, this self-imposed imprisonment which reduces their exposure to the threat explains in part why they are not victimized more often.

Because crime and youth are so strongly linked, perhaps our aging society foretells a steep decline in our overall rates of crime. Crime rates have already begun to fall as the bulge of the "baby boomers" continue to grow out of their most crime-prone years, but not as much as had been anticipated.

Various factors raise concern that we may not soon see a dramatic drop in crime—the growing gap between rich and poor, drugs, teenage pregnancy, illiteracy, high unemployment among minority youths, the continued proliferation of guns, and alarming rates of child abuse and neglect. Even if we are fortunate enough to see a substantially safer future during our lifetime, we can also expect that people will begin to demand more. For example, the police will be asked to pay more attention to other wants and needs that are now often ignored or given short shrift because of the current crisis posed by serious crime.

CONCLUSION

Community policing offers an important new tool to help heal the wounds caused by crime, fear of crime, and disorder. In one community that might mean a community police officer recruiting elderly volunteers from a senior center to help immigrant youths become more fluent in English. This offers the hope that those retirees will overcome their fears, while at the same time enhancing a young person's opportunity to perform well in school and on the job.

In a different neighborhood, the challenge could be for the CPO to encourage blacks, Hispanics, and Asians to cooperate together in persuading area businesses to help provide recreational activities for juveniles. The possibilities are bounded only by the imagination and enthusiasm of the officers and the people they are sworn to serve, if the police are given the resources, time, and opportunity to work with people where they live and work.

It would be naive to suggest that community policing is a panacea that can heal all the wounds in any community. But it has demonstrated its ability to make people feel safer and improve the overall quality of community life. Today's challenge is to find new ways for law enforcement to contribute to make the United States a place where all people have an equal chance to secure a piece of the American dream for themselves and their children. Therefore, the urgent message is that we must begin preparing now, so that we can do even more toward the worthy goal in the ever-changing future.

ENDNOTES

1. U.S. Census Bureau projections on future trends.
2. Thomas Exter, "Demographic Forecasts—On to Retirement," *American Demographics*, April 1989.
3. Reported on the NBC special, "The R.A.C.E.," hosted by Bryant Gumbel, September 6, 1989.
4. Joe Schwartz and Thomas Exter, "All Our Children," *American Demographics*, May 1989.
5. John Dillin, "Asian-American: Soaring Minority," *The Christian Science Monitor*, October 10, 1985.
6. Supra note 4.
7. Supra note 5.
8. Supra note 4.
9. "Immigration Statistics: Fiscal Years 1988–Advance Report," U.S. Department of Justice, Immigration and Naturalization Service, Series IMM 88, April 1989.
10. Supra note 5.
11. Thomas Exter, "How Many Hispanics?" *American Demographics*, May 1987.
12. Morton Kondracke, "Borderline Cases," *The New Republic*, April 10, 1989.
13. Ibid.
14. Supra note 9.
15. Ibid.
16. Ibid.
17. Supra note 12.
18. Supra note 9.
19. Supra note 12.
20. Charles E. Silberman, *Criminal Violence, Criminal Justice* (New York: Random House, 1978), also *Report to the Nation on Crime and Justice*—Second Edition, U.S. Department of Justice, Bureau of Justice Statistics, March 1988.
21. Samuel Walker, *Employment of Black and Hispanic Police Officers, 1983–1988: A Follow-up Study, Occasional Paper*, Center for Applied Urban Research, University of Nebraska at Omaha, February 1989.
22. David L. Carter, Allen Sapp, and Darrell Stephens, *The State of Police Education: Policy Direction for the 21st Century*, Police Executive Research Forum, Washington, DC, 1989.
23. Ibid.
24. Robert C. Trojanowicz and Dennis W. Banas, *Job Satisfaction: A Comparison of Foot Patrol Versus Motor Patrol Officers*, Community Policing Series No. 2, National Neighborhood Foot Patrol Center (now the Center for Community Policing), Michigan State University, East Lansing, MI, 1985.

QUESTIONS FOR THOUGHT AND DISCUSSION

1. What are the major shifts in the U.S. population forecast for the next century, and how will they affect crime?
2. How can community policing help solve some of the forecasted crime problems?

OPHELIA THE CCW

May 11, 2010

Todd R. Clear

Ophelia Edison awakened gently, brought slowly to awareness by the vibrations of her massage bed. She opened her eyes to look at the ceiling of her bedroom, where the tele-inform displayed the time 5:45 A.M. As she got up from her bed, the vibrations abruptly ceased, turned off by the body sensor, which felt her weight leave the bed's surface.

Walking to the lavatory center adjacent to the bedroom, she said in a firm tone, "Shower." Automatically, at the sound of her voice, the shower came on and the cascading water began to heat to a predetermined temperature. Because she wore no clothing to bed, she could walk right into the washing compartment of the lavatory, and she installed the VOICE-START system as a convenience. She loved their advert slogan: "A minute saved is a dollar earned."

Glancing back at the massage bed, she smiled slightly to herself, thinking it was one of her favorite indulgences. Actually, though, it was not an indulgence at all. Her union, the Middlesex Association of Community Control Workers, had negotiated them as part of last year's contract with COMCON, the firm that has the probation contract in her country. The COMCON contract specified merit bonuses for all employees whose performance scores were above the office average. Ophelia, who qualified easily, chose the massage bed instead of cash—inflation being what it was, it seemed a better investment.

Ophelia was a Community Control Specialist II, what used to be called a "probation officer" in the old days. She earned the "specialist" grade because she worked only with child sex offenders—it was her area of expertise. She was designated as "II" because she had been doing the work for five years, and every year her work performance scored out as "satisfactory"—within two standard deviations of the mean for the office.

She might not have said it publicly, but she was really glad she joined the union back when it first started up. Ever since COMCON got the contract for probation supervision services, there had been tension between the workers and the firm. COMCON was a wholly owned subsidiary of IBM, and it was in the money-making business. One way to make money, of course, was to keep salaries and wages down. In fact, the financial pressure to

From "Ophelia the C.C.W.: May 10, 2010," Todd R. Clear in J. Klofas and Stan Stojkovic, eds., *Crime and Justice in the Year 2010*, 1994, pp. 205–221. Belmont, CA: Wadsworth Publishing Company. Reprinted by permission of the publisher.

find ways to cut costs was worse now than in the old days, when government managed probation.

So no one could blame the CCWs (Community Control Workers) when they formed a union to protect their interests. After all, their work was difficult and dangerous, and they deserved to be well paid. Too bad the relations between the union and COMCON had been so vitriolic—there had been two strikes and a work slowdown in the first six months of the union. If the government hadn't stepped in and forced a settlement (by threatening to cancel the COMCON contract), things never would have calmed down.

She understood COMCON's problem very well, of course. With liability costs soaring (fighting civil suits and paying damage for lost suits had been more than 20 percent of last year's COMCON budget), the firm was even more pressed than ever. But the CCWs had the bosses between a rock and a hard place on this one: Suits were caused by failures to follow legally approved procedures and policy, and the slow-downs and strikes guaranteed more such failures.

"Let the management and union go after each other tooth and nail," she thought. "It doesn't bother me."

These were the sorts of things Ophelia pondered as she first showered, then dressed for work. She liked her job overall, and in the mornings it was good to reflect on that. The thoughts sort of warmed her up for the day ahead of her.

While drying her hair and dressing for the day, she turned on the audio news. "Good Morning America" was on, that old-time standard. The big news was the progress on talks of Ukraine and Mexico joining the United States, following Puerto Rico's lead. But this story interested her very little. She was waiting to hear about road conditions along the Eastern Seaboard, because today was a field day.

She chose her green flak-blouse for the day. It was hard to believe this stylishly cut material, which weighed only 2 pounds, could stop a bullet fired at point-blank range. All CCWs were required to wear flak-tops, ever since the massacre three years ago during a routine arrest and she certainly felt safer with one on. Typically, COMCON had resisted the policy, citing "absurd costs" of providing flak-clothes for everyone. In the end, the union won out by threatening to stop all arrests.

Strapped inside her field boots were a stun gun and an electric revolver. She checked to see that each was working. After finishing dressing, she pulled a breakfast tube from her pantry and microtoasted it. With coffee and orange juice it was a perfect 320 calories, just right to start the day but not too much for her exercise-health program guidelines.

When she walked out the door, the tele-inform said 6:05.

Ophelia needed to start early on field days. Policy standards required home contacts at certain intervals for offenders whose profiles fit the complicated criteria. It was good to start out early so she could catch as many as possible before they reported to work (or to their "service post" if they didn't have a job). On the normal working day—there were only five randomly scheduled field days a months—she would awaken at 8:30 A.M. and be at the office by 9:30. But the days when she was to be "in the field" were determined by the office computer in a random basis. Randomness prevented the offenders from being able to pick up a "routine" field time and arrange to be "out" when she came by. It also kept the bosses in charge of things, at least so she thought.

The way everything worked now, her entire daily schedule was handled by computer. This was a good thing, she felt, since she couldn't make heads or tails out of the supervision policies.

The whole thing ran on "profiles." Profiles were really a complicated, interlocking pattern of criteria that were applied to offenders to determine how they should be supervised. Some offenders were seen as often as daily in the field; these cases were handled by Community Control Specialist IIIs, who carried only the "intensive" cases. Since Ophelia's cases were sex offenders, she averaged seeing them fairly frequently, sometimes even twice weekly, depending on their profile.

According to what she had been told in her orientation training, the profiles were all determined by scientific research approaches called "actuarial tables" that predicted how offenders having certain backgrounds would behave and specified the best way to deal with them in order to prevent problems. She found the whole thing a bit confusing and a bit far-fetched, but the computer system made it all easy anyway, so she didn't mind. And they said it was based on literally thousands of case histories.

Stepping out into the sidewalk in front of her apartment building, Ophelia took a deep breath and looked around for the car she would be using. It was a company car and was in use nearly twenty-four hours a day. The carpool service would have delivered it to her street sometime in the night, after a night shift of CCWs had finished with it. It was never hard to find, since it was easily identifiable: military green, nondescript, and one of the few American-made cars on her street. She just looked around for a car nobody wanted to own. There it was, right across the street.

Getting into the car, she did a voice-start, saying simply, "Start." The engine softly hummed on, and the computer sitting under the dashboard engaged.

"Good morning," said the gender-neutral voice inside the machine. "Please identify yourself."

"Kiss my butt," said Ophelia with a sneer, as she punched in her ID. She knew this machine was deaf, and it amused her to be insolent to it.

"Good morning, Ophelia," the machine voice said. Ophelia winced and hit the function key that turned off the sound. The computer voice really annoyed her, and she preferred to read the instructions on the monitor rather than hear them.

On the monitor, the message appeared:

FIRST STOP: WALTER WILSON,
2721 LAKELAND BLVD., APT. 10G.

Ophelia remembered Wilson very well: He was on probation after being convicted of child sex abuse—fondling a neighbor's son. It was his first offense, but the profile indicated a "likelihood" of prior, unreported offenses. After meeting him, she thought the profile was dead-on.

These days he lived in an "iffy" neighborhood, and it made her uncomfortable to visit him there. He was a co-share case, and so she had only been out to see him a half-dozen times or so in the two years he had been on probation. A co-share case was one seen by more than a single CCW. Apparently, research had demonstrated that with certain cases, a joint-supervision approach was more effective, because one CCW might pick up on cues that another missed. She co-shared with Andy Rajandra, and about once a month or so the computer would set up a co-share conference between them to discuss this and other jointly supervised cases.

Ophelia liked sharing cases and she had a lot of respect for Andy's expertise. In the old days, a person had a caseload and was pretty much completely in charge of it. But this meant that offenders could learn officers' weaknesses and figure out ways to manipulate them—often with tragic consequences. Under joint supervision, she was paired with the other CCWs who specialized in sex offenders, and they reinforced each other's strengths while canceling out the weaknesses. She had grown so used to co-sharing her work that she didn't even think of herself as having a "caseload" anymore. She just had work assignments.

Today she was lucky. The first visit scheduled by the accountability system was along an "electric commuter" path from her apartment. She could let the transportation macrosystem drive the car for most of the way, and that would give her time to read the paper while in transit.

She used the computer to contact Transit and punched in her location and destination. Transit "accepted" her request (it almost always did, since government workers on duty had priority) and eased her into the morning traffic. She reached into the glovebox and pulled out the newspaper that was automatically printed there every morning. The front-page story made her chuckle: Congress had started the investigation of the report that thirty years ago three actors had impersonated Ronald Reagan during his presidency, because he had actually been secreted away in a coma off in some CIA basement room.

Twenty minutes later, she was across town and within a few blocks of Wilson's apartment. She reached down to the computer and hit the function key for "instructions." The monitor printed back:

WALTER WILSON, AGE: 53, ETHNICITY: WHITE.
PROFILE: SEX OFFENDER, TAPE A-2
DURING MOST RECENT CONTACT BY CCW
   RAJANDRA (MAY 3) SUSPICION OF ALCOHOL USE, BUT SKIN SCRATCH WAS
   NEGATIVE. PLEASE OBSERVE THE FOLLOWING PROTOCOL:

1. Take skin scratch.
2. Discuss job situation—supervisor relations.
3. Check angela (daughter, age 9) for marks.
4. Talk to Myra (co-inhabitant, age 47).

   CCW VIOLENCE RISK PROFILE, NEAR ZERO.

Ophelia made a mental note of the instructions, then took manual control of the car to drive up to Wilson's apartment. Moments later, she was facing him in his doorway.

"Good morning, Mr. Wilson," she began, "I hope I didn't awaken you."

"That's all right," he responded groggily. "Come on in."

Inside, they sat across from each other in the living room. Ophelia glanced about her, quickly taking in her whole surroundings. This was her habit, to see if anything struck her as amiss. It was a sixth sense she had developed about things and honed over her years on the job. This time her invisible antenna picked up nothing out of the ordinary.

Looking back at Wilson, she began. "I'd like to start with a skin scratch."

It was an abrupt way to start, she knew, and it made them both momentarily uncomfortable. But the computer system had been plain that this was the thing she would have to do, and if she deviated from specific instructions she would have to have a good reason, one her supervisor would accept. Her own preference would be to chat awhile before doing the test, but experience had taught her that a mere personal "preference" would not be enough to override "instructions," and then she would be liable for whatever happened.

And liability was a very big deal at COMCON. Workers who deviated from "instructions" too often or who did so without good, tangible reasons did not last long.

Wilson rolled up his sleeve. "Sure thing," he said. She pulled a styletometer from her bag and took a scratch. Three seconds later, the light on the styletometer showed green. A red or yellow reading would have required Wilson to give a full urine sample—a part of the job Ophelia disliked—and if that was positive, he would be arrested on the spot, since his violence profile was so low. The green reading meant he was clear.

"Good," said Ophelia, replacing the styletometer. "Let's talk about how you are doing."

They spent about 15 minutes talking about his comings and goings. Her aim was to help him relax and to gain a little rapport before getting on with the "instructions." This was one of Ophelia's skills—getting clients to relax in her presence—and she enjoyed being in control of her interaction style. All the while, she was watching him, looking for any cues that something might be wrong, that he might be trying to hide something.

Then she asked about his job, testing out how well he was doing with his supervisor. His answer was hesitant, and she realized this was an area to probe further.

With a bit of relief, he told her that his boss at the supermarket where he worked was giving him a hard time about his conviction. He wanted to quit. They talked about it for awhile, and she convinced him to stick it out for awhile longer. Mentally, she made a note to report the problem, knowing that a community relations specialist would follow up with the supervisor to try to head off any trouble. Wilson's job was a good one, and if he quit he would have trouble finding something in its place. Better to get the supervisor to stop the harassment.

After they had talked about the job for awhile, and Wilson seemed a bit more settled about it, Ophelia changed the subject.

"How's Angela? Could I talk to her?"

Wilson said he would have to wake her up, and when Ophelia said "Thanks," he realized that she intended to talk to his daughter anyway. So he went to get her.

A few minutes later, Angela walked out yawning and wearing her nightgown. She was a cutie—a redhead with big freckles.

Ophelia broke into a big smile and reached out, taking Angela's little hands into her own.

"Angela, how are you?" she asked sweetly. She and Angela had talked several times before, and she sensed that Angela liked her. By holding her hand, Ophelia would be able to talk to Angela for awhile and, without being obvious, check her arms for marks.

They talked about Angela's schoolwork and the play she was going to be in this term. Satisfied that there was no evidence of physical abuse, Ophelia gave Angela a hug and sent her back to bed.

It was routine to check for any evidence of violence for all child sex offenders who lived with children. Ophelia was very good at it—children seldom realized what she was doing. This was just another of the many ways that Ophelia had talents that justified being a specialist.

Being a specialist was very important, of course. Regular CCWs had a hard job. They got routine cases with mediocre profiles of risk and problems—and they got lots of them. It was not unusual for them to have as many as 300 cases to keep track of, and the compuwork, videophoning, and coordinations were a huge headache. And all they ever seemed to do was monitor payments of fines and performance of community service. No wonder turnover was so high for these jobs.

The specialists got better pay and better benefits and had much more interesting work organized into more reasonable workloads. There were three child-sex offender specialists in Middlesex County, and they co-shared a total of about seventy cases. Ophelia loved her work—and she was known to be good at it.

After Angela left the room, Ophelia complimented Wilson on how lovely a child she was. The she asked to talk with Myra. Alone.

Her conversations with Myra were always a little strained, for Myra had never gotten over her partner's arrest and conviction. But her willingness to stand behind him—that and the lack of evidence that sexual misconduct had occurred with Angela—persuaded the judge to put Wilson on Special Probation rather than sentence him to three years in prison. He would be on probation for a full decade, according to his profile. Myra would have plenty of time to get used to supervision, which would grow gradually less frequent as Wilson continued to show no new misconduct and continued to respond well to therapy.

The most discomfort between Ophelia and Myra came when she asked about Wilson's sexuality with her. Even though Ophelia was very good at handling this sensitive area, Myra was embarrassed to discuss it. But according to his profile, his heterosexual adjustment was a key indicator of his overall adjustment.

An hour after arriving, Ophelia left Wilson's apartment. She was satisfied that all was well there, and she felt good about it. Wilson, she thought, had a great chance to make it.

Back in the company car, she entered the data about her visit. It took just a minute or two because the accountability system was designed to record what were called "key indicators" very efficiently. While Ophelia was free to add anything she wished, her experience was that the system usually asked everything that was important. Profiles again!

Once done with the Wilson report, she again asked for "instructions." The computer routed her to her next case, one Florence Trueblood.

But halfway to the Trueblood house, the computer voice abruptly chimes out the words, "Override. Override. Override." Ophelia took manual control of the car and pulled over. The computer screen gave her information that one of her cases—a Vernon Granger—was being questioned by police about his daughter's accusation that he had beaten her up. The instruction was to go immediately to Granger's house to investigate and—according to office policies—consider making an arrest. She put on her siren and sped away to Granger's.

The override was itself office policy. Specialists took pride in making their own arrests: the saying was, "The specialists clean up after themselves." By making their own arrests, specialists reinforced the importance of their work and kept their credibility high with courts and the police. It was a matter of pride.

When Ophelia arrived at Granger's, the police were about to handcuff him. She recognized one of the officers and went to him to learn what had happened. She learned that the daughter had been reported missing by Mrs. Granger, and that an hour or so ago the girl had been found hiding in some bushes near the edge of the city's main park. She told the police she had run away because she was afraid of her dad. There were ugly bruises on her head and arms. Granger denied everything, but they decided to make an arrest anyway.

Ophelia asked permission to take over on the arrest, and the police agreed to let her. They had learned that the specialists handled these situations very well, and they could save a lot of police time by letting CCWs do the dirty work. She went over to Granger, read him his rights, handcuffed him, and put him in the back of her car.

The whole arrest process—taking him to the precinct, booking him, and filing the appropriate information with headquarters—took nearly two hours. By the time she was done, she was tired, hungry—and a bit angry. After talking to Granger's daughter, Ophelia had decided to ask for a semen exam. The results weren't in, but she was pretty sure they would be positive. If so, Granger was looking at a long sentence: He was already on parole for assaulting a daughter from a prior marriage. The shame of it was that the whole family—Granger, his wife, and the three daughters—had been watched closely and in continual therapy ever since the wedding—as a condition of parole. How did people get themselves into these problems?

Back in her car, she asked again for "instructions." The computer said mutely, "Well done, Ms. Edison." Ophelia answered back absently. "Kiss my butt" and requested her lunch break. It was approved.

Lunch improved her mood a little, and the next three hours went fairly smoothly. She made four routine home visits—unusually, all without a hitch. By 3 P.M., it was time for "group."

One of the job satisfactions for specialists was participation in treatment. It was an area where she was able to use her skills and knowledge regarding sex offenders to best effect. It was also one of the few areas left where the accountability system allowed her free rein. By office policy, she was left completely on her own during the hour and a half of group. She wasn't even interrupted for an arrest.

Her co-therapist was Dana Richardson, a clinical social worker who was experienced with sex offenders. They conducted a weekly group therapy program for eight probationers or parolees convicted of child sex offenses. During group, they discussed a wide range of feelings and reactions the offenders had, and they confronted the offenders about the rationalization they used to excuse their behavior.

The groups were one of the main reasons Ophelia liked the job. Much of her work involved monitoring offenders, and sometimes this work could get oppressive and heavy-handed. The group was a way to humanize her work, dealing with the lives of her clients and helping them work through their adjustment problems. It was also a great way for her to grow professionally. In addition to her contact with Dana, a man with whom she shared mutual respect, she had monthly meetings with a psychologist who consulted with Dana and her about the group's progress.

Today's particular group session was exhilarating. One of the members had made a new friendship with a divorcee who had a young son. The group spent a lot of time focusing on the issues surrounding disclosure of his past to the woman. By the time group was over at 4:30, Ophelia had overcome her anger about the Granger episode and accepted it as a part of the job.

Learning to live with failure—not internalizing it when it happened—was probably the most difficult aspect of the job for Ophelia. When her sex offenders failed, it was almost always a tragedy that damaged a child's life. That made it hard to get over the feeling that "she could have done something to prevent it," a common feeling among her peers.

That was why she felt compassion without sympathy when she arrested someone for violating the rules. On the regular probation caseloads, people were almost never revoked from probation for mere rules violations. There had to be a new arrest to force the system to take action. But for the specialists, the stakes were too high. The first indication that a person was sliding into misconduct was always met with swift and stern action. There could be no other way.

Sometimes, though, after she arrested one of her client for a new offense, she was tempted to leave the job. After all, there were plenty of correctional businesses out there she could work for: electronic monitoring, drug-control systems, work camps, and so on. In the last twenty years there had been a proliferation of nonprison programs for criminals, and they were all grouped together and called "intermediate sanctions." More than 40 percent of offenders were sent to one or another of these private programs. Only a handful were put on probation or parole and thereby assigned to community control.

By the end of her group session, she was pretty drained, which was typical. She and Dana talked for awhile about the clients in the group, after which she spent twenty minutes recording information about the session into the accountability system. It was important to record everything, because at the end of the year she would be evaluated. Her performance—arrests, groups, client progress, policy adherence, and so forth, all added together in a master formula—would be computed. Based on her score, and based on how the score compared to everyone else, she would receive a raise and a bonus. Ophelia was proud that she scored in the top 20 percent of staff every year on the job.

Her day had lasted nearly twelve hours, and she felt it was high time she left the office. On her way out the door, she inserted her index finger into the bioreader machine that stood at the end of the office hallway. The bioreader was a combined drug-testing device and physical checkup machine. It took her blood pressure, tested for illegal substances, and checked for developing infections. The machine, which helped prevent employee stress and work-related maladies, was another accomplishment of the work of the union.

The light burned green— "no problem"—and she unconsciously nodded a "thanks" to the inert device and headed out the door. Machines seemed to get better treatment than people these days.

She would make a stop at the health club; regular visits there reduced her health insurance costs and resulted in another work bonus. Then she would get a bite to eat on her way home. By now, the office car was in use by another CCW, so she would have to walk home from the health club. It was only a few blocks, and she didn't mind the stroll. The spring air smelled unusually clean, and she felt good about herself. She broke into a whistle.

EXPLANATION

Only people stupid enough to bet on the Baltimore Colts to defeat the New York Jets in the 1968 Super Bowl would try to predict the nature of community corrections in 2010. I did the former, and so I did the latter.

But the reader should be advised that it not only is hazardous to one's intellectual health to believe that one can foresee the future, but also a proven idiocy. In 1967, when the presidential commission ushered in an era called "reintegration," everyone foresaw the coming of a decade of community corrections. The prison was seen as an outdated and proven failure. Treatment methods in the community were seen as the only truly effective methods for dealing with crime as well as the certain wave of the future. Experts geared up for a generation of prison reform and community programming.

What then happened? During the 1970s and 1980s, America's prison population experienced a growth unprecedented in American history. The number of citizens locked up in prisons quadrupled, from fewer than 200,000 in 1967 to more than three-quarters of a million in 1990. The imprisonment rate per 100,000 citizens tripled from 97 in 1967 to 293 in 1990. Every failure should be successful.

The point is that, however confident one might feel that the future is clearly laid out before one's eyes, the future that eventually occurs is bound to disappoint. Bearing this in mind, I offer the above speculative leap to the year 2010. It was based on a few ideas about some things that I think are likely to happen over the next twenty years.

Before getting into the predictions, I need to clarify a couple of terms used throughout. Sometimes, I will use the term *traditional* probation or parole supervision. By this, I mean the regular agencies' practices, which have remained fairly stable over the last century. In the case of probation, this means offenders who are assigned to the oversight of an officer in lieu of a prison sentence. For parole, "traditional" programs are those where an offender is released by a parole board and is placed under the supervision of a parole officer. My use of the term "traditional" means that there are "nontraditional" versions of these programs: Intensive probation, electronically monitored supervision, and special early release programs are illustrations.

This distinction is important because, as my predictions make clear, community supervision is increasingly splitting into two, sometimes quite different versions. The traditional versions remain funded and respected about as much as they always have: not very well. The "new" versions are high-profile, ambitious attempts to be responsive to the main complaints people have lodged about traditional methods.

There is also one dominant force that will shape every aspect of the next two decades in corrections. The capacity of the prison system is finite. The rest of the criminal justice system can produce as many offenders as it can—and the capacity of law enforcement and the courts to produce them has accelerated—but prisons can absorb only so many offenders. The rest have to go to other correctional assignments.

Because of this, there will always be a powerful need for nonprison correctional alternatives. It is not merely a matter of justice—although for many, perhaps most, offenders a prison sentence is not just a punishment—it's a matter of economics.

With these points in mind, let us proceed to the predictions.

TEN PREDICTIONS

1. Specialized nontraditional supervision services will predominate in field services. In the 1980s, research and programming have both documented the complexity of criminality, from the general idea of criminal careers to the specific examples of drug-using offenders, sex offenders, and violent criminals. There is no way that a single person, carrying a heterogeneous caseload comprised of all types of felons, can be a fully capable "expert" in how to deal with all of them. Specializing caseloads into subgroups of more homogeneous types of problems is an idea that simply makes sense.

2. Intermediate sanctions options will grow in number and size. Intermediate sanctions are types of punishment that fall in severity between traditional probation and traditional parole. Since the mid-1980s, there has been a proliferation of correctional programs that are not as lenient as probation but not as severe as prison. Besides being politically popular, these programs are a public-relations godsend to community corrections. They advertise themselves as "tough," they cost far less than prison, and many have been shown to have very low recidivism. With a good "rep," a real demand, and a history of delivery on its promises, it is hard to see how intermediate sanctions are not the correctional growth industry of the future.

3. Traditional probation and parole supervision will handle a decreasing share of the offender population. It follows from the first two predictions that the future of the traditional supervision methods is not a bright one. This does not mean that community-based sanctions will be unimportant by 2010. Frankly, there is no way that corrections can survive without a strong, healthy nonprison component. Yet there is also no way that full funding of nonprison alternatives is feasible.

The likely scenario is that traditional types of community supervision—which have not enjoyed strong support in criminal justice since the 1960s—will languish. Instead, growing emphasis will be given to correctional approaches that are not as expensive as prison, but which do not align themselves with traditional techniques.

4. Private-sector involvement in community corrections will have grown to become a powerful factor in policy and program development. We already have seen a growth of privatization in community corrections. The profits have apparently been enough that new businesses are starting in many areas of the country. The conditions for new businesses are ideal. Correctional crowding guarantees a large pool of potential "customers." Disquiet about traditional methods guarantees a business environment sympathetic to new ideas and new businesses.

5. A probation officer will lose a civil liability suite for $5 million. The liability of probation and parole officers has grown dramatically in recent years. Some agencies now calculate liability settlements into their annual budgetary projections.

Civil liability occurs when a probation or parole officer fails to supervise a client according to established policies and procedures, enabling the client to commit a new crime. Already, there have been suits that resulted in awards to victims of more than $1 million. The only thing that will stop an eye-popping, multimillion-dollar award against a probation agency is a legislative cap on the size of allowable civil damages.

6. Accountability-oriented systems will dominate new technologies. In the last decade, the story about community corrections has been its growing reliance on systems of accountability. The most obvious example is the National Institute of Correction's Model Case Management System. This approach sets specific standards for supervision contracts and bases the distribution of cases among officers on time-study data about prior performance. There has also been an emphasis placed on managerial supervision of the work of line officers, especially as it relates to conformity with policy and procedure.

Two forces have spawned this wave of accountability measures: (1) the powerful threat of agency liability and (2) the fact that funding is increasingly dependent on showing that programs are effective. These forces will continue to grow in importance over the next twenty years, and so agencies will be even more inclined to remedy them by developing techniques of improved accountability.

7. The amount of "formal" discretion exercised by line workers in community corrections will diminish. Accountability systems, when they work well, have one main result: They reduce the range of decisions officers can make regarding their clients. They do so by reducing the amount of discretion that officers have concerning how to manage their cases.

The loss of discretion is an important change in the nature of the job for the officer. For many officers, what makes the job interesting and challenging is the chance to "work with people." The phrase, as they use it, connotes the ability to be creative in case management, to respond to cases with gut feelings and seat-of-the-pants decisions. It makes the officer feel like something of an artist—or maybe more like a cowboy or a "Lone Ranger"—in control of his or her own caseload as though it were a domain.

8. Treatment programs will make a comeback in the field, especially those based on a "partnership" between corrections and a treatment provider. Evidence is growing that treatment is one of the best ways to control clients' criminal behavior. It is a surprising circumstance, after all the criticism that has been applied to the concept, to find that in the mid-1990s, treatment programs appear to be more important than ever as a part of the correctional arsenal.

The nature of the treatments have changed, of course. They are no longer the general "counseling" approaches designed to generate "insight" into the causes of criminal behavior. They are much more structured interventions—treatment systems—that combine behavior monitoring and control with cognitive counseling. They presume a depth of knowledge about particular patterns of criminal behavior, so they are often done collaboratively with "experts."

9. The importance of information technologies will overwhelm traditional practices in virtually every way. It would be remarkable if the computer age, which has transformed the world of work, did not also change the nature of probation and parole work. The only real question is, "How will the work change?"

The description of the need for accountability systems has already shown how important information will be for parole and probation agencies. Critical to accountability is the ability to demonstrate what has been done about cases, and this requires recording information about actions. Moreover, it is information about offenders that provides treatment profiles, classification scores, and instructions for supervision from case-management systems. It is impossible to think of the future of community supervision without also thinking about information.

10. Labor-management relations in probation and parole will be increasingly vitriolic. If earlier predictions are correct, then the job will change a great deal in the coming years. Officers' discretion will be essentially eradicated, at least formally. All actions will be sifted through the "opinion" of a computerized prepackaged set of policies and procedures. Liability for failures to follow the procedures will be higher than ever.

In the face of these pressures, local professional organizations will be more and more inclined to focus on bread-and-butter labor issues instead of problems of the profession. Salaries, wages, benefits, and working conditions will be the area of contention between government and workers. Probation and parole organizations will become increasingly antagonistic about these issues.

FIVE MORE TENTATIVE PREDICTIONS

1. Caseloads will not be the only way in which probation and parole caseloads are organized. The caseload is an administrative convenience; it allows the "boss" to decide how to hand cases out and how to hold officers accountable. When there are new accountability systems available, the caseload will be valuable only to the degree that it manages cases well.

2. Revocation of community supervision status will become dual track: Regular cases will be revoked only for new arrests, and specialized cases will be revoked for rules violations. Already it is difficult to get a case revoked from traditional community supervision without evidence of a new crime. This has not been the case for the special programs, however: These normally have very high "technical" failure rates. There is no obvious reason why this trend would stop.

3. A completely private community corrections system will be tried somewhere on an experienced basis. Depending on how the privatization experiments turn out, this is a likely scenario. After all, private vendors provide medical services to government on a contractual basis. Why not extend this to community corrections? The promise will be pretty tempting: better service at less cost. Some jurisdiction somewhere is bound to try it. The only thing that would interfere would be a resounding failure of correctional privatization in other spheres. This seems unlikely.

4. Fines and community service will replace traditional probation for nonserious, low-risk offenders. These are cheap, effective, and popular sanctions.

5. Supervision role conflict will be considered unimportant. Evidence is mounting that far too much has been made of the "conflict" between law enforcement and social work in community supervision. Increasingly, it will be recognized that the role is not a duality of two ideas, but an integration of two themes: control and change.

FIVE DEFINITE PREDICTIONS (PROBABLY)

1. Risk prediction will not be more accurate. There are a few ways to improve profiling systems to increase prediction accuracy. But in the long run, prediction will not become more refined until people become more predictable. This is a problem of evolution and is not going to be resolved in two decades.

2. Every state will experience a "Willie Horton" case—a situation in which a serious offender who is released into the community commits a heinous crime. Failure—and its effects on the system—will continue to be uniform experience in community corrections. Nothing will eradicate it—the only solution is to prepare for it.

3. The probation or parole officer's task uncertainty will not diminish. All of the above means that the work of the probation officer will still contain a great deal of subtlety. Seeing how offenders act, making interpretations of their behavior, managing the interaction of supervision—this will be the main content of the job. No amount of performance structuring can eliminate it.

4. The use of "electronic monitoring" will have topped out. Such use is limited to only certain kinds of cases—those whose effective management is augmented by making sure they are home at certain times. The number of cases fitting this profile will be finite and will not feed an ever-expanding industry.

5. One or more of my predictions will not pan out. No comment.

QUESTIONS FOR THOUGHT AND DISCUSSION

1. How may new technology affect the delivery of probation and parole services in the future?
2. Out of all the predictions made by the author, which two do you think will have the greatest impact on crime control in the future?

A FUTURE OF UTOPIA OR DYSTOPIA?

Richard N. Holden
Allen D. Sapp

Science-fiction writers, by the very nature of their craft, are fascinated with the future. Whether by accident or by design no such writer appears able to envision a future in which few changes have taken place. There is no agreement on what shape the future will take. To study the future is to recognize one's own ineptitude. One simply cannot know the future; one must make the best guess possible and hope that guess is at least in the ball park.

Our first task is to define the limitations of the ball park in which we will play this game. We will identify the extreme limits of future societies and examine the likely police organization of such a society.

EXTREME VIEWS OF THE FUTURE

Futures research is limited in three significant ways: (1) the future is neither fixed nor predetermined; (2) the future is not predictable; and (3) individual choices and actions can influence and change the future (Tafoya, 1990). Some forecasts are too pessimistic while others are too optimistic. There seem to be two schools of thought on the future. We might call these the optimistic view of the future and the pessimistic view. Writers in that field have more scientific terms; the utopian school and the dystopian school.

Utopia

Utopia is where only good things happen. Those with strong religious convictions might call this Heaven, Eden, or Valhalla. The utopian view of the future envisions a world where there is no hunger, disease, or war. All people are engaged in useful and meaningful work. The popular television series *Star Trek: The Next Generation* is typical of this view. This is a society which must turn to deep space for adventure; all problems on Earth have been solved.

A paper presented to the Society of Police Futurists International, Symposium on "Police Leadership in the 21st Century," Baltimore, MD, May 2–5, 1993.

Dystopia

Dystopia provides a somewhat less optimistic view of the future. This is a future of chaos. One in which social institutions have collapsed. Crime, corruption, hunger, and suffering are the foundations of this world; endless war and institutionalized depravity its salient features. This view is most prevalent in the tandem of futuristic films *The Terminator* and *Terminator II*. This is also true, in a lesser degree, within the dark, foreboding Gotham City that represents the haunts of *Batman*. In this view of the future, the very survival of the human race is in doubt. Human institutions have long since failed.

EVOLUTIONARY DISSONANCE

Why are there such extreme views of the future? One reason is the unpredictability of the future. Either extreme view is supportable in theory. Moreover, such diverse views offer richer fields for the fertile mind of the fictional writer. A second reason is what we might refer to as evolutionary dissonance. This is the social friction generated by the different speeds at which the parts of the global societies move into the future (Toffler and Toffler, 1990). Time moves at a constant speed, but change does not. Various technical fields, for example, move rapidly; seeming to leap from one major breakthrough to another. Social change, however, is more spasmodic. At times social forces actually attempt to drive some elements of society backwards in time; others push forward more rapidly than the society can respond. One part of the world strives to place colonies on Mars; another seeks to return to the fourteenth century.

    Many of society's stress lines can be identified in a manner similar to that of locating fault lines in earthquake zones. Where elements within a civilization move at different speeds, there is social friction; there is evolutionary dissonance. This dissonance is ever-present and renders difficult any meaningful prediction of future societies. Future civilizations, therefore, may be either utopian, dystopian, or possess elements of both.

SOCIETAL HOMEOSTASIS

In nature there are built-in mechanisms that tend to hold environments stable. This is true of social environments as well. Societal homeostasis, therefore, is the tendency of the system to adapt to its surroundings. It is also, in many cases, a force that works against rapid change.

    There is a tendency to overestimate the amount of change that will occur over the next few centuries. Such overestimations will occur because few futurists take homeostasis into account. As in the laws of physics, where every action produces an equal and opposite reaction; so too does social change produce a reaction against that change.

    For example, at a time when technological developments are transforming the world, we are being confronted with a dramatic growth in fundamentalist religious movements attempting to block all or most of those changes. Increased political and economic gains by minorities in this country produce a growth in organized racist groups who wish to block those gains. As eastern European nations become more democratic, new Nazi movements are born; cultural supremacy and racial cleansing become the order of the day. The forces propelling society forward are held in check by equally compelling forces pulling society back. Any analysis of the future must, therefore, be tempered by the effects of homeostasis. The world is capable of changing very rapidly, but there are forces at work that will mitigate the speed at which those changes occur.

POLICING A UTOPIAN ENVIRONMENT

Assuming the future is bright and cheery, what role will law enforcement play in a perfect society? One might argue that a utopian society has no need of police. That might be true in an absolute utopia. Such a world, however, is not envisioned by anyone, even science-fiction writers. A more reasonable utopian vision is one in which the health, education, and housing needs have been reasonably met. There need be no hunger; access to economic opportunities are equally distributed.

There will still be crime, for even in a world of plenty there are those who will always want more. Moreover, while the economic needs of the society may be met, no society has envisioned how to meet the competing power needs of its members. There will always be some whose drive to be in command will override respect for custom and law.

Given that the police will still be needed, what are the likely features of a police organization within such a society? The most logical form of such an organization will be community-oriented policing in its purist form.

COMMUNITY-INSTITUTIONAL INTEGRATION

A society functioning in total harmony is one wherein all institutions work together for the common good. The police department will be an agency that is open and responsive to the needs of the community. It will be quick to identify community needs and equally quick to identify and address community problems (Trojanowicz and Carter, 1990). Citizens will have maximum access to the chief administrator and to other components of the department. Open and honest communication will be a salient feature of such organizations (Trojanowicz, 1989).

Utopian departments will have little tolerance for police abuse in any form. The officers will be professionalized to the degree that they will not tolerate unprofessional conduct on the part of their co-workers. Officers within the utopian organization will be educated and highly trained. Graduate degrees will be prevalent at all levels of the police organization; no one will be commissioned without the minimum level of a baccalaureate degree. Training will be intensive and on-going (Carter and Sapp, 1990). The organizational structure of the utopian department will be loosely defined with a decentralized command structure (Stamper, 1992). It will be flexible and able to rapidly adapt to changing social conditions. Its primary function will be maintaining social harmony.

The utopian society will also see an evaporation of the concept of multiple levels of government. The overlapping, redundancy of various police organizations will give way to the more systematized and professional single entity force. This force will be controlled at the national level, but will be sufficiently decentralized in its structure to be fine-tuned to the needs of the local communities.

MAINTAINING SOCIAL HARMONY

Some might argue that the term social harmony is just another way of saying order maintenance. There is, however, a difference. Order maintenance is a term that carries both a good and bad image. Too often order maintenance has meant curbside justice or extra-legal repression of dissent. Order maintenance, by definition, attacks symptoms rather than problems (Goldstein, 1990).

Social harmony is the degree to which all elements of the community are in synchronization with all the others. While order maintenance activities attempt to "keep the lid on" the community by suppressing conflict, maintaining social harmony depends on the ability to focus conflict into rational-legal modes of conflict resolution (Trojanowicz and Bucqueroux, 1990). Officers will identify the sources of the conflict and help to eliminate or reconcile the problems. The goal will be to solve the problems rather than to merely suppress the symptoms. Ideally, the police will attempt to identify a permanent solution (Eck and Spelman, 1987). The police will take responsibility for bringing all components of the community together regularly for the purpose of identifying problems and solutions (Maddox, 1993). Furthermore, the police in a utopian setting will orchestrate community interaction.

THE BLESSING OF TECHNOLOGY

The one certainty in predicting the future is the rapid development of technology. Technological innovations offer the greatest potential for increasing police effectiveness (Toffler and Toffler, 1990). Computer analysis of long term crime trends and short term criminal episodes are already improving the police investigative function. The same can be said of computerized fingerprint systems and genetic coding as a means of identification (O'Loughlin, 1992). Computers already possess more capacity than most users can comprehend. The equipment is years ahead of the software developers' imagination, which, in turn, is years ahead of the users' capability. Visual monitoring systems will also enhance police effectiveness. The ability to provide small cameras and transmitters to police units will enable dispatchers to visually monitor police activities. This, in turn, will provide police commanders and courts with a more accurate image of police-citizen interactions.

The police of the utopian future will be the finest equipped force ever conceived. Highly trained and educated, they will utilize technology to its fullest extent. These police agencies will be in tune with both the human and the technical components of their society.

POLICING A DYSTOPIAN ENVIRONMENT

A dystopian world will have a critical need for police organizations. The dystopian vision of the future is bleak indeed. This is a world of hunger, conflict, and social disintegration.

The problem, as it relates to the police, is that the demands for police service will be in direct conflict with the resources provided to the police. A dystopic society does not provide sufficient resources for any social service agency. A society of this nature will require its institutions to "operate on a shoestring." Social problems will far exceed solutions.

EXTREME FRAGMENTATION

The fragmented society is one in which components of the society vie for power and resources at the expense of society as a whole. During the next fifty years there will be four distinct cultures vying for control of our society. This should come as no surprise as these groups are already well represented in our nation. Their growth, both in population and political power, however, assures us that they will each play a significant role in the setting of national and local priorities. These are the Orientals (predominantly Japanese), Hispanics (from Mexico. Central America, and Cuba), Afro-Americans (Blacks), and Caucasians (Whites) (Holden and Sapp, 1991).

The dystopic view of the future is one of extreme fragmentation. This means sporadic episodes of racial cleansing or even a full blown race war, or wars. At a minimum it means that what few resources exist will be the object of intense competition. Each group will vie for economic and political power. Two party government may be replaced with multiple party politics leading to a coalition government structure; one of the least effective forms of government on Earth.

Social Fragmentation

Rather than American society being a melting pot; it will become a collection of armed fortresses. Business and industry will be structured along racial lines. In this view of the future, we will return to a form of paternalistic aristocracy where bloodlines form the basis for local government control. High tech weaponry and security systems may become the mechanisms for controlling large segments of one's population group. We may actually see a return to feudalism, albeit a twenty-first century version, complete with sophisticated weaponry and high tech espionage.

The dystopian view of the future is that society will return to the dark ages. The high tech aristocracy will be countered by an equally high tech theocracy. Fundamentalist religious movements will be locked in mortal combat with New Age religious movements. As family-racial groups vie for power they will align first with one religious movement, then another. Religious manipulation will become one more weapon in the struggle to control resources.

Police Fragmentation

Increased social fragmentation will require further fragmenting of police forces. Each community group will expect, or demand, its own police force; one that mirrors its racial-cultural value system. Internal strife within and between police agencies will increase. Each police force will become more isolated as the mistrust of federal and state government grows to paranoid dimensions.

Internally, racial and familial affiliations will supersede organizational loyalty. Indeed, personal goals will be the predominate determinate of officer behavior. The most important of the internal associations will be that of the officers' labor unions. These also will be fragmented along racial-cultural lines. Different racial groups will actually negotiate different contractual arrangements. Salary, benefits, and work assignments will, in some agencies, be dependent on one's race, sex, or religious-cultural affiliation. In cases of extreme fragmentation, promotion and selection will also be affected by these factors.

The police will mirror their society and will be a dysfunctional organization. Managing such a force will require tremendous patience and an ability to accept low levels of effectiveness as the norm. It will also require that the chief executive officer be of the appropriate race, sex, and cultural group. Political skill will be more important than administrative skill.

DEFENSIVE POLICING

There has been an array of terms denoting ineffective management techniques that focus on handling serious problems while the organization stumbles blindly along into the future. The terms, "brush-fire management," or "crisis management" both refer to the administrative style of reacting to crises within the organization while failing to plan for any future contingencies (Goldstein, 1990). Policing a dystopian society will, in effect, be this type of policing. It will not only be reactive, rather than proactive; it will be defensive.

Defensive policing is a style wherein the police organization responds to only those calls for service when the type of call or the person calling has the potential to affect future police resources or the incident involves an attack on the police organization or personnel.

The police, in other words, will act to perpetuate their own survival, but will be insensitive to the needs or demands of the community as a whole. Those police organizations that are created to provide police service to a particular group will respond to the specific needs of that group. Large, multi-cultural agencies will identify the power bases within the larger community and meet their needs.

Defensive policing will be the operational philosophy of dystopian public policing. As a result, American society will be inundated with private security forces as each community attempts to protect itself. Protection will be required from the attacks by other groups as well as from attacks by traditional criminals.

THE CURSE OF TECHNOLOGY

For every blessing there is a curse. It has been estimated that computers, originally introduced to reduce paperwork in organizations, have actually increased the amount of paper work in some organizations by a factor of ten. Each new technological innovation carries a price tag; it requires purchase, training, and upkeep (O'Loughlin, 1992). Even the good features of technological change carry a price. In a dystopian future, technology will be looked upon by many with dread.

The introduction of visual monitoring, so useful in a utopian society, will become the mechanism of autocratic control in the dystopian world. The ability to transmit visual images, complete with sound, live from the scene to the police department will allow the supervisor instant access to the scene. The supervisor will observe the situation and relay instructions to the officer. The officer will be reduced to a mobile secretary, doing the leg work while a command-level officer makes decisions over a cup of coffee.

There is another possibility with the above scenario. If live action can be transmitted from the scene of an incident, it can be intercepted by nonpolice organizations. Where we now have television shows using actual footage of police officers in action, it will be possible for these shows to provide live performances in the future. Police officers may become well known within their communities. Their evaluations may reflect their television ratings. Police departments may ultimately change the way they label shifts. These may become late night, daytime, and prime time. Prime time officers may reach a certain cult star status. Future contract negotiations may be tied to an officer's television rating.

Police officers in a dystopian society will be slaves to their technology. Automated decision-making will leave police officers without the need for creativity or initiative. The only avenue left for such officers is internal politics. The result will be increased secrecy, organizational sabotage, and open hostility toward the public.

REALITY AND THE FUTURE

Where is American Society really going? We know the human population mix will become exceedingly diverse (Schwartz and Exter, 1989). Religious movements of all kinds will rise, fragment into smaller groups, then rise again. The American family will become even more fragmented with family structure becoming increasingly non-traditional (Toffler and Toffler, 1990). Serial monogamy is likely to become the standard marital pattern. The normal family will be either single parent or multiple parent with a large array of step-parents, step-brothers and sisters, half brothers and sisters and multiple family grandparents, aunts, and uncles.

What do the changes mean for American society in the future? Quite likely they mean ever increasing crime rates (Toffler and Toffler, 1990). There are three factors that have been associated with low crime societies. These factors are homogeneity of the population, religiosity, and family structure.

Homogeneity refers to societies with a low cultural mix. Where people in a culture are all or mostly all alike, there are fewer conflicts and less crime. Religiosity refers to the absence or presence of a dominant religion. When the people of a society agree on the common values of a single religion, there are fewer conflicts and less crime. A strong multi-layered family structure controls behavior of family members. Fragmented families have less capacity for social control. Societies with strong family structures have less crime than those societies where such structures are weak.

Given the above information, it should come as no surprise that the United States is among the world leaders in criminal activity. Since we are becoming more heterogeneous, have an increased number of religious and anti-religious movements, and are experiencing extreme stress in the structure of our families, the prognosis is for increasing problems with crime and social disorganization. The future may be more dystopian than utopian.

The reality of policing, however, is more likely to be somewhere in the middle, regardless of how the future evolves. In all probability, with the exception of technology, the police will change very little over the next century.

The reasons for this are simple. First, American police agencies are severely fragmented and notoriously traditional. One cannot speak of the police in this country as a single entity. Instead we must always refer to the police as a generic plural. There are thousands of police agencies. Each has its own philosophy, size, and structure. When we speak of change, therefore, we are always referring to either the very large agencies or to those few agencies willing to experiment.

Second, police leadership is charismatic. The average tenure of the American police chief is approximately three years. A further complication is the fact that incumbent chiefs have no input into the selection of their successors. Often, successors are more apt to be chosen because of their differences with the incumbent chief rather than their similarities. Since many police administrators do not believe there is anything wrong with traditional policing, there will always be a large contingent of traditionalists to take over police agencies.

Third, in times of perceived social stress, when crime rates are high, the community and its elected leaders have a strong preference for traditional "war-on-crime" policing as opposed to the community oriented model which is seen more as "peace-time" policing. Rather than provide an impetus for police reform, as was the case in past decades, social crises now tend to create pressure for the opposite. This difference may lie in the social backlash created by several decades of reform in which the public saw the police as being unfairly restricted to the benefit of criminals. Or, it may be merely the fear generated by ever-rising levels of criminal activity.

Whatever the reason for this change in public attitude, the realities of the immediate future are a growing demand by the public for tougher laws, courts, and especially police officers. More officers, better guns, bigger nightsticks, and more police cars will likely be the strategy of crime control in the twenty-first century. The same was true in the twentieth and in the nineteenth centuries.

Overall, the future of policing in America remains uncertain. There are clouds on the horizon, and some would suggest that the storm will break soon. Others point out the positive changes taking place in law enforcement today and place trust in technology and the dedication of law enforcement officers (Sapp, 1992). However, neither technology nor dedicated officers can stem the trends that will affect policing in the future. What is needed is understanding and planning. Understanding of trends and events that will shape the future is required. Planning is required to effect the changes that are needed to influence the trends and future. The need for change is evident. Survival of law enforcement dictates change and only those willing to seek, find, and understand change will survive and succeed.

REFERENCES

CARTER, DAVID L. AND ALLEN D. SAPP. (1990). "The Evolution of Police Education: Preliminary Findings From a National Study." *Journal of Criminal Justice Education*, Vol. 1, No. 1, 59-86.

ECK, JOHN E. AND WILLIAM SPELMAN. (1987). *Problem Solving: Problem-Oriented Policing in Newport News*. Washington, DC: Police Executive Research Forum.

GOLDSTEIN, HERMAN. (1990). *Problem-Oriented Policing*. New York: McGraw-Hill.

HOLDEN, R. N. AND A. D. SAPP (1991). "The Evolution and Future of Bias Motivated Extremism in America." A paper presented at the First International Symposium on The Future of Policing, Quantico, Virginia.

MADDOX, JOSEPH H. (1993). "Community Sensitivity." *FBI Law Enforcement Bulletin*, Vol. 62, No. 2, 10-11.

O'LOUGHLIN, THOMAS J. (1992). "The Benefits and Pitfalls of Police Department Computerization." *The Police Chief*, Vol. LIX, No. 4, 29-34.

SAPP, ALLEN D. (1992). "Alternative Future." in Larry T. Hoover, (ed.) *Police Management: Issues and Perspectives*. Washington, DC: Police Executive Research Forum.

SCHWARTZ, JOE AND THOMAS EXTER. (1989). "All Our Children." *American Demographics*, May.

STAMPER, NORMAN H. (1992). *Removing Managerial Barriers to Effective Police Leadership*. Washington, DC: Police Executive Research Forum.

TAFOYA, W. L. (1990). "Futures Research: Implications for Criminal Investigations," in J. N. Gilbert, ed., *Criminal Investigation: Essays and Cases*. Columbus, OH: Merrill Publishing Company.

TOFFLER, ALVIN AND HEIDI TOFFLER. (1990). "The Future of Law Enforcement: Dangerous and Different." *FBI Law Enforcement Bulletin*, Vol. 59, No. 1, 2-5.

TROJANOWICZ, ROBERT. (1989). *Preventing Civil Disturbances: A Community Policing Approach*. Community Policing Series No. 18. East Lansing, MI: National Center for Community Policing, Michigan State University.

TROJANOWICZ, ROBERT AND BONNIE BUCQUEROUX. (1990). *Community Policing: A Contemporary Perspective*. Cincinnati, OH: Anderson Publishing.

TROJANOWICZ, ROBERT C. AND DAVID L. CARTER. (1990). "The Changing Face of America." *FBI Law Enforcement Bulletin*, Vol. 59, No. 1, 6-12.

QUESTIONS FOR THOUGHT AND DISCUSSION

1. How would policing be different in a utopian environment?
2. If the future brings us a dystopian social environment, how will this affect policing strategies?

SUGGESTIONS FOR FURTHER READING

JOHN CONRAD, "The Future Is Almost Here." *Federal Probation*. March 1989.

JOHN KLOFAS AND STAN STOJKOVIC, *Crime and Justice in the Year 2010*. Wadsworth Publishing Company, 1994.

ALVIN TOFFLER AND HEIDI TOFFLER, "Future of Law Enforcement: Different and Dangerous." *FBI Law Enforcement Bulletin*. January, 1990.

INDEX